# The General Biographical Dictionary: Containing an Historical and Critical Account of the Lives and Writings of the Most Eminent Persons in Every Nation
by Alexander Chalmers

Address:
HardPress
8345 NW 66TH ST #2561
MIAMI FL 33166-2626
USA
Email: info@hardpress.net

# THE GENERAL

# BIOGRAPHICAL DICTIONARY.

## A NEW EDITION.

———————

## VOL. XXXII.

Printed by NICHOLS, SON, and BENTLEY,
Red Lion Passage, Fleet Street, London.

# THE GENERAL

# BIOGRAPHICAL DICTIONARY :

## CONTAINING

## AN HISTORICAL AND CRITICAL ACCOUNT

### OF THE

## LIVES AND WRITINGS

### OF THE

## MOST EMINENT PERSONS

## IN EVERY NATION;

### PARTICULARLY THE BRITISH AND IRISH.

### FROM THE EARLIEST ACCOUNTS TO THE PRESENT TIME.

## A NEW EDITION,

### REVISED AND ENLARGED BY

## ALEXANDER CHALMERS, F. S. A.

## VOL. XXXII.

*LONDON:*

PRINTED FOR J. NICHOLS AND SON; F. C. AND J. RIVINGTON; T. PAYNE;
OTRIDGE AND SON; G. AND W. NICOL; G. WILKIE; J. WALKER; W.
LOWNDES; T. EGERTON; LACKINGTON, ALLEN, AND CO.; J. CARPENTER;
LONGMAN, HURST, REES, ORME, AND BROWN; CADELL AND DAVIES; LAW
AND WHITTAKER; J. BOOKER; J. CUTHELL; CLARKE AND SONS; J. AND
A. ARCH; J. HARRIS; BLACK, PARBURY, AND ALLEN ; J. BLACK; J. BOOTH;
J. MAWMAN; GALE AND FENNER; R. H. EVANS; J. HATCHARD; J. MURRAY;
BALDWIN, CRADOCK, AND JOY; R. BENTLEY ; OGLE AND CO.; W. GINGER;
RODWELL AND MARTIN; P. WRIGHT; J. DEIGHTON AND SON, CAMBRIDGE;
CONSTABLE AND CO. EDINBURGH; AND WILSON AND SON, YORK.

1817.

# A NEW AND GENERAL

# BIOGRAPHICAL DICTIONARY.

WHITGIFT (JOHN), archbishop of Canterbury in the reigns of queen Elizabeth and king James, and one of the most intrepid supporters of the constitution of the church of England, was descended of the antient family of Whitgift in Yorkshire. His grandfather was John Whitgift, gent. whose son was Henry, a merchant of Great Grimsby in Lincolnshire. Another of his sons was Robert Whitgift, who was abbot *de Wellow* or *Welhove juxta Grimsby* in the said county, a monastery of Black Canons dedicated to the honour of St. Augustin. He was a man memorable, not only for the education of our John Whitgift, but also for his saying concerning the Romish religion. He declared in the hearing of his nephew, that " they and their religion could not long continue, because," said he, " I have read the whole Scripture over and over, and could never find therein that our religion was founded by God." And as a proof of this opinion, the abbot alleged that saying of our Saviour, " Every plant that my heavenly Father hath not planted, shall be rooted up." Henry, the father of our archbishop, had six sons, of whom he was the eldest, and one daughter, by Anne Dynewel, a young gentlewoman of a good family at Great Grimsby. The names of the other five sons were William, George, Philip, Richard, and Jeffrey ; and that of the daughter Anne.

John was born at Great Grimsby in 1530, according to his biographers Strype and Paule, but according to Mr. Francis Thynne, quoted by Strype, in 1533 : the former, however, is most probably the right date. He was sent early for education to St. Antony's school, London, then a very eminent one, and was lodged in St. Paul's church-yard, at his aunt's, the daughter of Michael Shaller, a verger of that church. Imbibing very young a relish of the doctrine of the reformation, he had of course no liking to the mass; so that though his aunt had often urged him to go with her to mass, and procured also some of the canons of St. Paul's to persuade him to it, he still refused. By this she was so much exasperated, that she resolved to entertain him no longer under her roof, imputing all her losses and domestic misfortunes to her harbouring of such an heretic within her doors; and at parting told him, " that she thought at first she had received a saint into her house, but now she perceived he was a Devil."

He now returned home to his father in Lincolnshire; and his uncle, the abbot, finding that he had made some progress in grammatical learning, advised that he should be sent to the university. Accordingly he entered of Queen's college, Cambridge, about 1548, but soon after removed to Pembroke-hall, where the celebrated John Bradford, the martyr, was his tutor. He had not been here long before he was recommended by his tutor and Mr. Grindal (then fellow, and afterwards archbishop of Canterbury) to the master, Nicholas Ridley, by which means he was made scholar of that house, and chosen bible-clerk. These advantages were the more acceptable to him, as his father had suffered some great losses at sea, and was less able to provide for him. When Bradford left Cambridge in 1550, Whitgift was placed under the care of Mr. Gregory Garth, who continued his tutor while he remained at Pembroke-hall, which was until he took his degree of bachelor of arts in 1553-4. The following year, he was unanimously elected fellow of Peter-house, and commenced master of arts in 1557.

Soon after this, as he was recovering from a severe fit of sickness, happened the remarkable visitation of his university by cardinal Pole, in order to discover and expel the heretics, or those inclined to the doctrines of the reformation. To avoid the storm, Whitgift thought of going abroad, and joining the other English exiles; but Dr. Perne, master of his college, although at that time a professed papist, had such an esteem for him, that he undertook to screen him from the commissioners, and thus he was induced to remain; nor was he deceived in his confidence in Dr. Perne's friendship, who being then vice-chancellor, effectually protected him from all inquiry, notwithstanding the very strict severity of the visitation.

In 1560 Mr. Whitgift entered into holy orders, and preached his first sermon at St. Mary's with great and general approbation. The same year he was appointed chaplain to Cox, bishop of Ely, who gave him the rectory of Teversham in Cambridgeshire. In 1563 he proceeded bachelor of divinity, and Matthew Hutton, then fellow of Trinity-college, being appointed regius professor of divinity, the same year Whitgift succeeded him as lady Margaret's professor of divinity. The subject of his lectures was the book of Revelations and the whole Epistle to the Hebrews, which he expounded throughout. These lectures were prepared by him for the press; and sir George Paule intimates, that they were likely in his time to be published; but whatever was the reason, they have never appeared. Strype tells us, that he saw this manuscript of Dr. Whitgift's own hand-writing, in the possession of Dr. William Payne, minister of Whitechapel London; and that after his death it was intended to be purchased by Dr. John More, lord bishop of Ely. This manuscript contained likewise his thesis, when he afterwards kept his act for doctor of divinity, on this subject, that " the Pope is Antichrist."

Soon after this he joined his brother professor, Hutton, and several heads of colleges, in a petition to sir William Cecil, their chancellor, for an order to regulate the election of public officers, the want of which created great disturbance in the university at that time. Two years after this he distinguished himself so eminently in the pulpit, that sir Nicholas Bacon, then lord-keeper, sent for him to court to preach before the queen, who heard him with great satisfaction, and made him her chaplain. The same year (1565) being informed that some statutes were preparing to enjoin an uniformity of habits, particularly to order the wearing of surplices in the university, he promoted the writing of a joint letter privately to Cecil, earnestly desiring him to stop (if possible) the sending down any such orders, which he perceived would be very unacceptable to the university. But this letter gave so much offence at court, that he found it necessary to make an apology for the share he had in it. In the mean time he was so highly esteemed at Cambridge, both as a preacher and a restorer of order and discipline there, that in June of the following year, the university granted him a licence under their common seal, to preach throughout the realm, and in July following the salary of his professorship was raised, out of respect to him, from twenty marks to twenty pounds.

He had the year before been a considerable benefactor to Peter-house, where, in 1567, he held the place of president, but was called thence in April to Pembroke-hall, being chosen master of that house, and not long after was appointed regius professor of divinity. In both these preferments he succeeded his old friend Dr. Hutton, now made dean of York, and to the first was recommended, as Dr. Hutton had been, by Grindal, then bishop of London. But he remained at Pembroke-hall only about three months, for upon the death of Dr. Beauchamp, the queen promoted him to the mastership of Trinity-college. This place was procured for him, chiefly by the interest of sir William Cecil, who, notwithstanding some objections had been made to his age, secured the appointment. The same year he took his degree of doctor in divinity ; and in 1570, having first applied to Cecil for the purpose, he compiled a new body of statutes for the university, which were of great service to that learned community.

This work he finished in August, and the same month was the principal agent in procuring an order from the vice-chancellor and heads of houses, to prohibit the celebrated Cartwright (See CARTWRIGHT), who was now Margaret professor, from reading any more lectures without some satisfaction given to them of his principles and opinions. Dr. Whitgift informed the chancellor of this step, and at the same time acquainted him with Cartwright's principles, and the probable consequences of them, on which he received the chancellor's approbation of what had been done. Cartwright, having refused to renounce his opinions, was deprived of his professorship ; but as he gave out that those opinions were rather suppressed by authority, than refuted by reason, Dr. Whitgift took an effectual method to remove that objection. At the chancellor's request, he wrote a confutation of some of the chief of Cartwright's sentiments, and sent them to archbishop Parker, in a letter dated Dec. 29, with an intention to publish them, which, however, was not done until afterwards when they were combined in his " Answer to the Admonition, &c." hereafter noticed.

In 1671 Dr. Whitgift served the office of vice-chancellor. The same year an order was made by the archbishop and bishops, that all those who had obtained faculties to preach, should surrender them before the third of August; and that upon their subscription to the thirty-nine articles, and other constitutions and ordinances agreed upon, new licences should be granted. This being signified to the university, and an order sent, requiring them to call in all the faculties granted before, Whitgift surrendered his former licence, obtained in 1566, and had another granted him in September 1571, in which he was likewise constituted one of the university preachers. In June, in consequence of the queen's nomination, he had been appointed dean of Lincoln, and in October the archbishop granted him a dispensation to hold with it his prebend of Ely and rectory of Teversham, and any other benefice whatsoever; but in the following year he resigned the rectory of Teversham.

He was now, by particular appointment from the archbishop of Canterbury, writing his " Answer to the Admonition," which requiring more leisure than his office as master of Trinity college could admit, he desired to leave the university, but this the other heads of houses succeeded in preventing. He had a little before expelled Cartwright from his fellowship for not taking orders in due time, according to the statute; and before the expiration of the year 1572 published his " Answer to the Admonition to the Parliament," 4to. The " Admonition" was drawn up by Field, minister of Aldermary, London, and Mr. Wilcox. As archbishop Parker was the chief person who encouraged Whitgift to undertake the " Answer," he likewise gave him considerable assistance, and other prelates and learned men were also consulted, and every pains taken to make it, what it has been generally esteemed, as able a defence of the Church of England against the innovations of the puritans, as bishop Jewel's was against the doctrines of the Church of Rome. A second edition appeared in 1573, with the title " An answer to a certain libel, entitled An Admonition to the Parliament, newly augmented by the author, as by conference shall appear." To this a reply being published by Cartwright, Dr. Whitgift published his defence, fol. 1574. Cartwright published in 1574, 4to, " The second Reply of T. C. against Dr. Whitgift's second Answer touching Church-Discipline." What the opinion of Dr. Whitaker, who was thought to be a favourer of puritanism, was concerning this book of Mr. Cartwright, will appear from the following passage in a Latin letter of his preserved by Dr. Richard Bancroft and sir George Paule in his "Life of archbishop Whitgift." "I have read a great part of that book, which Mr. Cartwright hath lately published. I pray God I live not, if I ever saw any thing more loosely written, and almost more childishly. It is true, that for words he hath great store, and those both fine and new; but for matter, as far as I can judge, he is altogether barren. Moreover, he doth not only think perversely of the authority of princes in causes ecclesiastical, but also flyeth into the papists holds, from whom he would be thought to dissent with a mortal hatred. But in this point he is not to be endured, and in other points also he borroweth his arguments from the papists. To conclude, as Jerom said of Ambrose, he playeth with words, and is lame in his sentiments, and is altogether unworthy to be confuted by any man of learning." And Whitgift, being advised by his friends to let Cartwright's "Second Reply" pass as unworthy of his notice, remained silent.

About the same time, Dr. Whitgift appeared in opposition to a design then meditated, for abolishing pluralities, and taking away the impropriations and tithes from bishops and spiritual (not including temporal) persons, for the better provision of the poorer clergy. He did not, however, proceed farther in this than to express his sentiments in private to the bishop of Ely, who had proposed the scheme, which does not appear to have been brought forward in any other shape, probably in consequence of the arguments he advanced against it. In March 1577 he was made bishop of Worcester; and as this diocese brought him into the council of the marches of Wales, he was presently after appointed vice-president of those marches in the absence of sir Henry Sidney, lord president, and now lord-lieutenant of Ireland. In June following he resigned the mastership of Trinity college; and just before procured a letter from the chancellor, in order to prevent the practice then in use, of taking money for the resignation of fellowships.

The queen, as we noticed in our account of archbishop Grindal, had some thoughts of placing Whitgift in that worthy prelate's room, even in his life-time, and Grindal certainly would have been glad to resign a situation in which his conduct had not been acceptable to the court, and he had at the same time such an opinion of Whitgift as to be very desirous of him for a successor. But Whitgift could not be prevailed upon to consent to an arrangement of this kind, and requested the queen would excuse his acceptance of the office on any terms during the life of Grindal. Grindal, however, died in July 1583, and the queen immediately nominated Whitgift to succeed him as archbishop of Canterbury. On entering on this high office he found it greatly over-rated as to revenues, and was obliged to procure an order for the abatement of 100*l.* to him and his successors, on the payment of first fruits, and he shortly after recovered from the queen, as part of the possessions of the archbishopric, Long-Beach Wood, in Kent, which had been many years detained from his predecessor by sir James Croft, comptroller to her majesty's household. But that in which he was most concerned was to see the established uniformity of the church in so great disorder as it was from the non-compliance of the puritans, who, taking advantage of his predecessor's easiness in that respect, were possessed of a great many ecclesiastical benefices and preferments, in which they were supported by some of the principal men at court. He set himself, therefore, with extraordinary zeal and vigour, to reform these infringements of the constitution, for which he had the queen's express orders. With this view, in December 1583, he moved for an ecclesiastical commission, which was soon after issued to him, with the bishop of London, and several others. For the same purpose, in 1584, he drew up a form of examination, containing twenty-four articles, which he sent to the bishops of his province, enjoining them to summon all such clergy as were suspected of nonconformity, and to require them to answer those articles severally upon oath, *ex officio mero*, likewise to subscribe to the queen's supremacy, the book of Common Prayer, and the thirty-nine articles.

At the same time he held conferences with several of the puritans, and by that means brought some to a compliance; but when others appealed from the ecclesiastical commission to the council, he resolutely asserted his jurisdiction, and vindicated his proceedings, even in some cases against the opinion of lord Burleigh, who was his chief friend there. But as archbishop Whitgift's conduct has been grossly misrepresented by the puritan historians and by their successors, who are still greater enemies to the church, it may be necessary to enter more in detail on his correspondence

with Burleigh, &c. at this time.   Some ministers of Ely
being suspended for refusing to answer the examination
above mentioned, applied to the council, who wrote a letter to the archbishop in their favour, May 26, 1583.   To
this he sent'an answer, in the conclusion of which, so well
was he persuaded in his own mind of the propriety of his
conduct, he told the council, " that rather than grant them
liberty to preach, he would chuse to die, or live in prison
all the days of his life, rather than be an occasion thereof,
or ever consent unto it."   Lord Burleigh, thinking these
ministers hardly used in the ecclesiastical commission, advised them not to answer to the articles, except their con-
sciences might suffer them ; he at the same time informed
the archbishop that he had given such advice, and intimated his dislike of the twenty-four articles, and their
proceedings in consequence of them, in several letters.
To these the archbishop answered separately, in substance
as follows : In a letter dated June 14, from Croydon, he
declares himself content to be sacrificed in so good a cause;
and that the laws were with him, whatever sir Francis
Knollys (who, he said, had little skill) said to the contrary.
This alludes to a paper written by sir Francis, treasurer to
the queen's household, in defence of the recusants, and
sent to the archbishop.   Burleigh, in a second letter, dated
July 1, expressing himself in stronger terms against these
proceedings, concludes with saying that the articles were
branched out into so many circumstances, that he thought
the inquisitors of Spain used not so many questions to trap
others ; and that this critical sifting of ministers was not
to reform, but to insnare : but, however, upon his request,
he would leave them to his authority, nor " thrust his sickle
into another man's harvest."

To this the archbishop sent an answer, dated July 3, to
the following purport : That, as touching the twenty-four
articles, which his lordship seemed so much to dislike, as
written in a Romish style, and smelling of the Romish inquisition, he marvelled at his lordship's speeches, seeing
it was the ordinary course in other courts, as in the star-
chamber, the courts of the marches, and other places ; and
that the objection of encouraging the papists by these
courses, had neither probability nor likelihood.   That as
to his lordship's speech for the two ministers, viz. that they
were peaceable, observed the book, denied the things
wherewith they were charged, and desired to be tried, the

archbishop demanded, now they were to be tried, why they did refuse it *qui male egit odit lucem?* That the articles he administered unto them were framed by the most learned in the laws, and who, he dared to say, hated both the Romish doctrine and Romish inquisition; and that he ministered them to the intent only that he might truly understand whether they were such manner of men, or no, as they pretended to be, especially, seeing by public fame they were noted of the contrary, and one of them presented by the sworn men of his parish for his disorders, as he was informed by his official there. That time would not serve. him to write much; that he referred the rest to the report of the bearer, trusting his lordship would consider of things as they were, and not as they seemed to be, or as some would have them; that he thought it high time to put those to silence who were and had been the instruments of such great discontentment as was pretended; that conscience was no more excuse for them than it was for the papists or anabaptists, in whose steps they walked. He knew, he said, that he was especially sought, and many threatening words came to his ears to terrify him from proceeding; that the bishop of Chester (Chaderton) had wrote to him of late, and that in his letter a little paper was inclosed, the copy whereof he sent to his lordship. "You know (said the archbishop) whom he knoweth; but it moves me not; he can do no more than God will permit him. It is strange to understand what devices have been used to move me to be at some men's becks;" the particularities of all which he would one day declare to his lordship, and added, that he was content to be sacrificed in so good a cause, " which I will never betray nor give over, God, her majesty, all the laws, my own, conscience and duty, being with me." He concludes with beseeching Burleigh not to be discomfited, but continue; the cause was good, and the complaints being general, were vain, and without cause, as would appear when they descended to particularities.

To encourage his lordship farther, the archbishop, on June 24, sent him a schedule of the number of puritan preachers in his province, with their degrees, confronting them with the nonconformists, by which it appeared that there were seven hundred and eighty-six conformists, and only forty-nine recusants.

Lord Burleigh, in another letter, still insisting that he

would not call his proceedings rigorous and captious, but that they were scarcely charitable, the archbishop sent him, July 15, a defence of his conduct in a paper entitled " Reasons why it is convenient that those which are culpable in the articles ministered judicially by the archbishop of Canterbury and others, her majesty's commissioners for causes ecclesiastical, shall be examined of the same articles upon their oaths." In this paper he maintained, 1. That by the ecclesiastical laws remaining in force, such articles may be ministered : this is so clear by all, that it was never hitherto called into doubt. 2. That this manner of proceeding has been tried against such as were vehemently suspected, presented, and detected by their neighbours, or whose faults were notorious, as by open preaching, since there hath been any law ecclesiastical in this realm. 3. For the discovery of any popery it hath been used in king Edward's time, in the deprivation of sundry bishops at that time, as it may appear by the processes, although withal for the proof of those things that they denied, witnesses were also used. 4. In her majesty's most happy reign, even from the beginning, this manner of proceeding has been used against the one extreme and the other as general, against all the papists, and against all those who would not follow the Book of Common Prayer established by authority ; namely, against Mr. Sampson and others; and the lords of the privy council committed certain to the Fleet, for counselling sir John Southwood and other papists not to answer upon articles concerning their own facts and opinions, ministered unto them by her highness's commissioners for causes ecclesiastical, except a fame thereof were first proved. 5. It is meet also to be done *ex officio mero*, because upon the confession of such offences no pecuniary penalty is set down whereby the informer (as in other temporal courts) may be considered for his charge and pains, so that such faults would else be wholly unreformed. 6. This course is not against charity, for it is warranted by law as necessary for reforming of offenders and disturbers of the unity of the church, and for avoiding delays and frivolous exceptions against such as otherwise should inform, denounce, accuse, or detect them; and because none are in this manner to be proceeded against, but whom their own speeches or acts, the public fame, and some of credit, as their ordinary or such like, shall denounce, and signify to be such as are to be reformed in this behalf. 7. That the form of such proceedings by articles *ex officio mero* is usual; it may appear by all records in ecclesiastical courts, from the beginning; in all ecclesiastical commissions, namely, by the particular commission and proceedings against the bishops of London and Winton, in king Edward's time, and from the beginning of her majesty's reign, in the ecclesiastical commission, till this hour; and therefore warranted by statute. 8. If it be said that it be against law, reason, and charity, for a man to accuse himself, *quia nemo tenetur seipsum prodere aut propriam turpitudinem revelare*, I answer, that by all charity and reason, *Proditus per denunciationem alterius sive per famam, tenetur seipsum ostendere, ad evitandum scandalum, et seipsum purgandum. Prælatus potest inquirere sine prævia fama, ergo a fortiori delegati per principem possunt: ad hæc in istis articulis turpitudo non inquiritur aut flagitium, sed excessus et errata clericorum circa publicam functionem ministerii, de quibus ordinario rationem reddere coguntur.* (The purport of our prelate's meaning seems to be, that although no man is obliged to inform against himself, yet, if informed against by others, he is bound to come forwards, in order to avoid scandal, and justify himself; that a bishop may institute an inquiry upon a previous *fame*, much more delegates appointed by the sovereign; and besides, that in these articles no inquiry is made as to turpitude or criminality, but as to the irregularities and errors of the clergy, in matters relating to their ministerial functions, an account of which they are bound to render to their ordinary.) 9. Touching the substance of the articles, first, is deduced there being deacons and ministers in the church, with the lawfulness of that manner of ordering; secondly, the establishing the Book of Common Prayer by statute, and the charge given to bishops and ordinaries for seeing the execution of the said statute; thirdly, the goodness of the book, by the same words by which the statute of Elizabeth calls and terms it. Fourthly, several branches of breaches of the book being *de propriis factis*. Fifthly, is deduced detections against them, and such monitions as have been given them to testify their conformity hereafter, and whether they wilfully still continue such breaches of law in their ministration. Sixthly, Their assembling of conventicles for the maintenance of their factious dealings. 10. For the second, fourth, and sixth points, no man will think it unmeet they should be examined, if they would have them touched for any breach of the book. 11. The article for examination, whether they be deacon or minister, ordered according to the law of the land, is most necessary; first, for the grounds of the proceeding, lest the breach of the book be objected to them who are not bound to observe it; secondly, to meet with such schismatics, whereof there is sufficient experience, which either thrust themselves into the ministry without any lawful calling at all, or else to take orders at Antwerp, or elsewhere beyond the seas. 12. The article for their opinion of the lawfulness of their admission into the ministry is to meet with such hypocrites as, to be enabled for a living, will be content to be ordained at a bishop's hands, and yet, for the satisfaction of their factious humour, will afterwards have a calling of certain brethren ministers, with laying on of hands, in a private house, or in a conventicle, to the manifest slander of the Church of England, and the nourishing of a flat schism; secondly, for the detection of such as not by private, but by public speeches, and written pamphlets spread abroad, do deprave the whole order ecclesiastical of this church, and the lawfulness of calling therein; advouching no calling lawful but where their fancied monstrous signorie, or the assent of the people, do admit into the ministry. 13. The sequel that would follow of these articles being convinced or proved, is not so much as deprivation from ecclesiastical livings, if there be no obstinate persisting, or iterating the same offence; a matter far different from the bloody inquisition in time of popery, or of the six articles, where death was the sequel against the criminal. 14. It is to be considered, what encouragement and probable appearance it would breed to the dangerous papistical sacraments, if place be given by the chief magistrates ecclesiastical to persons that tend of singularity, to the disturbance of the good peace of the church, and to the discredit of that, for disallowing whereof the obstinate papist is worthily punished. 15. The number of these singular persons, in comparison of the quiet and conformable, are few, and their qualities are also, for excellence of gifts in learning, discretion, and considerate zeal, far inferior to those other that yield their conformity; and for demonstration and proof, both of the numbers, and also of the difference of good parts and learning in the province of Canterbury, there are but — hundred that refuse, and — thousands that had yielded their conformities.

These sentiments of the archbishop, although the detail of them may seem prolix, will serve to shew the nature of that unhappy dispute between the church and the puritans which, by the perseverance of the latter, ended in the fatal overthrow both of church and state in the reign of Charles I. They also place the character of Whitgift in its true light, and demonstrate, that he was at least conscientious in his endeavours to preserve the unity of the church, and was always prepared with arguments to defend his conduct, which could not appear insufficient in the then state of the public mind, when toleration was not known to either party. That his rigorous protection of the church from the endeavours of the puritans to new mould it, should be censured by them and their descendants, their historians and biographers, may appear natural, but it can hardly be called consistent, when we consider that the immediate successors of Whitgift, who censured him as a persecutor, adopted every thing that was contrary to freedom and toleration in his system, established a high commission-court by a new name, and ejected from their livings the whole body of the English clergy who would not conform to their ideas of church-government: and even tyrannized over such men as bishop Hall and others who were *doctrinal* puritans, and obnoxious only as loving the church that has arisen out of the ashes of the martyrs.

In 1585, we find Whitgift, by a special order from the queen, employed in drawing up rules for regulating the press, which were confirmed and published by authority of the Star-chamber in June. As he had been much impeded in his measures for uniformity by some of the privy-council, he attached himself in a close friendship with sir Christopher Hatton, then vice-chamberlain to the queen, to whom he complained of the treatment he had met with from some of the court. The earl of Leicester, in particular, not content with having made Cartwright master of his hospital, newly built at Warwick, attempted, by a most artful address, to procure a license for him to preach without the subscription; but the archbishop peremptorily refused to comply. About the beginning of next year, the archbishop was sworn into the privy-council, and the next month framed the statutes of cathedral-churches, so as to make them comport with the reformation. In 1587, when the place of lord-chancellor became vacant by the death of sir Thomas Bromley, the queen made the archbishop an offer of it, which he declined, but recommended sir Christopher Hatton, who was accordingly appointed.

On the alarm of the Spanish invasion in 1588, he procured an order of the council to prevent the clergy from being cessed by the lord-lieutenants for furnishing arms, and wrote circular letters to the bishops, to take care that their clergy should be ready, with a voluntary appointment of arms, &c. This year the celebrated virulent pamphlet, entitled " Martin Mar-prelate" was published, in which the archbishop was severely handled in very coarse language, but without doing him any injury in the eyes of those whom he wished to please. The same year, the university of Oxford losing their chancellor, the earl of Leicester proposed to elect Whitgift in his stead ; but this, being a Cambridge-man, he declined, and recommended his friend sir Christopher Hatton, who was elected, and thus the archbishop still had a voice in the affairs of that university. In 1590, Cartwright being cited before the ecclesiastical commission, for several misdemeanours, and refusing to take the oath *ex officio*, was sent to the Fleet-prison, and the archbishop drew up a paper containing several articles, more explicitly against the disciplinarians than the former, to be subscribed by all licensed preachers. The next year, 1591, Cartwright was brought before the Star-chamber; and, upon giving bail for his quiet behaviour, was discharged, at the motion of the archbishop, who soon after was appointed, by common consent, to be arbitrator between two men of eminent learning in a remarkable point of scripture-chronology. These were Hugh Broughton the celebrated Hebraist, and Dr. Reynolds, professor of divinity at Oxford. The point in dispute was, "Whether the chronology of the times from Adam to Christ could be ascertained by the holy Scriptures?" The first held the affirmative, which was denied by the latter. (See BROUGHTON, p. 82.)

In 1593, Dr. Bancroft published his " Survey of Discipline," in which he censured Beza's conduct in intermeddling with the English affairs in respect of church-government ; upon which the latter complained of this usage in a letter to archbishop Whitgift, who returned a long answer ; in which, he not only shewed the justice of Dr. Bancroft's complaint, but further also vindicated Saravia and Sutcliffe, two learned men of the English church, who

had written in behalf of the order of episcopacy, against
Beza's doctrine of the equality of ministers of the gospel,
and a ruling presbytery.   In 1594, fresh complaints being
made in parliament of the corruption of the ecclesiastical
courts, the archbishop made a general survey of those
courts, and their officers; and the same year he put a stop
to the passing of some new grants of concealed lands belonging to the cathedrals.

In 1595, when the disputes respecting church-discipline
appeared to be in a good measure appeased, the predes-
tinarian-controversy took place; and on this occasion, the
archbishop had the chief direction in drawing up the famous " Lambeth articles," in concert with Bancroft, then
bishop of London, Vaughan bishop of Bangor, Tindal dean
of Ely, Whitaker, and others.  Our readers are apprized
that these articles are favourable to the doctrines of Calvin.  The archbishop's declaration was, " I know them to
be sound doctrines, and uniformly professed in this church
of England, and agreeable to the articles of religion established by authority."  The archbishop of York made a
similar declaration, and the articles were forwarded to
Cambridge, accompanied by a letter from Whitgift, recommending that " nothing be publicly taught to the
contrary."

This year (1595) he obtained letters patent from her
majesty, and began the foundation of his hospital at Croydon.  The same year he protected the hospital of Har-
bledown, in Kent, against an invasion of their rights and
property: and the queen having made him a grant of all
the revenues belonging to the hospital of Eastbridge, in
Canterbury, he found out, and recovered next year, some
lands fraudulently withheld from it.  In 1599, his hospital
at Croydon being finished, was consecrated by bishop
Bancroft.  The founding of this hospital (then the largest
in the kingdom) having given rise to an invidious report
of the archbishop's immense wealth and large revenues, he
drew up a particular and satisfactory account of all his purchases since he had been bishop, with the sums given for
the same, and the yearly value of the lands, and to what
and whose uses, together with the yearly value of the arch-
bishoprick.

On the death of queen Elizabeth, in 1602, the archbishop sent Dr. Nevile, dean of Canterbury, into Scotland
to king James, in the name of the bishops and clergy of

England, to tender their allegiance, and to understand his majesty's pleasure in regard to the government of the church ; and though the dean brought a gracious message to him from the king, assuring his grace that he would maintain the settlement of the church as his predecessor left it, yet the archbishop was for some time not without his fears. The puritans, on the death of the queen, conceived fresh hopes of some countenance, and began to speak with more boldness of their approaching emancipation from ecclesiastical authority. A book had been printed the year before, by some of their party, entitled " The Plea of the Innocents," and in this year, 1603, appeared " The humble Plea of the thousand Ministers for redressing offences in the Church," at the end of which they required a conference. In October a proclamation was issued concerning a meeting for the hearing and determining things said to be amiss in the church. This issued in the famous conference held at Hampton-court, Jan. 14, 16, and 18, an account of which was drawn up by bishop Barlow. It only served to shew the puritans that the king was decidedly against them.

Archbishop Whitgift did not survive this conference long. He was not well in December before, but troubled with jaundice, which, together with his age, made him unfit to wait upon the king and court abroad the last summer. But soon after the conference at Hampton-court, going in his barge to Fulham in tempestuous weather, he caught cold ; yet the next Sunday, being the first Sunday in Lent, he went to Whitehall, where the king held a long discourse with him and the bishop of London, about the affairs of the church. His grace going thence to the council-chamber to dinner, after long fasting, he was seized with a paralytic stroke, and his speech was taken away. He was then carried to the lord treasurer's chamber, and thence, after a while, conveyed to Lambeth. On Tuesday he was visited by the king, who, out of a sense of the importance of his services at this particular juncture, told him, " that he would pray to God for his life; and that if he could obtain it, he should think it one of the greatest temporal blessings that could be given him in this kingdom." The archbishop would have said something to the king, but his speech failed him, so that he uttered only imperfect words. But so much of his speech was heard, repeating earnestly with his eyes and hands lifted up, " Pro Ecclesia Dei !"

Being still desirous to have spoken his mind to the king, he made two or three attempts to write to him; but was too far gone, and the next day, being February the 29th, he died. "Whether grief," says Strype, "was the cause of his death, or grief and fear for the good estate of the church under a new king and parliament approaching, mingling itself with his present disease, might hasten his death, I know not." But Camden says, "Whilst the king began to contend about the liturgy received, and judged some things fit to be altered, archbishop Whitgift died with grief." "Yet surely," says Strype, "by what we have heard before related in the king's management of the conference, and the letter he wrote himself to the archbishop, he had a better satisfaction of the king's mind. To which I may add, that there was a 'Directory,' drawn up by the Puritans, prepared to be offered to the next parliament, which, in all probability, would have created a great deal of disturbance in the house, having many favourers there; which paper the aged archbishop was privy to, and apprehensive of. And therefore, according to another of our historians, upon his death-bed, he should use these words, 'Et nunc, Domine, exaltata est Anima mea, quod in eo tempore succubui, quando mallem episcopatûs mei Deo reddere rationem, quam inter homines exercere: i. e. And now, O Lord, my soul is lifted up, that I die in a time, wherein I had rather give up to God an account of my bishoprick, than any longer to exercise it among men.'"

He was interred in the parish church of Croydon, where a monument was erected, with an inscription to his memory. He is described as being in person of a middle stature, a grave countenance, and brown complexion, black hair and eyes. He wore his beard neither long nor thick. He was small-boned, and of good agility, being straight and well shaped in all his limbs, to the light habit of his body, which began somewhat to spread and fill out towards his latter years. His learning seems to have been confined to the Latin language, as Hugh Broughton often objected to him, nor does he appear to have been much skilled in the deeper points of theology; but he was an admired and diligent preacher, and took delight in exercising his talent that way; it was, however, in ecclesiastical government that his *forte* lay, in the administration of which he was both indefatigable and intrepid. It is by his conduct in this that his character has been estimated by posterity, and has been variously estimated according to the writer's regard for, or aversion to, the constitution of the church of England.

In his expences it appears that he was liberal and even munificent. Both when bishop of Worcester and archbishop of Canterbury, he took for many years into his house a number of young gentlemen, several of quality, to instruct them, as their tutor, reading to them twice a day in mathematics and other arts, as well as in the languages, giving them good allowance and preferments as occasion offered. Besides these, he kept several poor scholars in his house till he could provide for them, and prefer them, and maintained others at the university. His charitable hospitality extended likewise to foreigners. He relieved and entertained at his house for many years together several distressed ministers (recommended by Beza and others) out of Germany and France, who were driven from their own homes, some by banishment, others by reason of war, shewing no less bounty to them at their departure. Sir George Paule assures us, that he remitted large sums of his own purse to Beza.

He was naturally of a warm temper, which however he learned to correct as he advanced in years. Cecil earl of Salisbury said of him, after his death, that "there was nothing more to be feared in his government, especially towards his latter time, than his mildness and clemency." The judicious Hooker confirms this opinion, by averring that "He always governed with that moderation, which useth by patience to suppress boldness." It does not appear that he printed any thing except what we have mentioned in the controversy with Cartwright, but in Strype's Life of him, are many of his letters, papers, declarations, &c. the whole, like all Strype's lives, forming an excellent history of the times in which he lived. [1]

WHITTINGHAM (WILLIAM), the puritan dean of Durham, the son of William Whittingham, esq. by a daughter of —— Haughton, of Haughton Tower, was born in the city of Chester, in 1524. In his sixteenth year he became a commoner of Brasenose college, Oxford, where he made great proficiency in literature. After taking his degree of bachelor of arts, he was elected fellow of All Souls in

[1] Strype's Life, fol.—Life by sir George Paule, 1699, 8vo.—The same with notes in Wordsworth's Biography.—Biog. Brit.—Fuller's Worthies, Church History, and Abel Redivivus.

1545, and two years afterwards was made one of the seniors of Christ-church, on the foundation of Henry VIII. In May 1550, having obtained leave to travel for three years, he passed his time principally at Orleans, where he married the sister of Calvin. He returned to England in the latter end of the reign of Edward VI. but, as he was a staunch adherent to the doctrines of the reformation, he found it necessary to leave home, when queen Mary came to the throne, and joined the exiles at Francfort. Here he became one of those who took part against the ceremonies of the Church of England being observed among the exiles, and afterwards became a member of the Church of Geneva. On the Scotch reformer, Knox, leaving that society to return to his own country, Whittingham was prevailed upon by Calvin to take orders in the Geneva form, and was Knox's successor. While here, he undertook, along with other learned men of the same society, an English translation of the Bible, which was not completed when those employed upon it had an opportunity to return to England, on the accession of queen Elizabeth. Whittingham, however, remained at Geneva to finish the work, during which time he translated into metre five of the Psalms, inscribed W. W. of which the 119th was one, together with the ten commandments, and a prayer, all which make part of the collection known by the names of Sternhold and Hopkins.

Soon after his return to England, he was employed to accompany Francis, earl of Bedford, on his embassy of condolence for the death of the French king, in 1560. And he attended Ambrose, earl of Warwick, to Havre de Grace, to be preacher there, while the earl defended it against the French; and Wood says, he preached nonconformity in this place. Warwick appears to have had a very high opinion of him, and it was by his interest that Whittingham was promoted to the deanery of Durham in 1563, which he enjoyed for sixteen years. During this time he was one of the most zealous opponents of the habits and ceremonies, and so outrageous in his zeal against popery, as to destroy some of the antiquities and monuments in Durham cathedral, and even took up the stone coffins of the priors of Durham, and ordered them to be used as troughs for horses to drink in.

Notwithstanding his opposition to the habits, when in 1564 the order issued for wearing them, he thought proper to comply, and being afterwards reproached for this by one who was with him at Geneva, he quoted a saying of Calvin's, "that for external matters of order, they might not neglect their ministry, for so should they, for tithing of mint, neglect the greater things of the law." It had been well for the church had this maxim more generally prevailed. Whittingham did essential service to government in the rebellion of 1569, but rendered himself very obnoxious at court, by a zealous preface, written by him, to Christopher Goodman's book, which denied women the right of government. He was probably in other respects obnoxious, generally as a nonconformist, which at last excited a dispute between him and Dr. Sandys, archbishop of York. In 1577 the archbishop made his primary visitation throughout the whole of his province, and began with Durham, where a charge, consisting of thirty-five articles, was brought against Whittingham, the principal of which was his being ordained only at Geneva. Whittingham refused to answer the charge, but denied in the first place the archbishop's power to visit the church of Durham. On this Sandys proceeded to excommunication. Whittingham then appealed to the queen, who directed a commission to the archbishop, Henry earl of Huntington, lord president of the north, and Dr. Hutton, dean of York, to hear and determine the validity of his ordination, and to inquire into the other misdemeanours contained in the articles; but this commission ended only in some countenance being given to Whitaker by the earl and by Dr. Hutton, the latter of whom went so far as to say, that "Mr. Whittingham was ordained in a better sort than even the archbishop himself." Sandys then obtained another commission directed to himself, the bishop of Durham, and lord president, the chancellor of the diocese, and some others. This was dated May 14, 1578, and may be seen in Rymer's Fœdera, vol. XV. Here, as Whittingham had nothing to produce but a certificate or call from the church of Geneva, it was objected to, but the lord president said that "it would be ill taken by all the godly and learned, both at home and abroad, that we allow of popish massing priests in our ministry, and disallow of ministers made in the reformed church." It does not appear that any thing was determined, and Whittingham's death put an end to the question. He died June 10, 1579, in the sixty-fifth year of his age, and his remains were interred in the cathedral of Durham, with a monumental inscription, which was afterwards destroyed by another set of innovators. He appears to have been a man of talents for business, as well as learning, and there was a design at one time of advancing him at court. He published little except some few translations from foreign authors to promote the cause of the reformation, and he wrote some prefaces. [1]

WHITTINGTON (ROBERT), one of our early grammarians, was born in Lichfield about 1480, and educated under the famous grammarian, John Stanbridge, in the school adjoining to Magdalen college, Oxford. He afterwards made a considerable progress in philosophy, but took more pleasure in classical and grammatical studies, in which he fancied himself destined to shine. In 1501 he began to teach a grammar-school, probably in London, as all his publications were dated thence. In the beginning of 1513, he supplicated the congregation of regents of the university of Oxford, by the name of Robert Whittington, a secular chaplain, and a scholar of the art of rhetoric, that whereas he had spent fourteen years in the study of the said art, and twelve years in teaching, " it might be sufficient for him that he might be laureated." This being granted, he composed an hundred verses which were stuck up in public places, especially on the doors of St. Mary's church, and was solemnly crowned with a wreath of laurel, &c. that is, he was made doctor of grammar, an unusual title and ceremony, and the last of the kind. This appears to have conferred no academical rank, for he was afterwards admitted to the degree of bachelor of arts. From this time, however, he called himself in several of his works *Protovates Angliæ*, an assumption which his fellow-grammarians, Horman and Lily, did not much relish. He appears indeed to have been very conceited of his abilities, and to have undervalued those who were at least his equals. Yet historians allow him to have been an excellent Greek and Latin scholar, and a man of a facetious turn, but too much given to personal satire both in conversation, and in his literary disputes with Lily, Aldridge, and others. He was alive in 1530, but how long afterwards does not appear. He wrote a great many grammatical treatises, some of which must have long been in use in schools, for they went through many editions. They are enumerated by

[1] Ath. Ox. vol. I.—Hutchinson's Hist. of Durham.—Strype's Life of Parker, pp. 135, 156.—Strype's Grindal, p. 170.—Strype's Annals.—Brook's Lives of the Puritans.

Wood, and, more correctly, by Mr. Dibdin in his Typographical Antiquities. Warton also mentions a few of them, and says that some of his Latin poetry is in a very classical style, and much in the manner of the earlier Italian poets.[1]

WHITWORTH (CHARLES, LORD), author of a very curious account of the Russian empire, was son of Richard Whitworth, esq. of Blowerpipe, in Staffordshire, who, about the time of the revolution, had settled at Adbaston. He married Anne Moseley, niece of sir Oswald Moseley, of Cheshire, by whom he had six sons and a daughter: Charles; Richard, lieutenant-colonel of the queen's own royal regiment of horse; Edward, captain of a man of war; Gerard, one of the chaplains to king George the First; John, captain of dragoons; Francis, surveyor-general of his majesty's woods, and secretary of the island of Barbadoes, father of Charles Whitworth, esq. member of parliament in the beginning of the present reign for Minehead in Somersetshire; and Anne, married to Tracey Pauncefort, esq. of Lincolnshire.

Charles, the eldest son, was bred under that accomplished minister and poet Mr. Stepney; and, having attended him through several courts of Germany, was, in 1702, appointed resident at the diet of Ratisbon. In 1704 he was named envoy-extraordinary to the court of Petersburgh, as he was sent ambassador-extraordinary thither on a more solemn and important occasion, in 1710. M. de Matueof, the Czar's minister at London, had been arrested in the public street by two bailiffs, at the suit of some tradesmen, to whom he was in debt. This affront had like to have been attended with very serious consequences. The Czar demanded immediate and severe punishment of the offenders, with threats of wreaking his vengeance on all English merchants and subjects established in his dominions. In this light the menace was formidable, and the Czar's memorials urged the queen with the satisfaction which she had extorted herself, when only the boat and servants of the earl of Manchester had been insulted at Venice. Mr. Whitworth had the honour of terminating this quarrel. In 1714, he was appointed plenipotentiary to the diet of Augsbourg and Ratisbon; in 1716, envoy-extraordinary and plenipotentiary to the king of Prussia; in 1717, envoy-extraordi-

[1] Ath. Ox. vol. I. new edit.—Warton's Hist. of Poetry.—Dibdin's Ames.—Dodd's Ch. Hist.

nary to the Hague. In 1719, he returned in his former character to Berlin; and in 1721 the late king rewarded his long services by creating him baron Whitworth of Galway, in the kingdom of Ireland. The next year his lordship was entrusted with the affairs of Great Britain at the congress of Cambray, in the character of ambassador-extraordinary and plenipotentiary. He returned home in 1724, and died the next year at his house in Gerard-street, London. His body was interred in Westminster-abbey.

His "Account of Russia, as it was in the year 1710," was published by the late lord Orford at Strawberry-hill, who informs us that besides this little piece, which must retrieve and preserve his character from oblivion, lord Whitworth left many volumes of state letters and papers in the possession of his relations. One little anecdote of him lord Orford was told by the late sir Luke Schaub, who had it from himself. Lord Whitworth had had a personal intimacy with the famous Czarina Catherine, at a time when her favours were not purchased, nor rewarded at so extravagant a rate as that of a diadem. When he had compromised the rupture between the court of England and the Czar, he was invited to a ball at court, and taken out to dance by the Czarjna. As they began the minuet, she squeezed him by the hand, and said in a whisper, " *Have you forgot little Kate ?* "

Lord Whitworth's MS Account of Russia was communicated to lord Orford, by Richard Owen Cambridge, esq. having been purchased by him in a very curious set of books, collected by Mons. Zolman, secretary to the late Stephen Poyntz, esq. This little library relates solely to Russian history and affairs, and contains, in many languages, every thing that perhaps has been written on that country.[1]

WHYTT (ROBERT), an eminent physician, born at Edinburgh Sept. 6, 1714, was the son of Robert Whytt, esq. of Beunochy, advocate. This gentleman died six months before the birth of our author, who was also deprived of his mother before he had attained the seventh year of his age. After receiving the first rudiments of school-education, he was sent to the university of St. Andrew's; and after the usual course of instruction there, in classical, philosophical, and mathematical learning, he came to Edinburgh, where he entered upon the study of medicine, under those emi-

---

[1] Lord Orford's preface to the " Account," &c.

nent teachers, Monro, Rutherford, Sinclair, Plummer, Alston, and Innes. After learning what was to be acquired in this university, he visited other countries in the prosecution of his studies, and after attending the most eminent teachers at London, Paris, and Leyden, he had the degree of M. D. conferred upon him by the university of Rheims in 1736, being then in the twenty-second year of his age. Upon his return to his own country, he had the same honour conferred upon him by the university of St. Andrews, where he had before obtained, with applause, the degree of M. A. In 1737, he was admitted a licentiate of medicine in the Royal College of Physicians of Edinburgh, and the year following he was raised to the rank of a fellow of the college. From the time of his admission as a licentiate, he practised physic at Edinburgh; and the reputation which he acquired for medical learning, pointed him out as a fit successor for the first vacant chair in the university. Accordingly, when Dr. Sinclair, whose eminent medical abilities, and persuasive powers of oratory, had contributed not a little to the rapid advancement of the medical school of Edinburgh, found that the talents which he possessed, could no longer be exerted consistently with his advanced age, he resigned his academical appointments in favour of Dr. Whytt.

This admission into the college took place June 20, 1746, and Dr. Whytt began his first course of the Institutions of Medicine at the commencement of the next winter session, in which the abilities he displayed were answerable to the expectations his fame had excited. The Latin tongue was then the language of the university of Edinburgh, and he both spoke and wrote in Latin with singular propriety, elegance, and perspicuity. At that time the system and sentiments of Boerhaave, which, notwithstanding their errors, must challenge the admiration of the latest ages, were very generally received by the most intelligent physicians in Britain. Dr. Whytt had no such idle ardour for novelties as to throw them entirely aside because he could not follow them in every particular. Boerhaave's "Institutions," therefore, furnished him with a text for his lectures; and he was no less successful in explaining, illustrating, and establishing the sentiments of the author, when he could freely adopt them, than in refuting them by clear, connected, and decisive arguments, when he had occasion to differ from him. The opinions which he himself proposed, were delivered and enforced with such acuteness of invention, such display of facts, and force of argument, as could rarely fail to gain universal assent from his numerous auditors, and he delivered them with becoming modesty and diffidence.

From the time that he first entered upon an academical appointment, till 1756, his prelections were confined to the institutions of medicine alone. But at that period his learned colleague, Dr. Rutherford, who was then professor of the practice of medicine, found it necessary to retire; and on this occasion, Dr. Whytt, Dr. Monro senior, and Dr. Cullen, each agreed to take a share in an appointment in which their united exertions promised the highest advantages to the university. By this arrangement, students who had an opportunity of daily witnessing the practice of three such teachers, and of hearing the grounds of that practice explained, could not fail to derive the most solid advantages. In these two departments the institutions of medicine in the university, and the clinical lectures in the royal infirmary (which were first begun by Dr. Rutherford) Dr. Whytt's academical labours were attended with the most beneficial consquences both to the students, and to the university. But not long after the period we have last mentioned, his lectures on the former of these subjects underwent a very considerable change. About this time the illustrious Gaubius, who had succeeded to the chair of Boerhaave, published his "Institutiones Pathologiæ." This branch of medicine had indeed a place in the text which Dr. Whytt formerly followed, but, without detracting from the character of Boerhaave, it may justly be said, that the attention he had bestowed upon it was not equal to its importance. Dr. Whytt was sensible of the improved state in which pathology now appeared in the writings of Boerhaave's successor; and he made no delay in availing himself of the advantages which were then afforded.

Accordingly, in 1762, his pathological lectures were entirely new modelled. Following the publication of Gaubius as a text, he delivered a comment, which was heard by every intelligent student with the most unfeigned satisfaction. For a period of more than twenty years, during which he was justly held in the highest esteem as a lecturer at Edinburgh, it may readily be supposed that the extent of his practice corresponded to his reputation. In fact he received both the first emoluments, and the highest honours, which could there be obtained. With extensive practice in Edinburgh, he had numerous consultations from other places. His opinions on medical subjects were daily requested by his most eminent contemporaries in every part of Britain. Foreigners of the first distinction, and celebrated physicians in the most remote parts of the British empire, courted an intercourse with him by letter. Besides private testimonies of esteem, many public marks of honour were conferred upon him both at home and abroad. In 1752, he was elected a fellow of the Royal Society of London; in 1761, he was appointed first physician to the king in Scotland; and in 1764, he was chosen president of the royal college of physicians at Edinburgh.

At an early period of life, soon after he had settled as a medical practitioner in Edinburgh, he married Miss Robertson, sister to general Robertson, governor of New York; by her he had two children, both of whom died in infancy, and their mother did not long survive them. A few years after he again entered into the married state with Miss Balfour, sister to James Balfour, esq. of Pilrig. By this lady he had fourteen children, six of whom only survived him. His wife died in 1764, and it is not improbable that the many deaths in his family, and this last loss had some share in hastening his own; for in the beginning of 1765 his health was so far impaired, that he became incapable of his former exertions. A tedious complication of chronical ailments, which chiefly appeared under the form of Diabetes, was not to be resisted by all the medical skill which Edinburgh could afford; and at length terminated in death, April 15, 1766, in the fifty-second year of his age.

Dr. Whytt's celebrity as an author was very great. His first publication was, "An Essay on the Vital and other Involuntary motions of animals," which was written fifteen years before publication in 1751. His next publication was his "Essay on the virtues of Lime-water and Soap in the cure of the stone," 1752, part of which had appeared several years before in the "Edinburgh Medical Essays." His "Physiological Essays," were first published in 1755. In 1764 appeared his principal work, entitled "Observations on the nature, causes, and cure of those disorders which are commonly called nervous, hypochondriac, and hysteric." The last of his writings, "Observations on the Dropsy of the Brain," did not appear till two years after his death,

when all his works were collected and published in one volume quarto, under the direction of his son, and of his intimate friend the late sir John Pringle. Besides these five
works, he wrote many papers which appeared in different
periodical publications; particularly in the Philosophical
Transactions, the Medical Essays, the Medical Observations, and the Physical and Literary Essays. [1]

WICKHAM. See WYKEHAM.

WICKLIFFE, WICLIFF, de WYCLIF, or WICLEF (JOHN),
a very learned English divine in the fourteenth century,
and the first champion of that cause which was afterwards
called Protestantism, was born at a village then called
Wickliffe, from which he took his surname, near Richmond
in Yorkshire, in 1324. Of the parents of one who lived in
so remote a period, it cannot be expected that we should
be able to procure any account. He was sent early to Oxford, and was first admitted commoner of Queen's college,
and afterwards of Merton, where he became probationer,
but not fellow, as has been usually reported. While he
resided here, he associated with some of the most learned
men of the age who were members of that college, and it
is said that Geoffry Chaucer was at one time his pupil.
Among his contemporaries, he was soon distinguished both
for study and genius. He acquired all the celebrity which
a profound knowledge of the philosophy and divinity then
in vogue could confer, and so excelled in wit and argument as to be esteemed more than human. Besides the
learning of the schools, he accumulated a profound knowledge of the civil and canon law, and of the municipal laws
of our own country, which have been rarely an object of
attention until the establishment of the Vinerian professorship. He also not only studied and commented upon the
sacred writings, but translated them into English, and
wrote homilies on several parts of them ; and to all this he
added an intimate acquaintance with the fathers of the
Latin church, with St. Austin and St. Jerome, St. Ambrose
and St. Gregory.

With these acquisitions, he did not hastily obtrude the
novel opinions to which they had given rise. He was
thirty-six years of age before his talents appeared to the
world, and even then they were called forth rather by necessity than choice. In 1360 he became the advocate for

[1] Encyclopædia Britannica.

the university against the incroachments made by the mendicant friars, who had been very troublesome from their first establishment in Oxford in 1230, and had occasioned great inquietude to the chancellor and scholars, by infringing their statutes and privileges, and setting up an exempt jurisdiction. Their misconduct had decreased the number of students from thirty thousand to six thousand, parents being afraid to send their children to the university, where they were in danger of being enticed by these friars from the colleges into convents; and no regard was paid to the determination of parliament in 1366, that the friars should receive no scholar under the age of eighteen. But Wickliffe now distinguished himself against these usurpations, and, with Thoresby, Bolton, Hereford, and other colleagues, openly opposed the justification which the friars had advanced in favour of their begging trade from the example of Christ and his apostles. Wickliffe also wrote several tracts against them, particularly "Of Clerks Possessioners," "Of the Poverty of Christ, against able Beggary," and "Of Idleness in Beggary." These were written, with an elegance uncommon in that age, in the English language, of which he may be considered as one of the first refiners, while his writings afford many curious specimens of old English orthography. His controversies gave him such reputation in the university, that, in 1361 he was advanced to be master of Baliol college; and four years after he was made warden of Canterbury-hall, founded by Simon de Islip, archbishop of Canterbury, in 1361, and now included in Christ-church. The letters of institution, by which the archbishop appointed him to this wardenship, were dated 14 Dec. 1365, and in them he is styled, " a person in whose fidelity, circumspection, and industry, his grace very much confided; and one on whom he had fixed his eyes for that place, on account of the honesty of his life, his laudable conversation, and knowledge of letters."

Wickliffe amply fulfilled these expectations, till the death of the archbishop in 1366, who was succeeded in the archiepiscopal dignity by Simon Langham. This prelate had been a monk, and being inclined to favour the religious against the seculars, was easily persuaded by the monks of Canterbury to eject Wickliffe in 1367 from his wardenship, and the other seculars from their fellowships. He also issued out his mandate, requiring Wickliffe and all the scholars to yield obedience to Wodehall as their warden. This Wodehall had actually been appointed warden by the founder, but he was at such variance with the secular scholars, that the archbishop was compelled to turn him and three other monks out of his new-founded hall, at which time he appointed Wickliffe to be warden, and three other seculars to be scholars. The scholars now, however, refused to yield obedience to Wodehall, as being contrary to the oath they had taken to the founder, and Langham, irritated at their obstinacy, sequestered the revenue, and took away the books, &c. belonging to the hall. Wickliffe, and his expelled fellows, appealed to the pope, who issued a bull, dated at Viterbo 28 May, 1370, restoring Wodehall and the monks, and imposing perpetual silence on Wickliffe and his associates. As this bull was illegal, and interfered with the form of the licence of mortmain, the monks in 1372 screened themselves by procuring the royal pardon, and a confirmation of the papal sentence, for which they paid 200 marks, nearly 800l. of our money.

About this time the pope (Urban) sent notice to king Edward, that he intended to cite him to his court at Avignon, to answer for his default in not performing the homage which king John acknowledged to the see of Rome; and for refusing to pay the tribute of 700 marks a-year, which that prince granted to the pope. The king laid this before the parliament, and was encouraged to resist the claim. One of the monks having endeavoured to vindicate it, Wickliffe replied; and proved that the resignation of the crown, and promise of a tribute made by king John, ought not to prejudice the kingdom, or oblige the present king, as it was done without consent of parliament. This introduced him to the court, and particularly to the duke of Lancaster, who took him under his patronage. At this time he styled himself *peculiaris regis clericus*, or the king's own clerk or chaplain, but continued to profess himself an obedient son of the Roman church. Shortly after he was presented, by the favour of the duke of Lancaster, to the living of Lutterworth in Leicestershire, but in the diocese of Lincoln, and it was here that he advanced in his writings and sermons, those opinions which entitle him to the rank of reformer. But as he did not in the most open manner avow these sentiments until he lost this living, his enemies then and since have taken occasion to impute them to a motive of revenge against the court of Rome which deprived him. This, however, is not strictly the truth, as he seems to have uttered and maintained some of his reforming opinions before he was turned out of the rectorship. This is evident from a tract entitled "Of the last age of the Church," published in 1356, fourteen years before, in which he censures the popish exactions and usurpations.

It must be allowed, however, that his boldness increased with his sufferings. In 1372 he took his degree as doctor of divinity, and read lectures with great applause, in which he more strongly opposed the follies and superstitions of the friars, exposed their corruptions, and detected their practices without fear or reserve. The conduct of the court of Rome in disposing of ecclesiastical benefices and dignities to Italians, Frenchmen, and other aliens, became so notorious and oppressive, that in 1374, the king issued out a commission for taking an exact survey of all the dignities and benefices throughout his dominions, which were in the hands of aliens. The number and value of them appeared enormous, and he determined to send seven ambassadors to require of the pope that he would not interfere with the reservation of benefices. He had tried a similar embassy the year before, which procured only an evasive concession. On the present occasion Wickliffe was the second person nominated, and, with the other ambassadors, was met at Bruges by the pope's nuncio, two bishops and a provost. This treaty continued two years, when it was concluded that the pope should desist from making use of reservations of benefices. But the very next year, the treaty was broken, and a long bill was brought into parliament against the papal usurpations, as the cause of all the plagues, injuries, famine, and poverty of the realm. They remonstrated that the tax paid to the pope amounted to five times as much as the tax paid to the king; and that God had given his sheep to the pope to be pastured, not fleeced. Such language encouraged Wickliffe, who boldly exposed the pride, avarice, ambition, and tyranny of the pope, in his public lectures and private conversation; and the monks complained to the pope that Wickliffe opposed the papal powers, and defended the royal supremacy; on which account, in 1376 they drew up nineteen articles against him, extracted from his public lectures and sermons, of which some notice will be taken hereafter. It may be sufficient to add in this place, that they tended to oppose the rights which the popes had assumed, and to justify the regal, in opposition to the papal pretensions of an ecclesiastical liberty, or an exemption of the persons of the clergy, and the goods of the church from the civil power. In advancing such opinions, he had the people on his side, and another powerful protector appeared for him in Henry Percy, earl-marshal. This alarmed the court of Rome, and Gregory XI. issued several bulls against Wickliffe, all dated May 22, 1377. One was directed to the archbishop of Canterbury and the bishop of London, whom he delegated to examine into the matter of the complaint; another was dispatched to the king himself, and a third to the university of Oxford. In the first, addressed to the two prelates, he tells them, " he was informed that Wickliffe had rashly proceeded to that detestable degree of madness, as not to be afraid to assert, and publicly preach, such propositions, as were erroneous and false, contrary to the faith, and threatening to subvert and weaken the estate of the whole church." He therefore required them to cause Wickliffe to be apprehended and imprisoned by his authority; and to get his confession concerning his propositions and conclusions, which they were to transmit to Rome; as also whatever he should say or write, by way of introduction or proof. But, if Wickliffe could not be apprehended, they were directed to publish a citation for his personal appearance before the pope within three months. The pope requested the king to grant his patronage and assistance to the bishops in the prosecution of Wickliffe. In the bull to the university, he says, the heretical pravity of Wickliffe tended " to subvert the state of the whole church, and even the civil government." And he orders them to deliver him up in safe custody to the delegates.

King Edward III. died before these bulls arrived in England, and the university seemed inclined to pay very little respect to the one addressed to them. The duke of Lancaster and the earl-marshal openly declared they would not suffer him to be imprisoned, and as yet, indeed, the bishops were not authorized by law to imprison heretics without the royal consent. The archbishop of Canterbury and the bishop of London, however, on the 19th Feb. 1378, issued out their mandate to the chancellor of the university of Oxford, commanding them to cite Wickliffe to appear before them in the church of St. Paul, London, within thirty days. But in such reputation was Wickliffe held at this time, that when, in the interval before his appearance, the first parliament of king Richard II. met, and debated "whether they might lawfully refuse to send the treasure out of the kingdom, after the pope required it on pain of censures, by virtue of the obedience due to him?" the resolution of this doubt was referred by the king and parliament to doctor Wickliffe, who undertook to prove the legality of their refusal.

Such confidence reposed in him by the higher powers augured ill for the success of the prelates who had summoned him to appear before them. On the day appointed, a vast concourse assembled, and Wickliffe entered, accompanied by the duke of Lancaster and the earl-marshal Percy, who administered every encouragement to him. But before the proceedings began, an altercation was occasioned by the bishop of London's opposing a motion of the earl-marshal, that Wickliffe should be allowed a seat. The duke of Lancaster replied to the bishop in warm terms, and said, although rather softly, that "rather than take such language from the bishop, he would drag him out of the church by the hair of his head." But this being overheard, the citizens present took part with their bishop, and such a commotion ensued that the court broke up without entering on the examination, while Wickliffe was carried off by his friends in safety. The Londoners, in revenge, plundered the duke of Lancaster's palace in the Savoy, and the duke turned the mayor and aldermen out of the magistracy for not restraining their violence. From these circumstances it would appear that at this time Wickliffe's principles had not been espoused by many of the lower classes, as is generally the case with innovations in religious matters; yet it was not long before he had a strong party of adherents even among them, for when he was a second time cited by the prelates to appear before them at Lambeth, the Londoners forced themselves into the chapel to encourage him, and intimidate his judges and accusers. On this occasion Wickliffe delivered a paper to the court, in which he explained the charges against him, but the proceedings were again stopped by the king's mother, who sent sir Lewis Clifford to forbid their proceeding to any definitive sentence against Wickliffe. This completely disconcerted them, and according to the evidence of their own historian, Walsyngham, changed their courage into pusillanimity. "Qui quam indevote," says he, "quam segniter commissa sibi mandata compleverint, melius est silere quam loqui." All they could do was to enjoin him silence, to which he paid no regard; his followers increased; the death of pope Gregory XI. put an end to the commission of the delegates; and when a schism ensued by the double election of two popes, Wickliffe wrote a tract, "Of the Schism of the Roman Pontiffs," and soon after published his book "Of the Truth of the Scripture," in which he contended for the necessity of translating the scriptures into the English language, and affirmed that the will of God was evidently revealed in two Testaments; that the law of Christ was sufficient to rule the church; and that any disputation, not originally produced from thence, must be accounted profane.

About this time, the fatigues he underwent in his attendance on the delegates, threw him into a dangerous illness on his return to Oxford. The mendicant friars took this opportunity to send a deputation to him, representing the great injuries he had done to them by his sermons and writings, and, as he was at the point of death, exhorting him to recant. Wickliffe, however, recovering his spirits at this unintended acknowledgment of the success of his writings, raised himself on his pillow, and replied, "I shall not die, but live to declare the evil deeds of the friars." On his recovery he embraced every opportunity in his lectures, sermons, or writings, of exposing the Romish court, and detecting the vices of the clergy, both religious and secular; and his efforts were supported by certain proceedings of the parliament, which in 1380 rendered foreign ecclesiastics incapable of holding any benefices in England; and at the same time petitioned the king to expel all foreign monks, lest they should instil notions into the people repugnant to the welfare of the state.

But what gave most uneasiness to his enemies, was his having undertaken to translate the Holy Scriptures into English. These had never been translated, except by Richard Fitz-ralph, archbishop of Armagh, and John de Trevisa, a Cornish-man, who both lived in the reign of Edward III. Mr. Lewis is of opinion that Wickliffe began his translation about 1379 or 1380. But it is more probable that it was his chief employment for the last ten years at least of his life, and he had the assistance of some of his followers. He translated from Latin into the vulgar tongue, the twenty-five canonical books of the Bible, which he reckoned in the following order, and we transcribe as a specimen of the style and spelling of his language. "1. Genesis. 2. Exodus. 3. Levitici. 4. Numeri. 5. Deuteronomi. 6. Josue. 7. Iudicum, that encloseth the story of Ruth. 8. 9. 10. 11. 12. 13. ben the 4 Bokes of Kyng and tweie Bokes of Paralipomenon. 14. Is Esdre, that comprehendeth Neemy. 15. Is Hester. 16. Is Job. 17. Psalter. 18. 19. 20, ben the 3 Bokes of Solomon. 21. 22. 23. 24, ben the four great prophets. 25. Is a Boke of 12 small Prophets, Osee, Joel, Amos, Abdie, Jonas, Michee, Nahum, Abacuc, Sophonie, Aggie, Zacharie, and Malachie." He adds, "That whatever boke is in the Olde Testament without these 25 aforesaid, shal be set among Apocrypha, that is, withouten autoritie of belive. Therefore as holie chirch redith Judith and Tobit, and the Bokes of Machabeis but receiveth not tho' amonge holi scriptures; so the chirch redith these 2 Bokes Ecclesiastici, and Sapieme to edifying of the people, not to confirme the autoritie of techyng of holi chirch. And that therefore he translated not the 3 ne 4 Boke of Esdree that ben Apocrypha." The books of the New Testament he reckons in this order. "The 4 Gospellers, Matthew, Mark, Luke, and John; 12 Epistles of Poule; 7 small Epistles; the Dedes of Apostles, and the Apocalyps, which ben fulli of autoritie of byleve." Mr. Lewis observes, he translated word for word, without always observing the idioms or proprieties of the several languages; by which means this translation in some places is not very intelligible to those who do not understand Latin. The reason why he made his version from the Vulgate was, not that he thought it the original, or of the same authority with the Hebrew and Greek text, but because he did not understand those languages well enough to translate from them.

Of this translation several manuscript copies are extant in the libraries of our universities, the British museum, and other public and private collections. The New Testament was published in 1731 fol. by Mr. John Lewis, minister of Margate; with a History of the English Translations of the Bible; which History was reprinted in 1739, 8vo, with large additions. Of the style we shall now exhibit a farther, and more perfect specimen, in these three verses of Romans viii. 28, 29, 30. "And we witen, that to men that louen God alle thing is worchen to gidre into good to hem that aftir purpose been clepid seyntis. For thilk that he knew bifore, he bifore ordeynyde bi grace to be maad lyk to the ymage of his Sone, that he be the firste bigeten among manye britheren. And thilke that he bifore ordeynyde *to blisse*, hem he clepide, and whiche he clepide hem he justifiede, and which he justifiede, and hem he glorifiede."

In 1381 we find Wickliffe attacking the doctrine of transubstantiation, which was first asserted by Radbertus about the year 820, and had been always propagated by the Romish church. Wickliffe offered to support his opinion in a public disputation, but as that was prohibited, he published it in a tract entitled " De Blasphemia," which was condemned by William de Barton, chancellor of the university, and eleven doctors, of whom eight were of the religious. Wickliffe maintained that they had not refuted his assertions, and appealed from their condemnation to the king. In the mean time William Courtney, bishop of London, succeeded archbishop Sudbury in the see of Canterbury, and was entirely devoted to the interest of his patron the pope. This prelate had before shewn himself a violent opposer of Wickliffe, and now proceeded against him and his followers. But as soon as the parliament met in 1382, Wickliffe presented his appeal to the king and both houses. Walsingham represents this as done with a design to draw the nobility into erroneous opinions, and that it was disapproved by the Duke of Lancaster, who ordered Wickliffe to speak no more of that matter. Others say that the duke advised Wickliffe not to appeal to the king, but submit to the judgment of his ordinary; upon which, the monks assert, he retracted his doctrine at Oxford in the presence of the archbishop of Canterbury, six bishops, and many doctors, surrounded with a great concourse of people. But the confession which he read, in Latin, was rather a vindication of his opinion of the sacrament, as it declares his resolution to defend it with his blood, and maintains the contrary to be heresy.

The persecution which followed plainly proves this to be the case. After the death of the queen, Anne of Luxemburg, in 1394, who was a favourer of the Wickliffites, the archbishop, Courtney, assembled a court of bishops, in the monastery of the preaching friars, London, who declared fourteen conclusions of Wickliffe and others, heretical and erroneous. It is said that Wickliffe was prevented from appearing at this court by his friends, who thought that a

plot was laid to seize him on the road.   His cause, however, was undertaken by the chancellor of Oxford, the two
proctors, and the greatest part of the senate, who, in a
letter, sealed with the university seal, and sent to the
court, highly commended his learning, piety, and orthodox faith.   His particular friends and followers, Dr. Nicholas Hereford, Dr. Philip Rapingdon, and John Ayshton,
M. A. defended his doctrines both in this court and in the
convocation.    The archbishop still persisted in his endeavours to punish the Wickliffites, but their doctrines increased, while Wickliffe himself, although obliged to quit
his professorship at Oxford, lived peaceably at Lutterworth,
still divulging his principles, and increasing the number of
his followers.   In 1382, soon after he left Oxford, he was
seized with the palsy ; and about the same time the pope
cited him to appear at Rome, to which he sent an excuse,
pleading, that "Christ had taught him to obey God rather than man."   He was seized with a second stroke of
palsy on Innocent's day 1384, as he was in his church of
Lutterworth, and soon after expired, in the sixtieth year
of his age.

On the 5th of May, 1415, the council of Constance condemned forty-five articles maintained by Wickliffe, as
heretical, false, and erroneous.   His bones were ordered
to be dug up and cast on a dunghill ; but this part of his
sentence was not executed till 1428, when orders were sent
by the pope to the bishop of Lincoln to have it strictly
performed.   His remains, which had now lain in the grave
forty-four years, were dug out and burnt, and the ashes
cast into an adjoining brook, called the Swift.   It is said
that the gown which Wickliffe wore now covers the communion-table of the church of Lutterworth.

The principles which this eminent reformer endeavoured
to introduce may be gathered from the nineteen articles
before-mentioned, which were extracted from his public
lectures and sermons, by the monks, and sent to the pope.
It appears that he held the doctrine of predestination in as
strong a sense as any who have since supported it, and, in
the opinion of a late writer, carries it much farther than
any modern or ancient writers have attempted.   He was,
indeed, an absolute necessitarian, and among certain articles extracted from his works by Thomas Netter (commonly called Thomas of Walden, who flourished about
1409) we find the following, "That all things come to pass

by fatal necessity; that God could not make the world otherwise than it is made; and that God cannot do any thing which he doth not do." Other less unguarded expressions have been laid to his charge, of which Fuller observes, that were all his works extant, " we might read the occasion, intention, and connection of what he spake, together with the limitations, restrictions, distinctions, and qualifications, of what he maintained. There we might see what was the overplus of his passion, and what the just measure of his judgment." He maintained, with the church in after-times, the doctrine of pardon and justification by the alone death and righteousness of Christ. The several points in which he differed from the then established popery were these; the reading of the bible in the vulgar tongue, and making them the sole rule of a Christian's faith and practice, without faith in tradition, or any human authority; his opposing the pope's supremacy and infallibility; his rejecting and condemning transubstantiation, indulgences, confession, and absolution, extreme unction; the celibacy of the clergy; forced vows of chastity; prayers to, and worship of saints, shrines and pilgrimages. But the opinions which rendered him most obnoxious in his day, were those which struck at the temporal dominion of the pope, and which occasioned many of his followers to be persecuted in the subsequent reigns of Richard II. Henry IV. and Henry V.

His works are very voluminous, yet he seems not to have engaged in any great work. They are, more properly speaking, tracts, some of which were written in Latin, and some in English; some were on school-questions; others on subjects of more general knowledge; but the greatest part on divinity. Mr. Gilpin has given a list of the more remarkable. Bale has a more particular account. Some are preserved in Trinity and Corpus colleges, Cambridge, a few in Trinity college, Dublin, in the Bodleian, and in the British museum. Mr. Baber, in his late edition of the New Testament, has given the fullest and most accurate account of these. The following list comprises all that have been printed: 1. "Trialogus," a dialogue in Latin, between Truth, Falsehood, and Wisdom," printed somewhere in Germany, about 1525, 4to, pp. 175. This is very scarce, having been mostly destroyed by the Romanists *, but a new edition of it was printed at Frank-

* See Ames Topog. Antiq. p. 1535. Mr. Ames purchased a copy at Dr Evans's sale for 3l. 14s.

fort, 1753, 4to. 2. "Wicklif's Wicket, or, a learned and godly treatise of the Sacrament," Norimberg, 1546, 8vo, and Oxford, 1612, 4to. 3. "The pathway to perfect knowledge, or Wickliffe's Prologue to the Bible," published by Robert Crowley, 1550, 12mo. 4. "The dore of the Holy Scripture," 1540, 8vo. 5. "De Christianorum villicatione," in English, published in 1582, under the name of R. Wimbledon. 6. "A Complaint of John Wickliffe, exhibited to the king and parliament." 7. "A Treatise of John Wickliffe against the order of Friars." These two were published together at Oxford in 1608, 4to, by Dr. James, from two MS copies, one in Bene't college, Cambridge, the other in the Bodleian library. 8. "Why poor Priests have no Benefices," published by Mr. Lewis in his life of Wickliffe, who has also published there, his Determination, Confessions, and large extracts from his works remaining in MS. together with his New Testament. His opinions are also particularly detailed in Dr. Thomas James's "Apologie for John Wickliffe, shewing his conformitie with the new Church of England;" collected chiefly out of his MS works in the Bodleian library, and printed at Oxford, 1608, 4to, now very scarce.

We have mentioned Lewis's edition of Wickliffe's New Testament. Of this a new, elegant, and very correct second edition was published in 1810 by the rev. Henry Hervey Baber, M. A. F. R. S. librarian of printed books in the British museum, in a 4to volume. To this are prefixed "Memoirs of the Life, opinions, and writings" of Wickliffe, to which we would refer our readers for much original information and ingenious research; and a very learned "Historical account of the Saxon and English versions of the Scriptures, previous to the opening of the fifteenth century." It was the intention of this excellent editor to have attempted an edition of Wickliffe's translation of the Old Testament, but no sufficient encouragement, we add with surprize and shame, has yet been offered to so important an addition to our translations of the Holy Scriptures. [1]

WICQUEFORT (ABRAHAM DE), famous for his embassies and his writings, was a Hollander, and born in 1598; but it is not certain at what place, though some have mentioned Amsterdam. He left his country very young, and

[1] Lewis's Life of Wickliffe.—Baber's Life prefixed to the New Testament.—Biog. Brit.—Fuller's Ch. History.—Gilpin's Life of Wickliffe.—Wood's Annals.

went and settled in France, where he applied himself diligently to political studies, and sought to advance himself by political services. Having made himself known to the elector of Brandenburg, this prince appointed him his resident at the court of France, about 1626; and he preserved this post two-and-thirty years, that is, till 1658. Then he fell into disgrace with cardinal Mazarin, who never had much esteem for him, and particularly disliked his attachment to the house of Condé. The cardinal accused him of having sent secret intelligence to Holland and other places; and he was ordered to leave the court and the kingdom: but, before he set out, he was seized and sent to the Bastille. M. le Tellier wrote at the same time to the elector of Brandenburg, to justify the action; which he did by assuring him that his minister was an intelligencer in the pay of several princes. The year after, however (1659), he was set at liberty, and escorted by a guard to Calais; whence he passed over to England, and thence to Holland. There De Witt, the pensionary, received him affectionately, and protected him powerfully: he had indeed been the victim of De Witt, with whom he had carried on a secret correspondence, which was discovered by intercepted letters. He reconciled himself afterwards to France, and heartily espoused its interests; whether out of spite to the prince of Orange, or from some other motive; and the count d'Estrades reposed the utmost confidence in him. For the present, the duke of Brunswic-Lunenburg made him his resident at the Hague; and he was appointed, besides this, secretary-interpreter of the States General for foreign dispatches.

The ministry of De Witt being charged with great events, the honour of the commonwealth, as well as of the pensionary, required that they should be written; and Wicquefort was selected as the properest person for such a work. He wrote this history under the inspection, as well as protection, of the pensionary, who furnished him with such memoirs as he wanted, and he had begun the printing of it when, being accused of holding secret correspondence with the enemies of the States, he was made prisoner at the Hague in March 1676; and, November following, condemned to perpetual imprisonment, and to the forfeiture of all his effects. His son published this sentence in Germany the year after, with remarks, which he addressed to the plenipotentiaries assembled then at Nimeguen to treat of peace : but these powers did not think proper to meddle with the affair. Wicquefort amused himself with continuing his history of the United Provinces, which he interspersed, as was natural for a man in his situation, with satirical strokes, not only against the prince of Orange, whom he personally hated, but also against the government and the court of justice who had condemned him. This work was published at the Hague in 1719, with this title, " L'Histoire des Provinces Unies des Pays-Bas, depuis le parfait établissement de cet Etat par la Paix de Munster:" it contains 1174 pages in folio, 246 of which were printed off when the author was thrown into prison.

He continued under restraint till 1679, and then contrived to escape by the assistance of one of his daughters, who ran the risk of her own liberty in order to procure his. By exchanging clothes with the lady, he went out, and took refuge at the court of the duke of Zell; from which he withdrew in 1681, disgusted, because that prince would not act with more zeal in procuring his sentence to be reversed at the Hague. It is not known what became of him after; but he is said to have died in 1682. His " L'Ambassadeur et ses Fonctions," printed at the Hague, 1681, in 2 vols. 4to, is his principal work, and is a very curious miscellany of facts and remarks, the latter not always profound, but often useful. He published also in 1677, during his imprisonment, " Mémoires touchant les Ambassadeurs et les Ministres publics." He translated some books of travels from the German into French ; and also from the Spanish, " L'Ambassade de D. Garcias de Silva Figueroa en Perse, contenant la Politique de ce grand Empire," &c. These works, which Wicquefort was at the pains to translate, are said to contain many curious and interesting things. [1]

WIDDRINGTON (Sir Thomas), an eminent lawyer, and speaker of the House of Commons, during the usurpation, was of an ancient family in Northumberland, and was educated partly at Oxford and partly at Cambridge. He afterwards entered of Gray's-inn, to study the law, in which he advanced with considerable rapidity, and was chosen recorder, first of Berwick-upon-Tweed, and secondly of York. He was knighted by Charles I. in 1639 at York, and, as recorder, congratulated his majesty both

[1] Niceron, vol. XXXIII.—Moreri.—Dict. Hist.

at York and Berwick, when he was on his way to be crowned king of Scotland. Both his addresses on this occasion are said to have been perfectly courtly and even fulsome, but he was soon to change his style as well as his opinions. Being returned member of parliament for Berwick, he became a warm advocate for the liberty then contested; avowed himself in religion, one of the independent sect, and took the covenant. In June 1647, he was so much a favourite with the parliament that they appointed him one of the commissioners of the great seal, which office he was to retain for one year, but held it till the king's death. The parliament also named him, in Oct. 1648, one in their call of serjeants, and soon after declared him king's serjeant. But far as he had gone with the usurping powers, he was by no means pleased with the commonwealth form of government, and immediately after the king's death, surrendered his office of keeper of the great seal, first upon the plea of bad health, and when that was not allowed, he set up some scruples of conscience. The parliament, however, as he continued to allow their authority, in requital of his former services, ordered that he should practice within the bar, and gave him a quarter's salary more than was due. His merit also recommended him to Cromwell, who heaped honours and great employments upon him. In April 1654, he was appointed a commissioner of the great seal and a commissioner of the treasury, for which he received a salary of 1000*l.*; and all his conscientious scruples seemed now at an end. In August of the same year, he was elected member of parliament for the city of York; and in the following year, became a committee-man for ejecting scandalous ministers in the north riding of that county.

In 1656, he represented both Northumberland and the city of York in parliament, and being chosen Speaker, was approved by Cromwell. His salary as speaker was 1829*l.* besides 5*l* for every private act, and the like sum for every stranger made a free denizen; when ill be appointed Whitelock for his deputy, as we noticed in the life of that statesman. In June 1658 he was appointed lord chief baron of the exchequer, and in Jan. 1660, one of the council of state and a commissioner of the great seal. He was returned both for Berwick and York in the parliament called in this year, and by some interest in the court of the restored king, Charles II. he was included in the call of serjeants, June 1, 1660. It was thought somewhat singular, and even mean that he should have submitted to this, as he had so long borne that title, had filled high offices in the state, was by no means a young man, and was possessed of a considerable fortune.    With regard to his fortune, however, he had suffered some loss.    He and Thomas Coghill, esq. had purchased the manor of Crayke, belonging to Durham cathedral, which was now ordered to revert to the church again. On the other hand, as some compensation, he was appointed temporal chancellor for life of that bishopric.    He died May 13, 1664, and was buried in the chancel of St. Giles's in the Fields, where a handsome monument against the north wall was placed by his four surviving daughters, ten years after, but it does not now exist.    Although sir Thomas had drank deep in the spirit of the times, we are told that his great abilities were only equalled by his integrity, and it was probably the latter which procured him favour after the restoration.    He married Frances, daughter of lord Fairfax, of Cameron, and sister of lord Fairfax, the parliamentary general; she died in 1649, and likewise lies buried in St. Giles's.

Mr. Noble, from whose " Memoirs of Cromwell" we have borrowed the above account, says that sir Thomas published in 1660 " Analecta *Eborensia,* or some remains of the ancient city of York," &c. but this is a mistake.    He only left a MS. account, under the title of " Analecta *Eboracentia :* or some remains of the ancient city of York, collected by a citizen of York."    Mr. Gough informs us that the above MS. was in the hands of Thomas Fairfax of Menston, esq. Sir Thomas began his researches in Charles I's time, and after the restoration offered to print this work, and dedicate it to the city of York, who seem to have refused it on account of the indifference he shewed to their interests when he represented them in Cromwell's parliament.    Upon this he is said to have expressly forbid his descendants to publish it.    Besides the Menston MS. there was another copy at Durham, in the Shaftoe family, one of whom married a daughter of the author    Mr. Drake had the use of one among the city records, and another from sir Richard Smyth of St. Edmund's Bury, which he thinks was prepared by the author himself for the press, and might have passed through different hands on the death of lord Fairfax, and dispersion of his effects.    Another copy, or perhaps one of those just mentioned, is among Mr. Gough's topographical treasures in the Bodleian library.    There are some of sir

Thomas's public speeches in Rushworth's "Collections," and others, according to Wood, were printed separately. [1]

WIDMANSTADIUS, JOHN. See JOHN ALBERTI, but ought to have been placed here, as we have since discovered by Chaufepie. His proper name was JOHN ALBERT WIDMANSTADT.

WIELAND (CHRISTOPHER MARTIN), a voluminous German writer who has been complimented with the title of the Voltaire of Germany, was born in 1733, at Biberach. Of his life no authentic account has, as far as we know, reached this country, but the following few particulars, gleaned from various sources, may perhaps be genuine. His father was a clergyman, who gave him a good education, and his attachment to the Muses discovered itself very early. At the age of fourteen, he wrote a poem on the destruction of Jerusalem. Two years after he was sent to Erfurt to study the sciences, where he became enamoured of Sophia de Gusterman, afterwards known by the name of Madame de la Roche. The youthful lovers swore eternal fidelity to each other, but Wieland's father thought proper to interrupt the connection, and sent his son to Tubingen to study law. For this he probably had little inclination, and employed most of his thoughts and time on poetry, producing at the age of eighteen an "Art of Love" in the manner of Ovid, and a poem "On the nature of things," in which we are told he combined the philosophy of Plato and Leibnitz. After this he appears to have devoted himself entirely to study and writing, and acquired considerable reputation as a poet of taste and fancy. For some time he appears to have resided in Swisserland, and in 1760 he returned to his native place, where he was appointed to the office of director of the chancery, and during his leisure hours wrote some of those works which completely established him in the opinion of his countrymen, as one of the greatest geniuses of the age, and honours were liberally bestowed upon him. The elector of Mentz made him professor of philosophy and polite literature at Erfurt, and he was soon after appointed tutor to the two young princes of Saxe Weimar; he was also aulic counsellor to the duke, who gave him a pension; and counsellor of government to the elector of Mentz. In 1765 he married a lady at Augs-

[1] Ath. Ox. vol. II.—Noble's Memoirs of Cromwell, vol. I. p. 427.—Gough's Topography, and Catalogue of the Library left to the Bodleian.

burgh, of whom he speaks so highly that we may conclude he had overcome or moderated his attachment to the object of his first love. In 1808 Bonaparte sent him the cross of the legion of honour, and after the battle of Jena, partook of a repast with Wieland, and, we are gravely told, "conversed with him at great length on the *folly* and *horrors* of war and on various projects for the establishment of a *perpetual peace!*" Wieland's latter days were employed in translating Cicero's Letters. A paralysis of the abdominal viscera was the prelude to his death, which took place at Weimar, in January 1813, in the eighty-first year of his age.

Wieland was the author of a prodigious number of works (of which there is an edition extending to forty-two volumes, quarto), both in prose and verse, poems of all kinds, and philosophical essays, dialogues, tales, &c. Of these, the "Oberon," (by Mr. Sotheby's elegant translation) the "Agathon," and some others, are not unknown, although they have never been very popular, in this country. In what estimation he is held in his own, may appear from one of the many panegyrics which German critics have pronounced on his merit: "No modern poet has written so much, or united so much deep sense with so much wit, such facility and sweetness. It may be truly said of him, that he has gone through the wide domain of human occupations, and knows all that happens in heaven and in earth. A blooming imagination and a creative wit; a deep, thinking, philosophical mind; fine and just sense, and a thorough acquaintance with both the moderns and ancients, are discernible in all his various writings. He knows how to make the most abstract metaphysical ideas sensible, by the magic of his eloquence; he can make himself of all times and all countries; he observes the customs of every country, and knows how to join truth with miracles, sensible with spirited imagery, and romance with the most profound morality. In the 'Agathon' he seems a Grecian; and in the 'Fairy Tales' a knight-errant, who wanders amidst fairies, vizards, and monsters. All his tales abound in portraits, comparisons, and parallels, taken from old and modern times, full of good sense and truth. The understanding, the heart, and the fancy, are equally satisfied. His verse is easy; there is not a word too much, or an idle false thought. He is as excellent in comical portraits as in the delineations of manners. The knowledge of Epicurus, the muses of frolic and satire, of romance and fairy land; the solidity of Locke, and the deep sense of Plato; Grecian eloquence, and Oriental luxuriance, what excites admiration in the writings of the best masters, are united in his immortal works." Such is the opinion of his countrymen; to which, however, it is our duty to add, that in many of his works the freethinking-system is predominant, and that the moral tendency of others is very doubtful. [1]

WIER (JOHN), an able physician, called in Latin WIERUS, and sometimes PISCINARIUS, was born in 1515, at Grave, on the Meuse, in the duchy of Brabant, of a noble family. He studied philosophy under the famous Henry Cornelius Agrippa; made several voyages even to Africa, but returned again into Europe, and was physician to the duke of Cleves during thirty years. Wier had so strong a constitution, that he frequently passed three or four days without eating or drinking, and found not the least inconvenience from it. He died suddenly Feb. 4, 1588, at Tecklenbourg, a German town in the circle of Westphalia, in the seventy-third year of his age. His works were printed at Amsterdam, 1660, one volume, quarto, which includes his treatise "De Prestigiis et Incantationibus," translated into French, by James Grevin 1577, 8vo. He maintains in this work, that those accused of witchcraft were persons whose brain was disordered by melancholy, whence they imagined falsely, and without any reason, that they had dealings with the devil, and were therefore deserving of pity rather than of punishment. It seems strange that, with this opinion, Wier should in other instances give the readiest credit to fabulous stories. The above mentioned book made much noise. [2]

WIGAND (JOHN), a learned divine of the reformed religion, was born at Mansfeld in Upper Saxony in 1523. His parents, who were of the middle rank, perceiving his love of learning, gave him a good education at school, whence he was sent to the university of Wirtemberg, where he studied the arts and languages for about three years; attending, at the same time, the lectures of Luther and Melancthon. He became also acquainted with other contributors to the reformation, as Cruciger, Justus Jonas, &c.

[1] Dict. Hist —Gent. Mag. &c. &c.
[2] Eloy Dict. Hist. de Medicine.—Dict. Hist.

and heard the Greek lectures of Vitus. In 1541, by the advice of his tutors and friends, he went to Noriberg, where he was made master of St. Lawrence-school, and taught there for three years; but being desirous of adding to his own knowledge, under the ablest instructors, he returned to Wirtemberg again. There he commenced M. A. before he was twenty-two years old, and begun the study of divinity, which he engaged in with great assiduity, until the events of the war dispersed the students of this university. He then was invited to his native place, Mansfeld, where he was ordained, and is said to have been the first who was ordained after the establishment of the Protestant religion. He soon became a very useful and popular preacher, and on the week-days read lectures to the youth in logic and philosophy. While here, at the request of the superintendent, John Spangenberg, he wrote a confutation of Sidonius's popish catechism, which was afterwards printed both in Latin and Dutch. He wrote also a confutation of George Major, who held that a man is justified by faith, but not saved, &c. He was one of those who strongly opposed the Interim.

His great delight, in the way of relaxation from his more serious engagements, was in his garden, in which he formed a great collection of curious plants. Haller mentions his publication " De succino Borussico, de Alce, de Herbis Borussicis, et de Sale," 1590, 8vo, which Freher and other biographers speak of as three distinct publications. In 1553 he was chosen superintendant of Magdeburg, but the count Mansfeld and his countrymen strongly opposed his removal from them, yet at last, in consequence of the application of the prince of Anhalt, consented to it. At Magdeburg, by his preaching and writings he greatly promoted the reformed religion, and had a considerable hand in the voluminous collection, entitled " The Magdeburg Centuries," which Sturmius used to say had four excellent qualities, truth, research, order, and perspicuity. In 1560, on the foundation of the university of Jena by the elector of Saxony, he was solicited by his highness to become professor of divinity, and performed the duties of that office until some angry disputes between Illyricus and Strigelius inclined him to resign. He was after a short stay at Magdeburg, chosen, in 1562, to be superintendant at Wismar. He now took his degree of doctor in divinity at the university of Rostock, and remained at Wismar seven years, at the end of which a negociation was set on foot for his return to Jena, where he was made professor of divinity and superintendant. Five years after he was again obliged to leave that university, when the elector Augustus succeeded his patron the elector William. On this he went to the duke of Brunswick who entertained him kindly, and he was soon after invited to the divinity-professorship of Konigsberg, and in two years was appointed bishop there. He died 1587, in the sixty-fourth year of his age. He wrote a prodigious number of works, principally commentaries on different parts of the Bible, and treatises on the controversies with the popish writers. He was esteemed a man of great learning, a profound theologian and no less estimable in private life. He ranks high among the promoters of the reformation in Germany.[1] .

WILCOCKS (JOSEPH), a late amiable and ingenious writer, was the only son of Dr. Joseph Wilcocks, of whom we have the following particulars. He was born in 1673, and was educated at Magdalen-college, Oxford, where he formed a lasting friendship with Mr. Boulter, afterwards primate of Ireland ; Mr. Wilcocks was chosen a demy of his college at the same election with Boulter and Addison, and from the merit and learning of the elect, this was commonly called by Dr. Hough, president of the college, " the *golden* election." He was ordained by bishop Sprat, and while a young man, went chaplain to the English factory at Lisbon ; where, as in all the other scenes of his life, he acquired the public love and esteem, and was long remembered with grateful respect. While here, such was his sympathy and his courage, that although he had not then had the small-pox, yet when that dreadful malady broke out in the factory, he constantly attended the sick and dying. On his return to England, he was appointed chaplain to George I. and preceptor to his royal granddaughters, the children of George II. He also had a prebend of Westminster, and in 1721 was made bishop of Gloucester, the episcopal palace of which he repaired, which for a considerable time before had stood uninhabited; and thus he became the means of fixing the residence of future bishops in that see. In 1731 he was translated to the bishopric of Rochester, with which he held the deanry of Westminster. Seated in this little diocese, he declined

[1] Melchior Adam.—Freheri Theatrum —Saxii Onomast.

any higher promotion, even that of the archbishopric of York, frequently using the memorable expression of bishop Fisher, one of his predecessors, "Though this my wife be poor, I must not think of changing her for one more opulent." The magnificence of the west-front of Westminster-abbey, during his being dean, is recorded as a splendid monument of his zeal for promoting public works, in suitable proportion to his station in life. He would doubtless have been equally zealous in adorning and enlarging his cathedral at Rochester, had there been ground to hope for national assistance in that undertaking; but its episcopal revenues were very inadequate to the expence. He was constantly resident upon his diocese, and from the fatigue of his last Visitation there, he contracted the illness which terminated his life by a gradual decay, March 9, 1756, aged eighty-three. He was buried in a vault in Westminster-abbey, under the consistory court, which he had built the year before, by permission from the Chapter. His son erected a monument for him next to that of Dr. Pearce. He married Jane, the daughter of John Milner, esq. sometime his Britannic majesty's consul at Lisbon, who died in her twenty-eighth year. By her he had Joseph, the more immediate subject of the present article.

Mr. Joseph Wilcocks was born in Dean's-yard, Westminster, Jan. 4, 1723, during the time his father was bishop of Gloucester, and a prebendary of Westminster. In 1736 he was admitted upon the foundation at Westminster-school, whence he was elected to Christ-church, Oxford in 1740, and proceeded regularly to the degree of M. A. in 1747. He very early distinguished himself at college, and obtained the second of three prizes before the end of the year he entered, the first of them being gained by his friend and contemporary, Mr. Markham, afterwards archbishop of York. As his estate was considerable he chose no particular profession, but devoted his property to various acts of beneficence, and his time to study. He was particularly attentive to biblical learning, and to every thing that could promote the cause of piety. His humility and diffidence were carried rather to an extreme; and from the same excess in the sensibility of his conscientious feelings, he forebore to act as a magistrate, having for a short time undertaken it as a justice, in the county of Berks. Having in early life paid his addresses to a lady whom his father deemed it imprudent for him to marry in point of circumstances, he submitted to parental authority, but continued unmarried ever after.

His mode of life, however, though exemplary in the highest degree, in point of conduct, is not one of those that furnish many or striking events; and we cannot better hold forth that example to the imitation of others, than in the following artless narrative of one of his old servants. "One of his very amiable qualities was to consider himself as a citizen of the world, and mankind in general as his brethren and friends; consequently, he endeavoured to do them all the good in his power. I think I may also safely say, the great rule of his life and conduct was to be a true disciple and follower of all the beneficent actions of our Saviour, and to interweave his examples into his daily exercise and practice. He used to rise early, and was a very great œconomist of his time; labouring to keep a most exact account of all his domestic concerns, and every thing that belonged to his receipts and expenditure. Even his numerous gifts and charities, I believe, were daily committed to paper, and all looked over in the evening, and balanced, noting every error and deficiency; and if he did not perceive he had done one or more acts of charity and beneficence, he thought he had lost a day. He was the most dutiful and affectionate son, the most kind nephew, cousin, or relation to all who stood in any degree of kindred. To servants, workmen, and tenants, the most gentle and beneficent; and to his poor neighbours an affectionate father, paying for schooling for their children, and even erecting schools, which is, perhaps, too well known to require mentioning. When travelling, he would inquire at the inns, who was in sickness or necessity in the place, leaving money for their relief. He frequently released debtors from prison, and had great charity to beggars. He frequently sent medical assistance to the sick, and gave large sums to hospitals; when abroad, he gave large sums also to poor convents, and to the necessitous of all countries and religions. He was always ready to assist every increase or improvement of learning, witness the very large and laborious share he took in assisting the collation of the Hebrew text of the Bible, by opening many of the foreign libraries in Europe, through his interest and labour, and employing professors to collate at his own expence. His humanity to the brute creation was very great, and his tenderness even to insects. He preserved a reverential respect for the place of his nativity, for the places where he had received his education, and for those who had been companions of his youth; likewise for the memory of those who had been in any way instrumental in forming his morals and perfecting his learning; and this was preserved even to their friends and posterity."

These, and many other acts of beneficence, both of a public and private nature, the latter always performed with the utmost delicacy, are specified at large in the very interesting memoirs prefixed to the last edition of his " Roman Conversations," by Mr. Bickerstaff, the successor of Mr. Brown, the bookseller, to whom he bequeathed that edition, with an express provision, " to indemnify him from any loss which might be incurred by the expences of the first edition." His classical taste, contracted by long reading, led him to Italy, and it appears to have been in the once " metropolis of the world," that he laid the foundation of the " Roman Conversations," his principal work, which may justly be recommended to the young, and indeed to readers in general. In it he separates the truth of Roman history from the errors which disfigure it, bestowing just praise on the real patriots of Rome, and equally just censure on those whose patriotism was only feigned ; and distinguishing between the insidious arts of demagogues, and the integrity of true friends to the public. In nice investigations of character, he appears to be free from prejudice, attentive to truth, and often strikingly original in his remarks. The chief defect is a want of regard to style, and a prolixity of remark and digression, which perhaps will be more easily pardoned by the old than the young, for whom the work was chiefly calculated ; yet it is a work which cannot fail to be perused by every student of Roman history with the greatest advantage. It is calculated to excite religious and moral reflections on that history, and to adapt and direct the study of it to the best and wisest purposes of a Christian education.

In the " Carmina Quadragesimalia" are many good verses written by Mr. Wilcocks, who also was the compiler of the " Sacred Exercises," now in use at Westminster-school. We are not informed of any other publication from his pen, except a little piece in the Philosophical Transactions, vol. liii. entitled " An Account of some subterraneous Apartments, with Etruscan Inscriptions and paintings, discovered at Civita Turchino, in Italy." These, we are told, were explored as here described, at the sole expence of our author.

Mr. Wilcocks died, of repeated attacks of the palsy, Dec. 23, 1791, at the close of his sixty-ninth year. He left behind him the "Roman Conversations" prepared for the press. They were composed by him, indeed, at an early period of his present majesty's reign; but modest diffidence would not allow him to publish them in his life-time, otherwise than by printing off a few copies, which he distributed among his intimate friends. With the hope, however, that the work might be more extensively useful, and particularly to younger minds, he gave directions that it should appear soon after his decease. Accordingly, in May 1792, the first volume was published; but, in conse-quence of a written injunction left by the worthy author, the second volume did not come out until a year after. In 1797, a new and much corrected edition was published by Mr. Bickerstaff, with memoirs of the author, to which we are indebted for the preceding sketch. Many particu-lars of Mr. Wilcocks's life are evidently, although under some disguise, interwoven in his "Roman Conversations." [1]

WILD (HENRY), a tailor, who, from an extraordinary love of study, became a professor of the Oriental lan-guages, was born in the city of Norwich about 1684, where he was educated at a grammar-school till he was almost qualified for the university; but his friends, wanting for-tune and interest to maintain him there, bound him ap-prentice to a tailor, with whom he served seven years, and afterwards worked seven years more as a journeyman. About the end of the last seven years, he was seized with a fever and ague, which continued with him two or three years, and at last reduced him so low as to disable him from working at his trade. In this situation he amused himself with some old books of controversial divinity, in which he found great stress laid on the Hebrew original of several texts of scripture; and, though he had almost lost the learning he had obtained at school, his strong de-sire of knowledge excited him to attempt to make himself master of that language. He was at first obliged to make use of an English Hebrew grammar and lexicon; but, by

---

[1] Memoirs as above.—Brit. Crit. vol. II. for 1793.—Manning and Bray's Hist. of Surrey, vol. I.

degrees, recovered the knowledge of the Latin tongue, which he had learned at school. On the recovery of his health, he divided his time between his business and his studies, which last employed the greatest part of his nights. Thus, self-taught, and assisted only by his great genius, he, by dint of continual application, added to the knowledge of the Hebrew that of all or most of the oriental languages, but still laboured in obscurity, till at length he was accidentally discovered. The worthy Dr. Prideaux, dean of Norwich, being offered some Arabic manuscripts in parchment, by a bookseller of that city, thinking, perhaps, that the price demanded for them was too great, declined buying them; but, soon after, Mr. Wild hearing of them, purchased them; and the dean, on calling at the shop and inquiring for the manuscripts, was informed of their being sold. Chagrined at this disappointment, he asked of the bookseller the name and profession of the person who had bought them; and, being told he was a tailor, he bad him instantly to run and fetch them, if they were not cut in pieces to make measures: but he was soon relieved from his fears by Mr. Wild's appearance with the manuscripts, though, on the dean's inquiring whether he would part with them, he answered in the negative. The dean then asked hastily what he did with them: he replied, that he read them. He was desired to read them, which he did. He was then bid to render a passage or two into English, which he readily performed, and with great exactness. Amazed at this, the dean, partly at his own expence, and partly by a subscription raised among persons whose inclinations led them to this kind of knowledge, sent him to Oxford; where, though he was never a member of the university, he was by the dean's interest admitted into the Bodleian library, and employed for some years in translating or making extracts out of Oriental manuscripts, and thus bad adieu to his needle. This appears to have been some time before 1718. At Oxford, he was known by the name of the Arabian tailor. He constantly attended the library all the hours it was open, and, when it was shut, employed most of his leisure-time in teaching the Oriental languages to young gentlemen, at the moderate price of half a guinea a lesson, except for the Arabic, for which he had a guinea, and his subscriptions for teaching amounted to no more than 20 or 30l. a year. Unhappily for him, the branch of learning in which he excelled was cultivated but by few; and the reverend Mr. Gagnier, a Frenchman, skilled in the Oriental tongues, was in possession of all the favours the university could bestow in this way, being recommended by the heads of colleges to instruct young gentlemen, and employed by the professors of those languages to read public lectures in their absence.

Mr. Wild's person was thin and meagre, and his stature moderately tall. He had an extraordinary memory; and, as his pupils frequently invited him to spend an evening with them, he would often entertain them with long and curious details out of the Roman, Greek, and Arabic, histories. His morals were good; he was addicted to no vice, but was sober, temperate, modest, and diffident of himself, without the least tincture of vanity. About 1720 he removed to London, where he spent the remainder of his life under the patronage of Dr. Mead. When he died is not known, but in 1734, which is supposed to have been after his death, was published his translation from the Arabic of " Mahomet's Journey to Heaven," which is the only piece of his that was ever printed. The writer of his life informs us that it was once suspected that he was a Jesuit in disguise, but for this there appears to have been no foundation. Before he went to Oxford, we have the following notice respecting him in a letter from Dr. Turner to Dr. Charlett, dated Norwich, March 4, 1714. " A taylor of this town, of about thirty years of age, has within seven years, mastered seven languages, Latin, Greek, Hebrew, Chaldaic, Syriac, Arabic, and Persic. Mr. Professor Ockley being here since Christmas has examined him, and given him an ample testimonial in writing of his skill in the Oriental languages. Our dean also thinks him very extraordinary. But he is very poor, and his landlord lately seized a Polyglot Bible (which he had made shift to purchase) for rent. But there is care taken to clear his debts, and if a way could be thought of to make him more useful, I believe we could get a subscription towards part of his maintenance." This we find by the above narrative was accordingly done.[1]

WILD (ROBERT), a nonconformist divine, poet, and wit, was born at St. Ives in Huntingdonshire in 1609, and was educated at the university of Cambridge. In 1642 he

[1] Gent. Mag. vol. XXV.—" Letters by Eminent Persons," 3 vols. 8vo. 1811.

was created bachelor of divinity at Oxford, and, probably had the degree of doctor there also, as he was generally called Dr. Wild. In 1646 he was appointed rector of Aynho in Northamptonshire, in the room of Dr. Longman, ejected by the parliamentary visitors; and on this occasion Calamy's editor gives us one of his witticisms. He and another divine had preached for the living, and Wild being asked whether he or his competitor had got it, he answered "We have divided it; I have got the AY, and he the NO." Wood says he was "a fat, jolly, and boon presbyterian," but Calamy asserts that those who knew him commended him not only for his facetiousness, but also his strict temperance and sobriety; and he was serious, where seriousness was wanted. He was ejected from Aynho at the restoration. He died at Oundle, in Northamptonshire in 1679, aged seventy. His works afford a curious mixture. 1. "The tragedy of Christopher Love at Tower-hill," Lond. 1660, a poem in one sheet 4to. 2. "Iter Boreale, attempting something upon the successful and matchless march of the L. Gen. George Monk from Scotland to London," ibid. 1660, 4to, in ridicule of the republican party. This was at that time a favourite subject, and Wood mentions three other *Iter Boreale's* by Eades, Corbet, and Master. 3. "A poem on the imprisonment of Mr. Edmund Calamy in Newgate," 1662, printed on a broad sheet, which produced two similar broadsheets in answer, the one "Antiboreale, an answer to a lewd piece of poetry upon Mr. Calamy, &c." the other "Hudibras on Calamy's imprisonment and Wild's poetry." These, with his Iter Boreale, and other pieces of a similar cast and very indifferent poetry, but with occasional flashes of genuine humour, were published together in 1668 and 1670. Wood mentions "The Benefice, a comedy," written in his younger years, but not printed till 1689. Wood adds, that there "had like to have been" a poetical war between Wild and Flaxman, but how it terminated he knows not. Wild had the misfortune to have some of his poems printed along with some of lord Rochester's. He has a few sermons extant.[1]

WILDBORE (CHARLES), an ingenious mathematician, was born in Nottinghamshire, and educated at the Blue

---

[1] Ath. Ox. vol. II.—Calamy by Palmer.—Restituta, vol. I. where is an extract from his "Iter Boreale."

Coat school of Nottingham. Of his early history we have little information, but it appears that he kept an academy at Bingham, in the above county, for some years, and afterwards was preferred to the living of Sulney, where he died at an advanced age, Oct. 30, 1802. In his latter days he had a remarkably strong and retentive memory, as a proof of which, he told a friend that he made a common practice of solving the most abstruse questions in the mathematics without ever committing a single figure, &c. to paper till finished; and, upon its being observed " how much pen and paper might assist him!" he replied, " I have to thank God for a most retentive memory; and so long as it is enabled to exercise its functions, it shall not have any assistance from art." When his mind was occupied in close study, he always walked to and fro in an obscure part of his garden, where he could neither see nor be seen of any one, and frequently paced, in this manner, several miles in a day.

Though so skilful in mathematics, he did not favour the world with any separate publication bearing his own name, and often used the signature of Eumenes; but he poured much light upon the regions of science through the medium of those periodical publications which are chiefly devoted to mathematical researches. He contributed a number of valuable articles to Martin's " Miscellaneous Correspondence," between the years 1755 and 1763, particularly an excellent paper, in which he made it his business to prove that the moon's orbit was always concave, with respect to the sun. He began his contributions to the " Gentleman's Diary" in 1759, when that performance was conducted by Mr. T. Peat. In the same year he commenced his communications to the " Ladies' Diary," which was edited by professor Simpson, of Woolwich. In 1773 and 1774 he carried on a spirited but amicable controversy, in Dr. Hutton's " Miscellanea Mathematica," with Mr. John Dawson, of Sedbergh, a gentleman well known at Cambridge, and the tutor of many pupils who have been senior-wranglers of that university. The subject of this controversy was " the velocity of water issuing from a vessel when put in motion." In 1780 his friend Dr. Hutton procured for him the editorship of the " Gentleman's Diary," an honour which he had long wished to attain, and he was highly gratified by the circumstance. From that period his valuable communications to this publication always appeared under the character of Eumenes, and those in the Ladies' Diary under that of Amicus. The prize-question in the Diary for 1803 is by Mr. Wildbore, and is a very curious and intricate question in the diophantine algebra.

At an early period of life he was a reviewer of the Philosophical Transactions, in which trust, as well as several others committed to his care and inspection, he so well acquitted himself, that he was solicited to become a member of the royal society; but this honour he very modestly declined, in a letter to the then president, remarking, amongst other things, " that his ambition had never led him to visit the metropolis; and if he accepted the honour of being one of that learned society, he should wish, not to be a passive, but an active member; to be which he supposed that it would be necessary for him to come forward in the world, which he had not the least inclination to do, preferring his village retirement infinitely beyond the ' busy hum of men,' and to be styled ' the humble village pastor,' without the addition of the initials F. R. S." He was intimately acquainted, by correspondence, with many learned men (for he scarcely ever saw any of them), particularly with Dr. Hutton, for whom he entertained a very high esteem. [1]

WILDE, or WYLD (JOHN), a lawyer, and a very prominent character during the usurpation, was the eldest son of a lawyer, as his father is said to have been serjeant George Wilde of Droitwich, in Worcestershire. He was of Baliol college, Oxford, and in 1610, when he took his degree of M. A. was a student in the Inner Temple. Of this society he became Lent reader 6 Car. I. afterwards a serjeant at law, one of the commissioners of the great seal in 1643, and in Oct. 1648, chief baron of the exchequer, and one of the council of state. In 1641 he drew up the impeachment against the bishops, and presented it to the House of Lords, and was prime manager not only in that, but on the trial of archbishop Laud. " He was the same also," says Wood, " who, upon the command, or rather desire, of the great men sitting at Westminster, did condemn to death at Winchester one captain John Burley, for causing a drum to be beat up for God and king Charles, at Newport, in the Isle of Wight, in order to rescue his captive

---

[1] Gent. Mag. vol. LXXII.

king in 1647." Wood adds, that after the execution of Burley, Wilde was rewarded with 1000*l.* out of the privy purse at Derby-house, and had the same sum for saving the life of major Edmund Rolph, who had a design to have murdered the king. When Oliver became protector " he retired and acted not," but after Richard Cromwell had been deposed he was restored to the exchequer. On the restoration he was of course obliged to resign again, and lived in retirement at Hampstead, where he died about 1669, and was buried at Wherwill, in Hampshire, the seat of Charles lord Delawar, who had married his daughter. Wilde married Anne, daughter of sir Thomas Harry, of Tonge castle, serjeant at law and baronet, who died in 1624, aged only sixteen, " being newly delivered of her first born." She lies buried in Tonge church, in Staffordshire.

Such are the particulars Wood has given of this lawyer, and they are in general supported by Clarendon and other contemporary authorities, and attempted to be contradicted only by Oldmixon and Neal. Oldmixon's evidence will not be thought to weigh much against Clarendon's. Neal calls him "A great lawyer, and of unblemished morals; and after the restoration of king Charles II. was made lord chief baron, and esteemed a grave' and venerable judge." But it is grossly improbable that such a man should have been thus promoted, and it is besides expressly contrary to fact, for sir Orlando Bridgeman was chief baron at the trial of the regicides, and was succeeded by judge Hale. It was the rump parliament only who bestowed the honour on Wilde.

Neal, perhaps, we know others have, confounded his favourite hero, serjeant Wilde, which was his only legitimate title, with sir William Wild, who was recorder of London in 1659, created a baronet Sept. 13, 1660, appointed king's serjeant Nov. 10, 1661, and made one of the justices of the common pleas in 1668. He was advanced to be a justice of the court of king's bench Jan. 21, 1672. In 1661 and 1674 he published "Yelverton's Reports," in French. He died Nov. 23, 1679, leaving issue sir Felix Wilde, of St. Clement Danes, in Middlesex, bart. The title is now extinct. Sir William Wilde was indeed " a grave and venerable judge," and it must not be forgot to his honour, that, because he disbelieved the evidence of the perjured Bedloe, in the popish plot, he was deprived of his office a few months before his death. [1]

WILKES (JOHN), a very singular political character in the early part of the present reign, was born Oct. 17, 1727, o. s. in St. John's street, Clerkenwell, where his father, Nathaniel, carried on in a very extensive way the trade of a distiller, and lived in the true style of ancient English hospitality, to which both he and his lady were always particularly attentive. Their house was consequently much frequented, particularly by many characters of distinguished rank in the commercial and literary world. It was in such society that their son John imbibed that taste for letters which he continued to cultivate through life. His education, therefore, though liberal, was domestic; and, though not severe, yet sufficiently sober. His philosophy (that of enjoying the world, and passing laughingly through it) was all his own, and adopted in compliance with his view of human nature. And this he was himself very willing to have believed. His parents (one of them at least) were not of the church of England; and Mr. Wilkes having passed his school years partly at Hertford, and partly in Buckinghamshire, was sent, not to either of our English universities, but with a private tutor, to the university of Leyden, where his talents attracted much notice.

In 1749 he married Miss Mead, heiress of the Meads of Buckinghamshire, from which marriage probably originated his connection with that county. This lady was about ten years older than himself, that is, about thirty-two. Their dispositions, we are told, were perfectly dissimilar, yet he treated her for a time with decent respect. Afterwards he became quite alienated from her, and a final separation took place in 1757. So depraved were his morals, and so destitute was he of a sense of honour, that amidst the distresses which his loose pleasures brought upon him, he endeavoured to defraud this lady of the annuity stipulated in the articles of separation; but this was prevented by a law-suit. In April 1754, he offered himself as a candidate to represent in parliament the borough of Berwick, and addressed the electors in terms not ill according with that political spirit which afterwards marked his public conduct. He was not, however, successful, but

[1] Ath. Ox. vol. I.—Gent. Mag. vols. LII. LIII. and LIV.—Neal's Puritans, and Grey's Examination, vol. III.—Heylyn's Examen Historicum.—Clarendon. —Burnet's Own Times.

in July 1757, was elected burgess for Aylesbury, and was again chosen at the general election in 1761 for the same place. Before this period he had formed connections with various men of rank, but not of the purest character for morals, who seem to have admitted him into their society as a companion who was not likely to lay them under any restraint. He had, however, formed some connections of a better stamp. It appears that as early as 1754 he was known to lord Temple, and to Mr. Pitt, afterwards lord Chatham.

In 1762 he began to engage in political discussion. In March of that year he published "Observations on the papers relative to the rupture with Spain, laid before both houses of parliament on Friday, Jan. 29, 1762." As much of his information on this subject was supplied by lord Temple (who, with Mr. Pitt, had retired from the cabinet in consequence of a negative being put upon their proposition for an immediate war with Spain) the success of this pamphlet is little to be wondered at. As he did not put his name to it, it was ascribed to Dr. Douglas, or Mr. Mauduit, by the sly suggestions of the real author. In the beginning of June following he commenced his celebrated paper called "The North Briton." The purpose of this was ostensibly to expose the errors of the then ministry, and hold them up to public contempt, but really, to give the author that sort of consequence that might lead to advantages which his extravagant mode of living had by this time rendered necessary. We have his own word that he had determined to take advantage of the times and to make his fortune, and that he soon formed an idea of what would silence and satisfy him. "If government," says he, "means peace or friendship with me, I then breathe no longer hostility. And, between ourselves, if they would send me ambassador to Constantinople, it is all I should wish."— Again, "It depends on them (the ministry) whether Mr. Wilkes is their friend or their enemy. If he starts as the latter, he will lash them with scorpions, and they are already prepared; I wish, however, we may be friends; and I had rather follow the plan I had marked out in my letter from Geneva," alluding to the embassy to Constantinople. In a subsequent letter he says, "If the ministers do not find employment for me, I am disposed to find employment for them." In these extracts we have anticipated the order of time, for they were written in 1764, when he was an exile, but they are necessarily introduced here to unfold the real character of Mr. Wilkes, and to determine to what species of patriots he belonged. We see at the same time here how very near the most popular character of the age was to dropping into comparative obscurity, and at what a cheap rate the ministry might have averted the hostility of Wilkes, and all its consequences, which we have always considered as more hurtful than beneficial to his country.

In the mean time he went on publishing his "North Britons," which, although written in an acute and popular style, and unquestionably very galling to ministers, had not produced any great commotion, nor seemed likely to answer the author's purpose. Ministerial writers were employed to write against him, and in this way a literary warfare might have gone on for years, without any of the consequences he expected. One duel, indeed, he had with lord Talbot, but neither party was hurt, and Wilkes was not benefited. At length, therefore, he began to think he had been too tame, or that ministers were become too callous, and with a view to a provocation, which could not fail to irritate, he made a rude attack on his majesty in No. 45 of the "North Briton," which appeared on the 23d of April 1763, and on the morning of the 30th Mr. Wilkes was served by a king's messenger with a *general warrant*, in consequence of which he was on the same morning conveyed to the Tower. That " a warrant to apprehend and seize, together with their papers, the authors, printers, and publishers of a work," without naming who those authors, printers, and publishers were even suspected to be, has an appearance of illegality, cannot be denied. But in justice to the secretaries of state who signed it, it should be remembered, that for a hundred years the practice of their office had been to issue such ; and that in so doing they did no more than what precedents seemed to justify. That they did not, however, in this case, act wisely the event shewed. Upon his commitment to the Tower, an application was instantly made to the court of common pleas for his habeas corpus, and he was brought up on the 3d of May. On the 4th he was dismissed from his situation as colonel of the Buckinghamshire militia. On the 6th the validity of his warrant of commitment was argued, his plea of privilege was allowed, and he was in consequence discharged. He immediately erected a printing-press in his house in George-street, published a narrative of the transactions in which he had been engaged, and renewed the publication of the " North Briton." He visited Paris a few months after, and was there challenged, in the month of August, by a captain Forbes, who, standing forth as the champion of Scotland, asked satisfaction of him, as the editor and conductor of the " North Briton," for the calumnies heaped upon his native country. Mr. Wilkes behaved on this occasion with much moderation, and declared himself no prize-fighter. Being again urged, however, though in terms. of politeness, he half complied, but being in the mean while put under an arrest, he pledged his honour not to fight on French ground. When set at liberty he proceeded to Menin, and there awaited his challenger, but no meeting took place.

The winter now advancing, Mr. Wilkes returned to England; previous to the opening of parliament, and resumed his labours in the " North Briton," which soon after involved him in another duel with Mr. Martin, member for Camelford, and late secretary to the treasury. In this Wilkes received a dangerous wound in the groin ; but appeared in parliament on the first day of the session, and had risen to address the chair of the speaker on the subject of his privilege, as a member of that house, having been violated. It had usually been considered as the established custom of parliament to enter upon the discussion of breaches of privileges before all other matters. In this instance the custom was overruled, and a message from the sovereign was conveyed to the commons, informing them, that J. Wilkes, esq. was the author of a most seditious and dangerous paper, and acquainting them with the measures which had been resorted to by the servants of the crown. The house, the proofs of the libel being entered upon, proceeded to vote, that No. 45 of the " North Britain" was, as it had been represented to be, a false, scandalous, and malicious libel, &c. and it was ordered to be burnt by the common hangman. A day having been appointed for the hearing of Mr. Wilkes's defence against the charge of being the author of the libel, he thought it proper to acquaint the house of the incapacity occasioned by his wound, and further time was in consequence allowed him. The house, however, suspecting some unnecessary delay, appointed Dr. Heberden and Mr. Hawkins to attend him, in addition to his own physician and surgeon ; and further, ordered them to report the state of his health. Mr. Wilkes politely rejected the offer of their visit. The house, he said, had desired them to visit him, but had forgotten to desire him to receive them, which he most certainly should not. At the same time, in vindication of the professional gentlemen whom he himself had employed, he sent for Dr. Duncan, one of his majesty's physicians in ordinary, and Mr. Myddleton, one of his majesty's serjeant-surgeons, humorously telling them, that as the House of Commons thought it fit that he should be watched, he himself thought two Scotchmen most proper for his spies. About a week after he suddenly withdrew to France; a retreat which prudence rendered very necessary, his circumstances being very much involved.

From Paris, where he sought an asylum, he certified to the speaker of the House of Commons, by the signatures of the physician of the king of France, and other gentlemen, his confinement to his room, and the impossibility, from his state of health, of his venturing to undertake the journey back to England. In the mean time, although the House of Commons had neglected his complaint of privilege, he derived his first considerable triumph from the verdict found for him in the court of common pleas. He had early brought his action against Robert Wood, esq. the under secretary of state, for the seizure of his papers, as the supposed author of the "North Briton." It was tried before a special jury on the 6th of December, and 1000l. damages were given. The charge to the jury, delivered by lord chief justice Pratt, concluded thus: "This warrant is unconstitutional, illegal, and absolutely void; it is a general warrant, directed to four messengers, to take up any persons, without naming or describing them with any certainty, and to apprehend them together with their papers. If it be good, a secretary of state can delegate and depute any of the messengers, or any even from the lowest of the people, to take examinations, to commit, or to release, and do every act which the highest judicial officers the law knows, can do or order. There is no order in our law-books that mentions these kinds of warrants, but several that in express words condemn them. Upon the maturest consideration, I am bold to say, that this warrant is illegal; but I am far from wishing a matter of this consequence to rest solely on my opinion; I am only one of twelve, whose opinions I am desirous should be taken in this matter, and I am very willing to allow myself to be the meanest of the twelve. There is also a still higher court, before which this matter may be canvassed, and whose determination is final ; and here I cannot help observing the happiness of our constitution in admitting these appeals, in consequence of which, material points are determined on the most mature consideration, and with the greatest solemnity. To this admirable delay of the law (for in this case the law's delay may be styled admirable) I believe it is chiefly owing that we possess the best digested, and most excellent body of law which any nation on the face of the globe, whether ancient or modern, could ever boast. If these higher jurisdictions should declare my opinion erroneous, I submit, as will become me, and kiss the rod ; but I must say, I shall always consider it as a rod of iron for the chastisement of the people of Great Britain."

We have already mentioned in our account of lord Camden how very popular this decision made him throughout the kingdom, and the same enthusiasm made it be considered as a complete triumph on the part of Mr. Wilkes, who, however, perhaps, thought differently of it, conscious that he had other battles to fight in which he might not be so ably supported. On Jan. 19, 1764, he was expelled from the House of Commons ; and on Feb. 21 was convicted in the court of King's Bench for re-publishing the " North Briton, No. 45," and also upon a second indictment, for printing and publishing an " Essay on Woman." This was an obscene poem which he printed at his private press, but can scarcely be said to have published it, as he printed only a very small number of copies (about twelve) to give away to certain friends. The great offence was (and this was complained of in the House of Lords), that he had annexed the name of bishop Warburton to this infamous poem, and it was hoped, by the ministry, that holding Mr. Wilkes forth as a profligate, might cure the public of that dangerous and overpowering popularity they were about to honour him with. But this was another of their erroneous calculations. The populace at this time, at least the populace of London, were more anxious about general warrants, which might affect one in ten thousand, than about morals, which are the concern of all ; and even some of the better sort could see no immediate connection between Wilkes's moral and political offences.

In the mean time being found guilty on both informations, and neglecting to make any personal appearance, when called upon to receive the judgment of the court of King's Bench, he was, towards the close of the year, outlawed. He had again repaired to France, whence he addressed a letter, in defence of his conduct, to the electors of Aylesbury, which, like all his publications, was read with much avidity. It was in this year (1764), and when at Paris, that he addressed those letters to his friends, of which we have already given extracts, to prove that, whatever his popularity, he had no very high expectations from it, and had sense enough to perceive that his deranged circumstances could be restored only by making peace with administration. His terms, we have seen, were not exorbitant, and might probably have been agreed to, had they been known, which it is doubtful whether they were.

The years 1765 and 1766 he passed in a journey through Italy. But as he knew too well the nature of the multitude, not to be aware that a long retirement would soon cause him to be forgotten, even by those whose sympathy in his favour was most warm, when the duke of Grafton became minister, towards the end of 1766, Mr. Wilkes solicited, in a letter to him, the clemency of his sovereign; and finding his address but faintly listened to, he, in a second letter to the same nobleman, again called the public attention to his case. He endeavoured also to keep his name alive, by publishing in 1767, "A collection of the genuine Papers, Letters, &c. in the Case of J. Wilkes, late member for Aylesbury in the county of Bucks; *à Paris, chez J. W. imprimeur, Rue du Columbier, Fauxburgh St. Germain, à l'Hotel de Saxe.*" In 1768 he again appeared *personally* upon the theatre of public action. On the 4th of March he addressed a letter of submission to the king, which was delivered by his servant at Buckingham Gate. This, like his first letter to the duke of Grafton, supplicated pardon, which one of his biographers says he was enabled to do without meanness, because "in no one syllable of his otherwise offensive publications had he offended against the personal respect due to the prince on the throne." But this writer surely forgets the obvious tenour of his No. 45, as well as the repeated and atrocious attacks he made on the princess dowager, his majesty's mother.

No attention was paid to this petition, and probably he had no great reliance on it, but as he had so long been the idol of the people of London, on the 16th of the same month, be offered himself a candidate to represent the city of London. In this he did not succeed, although at the close of the poll on the 23d he was found to have polled 1247 votes. Not disheartened at this failure, he immediately declared his intention of becoming a candidate for the county of Middlesex, and on the 28th was chosen by a vast majority. On the 27th of April he was taken up on a *capias utlagatum*, and committed to the King's Bench, and on the 18th of June was sentenced, on the two verdicts against him, to be imprisoned twenty-two months, to pay two fines of 500*l.* each, and to give security for his good behaviour for seven years, himself in 1000*l.* and two sureties in 500*l.* each. This judgment was far milder than had been expected by the public, and it is said that Mr. Wilkes might have made his peace with government at this time, but one condition was proposed to him in which he could not concur, namely, *not* to present a petition relative to his case, which he had told the freeholders of Middlesex he should present. He conceived that a public pledge had been given to the contrary, and from this public pledge he resolved not to withdraw. The petition was accordingly laid before the House on the following day by sir J. Mawbey, and was received as the declaration of a second war.

On the 10th of May, 1768, the populace had assembled in great numbers about the neighbourhood of the King's Bench prison, where Mr. Wilkes was in confinement. The riot-act was read by the justices of Surrey, and the mob not dispersing, the military was ordered to fire: several persons were slightly wounded, some more seriously, and one was killed on the spot. Lord Weymouth, the secretary of state, had written to the magistrates a letter dated April 17, exhorting them to firmness in the suppression of any popular tumult which might arise: and lord Barrington, the secretary at war, returned thanks, after the 10th of May, in the name of his majesty, to the officers and soldiers of that regiment of guards, which had been employed upon the occasion. These two letters were transmitted to the newspapers by Mr. Wilkes, accompanied with some prefatory remarks, in which he termed the unhappy transaction a massacre. Of these remarks he avowed himself, at the bar of the House of Commons, to be the author. The remarks were voted libellous, and he, as the

author of them, was expelled; but his conduct appearing
still more meritorious in the eyes of his constituents, he
was re-chosen on the 16th of February, 1769, without opposition.    On the following day he was declared by a majority of the House of Commons *incapable* of being elected
into that parliament, and the election was vacated, upon
the principle that the expulsion of a member of parliament
was equivalent to exclusion; but notwithstanding this resolution, he was a third time elected, again without opposition; a Mr. Dingley indeed offering himself as a candidate, but without the least success.   In April, Wilkes was
elected a fourth time by a majority of 1143 votes against
Mr. Luttrell, a new candidate who had only 296, and the
same day the House of Commons confirmed Mr. Luttrell's
election.    These proceedings were not carried on, however, without long discussions in the House, and a warm
controversy from the press, in which many eminent writers
took a part.
    In the mean time, Wilkes, now within the walls of the
King's Bench, was approaching nearer to those substantial
rewards which he valued more than the empty noise of a
triumph.    From the time of his first election for Middlesex
in March 1768, through the whole of 1769, and even far
into 1772, he was the sole unrivalled political idol of the
people, who lavished upon him all in their power to bestow, as if willing to prove that in England it *was* possible
for an individual to be great and important through *them
alone.*   A subscription was opened for the payment of his
debts, and 20,000*l.* are said in a few weeks to have been
raised for that purpose, and for the discharging his fine.
A newly established society for the support of the "Bill of
Rights" presented him with 300*l.*   Gifts of plate, of wine,
of household goods, were daily heaped upon him.   An
unknown patriot conveyed to him in a handsomely embroidered purse five hundred guineas.   Au honest chandler enriched him with a box containing of candles, the
magic number of dozens, forty-five.   High and low contended with each other who most should serve and celebrate
him.    Devices and emblems of all descriptions ornamented
the trinkets conveyed to his prison: the most usual was the
cap of liberty placed over his crest: upon others was a
bird with expanded wings, hovering over a cage, beneath
a motto, "I love liberty."   Every wall bore his name, and
every window his portrait.   In china, in bronze, in marble,

he stood upon the chimney-piece of half the houses in the metropolis: and he swung upon the sign-post of every village, and of every great road throughout the environs of London.

In November 1769, he brought his action, which had been prevented by his absence abroad, against lord Halifax, for false imprisonment, and the seizure of his papers, and obtained a verdict of 4000*l.* On the 17th of April, 1770, he was discharged from his imprisonment. On the 24th he was sworn as alderman of the ward of Farringdon Without. It was, however, soon discovered that there was a difference of opinion in many points between him and several of his former friends. Early in 1771 a rupture between him and Mr. Horne (afterwards Horne Tooke) produced hostilities in the newspapers, and both parties exerted their abilities in abusing each other with much acrimony, to the great entertainment of the public, though little to their own credit. After some time it was found that the world was perverse enough to believe both the gentlemen in their unfavourable representation of each other. Mr. Wilkes soon saw this effect of the controversy, and wisely withdrew from it on being chosen sheriff on the 3d of July, 1771. His antagonist also, being left to himself without an opponent, and feeling the disgrace which he had brought on himself, also prudently and silently quitted the field, discomfited and disappointed.

On the 8th of October, 1772, Mr. Wilkes was by the livery elected one of the persons to be selected for lord mayor, but was not chosen by the court of aldermen; and the same circumstance happened the succeeding year. On the third year (1774) he was again elected in the same manner, and approved by the court of aldermen. On the 20th of October he was again elected member for the county of Middlesex, and was permitted to take his seat without molestation. The popularity which he had hitherto enjoyed was now to suffer some diminution. In the beginning of 1776 sir Stephen Theodore Janssen resigned the office of chamberlain, and Mr. Wilkes was a candidate to succeed him; when, notwithstanding every exertion in his favour, and every art employed, he lost his election, and Mr. alderman Hopkins was chosen, by a majority of 177. He made another effort in the succeeding year with equal ill success; and on a third attempt in 1778, was again rejected, having only 287 votes against 1216. His situation at this time was truly melancholy: his interest in the city appeared to be lost; a motion to pay his debts had been rejected in the common council; he was involved in difficulties of various kinds; his creditors were clamorous; and such of his property which could be ascertained, and amongst the rest his books, had been taken in execution: those who formerly supported him were become cold to his solicitations, and languid in their exertions, and the clouds of adversity seemed to gather round him on every side, without a ray of light to cheer him. While in this forlorn state, Mr. Hopkins died in 1779, and Mr. Wilkes at length obtained an establishment, which, profiting by experience, rendered the remainder of his life easy and comfortable. On the 1st of December he was chosen chamberlain, by a majority of 1972 votes, and continued to fill the office with credit to himself, and to the satisfaction of his constituents, during the rest of his life, in spite of some feeble attempts at opposition to him.

In 1782, upon the dismission from office of the ministers who conducted the war against America, the obnoxious resolutions against him were, at length, upon his own motion, expunged from the journals. This was the crown of those political labours, which more immediately concerned his own personal actions. He thenceforward deemed himself " a fire burnt out." His popularity was fast decaying, and although he took the popular side in the contest betwixt Mr. Pitt and Mr. Fox in 1783, and thereby secured his election in 1784, he did not venture to be a candidate in the general election of 1790. That he was pretty well tired of " his followers," appears from a short letter to his daughter, written in 1784, in which he says, " yesterday was sacred to the powers of dullness, and the anniversary meeting of the Quintuple Alliance * when I was obliged to eat stale fish, and swallow sour port, with sir Cecil Wray, Mr. Martin the banker, Dr. Jebb, &c. to promote the grand reform of parliament. I was forced into the chair, and was so far happy as to be highly applauded, both for a long speech, and my conduct as president through an arduous day. I have not, however, authenticated to the public any account of the day's proceeding, nor given to the press the various new-fangled toasts which were the amusement of the hour, and should perish with it." This

* A political club not now existing.

insincerity he was at no pains to disguise, and after he had obtained his wishes as to situation, he appeared always sufficiently candid in ridiculing the persons who had brought him to it.

Though now far advanced in years, he shewed no decay of intellect. His short congratulatory addresses spoken as chamberlain to those public characters, who received between 1790 and 1797 the freedom of the city, were his last public exertions. He died Dec. 26, 1797, aged seventy, at his house in Grosvenor-square; and his remains were interred in a vault in Grosvenor chapel, South Audley-street, according to the directions of his will, being near to where he died. A hearse and three mourning-coaches, and Miss Wilkes's coach, formed the cavalcade; and eight labouring men, dressed in new black cloaths, bore the deceased to the place of interment, for which each man received a guinea besides the suit of cloaths. He has also directed a tablet to be placed to his memory, with these few lines:

THE REMAINS
OF
JOHN WILKES,
A FRIEND TO LIBERTY.
BORN AT LONDON, OCT. 17, 1727, O.S.
DIED IN THIS PARISH.

Mr. Wilkes left behind him a daughter, Mary, the offspring of his marriage with Miss Mead. Miss Wilkes survived her father but a few years, she died the 12th of March 1802, aged fifty-one. He left also two natural children, but scarcely any property.

Wilkes was perhaps the most popular political character that ever had been known, or perhaps will ever be known again, for, by imposing on the credulity, he has added to the experience of mankind, and it will be difficult, although we have seen it tried, for any other pretender to imitate Wilkes with equal effect. At one period of his life, he obtained a very dangerous influence over the minds of the people; his name was sufficient to blow up the flames of sedition, and excite the lower orders of the community to acts of violence against his opponents in a manner something allied to madness. After great vicissitudes of fortune, he found himself placed in a state of independence and affluence; gradually declined from the popularity he had acquired, and at last terminated a turbulent life in a state of neglected quiet. Reviewing the present state of the

country, and comparing it with that in which he began his
exertions, though some advantages may be placed to his
account, we hesitate in giving him credit for those beneficial consequences which his admirers are apt to ascribe
to him. We believe he was a patriot chiefly from accident,
a successful one it must be owned, but not originating in
principle. This was thought even in his life-time, but it
has been amply confirmed by two publications which have
since appeared; the one " Letters from the year 1774 to
the year 1796 of John Wilkes, esq. addressed to his daughter," 1804, 4 vols. 12mo, with a well-written memoir of his
life, of which we have occasionally availed ourselves; the
second, " The Correspondence of John Wilkes, esq. with
his friends, printed from the original manuscripts, in which
are introduced Memoirs of his Life, by John Almon," 1805,
5 vols. 8vo, a publication in which Mr. Almon is the greatest admirer and the greatest enemy to Mr. Wilkes's character he ever had.

Of Wilkes's private character, blackened, with no sparing
hand, in the latter of these publications, there are parts
which always conciliated esteem. He was a gentleman of
elegant manners, of fine taste, and of pleasing conversation. Amidst all the vicissitudes of his life, he spared some
hours for the cultivation of classical learning, and in 1790,
paid his worthy deputy (of the ward) John Nichols, esq.
whom he highly and deservedly esteemed, the compliment
of publishing from his press, for the use only of particular
friends, splendid editions of the characters of Theophrastus
and the poems of Catullus; and he had also made considerable
progress in a translation of Anacreon. His own letters and
speeches were collected in 1769, 3 vols. 12mo, his speeches,
by himself, in 1787, 1 vol. 8vo, to which, in 1788, he added
a single speech in defence of his excellent friend, Mr.
Hastings; on which he justly prided himself; it being,
perhaps, the ablest exculpation of that gentleman which has
appeared in print. Many other of his occasional effusions
are scattered through the newspapers and magazines of the
day, and the principal have been reprinted in Mr. Almon's
book. [1]

WILKES (RICHARD), an English antiquary and physician, was the eldest son of Mr. Richard Wilkes, of Willen-

[1] Almon's Correspondence.—and " Letters" above-mentioned.—Gent. Mag.
1798, &c.

hall, in the county of Stafford, a gentleman who lived upon his own estate, and where his ancestors had been seated since the time of Edward IV. His mother was Lucretia, youngest daughter of Jonas Asteley, of Woodeaton, in Staffordshire, an ancient and respectable family. He was born March 16, 1690-91, and had his school-education at Trentham. He was entered of St. John's college, Cambridge, March 13, 1709-10, and was admitted scholar in 1710. On April 6, 1711, he attended Mr. Saunderson's mathematical lectures, and ever after continued a particular friendship with that gentleman. In the preface to "Saunderson's Elements of Algebra," the reader is told, that whatever materials had been got together for publishing Saunderson's life, had been received, among other gentlemen, from Mr. Richard Wilkes. He took the degree of B. A. January 1713-14; and was chosen fellow Jan. 21, 1716-17; and April 11, 1716, was admitted into lady Sadler's Algebra Lecture, and took the degree of M.A. at the commencement of 1717; also July 4, 1718, he was chosen Linacre Lecturer. It does not appear that he ever took any degrees in medicine. He seems to have taken pupils and taught mathematics in the college from 1715 till the time that he left it. It is not known when he took deacon's orders, but a relation of his remembered his having preached at Wolverhampton. He also preached some time at Stow, near Chartley. The disgust he took to the ministry has been imputed to his being disappointed in the hope of preferment in the church, and he thought he could make his talents turn to better account, and accordingly began to practise physic at Wolverhampton, Feb. 1720, and became very eminent in his profession. On the 24th June 1725, he married Miss Rachel Manlove, of Lee's-hill, near Abbots Bromley in Staffordshire, with whom he had a handsome fortune, and from that time he dwelt with his father at Willenhall. In the beginning of 1747 he had a severe fit of illness, during which, among other employments, he composed a whimsical epitaph on himself, which may be seen in Shaw's History of Staffordshire. His wife dying in May 1756, he afterwards married in October the same year, Mrs. Frances Bendish (sister to the late Rev. sir Richard Wrottesley, of Wrottesley, bart.) who died Dec. 24, 1798, at Froxfield, Hampshire, at a very advanced age. Dr. Wilkes died March 6, 1760, of the gout in his stomach, greatly lamented by his tenants, to whom he had been an indulgent landlord, and by the poor to whom he had been a kind and liberal physician and friend.

He published an excellent "Treatise on the Dropsy," and during the time that the distemper raged in Staffordshire among the horned cattle, he published a pamphlet, entitled "A Letter to the Gentlemen, Farmers, and Graziers, in the county of Stafford," calculated to prevent, or cure that terrible plague. Among other things, he meditated a new edition of Hudibras, with notes, &c. As an antiquary he is principally known by his valuable collections for the history of Staffordshire. His chef-d'œuvre, says Mr. Shaw, is a general history from the earliest and most obscure ages to his own times, drawn up with great skill and erudition, which Mr. Shaw has made the basis of his own introduction. This, with his other manuscripts, were long supposed to have been lost, and were not indeed brought to light until 1792, when they fell into the hands of Mr. Shaw, who has incorporated them in his valuable history. [1]

WILKIE (WILLIAM), a Scotch poet of some fame in his day, was born in the parish of Dalmeny, in the county of West Lothian, Oct. 5, 1721. His father, although a small farmer, and poor and unfortunate, endeavoured to give him a liberal education, which he appears to have improved by diligence. At the age of thirteen, he was sent to the university of Edinburgh, where he made a rapid progress in learning, but before he completed his academical course, his father died, leaving him no other inheritance than his small farm, and the care of three sisters. Necessity thus turned his attention to the study of agriculture, which he cultivated with so much success, although upon a confined scale, that he acquired a solid reputation as a practical farmer, and was enabled to provide for himself and his sisters. He still, however, prosecuted his studies, and at the accustomed period was admitted a preacher in the church of Scotland.

For some years this made no alteration in his mode of life; and as a clergyman he only occasionally assisted in some neighbouring churches, while he devoted his principal time to his farm and his studies. He appears to have been early ambitious of the character of a poet, and having read Homer, as Don Quixote read romances, he determined

<hr>

[1] Shaw's Hist. of Staffordshire, vol. II. Part I. p. 147, 148, and Pref. to vol. I.

to sally forth as his rival, or continuator; and this enthusiasm produced "The Epigoniad," published in 1753. On this poem he is said to have employed fourteen years, which ill agrees with what his biographers tell us of his propensity to poetry, and the original vigour of his mind; for after so much labour it appeared with all the imperfections of a rough sketch. Its reception by the English public was not very flattering, but in his own country "The Epigoniad" succeeded so well, that a second edition was called for in 1759, to which he added a dream in the manner of Spenser. Yet, as this edition was slowly called for, an extraordinary appeal from the general opinion was made by the celebrated Hume, who wrote a very long encomium on the "Epigoniad," addressed to the editor of the Critical Review. This has been inserted in the late edition of the "English Poets," and those who knew Mr. Hume's taste, friendship, or sincerity, will be best able to determine whether he is serious.

A few years before the publication of the first edition, Wilkie was ordained minister of Ratho, and in 1759 was chosen professor of natural philosophy in the university of St. Andrew's. In 1766 the university conferred upon him the degree of doctor in divinity. In 1768, he published his "Fables," which had less success than even his "Epigoniad," although they are rather happy imitations of the manner of Gay, and the thoughts, if not always original, are yet sprightly and just. After a lingering illness, he died Oct. 10, 1772. The private character of Dr. Wilkie appears to have been distinguished for those singularities, which are sometimes found in men of genius, either from early unrestrained indulgence, or from affectation. His biographers have multiplied instances of his slovenly and disgusting manners, exceeding what we have almost ever heard of; yet we are told he preserved the respect of his contemporaries and scholars. His learning, according to every account, was extensive, and much of it acquired at a very early age. [1]

WILKINS (DAVID), a learned divine and editor, was born in 1685, but when, or where educated we are not told. His name does not appear among the graduates of either university, except that among those of Cambridge, we find he was honoured with the degree of D.D. in 1717. Two

[1] Encyclop. Brit.—English Poets, 1810, 21 vols. 8vo.

years before this, he was appointed by archbishop Wake to succeed Dr. Benjamin Abbot, as keeper of the archiepiscopal library at Lambeth; and in three years drew up a very curious catalogue of all the MSS. and printed books in that valuable collection. As a reward for his industry and learning, archbishop Wake collated him to the rectory of Mongham-Parva, in Kent, in April 1716, to that of Great Chart in 1719, and to the rectory of Hadleigh in the same year. He was also constituted chaplain to the archbishop and collated to the rectories of Monks-Ely and Bocking; appointed commissary of the deanery of Bocking, jointly and severally with W. Beauvoir; collated to a prebend of Canterbury in 1720, and collated to his grace's option of the archdeaconry of Suffolk in May 1724. In consequence of these last preferments, he resigned the former, and was only archdeacon of Suffolk and rector of Hadleigh and Monks-Ely at his death, which happened Sept. 6, 1745, in the sixtieth year of his age. He married, Nov. 27, 1725, the eldest daughter of Thomas lord Fairfax of Scotland, a lady who survived him, and erected a monument to his memory at Hadleigh.

Dr. Wilkins's publications were, 1. "Novum Testamentum Copticum," Oxon. 1716, 4to. 2. A fine edition, with additions, of the "Leges Saxonicæ," Lond. 1721, fol. 3. An edition of "Selden's works," begun in 1722, and finished in 1726, very highly to the credit of Dr. Wilkins, as well as of his learned printer, Bowyer, Lond. 3 vols. folio. This work was published by subscription, in a manner that would now be thought singular. The small paper copies were paid for at the rate of two-pence a sheet, which amounted to 6l. 14s. : the large paper at three-pence a sheet, amounting to 10l. 2s. 4. "Concilia Magnæ Britanniæ," 1736, 4 vols. fol. Besides these he wrote the preface on the literary history of Britain, which is prefixed to bishop Tanner's "Bibliotheca." [1]

WILKINS (JOHN), an ingenious and learned English bishop, was the son of Mr. Walter Wilkins, citizen and goldsmith of Oxford, and was born in 1614, at Fawsley, near Daventry, in Northamptonshire, in the house of his mother's father, the celebrated dissenter Mr. John Dod. He was taught Latin and Greek by Edward Sylvester, a teacher of much reputation, who kept a private school in

[1] Nichols's Bowyer.

the parish of All-Saints in Oxford; and his proficiency was such, that at thirteen he entered a student of New-inn-hall, in 1627. He made no long stay there, but was removed to Magdalen-hall, under the tuition of Mr. John Tombes, and there took the degrees in arts. He afterwards entered into orders; and was first chaplain to William lord Say, and then to Charles count Palatine of the Rhine, and prince elector of the empire, with whom he continued some time. To this last patron, his skill in the mathematics was a very great recommendation. Upon the breaking out of the civil war, he joined with the parliament, and took the solemn league and covenant. He was afterwards made warden of Wadham-college by the committee of parliament, appointed for reforming the university; and, being created bachelor of divinity the 12th of April, 1648, was the day following put into possession of his wardenship. Next year he was created D. D. and about that time took the engagement then enjoined by the powers in being. In 1656, he married Robina, the widow of Peter French, formerly canon of Christ-church, and sister to Oliver Cromwell, then lord-protector of England: which marriage being contrary to the statutes of Wadham-college, because they prohibit the warden from marrying, he procured a dispensation from Oliver, to retain the wardenship notwithstanding. In 1659, he was by Richard Cromwell made master of Trinity-college in Cambridge; but ejected thence the year following upon the restoration. Then he became preacher to the honourable society of Gray's-inn, and rector of St. Lawrence-Jewry, London, upon the promotion Dr. Seth Ward to the bishopric of Exeter. About this time, he became a member of the Royal-Society, was chosen of their council, and proved one of their most eminent members. Soon after this, he was made dean of Rippon; and, in 1668, bishop of Chester, Dr. Tillotson, who had married his daughter-in-law, preaching his consecration sermon. Wood and Burnet both inform us, that he obtained this bishopric by the interest of Villiers duke of Buckingham; and the latter adds, that it was no small prejudice against him to be raised by so bad a man. Dr. Walter Pope observes, that Wilkins, for some time after the restoration, was out of favour both at Whitehall and Lambeth, on account of his marriage with Oliver Cromwell's sister; and that archbishop Sheldon, who then disposed of almost all ecclesiastical preferments, opposed his promotion; that, however, when bishop Ward introduced him afterwards to the archbishop, he was very obligingly received, and treated kindly by him ever after. He did not enjoy his preferment long; for he died of a suppression of urine, which was mistaken for the stone, at Dr. Tillotson's house, in Chancery-lane, London, Nov. 19, 1672. He was buried in the chancel of the church of St. Lawrence Jewry; and his funeral sermon was preached by Dr. William Lloyd, then dean of Bangor, who, although Wilkins had been abused and vilified perhaps beyond any man of his time, thought it no shame to say every thing that was good of him. Wood also, different as his complexion and principles were from those of Wilkins, has been candid enough to give him the following character: "He was," says he, "a person endowed with rare gifts; he was a noted theologist and preacher, a curious critic in several matters, an excellent mathematician and experimentist, and one as well seen in mechanisms and new philosophy, of which he was a great promoter, as any man of his time. He also highly advanced the study and perfecting of astronomy, both at Oxford while he was warden of Wadham-college, and at London while he was fellow of the Royal Society; and I cannot say that there was any thing deficient in him, but a constant mind and settled principles."

Wilkins had two characteristics, neither of which was calculated to make him generally admired: first, he avowed moderation, and was kindly affected towards dissenters, for a comprehension of whom he openly and earnestly contended: secondly, he thought it right and reasonable to submit to the powers in being, be those powers who they would, or let them be established how they would. And this making him as ready to swear allegiance to Charles II. after he was restored to the crown, as to the usurpers, while they prevailed, he was charged with being various and unsteady in his principles; with having no principles at all, with Hobbism, and every thing that is bad. Yet the greatest and best qualities are ascribed to him, if not unanimously, at least by many eminent and good men. Dr. Tillotson, in the preface to some "Sermons of Bishop Wilkins," published by him in 1682, animadverts upon a slight and unjust character, as he thinks it is, given of the bishop in Mr. Wood's "Historia & Antiquitates Universitatis Oxoniensis;" "whether by the author," says he, "or by some other hand, I am not curious to know:" and concludes his animadversions in the following words : " Upon the whole, it hath often been no small matter of wonder to me, whence it should come to pass, that so great a man, and so great a lover of mankind, who was so highly valued and reverenced by all that knew him, should yet have the hard fate to fall under the heavy displeasure and censure of those who knew him not; and that he, who never did any thing to make himself one personal enemy, should have the ill fortune to have so many. I think I may truly say, that there are or have been very few in this age and nation so well known, and so greatly esteemed and favoured, by so many persons of high rank and quality, and of singular worth and eminence in all the learned professions, as our author was. And this surely cannot be denied him, it is so well known to many worthy persons yet living, and hath been so often acknowledged even by his enemies, that, in the late times of confusion, almost all that was preserved and kept up, of ingenuity and good learning, of good order and government in the university of Oxford, was chiefly owing to his prudent conduct and encouragement : which consideration alone, had there been no other, might have prevailed with some there to have treated his memory with at least common kindness and respect." The other hand, Dr. Tillotson mentions, was Dr. Fell, the dean of Christ church, and under whose inspection Wood's "Athenæ Oxonienses" was translated into Latin ; and who, among other alterations without the privity of that compiler, was supposed to insert the poor diminishing character of bishop Wilkins, to be found in the Latin version. The friendship which subsisted between our author and Dr. Tillotson is a proof of their mutual moderation, for Wilkins was in doctrine a strict and professed Calvinist. We need quote no more to prove this, than what has been already quoted by Dr. Edwards in his " Veritas Redux," p. 553. " God might (says Dr. Wilkins) have designed us for vessels of wrath ; and then we had been eternally undone, without all possible remedy. There was nothing to move him in us, when we lay all together in the general heap of mankind. It was his own free grace and bounty, that made him to take delight in us, to chuse us from the rest, and to sever us from those many thousands in the world who shall perish everlastingly." Gift of Prayer, c. 28. In his " Ecclesiastes," section 3, he commends to a preacher, for his best authors, Calvin, Junius, P. Martyr,

Musculus, Paræus, Piscator, Rivet, Zanchius, &c. as most eminent for their orthodox sound judgement." Burnet, in his Life of Sir Matthew Hale, printed in 1682, declares of Wilkins, that " he was a man of as great a mind, as true a judgement, as eminent virtues, and of as good a soul, as any he ever knew ." and in his " History" he says, that, though " he married Cromwell's sister, yet he made no other use of that alliance but to do good offices, and to cover the university of Oxford from the sourness of Owen and Goodwin. At Cambridge he joined with those who studied to propagate better thoughts, to take men off from being in parties, or from narrow notions, from superstitious conceits, and fierceness about opinions. He was also a great observer and promoter of experimental philosophy, which was then a new thing, and much looked after. He was naturally ambitious, but was the wisest clergyman I ever knew. He was a lover of mankind, and had a delight in doing good." The historian mentions afterwards another quality Wilkins possessed in a supreme degree ; and that was, says he, " a courage, which could stand against a current, and against all the reproaches with which ill-natured clergymen studied to load him."

All the works of bishop Wilkins are esteemed ingenious and learned, and many of them particularly curious and entertaining. His first publication was in 1638, when he was only twenty-four years of age, of a piece, entitled " The Discovery of a new World ; or, a Discourse tending to prove, that it is probable there may be another habitable World in the Moon ; with a Discourse concerning the possibility of a passage thither," in 8vo. The object of this singular work may appear from the fourteen propositions which he endeavours to establish, some of which have often been quoted in jest or earnest by subsequent wits * or philosophers. He contends, I. That the strangeness of this opinion is no sufficient reason why it should be rejected, because other certain truths have been formerly esteemed ridiculous, and great absurdities entertained by common consent. II. That a plurality of worlds does not contradict any principle of reason or faith. III. That the heavens do not consist of any such pure matter, which can

---

* Among others the famous duchess of Newcastle objected to Dr. Wilkins, the want of baiting-places in his way to the new world, when the doctor expressed his surprise that this objection should be made by a lady who had been all her life employed in building castles in the air.

privilege them from the like change and corruption, as these inferior bodies are liable unto. IV. That the moon is a solid compacted opacous body. V. That the moon hath not any light of her own. VI. That there is a world in the moon, hath been the direct opinion of many ancient, with some modern mathematicians, and may probably be deduced from the tenets of others. VII. That those spots and brighter parts, which by our sight may be distinguished in the moon, do shew the difference betwixt the sea and land in that other world. VIII. That the spots represent the sea, and the brighter parts the land. IX. That there are high mountains, deep vallies, and spacious plains in the body of the moon. X. That there is an atmosphere, or an orb of gross vaporous air immediately encompassing the body of the moon. XI. That as their world is our moon, so our world is their moon. XII. That it is probable there may be such meteors belonging to that world in the moon as there are with us. XIII. That it is probable there may be inhabitants in this other world; but of what kind they are, is uncertain. XIV. That it is possible for some of our posterity to find out a conveyance to this other world; and if there be inhabitants there, to have commerce with them. Under this head he observes, that " if it be here inquired, what means there may be conjectured for our ascending beyond the sphere of the earth's magnetical vigour; I answer, says he, 1. It is not perhaps impossible, that a man may be able to flye by the application of wings to his owne body; as angels are pictured, and as Mercury and Dædalus are fained, and as hath been attempted by divers, particularly by a Turke in Constantinople, as Busbequius relates. 2. If there be such a great *Ruck* in Madagascar, as Marcus Polus the Venetian mentions, the feathers in whose wings are twelve foot long, which can soope up a horse and his rider, or an elephant, as our kites doe a mouse; why then it is but teaching one of these to carry a man, and he may ride up thither, as Ganymed does upon an eagle. 3. Or if neither of these ways will serve, yet I doe seriously and upon good grounds affirme it possible to make a flying chariot; in which a man may sit, and give such a motion into it, as shall convey him through the aire. And this perhaps might be made large enough to carry divers men at the same time, together with foode for their *viaticum*, and commodities for traffique. It is not the bignesse of any thing in this kind, that can hinder its motion, if the motive faculty be answerable thereunto. We see a great ship swimme as well as a small corke, and an eagle flies in the aire as well as a little gnat. This engine may be contrived from the same principles by which Archytas made a wooden dove, and Regiomontanus a wooden eagle. I conceive it were no difficult matter, if a man had leisure, to shew more particularly the meanes of composing it. The perfecting of such an invention would be of such excellent use, that it were enough, not only to make a man, but the age also wherein he lives. For besides the strange discoveries, that it might occasion in this other world, it would be also of inconceivable advantage for travelling above any other conveiance that is now in use. So that notwithstanding all these seeming impossibilities, 'tis likely enough, that there may be a meanes invented of journying to the moone. And how happy shall they be, that are first successefull in this attempt?

‘ ——— Fœlicesq ; Animæ, quas nubila supra,
Et turpes fumos, plenumq ; vaporibus orbem,
Inseruit Cœlo sancti scintilla Promethei.’

Having thus finished this discourse, I chanced upon a late fancy to this purpose under the fained name of Domingo Gonzales, written by a late reverend and learned bishop (Godwin); in which (besides sundry particulars, wherein this later chapter did unwittingly agree with it) there is delivered a very pleasant and well contrived fancy concerning a voyage to this other world.”

Two years after, in 1640, appeared his “Discourse concerning a new Planet; tending to prove, that it is probable our Earth is one of the planets.” In this he maintains ; 1. That the seeming novelty and singularity of this opinion can be no sufficient reason to prove it erroneous. 2. That the places of Scripture, which seem to intimate the diurnal motion of the sun or heavens, are fairly capable of another interpretation. 3. That the Holy Ghost in many places of Scripture does plainly conform his expressions to the error of our conceits, and does not speak of sundry things as they are in themselves, but as they appear unto us. 4. That divers learned men have fallen into great absurdities, whilst they have looked for the grounds of philosophy from the grounds of Scripture. 5. That the words of Scripture in their proper and strict construction do not any where affirm the immobility of the earth. 6. That there is not any argument from the words of Scripture, principles of nature, or observations in astronomy, which can sufficiently evidence the earth to be in the center of the universe. 7. It is probable that the sun is the center of the world. 8. That there is not any sufficient reason to prove the earth incapable of those motions, which Copernicus ascribes unto it. 9. That it is more probable the earth does move, than the heavens. 10. That this hypothesis is exactly agreeable to common appearances.

His name was not put to either of these works; but they were so well known to be his, that Langrenus, in his map of the moon, dedicated to the king of Spain, calls one of the lunar spots after Wilkins's name. His third piece, in 1641, is entitled "Mercury; or, the secret and swift Messenger; shewing how a man may with privacy and speed communicate his thoughts to a friend at any distance," in 8vo. His fourth, in 1648, "Mathematical Magic; or, the Wonders that may be performed by Mechanical Geometry," in 8vo. All these pieces were published entire in one volume, 8vo, in 1708, under the title of "The Mathematical and Philosophical Works of the Right reverend John Wilkins," &c. with a print of the author and general title-page handsomely engraven, and an account of his life and writings. To this collection is also subjoined an abstract of a larger work, printed in 1668, folio, and entitled "An Essay towards a real Character and a philosophical Language." This he persuaded Ray to translate into Latin, which he did, but it never was published; and the MS. is now in the library of the Royal Society. These are his mathematical and philosophical works. He was also the inventor of the Perambulator, or Measuring wheel. His theological works are, 1. "Ecclesiastes; or, a Discourse of the Gift of Preaching, as it falls under the rules of Art," 1646. This no doubt was written with a view to reform the prevailing taste of the times he lived in; from which no man was ever farther than Wilkins. It has gone through nine editions; the last in 1718, 8vo. 2. "Discourse concerning the beauty of Providence, in all the rugged passages of it," 1649. 3. "Discourse concerning the Gift of Prayer, shewing what it is, wherein it consists, and how far it is attainable by industry," &c. 1653. This was against enthusiasm and fanaticism. These were published in his life-time; after his death, in 1675, Tillotson published two other of his works. 4. "Sermons preached on several occasions;"

and, 5. " Of the principles and duties of Natural Religion,"
both in 8vo.    Tillotson tells us, in the preface to the latter,
that " the first twelve chapters were written out for the
press in his life-time ; and that the remainder hath been
gathered and made up out of his papers." [1]

WILKINSON (HENRY), one of four divines of the name
of Wilkinson, who made considerable noise at Oxford
during the usurpation, was born in the vicarage of Halifax
in Yorkshire, Oct. 9, 1566, and came to Oxford in 1581,
where he was elected a probationer fellow of Merton college, by the interest of his relation Mr. afterwards sir
Henry Savile, the warden.    In 1586 he proceeded in arts,
and studying divinity, took his bachelor's degree in that
faculty.    In 1601 he was preferred to the living of Waddesdon in Buckinghamshire, which he held for forty-six
years.    He was a man of considerable learning and piety,
and being an old puritan, Wood says, he was elected one
of the assembly of divines in 1643.    He was the author of
" A Catechism for the use of the congregation of Waddesdon," 8vo, of which there was a fourth edition in 1647.
He published also " The Debt-Book ; or a treatise upon
Romans xiii. 8. wherein is handled the civil debt of money
or goods," Lond. 1625, 8vo ; and other things, the names
of which Wood has not mentioned.    He died at Waddesdon March 19, 1647, aged eighty-one, and was buried in
his own church, with a monumental inscription.    By his
wife Sarah, the daughter of Mr. Arthur Wake, another
puritan, he had six sons and three daughters.    One of his
sons, Edward, was born in 1607, and educated at Magdalen-hall, Oxford, which he entered when little more than
eleven years old, and completed his degrees in arts at the
age of eighteen.    He must have been of extraordinary
parts, or extraordinary interest, for in 1627, when only
twenty, he was chosen professor of rhetoric in Gresham
college.    All that Ward has been able to discover of him,
is, that he held this office upwards of eleven years, and
resigned it in 1638.    Another of the rector of Waddesdon's
sons, a more distinguished character, is the subject of our
next article. [2]

WILKINSON (HENRY), one of the sons of the preceding, and called LONG HARRY, to distinguish him from

[1] Biog. Brit.—Ath. Ox. vol. II.—Burnet's Own Times.—Birch's Life of Tillotson. &c.
[2] Ath. Ox. vol. II.—Watson's Halifax.

a contemporary and cousin of the same names, who was called DEAN HARRY, was born at Waddesdon in 1609, and in 1622 became a commoner of Magdalen-hall, where, making great proficiency in his studies, he took the degrees in arts, became a noted tutor, master of the schools, and divinity reader in his hall. In 1638, he was admitted B. D. and preached frequently in and near Oxford, "not," says Wood, "without girds against the actions, and certain men of the times," by which we are to understand that he belonged to that growing party which was hostile to the ecclesiastical establishment. Of this he gave so decided a proof in a sermon preached at St. Mary's in Sept. 1640, in which he inveighed against the ceremonies, &c. that he was ordered to recant, and a form drawn up accordingly. But as he peremptorily refused to sign this, well knowing that the power of the church was undermined, he was suspended from preaching, &c. within the university and its precincts, according to the statute. Immediately, however, on the meeting of the Long parliament, he complained to the House of Commons of the treatment he had met with from the vice chancellor: and the committee of religion not only took off his suspension, but ordered his sermon to be printed, as suiting their views.

With this encouragement Wilkinson went on preaching what he pleased without fear, but removed to London, as the better scene of action, where he was made minister of St. Faith's, under St. Paul's, and one of the assembly of divines. He was also a frequent preacher before the parliament on their monthly fasts, or on thanksgiving days. In 1645 he was promoted to the rectory of St. Dunstan's in the West*. Soon after he was constituted one of the six ministers appointed to go to Oxford (then in the power of parliament), and to establish preachings and lectures upon presbyterian principles and forms. He was also made one of the visitors for the ejection of all heads of houses, fellows, students, &c. who refused compliance with the now predominant party. For these services he was made a senior fellow of Magdalen college (which, Wood says, he kept till he married a holy woman called the Lady Carr), a canon of Christ church, doctor of divinity, and, after Cheynel's departure, Margaret professor. Of all this he was deprived at the restoration, but occasionally preached

* Calamy says, St. Dunstan's in the East.

in or about London, as opportunity offered, particularly
at Clapham, where he died in September 1675, and his
body, after lying in state in Drapers' hall, London, was
buried with great solemnity in the church of St. Dunstan's.
His printed works are entirely " Sermons" preached before
the parliament, or in the "Morning Exercise" at Cripplegate and Southwark, and seem to confirm part of the character Wood gives of him, that " he was a good scholar,
always a close student, an excellent preacher (though his
voice was shrill and whining)," yet, adds Wood, " his sermons were commonly full of dire and confusion, especially
while the rebellion lasted." [1]

WILKINSON (HENRY), denominated sometimes JU-
NIOR, but commonly called DEAN HARRY, to distinguish
him from the preceding, was the son of the rev. William
Wilkinson of Adwick, or Adwickstreet, in the West Riding
of Yorkshire, the brother of the first Henry Wilkinson,
rector of Waddesdon ; and consequently cousin to the preceding Long Harry.   He was born at Adwick in 1616, and
was educated in grammar at a school in All Saints parish,
Oxford.    He entered a commoner of Magdalen-hall in
1631, took the degrees in arts, was admitted into holy
orders, and became a noted tutor, and moderator or *dean*
of Magdalen-hall.    Being of the same principles with his
relations, he quitted the university in 1642, and going to
London, took the covenant, and became a frequent
preacher.    On the surrender of Oxford to the parliamentary forces, he returned thither, and was created bachelor
of divinity, and made principal of his hall, and moral philosophy reader of the university.    He also took the degree
of D. D. and became a frequent preacher at the different
churches in Oxford.    As the governor of a society, Wood
speaks of him very highly, and his character indeed in this
respect was so well established, that he might have remained principal, if he could have conformed.    He suffered
considerably afterwards for nonconformity, while endeavouring to preach at Buckminster in Leicestershire, Gos-
field in Essex, Sible-Headingham, and finally at Connard
near Sudbury in Suffolk, where he died May 13, 1690. He
was buried at Milding near Lavenham, in Suffolk.    Wood
says " he was a zealous person in the way he professed,
but overswayed more by the principles of education than

[1] Ath. Ox. vol. II.—Calamy.

reason. He was very courteous in speech and carriage, communicative of his knowledge, generous and charitable to the poor; and so public-spirited (a rare thing, adds Wood, in a presbyterian), that he always minded the common good, more than his own concerns." He was a considerable benefactor to Magdalen-hall, having built the library, and procured a good collection of books for it.

He published, in Latin, various "Conciones," and "Orationes," delivered at Oxford on public occasions; and several English sermons, besides the following, 1. "Catalogus librorum in Bibl. Aul. Magd. Oxon.", Oxford, 1661, 8vo. 2. "The doctrine of contentment briefly explained, &c." Lond. 1671, 8vo. 3. "Characters of a sincere heart, and the comforts thereof," ibid. 1674, 8vo. 4. "Two Treatises concerning God's All-Sufficiency, &c." ibid. 1681, 8vo. In this last work we find a singular anecdote, which he says was communicated to him by archbishop Usher, with whom he was well acquainted. Our readers probably know that the Marian persecution never reached Ireland, and if the following be true, the Irish protestants had a very narrow escape from that tyranny. "A commission *de Hæreticis comburendis* (for burning of heretics) was sent to Ireland from queen Mary, by a certain doctor, who, at his lodgings at Chester, made his boast of it. One of the servants in the inn, being a well-wisher to protestants, took notice of the words, and found out a method to get away the commission, which he kept in his own hands. When the commissioner came to Ireland, he was entertained with great respect. After some time he appeared before the lords of the council, and then opened his box to shew his commission, but there was nothing in it but a pack of cards. On this he was committed to prison and threatened exceedingly; but upon giving security he was released, returned to England, and obtained a new commission; as soon, however, as he came to Chester, the report arrived of queen Mary's death, which stopt his farther journey."[1]

WILKINSON (JOHN), brother of the rector of Waddesdon, first-mentioned, and uncle to the two Henrys, was born in Halifax, and educated at Oxford, where he was very celebrated. He became fellow of Magdalen college, and in 1605, when Henry, prince of Wales, was matricu-

[1] Ath. Ox. vol. II.—Calamy.

lated of Magdalen college, Mr. Wilkinson, then B. D. was appointed his tutor, as high a mark of respect as could well be paid, and a striking proof of the respect in which he was then held. In the same year Mr. Wilkinson was made principal of Magdalen-hall; and Wood says, that under his government, in 1624, and before, there were three hundred students in the hall, of which number were forty or more masters of arts, but, Wood adds, " all mostly inclining to Calvinism." On the commencement of the rebellion, being of the same sentiments as his relations beforementioned, he left Oxford in 1643, and joined the parliamentary party. After the surrender of the city of Oxford to the parliamentary forces in 1646, he returned to Magdalen-hall, and resumed his office as principal until 1648, when he resigned it on being advanced to be president of Magdalen-college. He had the year before been appointed one of the visitors of the university. He did not, however, live long to enjoy any of these honours, for he died Jan. 2, 1649, and was interred in the church of Great Milton in Oxfordshire. It does not appear that Dr. John Wilkinson published any thing; the greater part of his life he spent as the governor of the two societies of Magdalen-hall and Magdalen-college. Notwithstanding his reputation in his early years, Wood gives him the character of being " generally accounted an illiterate, testy, old creature, one that for forty years together had been the sport of the boys, and constantly yoked with Dr. Kettle : a person of more beard than learning, &c." It is unnecessary to copy more of this character, which agrees so ill with what Wood says of him in his account of Magdalen-hall, that we are almost inclined to think he is speaking of another person. There is much confusion in some of the accounts given of these Wilkinsons, and we are not quite sure that we have been enabled to dispell it ; but Wood so expressly mentions a John Wilkinson Magdalen-hall, as one of the visitors of Oxford, and afterwards a *physician*, that we suspect he has mixed the characters of the two. On this account the story of Dr. *John* Wilkinson having robbed the college of some money, which is related by Fuller and Heylin, must remain doubtful, for Wood attributes it to *Henry* Wilkinson, the vice-president.[1]

[1] Ath. Ox. vols. I and II.—Wood's Annals and History of Oxford.—Ward's Lives of the Gresham professors.—Fuller's Ch. Hist.

WILLAN (ROBERT), a learned physician, was born November 12, 1757, at the Hill, near Sedbergh in Yorkshire, where his father resided, in the enjoyment of extensive medical reputation and practice *. He was educated in the principles of the Quakers, and received his scholastic tuition exclusively at Sedbergh, at the grammar-school of that place, under the care of the reverend Dr. Bateman, and the celebrated Mr. Dawson. The medical profession had long been determined upon as the object of his future pursuit, and he commenced his studies in that science at Edinburgh, in the autumn of 1777. After the usual residence of three years in that university, he received the degree of doctor in 1780, when he published an inaugural dissertation, " De Jecinoris Inflammatione."

In the autumn of the same year, he repaired to the metropolis with the view of obtaining farther medical information, and attended lectures with great assiduity. An arrangement had been made some time previously with Dr. Trotter, a relative, and a physician of some eminence at Darlington, in the county of Durham, but advanced in life, in consequence of which he intended to decline practice in that place in favour of his young friend, as soon as he had completed his studies. When in London, Dr. Willan was introduced to Dr. Fothergill, who, from a just estimate of his talents and acquirements, recommended him to try his fortune in the metropolis, and offered him his assistance. Dr. Fothergill, however, died in the month of December, in that year; and in the commencement of the following year, 1781, the death of Dr. Trotter also occurred; upon which Dr. Willan immediately went to Darlington, where he remained about a year; during which period he analyzed the sulphureous water at Croft, a village about four miles from that place, and wrote a small treatise respecting its chemical and medicinal qualities, containing also a comparison of its properties with those of the Harrogate waters. This tract was published in 1782, with the title of " Observations on the Sulphur water at Croft, near Darlington:" and a second edition was printed a few years afterwards.

In the beginning of 1782, not succeeding in practice at Darlington, Dr. Willan determined to return to London,

* Dr. Robert Willan, senior, graduated at Edinburgh in 1745, and published an inaugural thesis, " De Qualitatibus Aëris." The Hill is now the residence of his eldest son, Richard Willan, esq.

where the Public Dispensary, in Carey-street, being opened
in the commencement of 1783, chiefly accomplished by
the exertions of some of his friends, he was appointed sole
physician to it; and under his humane and active superintendence, together with that of his able and benevolent
colleague, Mr. John Pearson, the surgeon to the institution, the new Dispensary speedily flourished, and became
one of the most extensive and respectable establishments
of its kind in London. In March 1785, having passed his
examinations before the College of Physicians with great
credit, he was admitted a licentiate of that body; on which
occasion he addressed some congratulatory Greek verses to
the board of censors.

About 1786 he engaged in the office of teacher, and
delivered lectures on the principles and practice of medicine at the Public Dispensary. But his success, we believe, in this undertaking, was inconsiderable. At a subsequent period he received, as pupils at the Dispensary,
young physicians who had recently graduated, and who
were initiated into actual practice, under his superintendence, among the patients of the institution; a mode of
tuition from which they derived much practical knowledge,
and were gradually habituated to the responsibility of their
professional duties. Upwards of forty physicians, almost
all of whom have subsequently attained professional reputation, or now occupy responsible situations, both in this
country and abroad, have received the benefit of this instruction.

From the moment when Dr. Willan settled in London,
he pursued his professional avocations with an indefatigable industry and attention, of which there are, perhaps, few
examples. He never quitted the metropolis for any consideration of health or pleasure, during a period of thirty
years. For many years he conducted the medical department of two dispensaries, (having subsequently been favoured with an appointment to the Finsbury Dispensary,
in addition to that of Carey-street), during which his unremitting attention to the progress of the diseases which
came under his care, is evinced by the prodigious collection of cases, which he has recorded in MS. mostly in a
neat Latin style, in which he wrote with great fluency.
During the whole of his career, he was not less assiduously
employed in examining the records of medicine, both ancient and modern, than in the actual observation of dis-

eases; of which the learning and critical acumen displayed in his publications, as well as the mass of manuscript collections which he has left behind, afford abundant proof. His habits of domestic privacy enabled him to dedicate a large portion of time to these researches; and indeed to the unabating ardour with which he applied himself to them, must be attributed that premature injury of his health, which shortened the period of his life.

Dr. Willan's advance to public reputation, and to the consequent emoluments of the profession, was regularly progressive, though slow; and his publications, especially his treatise on the diseases of the skin, upon which his posthumous reputation will principally rest, finally placed his professional character upon high ground. In the spring of 1791, he had the honour of being chosen a fellow of the Society of Antiquaries. He had been early attached to antiquarian researches, and in his juvenile days had, with considerable industry and accuracy, collected from the Odyssey a history of the manners of the primeval times of Greece. Latterly he communicated some papers to this society, of which, however, he declined the honour of publication; particularly, a collection of provincial words, and an elaborate essay on the practice of " Lustration by Need-fire," (scarcely extinct in some of the northern counties,) which led him into a curious and extensive research, respecting similar practices in ancient times, and the mythological superstitions connected with them. It was not until the month of February 1809, that he was elected a fellow of the Royal Society.

The increase of his professional avocations, which had compelled him some time before to resign his office in the Finsbury Dispensary, led him, in 1800, to wish to lessen the fatigue of his duties at the Public Dispensary; and accordingly his friend and pupil, Dr. T. A. Murray, was appointed his colleague in that year. This active and intelligent physician, through whose exertions, aided by the society for bettering the condition of the poor, the Fever institution of the metropolis was established, was unfortunately cut off in February 1802, by the contagion of fever, caught in the infected apartments of the first patients who were admitted into the institution. Dr. Willan, who had strenuously recommended this establishment, was nominated one of its physicians extraordinary. In December 1803, finding his private practice incompatible with a proper attention to the concerns of the Dispensary, which he had now superintended for the space of nearly twenty-one years, he resigned his office. The governors of the charity, in testimony of their gratitude for his services and esteem for his character, nominated him consulting physician, and made him a governor for life, and likewise presented him with a piece of plate, of the value of fifty guineas, inscribed with a testimonial of their attachment and respect *.

For several years previous to his resignation, Dr. Willan's fame and character had been fully established, and the emoluments derived from his practice very ample. He had during the preceding course of years, resided successively in Ely-place, Holborn, and in Red Lion-square, in connection with the family before-mentioned; and lastly, on his marriage in the spring of 1801, he settled in Bloomsbury-square. He was now not only generally consulted, especially by persons labouring under cutaneous diseases, but was also deferred to on all occasions by his professional brethren, as the ultimate appeal on these subjects: for, however generally skilled in every other department of medical practice, his reputation for peculiar knowledge on this point had certainly excluded him, in some measure, from that universal occupation in his profession, to which he was so well entitled.

From his childhood Dr. Willan had been of a delicate constitution; his complexion in early life being pale and feminine, and his form slender. His extremely regular and temperate mode of life, however, had procured him an uninterrupted share of moderate health, and latterly even a certain degree of corpulency of person, though without the appearance of robust strength. In the Winter of 1810, some of his friends had remarked a slight shrinking of bulk and change in his complexion; but it was not till the following spring that symptoms of actual disease manifested themselves, and increased rapidly. With a view to obtain some respite from professional fatigue, as well as the advantage of a better air, he took a house in

---

* This inscription was written by the late learned, and revereud Dr. Matthew Raine, one of the governors of the Dispensary, and was as follows. " Viro integerrimo, artis scientiæque suæ peritissimo, Roberto Willan, M. D. ob felicissimam operam, in morbis egenorum civium sanandis, viginti annos amplius gratuito et strenue navatam, ægrotantum apud Londinenses pauperum Patroni, amico amici, L. L. D. D. D. A. D. 1804, Preside Comite Sandvicense, collatæ pecuniæ Custode Gulielmo Waddington."

June 1811 at Craven-hill, about a mile from town, on the Uxbridge-road, where he spent his time, with the exception of two or three hours in the middle of the day, when he went to Bloomsbury-square, to receive the patients who came thither to consult him; but the probability of becoming phthisical, under the influence of an English winter, induced him to accede to the strenuous recommendation of some of his friends, and to undertake a voyage to Madeira. He accordingly embarked on the 10th of October, and arrived at Madeira on the 1st of December. By perseverance in an active course of medicine, after his arrival at Funchall, all his bad symptoms were considerably alleviated; insomuch that, in the month of February, he meditated a return to the south of England in April. But this alleviation was only temporary: his disease was again aggravated; the dropsy, and its concomitant obstruction to the functions, increased; and with his faculties remaining entire to the last, he expired on April 7, 1812, in the fifty-fifth year of his age.

By the death of Dr. Willan the profession was deprived of one of its bright ornaments, and of its zealous and able improvers; the sick, of a humane, disinterested, and discerning physician; and the world of an estimable and upright man, while in all the relations of domestic life, indeed, he was an object of general esteem and attachment.

As a professional writer, Dr. Willan appeared early, in his contributions to the periodical works. On his arrival in London, he became a member of a private medical society, which held its meetings at a coffee-house, in Cecil-street, and which published two volumes of papers, under the title of "Medical Communications," in 1784 and 1790. In the second of these volumes he published the history of "A remarkable case of Abstinence," in a hypochondriacal young man, which was uninterrupted for the space of sixty-one days, and terminated fatally. We believe that this was the only medical society of which he was ever a member. Several communications from him were also printed in the London Medical Journal, edited between the years 1781 and 1790 by Dr. Simmons. In the fourth volume, p. 421, a short letter of his appears, stating the character of a non-descript Byssus, found in the sulphureous waters of Aix; and in the sixth volume of the same Journal, he relates a fatal case of obstruction in the bowels, to which last he appended some useful reflections on the diagnostic symptoms of these obstructions, as occurring in the large or in the small intestines.   He has also some communications in the seventh and eighth volumes.   After the publication of the eleventh volume of this Journal, Dr. Simmons commenced a new series, under the title of " Medical Facts and Observations ;" in the third volume of which a paper of Dr. Willan's appeared, containing a description of several cases of iscuria renalis in children.

In the year 1796, Dr. Willan commenced a series of monthly reports, after the manner of those which Dr. Fothergill had formerly given to the publick *, containing a brief accouut of the state of the weather, and of the prevalent diseases in the metropolis.   These reports were published in the " Monthly Magazine," and were continued to 1800, when he collected them into a small volume, and published them in 1801, under the title of " Reports on the Diseases in London."   This little work is pregnant with important and original medical observations; but, from its unassuming pretensions, and desultory arrangement, has not been sufficiently known and valued by the profession.

We are unacquainted with the circumstances which originally drew the attention of Dr. Willan to the subject of cutaneous diseases ; but he was led so early as 1784 and 1785, to attend to the elementary forms of eruptions, if we may so speak, upon which he saw that a definite nomenclature could alone be founded, and upon which he erected the ingenious system developed in his large work.   At that period, in his notes of cases, he has seldom designated eruptions by their ordinary names ; but speaks of papulæ scorbuticæ, eruptio papulosa, &c.   In 1786, his notes exhibit still more decisive proofs of the careful attention which he was directing to this subject, in the minute descriptions (accompanied by slight sketches with the pen), of the forms, magnitude, and progress of eruptions. - The zeal with which he was at the same time investigating the original acceptation of the Greek, Roman, and Arabian terms, applied to eruptive diseases, is likewise manifested by his copious collections from authors, and by the occasional alterations of the nomenclature, applied in the

* In the Gentleman's Magazine, vol. XX. et seq.

cases, before he had finally determined on his arrangement. This was probably decided about 1789; as in the following year his classification was laid before the Medical Society of London, and honoured by the assignment of the Fothergillian gold medal of that year to the author.

It was not till the beginning of 1798, that the first part of this work, including the papulous eruptions, was published, in which, as in the subsequent parts, each variety was represented by a coloured engraving. In 1801 the second part, including the scaly diseases of the skin, appeared; in 1805 the third part, comprising only two genera of rashes, viz. measles and scarlet-fever; and in 1808 the fourth part, comprehending the remainder of the rashes, and the bullæ, or large vesications; the whole containing thirty-three plates, and comprising about half of the classification. Four orders, characterized by the appearance of pustules, vesicles, tubercles, and spots, remain unpublished. In the interim, however, from the temporary interest which the investigation of the vaccine question excited, Dr. Willan was induced so far to anticipate the order of vesicles, as to publish in 1806 a treatise " On Vaccination ;" in which he also introduced the subject of chicken-pox (another vesicular disease) in consequence of the mistakes which had been committed, in supposing that this was small-pox, when it occurred after vaccination.

In addition to the writings above mentioned, which have been committed to the press, Dr. Willan had left some others in an unfinished state. During three or four years previous to his death he had employed his leisure in a most extensive investigation of the antiquities of medicine, if we may so express ourselves, which he had conducted with his usual felicity of execution. His principal object was the illustration of four subjects, which are enveloped in no small degree of obscurity; namely, 1. The nature and origin of the epidemic or endemic ignis sacer, which was a frequent cause of much mortality in ancient times, and in the middle ages, and has been confounded with the plague, to which it had no resemblance but in its fatality : 2. The evidence of the prevalence of small-pox, measles, and scarlet fever, not only in the first ages of the Christian æra, but at still more ancient periods, of which he has brought together, with great ingenuity, a collection that appears incontrovertibly to establish the affirmative of the question : 3. The history of the leprosy of the middle ages : and 4. That of the lues venerea. The dissertations relative to the two first mentioned topics, Dr. Willan had nearly completed, having re-modelled the second, by the aid of a friendly amanuensis, during his residence in Madeira. They contain a very able and original view of the state of disease in the early ages of the world, not founded upon any fanciful explanation of terms, but deduced from a sagacious developement of facts, which have hitherto been concealed under perplexed and mistaken, but sufficiently intelligible language. He has likewise supported the conclusions which he has drawn by evidence collected from sources not usually resorted to in such researches.

Several years ago, Dr. Willan made a collection of observations in about two thousand patients, with a view to an investigation of medical physiognomy, or temperaments, chiefly in regard to the diseases to which each variety of temperament is peculiarly predisposed, and to the operation of medicines on them respectively. In the prosecution of this inquiry he procured several drawings (portraits) illustrative of the characteristic marks of the more striking varieties. He arrived at some interesting inferences respecting both the physical and moral constitutions connected with these external characters, but he did not deem the matter sufficiently matured to lay before the public.

In conclusion, we must not omit to mention a juvenile work published by Dr. Willan, on a theological subject ; namely, a " Life of Christ," related in the words of the evangelists, of whose details he selected those parts respectively which were most full and explicit; and he illustrated the whole by critical notes and explanations, which were particularly full in regard to the diseases mentioned by those sacred writers. A second edition of this work, with additional illustrations, was published in 1802.[1]

WILLET (ANDREW), a learned divine, was born in the city of Ely in 1562. His father, Mr. Thomas Willet, was sub-almoner to Edward VI. and a sufferer during the persecutions in queen Mary's reign ; but in that of queen Elizabeth, was preferred to the rectory of Barley in Hertfordshire, and to a prebend in the church of Ely. His son, who had been a very diligent and successful student while at school, was sent in his fourteenth year to Peter-house,

[1] Abridged from the Life of Dr. Willan, in the "Edinburgh Medical and Surgical Journal," No. 32; and obligingly communicated to us by the learned author, Dr. Bateman, of Bloomsbury-square.

Cambridge, whence he afterwards removed to Christ's college, and obtained a fellowship. After passing thirteen years in the university, during which he afforded many proofs of extraordinary application and talents, queen Elizabeth gave him his father's prebend in Ely, about 1598, the year his father died. One of his name was also rector of Reed, in Middlesex, in 1613, and of Chishall Parva, in Essex, in 1620, but it is doubtful whether this was the same person. It seems more certain, however, that he had the rectory of Childerley, in Cambridgeshire, and in 1597 that of Little Grantesden, in the same county, for which he took in exchange the rectory of Barley, vacant by his father's death. He was also chaplain to prince Henry. About this time he married a relation to Dr. Goad, by whom he had eleven sons and seven daughters.

Dr. Willet was usually called a living library, from the great extent of his reading and of his memory. He was also not less admired as a preacher, not only in his parish, but at court. He also obtained a great degree of celebrity by his numerous publications, particularly his "Synopsis Papismi; or a general view of papistrie," a work dedicated to the queen, which, although a folio of 1300 pages, passed through five editions, and was much admired in both universities, and by the clergy and laity at large, as the best refutation of popery, which had then appeared. He died of the consequences of a fall from his horse, at Hoddesdon, in Hertfordshire, Dec. 4, 1621, in the fifty-eighth year of his age. He was interred in the chancel of Barley church, where there is a representation of him at full length, in a praying attitude, and with an inscription, partly Latin and partly English.

Besides his "Synopsis Papismi," Dr. Willet was the author of many works, principally commentaries on the scriptures; as, 1. "Hexapla on Genesis and Exodus," fol. 1632. 2. "On Leviticus," 1631, fol. 3. "On Daniel," 1610, fol. 4. "On the Romans," 1611, fol. &c. 5. "Tractatus de Salomonis nuptiis, vel Epithalamium in nuptiis inter Comit. Palatinum et Elizabetham Jacobi regis filiam unicam," 1612, 4to. 6. "De Gratia generi humano in primo parente collata, de lapsu Adami," &c. Leyden, 1609, 8vo. 7. "Thesaurus Ecclesiae," Camb. 1604, 8vo. 8. "De animæ natura et viribus." 9. "Sacra Emblemata," &c. &c. with others, the titles of which are given very inaccurately by his biographers.

One of his descendants was the late Ralph Willet, esq. of Merly, in Dorsetshire, and founder and proprietor of the celebrated Merly library, which was disposed of by auction some months ago. [1]

WILLIAM of MALMSBURY.　See MALMSBURY.

WILLIAM of NANGIS.　See NANGIS.

WILLIAMS (ANNA), an ingenious English lady, was the daughter of a surgeon and physician in South Wales, where she was born in 1706.　Her father, Zachariah Williams, during his residence in Wales, imagined that he had discovered, by a kind of intuitive penetration, what had escaped the rest of mankind.　He fancied that he had been fortunate enough to ascertain the longitude by magnetism, and that the variations of the needle were equal, at equal distances, east and west.　The idea fired his imagination; and, prompted by ambition, and the hopes of splendid recompence, he determined to leave his business and habitation for the metropolis.　Miss Williams accompanied him, and they arrived in London about 1730; but the bright views which had allured him from his profession soon vanished.　The rewards which he had promised himself ended in disappointment; and the ill success of his schemes may be inferred from the only recompence which his journey and imagined discovery procured.　He was admitted a pensioner at the Charter-house.　When Miss Williams first resided in London, she devoted no inconsiderable portion of her time to its various amusements.　She visited every object that merited the inspection of a polished and laudably-inquisitive mind, or could attract the attention of a stranger.　At a later period of life she spoke familiarly of these scenes, of which the impression was never erased, though they must, however, have soon lost their allurements.　Mr. Williams did not long continue a member of the Charter-house.　A dispute with the masters obliged him to remove from this asylum of age and poverty.　In 1749 he published in 4to "A true Narrative," &c. of the treatment he had met with.　He was now exposed to severe trials, and every succeeding day increased the gloominess of his prospects.　In 1740 Miss Williams lost her sight by a cataract, which prevented her, in a great measure, from assisting his distresses, and alleviating

[1] Fuller's Abel Redivivus, and Barksdale's Remembrancer, in both of which is Dr. Willet's life by his son-in-law Dr. Peter Smith.—Strype's Whitgift, p. 435, 543.—Ath. Ox. vol. I.—Nichols's Bowyer, vol. VIII.

his sorrows. She still, however, felt her passion for literature equally predominant. She continued the same attention to the neatness of her dress; and, what is more extraordinary, continued still the exercise of her needle, a branch of female accomplishment in which she had before displayed great excellence. During the lowness of her fortune she worked for herself with nearly as much dexterity and readiness as if she had not suffered a loss so irreparable. Her powers of conversation retained their former vigour. Her mind did not sink under these calamities; and the natural activity of her disposition animated her to uncommon exertions:

> "Though fallen on evil days;
> On evil days though fallen;
> In darkness, and with dangers compass'd round,
> And solitude!"

In 1746, notwithstanding her blindness, she published the "Life of the emperor Julian, with notes, translated from the French of F. La Bleterie." In this translation she was assisted by two female friends, whose names were Wilkinson. This book was printed by Bowyer, in whose life, by Nichols, we are informed, that he contributed the advertisement, and wrote the notes, in conjunction with Mr. Clarke and others. The work was revised by Markland and Clarke. It does not appear what pecuniary advantages Miss Williams might derive from this publication. They were probably not very considerable, and afforded only a temporary relief to the misfortunes of her father. About this time, Mr. Williams, who imparted his afflictions to all from whom he hoped consolation or assistance, told his story to Dr. Samuel Johnson; and, among other aggravations of distress, mentioned his daughter's blindness. He spoke of her acquirements in such high terms, that Mrs. Johnson, who was then living, expressed a desire of seeing her; and accordingly she was soon afterwards brought to the doctor's house by her father; and Mrs. Johnson found her possessed of such qualities as recommended her strongly for a friend. As her own state of health, therefore, was weak, and her husband was engaged during the greater part of the day in his studies, she gave Miss Williams a general invitation: a strict intimacy soon took place; but the enjoyment of their friendship did not continue long. Soon after its commencement, Mrs. Johnson was attended by her new companion in an illness which terminated fatally.

Dr. Johnson still retained his regard for her, and in 1752, by his recommendation, Mr. Sharp, the surgeon, undertook to perform the operation on Miss Williams's eyes, which is usual in such cases, in hopes of restoring her sight. Her own habitation was not judged convenient for the occasion. She was, therefore, invited to the doctor's. The surgeon's skill, however, proved fruitless, as the crystalline humour was not sufficiently inspissated for the needle to take effect. The recovery of her sight was pronounced impossible. After this dreadful sentence, she never left the roof which had received her during the operation. The doctor's kindness and conversation soothed her melancholy situation: and her society seemed to alleviate the sorrows which his late loss had occasioned.

When Dr. Johnson, however, changed his residence, she returned to lodgings; and, in 1755, her father published a book, in Italian and English, entitled "An Account of an Attempt to ascertain the longitude at sea, by an exact Theory of the magnetical Needle."

In 1755, Mrs. Williams's circumstances were rendered more easy by the profits of a benefit-play, granted her by the kindness of Mr. Garrick, from which she received 200*l*. which was placed in the stocks. While Mrs. Williams enjoyed so comfortable an asylum, her life passed in one even tenour. It was chequered by none of those scenes which enliven biography by their variety. The next event of any consequence, in the history of Mrs. Williams, was the publication of a volume of "Miscellanies in Prose and Verse," in 1766. Her friends assisted her in the completion of this book, by several voluntary contributions; and 100*l*. which was laid out in a bridge-bond, was added to her little stock by the liberality of her subscribers. About 1766, Dr. Johnson removed from the Temple, where he had lived, for some time, in chambers, to Johnson's-court, Fleet-street, and again invited to his house the worthy friend of Mrs. Johnson. The latter days of Mrs. Williams were now rendered easy and comfortable. Her wants were few, and, to supply them, she made her income sufficient. She still possessed an unalterable friend in Dr. Johnson. Her acquaintance was select rather than numerous. Their society made the infirmities of age less intolerable, and communicated a cheerfulness to her situation, which solitary blindness would otherwise have rendered truly deplorable.

She died at the house of her friend, in Bolt-court, Fleet-street (whither they removed about 1775), on the 6th of September, 1783, aged seventy-seven years. She bequeathed all her little effects to a charity, which had been instituted for the education of poor deserted girls, and supported by the voluntary contributions of several ladies. [1]

WILLIAMS (CHARLES HANBURY), a statesman and wit of considerable temporary fame, was the third son of John Hanbury, esq. a South Sea Director, who died in 1734. Charles, who in consequence of the will of his godfather, Charles Williams, esq. of Caerleon, assumed the name of Williams, was born in 1709, and educated at Eton, where he made considerable progress in classical literature; and having finished his studies, travelled through various parts of Europe. Soon after his return he assumed the name of Williams, obtained from his father the estate of Coldbrook, and espoused, in 1732, lady Frances Coningsby, youngest daughter of Thomas, earl of Coningsby.

On the death of his father in 1733, he was elected member of parliament for the county of Monmouth, and uniformly supported the administration of sir Robert Walpole, whom he idolized; he received from that minister many early and confidential marks of esteem, and in 1739 was was appointed by him paymaster of the marines. His name occurs only twice as a speaker, in Chandler's debates: but the substance of his speech is given in neither instance. Sprightliness of conversation, ready wit, and agreeable manners, introduced him to the acquaintance of men of the first talents: he was the soul of the celebrated coterie, of which the most conspicuous members were, lord Hervey, Winnington, Horace Walpole, late earl of Orford, Stephen Fox, earl of Ilchester, and Henry Fox, lord Holland, with whom, in particular, he lived in the strictest habits of intimacy and friendship. At this period he distinguished himself by political ballads remarkable for vivacity, keenness of invective, and ease of versification. In 1746 he was installed knight of the Bath, and soon after, appointed envoy to the court of Dresden, a situation which he is said to have solicited, that its employments might divert his grief for the death of his friend Mr. Winnington. The votary of wit and pleasure was instantly transformed into a man of business,

[1] Gent. Mag. vols. XX. LIII. and LVII.—London Mag. 1784.—Hawkins's Life of Johnson.—Boswell's Life of Johnson.—Nichols's Bowyer.

and the author of satirical odes penned excellent dispatches. He was well adapted for the office of a foreign minister, and the lively, no less than the solid, parts of his character, proved useful in his new employment; flow of conversation, sprightliness of wit, politeness of demeanour, ease of address, conviviality of disposition, together with the delicacy of his table, attracted persons of all descriptions. He had an excellent tact for discriminating characters, humouring the foibles of those with whom he negociated, and conciliating those by whom the great were either directly or indirectly governed.

In 1749 he was appointed, at the express desire of the king, to succeed Mr. Legge as minister plenipotentiary at the court of Berlin; but in 1751 returned to his embassy at Dresden. During his residence at these courts, he transacted the affairs of England and Hanover with so much address, that he was dispatched to Petersburg, in a time of critical emergency, to conduct a negociation of great delicacy and importance. The disputes concerning the limits of Nova Scotia, and the possessions of North America threatened a rupture between Great Britain and France; hostilities were on the point of commencing in America, and France had resolved to invade the Low Countries, and the electorate of Hanover, and to excite a continental war. With this view the cabinet of Versailles proposed to the king of Prussia, to co-operate in invading the electorate, and attacking the dominions of the house of Austria, hitherto the inseparable ally of England. The British cabinet, alarmed at this aspect of affairs, formed a plan of a triple alliance between Great Britain, Austria, and Russia, and to promote the negociation, the king repaired to Hanover, accompanied by the earl of Holdernesse, secretary of state.

Sir Charles Hanbury Williams arrived at St. Petersburg in the latter end of June; the negociation had been already opened by Mr. Guy Dickins, who lately occupied the post of envoy to the court of Russia; but his character and manners were not calculated to ensure success. He was treated with coldness and reserve by the empress, and had rendered himself highly offensive to the great chancellor, count Bestucheff. On the first appearance of the new ambassador, things immediately wore a favourable aspect; at his presence all obstacles were instantly removed, and all difficulties vanished. The votary of wit and pleasure was well received by the gay and voluptuous Elizabeth; he attached to his cause the great duke, afterwards the unfortunate Peter the Third; and his consort, the princess of Anhalt Zerbst, who became conspicuous under the name of Catherine the Second. All the ministers vied in loading him with marks of attention and civility; he broke through the usual forms of etiquette, and united in his favour the discordant views of the Russian cabinet; he conciliated the unbending and suspicious Bestucheff; warmed the phlegmatic temper of the vice-chancellor, count Voronzoff; and gained the under agents, who were enabled, by petty intrigues and secret cabals, to thwart the intentions of the principal ministers. He fulfilled literally the tenor of his own expressions, that he would "make use of the honeymoon of his ministry," to conclude the convention as speedily as possible on the best terms which could be obtained: he executed the orders of the king, not to sign any treaty in which an attack on any of his majesty's allies, or on any part of his electoral dominions, was not made a *casus fœderis:* in six weeks after his arrival at St. Petersburg, he obtained the signature, without using all the full powers intrusted to him by the British cabinet, and instantly transmitted it to Hanover.

His sanguine imagination exaggerated the merit of his services; and he fondly expected an instantaneous answer filled with expressions of high applause. Some time, however, elapsed before any answer arrived; at length the expected messenger came; he seized the dispatches, and opened them with extreme impatience, in the presence of his confidential friend, count Poniatowski, afterwards king of Poland. In a few minutes he threw the letter which he was reading on the floor, struck his forehead with both his hands, and remained for some time absorbed in a deep reverie. Turning at length to count Poniatowski, he exclaimed, "Would you think it possible? Instead of receiving thanks for my zeal and activity in concluding the convention, I am blamed for an informality in the signature, and the king is displeased with my efforts to serve him." This interesting anecdote, Mr. Coxe, from whose "Tour in Monmouthshire" this life is abridged, received from the late king of Poland himself in 1785. To the same work we must refer for a particular detail of the intrigues which baffled the endeavours of sir Charles, and in-

duced him to make repeated and earnest entreaties, in consequence of which, permission was granted for his return,
but he was induced to continue in his post until all his
efforts proved unsuccessful, and the empress coalesced with
Austria and France.　In the midst of this arduous business
his health rapidly declined, his head was occasionally affected, and his mind distracted with vexation ; the irregularities of his life irritated his nerves, and a fatiguing journey exhausted his spirits.

Soon after his arrival at Hamburgh, in the autumn of
1757, he was suddenly smitten with a woman of low intrigue, gave her a note for 2000*l*. and a contract of marriage, though his wife was still living ; he also took large
doses of stimulating medicines, which affected his head,
and he was conveyed to England in a state of insanity.
During the passage, he fell from the deck into the hold,
and dangerously bruised his side ; he was blooded four
times on board, and four times immediately after his arrival in England.　In little more than a month he recovered,
and passed the summer at Coldbrook-house.　But towards
the latter end of 1759, he relapsed into a state of insanity,
and expired on the second of November, aged fifty.

His official dispatches, says Mr. Coxe, are written with
great life and spirit ; he delineates characters with truth
and facility ; and describes his diplomatic transactions with
minuteness and accuracy, but without tediousness or for-
mality.　His verses were highly prized by his contemporaries, but in perusing those which have been given to the
public, " Odes, 1775, 12mo," and those which are still in
manuscript, the greater part are political effusions, or licentious lampoons, abounding with local wit and temporary
satire, eagerly read at the time of their appearance, but
little interesting to posterity.　Three of his pieces, however, deserve to be exempted from this general character ;
his poem of " Isabella, or the Morning," is remarkable for
ease of versification, and happy discrimination of character ;
his epitaph on Mr. Winnington is written with great feeling ; and his beautiful " Ode to Mr. Pointz," in honour of
the duke of Cumberland, breathes a spirit of sublimity,
which entitles the author to the rank of a poet, and excites
our regret that his muse was not always employed on subjects worthy of his talents.

He wrote a very admirable paper in the World, No. 37,

not noticed by Mr. Coxe, but which from the date appears to have been the employment of a leisure hour when at St. Petersburg.

Sir Charles left by his wife two daughters; Frances, first wife of William Anne, late earl of Essex, and Charlotte, who espoused the honourable Robert Boyle Walsingham, youngest son of the earl of Shannon, a commodore in the navy. On his death without issue male, the estate and mansion of Coldbrook came to his brother George, who died in 1764, and now belongs to his son John Hanbury Williams, esq. the present proprietor. [1]

WILLIAMS (DANIEL), an eminent divine among the dissenters, and a munificent benefactor to their and other societies, both of the learned and charitable kind, was born about 1644, at Wrexham, in the county of Denbigh, in North Wales. No particulars are known of his parents, or of his early years, but it appears that he laboured under some disadvantages as to education, which, however, he surmounted by spirit and perseverance. He says of himself, that "from five years old, he had no employment, but his studies, and that by nineteen he was regularly admitted a preacher." As this was among the nonconformists, it is probable that his parents or early connections lay among that society. As he entered on his ministry about 1663, when the exercise of it was in danger of incurring the penalties of the law, he was induced to go to Ireland, and was there invited to be chaplain to the countess of Meath. Some time after he was called to be pastor to a congregation of dissenters assembling in Wood-street, Dublin, in which situation he continued for nearly twenty years, and was highly approved and useful. Here he married his first wife, a lady of family and fortune, which last, while it gave him a superior rank and consequence to many of his brethren, he contemplated only as the means of doing good.

During the troubles in Ireland, at the latter end of the reign of king James II. he found it necessary to return to London in 1687, and resided in London. Here he was of great use upon a very critical occasion. Some of the court agents at that time endeavoured to bring the dissenters in the city to address the king upon his dispensing with the penal laws. In a conference at one of their meetings

[1] Coxe's Tour in Monmouthshire.

upon that occasion, in the presence of some of the agents, Mr. Williams declared, "That it was with him past doubt, that the severities of the former reign upon the protestant dissenters were, rather as they stood in the way of *arbitrary* power, than for their *religious* dissent. So it were better for them to be reduced to their former hardships, than declare for measures destructive of the liberties of their country ; and that for himself, before he would concur in such an address, which should be thought an approbation of the *dispensing power*, he would choose to lay down his liberty at his majesty's feet." He pursued the argument with such clearness and strength, that all present rejected the motion, and the emissaries went away disappointed. There was a meeting at the same time of a considerable number of the city clergy, waiting the issue of their deliberation, who were greatly animated and encouraged by this resolution of the dissenting ministers. Very recent experience has shewn how much Mr. Williams differs in this matter from his descendants, many of whom have been the professed advocates for what is called catholic emancipation.

After the revolution, Mr. Williams was not only frequently consulted by king William concerning Irish affairs, with which he was well acquainted, but often regarded at court on behalf of several who fled from Ireland, and were capable of doing service to government. He received great acknowledgments and thanks upon this account, when, in 1700, he went back to that country to visit his old friends, and to settle some affairs, relative to his estate in that kingdom. After preaching for some time occasionally in London, he became pastor of a numerous congregation at Hand-alley in Bishopsgate-street in 1688, and upon the death of the celebrated Richard Baxter in 1691, by whom he was greatly esteemed, he succeeded him as one of those who preached the merchants'-lecture, at Pinners'-hall, Broad-street. But it was not long before the frequent clashings in the discourses of these lecturers caused a division. Mr. Williams had preached warmly against some antinomian tenets, which giving offence to many persons, a design was formed to exclude him from the lecture. Upon this he, with Dr. Bates, Mr. Howe, and Mr. Alsop, &c. retired and raised another lecture at Salter's-hall on the same day and hour. This division was soon after increased by the publication of some of Dr. Crisp's works,

(See Crisp) and a controversy took place as to the more or less of antinomianism in these works, which lasted for some years, and was attended with much intemperance and personal animosity. What is rather remarkable, the contending parties appealed to bishop Stillingfleet, and Dr. Jonathan Edwards of Oxford, who both approved of what Mr. Williams had done. Mr. Williams's chief publication on the subject was entitled "Gospel Truth stated and vindicated," 1691, 12mo. The controversy by his friends was called the antinomian, but by Dr. Crisp's advocates the *neonomian* controversy. Mr. Williams was not only reckoned a heretic, but attempts were even made to injure his moral character, which, however, were defeated by the unanimous testimony of all who knew him, or took the trouble to inquire into the ground of such accusations. In his congregation, it is said, he lost no friend.

Some time after the death of his wife, he married in 1701, as his second, Jane, the widow of Mr. Francis Barkstead, and the daughter of one Guill, a French refugee; by her also he had a very considerable fortune, which he devoted to the purposes of liberality. Of his political sentiments, we learn only, that he was an enemy to the bill against occasional conformity, and a staunch friend to the union with Scotland. When on a visit to that country in 1709, he received a diploma for the degree of D. D. from the university of Edinburgh, and another from Glasgow. One of his biographers gives us the following account of his conduct on this occasion. " He was so far from seeking or expecting this honour, that he was greatly displeased with the occasion. of it, and with great modesty he entreated Mr. Carstairs, the principal of the college at Edinburgh, to prevent it. But the dispatch was made before that desire of his could reach them. I have often heard him express his dislike of the thing itself, and much more his distaste at the officious vanity of some who thought they had much obliged him when they moved for the procuring it; and this, not that he despised the honour of being a graduate in form in that profession in which he was now a truly reverend father; nor in the least, that he refused to receive any favours from the ministers of the church of Scotland, for whom he preserved a very great esteem, and on many occasions gave signal testimonies of his respect; but he thought it savoured of an extraordinary vanity, that the English presbyterians should accept a nominal distinction, which the ministers of the church of Scotland declined for themselves, and did so lest it should break in upon that parity which they so severely maintained; which parity among the ministers of the gospel, the presbyterians in England acknowledged also to be agreeable to that scripture rule, 'Whosoever will be greatest among you let him be as the younger,' Luke xxii. 26; and Matt. xxiii. 8, ' Be ye not called Rabbi,' of which text a learned writer says, it should have been translated, ' Be ye not called doctors;' and the Jewish writers and expositors of their law, are by some authors styled Jewish Rabbins, by others, and that more frequently, doctors, &c. &c." Our readers need scarcely be told that this is another point on which Dr. Williams differs much from his successors, who are as ambitious of the honour of being called doctor, as he was to avoid it.

In the latter end of queen Anne's reign, our author appears to have had extraordinary fears respecting the protestant succession, and that he corresponded very freely with the earl of Oxford upon that subject, who, however, discovering that he had been yet more free in his sentiments in another and more private correspondence, withdrew his friendship from him. Soon after, the accession of George I. dispelled his fears, and he was at the head of a body of the dissenting ministers, who addressed his majesty on that auspicious occasion.

Dr. Williams died, after a short illness, Jan. 26, 1715-16, in the seventy-third year of his age. He appears to have been a man of very considerable abilities, and having acquired an independent fortune, had great weight both as a member of the dissenting interest, and as a politician in general. As he had spent much of his life in benevolent actions, at his death he fully evinced, that they were the governing principles of his character. The bulk of his estate he bequeathed to a great variety of charities. Besides the settlement on his wife, and legacies to his relations and friends, he left donations for the education of youth in Dublin, and for an itinerant preacher to the native Irish; to the poor in Wood-street congregation, and to that in Hand-alley, where he had been successively preacher; to the French refugees; to the poor of Shoreditch parish, where he lived; to several ministers' widows; to St. Thomas's hospital; to the London workhouse; to several presbyterian meetings in the country; to the college of Glasgow; to the society for the reformation of manners; to the society of Scotland for propagating Christian knowledge; to the society for New-England, to support two persons to preach to the Indians; to the maintaining of charity-schools in Wales, and the support of students; for the distribution of Bibles, and pious books among the poor, &c, He also ordered a convenient building to be purchased, or erected, for the reception of his own library, and the curious collection of Dr. Bates, which he purchased for that purpose, at the expence of between five and six hundred pounds. Accordingly, a considerable number of years after his death, a commodious building was erected by subscription among the opulent dissenters, in Redcross-street, Cripplegate, where the doctor's books were deposited, and by subsequent additions, the collection has become a very considerable one. It is also a depository for paintings of nonconformist ministers, which are now very numerous; of manuscripts, and other matters of curiosity or utility. In this place, the dissenting ministers meet for transacting all business relating to the general body. Registers of births of the children of protestant dissenters are also kept here with accuracy, and have been, in the courts of law, allowed equal validity with parish registers. The librarian, who resides in the house, is usually a minister, chosen from among the English presbyterians, to which denomination the founder belonged. Dr. Williams's publications, besides his " Gospel Truth stated," are chiefly sermons preached on occasion of ordinations, or funerals. These were published together in 1738, 2 vols. 8vo, with some account of his life.[1]

WILLIAMS (DAVID), a literary and religious projector of some note, was born at a village near Cardigan, in 1738, and after receiving the rudiments of education, was placed in a school or college at Carmarthen, preparatory to the dissenting ministry; which profession he entered upon in obedience to parental authority, but very contrary to his own inclination. His abilities and acquirements even then appeared of a superior order; but he has often in the latter part of his life stated to the writer of his memoirs, in the Gentleman's Magazine, that he had long considered it as a severe misfortune, that the most injurious impressions were made upon his youthful and ardent mind by the cold, austere, oppressive, and unamiable manner in which the doctrines and duties of religion were disguised in the stern and rigid habits of a severe puritanical master. From this college he took the office of teacher to a small congregation at Frome, in Somersetshire, and after a short residence was removed to a more weighty charge at Exeter. There the eminent abilities and engaging manners of the young preacher opened to him the seductive path of pleasure; when the reproof that some elder members of the society thought necessary, being administered in a manner to awaken resentment rather than contrition; and the eagle eye of anger discovering in his accusers imperfections of a different character indeed, but of tendency little suited to a public disclosure, the threatened recrimination suspended the proceedings, and an accommodation took place, by which Mr. Williams left Exeter, and was engaged to the superintendence of a dissenting congregation at Highgate. After a residence there of a year or two, he made his first appearance in 1770, as an author, by a " Letter to David Garrick," a judicious and masterly critique on the actor, but a sarcastic personal attack on the man, intended to rescue Mossop from the supposed unjust displeasure of the modern Roscius: this effect was produced, Mossop was liberated, and the letter withdrawn from the booksellers. Shortly after appeared " The Philosopher, in three Conversations," which were much read, and attracted considerable notice. This was soon followed by " Essays on Public Worship, Patriotism, and Projects of Reformation;" written and published upon the occasion of the leading religious controversy of the day; but though they obtained considerable circulation, they appear not to have softened the asperities of either of the contending parties. The Appendix to these Essays gave a strong indication of that detestation of intolerance, bigotry, and hypocrisy which formed the leading character of his subsequent life, and which had been gradually taking possession of his mind from the conduct of some of the circle of associates into which his profession had thrown him.

He published two volumes of " Sermons," chiefly upon Religious Hypocrisy, and then discontinued the exercise of his profession, and his connection with the body of dissenters. He now turned his thoughts to the education of youth, and in 1773, published "A Treatise on Education," recommending a method founded on the plans of Comменius and Rousseau, which he proposed to carry into effect. He took a house in Lawrence-street, Chelsea, married a young lady not distinguished either by fortune or connection, and soon found himself at the head of a lucrative and prosperous establishment. A severe domestic misfortune in the death of his wife blighted this prospect of fame and fortune : his fortitude sunk under the shock ; his anxious attendance upon her illness injured his own health, the internal concerns of the family became disarranged, and he left his house and his institution, to which he never again returned.

During his residence at Chelsea, he became a member of a select club of political and literary characters, to one of whom, the celebrated Benjamin Franklin, he afforded an asylum in his house at Chelsea during the popular ferment against him, about the time of the commencement of the American war. In this club was formed the plan of public worship intended to unite all parties and persuasions in one comprehensive form. Mr. Williams drew up and published, "A Liturgy on the universal principles of Religion and Morality ;" and afterwards printed two volumes of Lectures, delivered with this Liturgy at the chapel in Margaret-street, Cavendish-square, opened April 7, 1776. This service continued about four years, but with so little public support, that the expence of the establishment nearly involved the lecturer in the loss of his liberty. As the plan proposed to include in one act of public worship every class of men who acknowledged the being of a God, and the utility of public prayer and praise, it necessarily left unnoticed every other point of doctrine ; intending, that without expressing them in public worship, every man should be left in unmolested possession of his own peculiar opinions in private. This, however, would not satisfy any of the various classes and divisions of Christians; it was equally obnoxious to the churchman and to the dissenter ; and as even the original proposers, though consisting only of five or six, could not long agree, several of them attempting to obtain a more marked expression of their own peculiar opinions and dogmas, the plan necessarily expired. Mr. Williams now occupied his time and talents in assisting gentlemen whose education had been defective, and in forwarding their qualifications for the senate, the diplo-

macy, and the learned professions. In this employment
he prepared, and subsequently published, "Lectures on
Political Principles," and "Lectures on Education," in
3 vols. His abilities also were ever most readily and cheer-
fully employed in the cause of friendship and benevolence;
and many persons under injury and distress have to acknowledge the lasting benefit of his energetic and powerful pen.

During the alarm in 1780 he published a tract, entitled
"A Plan of Association on Constitutional Principles;"
and in 1782, on occasion of the county meetings and associations, he gave to the public his "Letters on Political
Liberty;" the most important perhaps of all his works; it
was extensively circulated both in England and France,
having been translated into French by Brissot, and was the
occasion of its author being invited to Paris, to assist in
the formation of a constitution for that country. He continued about six months in Paris; and on the death of the
king, and declaration of war against this country, took leave
of his friends of the Girondist party, with an almost prophetic intimation of the fate that awaited them. He
brought with him on his return a letter from the minister of
war, addressed to lord Grenville, and intended to give Mr.
Williams, who was fully and confidentially entrusted with
the private sentiments and wishes of the persons then in
actual possession of the government of France, an opportunity of conveying those sentiments and wishes to the
British ministry. Mr. Williams delivered the letter into
the hands of Mr. Aust, the under secretary of state, but
never heard from lord Grenville on the subject. Some
further curious circumstances relating to this transaction
are detailed in a page or two, corrected by Mr. Williams
himself, in Bisset's "History of George III."

Previously to receiving this invitation he had removed
from Russell-street to Brompton, for the purpose of executing an engagement he had formed with Mr. Bowyer, to
superintend the splendid edition of Hume, and write a
continuation of the history; but after his return from
France he found himself in an extraordinary situation, for
at the very time he had been denounced in France as a
royalist, he had been branded in his own country as a democrat; and he was informed that his engagement respecting the History of England could not be carried into effect,
in consequence, as it was stated, of an intimation having

been given that the privilege of dedication to the crown would be withdrawn if he continued the work. About this time he published the " Lessons to a young Prince," and engaged in, and afterwards executed, the " History of Monmouthshire," in one vol. 4to, with plates by his friend the rev. John Gardnor.

With regard to the circumstance upon which he always seemed inclined to rest his fame, and which was most dear to his heart—the establishment of the Literary Fund, he had, so far back as the time of his residence at Chelsea, projected a plan for the assistance of deserving authors in distress; and after several ineffectual attempts, he so far succeeded in 1788 and 1789 as to found the institution, and commence its benevolent operations, and with unremitting zeal and activity devoted the full force of his abilities, and the greater part of his time and attention, to foster and support the infant institution. He had the heartfelt satisfaction of seeing it continually rise in public estimation, and at length honoured with the illustrious patronage of his royal highness the prince of Wales, who generously bestowed an annual donation for the purpose of providing a house for the use of the society, and expressly desired that Mr. Williams should reside in it. A singular and striking work, written by Mr. Williams and several of his zealous and able coadjutors, who each put their names to their own several productions, was given by the public under the title of " The Claims of Literature; explanatory of the Nature, Formation, and Purposes of the Institution."

During the peace of Amiens Mr. Williams again visited Paris, and is supposed to have been then intrusted with some confidential mission from the government of his own country, his remarkable figure having previously been noticed entering the houses of several of the higher members of the then administration. On his return he published a much enlarged edition of a little work which the alarm of invasion had induced him to write, entitled " Regulations of Parochial Police;" and he is thought to have been the author of a sort of periodical publication which appeared about that time in numbers, " Egeria; or Elementary Studies on the Progress of Nations in Political Economy, Legislation, and Government;" but which does not appear to have been continued beyond the first volume. The last acknowledged work that proceeded from his prolific pen was, " Preparatory Studies for Political Reformers." It is curious and instructive to observe the marked and striking effect produced by his experience of reform and reformers in the struggles of, and consequent upon, the French revolution; his diction retains its full vigour, but his anticipations are much less sanguine, and his opinions on the pliability of the materials on which reformers are to operate, or in other words, on the real character of human nature, seem much changed. About five years before his death he was seized with a severe paralytic affection, from which he partially recovered, but continued to suffer the gradual loss of his corporeal and mental powers; his memory became very considerably impaired, and for some length of time preceding his decease he was unable to walk or move without assistance. The tender assiduities of an affectionate niece soothed the sorrows of declining nature, and received from him the most affecting and frequent expressions of gratitude. The state of his mind cannot be so well depicted as by himself in the following letter, one of the last he ever wrote, and addressed to a clergyman of the church of England, in the country:

"Dear Sir,

"I am now drawing near my end, and am desirous to conclude my days in peace. I have outlived almost all my relations and all my acquaintance; and I am desirous to exchange the most sincere and cordial forgiveness with those I have in any sort offended. I had once a great regard for you; why it was not continued I have forgotten. Indeed, a paralytic stroke has greatly destroyed my memory, and will soon destroy me. I take leave of my friends and acquaintance; among others I take leave of you. I greatly esteemed you and your worthy father, and I hope you will only remember what you saw commendable and good in me, and believe me very sincerely yours. D. W."

It will readily be supposed that this letter brought the gentleman immediately to town; and his friendly offices of kindness contributed very much during the last two years to the comfort and consolation of his suffering friend, who breathed his last on Saturday morning, the 29th of June 1816, and was interred the Saturday following, in St. Anne's church, Soho, under this inscription:

David Williams, esq. aged 78 years;
Founder of the Literary Fund.

In the words of his friend, captain Thomas Morris, "The

distinguishing traits of Mr. Williams's character were, a boundless philanthropy and disinterestedness; studious of every acquisition that forms the taste, but applying the strength of his genius to the arts of government and education as objects of the highest importance to the welfare of nations and the happiness of individuals. In his dress elegantly plain; in domestic life attentive to the niceties of decorum; in public politely ceremonious; in all his manners dignified and distinguished; in conversation elevated; in his person tall and agreeable, having a commanding look softened with affability."

A review of the life and writings of this remarkably gifted man strongly illustrates the observation, that political and moral philosophy, theories of government and education, even when displayed with splendid ability, and enforced with the most engaging benevolence, and with the best and most earnest motives of doing good, are found by a painful experience to be wholly inadequate to the task of reforming mankind, if employed without the aid of Christianity; it is the Gospel alone that can reach the weak and erring heart of man, and found the reformation and improvement of societies upon the purity, the virtue, and the piety of individuals. But to this very necessary knowledge Mr. Williams was a stranger. In early life he appears to have formed himself on the model of the Voltaires, Rousseaus, D'Alemberts, and other French writers of a similar stamp. They unfortunately had to operate on weak minds, and produced incalculable mischief. David Williams, by bringing forward his opinions and his schemes in a country where genuine religion is understood, and at all times ably defended, sunk under the argument and ridicule which he had to encounter, and became a harmless visionary. [1]

WILLIAMS (GRIFFITH), bishop of Ossory, in Ireland, was born at Caernarvon, in North Wales, about 1589. In 1603 he was sent to Oxford by his uncle; but this relation failing to support him, he was, after two years, received at Cambridge by the kindness of a friend, and admitted of Jesus college, where he took his degrees in arts, and after entering into holy orders, was appointed curate of Hanwell, in Middlesex. Afterwards the earl of Southampton gave him the rectory of Foscot, in Buckinghamshire; and he was for some years lecturer of St. Peter's, Cheapside,

1 Gent. Mag. vol. LXXXVI.

London. While in this situation, he informs us, "his persecutions began from the puritans," who took offence at something he had preached and printed; and it was now he published his first book, called "The Resolution of Pilate," which neither Harris nor Wood mention among his works; and another called "The Delight of the Saints. A most comfortable treatise of grace and peace, and many other excellent points, whereby men may live like saints on earth, and become true saints in heaven," Lond. 1622, fol. reprinted 1635. His boldness in the pulpit raised him many enemies, but their persecutions were for some time of no avail, until at length they prevailed on the bishop of London to suspend him. This appears to have been in his twenty-seventh year, when, notwithstanding, he went back to Cambridge and took his degree of B. D. On his return to London he found friends in Abbot, archbishop of Canterbury, and in the chancellor Egerton, who gave him the living of Llan-Lecbyd, in the diocese of Bangor, worth 100*l.* and a better rectory than what he was suspended from by the bishop of London. He now found a new enemy. Refusing another living in exchange for what he had just got, the bishop of Bangor presented certain articles against him *ex officio*, and he was again obliged to appeal to the Arches. The bishop of Bangor being in town, the archbishop of Canterbury sent for them both, and checked the bishop for his prosecution, and gave Mr. Williams a licence to preach through several dioceses of his province.

After remaining four years in the diocese of Bangor, in which the bishop's conduct made him uneasy, he went to Cambridge, and took his degree of D. D. and returning to London became domestic chaplain to the earl of Montgomery (afterwards earl of Pembroke) and tutor to his children, and was promoted to be chaplain to the king, prebendary of Westminster, and dean of Bangor, to the last of which preferments he was instituted March 28, 1634; and he held this deanery in commendam till his death. He says that, "before he was forty years old, he *narrowly escaped* being elected bishop of St. Asaph." He remained in the enjoyment of these preferments about twelve years, and in 1641 was advanced to the bishopric of Ossory, but the Irish rebellion breaking out in less than a month after his consecration, he was forced to take refuge in England, and joined the court, being in attendance on his majesty, as one of his chaplains, at the battle of Edge-hill, Oct. 23,

1642. He remained also with the king during the greater part of the winter at Oxford, and then retired to Wales to be at more leisure to write his " Discovery of Mysteries, or the plots of the parliament to overthrow both church and state," published at Oxford, 1643, 4to. In the following year he published his " Jura majestatis; the rights of kings both in church and state, granted, first by God, secondly, violated by rebels, and thirdly, vindicated by the truth," Oxford, 4to. He had also published in 1643, at the same place, "Vindiciæ regum, or the Grand Rebellion," &c.

In the mean time he was employed to go to London to try to bring over the earl of Pembroke to the royal cause (two of whose sons were with the king at Oxford, and had been the bishop's pupils). This task he undertook, surrounded as it was with danger, and obnoxious as he knew himself to be by his publications. The negociation failed, and the earl was so incensed, that Dr. Williams had reason to think he would deliver him up to parliament, who had recently ordered his last mentioned publication to be burnt. He contrived, therefore, and not without some difficulty, to obtain a pass from the lord mayor of London, "as a poor pillaged preacher of Ireland," and by this means got to Northampton, and thence to Oxford, whence he went first to Wales, and then to Ireland, where he remained until after the battle of Naseby, in 1645.

After this he underwent a series of hardships for his loyalty, and lived sometimes in Wales and sometimes in Ireland, in a very precarious way, until the restoration. As soon as he heard the first news of that event he went to Dublin, and preaching on the day of his arrival at St. Bride's, was the first man in Ireland who publicly prayed for the king. He then repaired to his diocese, and finding his palace as well as his cathedral in ruins, set himself to repair both, but found many difficulties, and was involved in many law-suits before he could recover the revenues belonging to the see. He appears to have been perfectly disinterested, for, besides what he laid out on these repairs, he devoted the greater part of his income to charitable purposes. He died at Kilkenny, March 29, 1672, in the eighty-third year of his age, and was buried on the south-side of the chancel of the cathedral.

Bishop Williams's other works were, 1. " Seven golden candlesticks, holding the seven greatest lights of Christian

Religion," Lond. 1627, 4to.   2. " The True Church shewed
to all men that desire to be members of the same : in six
books, containing the whole body of divinity," ibid. 1629,
fol.   3. " The right way to the best Religion ; wherein is
largely explained the sum and principal heads of the Gospel,
in certain sermons and treatises," ibid. 1636, fol.   4. " The
great Antichrist revealed," ibid. 1660, fol.   In this he attempted to prove that Antichrist was neither pope, nor
Turk, nor any one person, but the party which overthrew
the church and state.   He published also some other treatises arising from the circumstances of the times, and many
sermons afterwards published collectively, in 1662, fol.
and 1666, 4to.   His most curious production, and from
which the preceding circumstances of his life are taken, is
entitled " The persecution and oppression of John Bale,
and Griffith Williams, bishops of Ossory," Lond. 1664,
4to.   In this he institutes a parallel between bishop Bale
and himself, as promoted to the same see at the mere motion of kings, without any interest or application ; both
violently expelled from the same house ; both their persecutions occasioned by their pulpit performances ; the one
by popish, the other by puritan adversaries ; both their
dangers by sea were great ; both persecuted by false accusers ; to which Mr. Harris adds, " the same licentious
spirit of railing appears in their writings, which no apology
can excuse." [1]

WILLIAMS (JOHN), an English prelate of great abilities
and very distinguished character, was the youngest son of
Edward Williams, esq. of Aber-Conway, in Caernarvon-
shire, in Wales, where he was born March 25, 1582.   He
was educated at the public school at Ruthin, in 1598, and
at sixteen years of age admitted at St. John's college, in
Cambridge.   His natural parts were very uncommon, and
his application still more so ; for he was of so singular and
happy a constitution, that from his youth upwards he never
required more than three hours sleep out of the twenty-
four for the purposes of perfect health.   He took the degree of A. B. in 1602, and was made fellow of his college ;
yet this first piece of preferment was obtained by a mandamus from James I.   His manner of studying had something
particular in it.   He used to allot one month to a certain
province, esteeming variety almost as refreshing as cessa-

  [1] Ath. Ox. vol. II.—Harris's edition of Ware's Works.

tion from labour; at the end of which he would take up
some other subject, and so on, till he came round to his
former courses. This method he observed, especially in
his theological studies; and he found his account in it. He
was also an exact philosopher, as well as an able divine,
and admirably versed in all branches of literature. In 1605,
when he took his master's degree, he entertained his friends
at the commencement in a splendid manner, for he was
naturally generous, and was liberally supplied with money
by his friends and patrons John lord Lumley often furnished him both with books and money; and Dr. Richard
Vaughan, bishop of London, who was related to him, gave
him an invitation to spend his time at his palace at vacation
times. Being thus introduced into the best company, contributed greatly towards polishing his manners.

He was not, however, so much distinguished for his
learning, as for his dexterity and skill in business. When
he was no more than five and twenty, he was employed by
the college in some concerns of theirs; on which occasions
he was sometimes admitted to speak before archbishop
Bancroft, who was exceedingly taken with his engaging
wit and decent behaviour. Another time he was deputed,
by the masters and fellows of his college, their agent to
court, to petition the king for a mortmain, as an increase
of their maintenance; on this occasion he succeeded in his
suit, and was taken particular notice of by the king; for,
there was something in him which his majesty liked so well,
that he told him of it long after when he came to be his
principal officer. He entered into orders in his twenty-
seventh year; and took a small living, which lay beyond
St. Edmund's Bury, upon the confines of Norfolk. In
1611 he was instituted to the rectory of Grafton Regis, in
Northamptonshire, at the king's presentation; and the
same year was recommended to the lord-chancellor Egerton for his chaplain, but obtained leave of the chancellor
to continue one year longer at Cambridge, in order to
serve the office of proctor of the university. While Mr.
Williams was in this post, the duke of Wirtemberg and his
train happened to pay a visit to the university. The duke
having the reputation of a learned prince, it was thought
proper to entertain him with learned disputations. Mr.
Williams being on this occasion president or moderator,
performed his part with equal skill and address. Out of
compliment to the duke he confirmed all his reasons with

quotations from the eminent professors of the German universities, which was so acceptable to the duke and his retinue, that they would not part with Mr. Williams from their company while they continued at Cambridge, and afterwards carried him with them to the palace at Newmarket, and acquainted the king with the honour he had done to the literati of their country. The following year Mr. Williams took the degree of B. D. and afterwards chiefly resided in the house of his patron, lord Egerton, who advised with him on many occasions, and testified his regard for him by various promotions, particularly the rectory of Grafton Underwood, in Northamptonshire; and in 1613 he was made precentor of Lincoln; rector of Waldgrave, in Northamptonshire, in 1614; and between that year and 1617 was collated to a prebend and residentiaryship in the church of Lincoln, and to prebends in those of Peterborough, Hereford, and St. David's, besides a sinecure in North Wales.

The chancellor Egerton dying the 15th of March, 1616-17, gave Williams some books and papers, all written with his own hand. His lordship, upon the day of his death, called Williams to him, and told him "that if he wanted money he would leave him such a legacy in his will as should enable him to begin the world like a gentleman." "Sir," says Williams, "I kiss your hands: you have filled my cup full; I am far from want, unless it be of your lordship's directions how to live in the world if I survive you." "Well," said the chancellor, "I know you are an expert workman; take these tools to work with; they are the best I have;" and so gave him the books and papers. Bishop Hacket says that he saw the notes; and that they were collections for the well-ordering the high court of parliament, the court of chancery, the star-chamber, and the council-board: so that he had a good stock to set up with; and Hacket does not doubt but his system of politics was drawn from chancellor Egerton's papers.

When sir Francis Bacon was made lord keeper, he offered to continue Williams his chaplain; who, however, declining it, was made a justice of the peace by his lordship for the county of Northampton. He was made king's chaplain at the same time, and had orders to attend his majesty in his northern progress, which was to begin soon after; but the bishop of Winchester got leave for him to stay and to take his doctor's degree, for the sake of giving entertainment to Marco Antonio de Dominis, archbishop of Spalato, who was lately come to England, and designed to be at Cambridge the commencement following. The questions which he maintained for his degree were, " Supremus magistratus non est excommunicabilis," and "Subductio calicis est mutilatio sacramenti et sacerdotii." Dr. Williams now retired to his rectory of Waldgrave, where he had been at the expence, before he came, of building, gardening, and planting, to render it an agreeable residence. He had also provided a choice collection of books, which he studied with his usual diligence. As a minister he was very attentive to the duties of his function. He read prayers constantly on Wednesdays and Fridays, and preached twice every Sunday at Waldgrave, or at Grafton; performing in his turn also at Kettering, in a lecture preached by an association of the best divines in that neighbourhood. It was a common saying with him, that " the way to get the credit from the nonconformists was, to out-preach them." And his preaching was so much liked that his church used to be thronged with the gentry of the neighbouring parishes as well as his own. In the mean time, he was most of all distinguished for his extensive charities to the poor; the decrepid, the aged, the widow, and the fatherless, were sure of a welcome share in his hospitality.

In 1619 Dr. Williams preached before the king on Matth. ii. 8, and printed his sermon by his majesty's order. The same year he was collated to the deanery of Salisbury, and the year after removed to the deanery of Westminster. He obtained this preferment by the interest of the marquis of Buckingham, whom for some time he neglected to court, says bishop Hacket, for two reasons; first, because he mightily suspected the continuance of the marquis in favour at court; secondly, because he saw that the marquis was very apt suddenly to look cloudy upon his creatures, as if he had raised them up on purpose to cast them down. However, once, when the doctor was attending the king, in the absence of the marquis, his majesty asked him abruptly, and without any relation to the discourse then in hand, " When he was at Buckingham ?" " Sir," said the doctor, " I have had no business to resort to his lordship." " But," replied the king, " wheresoever he is, you must go to him about my business;" which he accordingly did, and the marquis received him courteously. He took this as a hint from the king to visit the marquis, to whom he was afterwards serviceable in furthering his marriage with the great heiress, the earl of Rutland's daughter.    He re-claimed her ladyship from the errors of the Church of Rome to the faith and profession of the Church of England; in order to which he drew up the elements of the true re-ligion for her use, and printed twenty copies of it with no name, only, " By an old prebend of Westminster."

The lord chancellor Bacon being removed from his office in May 1621, Williams was made lord keeper of the great seal of England, the 10th of July following; and the same month bishop of Lincoln, with the deanery of Westminster, and the rectory of Waldgrave, in commendam.    When the great seal was brought to the king from lord Bacon, his majesty was overheard by some near him to say, upon the delivery of it to him, " Now by my soule, I am pained at the heart where to bestow this; for, as to my lawyers, I thinke they be all knaves."    In this high office bishop Wil-liams discharged his duties with eminent ability, and with extraordinary diligence and assiduity.    It is said by Hac-ket, that when our prelate first entered upon the office, he had such a load of business, that he was forced to sit by candle-light in the court of chancery two hours before day, and to remain there till between eight and nine; after which he repaired to the House of Peers, where he sat as speaker till twelve or one every day.    After a short repast at home, he then returned to hear the causes in chancery, which he could not dispatch in the morning; or if he attended the council at Whitehall, he came back towards evening, and followed his chancery business till eight at night, and later.    After this when he came home, he perused what papers his secretary brought to him; and when that was done, though late in the night, he prepared himself for the business which was to be transacted next morning in the House of Lords.    And it is said that when he had been one year lord keeper, he had finally concluded more causes than had been decided in the preceding seven years.    In the Star-chamber he behaved with more lenity and moderation in general, than was usual among the judges of that court.    He would excuse himself from in-flicting any severe corporal punishment upon an offender, by saying that "councils had forbidden bishops from med-dling with blood in a judicial form."    In pecuniary fines he was also very lenient, and very ready to remit his own share in fines. Of this we have the following instance. Sir Francis Inglefield had asserted before witnesses, that "he could prove this holy bishop judge had been bribed by some that had fared well in their causes." The lord keeper immediately called upon sir Francis to prove his assertion, which he being unable to do, was fined some thousand pounds to be paid to the king and the injured party. Soon after bishop Williams sent for sir Francis, and told him he would give him a demonstration that he was above a bribe; and "for my part," said he, "I forgive you every penny of my fine, and will beg of his majesty to do the same." This piece of generosity made sir Francis acknowledge his fault, and he was afterwards received into some degree of friendship and acquaintance with the lord keeper. Weldon's charge of corruption against Williams seems to be equally ill founded, nothing of the kind having ever been proved.

Bishop Williams was very desirous of keeping upon good terms with the favourite Buckingham, but it appears, notwithstanding, that he withstood him when he had just reason for it. He sometimes also gave Buckingham good advice, which being delivered with freedom, could not be very acceptable to the haughty favourite. His resolution in opposing Buckingham's designs, when he saw weighty reasons for it, was so remarkable that the king used to say, that "he was a stout man, and durst do more than himself." James sometimes really appeared afraid of openly expressing his dislike at such of Buckingham's actions as he really disapproved; and we are told that his majesty thanked God, that he had put Williams into the place of lord keeper; "for," said he, "he that will not wrest justice for Buckingham's sake, whom he loves, will never be corrupted with money which he never loved." And because the lord keeper had lived for the space of three years upon the bare revenues of his office, and was not richer by the sale of one cursitor's place in all that time, his majesty gave him a bountiful new-year's gift, thinking that it was but reasonable to encourage, by his liberality, a man who never sought after wealth by the sordid means of extortion or bribery.

The lord keeper made use of his influence with the king, in behalf of several noblemen who were under the royal displeasure and in confinement. He prevailed with his majesty to set at liberty the earl of Northumberland, who had been fifteen years a prisoner in the Tower. He procured also the enlargement of the earls of Oxford and Arundel, both of whom had been a considerable time under confinement. He employed likewise his good offices with the king, in behalf of many others of inferior rank, particularly some clergymen who offended by their pulpit freedoms. One instance we shall extract from his principal biographer, as a proof of his address, and knowledge of king James's peculiar temper. A Mr. Knight, a young divine at Oxford, had advanced in a sermon somewhat which was said to be derogatory to the king's prerogative. For this he was a long time imprisoned, and a charge was about to be drawn up against him, to impeach him for treasonable doctrine. One Dr. White, a clergyman far advanced in years, was likewise in danger of a prosecution of the same kind. Bishop Williams was very desirous of bringing both these gentlemen off, and hit on the following contrivance. Some instructions had been appointed to be drawn up by his care and direction, for the performance of useful and orderly preaching; which being under his hand to dispatch, he now besought his majesty that this proviso might pass among the rest, that none of the clergy should be permitted to preach before the age of thirty years, nor after three-score. "On my soul," said the king, "the devil, or some fit of madness is in the motion; for I have many great wits, and of clear distillation, that have preached before me at Royston and Newmarket to my great liking, that are under thirty. And my prelates and chaplains, that are far stricken in years, are the best masters of that faculty that Europe affords." "I agree to all this," answered the lord keeper, "and since your majesty will allow both young and old to go up into the pulpit, it is but justice that you shew indulgence to the young ones if they run into errors before their wits be settled (for every apprentice is allowed to mar some work before he be cunning in the mystery of his trade), and pity to the old ones, if some of them fall into dotage when their brains grow dry. Will your majesty conceive displeasure, and not lay it down, if the former set your teeth on edge sometimes, before they are mellow-wise; and if the doctrine of the latter be touched with a blemish, when they begin to be rotten, and to drop from the tree?" "This is not unfit for consideration," said the king, "but what do you drive at?" "Sir," replied Williams, "first to beg your pardon for mine own boldness; then to remember you that Knight is a beardless boy, from whom exactness of judgment could not be expected. And that White is a decrepit, spent man, who had not a fee-simple, but a lease of reason, and it is expired. Both these that have been foolish in their several extremes of years, I prostrate at the feet of your princely clemency." In consequence of this application, king James readily granted a pardon to both of them.

Bishop Williams continued in favour during this reign, and attended king James at his death, and preached his funeral-sermon, on 2 Chron. ix. 29, 30, 31, which was afterwards printed. That king had promised to confer upon him the archbishopric of York at the next vacancy; but his lordship's conduct in many points not being agreeable to the duke of Buckingham, he was removed by Charles I. from his post of lord keeper, Oct. 1626. He was ordered also not to appear in parliament, but refused to comply with that order, and taking his seat in the House of Peers, promoted the petition of right.

For four years after Williams was consecrated bishop of Lincoln, the multiplicity of his affairs prevented his visiting his clergy, yet his government, it is said, was such as to give content to his whole diocese. He managed the affairs of it with the greatest exactness by faithful substitutes, who gave him a just account of all matters, so that he knew the name and character of every one of his clergy, and took care to encourage the deserving. When now, however, he came to Bugden, he found it necessary to repair his house, and the chapel, which he did at a great expence, and in a magnificent manner. The concourse that resorted to this chapel was very great; and his table was generally well filled with gentry, so that the historian Sanderson, who is no friend to Williams, said, that " he lived at Bugden more episcopally than any of his predecessors." All the great persons and nobility who had occasion to travel that way, used to call upon his lordship, from whom they and their retinue were sure of a hearty welcome, and the best entertainment. All the neighbouring clergy also, and many of the yeomanry, were free to come to his table, and, indeed, he seldom sat down without some of the clergy. He was also extremely charitable to the poor, and used to say, that " he would spend his own while he had it; for he thought his adversaries would not permit him long to enjoy it." Had he not lived in this hospitable manner, yet his conversation, and agreeable manner of accommodating himself to his guests, were so generally pleasing, that he was not likely to be much alone. Many members of both universities, the most distinguished for their wit and learning, made him frequent visits; so that very often, taking the company and entertainment together, Bugden was said to resemble one of the universities in commencement time. It was his custom, at his table, to have a chapter in the English Bible read daily at dinner by one of the choristers, and another at supper in Latin by one of his gentlemen.

This hospitable and splendid manner of living gave offence to the court, as he was publicly known to be out of favour there. It was said, that such a mode of living was very improper for a man in disgrace. To which he replied, that " he knew not what he had done, to live the worse for their sakes, who did not love him." His family was the nursery of several noblemen's sons; particularly those of the marquis of Hertford, and of the earls of Pembroke, Salisbury, and Leicester. These, together with many other young gentlemen, had tutors assigned them, of whom our prelate took an account, how their pupils improved in virtue and learning. To those who were about to be removed to the universities, before he parted with them, he read himself a brief system of logic, which lectures even his own servants might attend who were capable of such instruction : and he took particular care that they should be thoroughly grounded in the principles of religion. He was exceedingly liberal to poor scholars in both universities; and his disbursements this way are said every year to have amounted to a thousand, and sometimes to twelve hundred pounds. He was also very generous to learned foreigners. When Dr. Peter du Moulin fled to England, to avoid persecution in France, bishop Williams hearing of him, sent his chaplain, Dr. Hacket, to pay him a visit, and supposing that he might be in want, bade him carry him some money, not naming any sum. Hacket said, that he supposed he could not give him less than twenty pounds. " I did demur upon the sum," said the bishop, " to try you. Is twenty pounds a fit gift for me to give to a man of his parts and deserts ? Take an hundred, and present it from me, and tell him, he shall not want, and I will come shortly and visit him myself;" which he afterwards did, and supplied Du Moulin's wants while he was in England. He was also a liberal patron of his countryman John Owen, the epigrammatist, whom he maintained for several years, and when he died he buried him, and erected a monument for him at his own expence.

In the mean time, the duke of Buckingham was not content with having removed our prelate from all power at court, but for a long time laboured to injure him, although some time before his death he appears to have been rather reconciled to him. With Laud, however, Williams found all reconciliation impossible, for which it is not easy to assign any cause, unless that their political principles were in some respects incompatible, and that Laud was somewhat jealous of the ascendancy which Williams might acquire, if again restored at court. In consequence of this animosity, besides being deprived of the title of privy-counsellor, Williams was perpetually harassed with law-suits and prosecutions; and though nothing criminal could be proved against him, yet he was, by these means, put to great trouble and expence. Amongst other prosecutions, one arose from the following circumstances, as related by his biographer Hacket. "In the conference which the bishop had with his majesty, when he was admitted to kiss his hand, after the passing of the petition of Right, the king conjuring his lordship to tell him freely, how he might best ingratiate himself with the people, his lordship replied, 'that the Puritans were many and strong sticklers; and if his majesty would give but private orders to his ministers to connive a little at their party, and shew them some indulgence, it might perhaps mollify them a little, and make them more pliant; though he did not promise that they would be trusty long to any government.' And the king answered, that 'he had thought upon this before, and would do so.' About two months after this, the bishop at his court at Leicester acted according to this counsel resolved upon by his majesty; and withal told sir John Lamb and Dr. Sibthorp his reason for it, 'that it was not only his own, but the Royal pleasure.' Now Lamb was one, who had been formerly infinitely obliged to the bishop: but, however, a breach happening between them, he and Sibthorp carried the bishop's words to bishop Laud, and he to the king, who was then at Bisham. Hereupon it was resolved, that upon the deposition of these two, a bill should be drawn up against the bishop for revealing the king's secrets, being a sworn counsellor. That information, together with some others, being transmitted to the council-table, was ordered for the present to be sealed up, and committed to the custody of Mr. Trumbal, one of the clerks of the council. Nevertheless the bishop made a shift to procure a copy of them. And so the business rested for some years. However, the bishop was still more and more declining in favour, by reason of a settled misunderstanding between him and bishop Laud, who looked upon Williams as a man who gave encouragement to the Puritans, and was cool with respect to our church-discipline; while, on the other hand, Williams took Laud to be a great favourer of the papists. Laud's interest at court was now so great, that in affairs of state, as well as of the church, he governed almost without controul; so that a multitude of lesser troubles surrounded bishop Williams, and several persons attacked him with a view to ingratiate themselves at court. Abundance of frivolous accusation and little vexatious law-suits were brought against him daily; and it was the height of his adversaries policy to empty his purse, and clip his wings, by all the means they could invent, that so at last he might lie wholly at their mercy, and not be able to shift for himself. Notwithstanding all which, what with his innocency, and what with his courage springing from it, he bore up against them all, and never shewed any grudge or malice against them. But his lordship, perceiving himself to be thus perpetually harassed, asked the lord Cottington, whether he could tell him, what he should do to procure his peace, and such other ordinary favours as other bishops had from his majesty. To which the lord Cottington answered, that the splendor in which he lived, and the great resort of company which came to him, gave offence; and that the king must needs take it ill, that one under the height of his displeasure should live at so magnificent a rate. In the next place, his majesty would be better satisfied, if he would resign the deanery of Westminster, because he did not care that he should be so near a neighbour at White-hall. As for the first of these reasons, his natural temper would not suffer him to comply with it, and to moderate his expences in house-keeping; and he was not so short-sighted as to part with his deanery upon such precarious terms; "for," said he, "what health can come from such a remedy? Am I like to be beholden to them for a settled tranquillity, who practise upon the ruin of my estate, and the thrall of my honour? If I forfeit one preferment for fear, will it not encourage them to tear me in piecemeal hereafter? It is not my case alone, but every man's; and if the law cannot maintain my right, it can maintain no man's." So, in spite of all their contrivances to out him, he kept the deanery till the king received it from him at Oxford in 1644. But they did all they could, since he was resolved to hold it, to make him as uneasy as possible in it. In this uneasy situation he continued several years; and now it was sufficiently known to all people how much he was out of favour; so that it was looked upon as a piece of merit to assist in his ruin. And this perhaps might be some incitement to what sir Robert Osborn, high sheriff of Huntingdonshire, acted against him in the levying of the ship-money. The bishop, for his part, was very cautious to carry himself without offence in this matter; but sir Robert, laying a very unequal levy upon the hundred wherein Bugden was, the bishop wrote courteously to him to rectify it, and that he and his neighbours would be ready to see it collected. Upon this sir Robert, catching at the opportunity, posts up to the court, and makes an heavy complaint against the bishop, that he not only refused the payment of ship-money himself, but likewise animated the hundred to do so too. And yet for all that, when the bishop afterwards cleared himself before the lords of the council, and they were satisfied that he had behaved himself with duty and prudence, sir Robert was not reprehended, nor had the bishop any satisfaction given him, nor was the levy regulated. After this, was revived the long and troublesome trial against the bishop in the Star-chamber, which commenced in the fourth year of king Charles I. upon some informations brought against him by Lamb and Sibthorp. Here he made so noble a defence of himself, that the attorney-general, Noy, grew weary of the cause, and slackened his prosecution; but that great lawyer dying, and the information being managed by Kilvert a solicitor, the bishop, when the business came to a final determination, was fined 10,000*l.* to the king, and to suffer imprisonment during his majesty's pleasure, and withal to be suspended by the high commission court from all his dignities, offices, and functions. In his imprisonment in the Tower, hearing that his majesty would not abate any thing of his fine, he desired that it might be taken up by 1000*l.* yearly, as his estate would bear it, till the whole should

be paid ; but he could not have so small a favour granted.
Upon which Kilvert, the bishop's avowed enemy, was ordered to go to Bugden and Lincoln, and there to seize
upon all he could, and bring it immediately into the exchequer. Kilvert, being glad of this office, made sure of all
that could be found ; goods of all sorts, plate, books, and
such like, to the value of 10,000*l.* of which he never gave
account but of 800*l.* The timber he felled ; killed the
deer in the park ; sold, an organ, which cost 120*l.* for 10*l.* ;
pictures, which cost 400*l.* for 5*l.* ; made away with what
books he pleased, and continued revelling for three sum-
mers in Bugden-house. For four cellars of wine, cyder,
ale, and beer, with wood, hay, corn, and the like, stored
up for a year or two, he gave no account at all. And thus
a large personal estate was squandered away, and not the
least part of the king's fine paid all this while ; whereas if
it had been managed to the best advantage, it would have
been sufficient to discharge the whole. It were endless to
repeat all the contrivances against his lordship during his
confinement ; the bills which were drawn up, and the suits
commenced against him, as it were on purpose to impo-
verish him, and to plunge him into debt, that so, if he
procured his enlargement from this prison, he might not
be long out of another. However, he bore all these afflictions with the utmost patience ; and if a stranger had
seen his lordship in the Tower, he would never have taken
him for a prisoner, but rather for the lord and master of
the place. For here he lived with his usual cheerfulness
and hospitality, and wanted only a larger allowance to
give his guests an heartier welcome ; for now he was confined to bare 500*l.* a year, a great part of which was consumed in the very fees of the Tower. He diverted himself,
when alone, sometimes with writing Latin poems ; at other
times with the histories of such as were noted for their
sufferings in former ages. And for the three years and a
half that he was confined, he was the same man as elsewhere, excepting that his frequent law-suits broke his
studies often ; and it could not be seen that he was the least
altered in his health or the pleasantness of his temper."

At length when the parliament met in November 1640,
bishop Williams petitioned the king for his enlargement,
and to have his writ of summons to parliament, which his
majesty thought proper to refuse ; but about a fortnight
after, the House of Lords sent the gentleman-usher of the

black rod to demand him of the lieutenant of the Tower, in consequence of which he took his seat among his brethren. Some being set on to try how he stood affected to his prosecutors, he answered, that " if they had no worse foes than him, they might fear no harm ; and that he saluted them with the charity of a bishop ;" and when Kilvert came to him to crave pardon and indemnity for all the wrongs he had done, " I assure you pardon," said the bishop, " for what you have done before ; but this is a new fault, that you take me to be of so base a spirit, as to defile myself with treading upon so mean a creature. Live still by petty-fogging and impeaching, and think that I have forgotten you." And now the king, understanding with what courage and temper he had behaved himself under his misfortunes, was pleased to be reconciled to him ; and commanded all orders, filed or kept in any court or registry upon the former informations against him, to be taken off, razed, and cancelled, that nothing might stand upon record to his disadvantage.

When the earl of Strafford came to be impeached in parliament, Williams defended the rights of the bishops, in a very significant speech, to vote in case of blood, as Hacket relates ; but lord Clarendon relates just the contrary. He says, that this bishop, without communicating with any of his brethren, very frankly declared his opinion, that " they ought not to be present ; and offered, not only in his own name, but for the rest of the bishops, to withdraw always when that business was entered upon :" and so, adds the noble historian, betrayed a fundamental right of the whole order, to the great prejudice of the king, and to the taking away the life of that person, who could not otherwise have suffered. Shortly after, when the king declared, that he neither would, nor could in conscience, give his royal assent to that act of attainder ; and when the tumultuous citizens came about the court with noise and clamour for justice ; the lord Say desired the king to confer with his bishops for the satisfaction of his conscience, and with bishop Williams in particular, who told him, says lord Clarendon, that " he must consider, that as he had a private capacity and a public, so he had a public conscience as well as a private : that though his private conscience, as a man, would not permit him to do an act contrary to his own understanding, judgment, and conscience, yet his public conscience as a king, which obliged him to do all things for the good of his

people, and to preserve his kingdom in peace for himself
and his posterity, would not only permit him to do that,
but even oblige and require him; that he saw in what commotion the people were; that his own life, and that of the
queen and the royal issue, might probably be sacrificed to
that fury : and it would be very strange, if his conscience
should prefer the right of one single private person, how
innocent soever, before all those other lives and the preservation of the kingdom. This," continues lord Clarendon, "was the argumentation of that unhappy casuist,
who truly, it may be, did believe himself:" yet he reveals
another anecdote, which shews, at least if true, that bishop
Williams could have no favourable intentions towards the
unfortunate earl of Strafford. It had once been mentioned
to the bishop, when he was out at court, whether by authority or no was not known, says the historian, that "his
peace should be made there, if he would resign his bishopric and deanery of Westminster, and take a good
bishopric in Ireland :" which he positively refused, and
said, " he had much to do to defend himself against the
archbishop (Laud) here; but, if he was in Ireland, there
was a man (meaning the earl of Strafford) who would cut
off his head within one month."

In 1641, he was advanced to the archbishopric of York;
and the same year opposed, in a long speech, the bill for
depriving the bishops of their seats in the House of Lords;
which had this effect, that it laid the bill asleep for five
months. Then the mob flocked about the parliament-house,
crying out, "No bishops, no bishops;" and insulted the
prelates, as they passed to the House. Williams was one
of the bishops who was most rudely treated by the rabble;
his person was assaulted, and his robes torn from his back.
Upon this, he returned to his house, the deanery of Westminster; and sending for all the bishops then in the town,
who were in number twelve, proposed, as absolutely necessary, that " they might unanimously and presently prepare a protestation, to send to the House, against the force
that was used upon them; and against all the acts which
were or should be done during the time that they should
by force be kept from doing their duties in the House;"
and immediately, having pen and ink ready, himself prepared a protestation, which was sent. But the politic
bishop Williams is here represented to have been transported by passion into impolitic measures; for, no sooner

# WILLIAMS.

was this protestation communicated to the House than the governing Lords manifested a great satisfaction in it; some of them saying, that "there was *digitus Dei* to bring that to pass, which they could not otherwise have compassed:" and, without ever declaring any judgment or opinion of their own upon it, sent to desire a conference with the Commons, who presently joined with them in accusing the protesters of high treason, and sending them all to the Tower; where they continued till the bill for putting them out of the House was passed, which was not till many months after. Lord Clarendon says, there was only one gentleman in the House of Commons that spoke in the behalf of these prelates; who said, among other things, that "he did not believe they were guilty of high treason, but that they were stark-mad, and therefore desired they might be sent to Bedlam."

In June 1642, the king being at York, our archbishop was enthroned in person in his own cathedral, but, soon after the king had left York, which was in July following, was obliged to leave it too; the younger Hotham, who was coming thither with his forces, having sworn solemnly to seize and kill him, for some opprobrious words spoken of him concerning his usage of the king at Hull. He retired to his estate at Aber Conway, and fortified Conway-castle for the king; which so pleased his majesty, that by a letter, Oxford, Aug. the 1st, 1643, the king "heartily desired him to go on with that work, assuring him, that, whatever moneys he should lay out upon the fortification of the said castle should be repayed unto him before the custody thereof should be put into any other hand than his own, or such as he should command." By virtue of a warrant, Jan. 2, 1643-4, the archbishop deputes his nephew William Hooks, esq. to have the custody of this castle; and, some time after, being sent for, set out to attend the king at Oxford, whom he is said to have cautioned particularly against Cromwell, who, "though then of but mean rank and use in the army, yet would be sure to rise higher. I knew him," says he, "at Buckden; but never knew his religion. He was a common spokesman for sectaries, and maintained their parts with stubbornness. He never discoursed as if he were pleased with your majesty and your great officers; indeed he loves none that are more than his equals. Your majesty did him but justice in repulsing a petition put up by him against sir Thomas Steward, of the Isle of Ely; but

he takes them all for his enemies that would not let him
undo his best friend; and, above all that live, I think he
is *injuriarum persequentissimus*, as Portius Latro said of
Catiline.. He talks openly, that it is fit some should act
more vigorously against your forces, and bring your person into the power of the parliament. He cannot give a
good word of his general the earl of Essex; because, he
says, the earl is but half an enemy to your majesty, and
hath done you more favour than harm. His fortunes are
broken, that it is impossible for him to subsist, much less
to be what he aspires to, but by your majesty's bounty, or
by the ruin of us all, and a common confusion; as one
said, ' Lentulus salva republica salvus esse non potuit.' In
short, every beast hath some evil properties; but Cromwell hath the properties of all evil beasts. My humble
motion is, either that you would win him to you by promises of fair treatment, or catch him by some stratagem,
and cut him off."

. After some stay at Oxford, he returned to his own country, having received a fresh charge from his majesty to
take care of all North Wales, but especially of Conway-
castle, in which the people of the country had obtained
leave of the archbishop to lay up all their valuables. A
year after this, sir John Owen, a colonel for the king,
marching that way after a defeat, obtained of prince Ru-
pert to be substituted under his hand commander of the
castle; and so surprising it by force entered it, notwithstanding it was before given to the bishop under the king's
own signet, to possess it quietly, till the charges he had
been at should be refunded him, which as yet had never
been offered. The archbishop's remonstrances at court
meeting with no success, he being joined by the country-
people, whose properties were detained in the castle, and
assisted by one colonel Mitton, who was a zealous man for
the parliament, forced open the gates, and entered it. The
archbishop did not join the colonel with any intention to
prejudice his majesty's service, but agreed to put him into
the castle, on condition that every proprietary should possess his own, which the colonel saw performed.

After the king was beheaded, the archbishop spent his
days in sorrow, study, and devotion; and is said to have
risen constantly every night out of his bed at midnight, and
to have prayed for a quarter of an hour on his bare knees,
without any thing but his shirt and waistcoat on. He lived

not much above a year after, dying the 25th of March 1650: he was buried in Llandegay church, where a monument was erected to him by his nephew and heir, sir Griffith Williams. Besides several sermons, he published a book against archbishop Laud's innovations in church-matters and religious ceremonies, with this title, "The Holy Table, Name, and Thing, more antiently, properly, and literally, used under the New Testament, than that of Altar. Written long ago by a minister in Lincolnshire, in answer to D. Coel, a judicious divine of queen Marie's dayes. Printed for the diocese of Lincoln, 1637;" in quarto. Lord Clarendon, though far from being favourable to this prelate, yet represents this "book so full of good learning, and that learning so closely and solidly applied, though it abounded with too many light expressions, that it gained him reputation enough to be able to do hurt; and shewed, that in his retirement he had spent his time with his books very profitably. He used all the wit and all the malice he could, to awaken the people to a jealousy of these agitations, and innovations in the exercise of religion; not without insinuations that it aimed at greater alterations, for which he knew the people would quickly find a name: and he was ambitious to have it believed, that the archbishop Laud was his greatest enemy, for his having constantly opposed his rising to any government in the church, as a man whose hot and hasty spirit he had long known."

In the mean time, there have not been wanting those, who, without disguising his infirmities, have set archbishop Williams in a better light than we find him represented by the earl of Clarendon, who seems by no means to have loved the man. Arthur Wilson tells us, that, "though he was composed of many grains of good learning, yet the height of his spirit, I will not say pride, made him odious even to those that raised him; haply because they could not attain to those ends by him, that they required of him. But being of a comely and stately presence, and that animated with a great mind, made him appear very proud to the vulgar eye; but that very temper raised him to aim at great things, which he affected: for the old ruinous body of the abbey-church at Westminster was new clothed by him; the fair and beautiful library of St. John's in Cambridge was a pile of his erection; and a very complete chapel built by him at Lincoln-college in Oxford, merely for the name of Lincoln, having no interest in nor relation to that university. But that which heightened him most in the opinion of those that knew him best, was his bountiful mind to men in want; being a great patron to support, where there was merit that wanted supply: but these great actions were not publicly visible: those were more apparent that were looked on with envious, rather than with emulous eyes."

Hacket likewise, after observing that he was a man of great hospitality, charity, and generosity, especially to gentlemen of narrow fortunes, and poor scholars in both universities, informs us that his disbursements this way every year amounted to 1000*l.* or sometimes 1200*l.* Hacket had reason to know his private character; for he was his chaplain, and although he may be supposed partial to so eminent a benefactor, the character he gives of archbishop Williams is, in general, not only consistent with itself, but with some contemporary authorities. He appears, amidst all his secular concerns, to have entertained a strong sense of the importance of religion. When a divine once came to him for institution to a living, Williams expressed himself thus; "I have passed through many places of honour and trust, both in church and state, more than any of my order in England these seventy years before. But were I but assured, that by my preaching I had converted but one soul unto God, I should take therein more spiritual joy and comfort, than in all the honours and offices which have been bestowed upon me."

Archbishop Williams undertook a Latin Commentary on the Bible; and the notes collected from various authors by his own hand were formerly in the custody of Mr. Goulaud, keeper of Westminster-college library. His lordship knowing well, that to perform such a task completely was above the abilities of any one man, intended to leave it to be finished by twelve or more of the best scholars in the nation, whom he had in his eye, and was willing to give them twenty thousand pounds rather than it should be left unfinished. He likewise resolved, as noticed by Dr. Pegge, in his valuable life of that prelate, to publish the works of his predecessor bishop Grosthead, which were scattered in several libraries at home and abroad, and he digested what he could procure of them, and wrote arguments upon various parts of them. '

1 Hacket's Life of Abp. Williams. fol.—Phillips's and Steevens's Lives, 8vo.—Clarendon's Hist.—Lloyd's Worthies,—Biog. Brit.

WILLIAMS (JOHN), an able divine, and bishop of Chichester, was born in Northamptonshire in 1634. In 1651 he entered a commoner of Magdalen-hall, Oxford, where in 1658 he completed his degrees in arts, and was ordained. In 1673 he was collated to the rectory of St. Mildred in the Poultry, London, and in 1683 to the prebend of Reymere in the cathedral of St. Paul. After the revolution he became chaplain to king William and queen Mary, and was preferred to a prebend of Canterbury, and in December 1696 advanced to the bishopric of Chichester, in which he died in 1709. He was a considerable writer in the controversies with the papists and dissenters, and preached the lectures founded by Mr. Boyle, his sermons on that occasion being published in 1695, 4to, under the title of "The characters of Divine Revelation." He wrote also a "History of the Gunpowder Treason," and many controversial pamphlets enumerated by Wood. He lived in great intimacy with Tillotson, who says of him, "Mr. Williams is really one of the best men I know, and most unwearied in doing good, and his preaching is very weighty and judicious." When Firmin, the Socinian, published his "Considerations on the explications of the doctrine of the Trinity," Dr. Williams wrote the same year (1694) a "Vindication of archbishop Tillotson's Four Sermons (concerning the divinity and incarnation of our blessed Saviour) and of the bishop of Worcester's sermon on the mysteries of the Christian faith." In this, which was not published till 1695, after Tillotson's death, Dr. Williams observes that it was not without the archbishop's direction and encouragement, that he entered upon it, and that had he lived to have perused the whole, as he did a part of it a few days before his last hours, it had come with greater advantage into the world, &c. [1]

WILLIAMS (ROGER), a brave officer in the reign of queen Elizabeth, was the son of Thomas Williams, of Penrose in Monmouthshire, and educated at Oxford, probably in Brasenose college. After leaving the university, he became a volunteer in the army, and served under the duke of Alva. In 1581, he was in the English army commanded by general Norris in Friesland, where Camden says the enemy's troops were defeated by sir Roger Williams at Northorn, who probably therefore was knighted for his gallant exploits before this time, although Wood says that honour was not conferred upon him until 1586. In this last-mentioned year he appears again in the army commanded by the earl of Leicester in Flanders. When the prince of Parma laid siege to Venlo in Guelderland, Williams, with one Skenk, a Frieslander, undertook to pierce through the enemy's camp at midnight, and enter the town. They penetrated without much difficulty, as far as the prince of Parma's tent, but were then repulsed. The attempt, however, gained them great reputation in the army. In 1591, Williams was sent to assist in the defence of Dieppe, and remained there beyond August 24, 1593. What other exploits he performed, we know not, but it is probable that he continued in the service of his country during the war in the Low Countries, of which war he wrote a valuable history. He died in London in 1595, and was buried in St. Paul's, attended to his grave by the earl of Essex, and other officers of distinction. "He might," says Camden, "have been compared with the most famous captains of our age, could he have tempered the heat of his warlike spirit with more wariness and prudent discretion." Wood calls him a colonel, but it does not clearly appear what rank he attained in the army. From his writings, which are highly extolled by Camden, he appears to have been a man of strong natural parts, and sound judgment. His principal writing is entitled "The Actions of the Low Countries," Lond. 1618, 4to, which has lately been reprinted in Mr. Scott's new edition of the Somers's Tracts. He wrote also "A brief discourse of War, with his opinion concerning some part of military discipline," ibid. 1590, 4to, in which he defends the military art of his country against that of former days. He mentions in his "Actions of the Low Countries," a "Discourse of the Discipline of the Spaniards;" and in Rymer's Fœdera is his "Advice from France, Nov. 20, 1590." Some of his MSS. and Letters are in the Cotton Library in the British Museum. [1]

WILLIAMSON (Sir Joseph), an eminent statesman and benefactor to Queen's college, Oxford, was son of Joseph Williamson, vicar of Bridekirk in Cumberland from 1625 to 1634. At his first setting out in life he was employed as a clerk or secretary by Richard Tolson, esq.; representative in parliament for Cockermouth; and, when

[1] Ath. Ox. vol. I. new edit.—Camden's Queen Elizabeth.—Restituta, vol. I.

at London with his master, begged to be recommended to Dr. Busby, that he might be admitted into Westminster-school, where he made such improvement that the master recommended him to the learned Dr. Langbaine, provost of Queen's college, Oxford, who came to the election at Westminster. He admitted him on the foundation, under the tuition of Dr. Thomas Smith (for whom sir Joseph after-wards procured the bishopric of Carlisle), and provided for him at his own expence; and when he had taken his ba-chelor's degree, February 2, 1653, sent him to France as tutor to a person of quality. On his return to college he was elected fellow, and, as it is said, took deacon's orders. In 1657 he was created A. M. by diploma. Soon after the restoration he was recommended to sir Edward Nicholas, and his successor Henry earl of Arlington, principal secre-tary of state, who appointed him clerk or keeper of the paper-office at Whitehall (of which he appointed Mr. Smith deputy), and employed him in translating and writing me-morials in French; and June 24, 1677, he was sworn one of the clerks of the council in ordinary, and knighted. He was under-secretary of state in 1665; about which time he procured for himself the writing of the Oxford Gazettes then newly set up, and employed Charles Perrot, fellow of Oriel college, who had a good command of his pen, to do that office under him till 1671. In 1678, 1679, 1698, 1700, he represented the borough of Thetford in parlia-ment. In 1685, being then recorder of Thetford, he was again elected, but Heveningham the mayor returned him-self, and on a petition it appeared that the right of elec-tion was in the select body of the corporation before the charter; and in 1690 he lost his election by a double re-turn. Wood says he was a recruiter for Thetford to sit in that parliament which began at Westminster May 8, 1661.

At the short treaty of Cologne, sir Joseph was one of the British plenipotentiaries, with the earl of Sunderland and sir Leolin Jenkins, and at his return was created LL.D. June 27, 1674, sworn principal secretary of state Septem-ber 11, on the promotion of the earl of Arlington to the chamberlainship of the household, and a privy counsellor. On November 18, 1678, he was committed to the Tower by the House of Commons, on a charge of granting com-missions and warrants to popish recusants; but he was the same day released by the king, notwithstanding an address from the House. He resigned his place of secretary February 9, 1678, and was succeeded by the earl of Sunderland; who, if we believe Rapin, gave him 6000*l.* and 500 guineas to induce him to resign. In December that year he married Catherine Obrien, baroness Clifton, widow of Henry lord Obrien, who died in August. She was sister and sole heiress to Charles duke of Richmond, and brought sir Joseph large possessions in Kent and elsewhere, besides the hereditary stewardship of Greenwich. Some ascribe the loss of the secretary's place to this match, through the means of lord Danby, who intended this lady for his son. She died November 1702. Sir Joseph was president of the Royal Society in 1678. Under 1674, Wood says of him that "he had been a great benefactor to his college, and may be greater hereafter if he think fit." Upon some slight shewn by the college, he had made a will by which he had given but little to it, having disposed of his intended benefaction to erect and endow a college at Dublin, to be called Queen's college, the provosts to be chosen from its namesake in Oxford. But soon after his arrival in Holland 1696, with Mr. Smith, his godson and secretary, (afterwards, 1730, provost of Queen's college, Oxford,) being seized with a violent fit of the gout, he sent for his secretary, who had before reconciled him to the place of his education, and calling him to his bedside, directed him to take his will out of a drawer in the bureau, and insert a benefaction of 6000*l.* When this was done and ready to be executed, before the paper had been read to him, "in comes sir Joseph's lady." The secretary, well knowing he had no mind she should be acquainted with it, endeavoured to conceal it; and on her asking what he had got there, he answered, "nothing but news, Madam;" meaning, such as she was not to know: and by this seasonable and ready turn prevented her further inquiries.

Dr. Lancaster, the provost, applied this benefaction towards erecting the south-side of the college. Sir Joseph also gave to the library a valuable collection of MSS. especially heraldic, and memoirs of his foreign negociations. His benefactions to this college in his life-time, and at his death, in plate, books, buildings, and money, amounted to 8000*l.* He left by will 500*l.* to the grandchildren of his patron Dr. Langbaine; and to the parish of Bride-kirk gilt bibles and prayer-books, communion-plate, &c. He was also a benefactor to the cloth-workers' company, of which he had been master, and left 5000*l.* to found a mathematieal school for freemen's sons at Rochester, which city he had represented in 1689, 1695, 1698, and 1700. He died in 1701, and was buried in Westminster-abbey. [1]

WILLIS (THOMAS), an illustrious English physician, was of a reputable family, and born at Great Bedwin, in Wiltshire, Jan. 27, 1621, in a house that was often visited by his grandson Browne Willis, and of which there is an engraving in the Gentleman's Magazine for 1798. He was instructed in grammar and classical literature by Mr. Edward Sylvester, a noted schoolmaster in the parish of All-Saints, Oxford; and, in 1636, became a member of Christ church. He applied himself vigorously to his studies, and took the degrees in arts; that of bachelor in 1639, that of master in 1642. About this time, Oxford being turned into a garrison for the king, he with other scholars bore arms for his majesty, and devoted his leisure hours to the study of physic; in which faculty he took a bachelor's degree in 1646, when Oxford was surrendered to the parliament. He pursued the business of his profession, and kept Abingdon market. He settled in an house over against Merton college, and appropriated a room in it for divine service, where Mr. John Fell, afterwards dean of Christ church, whose sister he had married, Mr. John Dolben, afterwards archbishop of York, and sometimes Mr. Richard Allestree, afterwards provost of Eton college, exercised the liturgy and sacraments according to the church of England, and allowed to others the privilege of resorting thither. This measure of theirs is commemorated by a painting in the hall of Christ church, Oxford.

In 1660, he was made Sedleian professor of natural philosophy; and the same year took the degree of doctor of physic. Being sent for to most of the people of quality about Oxford, and even at great distances, he visited the lady Keyt in Warwickshire; and is supposed to have been going to her in April 1664, when he discovered, and made experiments upon, the famous medicinal spring at Alstrop, near Brackley. Willis and Lower first recommended these waters, which were afterwards decried by Radcliffe. The reason which Granger heard assigned for his decrying them was, because the people of the village insisted upon his keeping a bastard child, which was laid to him by an infa-

1 Martin's Hist. of Thetford.—Burn's Cumberland and Westmoreland—and Hutchinson's Cumberland.

mous woman of that place. Upon this the doctor declared "that he would put a toad into their well," and accordingly cried down the waters, which soon lost their reputation.

Dr. Willis was one of the first members of the Royal Society, and soon made his name as illustrious by his writings as it was already by his practice. In 1666, after the fire of London, he removed to Westminster, upon an invitation from archbishop Sheldon, and took a house in St. Martin's-lane. As he rose early in the morning, that he might be present at divine service, which he constantly frequented before he visited his patients, he procured prayers to be read out of the accustomed times while he lived, and at his death settled a stipend of 20*l*. per annum to continue them. He was a liberal benefactor to the poor wherever he came, having from his early practice allotted part of his profits to charitable uses. He was a fellow of the college of physicians, and refused the honour of knighthood. He was regular and exact in his hours ; and his table was the resort of most of the great men in London. After his settlement there, his only son Thomas falling into a consumption, he sent him to Montpellier in France for the recovery of his health, which proved successful. His wife also labouring under the same disorder, he offered to leave the town; but she, not suffering him to neglect the means of providing for his family, died in 1670. He died, at his house in St. Martin's, Nov. 11, 1675, and was buried near her in Westminster-abbey. His son Thomas, above mentioned, was born at Oxford in Jan. 1657-8, educated some time in Westminster-school, became a student a Christ church, and died in 1699. He was buried in Bletchley church, near Fenny-Stratford, the manors of which places his father had purchased of the duke of Buckingham, and which descended to his eldest son Browne Willis of Whaddon-hall, esq. eminent for his knowledge in antiquities, and of whom some memoirs will be given. Wood tells us, that " though Dr. Willis was a plain man, a man of no carriage, little discourse, complaisance, or society, yet for his deep insight, happy researches in natural and experimental philosophy, anatomy, and chemistry, for his wonderful success and repute in his practice, the natural smoothness, pure elegancy, delightful unaffected neatness of Latin style, none scarce hath equalled, much less outdone, him, how great soever. When at any time he is mentioned by authors, as he is very often, it is done in words expressing their highest esteem of his great worth and excellency, and placed still as first in rank among physicians. And, further, also, he hath laid a lasting foundation of a body of physic, chiefly on hypotheses of his own framing." These hypotheses, by far too numerous and fanciful for his reputation, are contained in the following works : 1. " Diatribæ duæ Medico-philosophicæ de fermentatione, altera de febribus," Hague, 1659, 8vo, London, 1660, 1665, &c. 12mo. This was attacked by Edm. de Meara, a doctor of physic of Bristol, and fellow of the college of physicians, but defended by Dr. Richard Lower in his " Diatribæ Thomæ Willisii Med. Doct. & Profess. Oxon de Febribus Vindicatio contra Edm. de Meara," London, 1665, 8vo. 2. " Dissertatio Epistolica de Urinis :" printed with the Diatribæ above mentioned. 3. " Cerebri Anatome," London, 1664, 8vo, Amsterdam, 1667, in 12mo. 4. " De ratione motus musculorum," printed with the " Cerebri Anatome." 5. " Pathologiæ Cerebri & nervosi generis specimina, in quo agitur de morbis convulsivis & de scorbuto," Oxford, 1667, 4to, London, 1668, Amsterdam, 1669, &c. 12mo. 6. " Affectionum quæ dicuntur hystericæ & hypochondriacæ Pathologia spasmodica, vindicata contra responsionem Epistolarem Nath. Highmore, M. D." London, 1670, 4to, Leyden, 1671, 12mo, &c. 7. " Exercitationes Medico-physicæ duæ, 1. De sanguinis accensione. 2. " De motu musculari," printed with the preceding book. 8. " De animâ Brutorum, quæ hominis vitalis ac sensativa est, exercitationes duæ, &c." London, 1672, 4to and 8vo, Amsterdam, 1674, 12mo. All these books, except " Affectionum quæ dicuntur hystericæ, &c." and that " de animâ Brutorum," were translated into English by S. Pordage, esq. and printed at London, 1681, folio. 9. " Pharmaceutice Rationalis : sive Diatriba de medicamentorum operationibus in humano corpore." In two parts, Oxford, 1674 and 1675, 12mo, 4to. Published by Dr. John Fell. In the postscript to the second part is the following imprimatur put to it by Dr. Ralph Bathurst, the author dying the day before.

" Imprimatur.

" Amicissimo Authori post tam immortale opus nihil mortale facturo, tanquam lumina morienti claudens, extremum hoc officium præstat

" Rad. Bathurst, Oxon.
Oxon, Nov. 12, 1675.                                 Vice-Cancell."

This book was translated into English by an anonymous

person, and printed at London, in 1679, in folio; but this
translation being very faulty, it was corrected by S. Pordage, esq. above mentioned, and published in his version
of Dr. Willis's Works in 1681. In 1685 there came out
at London, in 8vo, "The London practice of Physic; or
the whole practical part of physic contained in the works
of Dr. Willis, faithfully made English, and printed together
for the public good." This contains, I. the first and second parts of our author's Pharmaceutice rationalis; II. his
treatise of convulsive diseases; III. that of the scurvy; IV.
that of the diseases of the brain and genus nervosum; V.
that of fevers. 10. A plain and easy method of preserving
those that are well from the infection of the plague, or any
contagious distemper, in city, camp, country, fleet, &c. and
for curing such as are infected with it. Written in 1666,
but not published till the end of 1690. All our author's
Latin works were printed in two volumes in 4to at Geneva
in 1676, and Amsterdam in 1682 in 4to.

Although Dr. Willis's works abound with the reveries of
the chemical philosophy, and consequently have fallen into
considerable neglect, there are many useful and curious
things to be found in them. His "Cerebri Anatome" is
the best of his works; but even here, although his anatomical descriptions be good, yet his physiological opinions
must be acknowledged to be altogether extravagant and
absurd. For example, he lodges common sense in the
corpus striatum of the brain, imagination in the corpus cal-
losum, and memory in the cineritious matter which en-
compasses the medullary. Yet, after all, what is this to
the more monstrous absurdities of that modern piece of
quackery, called Craniology? Vieussens, who in his "Neu-
rographia," animadverted on Willis, is notwithstanding
under great obligations to him, and Willis's enumeration of
the nerves is still adhered to by anatomists.

A Dutch physician, named Schelhammer, in a book
"De Auditu," printed at Leyden in 1684, took occasion to
animadvert upon a passage in Dr. Willis's book "de Anima
Brutorum," printed in 1672; and in such a manner as reflected not only upon his skill, but also upon his integrity.
But Dr. Derham observes, "that this is a severe and unjust
censure of our truly-famous countryman, a man of known
probity, who hath manifested himself to have been as curious and sagacious an anatomist, as great a philosopher, and
as learned and skilful a physician as any of his censurers;

and his reputation for veracity and integrity was no less than any of theirs too." It remains to be noticed, that his "Cerebri Anatome" had an elegant copy of verses written in it by Mr. Phillip Fell, and the drawings for the plates were done by his friend Dr. Christopher Wren, the celebrated architect.[1]

WILLIS (BROWNE), an eminent antiquary, was born Sept. 14, 1682, at Blandford in Dorset. He was grandson to the preceding Dr. Willis, and eldest son of Thomas Willis, esq. of Bletchley, in Bucks. His mother was daughter of Robert Browne, esq. of Frampton, in Dorsetshire. He had the first part of his education under Mr. Abraham Freestone at Bechampton, whence he was sent to Westminster-school, and during his frequent walks in the adjoining abbey imbibed that taste for architectural, particularly ecclesiastical, antiquities, which constituted the pleasure and employment of his future life. At the age of seventeen he was admitted a gentleman commoner of Christ church, Oxford, under the tuition of the famous geographer Edward Wells, D. D. and when he left Oxford, he lived for three years with the famous Dr. Will. Wotton. In 1702, he proved a considerable benefactor to Fenny-Stratford, by reviving the market of that town. In 1705, he was chosen for the town of Buckingham; and, during the short time he was in parliament, was a constant attendant, and generally upon committees. In 1707, he married Catharine, daughter of Daniel Elliot, esq. of a very ancient family in Cornwall, with whom he had a fortune of 8000l. and by whom he had a numerous issue. She died Oct. 2, 1724. This lady had some literary pretensions. She wrote a book entitled "The established Church of England the true catholick church, free from innovations, or diminishing the apostolic doctrines, the sacraments, and doctrines whereof are herein set forth," Lond. 1718, 8vo. What the merit of this work may be, we know not; but her husband often made a joke of it, and in his own copy wrote the following note, "All the connexion in this book is owing to the book-binder." Between 1704 and 1707 he contributed very largely towards the repairing and beautifying Bletchley church, of which he was patron, and to which he gave a set of communion-plate. In 1717-18, the

[1] Ath. Ox. vol. II.—Biog. Brit.—Letters by Eminent Persons, 1813, 3 vols. 8vo.—Thomson's Hist. of the Royal Society.—Granger.—Birch's Lives.—Dean Barwick's Life.

Society of Antiquaries being revived, Mr. Willis became a
member of it, and Aug. 23, 1720, the degree of M. A. and
1749, that of LL. D. were conferred on him, by diploma,
by the university of Oxford. From some of his letters in
1723, it would appear that at that time he had some employment in the Tower, or perhaps had only gained access
to the archives preserved there. At his solicitation, and in
concurrence with his cousin Dr. Martin Benson, afterwards
bishop of Gloucester, rector of that parish, a subscription
was raised for building the beautiful chapel of St. Martin's
at Fenny-Stratford, which was begun in 1724, and consecrated May 27, 1730. A dreadful fire having destroyed
above fifty houses and the church at Stoney-Stratford,
May 19, 1746, Mr. Willis, besides collecting money among
his friends for the benefit of the unhappy sufferers, repaired, at his own expence, the tower of the church, and
afterwards gave a lottery ticket towards the re-building of
that church, which came up a prize. In 1741 he presented the university of Oxford with his fine cabinet of
English coins, at that time looked upon as the most complete collection in England, and which he had been upwards of forty years in collecting; but the university
thinking it too much for him, who had then a large
family, to give the gold ones, purchased them for 150
guineas, which were paid to Mr. Willis for 167 English
gold coins, at the rate of four guineas per ounce weight;
and even in this way the gold coins were a considerable
benefaction. This cabinet Mr. Willis annually visited 19
Oct. being St. Frideswide's day, and never failed making
some addition to it. He also gave some MSS. to the Bodleian
library, together with a picture of his grandfather, Dr.
Thomas Willis. In 1752 he laid out 200l. towards the repairs of the fine tower at Buckingham church, which fell
down some years ago, and he was, upon every occasion, a
great friend to that town. In 1756, Bow Brickhill church,
which had been disused near 150 years, was restored and
repaired by his generosity. In 1757 he erected, in Christ
church, Oxford, a handsome monument for Dr. Iles, canon,
of that cathedral, to whose education his grandfather had
contributed; and in 1759, he prevailed upon University
college to do the same in Bechampton church, for their
great benefactor sir Simon Benet, bart. above 100 years
after his death: he also, at his own expence, placed a marble stone over him, on account of his benefactions at Be-

champton, Buckingham, Stoney-Stratford, &c. Dr. Willis died at Whaddon-hall, Feb. 5, 1760, in the seventy-eighth year of his age, and was buried in Fenny-Stratford chapel, where is an inscription written by himself.

The rev. Mr. Gibberd, curate of Whaddon, gives him the following character. "He was strictly religious, without any mixture of superstition or enthusiasm. The honour of God was his prime view in every action of his life. He was a constant frequenter of the church, and never absented himself from the holy communion; and, as to the reverence he had for places more immediately set apart for religious duties, it is needless to mention what his many public works, in building, repairing, and beautifying churches, are standing evidences of. In the time of health he called his family together every evening, and, besides his private devotions in the morning, he always retired into his closet in the afternoon at about four or five o'clock. In his intercourse with men he was in every respect, as far as I could judge, very upright. He was a good landlord, and scarce ever raised his rents; and that his servants likewise had no reason to complain of their master is evident from the long time they generally lived with him. He had many valuable and good friends, whose kindness he always acknowledged. And though perhaps he might have some disputes with a few people, the reason of which it would be disagreeable to enter into, yet it is with great satisfaction that I can affirm that he was perfectly reconciled with every one. He was, with regard to himself, peculiarly sober and temperate; and he has often told me, that he denied himself many things, that he might bestow them better. Indeed, he appeared to me to have no greater regard to money than as it furnished him with an opportunity of doing good. He supplied yearly three charity schools at Whaddon, Bletchley, and Fenny Stratford; and besides what he constantly gave at Christmas, he was never backward in relieving his poor neighbours with both wine and money when they were sick, or in any kind of distress. He was a faithful friend where he professed it, and always ready to contribute any thing to their advantage."

Many other curious particulars of Dr. Willis's character and singularities may be seen in Mr. Nichols's "Literary Anecdotes," vols. VI. and VIII. and many extracts from his correspondence. It is now necessary to give some account of his labours as an antiquary, which, in general, do the highest credit to his talents, industry, and perseverance, yet perhaps, could not have been carried on without a considerable proportion of that enthusiasm which sometimes embarrassed his fortune, and created many oddities of character and behaviour.

In 1710, when Mr. Gale published his " History and Antiquities of Winchester Cathedral," Willis supplied him with the history of Hyde abbey, and lists of the abbots of Newminster and Hyde, published in that work. In 1715 and 1716 he published his " Notitia Parliamentaria, or an History of the Counties, cities and boroughs in England and Wales," 2 vols. 8vo, to which he added a third in 1730. The first volume was reprinted in 1730, with additions; and a single sheet, as far as relates to the borough of Windsor, was printed in 1733, folio. In 1717, he published, without his name, a kind of abridgment of " The Whole Duty of Man," " for the benefit of the poorer sort." In the same year, " A Survey of the Cathedral Church of St. David's, and the edifices belonging to it, as they stood in the year 1715," 8vo. In 1718 and 1719, " An History of the mitred Parliamentary abbies and conventual cathedral churches," 2 vols. 8vo. In 1719, 20, and 21, " Surveys of the Cathedral churches of Llandaff, St. Asaph, and Bangor, &c." 8vo. This led to his greatest and most important work, " Survey of the Cathedrals of England, with the *Parochiale Anglicanum*, illustrated with draughts of the cathedrals," 3 vols. 4to, 1727, 1730, and 1733. These volumes contain the history of the cathedrals of York, Durham, Carlisle, Chester, Man, Lichfield, Hereford, Worcester, Gloucester, Bristol, Lincoln, Ely, Oxford, and Peterborough. These were first published by Mr. Francis Gosling, afterwards the banker and founder of the well-known and highly respected firm of that name, who, on giving up the bookselling business, sold the remaining copies to Osborne, who prefixed a title with the date 1742, and advertised them as containing a history of *all* the cathedrals. Against this roguish trick, Willis thought proper to guard the public in an advertisement in the public papers. It is to be regretted, however, that he did not extend his labours to all the cathedrals, for he had during his long life visited every cathedral in England and Wales except Carlisle, which journies he used to call his pilgrimages.

In 1733 he published " A Table of the Gold Coins of the Kings of England," in one sheet folio, which is in the

" Vetusta Monumenta." Before 1752 he printed an " Address to the patrons of ecclesiastical livings," 4to, with the view to prevent pluralities and non-residence; and in 1754, an improved edition of " Ecton's Thesaurus rerum ecclesiasticarum," 4to. His last publication was the " History and antiquities of the Town, hundred, and deanry, of Buckingham," London, 1755, 4to. His large collections for the whole county are now among his MSS. in the Bodleian library; and his MS. of the " History of the Hundreds of Newport and Cotslow," transcribed and methodized by Mr. Cole, are now among Mr. Cole's valuable MSS. in the British Museum. Willis was not much a gainer by any of his publications, the sale being generally very tardy, of which he makes many complaints in his private correspondence. They have all, however, since, borne a price more suited to their merits.[1]

WILLUGHBY (FRANCIS), a celebrated natural historian, was the only son of sir Francis Willughby, knt, and was born in 1635. His natural advantages, with regard to birth, talents, and fortune, he applied in such a manner as to procure to himself honours that might more truly be called his own. He was addicted to study from his childhood, and was so great an œconomist of his time, that he was thought by his friends to have impaired his health by his incessant application. By this means, however, he attained great skill in all branches of learning, and got deep insight into the most abstruse kinds of knowledge, and the most subtle parts of the mathematics. But observing, in the busy and inquisitive age in which he lived, that the history of animals was in a great measure neglected by his countrymen, he applied himself particularly to that province, and used all diligence to cultivate and illustrate it. To prosecute this purpose more effectually, he carefully read over what had been written by others on that subject; and in 1660, we find him residing at Oxford for the benefit of the public library. But he had been originally a member of Trinity college, Cambridge, where he took his degree of A. B. in 1656, and of A. M. in 1659. After leaving Oxford, he travelled, in search of natural knowledge, several times over his native country; and afterwards to France, Spain, Italy, Germany,

[1] Life prefixed to his Cathedrals.—Nichols's Bowyer.—Hutchins's Hist. of Dorsetshire.—Cole's MS Athenæ in Brit. Mus.—Biog. Brit.

and the Low-Countries, attended by his ingenious friend
Mr. John Ray, and others ; in all which places, says Wood,
he was so inquisitive and successful, that not many sorts
of animals, described by others, escaped his diligence.
He died July 3, 1672, aged only thirty-seven ; to the great
loss of the republic of letters, and much lamented by those
of the Royal Society, of which he was an eminent member
and ornament.   He left to Mr. Ray the charge of educating his two infant sons, with an annuity of 70l, which constituted ever after the chief part of Ray's income.   A most
exemplary character of him may be seen in Ray's preface
to his " Ornithology ;" whence all the particulars are con-
cisely and elegantly summed up in a Latin epitaph, on a
monument erected to his memory in the church of Middleton in Warwickshire, where he is buried with his ancestors.
His works are, " Ornithologiæ libri tres: in quibus aves
omnes bactenus cognitæ in methodum naturis suis conveni-
entem redactæ accurate describuntur, descriptiones iconi-
bus elegantissimis, & vivarum avium simillimis, æri incisis
illustrantur," 1676, folio.   This was prepared for the press,
corrected and digested into order, by Ray, afterwards by
him also translated into English, with an appendix, and
figures engraved at the expense of Mr. Willughby, but of
inferior merit, 1678, folio.   2. " Historiæ Piscium libri
quatuor, &c." 1686, folio.   This was revised and digested
by Ray, with engravings of many species, not then known
in England.   3. " Letter containing some considerable
observations about that kind of wasps called Ichneumones,
&c. dated Aug. 24, 1671."   See the Phil. Trans. N° 76.
4. " Letter about the hatching a kind of bee lodged in old
willows, dated July 10, 1671."   Trans. N° 47.   5. " Letters of Francis Willughby, esq." added to " Philosophical
Letters between the late learned Mr. Ray and several of
his correspondents," 8vo.   By William Derham. [1]

WILLYMOT (WILLIAM), a teacher of considerable
note, and a publisher of some school-books of reputation,
was the second son of Thomas Willymot of Royston, in the
county of Cambridge, by his wife Rachel, daughter of Dr.
Pindar of Springfield in Essex.   He was born, we are not
told in what year, at Royston, and admitted scholar of
King's-college, Cambridge, Oct. 20, 1692.   He proceeded

[1] Birch's Hist. of the Royal Society, vol. III. p. 66.—Ath. Ox. vol. II.—Biog.
Brit.—Derham's Life of Ray.—Ray's Life, vol. XXVI. of this work.

A. B. in 1697, A. M. in 1700, and LL.,D. in 1707. After
taking his master's degree he went as usher to Eton, where
Cole says "he continued not long, but kept a school at
Isleworth in Middlesex:" Harwood, however, says that
he was many years an assistant at Eton, and was the editor
of several books for the use of boys educated there. Harwood adds that he was tutor, when at King's college, to
lord Henry and lord Richard Lumley, sons of the earl of
Scarborough; and Cole informs us that he was private
tutor in the family of John Bromley, of Horseheath-hall
in Cambridgeshire, esq. father of Henry lord Montfort;
" but here endeavouring to pay his addresses to one of the
ladies of the family, he was dismissed." When he left
Eton is uncertain, but in 1721 we find him master of a
private school at Isleworth, and at that time one of the
candidates for the mastership of St. Paul's school, in which
he did not succeed. By an advertisement then published
by him, it would appear that his failure arose in some
measure from his being suspected of an attachment to the
pretender, which he denies. Some time before this he had
studied civil law, and entered himself of Doctors'-com-
mons, but changing his mind, returned to college, took
holy orders, and was made vice-provost of King's college
in the above year, 1721, at which time he was senior fellow.
In 1735 he was presented to the rectory of Milton near
Cambridge, after a contest with the college, which refused
him, in consideration of his not having remained and performed the requisite college exercises. Even with this,
Cole says, he was soon dissatisfied, and would have returned to his fellowship had it been possible. He died
June 7, 1737, of an apoplexy, at the Swan Inn, at Bedford, on his return from Bath. Among his publications for
the use of schools are, 1. "The peculiar use and signification of certain words in the Latin tongue," &c. 1705, 8vo.
2. "Particles exemplified in English sentences, &c." 1703,
8vo. 3. "Larger examples, fitted to Lilly's grammar-
rules." 4. "Smaller examples, &c." 5. "Three of Te-
rence's comedies, viz. the Andria, the Adelphi, and the
Hecyra, with English notes," 1706, 8vo. 6. "Select
stories from Ovid's Metamorphoses, with English notes."
7. "Phædrus Fables, with English notes," &c. &c. He
published also "A collection of Devotions for the Altar,"
2 vols. 8vo; "Lord Bacon's Essays," 2 vols. 8vo. and "A
new translation of Thomas à Kempis," 1722. The com-

mon copies are dedicated " To the Sufferers by the South Sea." It was originally dedicated to Dr. Godolphin, provost of Eton, but as he had abused the fellows of the college in it, upon recollection he called it in, " so," says Cole, " this curious dedication is rarely to be met with."[1]

WILMOT (JOHN, EARL OF ROCHESTER), a noted wit in the reign of Charles II. was the son of Henry earl of Rochester; who bore a great part in the civil wars, and was the chief manager of the king's preservation after the battle of Worcester. He was born April 10, 1647, at Ditchley in Oxfordshire; and was educated in grammar and classical literature in the free-school at Burford. Here he acquired the Latin to such perfection, that to his dying day he retained a quick relish for the beauties of that tongue; and afterwards became exactly versed in the authors of the Augustan age, which he often read. In 1659, when only twelve years old, he was admitted a nobleman of Wadham college in Oxford, under the inspection of Dr. Blandford, afterwards bishop of Oxford and Worcester; and, in 1661, was with some other persons of rank created master of arts in convocation: at which time, Wood says, he and none else was admitted very affectionately into the fraternity by a kiss from the chancellor of the university, Clarendon, who then sate in the supreme chair. Afterwards he travelled into France and Italy; and at his return frequented the court, which, Wood observes, and there is reason to believe very truly, not only corrupted his morals, but made him a perfect Hobbist in principle. In the mean time, he became one of the gentlemen of the bed-chamber to the king, and comptroller of Woodstock-park. In 1665 he went to sea with the earl of Sandwich, who was sent to lie in wait for the Dutch East-India fleet; and was in the Revenge, commanded by sir Thomas Tiddiman, when the attack was made on the port of Bergen in Norway, the Dutch ships having got into that port. It was a desperate attempt; and, during the whole action, the earl of Rochester shewed the greatest resolution, and gained a high reputation for courage. He supported his character for bravery in a second expedition, but afterwards lost it in an adventure with lord Mulgrave; of which that noble author, in the memoirs of himself, gives a par-

---

[1] Cole's MS Collections in Brit. Mus. vol. XVI.—Harwood's Alumni Etonenses.—Nichols's Bowyer.

ticular account. It exhibits some traits of the earl of Rochester's character; and therefore, though somewhat tedious and wordy, may not be unacceptable. " I was informed," says lord Mulgrave, " that the earl of Rochester had said something of me, which, according to his custom, was very malicious. I therefore sent colonel Aston, a very mettled friend of mine, to call him to account for it. He denied the words, and indeed I was soon convinced he had never said them ; but the mere report, though I found it to be false, obliged me, as I then foolishly thought, to go on with the quarrel ; and the next day was appointed for us to fight on horseback, a way in England a little unusual, but it was his part to chuse. Accordingly, I and my second lay the night before at Knightsbridge privately, to avoid the being secured at London upon any suspicion ; and in the morning we met the lord Rochester at the place appointed, who, instead of James Porter, whom he assured Aston he would make his second, brought an errant lifeguard man, whom nobody knew. To this Mr. Aston took exception, upon the account of his being no suitable adversary; especially considering how extremely well he was mounted, whereas we had only a couple of pads : upon which, we all agreed to fight on foot. But, as my lord Rochester and I were riding into the next field in order to it, he told me, that he had at first chosen to fight on horseback, because he was so much indisposed, that he found himself unfit at all any way, much less on foot. I was extremely surprised, because at that time no man had a better reputation for courage; and I took the liberty of representing what a ridiculous story it would make, if we returned without fighting, and therefore advised him for both our sakes, especially for his own, to consider better of it, since I must be obliged in my own defence to lay the fault on him, by telling the truth of the matter. His answer was, that he submitted to it; and hoped, that I would not desire the advantage of having to do with any man in so weak a condition. I replied, that by such an argument he had sufficiently tied my hands, upon condition that I might call our seconds to be witnesses of the whole business ; which he consented to, and so we parted. When we returned to London, we found it full of this quarrel, upon our being absent so long ; and therefore Mr. Aston thought himself obliged to write down every word and circumstance of this whole matter, in order to spread every where the true reason of our returning without having fought. This, being never in the least contradicted or resented by the lord Rochester, entirely ruined his reputation as to courage, of which I was really sorry to be the occasion, though nobody had still a greater as to wit; which supported him pretty well in the world, notwithstanding some more accidents of the same kind, that never fail to succeed one another, when once people know a man's weakness.''

The earl of Rochester, before he travelled, had given somewhat into that disorderly and intemperate way of living which the joy of the whole nation, upon the restoring of Charles II. had introduced; yet during his travels he had at least acquired a habit of sobriety. But, falling into court-company, where excesses were continually practised, he soon became intemperate, and the natural heat of his fancy, being inflamed with wine, made him so extravagantly pleasant, that many, to be more diverted by that humour, strove to engage him deeper and deeper in intoxication. This at length so entirely subdued him, that, as he told Dr. Burnet, he was for five years together continually drunk: not all the while under the visible effect of liquor, but so inflamed in his blood, that he was never cool enough to be master of himself. There were two principles in the natural temper of this lively and witty earl, which carried him to great excesses; a violent love of pleasure, and a disposition to extravagant mirth. The one involved him in the lowest sensuality, the other led him to many odd adventures and frolics. Once he had disguised himself so, that his nearest friends could not have known him, and set up in Tower-street for an Italian mountebank, where he practised physic for some weeks. He disguised himself often as a porter, or as a beggar; sometimes to follow some mean amours, which, for the variety of them, he affected. At other times, merely for diversion, he would go about in odd shapes; in which he acted his part so naturally, that even those who were in the secret, and saw him in these shapes, could perceive nothing by which he might be discovered. He is said to have been a generous and good-natured man in cold blood, yet would go far in his heats after any thing that might turn to a jest or matter of diversion; and he laid out himself very freely in libels and satires, in which he had so peculiar a talent of mixing wit with malice, that all his compositions were easily known. Andrew Marvell, who was himself a great wit, used to say, "that Rochester was the only man in England who had the true vein of satire."

"Thus," says Dr. Johnson, "in a course of drunken gaiety, and gross sensuality, with intervals of study perhaps yet more criminal, with an avowed contempt of all decency and order, a total disregard to every moral, and a resolute denial of every religious obligation, he lived worthless and useless, and blazed out his youth and his health in lavish voluptuousness; till, at the age of one and thirty, he had exhausted the fund of life, and reduced himself to a state of weakness and decay."

In Oct. 1679, when he was slowly recovering from a severe disease, he was visited by Dr. Burnet, upon an intimation that such a visit would be very agreeable to him. With great freedom he laid open to that divine all his thoughts both of religion and morality, and gave him a full view of his past life: on which the doctor visited him often, till he went from London in April following, and once or twice after. They canvassed at various times the principles of morality, natural and revealed religion, and Christianity in particular; the result of all which, as it is faithfully related by Dr. Burnet in a book, which, Dr. Johnson observes, "the critic ought to read for its elegance, the philosopher for its arguments, and the saint for its piety," was, that this noble earl, though he had lived the life of an atheist and a libertine, yet died the death of a sincere penitent. The philosophers of the present age will naturally suppose, that his contrition and conviction were purely the effects of weakness and low spirits, which scarcely suffer a man to continue in his senses, and certainly not to be master of himself; but Dr. Burnet affirms him to have been " under no such decay as either darkened or weakened his understanding, nor troubled with the spleen or vapours, or under the power of melancholy." The reader may judge for himself from the following, which is part of a letter from the earl to Dr. Burnet, dated " Woodstock-park, June 25, 1680, Oxfordshire." There is nothing left out, but some personal compliments to the doctor.

"My most honoured Dr. BURNET,

"My spirits and body decay so equally together, that I shall write you a letter as weak as I am in person. I begin to value churchmen above all men in the world, &c. If God be yet pleased to spare me longer in this world, I hope in your conversation to be exalted to that degree of piety, that the world may see how much I abhor what I so long loved, and how much I glory in repentance, and in God's service. Bestow your prayers upon me, that God would spare me, if it be his good will, to shew a true repentance and amendment of life for the time to come; or else, if the Lord pleaseth to put an end to my worldly being now, that he would mercifully accept of my death-bed repentance, and perform that promise he hath been pleased to make, that 'at what time soever a sinner doth repent, he would receive him.' Put up these prayers, most dear doctor, to Almighty God, for your most obedient and languishing servant,                    ROCHESTER."

He died July 26 following, without any convulsion, or so much as a groan: for, though he had not completed his thirty-third year, he was worn so entirely down, that all the powers of nature were exhausted. He left behind him a son named Charles, who died Nov. 12, 1681; and three daughters *. The male line ceasing, Charles II. conferred the title of Rochester on Laurence viscount Killingworth, a younger son of Edward earl of Clarendon.

The earl of Rochester was a graceful and well-shaped person, tall, and well-made, if not a little too slender, as Burnet observes. "He was," says Johnson, "eminent for the vigour of his colloquial wit, and remarkable for many wild pranks and sallies of extravagance. The glare of his general character diffused itself upon his writings; the compositions of a man whose name was heard so often were certain of attention, and from many readers certain of applause. This blaze of reputation is not yet quite extinguished; and his poetry still retains some splendour beyond that which genius has bestowed.

"Wood and Burnet give us reason to believe, that much was imputed to him which he did not write. It is not known by whom the original collection was made, or by what authority its genuineness was ascertained. The first edition was published in the year of his death, with an air of concealment, professing in the title-page to be printed

---

* In the London Chronicle for Feb. 11, 1765, and probably in other papers, we read the following: " Yesterday morning died, in an advanced age, at her lodgings in Fleet-street, Mrs. Arabella Wilmot, a natural daughter of the famous earl of Rochester, the celebrated wit in the reign of Charles II."

at Antwerp.    Of some of the pieces, however, there is no
doubt.    The Imitation of Horace's Satire, the Verses to
lord Mulgrave, the Satire against Man, the verses upon
Nothing, and perhaps some others, are I believe genuine,
and perhaps most of those which the collection exhibits.
As he cannot be supposed to have found leisure for any
course of continued study, his pieces are commonly short,
such as one fit of resolution would produce.    His songs
have no particular character ; they tell, like other songs,
in smooth and easy language, of scorn and kindness, dismission and desertion, absence, and inconstancy, with the
common-places of artificial courtship.    They are commonly
smooth and easy ; but have little nature, and little sentiment.    His imitation of Horace on Lucilius is not inele-
gant or unhappy.    In the reign of Charles the Second began that adaptation, which has since been very frequent,
of ancient poetry to present times ; and perhaps few will
be found where the parallelism is better preserved than in
this.    The versification is indeed sometimes careless, but
it is sometimes vigorous and weighty.    The strongest effort
of his muse is his poem upon " Nothing."    Another of his
most vigorous pieces is his lampoon upon sir Carr Scrope.
Of the satire against Man, Rochester can only claim what
remains when all Boileau's part is taken away.    In all his
works there is sprightliness and vigour, and every where
may be found tokens of a mind which study might have
carried to excellence.    What more can be expected from
a life spent in ostentatious contempt of regularity, and
ended before the abilities of many other men began to be
displayed?"    The late George Steevens, esq. made the selection of Rochester's poems which appears in Dr. Johnson's edition ; but Mr. Malone observes, that the same task
had been performed in the early part of the last century
by Jacob Tonson. '

WILMOT (JOHN EARDLEY), a learned lawyer, and lord
chief justice of the court of common pleas, was the second
son of Robert Wilmot, of Osmaston in the county of Derby,
esq. and of Ursula, one of the daughters and coheiresses of
sir Samuel Marow, of Berkswell, in the county of Warwick,
bart.    He was born Aug. 16, 1709, at Derby, where his father then lived, and after having acquired the rudiments

Life by Bp. Burnet.—Johnson's Poets.—Biog. Brit.—Park's Edition of the
Royal and Noble Authors.

of learning at the free-school in that town, under the **Rev.**
Mr. Blackwell, was placed with the Rev. Mr. Hunter at
Lichfield, where he was contemporary with Johnson and
Garrick. At an after period of his life it could be remarked
that there were then five judges upon the bench who had
been educated at Lichfield school, viz. Willes, Parker,
Noel, Lloyd, and Wilmot. In Jan. 1724, he was removed
to Westminster-school, and placed under Dr. Freind; and
here, and at Trinity-hall, Cambridge, where he resided
until Jan. 1728, he laid the foundation of many friendships,
which he preserved through a long life. At the university
he contracted a passion for study and retirement that never
quitted him, and he was often heard to say, that at this
time the height of his ambition was to become a fellow of
Trinity-hall, and to pass his life in that learned society.
His natural disposition had induced him to give the preference to the church; but his father, who was a man of
sagacity as well as of reading, had destined him to the
study of the law, which he accordingly prosecuted with
much diligence at the Inner Temple, and was called to the
bar in June 1732. In 1743 he married Sarah, daughter of
Thomas Rivett, of Derby, esq.

We are not acquainted with any interesting particulars
of Mr. Wilmot's life between the period of his leaving the
university and his being in a considerable degree of practice as a barrister: but as duty and filial piety, more than
inclination, had induced him to embrace the profession of
the law, his pursuit after its emoluments was not eager,
though his study of it was unremitted. He was regular in
his attendance on the terms, but his practice was at this
time chiefly confined to the county of Derby, where he
was much respected. In town his business was not great;
yet in those causes in which he was engaged, his merit,
learning, and eloquence, were universally acknowledged,
and gained him the esteem and approbation of some of
the greatest ornaments of the profession, among whom
were sir Dudley Ryder, then attorney-general, and the
lord chancellor Hardwicke. In 1753, the chancellor proposed to make him one of his majesty's counsel, and afterwards king's serjeant: but both these he declined, chiefly
from a disinclination to London business, and a wish, that
never left him, of retiring altogether into the country. On
this he was so determined that in 1754, he actually made
what he called his farewell speech in the court of exchequer,

which he had of late years attended more than any other. Perhaps his disposition was not calculated for forensic disputation, though his profound knowledge and indefatigable labour, as well as ability and penetration, had made him, in the opinion of those who knew him, one of the best lawyers of his time. He had more than one offer of a seat in the House of Commons about this period, but he uniformly declined every temptation of this kind. He had not however long enjoyed his retirement in Derbyshire before he received a summons to town to succeed sir Martin Wright, as judge of the court of King's Bench. With much persuasion, aided perhaps by the increase of his family, consisting now of five children, he was induced to accept this preferment in February 1755, which was accompanied, as usual, with the honour of knighthood. It is not known to what interest he owed this promotion, and it seems most fair to conclude that a sense of his merit only must have induced his patrons to send to the country for one so resolute on retirement, when so many, at hand, would have been glad to accept the office.

In the autumn of 1756, lord Hardwicke resigned the great seal, which continued for about a year in the hands of three lords commissioners, chief justice Willes, sir S. S. Smythe, and sir John Eardley Wilmot. In March 1757, sir Eardley had a most providential escape from being destroyed at Worcester by the fall of a stack of chimneys through the roof into court. His first clerk was killed at his feet, also the attorney in the cause then trying, two of the jurymen, and some others. Sir Eardley was beginning to sum up the evidence when the catastrophe happened. Sir Eardley continued about nine years longer, as one of the puisne judges of the court of King's Bench. The King's Bench was at this time filled with men of distinguished talents, and it is no small honour to sir Eardley Wilmot that he sat for a long period as the worthy colleague of Mansfield, Dennison, and Foster. Though the part he took was not a very conspicuous one, from his situation on the bench, and from his native modesty, yet his brethren, and those who were acquainted with Westminster-hall at that period, bore testimony that his active mind was always engaged, either in or out of court, in elucidating some obscure point, in nicely weighing questions of the greatest difficulty, and in contributing his share towards expediting and deciding the important suits then under discussion;

nor was he less eminent in that important branch of his judicial office, the administration of the criminal justice of the kingdom; and while his pervading mind suffered few crimes to escape detection and punishment, his humanity and compassion were often put to the severest trials.

Among many other parts of this laborious profession, to which sir Eardley had given unremitting attention, is that of taking notes, to which he had invariably accustomed himself both before and after he was called to the bar. These notes were transcribed by his clerk, and he thus by degrees became possessed of many volumes of MS. notes, both in law and equity. The same practice he continued after he was raised to the bench, till he heard that Mr. (afterwards sir James) Burrow intended to publish his notes from the time of lord Mansfields being appointed chief justice; but he uniformly lent Mr. Burrow his papers from this period, and with such short notes as he took himself. We may here mention that the "Notes of Opinions delivered in different courts," by sir John Eardley Wilmot, were published in 1802, 4to, by his son, with a memoir of his life, from which we have extracted the present account.

Although sir Eardley persevered unremittingly in the discharge of his duty, it was not without a frequent sigh for a more quiet and retired station than that of the court of King's Bench. In 1765, a serious treaty was set on foot by him, to exchange his present office for one, not less honourable indeed, but undoubtedly at that time less lucrative and less conspicuous, that of chief justice of Chester, which was then held by Mr. Morton; but the treaty was at length broken off, and when in the summer of 1766, lord Camden, who had been chief justice of the common pleas about four years, was appointed lord chancellor, sir Eardley was promoted to the chief justiceship in his room. Here, however, as in former instances, his friends had no little trouble in overcoming his repugnance to a more elevated situation. It is believed, that next to his character for learning and integrity, he was indebted for this preferment, to the high opinion and esteem of both the old and new chancellor, and also to the friendship of lord Shelburne, appointed at that time one of the secretaries of state. His lordship, though a much younger man, had ever since his first acquaintance with him, several years before, conceived so great an admiration of his talents, and esteem for his virtues, that he had long lived with him in habits of the greatest intimacy and friendship. In the evening of the day that sir Eardley kissed hands on being appointed chief justice, one of his sons, a youth of seventeen, attended him at his bed-side. "Now," said he, "my son, I will tell you a secret worth your knowing and remembering; the elevation I have met with in life, particularly this last instance of it, has not been owing to any superior merit or abilities, but to my humility, to my not having set up myself above others, and to an uniform endeavour to pass through life, void of offence towards God and man." Sir Eardley was now called to preside in a court where he had many seniors on the bench; but the appointment gave general satisfaction, and his acknowledged abilities, his unaffected modesty and courtesy, soon made him as much esteemed and beloved in his new court, as he had been before in his old one.

In 1768, bishop Warburton, who had the highest opinion of sir Eardley, requested him to become one of the first trustees of his lectureship at Lincoln's-inn chapel, along with lord Mansfield and Mr. Yorke; and this being complied with, in 1769, sir Eardley requested his assistance and advice on the occasion of one of his sons preparing himself for the church. The bishop complied, and sent him the first part of some "Directions for the study of Theology," which have since been printed in Warburton's works, being given to his editor, Dr. Hurd, by the son to whom they were addressed, the late John Eardley Wilmot, esq. Circumstances afterwards induced this son to go into the profession of the law, on which sir Eardley, in 1771, made the following indorsement on the bishop's paper. "These directions were given me by Dr. Warburton, bishop of Gloucester, for the use of my son, when he proposed to go into orders; but, in the year 1771, he *unfortunately* preferred the bar to the pulpit, and, instead of lying upon a bed of roses, ambitioned a crown of thorns. *Digne puer meliore flamma!*" This shews how uniform sir Eardley was, from his earliest youth, in his predilection for the church, a predilection which probably influenced, more or less, every act of his life. It was about this time, viz. 1769, that sir Eardley presided in the memorable cause of Mr. Wilkes against lord Halifax and others, a period of great heat and violence, both in parliament and in the nation; but he was so entirely free from all political bias, that his conduct gave universal satisfaction. It was an action of trespass for false imprisonment, damages laid at 20,000*l.* ; Mr. Wilkes having been taken up and confined in the Tower, and his papers seized and taken away, by virtue of a general warrant from lord Halifax, one of his majesty's secretaries of state. Sir Eardley's speech is published in his Life, and does great credit to his impartiality. The jury gave 4000*l.* damages.

On the resignation of lord Camden, and the subsequent death of Mr. Yorke, in January 1770, the great seal, with other honours, was offered to sir Eardley by the duke of Grafton, and was again pressed upon him in the course of that year by lord North, the duke's successor, but in vain. He was at this time too fixed in his resolution of retiring alto-gether from public business, and it seemed to him a good opportunity to urge the same reason for resigning the office he held, as for declining the one that was offered him, namely, ill health, which had prevented him occasionally from attending his court. His intention was to have re-signed without receiving any pension from the crown ; but when his resignation was accepted in 1771, he was much surprised and disconcerted to find, that he was to receive a pension for life. This he withstood in two several inter-views with the first lord of the treasury ; but his majesty having desired to see him at Buckingham house, was pleased to declare, that he could not suffer so faithful a servant to the public to retire, without receiving this mark of appro-bation and reward for his exemplary services. After this, sir Eardley thought it would be vanity and affectation to contend any longer ; and certainly his private fortune would not have enabled him to live in the manner to which he had been accustomed. But as he was thus liberally provided for by his majesty's bounty, he thought the least he could do was to make every return in his power ; and having the honour of being one of his majesty's privy council, he, in conjunction with the venerable sir Thomas Parker, who had been chief baron of the exchequer, uni-formly attended the appeals to the king in council till 1782, when his increasing infirmities obliged him to give up this last part of what he thought his public duty. Of his infir-mities he gives a most affecting proof in a short letter to earl Gower, dated Jan. 12 of that year. " My sight and hearing are extremely impaired ; but my memory is so shook, that if I could read a case over twenty times, I could neither understand nor remember it ; and as my attendance at council would only expose my infirmities, without being of any service to the public, I cannot think of ever putting myself into such a disagreeable situation."

He now retired totally from public business, and saw very little company during the remainder of his life, except a few friends, whom time had hitherto spared. His retreat from business not only procured him ease and health, but probably lengthened his life. He died Feb. 5, 1792, aged eighty-two. He left his eldest surviving son his sole executor, with express directions, in his own hand-writing, for a plain marble tablet to be put up in the church of Berkswell, in the county of Warwick, with an inscription, containing an account of his birth, death, the dates of his appointments, and names of his children, "without any other addition whatever."

Sir Eardley's person was of the middle size : his countenance commanding and dignified ; his eye lively, tempered with sweetness and benignity ; his knowledge extensive and profound ; and perhaps nothing but invincible modesty prevented him from equalling the greatest of his predecessors, and fettered his abilities and learning. Though not fond of the law as a profession, he always declared his partiality for the study of it, and he was also well versed in the civil law ; a general scholar, but particularly conversant with those branches which had a near connexion with his legal pursuits, such as history and antiquities, and he was one of the first fellows of the Society of Antiquaries, incorporated in 1750. In private life he excelled in all those qualities which render a man respected and beloved. Genuine and uniform humility was one of his most characteristic virtues.[1]

WILMOT (JOHN EARDLEY), second son of the preceding, was born in 1748, and received the first rudiments of education at Derby and at Westminster schools, at both which places he remained but a very short time. From thence he was placed at the academy at Brunswick ; and having remained there till he was seventeen, he went to University college, Oxford, where he was contemporary with many men who have since distinguished themselves in public and private life. He was at first intended for the church, as we have seen in our account of his father ; but, upon the death of his elder brother in the East Indies, and

[1] Memoirs as above.

upon the elevation of his father to one of the highest judicial situations, his intended pursuits were changed, and the
profession of the law was ultimately fixed upon.    From All
Souls college, of which he had been elected a fellow, he
removed to the Temple, and studied the law under the
superintendance of sir Eardley.    He was at the usual time
called to the bar, and went the Midland circuit.    He soon
after married the only daughter of S. Sainthill, esq. by
whom he had four daughters and one son, all of whom survived him.

In 1783, he was made a master in chancery, having been
chosen for Tiverton, in Devonshire, in the two preceding
parliaments.    Though seldom taking an active part in the
debates of those times, he was always attentive to the important duties of a member of parliament, and constant in
his attendance in the House.    He uniformly opposed the
American war, and though at the termination of that contest, when the claims of the American loyalists were to be
inquired into, and satisfied, it was most natural to suppose
that some gentleman on the other side of the House would
have been appointed commissioner for that purpose, yet
Mr. Wilmot's known abilities, integrity, and benevolence,
were so universally acknowledged, that his nomination to
that arduous office gave perfect satisfaction.    How far the
labours of himself and colleagues were crowned with success, the universal approbation of this country, and of
America, sufficiently testify.

In 1784 he was elected, with lord Eardley, his brother-
in-law, member for Coventry, in opposition to lord Shef-
field and Mr. Conway, now marquis of Hertford, whither
they had gone to add to the triumphant majority which
ultimately secured Mr. Pitt in his situation as prime minister.

It was in the summer of 1790, that the revolutionary
storm, so long collecting in France, suddenly discharged
itself; and an immense number of French clergy and laity
took refuge in this country.    The subject of these memoirs
was then in town; and the continual scenes of distress he
was daily witnessing in the streets, added to particular instances of misery which came under his own immediate observation, induced him alone, without previous communication with any one, to advertize for a meeting of the gentlemen then in town, at the Freemason's Tavern, to take
into consideration some means of affording relief to their
Christian brethren.    The meeting was most numerous and

respectable; the archbishop of Canterbury, many bishops, and most of the nobility then in London, attending; and Mr. Wilmot being called to the chair, and having stated his object in calling them together, subscriptions to a large amount were immediately entered into; and a fund created, which, with the assistance of parliament, and the contributions of every parish in the kingdom, relieved, and continued to relieve until the late prosperous events rendered a continuance unnecessary, those unhappy exiles from their native country. Mr. Wilmot continued, till he retired into the country a few years before his death, to dispense under government this national bounty; a task well suited to that universal benevolence and kindness of heart which so eminently distinguished him, and in which he had few equals, and none superior.

In 1793 he married a second wife, Sarah Anne, daughter of col. Haslam; by whom he had a son and a daughter, both of whom died in their infancy.

It was in the spring of 1804, that, finding himself ill able, from bodily infirmity, to continue the various employments he had so long zealously fulfilled, as also from an innate and hereditary love of retirement and study, he resolved to quit London entirely, and live in the country. He accordingly resigned his mastership in chancery, his situation as distributor of relief to the French refugees, and some of the many important trusts which his own kindness and the importunity of friends had induced him to accept. He bought Bruce castle, formerly the seat of the Coleraine family, situated at Tottenham, about five miles from London; near enough to town to continue what remained of the duty of commissioner of American claims, and to discharge several trusts, which were of a family nature. Here he passed a considerable part of his time in reading and study, and prepared his father's notes and reports for the press, with the Memoirs of his life already mentioned. The " Memoirs" were sold separately, with a fine engraving of sir Eardley, from a painting by Dawe. Soon after, he engaged on the Life and Letters of bishop Hough, which appeared in a very splendid 4to volume in 1812. Besides these, he published in 1779 " A short Defence of the Opposition," in answer to a pamphlet entitled " A short History of the Opposition;" and in 1780 he collated " A treatise of the Laws and Customs of England," written by Ranulf Glanvil, in the time of Henry II. with the MSS. in the Harleian, Cottonian, Bodleian, and Dr. Mills's libraries, and printed it in Latin, 12mo. His last labour was a "History of the Commission of American Claims," printed in 1815.

Mr. Wilmot died at Tottenham, June 23, 1815, in the sixty-seventh year of his age, lamented by all who knew the virtues of his public and private character. [1]

WILSON (ARTHUR), an English historian, was the son of Richard Wilson, of Yarmouth, in the county of Norfolk, gentleman; and was born in that county, 1596. In 1609 he went to France, where he continued almost two years; and upon his return to England was placed with sir Henry Spiller, to be one of his clerks in the exchequer office; in whose family he resided till having written some satirical verses upon one of the maid-servants, he was dismissed at lady Spiller's instigation. In 1613 he took a lodging in Holborn, where he applied himself to reading and poetry for some time; and, the year after, was taken into the family of Robert earl of Essex, whom he attended into the Palatinate in 1620; to the siege of Dornick, in Holland, in 1621; to that of Rees in 1622; to Arnheim, in 1623; to the siege of Breda in 1624; and in the expedition to Cadiz in 1625. In 1630 he was discharged the earl's service, at the importunity of his lady, who had conceived an aversion to him, because she had supposed him to have been against the earl's marrying her. He tells us, in his own life, that this lady's name, before she married the earl, was Elizabeth Paulet; that "she appeared to the eye a beauty, full of harmless sweetness; that her conversation was affable and gentle; and, as he was firmly persuaded, that it was not forced, but natural. But the height of her marriage and greatness being an accident, altered her very nature; for," he says, "she was the true image of Pandora's box," nor was he much mistaken, for this lady was divorced for adultery two years after her marriage. In 1631 he retired to Oxford, and became gentleman commoner of Trinity college, where he stayed almost two years, and was punctual in his compliance with the laws of the university. Then he was sent for to be steward to the earl of Warwick, whom he attended in 1637 to the siege of Breda. He died in 1652, at Felstead, in Essex, and his will was proved in October of that year. The earl

[1] Gent. Mag. vol. LXXXV.

and countess of Warwick received from him the whole of
his library, and 50*l.* to be laid out in purchasing a piece of
gold plate, as a memorial, particularly applying to the
latter, " in testimony," as he adds, " of my humble duty
and gratitude for all her noble and undeserved favours to
me." Gratitude seems to have been a strong principle
with Wilson, as appears from his life, written by himself,
and printed in Peck's " Desiderata." Wood's account of
him is, that " he had little skill in the Latin tongue, less
in the Greek, a good readiness in the French, and some
smattering in the Dutch. He was well seen in the mathematics and poetry, and sometimes in the common law
of the nation. He had composed some comedies, which
were acted at the Black Friars, in London, by the king's
players, and in the act-time at Oxford, with good applause,
himself being present ; but whether they are printed I cannot yet tell ; sure I am, that I have several specimens of
his poetry printed in divers books. His carriage was very
courteous and obliging, and such as did become a well-
bred gentleman. He also had a great command of the
English tongue, as well in writing as speaking ; and, had
he bestowed his endeavours on any other subject than that
of history, they would without doubt have seemed better.
For, in those things which he hath done, are wanting the
principal matters conducing to the completion of that faculty, viz. matter from record, exact time, name, and
place, which, by his endeavouring too much to set out his
bare collections in an affected and bombastic style, are
much neglected." The history here alluded to by Wood,
is " The Life and Reign of king James I." printed in London in 1653, folio ; that is, the year after his death ; and
reprinted in the 2d volume of " The complete History of
England," in 1706, folio. This history has been severely
treated by many writers. Mr. William Sanderson says, that,
" to give Wilson his due, we may find truth and falsehood
finely put together in it." Heylin, in the general preface
to his " Examen," styles Wilson's history " a most famous
pasquil of the reign of king James ; in which it is not easy to
judge whether the matter be more false, or the style more
reproachful to all parts thereof." Mr. Thomas Fuller, in his
" Appeal of injured Innocence," observes, how Robert
earl of Warwick told him at Beddington, that, when Wilson's
book in manuscript was brought to him, his lordship expunged more than an hundred offensive passages : to which

Mr. Fuller replied, " My lord, you have done well ; and you had done better if you had put out a hundred more." Mr. Wood's sentence is, " that, in our author's history, may easily be discerned a partial presbyterian vein, that constantly goes through the whole work : and it being the genius of those people to pry more than they should into the courts and comportments of princes, they do take oc-casion thereupon to traduce and bespatter them. Further also, our author, having endeavoured in many things to make the world believe that king James and his son after him were inclined to Popery, and to bring that religion into England, hath made him subject to many errors and misrepresentations." On the other hand, archdeacon Echard tells us, that " Wilson's History of the life and reign of king James, though written not without some prejudices and rancour in respect to some persons, and too much with the air of a romance, is thought to be the best of that kind extant :" and the writer of the notes on the edition of it in the " Complete History of England" re-marks, that, as to the style of our author's history, " it is harsh and broken, the periods often obscure, and sometimes without connection ; faults, that were common in most wri-ters of that time. Though he finished that history in the year 1652, a little before his death, when both the monar-chy and hierarchy were overturned, it does not appear he was an enemy to either, but only to the corruptions of them ; as he intimates in the picture he draws of himself before that book."

The plays mentioned by Wood were " The Switzer," " The Corporal," and the " Inconstant Lady," all which were entered in Stationers'-hall in 1646 and 1653, but it does not appear that they were printed. " The Inconstant Lady," however, was lately printed at Oxford in 1814, 4to, from a manuscript bequeathed in 1755 to the Bodleian library by Dr. Rawlinson, with curious notes by the editor, and many circumstances of Wilson's life and character. [1]

WILSON (BERNARD), an English divine and writer, was born in 1689, and became a member of Trinity-college, Oxford, where he took his degree of B. A. in 1712, and that of A. M. in 1719. In the following year he was pre-bendary of Lowth, and afterwards of Scamblesbey in the church of Lincoln in 1727, about which time he was also

---

[1] Life by himself in Peck.—Ath. Ox. vol. II.

vicar of Newark in Nottinghamshire, master of the hospital there, and an alderman. He is thought to have owed his preferments chiefly to bishop Reynolds of Lincoln. From the crown he had a prebend of Worcester, and another of Carborough in Lichfield, where he had a house given him by bishop Chandler. In July 1735, he was presented to Bottesford in Leicestershire, but never took possession of it. In 1737 he took his degree of D. D. He died April 30, 1772, aged eighty-three, and was interred in the church of Newark with an inscription, extolling his extensive benevolence, by his nephew Robert Wilson Cracroft, esq.

Although a man of learning and address, of a very charitable disposition, and enjoying distinguished patronage, he seems frequently to have been involved in disputes which cast some shade on his character. At one time he received a great accession of property, by the will of sir George Markham, but was obliged to publish a defence of himself, in a quarto pamphlet, against the insinuations of sir George's relations. In 1747 he was prosecuted for breach of promise of marriage by a Miss Davids of Castleyard, Holborn, and the case appeared to the jury in such a light, that they gave 7000*l.* damages, yet we see that he was at this time fifty-eight years of age. Some pamphlets were also published concerning his disputes with the parish of Newark, to which he left ample benefactions, but these were lost to the poor by the Mortmain act. He translated some parts of Fleury, but his greatest undertaking was a translation of Thuanus, of which he published vol. I. in 1729, and vol. II. in 1730. It is perhaps to be regretted that want of encouragement obliged him to desist, for these are two elegantly printed folios, and the completion would have done credit to the age. [1]

WILSON (FLORENCE), known in his own time, among scholars, by the name of FLORENTIUS VOLUSENUS, was born at Elgin, in Scotland, about the beginning of the sixteenth century, and was educated in his native place, whence he removed for academical studies to the university of Aberdeen. On quitting college, he went to England, where his talents recommended him to the notice of cardinal Wolsey, who made him preceptor to his nephew, whom he afterwards accompanied to Paris for education, and remained with him till the death of Wolsey, which for a

[1] Nichols's Bowyer.

time eclipsed his prospects.    He was soon afterwards taken under the protection of the learned cardinal du Bellai, archbishop of Paris, but here again the disgrace at court of this second patron proved a severe disappointment. Wilson, however, adhered to the cardinal, and would have accompanied him to Rome, but he fell sick at Avignon, and the cardinal being obliged to leave him, his finances were too much exhausted to allow any thoughts of his accomplishing the journey alone, and his patron's change of fortune having probably put the offer of sufficient assistance out of his power, Mr. Wilson found himself compelled to abandon a project, in which both affection and curiosity had so warmly interested his heart.

At this time the cardinal Sadolet was in residence upon his bishopric of Carpentras.    His name in the republic of letters was inferior to very few in the fifteenth and sixteenth centuries ; nor was he less celebrated for his liberality towards learned men in circumstances of want and distress.    Mr. Wilson, as soon as the re-establishment of his health permitted, took the resolution of paying him a visit.    Although it was night at Mr. Wilson's arrival, the courtesy of the cardinal, then engaged in study, gave him immediate access.    He first learned from the stranger, that his visit was occasioned, partly by his desire of seeing a person not less illustrious by his learned writings than the eminence of his station, and partly by his wish to recommend himself, through the cardinal's interest, to the employment of teaching the Greek and Latin languages to the youth of the city.    Mr. Wilson's eloquent command of the Latin tongue, and the proof which he soon gave of superior understanding and knowledge, inspired the cardinal with such prepossession in his favour, that he was unwilling to part with him, till he had learnt the particulars of the stranger's country, his parentage, his education, and the different scenes of life through which he had passed.    Greatly interested by the narrative, he rose early the next morning, and, demanding a conference with the magistrates, consulted them on Mr. Wilson's proposition ; but not wishing their decision to be solely the result of his recommendation, he invited them on a certain day to an entertainment, a kind of symposium at his palace ; during which he contrived to engage Mr. Wilson in disputation with a learned physician on certain points of Natural Philosophy.

It does not appear, that his learning and accomplishments ever procured him any thing better from this period than his laborious though honourable employment of teaching the ancient languages at Carpentras. It was perhaps to reconcile himself to the mediocrity of his lot, that during his residence in that city he composed his excellent book " De Tranquillitate Animi." If he possessed that contentment and peace of mind which made the subject of these contemplations, the first blessing of life was his, and which wealth and station only have never bestowed on man.

This work is written in dialogue. The speakers are, Franciscus Michaelis, a patrician of Lucca, Demetrius, Caracalla, and the author himself. The first part of the work, and about one third of the whole, is taken up with proving, partly from the sentiments of the author, but chiefly from those of the ancient philosophers, moralists, and poets, that tranquillity of mind is a practicable acquisition, in answer to the doubts and objections of the other interlocutors. In this part, and indeed throughout the whole work, Mr. Wilson displays a vast compass of learning, and an intimate acquaintance with all the Greek and Latin classics; many apt and beautiful quotations from them adorn his treatise; not to mention several little poems of his own composition interspersed, which at once enliven the piece, and give the reader a very advantageous idea of the author's poetic genius and talent for Latin versification. This work was first printed by Gryphius, at Leyden, 1543, and reprinted at Edinburgh in 1571, 8vo. A third edition was printed at Edinburgh in 1707, corrected by Ruddiman; and there is a fourth, 1751, with a preface by Dr. John Ward.

About 1546, the tenth year of Mr. Wilson's residence at Carpentras, after having taught the belles lettres with great reputation, and established the character of a very learned, ingenious, and worthy man, he felt a strong desire to revisit his native country. But the doctrines of the Reformation having now got some footing in Scotland, Mr. Wilson was aware of the difficulties which he should have to contend with on his return. He had therefore recourse to his friend and patron the cardinal Sadolet, at that time at Rome. He wrote to request his advice, in what manner he should conduct himself betwixt religious parties in his own country. We find the answer in the sixteenth book of Sadolet's Epistles, dated 1546, and the substance of it is to recommend an adherence to the religion of his forefathers. From a Romish cardinal no other could be expected. Wilson now determined upon his journey to Scotland, but falling sick at Vienne in Dauphiny, his progress was suddenly stopped. His disorder increased beyond the power of medical relief; and he expired on the banks of the Rhone 1547.

Besides the work mentioned in the course of Mr. Wilson's life, he wrote a book of Latin poems, printed in London 1619, 4to; also "Commentatio Theologica, in Aphorismos dissecta, per Sebast. Gryphæum," 1539, 8vo; and "Philosophiæ Aristotelicæ Synopsis," Lib. IV. Whether this last article ever appeared in print is doubtful. [1]

WILSON (RICHARD), a very distinguished artist of the last century, was born in 1714, and was the son of the rector of Pineges, in Montgomeryshire, who was afterwards collated to the living of Mould in Flintshire. Edwards says, that " his connections were highly respectable, being maternally related to the late lord chancellor Camden, who was pleased to acknowledge him as his cousin." His father gave him a good education, and as he early discovered a taste for painting, sent him to London, and placed him under the tuition of one Thomas Wright, a portrait-painter of very slender abilities. Wilson, therefore, began his career as a portrait-painter but with a mediocrity that afforded no luminous hopes of excellence; yet he must have acquired some rank in his profession, for we find, that in 1749, he painted a large picture of his present majesty, and of his brother the late duke of York. After having practised some years at London, he went to Italy, and continued the study of portrait-painting, until a small landscape of his, executed with a considerable share of freedom and spirit, casually meeting the eye of Zuccarelli, so pleased the Italian, that he strenuously advised him to follow that mode of painting, as most congenial to his powers, and therefore most likely to obtain for him fame as well as profit.

This flattering encomium from an artist of Zuccarelli's knowledge and established reputation, produced such an

[1] Life by Dr. Lettice.—Europ. Mag. 1795.—Mackenzie's Scotch Writers, vol. III.—Chalmers's Life of Ruddiman.

influence on Wilson, as to determine him at once to turn from portrait to landscape, which he pursued with vigour and success. To this fortunate accident is owing the splendour diffused by his genius over this country, and even over Italy itself, whose scenes have been the frequent subjects of his pencil. His studies, indeed, in this branch of the art, must have been attended with rapid success, for he had some pupils in landscape while at Rome, and his works were so much esteemed that Mengs painted his portrait, for which Wilson, in return, painted a landscape.

It is not known at what time he returned to England, but he was in London in 1758, and resided over the north arcade of the piazza, Covent-garden, at which time he had gained great celebrity as a landscape-painter. To the first exhibition of 1760, he sent his picture of Niobe, which is now in the possession of his royal highness the duke of Gloucester. Sir Joshua Reynolds, in his last lecture but one, has offered some strictures on the figures introduced in this celebrated picture, in which Mr. Fuseli seems to agree, but which Edwards labours to oppose; and even to trace sir Joshua's opinion to private pique. In 1765, Wilson exhibited, with other pictures, a view of Rome, from the villa Madama, a capital performance, which was purchased by the late marquis of Tavistock, and is probably in the collection of the duke of Bedford. When the Royal Academy was instituted, he was chosen one of the founders, and, after the death of Hayman, was made librarian; an office which his necessities rendered desirable, and which he retained until his decayed health compelled him to retire to his brother's in Wales, where he died in May 1782. Mr. Opie says, in his "Lectures," that Wilson, though second to no name of any school or country in classical and heroic landscape, succeeded with difficulty, by pawning some of his works at the age of seventy (sixty-seven or sixty-eight), in procuring ten guineas to carry him to die in unhonoured and unnoticed obscurity in Wales." Edwards informs us, that "though he had acquired great fame, yet he did not find that constant employment which his abilities deserved. This neglect might probably result from his own conduct; for it must be confessed, that Mr. Wilson was not very prudentially attentive to his interest; and though a man of strong sense, and superior education to most of the artists of his time, he certainly did not possess that suavity of manners which distinguished many of his contemporaries. On this account, his connexions and employment insensibly diminished, and left him, in the latter part of his life, in comfortless infirmity." This appears to us but a sorry excuse for the neglect Wilson met with; for what has patronage to do with the temper of an artist? Wilson's taste was so exquisite, says Fuseli, and his eye so chaste, that whatever came from his easel bore the stamp of elegance and truth. The subjects he chose were such as did credit to his judgment. They were the selections of taste; and whether of the simple, the elegant, or the sublime, they were treated with an equal felicity. Indeed, he possessed that versatility of power, as to be one minute an eagle sweeping the heavens, and the next, a wren twittering a simple note on the humble thorn. His colouring was in general vivid and natural; his touch, spirited and free; his composition, simple and elegant; his lights and shadows, broad and well distributed; his middle tints in perfect harmony, while his forms in general produced a pleasing impression. Wilson has been called the English Claude; a comparison which Mr. Fuseli cannot admit, from the total dissimilarity of their style. "Claude," he adds, "little above mediocrity in all other branches of landscape-painting, had one great prerogative, sublimity; but his powers rose and set with the sun, he could only be serenely sublime or romantic. Wilson, without so great a feature, had a more varied and more proportionate power: he observed nature in all her appearances, and had a characteristic touch for all her forms. But though in effects of dewy freshness and silent evening lights few equalled, and fewer excelled him, his grandeur is oftener allied to terror, bustle, and convulsion, than to calmness and tranquillity. Figures, it is difficult to say, which of the two introduced or handled with greater infelicity: treated by Claude or Wilson, St. Ursula with her Virgins, and Æneas Landing, Niobe with her family, or Ceyx drawn on the shore, have an equal claim to our indifference or mirth." [1]

WILSON (THOMAS), a statesman and divine in the reign of queen Elizabeth, celebrated for the politeness of his style and the extent of his knowledge, was the son of Thomas Wilson of Stroby in Lincolnshire, by Anne daughter and heir of Roger Comberworth, of Comberworth in

----

[1] Edwards's Anecdotes of Painters.—Pilkington by Fuseli.

the same county. He was educated at Eton, and at King's-college, Cambridge; and went thence into the family of Charles Brandon, duke of Suffolk, who intrusted him with the education of his two sons. During the reign of Mary, to whose persecution many fugitives owed their qualifications for future honours, he lived abroad, received the degree of doctor of laws at Ferrara, and was for some time imprisoned by the inquisition at Rome, on account of his two treatises on rhetoric and logic, which he had published in England, and in the English language, several years before. He is said to have suffered the torture, and would have been put to death, on refusing to deny his faith, had not a fire happened, which induced the populace to force open the prison, that those confined there might not perish, by which means he escaped; and, returning to England, after queen Mary's death, was appointed one of the masters of requests, and master of St. Katherine's hospital near the Tower. This was in the third year of queen Elizabeth, at which time he was her majesty's secretary; but finding his patent for the mastership of St. Katherine's void, because he was not a priest, according to queen Philippa's charter, he surrendered the office, and had a new patent, with a *non obstante*, Dec. 7, 1563. According to Dr. Ducarel, his conduct in this office was somewhat objectionable, as he sold to the city of London the fair of St. Katherine's, for the sum of 700 marks, surrendered the charter of Henry VI. and took a new one 8. Elizabeth, leaving out the liberty of the aforesaid fair; and did many other things very prejudicial to his successors. In 1561 he had been admitted a civilian; and in 1576 he was sent on an embassy to the Low Countries, where he acquitted himself so well, that in the following year he was named to succeed sir Thomas Smith as secretary of state; and in 1579 obtained a deanery of Durham. He died in 1581, and was buried in St. Katherine's church. He was endowed with an uncommon strength of memory, which enabled him to act with remarkable dispatch in his negociations. Yet he was more distinguished as a scholar than as a minister, and was perhaps unfortunate in having served jointly with the illustrious Walsingham, whose admirable conduct in his office admitted of no competition. Sir Thomas Wilson married Anne, daughter of sir William Winter, of Lidney in Gloucestershire, and left three children : Nicholas, who settled at Sheepwash in Lincolnshire; Mary, married, first, to Robert Burdett, of Bramcote in Warwickshire, secondly to sir Christopher Lowther, of Lowther in Westmoreland ; and Lucretia, wife of George Belgrave, of Belgrave in Leicestershire.

Sir Thomas Wilson wrote, 1. " Epistola de vita et obitu duorum fratrum Suffolciensium, Henrici et Caroli Brandon," Lond. 1552, 4to, prefixed to a collection of verses written on their deaths by several scholars of Oxford and Cambridge. Of this rare book there are only three copies known, one in the Bodleian, another in the British museum, and a third in the magnificent library of earl Spencer. 2. "The rule of Reason, containing the art of Logic," 1551, 1552, 1553, 1567, 4to. 3. " The art of Rhetoric," 1553, 4to, often reprinted. 4. " Discourse upon Usury," Lond. 1572, a work much praised by Dr. Lawrence Humphrey, the queen's professor of divinity at Oxford, in his life of Jewell. Wilson also translated from Greek into English, " The three Orations of Demosthenes, chief orator among the Grecians," Lond. 1570. Of his " Art of Logic," Mr. Warton says that such a " display of the venerable mysteries of this art in a vernacular language, which had hitherto been confined within the sacred pale of the learned tongues, was esteemed an innovation almost equally daring with that of permitting the service of the church to be celebrated in English ; and accordingly the author, soon afterwards happening to visit Rome, was incarcerated by the inquisitors of the holy see, as a presumptuous and dangerous heretic." Of his " Art of Rhetoric," Mr. Warton says, it is liberal and discursive, illustrating the arts of eloquence by example, and examining and ascertaining the beauties of composition with the speculative skill and sagacity of a critic. It may therefore be justly considered as the first book or system of criticism in our language. This opinion Mr. Warton confirms by very copious extracts. [1]

WILSON (Thomas) a puritan divine, of the sixteenth century, was minister of St. George's church, in Canterbury, one of the six preachers in that city, chaplain to lord Wotton, and a man of high reputation. We have, however, no particulars of his early life. He preached at Canterbury thirty-six years, and was assiduous and indefati-

[1] Tanner.—Ath. Ox. vol. II. new edit.—Strype's Annals.—Lodge's Illustrations, vol. II.—Warton's Hist. of Poetry.—Hutchinson's Hist. of Durham, vol. II. p. 152.—Ducarel's Hist. of St. Katherine's.

gable in all the duties of his sacred office.  He died in Jan. 1621, on the 25th of which month his funeral sermon, which has been printed, was preached by William Swift, minister of St. Andrew's, at Canterbury, and great grandfather of dean Swift.  His works are, 1. " A Commentary on the Romans," 1614, a work much approved. 2. " Christ's farewell to Jerusalem," 1614.  3. " Theological Rules," 1615.  4. " A complete Christian Dictionary," fol. of which the sixth edition, with a continuation by Bagwell and Symson, was published in 1655.  This was one of the first attempts, in English, towards a concordance of the Bible.  Mr. Wilson wrote some other pieces of less note. [1]

WILSON (THOMAS), the pious and venerable bishop of Sodor and Man, was born at Burton, a village in the hundred of Wirrel, in the county Palatine of Chester, in 1663.  He was educated in the city of Chester until qualified for the university, when he was entered of Trinity college, Dublin.  During his residence there he made great proficiency in academical studies, and had at first an intention of devoting himself to that of physic as a profession, but he was soon persuaded by a dignitary of the church to turn his thoughts to divinity.  He continued at college till 1686, when he was ordained a deacon by the bishop of Kildare, soon after which he left Ireland, partly owing to the confusions which prevailed under the unhappy reign of king James II. ; and in the latter end of the same year, became curate of New Church, in the parish of Winwick, in Lancashire, of which his maternal uncle, Dr. Sherlock, was then rector, and here he first displayed his affectionate and conscientious regard for the poor, by setting apart a tenth of his income (which was only 30l. a year) to charitable purposes.

In 1689 he entered into priest's orders, and it was not long before his excellent character recommended him to the notice of the earl of Derby, who, in 1692, appointed him his domestic chaplain, and preceptor to his son, lord Strange, with a salary of 30l. and he being appointed about the same time master of the alms-house at Latham, worth 20l. a year more, he set apart a fifth part of the whole for pious uses.  In this situation he remained till 1697, when, to use his own words, " he was forced into the bishopric of

[1] Brook's Lives of the Puritans.—Granger.

the Isle of Man," a promotion for which he was in all respects eminently qualified. Being first created doctor of laws by the archbishop of Canterbury, he was confirmed bishop of Man at Bow church, Jan. 15, 1697-8, and next day was consecrated at the Savoy church, by Dr. Sharp, archbishop of York.

In the beginning of April following he landed in the Isle of Man, and was enthroned in the cathedral of St. Germain's in Peel Castle. His palace he found almost a ruin. It had not been inhabited for eight years, and nothing but an ancient tower and chapel remained entire. He was, therefore, obliged to rebuild it, and the expence, which amounted to 1400*l.* interrupted, in some measure, his charity to the poor, but this he soon resumed, and his beneficence ever afterwards increased with his income. About this time the earl of Derby offered him the valuable living of Baddesworth, in Yorkshire, to hold *in commendam,* probably as a compensation for the expences he had been at ; but he declined the offer, as being incompatible with his resolution never to take two ecclesiastical preferments with cure of souls, especially when he must necessarily be absent from one of them.

In 1699 bishop Wilson published a small tract in Manks and English, the first work ever printed in the former language, entitled "The Principles and Duties of Christianity, for the use of the island," where a great degree of ignorance prevailed, and where it was necessary to diffuse elementary treatises written in the plainest manner, which is the characteristic of most of our prelate's writings, and predominated also in his sermons. By the advice, and with the assistance of Dr. Bray, he likewise began to found parochial libraries throughout his diocese, giving to each a proper book-case, and furnishing them with Bibles and such other books as were calculated to instruct the people in the great truths and duties of religion. In the beginning of 1707 the degree of D. D. was conferred upon him by the universities of Oxford and Cambridge. About this time also he was admitted a member of the society for promoting Christian knowledge, and in the same year he had the church catechism printed in Manks and English, for the use of the schools which he had established in various parts of his diocese, and which he superintended with the greatest care. Indeed he applied himself with singular diligence to all the duties of his sacred function, and also endeavoured, both by his exhortations and example, to animate the clergy of the island to a regular and faithful discharge of their pastoral office. With this view they were occasionally assembled in convocation at Bishop's court (the name of the episcopal palace), where our prelate delivered such charges as circumstances required, earnestly pressing them at all times to attend to the care of their flocks, and to endeavour, by all possible methods, to plant the fear of God in the hearts of the people. One of his leading objects was to maintain and preserve, in their full force, those ecclesiastical constitutions which he had established in 1703, and by which he hoped to revive in some measure the primitive discipline of the church. The lord chancellor King was so much pleased with these constitutions as to declare, that "if the ancient discipline of the church were lost, it might be found in all its purity in the Isle of Man."

From this time our prelate continued to perform all the offices of a good bishop and a good man; and we hear little more of him till 1721 and 1722, when the orthodoxy of his spirit, and zeal for church-discipline, seem to have involved him in altercations and difficulties. When the famous work called "The Independent Whig," came into the diocese of Man, the bishop immediately issued an act against it, dated Jan. 27, 1721, declaring its purpose to be subversive of the doctrine, discipline, and government, of the church, as well as undermining the Christian religion. But his zeal against it did not stop here, for he took it upon him to seize it wherever he found it: and accordingly, when Mr. Worthington sent it as a present to the public library of the island, the bishop commanded one Stevenson to take and keep it; so that it should neither be deposited in the library, nor yet restored to the right owner. Complaint was made to the governor of the island, who committed Stevenson to prison till he should make reparation. The bishop remonstrated; and the governor replied, in which reply he charged the bishop, who had pleaded obedience to the king's commands in his attempts to suppress irreligion, with having neglected to use the prayers composed in the time of the rebellion in 1715, which was also an equal object of obedience. The issue of this affair was, that the book was restored, and Stevenson set at liberty.

But there happened another dispute between the bishop

and the governor, which, so far as the bishop was personally concerned, was much more serious; and it is related thus: Mrs. Horne, the governor's wife, had defamed Mrs. Puller and sir James Pool with a false charge of criminal conversation; and, in consequence of being contumacious, and refusing to ask pardon of the persons injured, was by the bishop interdicted from the holy communion. But Mr. Horribin, his archdeacon, who was chaplain to captain Horne, received Mrs. Horne to the communion, and was suspended by the bishop. Upon this, the governor, conceiving that the bishop had acted illegally, fined him 50*l.* and his two vicars-general 20*l.* each; and, on their refusing to pay this fine, committed them all, June 29, 1722, to Castle Rushin, a damp and gloomy prison, where they were closely confined, and no persons were admitted within the walls to see or converse with them, and where Dr. Wilson was treated with a rigour which no protestant bishop had experienced since the reformation.

The concern of the people was so great when they heard of this tyrannical treatment of their beloved pastor and friend, that they assembled in crowds, and it was with difficulty they were restrained from proceeding to violence and outrage against the governor, by the bishop himself, who, being permitted to speak to them through a grated window, exhorted them to peace, and told them that he intended to appeal to the king, and did not doubt but his majesty would vindicate his cause. He also sent a circular letter to his clergy, drawn up in such terms as seemed most proper for appeasing the people, and desired it might be generally communicated throughout the island. After some delays, owing to the technical formalities of law, the bishop's appeal was heard before the lords justices in council, July 18, 1723, and the proceedings of the governor were reversed, as extrajudicial and irregular, and the fines were ordered to be restored to the bishop and his vicars-general. This was accordingly done, and upon the bishop's application for costs, the king, by the president of the council, and sir Robert Walpole, promised that he would see him satisfied. In consequence of this engagement, the king, some time after, offered him the bishopric of Exeter, then, vacant, to reimburse him, but our unambitious prelate could not be prevailed upon to quit his own diocese; upon which his majesty promised to defray his expences out of the privy purse, and gave it in charge to lord Townsend, lord Carleton, and sir Robert Walpole, to remind him of it; but the king going soon afterwards to Hanover, and dying before his return, this promise was never fulfilled. The only recompense he had was by a subscription set on foot by the archbishop of York, amounting tò 300*l.* not a sixth part of the expences of his application to the crown. To add to the indignation which we are confident every reader will feel, it may be mentioned, that from the dampness of the prison in which the bishop was confined by the brutal governor, he contracted a disorder in his right hand, which disabled him from the free use of his fingers, and he ever after wrote with his whole hand grasping the pen. He was advised to prosecute the governor, &c. in the English courts of law, to recover damages; but to this he could not be persuaded, and extended his forgiveness to those who had ill-used him, in the most sincere and liberal manner.

After this absence from his diocese of eighteen months, which he had spent mostly in London, where he was beloved and admired to a degree of enthusiasm by all classes of people, he returned to the island, and resumed his exemplary course. In 1735 he came to England for the last time, to visit his son, the subject of the following article; and being introduced at the court of George II. he was much noticed by their majesties, and particularly by queen Caroline, who was very desirous of keeping him in England, but he could not be prevailed upon to quit his poor diocese, the value of which did not exceed 300*l.* a year. On his return he visited the province of York at the request of archbishop Blackburn, and confirmed upwards of fifteen thousand persons.

In 1739 the clergy of the Isle of Man were much alarmed by the death of the earl of Derby, who dying without issue, the lordship of Man, as a barony in fee, became the property of the duke of Athol, who had married the heiress of a late earl of Derby. This threatened to deprive the clergy of their subsistence, for the livings of the Isle of Man consist of a third of the impropriations, which had been originally purchased of a former earl of Derby by bishop Barrow, in the reign of Charles II.; but now the duke of Athol claimed the impropriations as an inseparable appendage of his estate and royalty. The clergy were now in danger of losing all their property, for the deeds of conveyance from the earl of Derby to bishop Barrow were lost from the records of the island, and the affair became every year more difficult, until at length, by the care and diligence of the bishop and his son, the deeds were discovered in the Rolls chapel, where they had been deposited for safe custody. This discovery put an end to the dispute, and in 1745 the deeds were exemplified under the great seal of England, and every precaution taken for the future payment of the money.

In his latter days bishop Wilson formed a plan for translating the New Testament into the Manks language, but did not live to make a further progress than to translate the four gospels, and print that of St. Matthew. This important work was completed by his successor (See HILDESLEY). This seems to have been the last concern of a public nature in which he was engaged, beyond the immediate duties of his bishopric, which he continued to execute to the latest period of his life, notwithstanding the infirmities naturally attending his great age. He had attained his ninety-third year, when, in consequence of a cold caught by walking in his garden in very cold weather, after reading evening prayers in his own chapel, he was confined for a short time to his bed, and expired March 7, 1755. He was interred in the church-yard of Kirk-Michael, almost the whole population of the island attending the funeral, and lamenting their loss.

Bishop Wilson's life was an uniform display of the most genuine and active benevolence. Considering himself as the steward, not the proprietor, of the revenues of the bishopric, he devoted his income to what he esteemed its proper use. The annual receipts of the bishopric, as we have just mentioned, did not exceed 300*l.* in money; some necessaries in his house were of course to be paid for in money; distressed or shipwrecked mariners, and some other poor objects, it was also requisite to relieve with money; but the poor of the island were fed and clothed, and the house in general supplied from his demesnes by exchange, without money. The poor who could spin or weave, found the best market at Bishop's-court, where they bartered the produce of their labour for corn. Taylors and shoemakers were kept in the house constantly employed, to make into garments,or shoes that cloth or leather which his corn had purchased; and the aged and the infirm were supplied according to their several wants. At the same time he kept an open hospitable table, covered with the produce of

his own demesnes, at which he presided with equal affability and decorum. His manners, though always consistently
adorned with Christian gravity, were ever gentle and polite; and in his conversation he was one of the most entertaining and agreeable, as well as instructive of men. With
these qualities of the gentleman, the bishop united the accomplishments and virtues of the scholar and the divine.
He was well skilled in the Hebrew, Greek, and Latin
languages; and there was hardly any part of science that
could be serviceable in his diocese which he did not understand. In his younger days he had a poetical turn, but
afterwards laid aside such amusements, as thinking them
inconsistent with his episcopal character. During the fifty-
eight years that he held the bishopric, he never failed,
unless on occasions of sickness, to expound the scripture,
to preach, or to administer the sacrament, every Sunday,
at one or other of the churches in his diocese, and, if
absent from the island, he always preached at the church
where he resided for the day. He alternately visited the
different parishes of his diocese on Sundays (which the
dimensions of the island will permit in a carriage) without
giving them notice, and, after doing the duty of the day,
returned home to dinner. His family prayers were as regular as his public duties. Every summer morning at six,
and every winter morning at seven o'clock, his whole
household attended him in his chapel, where he himself,
or one of those divinity-students whom he maintained in
his house, performed the service of the day; and in the
evening they did the same. Thus it was that he formed
his young clergy for the pulpit, and for a graceful delivery.
He was so great a friend to toleration, that the papists who
resided in the island, loved and esteemed him, and not
unfrequently attended his ministrations. Dissenters likewise even attended the communion-service, as he admitted
them to receive the sacrament, either standing or sitting,
at their own option, so that there was neither schism nor
separate congregation in his diocese. The few quakers
also, who were resident on the island, visited and respected
him. Many other amiable, and some singular traits of the
character of this excellent prelate may be seen in the
work from which the above particulars are taken.

His works, consisting of religious tracts, most of which
have been repeatedly printed separately, and extensively
circulated, and of sermons, were collected by his son and

published in 1780, 2 vols. 4to, and reprinted in 2 handsome volumes, folio, by the editor, the late Rev. Clement Cruttwell, who also edited, a few years after, a splendid edition of the Bible in 3 vols. 4to, with notes by bishop Wilson. [1]

WILSON (THOMAS), D. D. only surviving son of the preceding, was born Aug. 24, 1703, in the parish of Kirk-Michael, in the Isle of Man, and after such an institution there as he must have received under the eye of so excellent a father, was entered of Christ Church, Oxford, where he took the degree of M. A. Dec. 16, 1727. On the 10th of May, 1739, having previously become possessed of his mother's jointure, which devolved to him on her decease, he accumulated the degrees of B. and D. D. May 10, 1739, when he went out grand compounder. He was many years senior prebendary of Westminster, and minister of St. Margaret's there; and rector of St. Stephen's, Walbrook, forty-six years; in which last he succeeded Dr. Watson, on the presentation of lord-chancellor Hardwicke. In 1761 was published a pamphlet entitled "The Ornaments of Churches considered; with a particular view to the late decoration of the parish church of St. Margaret, Westminster. To which is subjoined an appendix, containing the history of the said church, an account of the altar-piece and stained glass window erected over it, a state of the prosecution it has occasioned, and other papers," 4to. To the second edition of this pamphlet was prefixed a view of the inside of St. Margaret's church, with the late excellent speaker, Arthur Onslow, in his seat. This pamphlet has been by some ascribed to a son of Dr. Shebbeare, as published under Dr. Wilson's inspection. The reason for such conjecture is not given, and the fact is therefore doubtful. We know of no son of Dr. Shebbeare's, and at this time Dr. Shebbeare himself was a well-known writer, and sufficiently practised in deceptions, had any been necessary. Another report is that the work was chiefly the composition of the *late* archdeacon Hole; Dr. Wilson having borrowed a MS treatise on the subject written by the archdeacon, and then printed almost the whole of it, inserting here and there a few notes, &c. of his own. This assertion is made by an anonymous writer in the Gent. Mag. for 1786, but who the *late* archdeacon Hole was, we have not been able to dis-

[1] Life prefixed to his works.

edver; Mr. William Hole, *archdeacon* of Sarum, was then alive, and died in 1791. Another pamphlet ascribed to Dr. Wilson was, " A review of the project for building a new square at Westminster, said to be for the use of Westminster-school. By a Sufferer. Part I." 1757, 8vo. The injury here complained of was the supposed undervaluation of the doctor's prebendal house, which was to have made way for the project alluded to. He was also the supposed author of a pamphlet entitled " Distilled Liquors the bane of the nation ;" which recommended him to sir Joseph Jekyll, then/master of the rolls, who interested himself in procuring him his rectory. Even concerning this a doubt has been suggested, as Dr. Hales printed a pamphlet with exactly the same title. That elaborate and excellent work of Dr. Leland's, entitled " A view of the principal Deistical Writers," was originally addressed in a series of letters, in the form they now appear, to Dr. Wilson, who finding that the booksellers would not give the author any adequate remuneration (50*l.* only were offered) printed the first edition at his own risk.

Dr. Wilson died at Alfred House, Bath, April 15, 1784, in the eighty-first year of his age, and on the 27th was interred, with great funeral pomp, in Walbrook church; where he had in his life-time put up a tablet undated. His tenacity in the cause he espoused was no less conspicuous in his opposition to the building of the intended square in Westminster, than in his attachment to the noted Mrs. Macaulay, to whom, when living, he erected a statue in his church, which, with his other marks of high regard for this lady, created much ridicule. By her second marriage, however, he was completely cured, and diverted his testamentary remembrances into more proper channels. Dr. Wilson adopted the modest motto of " Sequitur patrem, *non* passibus æquis," and in his adherence to the turbulent politics of Wilkes and his party, certainly departed from his father's example, but in acts of benevolence was by no means behind him. He often employed the Rev. Clement Cruttwell, whom we have mentioned as the editor of bishop Wilson's works, as his almoner, who, among many other instances of his liberality and prompt attention to the wants of the distressed, used to relate the following. One day Dr. Wilson discovered a clergyman at Bath, who he was told was sick, poor, and had a numerous family. In the evening of the same day he gave Mr. Cruttwell a considerable sum (50*l.* if we have not forgot) requesting he would deliver it to the clergyman in the most delicate manner, and as from an unknown person. Mr. Cruttwell said, " I will call upon him early in the morning."—" You will oblige me by calling directly. Think, sir, of what importance a good night's rest may be to that poor man." Dr. Wilson had accumulated a very copious historical library for the use of Mrs. Macaulay, which he bequeathed to Mr. Cruttwell, along with the copy-right of his father's works. This curious library, after Mr. Cruttwell's death, came into the possession of one of his nephews at Bath. [1]

WINCHELSEA, ANNE. See FINCH.

WINCHESTER (THOMAS), a learned English divine, was the son of a reputable surgeon at Farringdon, in the county of Berks, where he was born. He was educated at Magdalen-college, Oxford, as a chorister and demy; proceeded M. A. in 1736, B. D. in 1747, and D. D. in 1749. In July 1747 he was elected fellow, having been for some years before, as he was afterwards, a considerable tutor in the college. In 1761 he resigned his fellowship, on being presented by the society to the rectory of Appleton, Berkshire, at a small distance from his native place; and in the same year, June 10, he married Lucretia Townson, sister of Thomas Townson, rector of Malpas, Cheshire, who had also been fellow of Magdalen-college. She died at Appleton, greatly esteemed and lamented, Jan. 26, 1772. Five years afterwards he married Jennett, widow of his fellow-collegian, Richard Lluellyn, B. D. and sister of the late Thomas Lewis, esq. of Frederick's-place, London, one of the directors of the Bank of England. To the sincere and lasting regret of all who knew him, he was seized with a paralytic stroke, which proved fatal May 17, 1780, and was buried in the chancel of his own church, near the remains of his wife. His only preferment, besides the rectory of Appleton, was the curacy of Astley-chapel, near Arbury, Warwickshire, a donative given him by his esteemed friend sir Roger Newdigate, bart.

" His talents," says his biographer, " if not splendid, were sound and good, his attainments various and useful; and he was a true son of the Church of England. He resided constantly on his living; where by his preaching and example, he brought to conformity some of the very few

1 Butler's Life of Hildesley.—Private information.—Gent. Mag. vol. LVI.

dissenters in his parish. He took a most cordial interest in the temporal and spiritual concerns of his parishioners; and having studied anatomy, and being well skilled in medicine, he was, according to the pattern of the excellent Mr. Herbert's ' Country Parson,' physician of the body as well as the soul, to his flock."

Dr. Winchester paid great attention to such controversies in his time as concerned the doctrine and discipline of the church, and contributed some valuable remarks to contemporary writers who were more particularly involved in these disputes. He also wrote some letters in the Gentleman's Magazine on the Confessional controversy, and topics arising from it. The only separate publication from his pen was published, but without his name, in 1773, under the title of "A Dissertation on the XVIIth article of the Church of England; wherein the sentiments of the compilers, and other contemporary reformers, on the subject of the divine decrees, are fully deduced from their own writings, to which is subjoined a short tract, ascertaining the reign and time in which the royal declaration before the XXXIX articles was first published." This work was reprinted in 1805, on occasion of the controversy being revived by Mr. Overton, " with emendations from the author's corrected copy, and the addition of a biographical preface." The latter is written by the rev. archdeacon Churton, and to it we are indebted for the preceding particulars. [1]

WINDER (HENRY), a learned dissenting divine, was born May 15, 1693, at Hutton-John, in the parish of Graystock, in Cumberland, where his father was a farmer. He was educated in grammatical learning at Penruddock, and in his fifteenth year began his divinity and philosophy studies at a dissenting academy at Whitehaven, where he had for his contemporaries Dr. Rotheram of Kendal, and Mr. John Taylor of Norwich, author of the Hebrew-English Concordance. From Whitehaven, Mr. Winder removed to Dublin, where for two years he applied very closely to the study of divinity under the rev. Mr. Boyse. After passing the usual examinations, he became a preacher, but returned to England, and in 1714, when only twenty-two years of age, succeeded Mr. Edward Rothwell, as pastor of a congregation at Tunley in Lancashire, and in 1716 was

---

[1] Biog. Preface, as above.

ordained. In 1718 he was chosen pastor of the meeting at Castle-hey in Liverpool, where it appears that he had some trouble with his congregation, during certain disputes on liberty, charity, and the rights of conscience, which he endeavoured to compose by referring them to the Bible as the only standard of orthodoxy, not sufficiently adverting to the fact that this is what all sects profess to do, without any approach towards harmony of sentiment. In 1740, when he was on a visit at Glasgow, the degree of D. D. was conferred upon him by that university. He continued to preside over his congregation at Liverpool, with great approbation, until his death, Aug. 9, 1752. As a testimony of his esteem for his people, he bequeathed his well-chosen library for the use of his successors. Dr. Winder is known in the literary world by an ingenious and elaborate work, published a second time in 1756, 2 vols. 4to, entitled "A critical and chronological History of the Rise, Progress, Declension, and Revival of Knowledge, chiefly religious; in two periods, the period of tradition from Adam to Moses, and the period of Letters from Moses to Christ." To this are prefixed memoirs of his life by the rev. Dr. George Benson. [1]

WINDHAM (JOSEPH), an artist and antiquary of great taste and talents, was born August 21, 1739, at Twickenham, in the house afterwards the residence of Richard Owen Cambridge, esq. He was educated at Eton school, from which he went to Christ's-college, Cambridge, but took no degree. He returned from an extensive tour through France, Italy, Istria, and Switzerland, in 1769; and soon after married the honourable Charlotte De Grey, sister to the lord Walsingham; by whom he has left no issue. In all which is usually comprehended under the denomination of *Belles Lettres*, Mr. Windham may claim a place among the most learned men of his time. To an indefatigable diligence in the pursuit of knowledge, he joined a judgment clear, penetrating, and unbiassed, and a memory uncommonly retentive and accurate. An ardent love for truth, a perfect freedom from prejudice, jealousy, and affectation, an entire readiness to impart his various and copious information, united with a singular modesty and simplicity, marked his conversation and manners. Few men had a more critical knowledge of the Greek and Latin

[1] Memoirs as above.

languages, or a deeper feeling for the beauties of style and sentiment in the classic writers ; but in his minute and comprehensive acquaintance with every thing in them illustrative of human life and manners, especially all that relates to the fine arts, he scarcely had an equal.    The history of art in the middle ages, and every circumstance relative to the revival of literature and the arts, from the fourteenth century to the present time, were equally familiar to him ; and his acquaintance with the language of modern Italy was surpassed by few.    He had very particularly studied the antiquities of his own country, and was eminently skilled in the history of English architecture. His pencil, as a draftsman from nature, was exquisite.    His portraits of mere natural scenery were peculiarly spirited and free, and his drawings of architecture and antiquities most faithful and elegant.    During his residence at Rome, he studied and measured the remains of ancient architecture there, particularly the baths, with a precision which would have done honour to the most able professional architect.    His numerous plans and sections of them he gave to Mr. Cameron, and they are engraved in his great work on the Roman baths.    To this work he also furnished a very considerable and valuable part of the letter-press. He also drew up the greater portion of the letter-press of the second volume of the " Ionian Antiquities," published by the society of Dilettanti ; and Mr. Stuart received material assistance from him in the second volume of his Athens.    In his own name he published very little *.    His accuracy of mind rendered it difficult to him to please himself ; and, careless of the fame of an author, he was better content that his friends should profit by his labours, than that the public should know the superiority of his own acquirements.    He had been long a fellow of the Royal and Antiquarian Societies ; and in the latter, was for many years of the council, and one of the committee for the publication of the Cathedrals of England.    He more than once declined the honourable office of vice-president.    Of the society of Dilettanti he was one of the oldest members ; and to his zeal it was principally owing that the publications of that society were continued, after a suspension of many years.

* We know only of his " Observations upon a passage in Pliny's Natural History, relative to the Temple of Diana at Ephesus," printed in the Archæologia, vol. VI. with two plates.

Mr. Windham died at Earsham-house, Norfolk, Sept. 21, 1810. In private life, he was the most amiable of men. Benevolent, generous, cheerful, without caprice, above envy, his temper was the unclouded sun-shine of virtue and sense. If his extreme modesty and simplicity of character prevented his striking at the first acquaintance, every hour endeared him to those who had the happiness of his intimacy. In every relation of life he was exemplary. A kind husband, a firm friend, a generous landlord, an indulgent master. [1]

WINDHAM (WILLIAM), a late distinguished statesman, was descended of an ancient family in Norfolk, and was born in Golden-square, London, May 3, 1750. His father was colonel William Windham, of Felbrigg in Norfolk, a man of versatile talents and an ardent mind. He was the associate of the wits of his time, the friend and admirer of Garrick, and the distinguished patron of all manly exercises. In his father's (Ash Windham's) life-time, he had lived much on the continent, particularly in Spain, and of his proficiency in the language of that country, he gave proof in some printed observations on Smollett's translation of Don Quixote. At home he had devoted his attention to the improvement of the militia, of which he became lieutenant-colonel, and was the author of a " Plan of Discipline composed for the use of the militia of the county of Norfolk," 1760, 4to, which was much esteemed, and generally adopted by other corps of the establishment. He died of a consumptive disorder in the following year, leaving one son, the subject of the present article.

At seven years of age young Mr. Windham was placed at Eton, where he remained until he was about sixteen, distinguishing himself by the vivacity and brilliancy of his talents. On leaving Eton in 1766, he went to the university of Glasgow, where he resided for about a year in the house of Dr. Anderson, professor of natural philosophy, and diligently attended his lectures and those of Dr. Robert Simson, professor of mathematics. For this study Mr. Windham had an early predilection, and left behind him three treatises on mathematical subjects. In Sept. 1767 he was entered a gentleman commoner of University-college, Oxford, Mr. (afterwards sir Robert) Chambers being his tutor. While here he took so little interest in public affairs, that it became the standing joke of one of his contemporaries, that "Windham would never know who was prime minister." This disinclination to a political life, added to a modest diffidence, in his own talents, led him about this period, to reject an offer which, by a youth not more than twenty years of age, might have been considered as a splendid one, that of being named secretary to his father's friend, lord Townshend, who had been appointed lord-lieutenant of Ireland.

After four years residence, he left Oxford in 1771; he always retained feelings of gratitude towards his *alma mater*, and preserved to the last an intimate acquaintance and correspondence with some of the most distinguished resident members. He probably took his degree of B. A. while at college, but did not obtain that of A. M. until 1782, and then by creation, as he did that of LL. D. in 1793 at the installation of the duke of Portland. It is related that on this occasion, almost the whole assembly rose from their seats, when he entered the theatre, and received him with acclamations of applause. Nor was his memory forgotten at the late installation of lord Grenville; for in the recitations made on that occasion, due honours were paid to the genius, taste, and acquirements of which the public had recently been deprived.

In 1773, when he was but twenty-three years old, his love of adventure and his thirst of knowledge, induced him to accompany his friend, Constantine lord Mulgrave, in his voyage towards the North Pole; but he was so harassed with sea-sickness, that he was under the necessity of being landed in Norway, and of wholly abandoning his purpose. His earliest essay as a public speaker was occasioned by a call which was made on the country, for a subscription in aid of government, to be applied towards carrying on the war with our American colonies. A meeting for this purpose was held at Norwich, and his speech, which has been preserved by his biographer, though it must not be compared with later specimens of his eloquence, may be allowed to exhibit some proofs of acuteness, dexterity, and vigour. He opposed the subscription, as well as the war itself. Some time before this he had entered himself as an officer in the western battalion of Norfolk militia, and when quartered at Bury in Suffolk, by his intrepidity and personal exertion, he quelled a dangerous mutiny which had broke out, notwithstanding he was highly beloved by the regiment. Soon afterwards, in consequence of remaining several hours in wet cloaths, he was seized with a dangerous bilious fever, which nearly deprived him of his life. In the autumn of that year, partly with a view of restoring his health, he went abroad, and spent the two following years in Switzerland and Italy.

Previously to his leaving England, he was chosen a member of the Literary club founded by sir Joshua Reynolds and Dr. Johnson, who had the greatest esteem for Mr. Windham; and, notwithstanding his engagements in consequence of his parliamentary business, and the important offices which he filled, he was a very frequent attendant at the meetings of that society, for which he always expressed the highest value, from 1781 to near the time of his death. In 1782 he came into parliament, where he sat for twenty-eight years, at first for Norwich, and afterwards for various boroughs; and he so early distinguished himself in the House of Commons, that he was selected by Mr. Burke in 1784 to second his motion for a representation to his majesty on the state of the nation. He was at this time in the ranks of the opposition, created by the appointment of Mr. Pitt to be prime-minister, and may have been said to be particularly of the school of Burke, with whom he afterwards thought and acted on many important occasions. In the preceding year, he had been appointed principal secretary to the earl of Northington, then constituted lord-lieutenant of Ireland; and in that capacity he visited Dublin in the spring of 1783, and intended to have accompanied his excellency, when he afterwards opened the session of parliament there in October *, but being prevented by illness, he relinquished the office.

---

* When about to visit that country in his official capacity, he called on Dr. Johnson; and in the course of conversation lamented that he should be under the necessity of sanctioning practices of which he could not approve. "Don't be afraid, sir," said the doctor, with a pleasant smile, "you will soon make a very pretty rascal."—Dr. Johnson in a letter to Dr. Brocklesby, written at Ashbourne in 1784, says: "Mr. Windham has been here to see me—he came, I think, forty miles out of his way, and staid about a day and a half; perhaps I make the time shorter than it was. Such conversation I shall not have again till I come back to the regions of Literature, and there Windham is *inter stellas luna minores.*" Although we have said that illness was the cause of Mr. Windham's resignation, his biographer affords some reason to think that it really arose from the conscientious scruples which Dr. Johnson thought might soon vanish, and that it was owing to his being dissatisfied with some part of the lord lieutenant's conduct.

Although from the time of his coming into parliament, he usually voted with the opposition of that day, he never was what is called a thorough party-man, frequently deviating from those to whom he was in general attached, when, in matters of importance, his conscience directed him to take a different course from them; on which account his virtues and talents were never rightly appreciated by persons of that description, who frequently on this ground vainly attempted to undervalue him. After the rupture between Mr. Fox and Mr. Burke, in consequence of the French revolution, Mr. Windham attached himself wholly to the latter, with whom he had for many years lived in the closest intimacy; and of whose genius and virtues he had always the highest admiration. Being with him thoroughly convinced of the danger then impending over his country from the measures adopted by certain classes of Englishmen, in consequence of that tremendous convulsion, he did not hesitate to unite with the duke of Portland, lord Spencer, and others, in accepting offices under the administration in which Mr. Pitt then presided. On this arrangement Mr. Windham was appointed secretary at war, with a seat in the cabinet, an honourable distinction which had never before been annexed to that office. This station he continued to fill with the highest reputation from that time (1794) till 1801, when he, lord Spencer, lord Grenville, and Mr. Pitt, resigned their offices; and shortly afterwards Mr. Addington (now lord viscount Sidmouth) was appointed chancellor of the exchequer and first lord of the treasury. On the preliminaries of peace with France being acceded to by that statesman and his coadjutors, in 1801, Mr. Windham made his celebrated speech in parliament, which was afterwards (April 1802) published, with an Appendix, containing a character of the Usurper of the French throne, which will transmit to posterity the principal passages of his life up to that period, in the most lively colours. On Mr. Addington being driven from the helm, in 1805, principally by the battery of Mr. Windham's eloquence, a new administration was again formed by Mr. Pitt, which was dissolved by his death, in 1806; and shortly afterwards, on lord Grenville's accepting the office of first lord of the Treasury, Mr. Windham was appointed secretary of state for the war department, which he held till his majesty in the following year thought fit to constitute a new administration. During this period he carried into a law his bill for the limited service of those who enlist in our regular army ; a measure which will ever endear his name to the English soldiery. But it is not our purpose to detail the particular measures which either originated from him, or in which he took a part. This indeed would be impossible within any prescribed limits ; and would involve the history of perhaps the whole of the war. It may suffice to notice that his genius and talents were universally acknowledged. He was unquestionably not inferior, in many respects, to the most admired characters of the age that is just gone by. He had been in his earlier years a very diligent student, and was an excellent Greek and Latin scholar. In his latter years, like Burke and Johnson, he was an excursive reader, but gathered a great variety of knowledge from different books, and from occasionally mixing, like them, with very various classes and descriptions of men. His memory was most tenacious. In his parliamentary speeches his principal object always was to convince the understanding by irrefragable argument, which he at the same time enlivened by a profusion of imagery, drawn sometimes from the most abstruse parts of science, but oftener from the most familiar objects of common life. But what gave a peculiar lustre to whatever he urged, was his known and uniform integrity, and a firm conviction in the breasts of his hearers, that he always uttered the genuine and disinterested sentiments of his heart. His language, both in writing and speaking, was always simple, and he was extremely fond of idiomatic phrases, which he thought greatly contributed to preserve the purity of our language. He surveyed every subject of importance with a philosophic eye, and was thence enabled to discover and detect latent mischief, concealed under the plausible appearance of public advantage. Hence all the clamourers for undefined and imaginary liberty, and all those who meditate the subversion of the constitution under the pretext of *Reform*, shrunk from his grasp ; and persons of this description were his only enemies. But his dauntless intrepidity, and his noble disdain of vulgar popularity, held up a shield against their malice ; and no fear of consequences ever drove him from that manly and honourable course, which the rectitude and purity of his mind induced him to pursue. As an orator, he was simple, elegant, prompt, and graceful. His genius was so fertile, and his reading so extensive, that there were few subjects on which he could not instruct, amuse, and persuade. He was frequently (as has justly been observed) " at once entertaining and abstruse, drawing illustrations promiscuously from familiar life, and the recondite parts of science ; nor was it unusual to hear him through three adjoining sentences, in the first witty, in the second metaphysical, and in the last scholastic." But his eloquence derived its principal power from the quickness of his apprehension, and the philosophical profundity of his mind. In private life no man perhaps of any age had a greater number of zealous friends and admirers. In addition to his extraordinary talents and accomplishments, the grace and happiness of his address and manner gave an irresistible charm to his conversation ; and few, it is believed, of either sex (for his address to ladies was inimitably elegant and graceful) ever partook of his society without pleasure and admiration, or quitted it without regret. His brilliant imagination, his various knowledge, his acuteness, his good taste, his wit, his dignity of sentiment, and his gentleness of manner (for he never was loud or intemperate) made him universally admired and respected. To crown all these virtues and accomplishments, it may be added, that he fulfilled all the duties of life, the lesser as well as the greatest, with the most scrupulous attention ; and was always particularly ardent in vindicating the cause of oppressed merit. But his best eulogy is the general sentiment of sorrow which agitated every bosom on the sudden and unexpected stroke which terminated in his death. During the nineteen days of his sickness, his hall was daily visited by several hundred successive inquirers concerning the state of his health ; and that part of Pall Mall in which his house was situated, was thronged with carriages filled with ladies, whom a similar anxiety brought to his door. Every morning, and also at a late hour every evening, when his physicians and surgeons attended, several apartments in his house were filled with friends, who anxiously waited to receive the latest and most accurate accounts of the progress or abatement of his disorder. This sympathetic feeling extended almost through every class, and even reached the throne, for his majesty frequently inquired concerning the state of his health, pronouncing on him this high eulogy, that " he was a genuine patriot, and a truly honest man." Of the fatal malady which put an end to his invaluable life, erroneous accounts have been published, but the fact was, that on the 8th of July 1809, Mr. Windham, returning on foot at twelve o'clock at night from the house of a friend, as he passed by the end of Conduit-street, saw a house on fire, and instantly hastened to the spot, with a view to assist the sufferers; and soon observed that the house of the Hon. Mr. Frederic North was not far distant from that which was then on fire. He therefore immediately undertook to save his friend's library, which he knew to be very valuable. With the most strenuous activity he exerted himself for four hours, in the midst of rain and the playing of the fire-engines, with such effect that, with the assistance of two or three persons whom he had selected from the crowd assembled on this occasion, he saved four parts out of five of the library; and before they could empty the fifth book-room, the house took fire. The books were immediately removed, not to Mr. Windham's house, but to the houses of the opposite neighbours, who took great care of them. In removing some heavy volumes he accidentally fell, and suffered a slight contusion on his hip, of which, however, he unfortunately took no notice for some months, when an indolent encysted tumour was formed, which, after due consultation, it was judged proper to cut out. The operation was accordingly performed apparently with success on May 17, 1810, but soon after unfavourable symptoms came on, and terminated fatally June 4, to the unspeakable regret of all who knew him.[1]

WINDHAM. See WYNDHAM.

WILFRID or WINFRID. See BONIFACE, St.

WINGATE (EDMUND), whom Dr. Hutton pronounces one of the clearest writers on arithmetic, &c. in the English language, was the son of Roger Wingate, esq. of Bornend and Sharpenhoe, in Bedfordshire, but was born in Yorkshire in 1593. In 1610 he became a commoner of Queen's-college, Oxford, and after taking a degree in arts, removed to Gray's-Inn, London, where he studied the law. His chief inclination, however, was to the mathematics, which he had studied with much success at college. In 1624 he was in France, where he published the scale, or rule of proportion, which had been invented by Gunter, and while in that country gave instructions in the English language to the princess Henrietta Maria, afterwards wife

---

[1] Gent. Mag. vol. LXXX.—Speeches in Parliament, with an excellent account of Mr. Windham's Life by Thomas Amyot, esq. 1812, 3 vols. 8vo.

of Charles I. and to her ladies. After his return to England, he became a bencher of Gray's-Inn; and on the breaking out of the great rebellion, he joined the popular party, took the covenant, was made justice of the peace for the county of Bedford, where he resided at Woodend in the parish of Harlington. His name occurs in the register of Ampthill church, as a justice, in 1654, at which period, according to the republican custom, marriages were celebrated by the civil magistrate. In 1650 he took the oath, commonly called the engagement, became intimate with Cromwell, and was chosen into his parliament for Bedford. He was also appointed one of the commissioners, for that county, to eject from their situations those loyal clergymen and schoolmasters who were accused as being scandalous and ignorant. He died in Gray's-Inn, in 1656, and was buried in the parish church of St. Andrew Holborn.

His works are, 1. "The use of the proportional Rules in Arithmetic and Geometry; also the use of Logarithms of numbers, with those of sines and tangents;" printed in French, at Paris, 1624, 8vo, and at London, in English, 1626, 1645, and 1658. In this book, Mr. Wingate speaks of having been the first who carried the logarithms to France; but an edition of Napier's "Description and construction of Logarithms" was printed at Lyons in 1620, four years earlier than Wingate's publication. 2. "Of Natural and Artificial Arithmetic, or Arithmetic made easy," Lond. 1630, 8vo, which has gone through numerous editions; the best is that by Mr. Dodson. 3. "Tables of Logarithms of the signs and tangents of all the degrees and minutes of the Quadrant; with the use and application of the same," ibid. 1633, 8vo. 4. "The Construction and use of Logarithms, with the resolution of Triangles, &c." 5. "Ludus Mathematicus: or an Explanation of the description, construction, and use of the numerical table of proportion," ibid. 1654, 8vo. 6. "Tacto-metria, seu Tetagne-nometria, or the Geometry of regulars, &c." * 8vo. 7. "The exact Surveyor of Land, &c." 8vo. 8. "An exact abridgment of all the statutes in force and use from the Magna Charta to 1641," 1655, 8vo, reprinted and continued to 1663, 1680, 1681, and 1684. 9. "The body of the common

* This was probably a republication of John Wyberd's, which appeared under the same title in 1650. Wyberd was a physician, and is slightly noticed by Wood in Ath. Ox. vol. II.

law of England," 1655, &c. 8vo. 10. " Maxims of reason, or the Reason of the Common Law of England," 1658,
fol. 11. " Statuta Pacis ; or, the Table of all the Statutes
which any way concern the office of a justice of peace,
&c." 12mo. 12. An edition of Britton, 1640, 12mo. He
was supposed to be the editor of some other law books,
which show equal judgment and industry, but he is now
remembered only as a mathematician.[1]

WINKELMAN (Abbé JOHN), an eminent antiquary,
was born at Stendall, in the old Marche of Brandenbourg,
in the beginning of 1718. He was the son of a shoemaker,
but although to all appearance destined by his birth to superintend a little school in an obscure town in Germany,
be raised himself to the office of president of antiquities in
the Vatican. After having been seven years professor in
the college of Seehausen near Salswedel, he went into
Saxony, where he resided seven years more, and was librarian to count Bunau at Nothenitz. The count was author of an " History of the Empire," and died 1762. His
fine library, valued in 1749 at 15,000 English crowns, has
been since added to the public library of Dresden. Mr.
Winkelman, in 1748, made a most methodical and informing catalogue of it, in 4 vols. When he left this place in
1754, he went to Dresden, where he formed an acquaintance with the ablest artists, and particularly with M. Oëser,
an excellent painter, and one of the best draughtsmen of
the age. In that year he abjured Lutheranism, and embraced the Roman catholic religion. In Sept. 1755, he
set out for Italy, and arrived at Rome in December following. His principal object was to see the Vatican library,
and to examine the ruins of Herculaneum. While engaged, as he tells us, in teaching some dirty boys their
A B C, he aspired to a knowledge of the beautiful, and
silently meditated on the comparisons of Homer's Greek
with the Latin literature, and a critical acquaintance with
the respective languages, which were more familiar to him
than they had ever been to any former lover of antiquity,
both by his application in studying them, and his public
lectures as professor of them. His extensive reading was
improved in the noble and large library which he afterwards
superintended. The solitude and the beauty of the spot
where he lived, and the Platonic reveries which he in-

[1] Ath. Ox. vol. II.—Hutton's Dictionary, new edit.

dulged, all served to prepare the mind for the enthusiasm which he felt at the sight of the master-pieces of art. His first steps in this career bespoke a man of genius; but what a concurrence of circumstances were necessary to develope his talents! The magnificent gallery of paintings and the cabinet of antiquities at Dresden, the conversation of artists and amateurs, his journey to Rome, his residence there, the friendship of Mengs the painter, his residence in the palace and villa of cardinal Albani, his place of writer in the Vatican, and that of president of antiquities, were so many advantages and helps to procure him materials, and to facilitate to him the use of them for the execution of the design which he had solely in view. Absolute master of his time, he lived in a state of perfect independence, which is the true source of genius, contenting himself with a frugal and regular life, and knowing no other passions than those which tended to inflame his ardent pursuit. An active ambition urged him on, though he affected to conceal it by a stoical indifference. A lively imagination, joined to an excellent memory, enabled him to derive great advantages from his study of the works of the ancients, and a steady indefatigable zeal led him naturally to new discoveries. He kindled in Rome the torch of sound study of the works of the ancients. His intimate acquaintance with them enabled him to throw greater certainty upon his explanations, and even upon his conjectures, and to overthrow many arbitrary principles and ancient prejudices. His greatest merit is, to have pointed out the true source of the study of antiquity, which is the knowledge of art, to which no writer had before attended. Mr. Winkelman carried with him into Italy a sense of beauty and art, which led him instantly to admire the master-pieces of the Vatican, and with which he began to study them. He soon increased his knowledge, and it was not till after he had thus purified his taste, and entertained conceptions of ideal beauty, which transported him to inspiration, and led him into the greatest secrets of art, that he began to think of the explanation of other monuments, in which his great learning could not fail to distinguish him. At the same time another immortal scholar treated the science of antiquity in the same manner on this side the Alps. Count Caylus had a profound and extensive knowledge of the arts, was master of the mechanical part, and drew and engraved in a capital style. Winkelman was

not endowed with these advantages, but in point of classical erudition surpassed the count; and while the latter
employed himself in excellent explications of little objects,
the former had continually before him at Rome the greatest
monuments of ancient art.    This erudition enabled him to
fill up his principal plan of writing the " History of Art."
In 1756 he planned his " Restoration of Ancient Statues,"
and a larger work on the " Taste of the Greek Artists;"
and designed an account of the galleries of Rome and Italy,
beginning with a volume on the Belvedere statues, in the
manner of Richardson, who, he says, only ran over Rome.
In the preface he intended to mention the fate of these
statues at the sacking of Rome in 1527, when the soldiers
made a fire in Raphael's lodge, which spoiled many things.
He also intended a history of the corruption of taste in art,
the restoration of statues, and an illustration of the obscure
points of mythology.    All these different essays led him to
his " History of Art," and his " Monumenti Inediti."    It
must, however, be confessed, that the first of these works
has not all the clearness and precision that might be expected in its general plan, and division of its parts and objects; but it has enlarged and extended the ideas both of
antiquaries and collectors.    The description of the gems
and sulphurs of the Stosch cabinet contributed not a little
to extend Mr. Winkelman's knowledge.    Few persons have
had opportunities of contemplating such vast collections.
The engravings of Lippet and count Caylus are all that
many can arrive at.    Mr. Winkelman's " Monumenti Inediti," of which he had begun the third vol. 1767, seem to
have secured him the esteem of antiquaries.    He there explained a number of monuments, and particularly bas reliefs till then accounted inexplicable, with a parade of
learning more in compliance with the Italian fashion than
was necessary.    Had he lived, we should have had a work
long wished for, a complete collection of the bas reliefs
discovered from the time of Bartoli to the present, the
greater part of which are in the possession of cardinal Albani.    But however we may regret his tragical end, the
intenseness of his application, and the eagerness of his
pursuit after ancient monuments, had at last so bewildered
him in conjectures, that, from a commentator on the works
of the ancients, he became a kind of seer or prophet.
His warm imagination outran his judgment.    As he proceeded in his knowledge of the characters of art in monu-

ments, he exhausted his fund of observations drawn from the ancients, and particularly from the Greeks.  He cited early editions, which are frequently not divided into chapters; and he was entirely unacquainted with the publications in the rest of Europe on the arts and antiquity. Hence his "History of Art" is full of anachronisms.

In one of his letters, dated 1754, he gives an account of his change of religion, which too plainly appears to have been guided by motives of interest, in order to make his way to Rome, and gain a better livelihood.  At Dresden he published, 1755, "Reflections on the Imitation of the Works of the Greeks," 4to, translated into French the same year, and republished 1756, 4to.  At Rome he made an acquaintance with Mengs, first painter to the king of Poland, afterwards, in 1761, appointed first painter to the house of Spain, with an appointment of 80,000 crowns, a house, and a coach; and he soon got access to the library of cardinal Passionei, who is represented as a most catholic and respectable character, who only wanted ambition to be pope.  His catalogue was making by an Italian, and the work was intended for Winkelman.  Giacomelli, canon of St. Peter, &c. had published two tragedies of Æschylus and Sophocles, with an Italian translation and notes, and was about a new edition of " Chrysostom de Sacerdotio;" and Winkelman had joined with him in an edition of an unprinted Greek oration of Libanius, from two MSS. in the Vatican and Barberini libraries.  In 1757 he laments the calamities of his native country, Saxony, which was then involved in the war between the emperor and the king of Prussia.  In 1758 he meditated a journey over the kingdom of Naples, which he says could only be done on foot, and in the habit of a pilgrim, on account of the many difficulties and dangers, and the total want of horses and carriages from Viterbo to Pisciota, the ancient Velia.  In 1768 we find him inraptured with the idea of a voyage to Sicily, where he wished to make drawings of the many beautiful earthen vases collected by the Benedictines at Catana.  At the end of the first volume of his letters, 1781, were first published his remarks on the ancient architecture of the temple of Girgenti.  He was going to Naples, with 100 crowns, part of a pension from the king of Poland, for his travelling charges, and thence to Florence, at the invitation of baron Stosch.  Cardinal Archinto, secretary of state, employed him to take care of his library.

His " Remarks on Ancient Architecture" were ready for a second edition. He was preparing a work in Italian, to clear up some obscure points in mythology and antiquities, with above fifty plates ; another in Latin, explanatory of the Greek medals that are least known ; and he intended to send to be printed in England " An Essay on the Style of Sculpture before Phidias." A work in 4to appeared at Zurich, addressed to Mr. Winkelman, by Mr. Mengs, but without his name, entitled, " Thoughts on Beauty and Taste in Painting," and was published by J. C. Fuesli. When Cardinal Albani succeeded to the place of librarian of the Vatican, he endeavoured to get a place for the Hebrew language for Winkelman, who refused a canonry because he would not take the tonsure. The elector of Saxony gave him, 1761, unsolicited, the place of counsellor Richter, the direction of the royal cabinet of medals and antiquities at Dresden. Upon the death of the abbé Venuti, 1762, he was appointed president of the antiquities of the apostolic chamber, with power over all discoveries and exportations of antiquities and pictures. This is a post of honour, with an income of 160 scudi per annum. He had a prospect of the place of president of antiquities in the Vatican, going to be created at 16 scudi per month, and was named corresponding member of the academy of inscriptions. He had thoughts of publishing an " Essay on the Depravation of Taste in the Arts and Sciences." The king of Prussia offered him by Col. Quintus Icilius the place of librarian and director of his cabinet of medals and antiquities, void by the death of M. Gautier de la Croze, with a handsome appointment. He made no scruple of accepting the offer ; but, when it came to the pope's ears, he added an appointment out of his own purse, and kept him at Rome. In April 1768 he left Rome to go with M. Cavaceppi over Germany and Switzerland. When he came to Vienna he was so pleased with the reception he met with that he made a longer stay there than he had intended. But, being suddenly seized with a secret uneasiness, and extraordinary desire to return to Rome, he set out for Italy, putting off his visits to his friends in Germany to a future opportunity. It was the will of Providence, however, that this opportunity should never come, he being assassinated in June of that year, by one Arcangeli, of whom, and of his crime, the following narrative was published :

" Francis Arcangeli was born of mean parents, near the city of Pistoia, and bred a cook, in which capacity he served in a respectable family at Vienna, where, having been guilty of a considerable robbery, he was condemned to work in fetters for four years, and then to be banished from all the Austrian dominions, after being sworn never to return. When three years of his slavery were expired, he found friends to intercede in his favour, and he was released from serving the fourth, but strictly enjoined to observe the order of banishment; in consequence of which he left Vienna, and retired to Venice with his pretended wife, Eva Rachel. In August 1767, notwithstanding his oath, he came to Trieste with a view to settle; but afterwards changed his mind, and returned to Venice, where, being disappointed of the encouragement he probably expected, he came again to Trieste in May 1768. Being almost destitute of money, and but shabbily dressed, he took up his lodging at a noted inn (probably with a view of robbing some traveller). In a few days the abbé Winkelman arrived at the same inn in his way from Vienna to Rome, and was lodged in the next apartment to that of Arcangeli. This circumstance, and their dining together at the ordinary, first brought them acquainted. The abbé expressed a desire of prosecuting his journey with all possible expedition, and Arcangeli was seemingly very assiduous in procuring him a passage, which the abbé took very kindly, and very liberally rewarded him for his services. His departure, however, being delayed by the master of the vessel which was to carry him, Arcangeli was more than ordinarily diligent in improving every opportunity of making himself acceptable to the abbé, and their frequent walks, long and familiar conversations, and the excessive civility and attention of Arcangeli upon all occasions that offered, so improved the regard which the abbé had begun to conceive for him, that he not only acquainted him in the general run of their discourse with the motives and the event of his journey to Vienna, the graces he had there received, and the offers of that ministry; but informed him also of the letters of credit he had with him, the medals of gold and silver which he had received from their imperial majesties, and, in short, with all the things of value of which he was possessed.

" Arcangeli expressed an earnest desire to see the medals, and the abbé an equal eagerness to gratify his curiosity; but the villain no sooner beheld the fatal coins, than yielding to the motions of his depraved heart, he determined treacherously to murder and rob the possessor. Several days, however, elapsed before he put his cruel design into execution, in which time he so officiously and courteously conformed himself to the temper and situation of his new friend, that he totally disarmed the abbé of all mistrust, and had actually inspired him with a sincere friendship.

"In the morning of the 7th of June, being determined no longer to delay his bloody purpose, he bought a sharp pointed knife, the instrument he intended to use in the execution, and then going to the coffee-house, he there found the abbé, who paid for him as usual, and continued with him in conversation till they both went home to dinner. After dinner they went again abroad together: but the villain having meditated a new scheme, he parted from the abbé and went and purchased some yards of cord, with which he returned home and retired to his chamber. Till the abbé came home, he employed himself in twisting the cord and forming a noose; and having prepared it to his mind, he placed that and the knife in a chair, ready. Soon after this the abbé came in, and, as his custom was, invited Arcangeli to supper. The cheerfulness of the abbé, and the frankness and cordiality with which he received and treated him, staggered him at first; and the sentiments of humanity so far took place, that his blood ran cold with the thoughts of his cruel intention, nor had he at this time courage to execute it. But the next morning, June the 8th, both going out of the inn together, and drinking coffee at the usual house, after Arcangeli had pretended in vain to hire a vessel to carry the abbé to Bagni, they returned to the inn, and each going into his own room, Arcangeli pulled off his coat (probably to prevent its being stained with blood) and putting the knife unsheathed, and the cord into his waistcoat pocket, about nine he went into Winkelman's chamber, who received him with his accustomed frankness, and entered into chat about his journey and about his medals; and, as he was upon the point of his departure, he invited the man, who was that instant to be his murderer, in the most affectionate manner, to Rome, where he promised him his best assistance. Full of those friendly sentiments, the abbé sat himself down in his chair, when instantly the assassin, who stood behind him, threw the cord over his head and drew it close. The abbé with both his hands endeavoured to loosen the cord, but the murderer with his knife already unsheathed stabbed him in several places. This increased the struggle, and the last efforts of the unhappy victim brought both of them to the ground; the murderer, however, was uppermost, and having his knife still reeking with blood in his hand, plunged it five times into the bowels of his wounded friend. The noise of the fall, and the groans of the abbé, alarmed the chamberlain of the house, who hastily opening the door, was witness to the bloody conflict. The assassin, surprised in the fact, dropped the bloody knife, and in his waistcoat only, without a hat, his breast open, and his shirt covered with blood, he escaped out of the inn.

" With the cord about his neck, and his wounds streaming, the abbé had still strength to rise, and descending from the second floor to the first, he placed himself against the balustrade, and called for assistance. Moved with compassion, those who heard his cries hastened to his relief, and helping him to his room, laid him upon his bed, where, having no hope of recovery, he received the sacraments, and made his will. After suffering a great deal with heroic constancy, and truly Christian piety, not complaining of his murderer, but most sincerely pardoning him, he calmly breathed his last about four in the afternoon.

" In the mean time the assassin had escaped into the Venetian territories, where, not thinking himself safe, he pursued his way to Pirano, with a design to embark in whatever ship was ready to sail, to whatever place; but expresses being every where dispatched with an account of the murder, and a description of the murderer, he found himself surrounded with dangers on all sides. Having found means, however, to change his cloaths, he quitted the high road, and passing through forests, and over mountains unknown to him, he at length came to a road that led to Labiana, and had already reached Planina, when a drummer, mistaking him for a deserter, caused him to be apprehended. Upon his examination, not being able to give a satisfactory account of himself, and being threatened by the magistrates of Aldesperg, he voluntarily confessed the murder, and eight days after committing the fact, was brought back to Trieste, heavily ironed, and under a strong guard. Here he was tried, and being found guilty, as well on his own confession as on the clearest evidence, he was sentenced by the emperor's judges to be broken on the wheel opposite to the inn where he had perpetrated the murder, and his body to be exposed in the usual place of executions. On the 18th of June he was informed of his sentence, and on the 20th of the same month it was executed in all its points, in the presence of an innumerable multitude, who flocked from all parts to see the execution."

Some of Winkelman's MSS. got to Vienna, where the new edition of his "History of Art" was presently advertised. He intended to have got this work translated into French at Berlin, by M. Toussaint, that it might be printed under his own inspection at Rome. It was translated by M. Hubert, so well known in the republic of letters, who has since published it in 3 vols. 4to, with head and tail-pieces from designs of M. Oëser. An Italian translation of it by a literary society has been published at Milan.

Abbé Winkelman was a middle-sized man; he had a very low forehead, sharp nose, and little black hollow eyes, which gave him an aspect rather gloomy than otherwise. If he had any thing graceful in his physiognomy, it was his mouth, yet his lips were too prominent; but, when he was animated, and in good humour, his features formed an ensemble that was pleasing. A fiery and impetuous disposition often threw him into extremes. Naturally enthusiastic, he often indulged an extravagant imagination; but, as he possessed a strong and solid judgment, he knew how to give things a just and intrinsic value. In consequence of this turn of mind, as well as a neglected education, a cautious reserve was a quality he little knew. If he was bold in his decisions as an author, he was still more so in his conversation, and has often made his friends tremble for his temerity. If ever man knew what friendship was, that man was Mr. Winkelman, who regularly practised all its duties, and for this reason he could boast of having friends among persons of every rank and condition. People of his turn of thinking and acting seldom or ever indulged suspicions: the abbé's fault was a contrary extreme. The frankness of his temper led him to speak his sentiments on all occasions; but, being too much addicted to that species of study which he so assiduously cultivated, he was not always on his guard to repress the sallies of self-love. His picture was drawn half length, sitting, by a German lady born at Kostnitz, but carried when young into Italy by her father, who was a painter. She etched it in a 4to size, and another artist executed it in mezzotinto. This lady was Angelica Kauffman. The portrait is prefixed to the collection of his letters published at Amsterdam, 1781, 2 vols. 12mo. Among his correspondents were Mr. Heyne, Munchausen, baron Reidesel (whose travels into Sicily, translated into English by Dr. Forster, 1773, 8vo, are addressed to him, and inspired him with an ardent longing to go over that ground), count Bunau, C. Fuesli, Gesner, P. Usteri, Van Mechlen, the duke de Rochfoucault, lord (alias Mr. Wortley) Montague, Mr. Wiell; and there are added extracts from letters to M. Clerisseaux, while he was searching after antiquities in the South of France; a list of the principal objects in Rome, 1766, &c.; and an abstract of a letter of Fuesli to the German translators of Webb on the " Beauties of Painting." [1]

WINSLOW (JAMES BENIGNUS), a skilful anatomist who settled in France, was born in 1669, at Odensee, in Denmark, where his father was minister of the place, and intended him for his own profession, but he preferred that of medicine, which he studied in various universities in Europe. In 1698 he was at Paris, studying under the celebrated Duverney, and here he was induced by the writings of Bossuet to renounce the protestant religion, a change which, it is rather singular, happened to his granduncle Stenonius (See STENONIUS) by the same influence. He now settled at Paris, was elected one of the college of physicians, lecturer at the royal garden, expounder of the Teutonic language at the royal library, and member of the academy of sciences. According to Haller, who had been his pupil, his genius was not so remarkable as his industry, but by dint of assiduity he became an excellent anatomist; and his system of anatomy, or " Exposition Anatomique," has long been considered as a work of the first reputation and utility, and has been translated into almost all the European languages, and into English by Douglas, 1734, 2 vols. 4to. He was also the author of a great number of anatomical dissertations, some of which were published separately, but they mostly appeared in the Memoirs of the French academy. He died in 1760, at the advanced age of ninety-one. [2]

[1] Prof. Heyne's Eloge, and Letters.—Gent. Mag. vols. XXXVIII. and LIV. drawn up by Mr. Gough. [2] Eloy, Dict. Hist. de Medecine.—Haller.

WINSTANLEY (WILLIAM), originally a barber, was author of the "Lives of the Poets;" of "Select Lives of England's Worthies;" "Historical Rarities;" "The Loyal Martyrology;" and some single lives; all in 8vo. Granger says he is a fantastical writer, and of the lowest class of biographers: but we are obliged to him for many notices of persons and things, which are mentioned by no other writer, which must account for his "England's Worthies" being a book still in request; and, as some of the vampers think, even worthy of being illustrated by prints. It is not, however, generally known, that it is necessary to have both editions of this work; those of 1660 and 1684, in order to possess the whole of his biographical labours: Winstanley, who could *trim* in politics as well as trade, omitted from the latter all the republican lives, and substituted others in their room. He *flourished* in the reigns of Charles I. II. and James II. and was probably alive at the publication of his second edition, in which he changed his dedication, adopting new patrons. In the "Censura Literaria," vol. V. is an account of "The Muses Cabinet," 1655, 12mo, containing his original poetry, which is called in the title-page "both pleasant and profitable;" but now we are afraid will not be thought either. He was a great plagiary, and took his character of the English poets from Phillips's "Theatrum," and much from Fuller and others, without any acknowledgment. [1]

WINSTON (THOMAS) an eminent physician, was born in 1575, and educated in Clare-hall, Cambridge, of which he became fellow. He took the degree of M. A. in 1602, and then visited the continent for improvement in the study of physic. He attended the lectures of Fabricius ab Aquapendente and Prosper Alpinus at Padua, and of Caspar Bauhine at Basil, and took the degree of doctor at Padua. He returned to England, graduated again at Cambridge in 1607, and settled in London; and in 1613 was admitted a candidate of the college of physicians, and the next year was made fellow. On the death of Dr. Mounsel, professor of physic in Gresham-college, he was chosen October 25, 1615, to succeed him, and held his professorship till 1642; when, by permission of the House of Lords, he went over to France, where he staid about ten years, and returned when the troubles were over. He did not

1 Granger.—Ath. Ox. vol. II. &c.

live long to enjoy a well acquired fortune; for he died October 24, 1655, aged eighty. He published nothing in his life-time; but after his death, his "Anatomical Lectures" were printed in 1659, 1664, 8vo, and were supposed the most complete then in the English language. [1]

WINTERTON (RALPH), an eminent Greek scholar, was the son of Francis Winterton of Lutterworth in Leicestershire, A. M. where he was born. That he was an excellent Greek scholar appears from many of his productions in that language, which entitled him to be a competitor, though an unsuccessful one, in 1627, for the Greek professorship at Cambridge, on the death of Andrew Downes, with four other candidates, who all read solemn lectures in the schools on a subject appointed them by the electors. He was educated at King's-college, Cambridge, where he had the misfortune, during the early part of his residence, to be somewhat disordered in his intellects; but, recovering, he took to the study of physic, and was allowed to excel all of that profession in his time. In 1631 he published the first book of Hippocrates's Aphorisms in a Greek metrical version at Cambridge, in quarto, and the year following the whole seven books together, in the same manner. In 1633, by the advice of Dr. John Collins, regius professor of physic, he published an edition of the Aphorisms in octavo at Cambridge, with Frere's Latin poetical translation, and his own Greek version, with a Latin prose translation by John Heurnus of Utrecht. At the end is annexed a small book of epigrams and poems, composed by the chiefest wits of both universities, but chiefly of Cambridge, and of King's-college in particular. In 1631 he printed, in octavo, at Cambridge, a translation of "Gerard's Meditations," which went through six editions in about nine years. In 1632 he published likewise at Cambridge, in octavo, Gerard's "Golden Chain of Divine Aphorisms." He published also, for the use of Eton-school, an edition of "Dionysius de situ Orbis," with some Greek verses at the end of it, addressed to the scholars, and exhorting them to the study of geography. This was reprinted at London in 1668, 12mo. In the above year (1632), he translated "Drexelius on Eternity," which was printed at Cambridge. In the preface to this, he has some sentiments which shew that he was of a pious but

somewhat singular turn of mind. In 1634, being **M. D.**
he was nominated by the king his professor of physic for
forty years, if he should live so long. The year following
he published at Cambridge in octavo an edition of the
" Minor Greek Poets," with observations upon Hesiod.
This has passed through many editions. His advancement
to the professorship appears to have interrupted his employment as an author ; but he did not survive that honour
long, dying in the prime of life Sept. 13, 1636. He was
buried at the east end of King's-college chapel, but without any memorial. After his death was published a translation by him of Jerome Zanchius's " Whole Duty of the
Christian Religion," Lond. 1659, 12mo. He appears to
have contributed his assistance in the publication of many
learned works, which have escaped our research. His
character was that of an industrious and judicious scholar,
an able physician, and a just and upright man. [1]

WINTLE (THOMAS), a learned divine, of whom our
memorial is but scanty, was born at Gloucester 28th April
1737. He was educated chiefly in his native city, and
distinguished by his thirst after knowledge, and his diligent
application to school-exercises. Obtaining an exhibition
at Pembroke-college, Oxford, he there became scholar,
fellow, and tutor, taking his degree of M. A. in 1759. In
1767, archbishop Secker made him rector of Wittrisham
in Kent, and called him to be one of his domestic chaplains ; and the following year he went to Oxford, and took
his degree of bachelor of divinity. After the death of his
grace, in the following year, he resided at Wittrisham, or
on the small living of St. Peter, in Wallingford ; until, in
1774, relinquishing these preferments, he was presented,
by the late bishop of Winchester, to the rectory of Brightwell, Berks. At Brightwell he lived constantly forty years,
and at Brightwell he died, July 29, 1814, leaving a widow, two sons, and one grand-daughter. In early life
Mr. Wintle was unremitting in the attainment of useful
learning, and in the practice of religion and virtue; and
in his more mature and later years he ceased not, by precept and example, to set forth the expediency and advantages of religion, while his fame in the literary world was
not inconsiderable. He published, 1st, "An improved
Version of Daniel attempted, with a Preliminary Disserta-

[1] Cole's MS Collectanea, in Brit. Mus. vol. XV.

tion, and Notes critical, historical, and explanatory." 2. "A Dissertation on the Vision contained in the second chapter of Zechariah." 3. " Eight Sermons on the Expediency, Prediction, and Accomplishment, of the Christian Redemption, preached at the Bampton Lecture." 4. " Christian Ethics, or Discourses on the Beatitudes, with some preliminary and subsequent Discourses ; the whole designed to explain, recommend, or enforce, the Duties of the Christian Life." 5. " A Letter to the Lord Bishop of Worcester, occasioned by his Strictures on Archbishop Secker and Bishop Lowth, in his Life of Bishop Warburton." The two first of these publications will class Mr. Wintle with the most distinguished Biblical scholars, and the Bampton Lectures and Christian Ethics are not less valuable, as illustrations of the Christian system. [1]

WINTON. See WYNTON.

WINTRINGHAM (CLIFTON), an eminent physician, was the son of Dr. Clifton Wintringham, also a physician, who died at York, March 12, 1748, and was an author of reputation, but rather of the mechanical school, as appears by his first publication, "Tractatus de Podagra, in quo de ultimis vasis et liquidis et succo nutritio tractatur," York, 1714, 8vo. In this he assigns, as the causes of the gout, a certain acrimonious viscosity in the nervous fluid, the rigidity of the fibres, and a straitness in the diameter of the vessels that are near the joints. His second publication was entitled " A Treatise of endemic diseases," ibid. 1718, 8vo, which was followed by his most important publication, "Commentarium nosologicum morbos epidemicos et aeris variationes in urbe Eboracensi, locisque vicinis, ab anno 1715 ad anni 1725 finem grassantes complectens," Lond. 1727, 1733, 8vo. This last edition was edited by his son. He published also "An experimental inquiry on some parts of the animal structure," ibid. 1740, 8vo, and " An inquiry into the exility of the vessels of a human body," ibid. 1743, 8vo.

His son, the more immediate subject of this brief notice, was born in 1710, and educated at Trinity college, Cambridge, where he took his degree of bachelor of medicine in 1734, and that of doctor in 1749. During the interval it is not improbable that he studied the art at Leyden, as was usual at that time. He settled however at London,

[1] Gent. Mag. vol. LXXXIV.

where he became a fellow of the college of physicians, and in 1742 of the Royal Society, in 1759 physician extraordinary, and afterwards physician general to the army. In 1749 he had been appointed chief physician to the duke of Cumberland, and in 1762 was nominated physician to his present majesty, and received the honour of knighthood. He attained considerable practice during a very long life, and was much respected both for his private and public character. He died at Hammersmith, after a lingering illness, Jan. 9, 1794, at the age of eighty-four. In 1774 he had been created a baronet, with remainder to Jarvis Clifton, esq. second son of sir Jarvis Clifton, bart. of Clifton, Nottinghamshire, who however died before him, and the title became extinct. By his will, sir Clifton left to Trinity college, where he had been educated, a small marble image of Esculapius found near Rome, which was accordingly deposited there by his widow.

Sir Clifton published an edition, with annotations, of Mead's " Monita et præcepta medica," and an edition of his father's works, 1752, 2 vols. 8vo. The only production from his own pen was entitled " De morbis quibusdam commentarii," 1782 and 1790, 2 vols. [1]

WINWOOD (Sir RALPH), secretary of state in the reign of James I. was son of Mr. Lewis Winwood, some time secretary to Charles Brandon, duke of Suffolk; and was born about 1565, at Aynho, in Northamptonshire. He was at first sent to St. John's college, Oxford, whence he was elected a probationer-fellow of Magdalen college in 1582. He took both the degrees in arts, and that of bachelor of law; and in 1692, was proctor of the university. Afterwards he travelled on the continent, and returned a very accomplished gentleman. In 1599, he attended sir Henry Neville, ambassador to France, as his secretary; and, in the absence of sir Henry, was appointed resident at Paris: whence he was recalled in 1602-3, and sent that year to the States of Holland by James I. In 1607, he was knighted; and the same year appointed ambassador jointly with sir Richard Spencer to Holland. He was sent there again in 1609, when he delivered the remonstrance of James I. against Vorstius (See VORSTIUS) the Arminian, to the assembly of the States, to which they seemed to pay very little attention. Upon this the king proceeded to

[1] Eloy, Dict. Hist. de Medecine.—Nichols's Bowyer.

threaten them with his pen; and plainly told them, that if they had the hardiness to " fetch again from hell ancient heresies long since dead, &c. he should· be constrained to proceed publicly against them." It is certain that his majesty wrote a pamphlet against Conr. Vorstius, which was printed in 1611.

In 1614, Winwood was made secretary of state; in which office he continued till his death, which happened Oct. 27, 1617. He was interred in the parish church of St. Bartholomew the Less, London. Lloyd tells us, that "he was a gentleman well seen in most affairs, but most expert in matters of trade and war." But although others acknowledge his abilities and integrity, they add that he was not sufficiently polished as a courtier, as there was something harsh and supercilious in his demeanour. He left a son named Richard, afterwards of Ditton Park in Bucks, who dying without issue in 1688, his estate went to a son of Edward earl of Montague, who had married his sister. In 1725, were published at London, in 3 vols. folio, " Memorials of Affairs of State in the Reigns of queen Elizabeth and king James I. collected chiefly from the original papers of the right honourable sir Ralph Winwood, knight, some time one of the principal secretaries of state. Comprehending likewise the negotiations of sir Henry Neville, sir Charles Cornwallis, sir Dudley Carlton, sir Thomas Edmonds, Mr. Trumble, Mr. Cottington, and others, at the courts of France and Spain, and in Holland, Venice, &c. wherein the principal transactions of those times are faithfully related, and the policies and the intrigues of those courts at large discovered. The whole digested in an exact series of time. To which are added two tables, one of the letters, the other of the principal matters. By Edmund Sawyer, esq." then one of the masters in chancery. [1]

WIRLEY. See WYRLEY.

WIRZ (JOHN), an artist, whom, Fuseli says, situation, temper, and perhaps circumstances, have deprived of the celebrity he deserved, was a native of Zuric, born in 1640, the son of a canon, and professor of divinity in its college, and appears to have had a liberal education. Though, when a youth, he lost one eye, he was bound to Conrad Meyer, of whom, with the elements of painting, he ac-

---

[1] Gen. Dict.—Biog. Brit. Supplement.—Lloyd's State Worthies.—Ath. Ox. vol. I.—Granger.

quired the mystery of etching. As a painter he devoted
himself to portraiture, which he exercised with success,
and in a style little inferior and sometimes equal to that of
S. Hofmann ; but the imitation of dormant or insipid coun-
tenances, unable to fill a mind so active and open to impression, in time gave way to composition in art and writing, both indeed devoted to the most bigoted superstition,
and theologic rancour, for in his Dialogues on the Apoca-
lypsis of S. John, blind zeal, legendary falsehood, and bar-
barism of style, go hand in hand with shrewdness of observation, controversial acuteness, and blunt naiveté : a heterogeneous mass, embellished by an etched series of poetic
and historic subjects, in compositions dictated by the most
picturesque fancy, original, magnificent, various, romantic,
terrible, and fantastic ; though in small, on a scale of arrangement and combinations to fill the pompous scenery of
Paolo, or challenge the wildest caprice of Salvator ; and in
the conception of the Last Judgment, for sublimity far superior to Michael Agnolo. With these prerogatives, and
neither insensible to beauty nor form, the artist is often
guilty of ludicrous, nay, even premeditated incorrectness,
and contortions which defy possibility. His style of etching, free, spirited, and yet regular, resembles that of Wil-
helm Baur ; and though no vestiges remain of his having
seen Italy, it is difficult to conceive by what other means
he could acquire that air of Italian scenery, and that minute acquaintance with the architecture, the costume, and
ceremonies, of that country, without having visited it himself. His dialogues, above mentioned, were published in
1677, 8vo, entitled "J. Wirzii Romæ animale exemplum,
&c." with 42 plates. Wirz resided and died in 1709, at
a small villa which he possessed near Zuric. [1]

WISE (FRANCIS), a learned antiquary, and Radcliffe librarian at Oxford, was born in the house of his father
Francis Wise, a mercer at Oxford, June 3, 1695. He received the first part of his education in New college school,
under the care of Mr. James Badger, a man very eminent
as a schoolmaster. In January 1710-11 he was admitted
a member of Trinity college, and in the summer following
was elected scholar of that house. He took the degree of
M. A. in 1717, and about this period was employed by
Mr. Hudson, as an underkeeper or assistant in the Bodleian

---

[1] Pilkington by Fuseli.

library, an admirable school for Mr. Wise, who had a turn for literary history and antiquities. In 1718 he became probationer, and in the following year actual fellow of his college. In 1722 he published "Asser Menevensis de rebus gestis Alfredi magni," 8vo, very elegantly printed, and with suitable engravings, &c. The year preceding this, (1721) the hon. Francis North, afterwards earl of Guildford, entered of Trinity college under the tuition of Mr. Wise, for whom he entertained a great esteem through life. From this nobleman he received the living of Ellesfield near Oxford, a very small piece of preferment, and not worth above 25l. a year at most, but peculiarly agreeable to our author, who contrived to make it a place of some importance to curious visitors. He took a small estate there, on a long lease, under lord Guildford, and converted a cottage upon it into an agreeable retirement, by building one or two good rooms, and laying out a garden with a piece of ground adjoining, scarcely before of any use, in a very whimsical but pleasing manner. In this little spot of a few acres, his visitors were surprised to meet with ponds, cascades, seats, a triumphal arch, the tower of Babel, a Druid temple, and an Egyptian pyramid. These buildings, which were designed to resemble the structures of antiquity, were erected in exact scale and measure, to give, as far as miniature would permit, a just idea of the edifice they were intended to represent. From the time that his illustrious pupil left Oxford, Mr. Wise constantly resided in his family at intervals, and divided his time between the seat of the Muses, and the elegant mansion of his friend and patron. In 1726 he was elected custos archivorum; and in 1727 took his degree of bachelor of divinity.

In 1738, Mr. Wise published a Letter to Dr. Mead concerning some antiquities in Berkshire, particularly showing that the White Horse was a Saxon monument, 4to. This pamphlet was answered by an anonymous person (supposed to be one Asplin, vicar of Banbury) who in his pamphlet, entitled "The Impertinence and Imposture of Modern Antiquaries displayed," insinuated a suspicion that Mr. Wise was no friend to the family on the throne. This insinuation gave Mr. Wise great uneasiness, as he then had in view some preferment from the officers of state (the place of Radcliffe Librarian). He therefore drew up in 1742, another treatise, called "Further Observations upon the White Horse, &c." and was vindicated also both in his political principles and antiquarian conjectures by a friend (the Rev. Mr. North, F.S.A.) who then concealed his name. (See NORTH, GEORGE).

In 1745, he was presented by Trinity college to the rectory of Rotherfield Greys, in the county and diocese of Oxford; and on May 10, 1748, he was appointed Radcliffe librarian. In 1750, he published his " Catalogue of the Coins in the Bodleian library," folio, which he had designed, and taken subscriptions for, above twenty years before, but through the smallness of his income he was unable to bear the expense of engravings, &c. This work he dedicated to his friend and patron the earl of Guildford, and in it has given some views of his house and gardens at Ellesfield. After this period he resided chiefly in this pleasing retreat, and pursued his researches into antiquity. In 1758, he printed in 4to, " Some Enquiries concerning the first inhabitants, learning, and letters of Europe, by a member of the Society of Antiquaries, London ;" and in 1764, another work in 4to, entitled " History and Chronology of Fabulous Ages considered." No name is prefixed to these performances, but at the end of each we have the initials F. W. R. L. (Francis Wise, Radcliffe librarian). .These were his last publications. He was after this period much afflicted with the gout, and lived quite retired at Ellesfield till his death, which happened Oct. 6, 1767. He was buried in the churchyard of that place, and by his own direction, no stone or monument perpetuates his memory. In his life-time he had been a benefactor to the Bodleian library by supplying from his own collections many deficiencies in the series of their coins ; and after his death, his surviving sister, who resided at Oxford, and was his executrix, generously gave a large and valuable cabinet of his medals, &c. to the Radcliffe library.[1]

WISHART (GEORGE), one of the first martyrs for the protestant religion in Scotland, and a person of great distinction in the ecclesiastical history of that country, was born in the beginning of the sixteenth century, and appears to have very early felt the consequences of imbibing the spirit of the reformers. He was descended of the house of Pitarrow in the Mearns, an illustrious family in Scotland,

[1] Memoirs drawn up by Mr. Huddesford of Trinity college, for Dr. Ducarel, and transcribed from the Doctor's MS Collections, vol. K. now in the possession of our obliging friend John Nichols, esq. See also his Literary Anecdotes.

and is said to have travelled into Germany, where he became acquainted with the opinions of Luther.   Other accounts mention his having been banished from his own
country by the bishop of Brechin, for teaching the Greek
Testament in the town of Montrose, and that after this he
resided for some years in the university of Cambridge.   Of
this latter circumstance there is no reason to doubt, for
besides an account of him while there by one of his pupils,
printed by Fox, the historian of Bene't or Corpus Christi
college has inserted a short account of him, as one of the
members of that house.   In 1544, he returned to his native
country, in the company of the commissioners who had
been sent to negociate a treaty with Henry VIII. of England.   At this time he was allowed to excel all his countrymen in learning, and to be a man of the most persuasive
eloquence, irreproachable in life, courteous and affable in
manners.   His fervent piety, zeal, and courage, in the
cause of truth, were tempered with uncommon meekness,
modesty, patience, prudence, and charity.   With these
qualifications he began to preach in a very bold manner,
against the corruptions of the Romish church, and the vices
of the clergy.   He met with a most favourable reception
wherever he appeared, and was much followed and eagerly
listened to, which so excited the indignation of cardinal
Beaton, and the popish clergy in general, that a resolution
was formed to take away his life by some means or other.

Two attempts were made to cut him off by assassination;
but he defeated the first by his courage, and the second
by his caution.   On the first of these attempts he behaved
with great generosity.   A friar named Weighton, who had
undertaken to kill him when he was in Dundee (where he
principally preached), knowing that it was his custom to
remain in the pulpit after sermon, till the church was
empty, skulked at the bottom of the stairs with a dagger in
his right hand under his gown.   Wishart (who was remarkably quick-sighted), as he came down from the pulpit, observing the friar's countenance, and his hand with something in it under his gown, suspected his design, sprung
forward, seized his hand, and wrenched the dagger from
him.   At the noise which this scuffle occasioned, a crowd
of people rushed into the church, and would have torn the
friar in pieces; but Mr. Wishart clasped him in his arms, and
declared that none should touch him but through his body.
"He hath done me no hurt," said he, "my friends; he

hath done me much good ; he hath taught me what I have to fear, and put me upon my guard." And it appeared that he defeated the second attempt on his life by the suspicion which the first had inspired. When he was at Montrose, a messenger came to him with a letter from a country gentleman, acquainting him that he had been suddenly taken ill, and earnestly intreating him to come to him without delay. He immediately set out, accompanied by two or three friends, but when they were about half a mile from the town, he stopped, saying, " I suspect there is treason in this matter. Go you (said he to one of his friends) up yonder, and tell me what you observe." He came back and told him, that he had seen a company of spearmen lying in ambush near the road. They then returned to the town, and on the way he said to his friends ; " I know I shall one day fall by the hands of that blood-thirsty man (meaning cardinal Beaton), but I trust it shall not be in this manner."

These two plots having miscarried, and Wishart still continuing to preach with his usual boldness and success, the cardinal summoned a synod of the clergy to meet Jan. 11, 1546, in the Blackfriars church, Edinburgh, and to consider of means for putting a stop to the progress of heresy, and while thus employed, he heard that Wishart was in the house of Ormiston, only about eight miles from Edinburgh, where he was seized by treachery, and conducted to the castle of Edinburgh, and soon after to the castle of St. Andrew's. Here, being completely in the hands of the cardinal, he was put upon his trial March 1, before a convocation of the prelates and clergy assembled for that purpose in the cathedral, and treated with the utmost barbarity, every form of law, justice, or decency, being dispensed with. He endeavoured to answer the accusations brought against him, and to shew the conformity between the doctrines he had preached and the word of God; but this was denied him, and he was condemned to be burnt as an obstinate heretic, which sentence was executed next day on the castle green. The cardinal seems to have been sensible that the minds of men would be much agitated by the fate of this amiable sufferer, and even to have apprehended that some attempt might be made to rescue him from the flames. He commanded all the artillery of the castle to be pointed towards the scene of execution ; and, either to watch the ebullitions of popular indignation, to display his contempt of the reformers, or to satiate himself by contemplating the destruction of a man, in whose grave he hoped that their principles would be buried, he openly, with the prelates who accompanied him, witnessed the melancholy spectacle. In many accounts which we have of Wishart's death, it is mentioned that, looking towards the cardinal, he predicted, "that he who, from yonder place (pointing to the tower where he sat), beholdeth us with such pride, shall, within a few days, lie in the same as ignominiously as now he is seen proudly to rest." In our account of Beaton we have noticed the evidence for this fact, and the opinion of historians upon it, to which may now be added the opinions of some able writers (noticed in our references) who have appeared since that article was drawn up. Concerning Wishart, we may conclude, with Dr. Henry, that his death was a loss to his persecutors as well as to his friends. If he had lived a few years longer, the reformation, it is probable, would have been carried on with more regularity and less devastation. He had acquired an astonishing power over the minds of the people; and he always employed it in restraining them from acts of violence, inspiring them with love to one another, and with gentleness and humanity to their enemies.[1]

WISHART, or WISCHEART (GEORGE), bishop of Edinburgh, was born in East Lothian in 1609, and educated in the university of Edinburgh; where he took his degrees, and entered into holy orders. He became minister of North Leith, but was deposed in 1638, for refusing to take the covenant, and was also imprisoned for his loyalty. On his release he accompanied the marquis of Montrose as his chaplain. When the marquis was defeated by general Lesley in 1645, Wishart was taken prisoner, and would have suffered death along with several noblemen and gentlemen whom the covenanters condemned, had not his amiable character endeared him to some of the leading men of the party. He then went abroad, and became chaplain to Elizabeth, queen of Bohemia, sister to Charles I. with whom he came over into England in 1660, to visit her royal nephew Charles II. Soon after, Mr. Wishart had the rectory of Newcastle upon Tyne conferred upon him; and upon the restoration of episcopacy in Scotland, was

[1] Mackenzie's Scotch Writers.—Buchanan's History. — Spotswood's and Knox's Histories.—Henry's Hist.—Cook's Hist. of the Reformation.—M'Crie's Life of Knox.—Masters's Hist. of C.C.C.C.

consecrated bishop of Edinburgh, June 1, 1662. In that station he gave a most striking proof of that benevolence which should ever characterise a real Christian ; for, when some of the presbyterians who had persecuted him were committed to prison for rebellion, he assisted them with every necessary, and procured them a pardon. He died in 1671, and was buried in the abbey of Holyrood-house, under a magnificent tomb, with a long Latin inscription. Keith says, " he was a person of great religion ; and having been a prisoner himself, it is reported of him that he was always careful at each dinner, to send off the first mess to the prisoners." He wrote the history of the war in Scotland under the conduct of the marquis of Montrose, in elegant Latin, under the title of " J. G. de rebus auspiciis serenissimi et potentissimi Caroli, Dei gratia Mag. Brit. regis, &c. sub imperio illustrissimi Montisrosarum marchionis, &c. anno 1644, et duobus sequentibus, præclare gestis, commentarius, interprete A. S." This was first published in 1646, and there have been several English translations of it from that time to 1720, when it was printed with a second part, which Keith says the author left in manuscript.[1]

WISSING (WILLIAM), an excellent portrait painter, was born at Amsterdam in 1656, and bred up under Dodaens, an historical painter at the Hague. On coming to England, he worked some time for sir Peter Lely, whose manner he successfully imitated, and after whose death he came into fashion. He painted Charles II. and his queen, James II. and his queen, and the prince and princess of Denmark ; and was sent over to Holland, by king James, to draw the prince and princess of Orange. What recommended him to the esteem of Charles II. was his picture of the duke of Monmouth, whom he drew several times and in several attitudes. He drew most of the then court, and became competitor with sir Godfrey Kneller, whose fame was at that time increasing every day. It is said that, in drawing portraits of the fair sex, when any lady came to sit, whose complexion was rather pale, he would commonly take her by the hand, and dance about the room till she became warmer and her colour increased. This painter died much lamented at Burleigh-house, in Northampton-

[1] Keith's Catalogue of the Scotch bishops.—Wood's Fasti, vol. II —Cens. Lit. vol. II.

shire, Sept. 10, 1687, aged only thirty-one; and was buried in St. Martin's church, Stamford, where a marble tablet, with a Latin inscription, was placed by John earl of Exeter. There is a mezzotinto print of him, under which are these words, " Gulielmus Wissingus, inter pictores sui sæculi celeberrimus, nulli secundus, artis suæ non exiguum decus & ornamentum.——Immodicis brevis est ætas." [1]

WITCHELL (George), a good astronomer and mathematician, was born in 1728. He was maternally descended from the celebrated clock and watchmaker, Daniel Quare, in which business he was himself brought up, and was educated in the principles of the Quakers, all his progenitors for many generations having been of that community, whose simplicity of manners he practised through life. It appears that he cultivated the study of astronomy at a very early age, as he had a communication on that subject in the " Gentleman's Diary" for 1741, which must have been written when he was thirteen years of age. Soon after this he became a frequent writer both in the Diaries and in the Gentleman's Magazine, sometimes under his own name, but oftener with the initials G. W. only. In 1764 he published a map, exhibiting the passage of the moon's shadow over England in the great solar eclipse of April 1, that year; the exact correspondence of which to the observations gained him great reputation. In the following year he presented to the commissioners of longitude a plan for calculating the effects of refraction and parallax, on the moon's distance from the sun or a star, to facilitate the discovery of the longitude at sea. Having taught mathematics in London for many years with much reputation, he was in 1767 elected F. R. S. and appointed head master of the royal naval academy at Portsmouth, where he died of a paralytic stroke in 1785, aged fifty-seven. [9]

WITHER (George), a name well known among the readers of old English poetry, and revived, of late, by the taste and judgment of some eminent poetical antiquaries, was born at Bentworth, near Alton in Hampshire, June 11, 1588. He was the only son of George Wither of Bentworth (by Anne Serle), who was the second son of John Wither of Manydowne near Wotton St. Lawrence in that

[1] First edit. of this Dict.—Walpole's Anecdotes.—Pilkington.
[9] Hutton's Dict. new edit.

county, at which seat Mr. Bigg Wither, the heir (not the
heir male, but the heir female, who has taken the name),
still resides.    The poet was educated under John Greaves
of Colemore, a celebrated schoolmaster, whom he afterwards commemorated with gratitude in a poem published
in 1613.    About 1604 he was sent to Magdalen college,
Oxford, under the tuition of John Warner, afterwards
bishop of Rochester.    Here he informs us, in the proë-
mium to his " Abuses stript and whipt," that he found the
art of logic, to which his studies were directed, first dull
and unintelligible ; but at the moment it began all at once
to unfold its mysteries to him, he was called home " to
hold the plough."    He laments that he was thus obliged
to forsake " the Paradise of England" to go " in quest of
care, despair, and discontent."

After he had remained some time in his own country,
certain malicious advisers, under the mask of friendship,
pretending that nothing was to be got by learning, endeavoured to persuade his father to put him to some mechanic
trade; but our poet, finding that country occupations were
not fitted to his genius, determined, on some slight gleam
of hope, to try his fortune at court, and therefore entered
himself as a member of Lincoln's-inn.    The world now
opened upon him in characters so different from his expectations, that, having been probably educated in puritanical
principles, he felt that disgust which perhaps made him a
satirist for life.    The first thing which appeared to fill him
with dislike and anger, was the gross flattery and servility
which seemed necessary to his advancement.    If, however,
his manners did not procure him favour with the courtiers,
his talents obtained him the acquaintance and friendship of
many men of genius.    William Browne, the pastoral poet,
who was of the Inner Temple, was an early familiar of
his.    And some of his verses having got abroad, began to
procure the name of a poet for himself.    His " Philarete's
Complaint, &c." formed a part of his " Juvenilia," which
are said to have been his earliest compositions.    He also
wrote elegies in 1612 on that general subject of lamenta-
tion, the death of prince Henry.

In 1613 first appeared his celebrated satires, entitled
" Abuses stript and whipt," for which so much food was
furnished by the motley and vicious manners of the nation.
Wither, therefore, bursting with indignation at the view of
society which presented itself to his young mind, took this

opportunity to indulge in a sort of publication to which the prosaic taste of the times was well adapted; but he disdained, and perhaps felt himself unqualified, to use that glitter of false ornament, which was now substituted for the true decorations of the muse. "I have strived," says he, " to be as plain as a pack-saddle," and in these satires he is indeed excessively plain, and excessively severe, and they gave so much offence that he was committed to the Marshalsea, where he continued several months. In 1615 he published "The Shepherd's Hunting: being certain eglogues written during the time of the author's imprisonment in the Marshalsea;" which book, Wood observes, is said to contain more of poetical fancy than any other of his writings. Of this interesting poem, sir Egerton Brydges has lately published a beautiful edition in 12mo, and in the preface observes, with a decision which every man of taste will respect, that "The Shepherd's Hunting has so much merit, and is so abundant in a natural vein of simple, affecting, and just sentiment, as well as imagery, that he who can read it, and doubt the author's genius, is insensible to all the features which bespeak the gifts of the muse." When in prison, Wither not only also wrote but published his "Satire to the King," 1614. He terms this an apology for former errors, proceeding from the heat of youth, but part of it is a vindictive appeal to the king from the restraint put upon his person, and part of it is a monologue conducted by the author between the impulses of supplication and disdain. It is thought, however, to have procured his release.

After this time he continued to write and publish both poetry and prose without intermission to the day of his death, which yet was at a great distance. Wood remarks, with more correctness of judgment and expression than he usually attains, that our poet was now cried up, " especially by the puritan party, for his profuse pouring forth of English rhyme," which abundant facility has certainly tempted him into an excess that has totally buried the effusions of his happier moments. Such a superfluity of easy but flat and insipid narrative, and trite prosaic remarks, scarce any writer has been guilty of. On, his pen appears in general, to have run, without the smallest effort at excellence ; and therefore subjected him too justly to Wood's stigma of being a scribbler. But let it be observed, this was the fault of his will, and not of his genius. When the examples of real poetry, which he has given, are selected from his multitudinous rhymes, they are in point both of quality and quantity sufficient to stamp his fame.

Another cause of the depression of Wither's reputation was the violent party spirit, by which a large portion of his works was dictated and degraded, as well as the active part which he took on the side of the parliament. In 1639, he had been a captain of horse in the expedition against the Scots, and quarter-master-general of his regiment, under the earl of Arundel. But as soon as the civil wars broke out in 1642, he sold his estate to raise a troop of horse for the parliament; and soon afterwards rose to the rank of major; but being taken prisoner by the royalists, " Sir John Denham the poet," says Wood, " some of whose estate at Egham, in Surrey, Wither had got into his clutches, desired his majesty not to hang him, because so long as Wither lived, Denham would not be accounted the worst poet in England. About that time," continues Wood, " he was constituted by the Long Parliament a justice of peace in quorum for Hampshire, Surrey, and Essex, which office he kept six years, and afterwards was made by Oliver, major-general of all the horse and foot in the county of Surrey, in which employment he licked his fingers sufficiently, gaining thereby a great odium from the generous loyalists."

At the restoration in 1660, the spoils which he had amassed from the adherents of the king, and from the church, were taken from him. His principles, and especially a libel entitled " Vox vulgi," which he had dispersed, and which was deemed seditious, rendered him obnoxious to the new government, and he was now committed to Newgate; and afterwards, by order of the House of Commons, was sent close prisoner to the Tower, to be debarred of pen, ink, and paper; and about the same time (March 1661-2), an impeachment was ordered to be drawn up against him. In this confinement he continued more than three years, and here he wrote several things by connivance of the keeper, of which some were afterwards published, " yet never," adds Wood, " could refrain from shewing himself a presbyterian satirist." When he was released is not mentioned, but he reached the age of seventy-nine, and died May 2, 1667, and was interred in the Savoy church in the Strand.

That Wither was a poet, and a poet deserving to be better known, has been sufficiently proved by the selection from his "Juvenilia," printed by the late Alexander Dalrymple, esq. in 1785, and particularly by the more recent republications of his "Shepherd's Hunting," 1814, his "Fidelia," 1815, and his "Hymns and Songs of the Church," 1815, by sir Egerton Brydges, whose prefaces and remarks add no small value to these beautiful volumes, and whose judgment and taste in the revival of works of neglected merit cannot be too highly appreciated. It is to this learned baronet also that the reader is indebted for all that is valuable in the present sketch of Wither, taken from a more copious life of the poet in the "Bibliographer." In the same work, the reader may be referred to a very accurate list, and history, by Mr. Park, of all Wither's writings, amounting to 112 articles in prose and verse, from which very pleasing selections may yet be made. They are almost all of rare occurrence, and expensive in proportion, since the attention of the public has been drawn to them by the various critics mentioned in our references.[1]

WITHERING (WILLIAM), an able physician and botanist, was born in 1741, at Willington in Shropshire, where his father was an apothecary. After being initiated in pharmacy and medicine under his father, he was sent to the university of Edinburgh, where he studied the usual time, and took the degree of doctor of physic in 1766. Not long after he left the university, he settled at Stafford, where meeting with little encouragement, he removed in 1774 to Birmingham; and here his abilities were soon called into action; and in a few years his practice became very extensive, and having a studious turn, he devoted those hours which remained after the business of the day, to philosophical and scientific pursuits. In 1776 he published, in 2 vols. 8vo, the first edition of his "Botanical Arrangement;" a work which, at that time, could be considered as little more than a mere translation from Linnæus of such *genera* and species of plants as are indigenous in Great Britain; and in which Ray's "Synopsis Methodica Stirpium Britannicarum," and Hudson's "Flora Anglica," could not fail to afford him great assistance; but, in the course of the two other editions of it (the last of which, in 4 vols. 8vo, was published in 1796), this "Arrangement" has been so much improved and enlarged, as to have become, in a great measure, an original work; and certainly, as a national Flora, it must be allowed to be a very elaborate and complete performance. Botany, however, did not engross all our author's attention: many of his leisure hours he devoted to chemistry and mineralogy. In 1783, he translated Bergman's "Sciagraphia Regni Mineralis," under the title of "Outlines of Mineralogy;" and, before and since that time, he addressed to the Royal Society several communications relative to those branches of knowledge. Thus, in 1773, we find inserted in the Philosophical Transactions his experiments on different kinds of marle found in Staffordshire. In the same Transactions for 1782, his analysis of the toad-stone, a fossil met with in Derbyshire. In the same work for 1784, his experiment on the *terra ponderosa.* And lastly, in 1798, his analysis of a hot mineral spring in Portugal. Amidst these diversified pursuits he did not relax in his professional studies. In 1779, he published an "Account of the Scarlet Fever and Sore Throat;" and, in 1785, appeared his account of the fox-glove; wherein he laid before the public a very satisfactory body of evidence in favour of the diuretic virtues of this vegetable in various kinds of dropsies. From early life Dr. Withering was of a slender and delicate habit of body; and, not long after his first establishment in practice, he became subject to attacks of peripneumony. By these repeated attacks his lungs were at length so much injured, and his whole frame so much debilitated, that he found it necessary to repair to a warmer climate. Accordingly, in the autumn of 1793, he made a voyage to Lisbon, where he passed the winter, returning to England the following spring. Thinking he had received benefit from the climate of Portugal, he made a second voyage to Lisbon the following winter, and returned home again 1795. While he was in Portugal, he analyzed the hot mineral waters, called the Caldas. This analysis was published in the Memoirs of the royal academy of sciences at Lisbon; and since in the Philosophical Transactions of the Royal Society in London. After his return from his last voyage to Lisbon, his health remained in a very fluctuating state, sometimes so tolerable as to allow going out in a carriage; at other times, so bad as to confine him to his room. In this manner his existence was protracted until Sept. 1799, when he removed from Edgbaston-hall, where he had resided (under a lease granted by the late lord Calthorpe) for several years, to a house, which he had recently purchased, and had named the Larches, and where he died Oct. 6, 1799. To the distinguished rank which he held in the medical profession, Dr. Withering was raised wholly by personal merit. He possessed great clearness of discernment, joined with a most persevering application. He was of a humane and mild disposition. With his family and among his friends he was cheerful and communicative; but with the world at large, and even in his professional character, he was shy and reserved.[1]

WITHERSPOON (JOHN), an eminent divine in Scotland and America, and a lineal descendant from Knox the celebrated Scotch reformer, was born Feb. 5, 1722, at Yester near Edinburgh, of which parish his father was minister. After some previous education at the public school at Haddington, he was, at the age of fourteen, sent to the university of Edinburgh, and having gone through the usual course of academical studies, was licensed to preach, and soon after was ordained minister of the parish of Beith, in the west of Scotland, whence, in a few years, he was removed to be minister at the large and flourishing town of Paisley. During his residence here he was much admired for his general learning, his abilities in the pulpit, and for his writings, one of which, his " Ecclesiastical Characteristics," is perhaps one of the most humorous satires ever written on a subject which apparently did not admit of that mode of treatment. No satire in our time was read with more approbation and interest than Witherspoon's " Characteristics" for many years in Scotland. It is levelled at the party in the general assembly of Scotland, who were called the *moderate* men, in contradistinction to those called the *orthodox*, or who adhered strictly to the doctrines contained in their national " Confession of Faith." From this publication, and from his speeches in the general assembly, Witherspoon acquired much influence, but he had to contend with almost all the literary force of the assembly, the Blairs, Gerards, Campbells, and Robertsons, who were considered as the leaders of the moderate party. One day, after carrying some important questions against Dr. Robertson, the latter said in his pleasant manner, " I think you have your men better disciplined than formerly." " Yes," replied Witherspoon, " by urging your politics too

[1] Gent. Mag. vol. LXIX.

far, you have compelled us to beat you with your own weapons."

During Dr. Witherspoon's residence at Paisley, he had eligible offers from Dublin, from Dundee, and from Rotterdam, which he rejected, but at length his reputation having reached that continent, he was induced to accept an offer from America, and on his arrival at Prince-town in 1768, was appointed president of the college there, the prosperity of which was greatly augmented under his administration, not only with respect to its funds and the number of students, but from his introducing every improvement in education and science, which had been adopted in Europe. When the revolutionary war was approaching, he became a decided friend to the cause of America, and was for seven years a member of the congress. After the peace he paid a visit to England, and returning soon after to Prince-town, died there Nov. 15, 1794, in his seventy-third year. His printed works, very superior in point of style and manner, consist of "Essays" in 3 vols. 8vo, on theological topics, and two volumes of "Sermons," besides the "Characteristics," already noticed, and a work " On the nature and effects of the Stage," which at one time made a great noise. Bishop Warburton mentions " The Characteristics" with particular approbation.[1]

WITSIUS, or WITS (HERMAN), a very learned and eminent divine of North Holland, was born at Enckhuisen, Feb. 12, 1636. He was trained to the study of divinity, and so distinguished himself by his uncommon abilities and learning, that he was chosen theological professor, first at Franeker, afterwards at Utrecht, and lastly at Leyden. He applied himself successfully to the study of the Oriental tongues, and was not ignorant in any branch of learning which is necessary to form a good divine. He died Oct. 22, 1708, in the seventy-third year of his age, after having published several important works, which shew great judgment, learning, and piety. One of the principal of these is " Egyptiaca;" the best edition of which, at Amsterdam, 1696, in 4to, has this title : " Ægyptiaca, et Decaphylon ; sive, de Ægyptiacorum Sacrorum cum Hebraicis collatione Libri tres. Et de decem tribubus Israelis Liber singularis. Accessit Diatribe de Legione Fulminatrice Christianorum, sub Imperatore Marco Aurelio Antonino," Amst. 1683, and

[1] Funeral Sermon by Dr. Rodgers, in Prot. Diss. Mag. vol. II.

1696, 4to. Witsius, in this work, not only compares the religious rites and ceremonies of the Jews and Egyptians, but he maintains particularly, against our sir John Marsham and Dr. Spencer, that the former did not borrow theirs, or any part of them, from the latter, as these learned and eminent writers had asserted in their respective works, " Canon Chronicus," and " De Legibus Hebræorum." " The Oeconomy of the Covenants between God and Man" is another work of Witsius, and the best known in this country, having been often printed in English, 3 vols. 8vo. Of this and its author, Hervey, in his " Theron and Aspasia," has taken occasion to speak in the following terms : " The Oeconomy of the Covenants," says he, " is a body of divinity, in its method so well digested, in its doctrine so truly evangelical, and, what is not very usual with our systematic writers, in its language so refined and elegant, in its manner so affectionate and animating, that I would recommend it to every student in divinity. I would not scruple to risk all my reputation upon the merits of this performance ; and I cannot but lament it, as one of my greatest losses, that I was no sooner acquainted with this most excellent author, all whose works have such a delicacy of composition, and such a sweet savour of holiness, that I know not any comparison more proper to represent their true character than the golden pot which had manna, and was outwardly bright with burnished gold, inwardly rich with heavenly food." [1]

WITT. See DE WITT.

WITTE DE. See CANDIDO.

WITTE, or WITTEN (Henningus), a German biographer, was born in 1634. We find very few particulars of him, although he has contributed so much to our knowledge of other eminent men. He was a divine and professor of divinity at Riga, where he died Jan. 22, 1696. Morhoff bestows considerable praise on his biographical labours, which were principally five volumes of memoirs of the celebrated men of the seventeenth century, as a sequel to those of Melchior Adam. They were octavo volumes, and published under the titles of " Memoria Theologorum nostri seculi," Franc. 1674, reprinted in 1685, 2 vols. ; " Memoria Medicorum ;" " Memoria Jurisconsultorum ;"

[1] Life prefixed to the " Oeconomy of the Covenants," edit. 1762.—Burman Traject. Erudit.—Saxii Onomasticon.

" Memoria Philosophorum," &c. which last includes poets and polite scholars. The whole consist of original lives, or eloges collected from the best authorities. The greater part are Germans, but there are a few French and English. In 1688 he published, what we have often found very useful, his " Diarium Biographicum Scriptorum seculi xvii." vol. I. 4to, 1688, vol. II. 1691. It appears that Witte paid a visit to England in 1666, and became acquainted with the celebrated Dr. Pocock, to whom he sent a letter ten years afterwards, informing the doctor that he had for some time been engaged in a design of writing the lives of the most famous writers of that age in each branch of literature, and had already published some decades, containing memoirs of divines, civilians, and physicians; " that he was now collecting eloges on the most illustrious philologers, historians, orators, and philosophers; but wanted memoirs of the chief Englishmen who, in the present (seventeenth) century, have cultivated these sciences, having no relation of this sort in his possession, except of Mr. Camden ; he begs, therefore, that Dr. Pocock, would, by the bearer, transmit to him whatever he had to communicate in this way." [1]

WODHULL (MICHAEL), the first translator into English verse of all the tragedies and fragments of Euripides which are extant, was born Aug. 15, 1740, at Thenford, in Northamptonshire, and was sent first to Twyford, in Buckinghamshire, to the school of the rev. William Cleaver. This preceptor had three sons, William, bishop of St. Asaph, Eusebius, archbishop of Dublin, and John, student of Christ Church, Oxford, who were all attached to Mr. Wodhull with the sincerest friendship through life. To John, one of his poetical epistles (the ninth) is addressed, in which honourable mention is made of the father.

> " Beneath whose auspices his earlier age
>   Imbibed the dictates of the good and sage."

From Twyford he was removed to Winchester school, and afterwards to Brasennose college, Oxford. He inherited from his father, who died while he was at school, a large fortune, of which the first use that he made was to build a handsome mansion on his patrimonial inheritance. In 1761 he married a lady of great personal accomplishments, and universally loved and respected, Miss Cathe-

---

[1] Baillet Jugemens.—Morhoff Polyhist.—Saxii Onomast.

rine Milcah Ingram, of an ancient family situated at Wolford, in Warwickshire, who left him a widower without family in 1808. In 1803 he took advantage of the short peace to gratify his curiosity in the libraries of Paris, and was one of the English detained by Bonaparte, but was afterward released on account of his age. He returned home an invalid and alone, and it was a source of great distress to him to be compelled to leave behind him in France his faithful servant. From that period his bodily infirmities gradually increased, his sight at length failed, and his voice became scarcely audible, but his senses and his memory, which was most singularly retentive, continued unimpaired to the last. He died without a struggle or groan, Nov. 10, 1816, in the seventy-seventh year of his age.

Of his politics, Mr. Wodhull says they were " those of a British whig, not run away with by national prejudices;" but he never entered into public life; his chief occupation and amusement being the study of books, of which he was celebrated as a collector. He disposed during his life of many which he had purchased, but left behind him above 4000 volumes, consisting principally of first editions and rare specimens of early printing. The duties of private and social life no man discharged with more fidelity or exactness. As a son, a husband, a friend, a master, a landlord, few could excel him, and his charities, which were numerous, were known generally to those only whom he benefited.

As to his religious sentiments, although he was an advocate for toleration, he invariably asserted the principle of conformity to the sound and apostolic establishments of the land. His practice, even when very infirm, was to attend divine service in his parish church, to read or procure some friend to read a sermon and prayers to his family and domestics every Sunday evening. He never spoke an unkind word to his servants, and there was hardly an instance known of any one quitting his service for that of another master. He never complained, nor uttered a peevish expression under the greatest privations and the most severe pain. His funeral was, by his own desire, as his life had been, without parade or ostentation, and the monumental stone declares no more than the name and age of him whose mortal reliques lie near it.

The first edition of Mr. Wodhull's translation of " Euri-

pides" appeared in 1782, 4 vols. 8vo, since reprinted in 3
vols. 8vo.　Whoever considers the number of dramas composed by the Greek tragedian, the variety of allusions which
they contain to ancient manners, and to the tenets of philosophers; and the peculiar force of the language in which
they were written, will acknowledge that the attempt to
render them into English verse must have failed altogether
without a rare union of perseverance, knowledge, and ability.　Original composition is the surest test of genius, but
the poetical images and ideas of one man cannot adequately
be represented or expressed by another who does not himself possess the imagination and fancy of a poet.　In his
translation of Euripides, Mr. Wodhull has selected blank
verse as the best adapted for the dialogue, and has rendered
the chorusses for the most part in a Pindaric ode.　The
difference therefore both of the subject and versification is
such that no comparison can fairly be instituted with the
poetical versions of the Æneid and the Iliad.　But as Dryden and Pope have secured to themselves a high rank in
the list of British Classics by their translations, an honourable post will also be assigned to Mr. Wodhull, who has
contributed no mean addition to the stock of British Literature, and naturalized among us him, whom he entitles
"The Philosophic Bard."

　Mr. Wodhull's poetical fame, however, does not rest
merely on translations; he was the author of several poems
published at different periods, which he collected in 1804,
and printed with several alterations for the use of his friends
in an elegant octavo volume, to which his portrait was prefixed.　The poems consist of five odes, two songs, "The
Equality of Mankind;" "On Mr. Hollis's print of Dr. May-
hew;" "The Use of Poetry," and thirteen epistles addressed to different friends.　When a very young man he
wrote an "Ode to Criticism," which is not found in this
collection.　It was intended as an attack on certain pecu-
liarities in the writings of Thomas Warton.　Warton took
a singular mode of avenging himself, by inserting the ode
in "The Oxford Sausage" among poems of a very different sort.　This proceeding may perhaps be considered as
a proof of humour in the laureate; but it is to be regretted
that it has been the means of perpetuating a composition
which its author would long ago have consigned to oblivion.[1]

　　　　[1] Private communication.

WODROW (ROBERT), a Scotch ecclesiastical historian, son to the rev. James Wodrow, professor of divinity in the university of Glasgow, was born there in 1679, and after passing through his academic course, was chosen in 1698 librarian to the university. He held this office for four years, during which he had many valuable opportunities for indulging his taste in the history and antiquities of the church of Scotland. In 1703 he was ordained minister of the parish of Eastwood, in which humble station he continued all his life, although he had encouraging offers of greater preferment in Glasgow and Stirling. He died in 1734, at the age of fifty-five. He published in 1721, in 2 vols. folio, a " History of the singular sufferings of the Church of Scotland, during the twenty-eight years immediately preceding the Revolution,"-written with a fidelity which has seldom been disputed, and confirmed, at the end of each volume, by a large mass of public and private records. In England this work has been little known, except perhaps by an abridgment in 2 vols. 8vo. by the Rev. Mr. Cruickshanks, but since the publication of the historical work of the Hon. Charles James Fox, as well as by the writings of Messrs. Sommerville and Laing, it has greatly risen in reputation as well as price. " No historical facts," Mr. Fox says, " are better ascertained than the accounts which are to be found in Wodrow. In every instance where there has been an opportunity of comparing these accounts with the records and authentic monuments, they appear to be quite correct." Mr. Wodrow also left a great many biographical memoirs of the Scotch reformers and presbyterian divines, which are preserved in the university library of Glasgow. [1]

WOIDE (CHARLES GODFREY), a name worthy to be preserved on account of his valuable edition of the Alexandrine MS. of the New Testament, was a native of Holland, but of his early history we have no account. His first preferment in this country was to the preachership of the Dutch chapel-royal at St. James's, about 1770, to which he was afterwards appointed reader also. At the time of his death he was reader and chaplain at the Dutch chapel in the Savoy. In 1778 he was elected a fellow of the society of antiquaries, and in that year distinguished himself by revising, through the Clarendon press, Scholtz's " Egyptian Gram-

[1] Encyclop. Britannica, last edition.

mar," written in 1750, in 2 vols. 4to, and also La Croze's
" Lexicon Egyptiaco-Latinum." It had long been the
wish of the learned that both these works, left in MS. by
their respective authors, might be published, but they could
not find a printer furnished with Egyptian types, or who
would hazard the undertaking, until at last the university
of Oxford, with its usual munificent spirit, determined to
bear the expense. When the Lexicon was printing, Mr.
Woide was desired to make some additions to it, but this
not being proposed till more than half the work was printed,
he could extend his remarks to three letters only, and to
render the undertaking more useful, he added an index.
It was intended to print Scholtz's Grammar in 2 quarto
vols. immediately after the Dictionary, which consists of
one vol. quarto; but it being found too voluminous, Woide
very properly abridged it, and has improved it by carefully
examining and correcting it by means of MSS. unknown to
Scholtz. The Sahidic part was entirely supplied by Dr.
Woide.

In 1782 Dr. Woide was appointed an assistant librarian
at the British Museum, at first in the department of natural history, but soon after in one more congenial to his
studies, that of printed books. He had before obtained
the degree of D. D. from the university of Copenhagen,
and in 1786 was created doctor of laws at Oxford. In this
year appeared his truly valuable work, the " Novum Testamentum Græcum, e codice MS. Alexandrino, qui Londini in Bibl. Musei Britannici asservatur, &c. Ex prelo
Joannis Nichols, Typis Jacksonianis," fol. The history
of this MS. thus preserved and perpetuated by an accurate
fac-simile, is contained in the editor's learned preface, which
was reprinted at Leipsic in 1790, in an octavo volume, with
notes by Gottliebb Leberecht Spohn. Dr. Woide was
seized with an apoplectic fit, May 6, 1790, while at sir
Joseph Banks's *converzations*, of which he died next day at
his apartments in the British Museum. [1]

WOLFE, or WOLFIUS, (CHRISTIAN), baron of the Roman empire, privy-counsellor to the king of Prussia, and
chancellor of the university of Hall in Saxony, was born at
Breslau, Jan. 24, 1679. To the college of this city he was
indebted for his first studies : after having passed his lessons in philosophy, he applied himself assiduously to the

! Nichols's Bowyer, vol. IX.

mathematics. The "Elementa Arithmeticæ, vulgaris et literalis," by Henry Horch, were his earliest guides; by a frequent perusal of these, he was at length enabled to enrich them with additional propositions of his own. So rapid a progress did him great honour; whilst the different disputes, in which he was engaged with the canons of Breslau, laid the permanent foundation of his increasing fame. In 1699, he repaired to the university of Jena, and chose John Philip Treuner for his master in philosophy, and George Albert Hamberger for the mathematics; whose lessons he received with so happy a mixture of attention and advantage, that he became afterwards the able instructor of his fellow-students.

From Philip Muller, and Frederic Beckman, he received his knowledge of theology : a treatise written by Tschirnhausen, entitled "Medicina Mentis & Corporis," engaged him for some time; in consequence of which, in 1702, he had a conference with the author, to clear up some doubts concerning particular passages. The detail into which Tschirnhausen had the complaisance to enter with this young philosopher, enabled him to model the whole on a more extensive plan. Having finished that part of his education which he was destined to receive at Jena, he went to Leipsic in 1702; and, having obtained a permission to give lectures, he began his new employment, and, in 1703, opened with a dissertation called "Philosophia practica universalis, methodo mathematica conscripta;" which first attempt served greatly to enhance the reputation of his talents. Wolfe chose, for the foundation of his lessons, the method followed by Tschirnhausen. His philosophy bore as yet a very strong resemblance to that of Descartes, as may be seen in his dissertation "De loquela," which he published in 1703. Leibnitz, to whom he sent it, told him, that he plainly perceived, that his hypothesis concerning the union of the soul and body was not hitherto sufficiently just and explicit. These objections made him review the whole, which afterwards went through several material alterations.

Two dissertations which he published at the end of 1703, the first, "De rotis dentatis," and the second, "De Algorithmo infinitesimali differentiali," obtained him the honourable appellation of assistant to the faculty of philosophy at Leipsic. The universities of Giessen and Hall having invited him to be their professor in mathematics, he accepted of the offer of the last, and went thither in 1707. The same year he was admitted into the society at Leipsic, which was at that time engaged in the publication of the "Acta eruditorum." After having inserted in this work many important pieces relating to physic and the mathematics, he undertook, in 1709, to teach all the various branches of philosophy, and began with a little logical Latin treatise, which made its appearance afterwards in the German language, under the title of "Thoughts on the Powers of the human Understanding." While he was carrying on these great pursuits with assiduity and ardour, the king of Prussia rewarded him with the post of counsellor to the court on the decease of Bodinus in 1721, and augmented the profits of that office by very considerable appointments: he was also chosen a member of the Royal Society of London and Prussia.

In the midst of this prosperity he raised a storm against himself. He had, on the 12th of July, 1721, delivered a Latin oration, the subject of which was the morality of the Chinese: he loaded their philosophy with applause, and endeavoured to prove how similar its principles were to those which he had advanced in doctrines of his own. The divines at Hall were so exasperated at this attempt to undervalue their tenets, that on the day following every pulpit resounded with censures of Wolfe, and the opposition to him continued till 1722, when the faculty of theology were determined strictly to examine each production of our extraordinary philosopher. Daniel Strathler, whose province was to scrutinize the "Essay on Metaphysics," published a refutation of it. Wolfe made his complaints to the academic council, who issued out an order, that no one should presume to write against him: but the faculty having sent their representation to the court, which were all backed by the most strenuous assertions, that the doctrine which Wolfe taught, particularly on the subject of liberty and necessity, was dangerous to the last degree, an order at length arrived, Nov. 18, 1723, not only displacing Wolfe, but commanding him (under pain of being severely punished if he presumed to disobey) to leave Hall and the States in twenty-four hours at the farthest.

Wolfe retired now to Cassel, where he obtained the professorship of mathematics and philosophy in the university of Marbourg, with the title of counsellor to the court of the landgrave of Hesse, to which a profitable pension was annexed. Here he reassumed his labours with redoubled ardour; and it was in this retreat that he published the best parts of his numerous works. In 1725 he was declared an honorary professor of the academy of sciences at St. Petersburgh, and, in 1733, was admitted into that at Paris. The king of Sweden also declared him one of the council of regency: the pleasing situation of his new abode, and the multitude of honours which he had received, were too alluring to permit him to accept of many advantageous offers; amongst which was the post of president of the academy at St. Petersburgh. The king of Prussia, who was now recovered from the prejudices he had been made to conceive against Wolfe, wished to re-establish him in the university of Hall in 1733, and made another attempt to effect it in 1739. Wolfe met these advances with all that respectful deference which became him, but took the liberty to insinuate, that he did not then believe it right for him to comply. At last, however, he submitted; and the prince offered him, in 1741, an employment which threw every objection that he could make aside. Wolfe, still mindful of his benefactors, took a gracious leave of the king of Sweden; and returned to Hall, invested with the characters of privy-counsellor, vice-chancellor, and professor of the law of nature and of nations. After the death of Ludwig, the king raised him to the dignity of chancellor of the university, and the elector of Bavaria created him a baron of the empire (whilst he was exercising the vicarship of it), from his own free unbiassed inclination.

He died at Hall in Saxony, of the gout in his stomach, April 9, 1754, in his seventy-sixth year; after having composed in Latin and German more than sixty distinct pieces. The chief of his mathematical compositions is his "Elementa Matheseos Universæ," the best edition of which is that of 1732, 5 vols. 4to, printed at Geneva; which does not, however, comprise his Mathematical Dictionary in the German language, nor many other distinct works on different branches of the mathematics. His "System of Philosophy" is contained in 23 vols. 4to.

Brucker says, that Wolfe "possessed a clear and methodical understanding, which by long exercise in mathematical investigations was particularly fitted for the employment of digesting the several branches of knowledge into regular systems; and his fertile powers of invention enabled him to enrich almost every field of science, in which he laboured, with some valuable additions. The lucid order which appears in all his writings enables his reader to follow his conceptions, with ease and certainty, through the longest trains of reasoning. But the close connection of the several parts of his works, together with the vast variety and extent of the subjects on which he treats, renders it impracticable to give a summary of his doctrines." A French critic remarks that all the German works of this author are "extremely well written, and he has also been very happy in finding words, in that language, answering to the Latin philosophical terms which had till then been adopted; and as this renders a small dictionary necessary for understanding his phrases, he has placed one at the end of such books as require it. As to his Latin works, they are very ill written; his words are ill chosen, and frequently used in a wrong sense; his phrases too perplexed and obscure, and his style in general too diffuse." An abridgment of his great Latin work, "On the Law of Nature and Nations," has been published in French, three small vols. 12mo, by Formey; to which is prefixed, a life of Wolfe, and a chronological list of all his writings. He was, doubtless, one of the most learned philosophers and mathematicians Germany has produced; but his eulogy seems to us to be carried too far, when he is compared to Descartes and Leibnitz for his genius and writings, in both which he was certainly much inferior to them.[1]

WOLFE (Major-General JAMES), a brave English officer, was the son of lieutenant-general Edward Wolfe, and was born at Westerham, in the county of Kent, where he was baptised the 11th of Jan. 1726. He seemed by nature formed for military greatness: his memory was retentive, his judgment deep, and his comprehension amazingly quick and clear: his constitutional courage was not only uniform and daring, perhaps to an extreme, but he possessed that higher species of it, that strength, steadiness, and activity, of mind, which no difficulties could obstruct, or dangers deter. With an universal liveliness, almost to impetuosity of temper, he was not subject to passion; with the greatest independence of spirit, free from pride. Generous, almost to profusion, he contemned every little art for the acquisition of wealth; whilst he searched after objects for

1 Life by Formey.—Moreri.—Dict. Hist.—Brucker.—Saxii Onomast.

his charity and beneficence, the deserving soldier never went unrewarded, and even the needy inferior officer frequently tasted of his bounty : constant and distinguishing in his attachment, manly and unreserved, yet gentle, kind, and conciliating in his manners. He enjoyed a large share of the friendship, and almost the universal good-will, of mankind ; and, to crown all, sincerity and candour, a true sense of honour, justice, and public liberty, seemed the inherent principles of his nature, and the uniform rule of his conduct. He betook himself, when very young, to the profession of arms ; and with such talents, joined to the most unwearied assiduity, he was soon singled out as a most rising military genius. Even so early as the battle of Lafeldt, when scarcely twenty, he exerted himself in so masterly a manner, at a very critical juncture, that it drew the highest encomiums from the great officer then at the head of the army. During the whole war, he went on, without interruption, forming his military character; was present at every engagement, and never passed undistinguished. Even after the peace, whilst others lolled on pleasure's downy lap, he was cultivating the arts of war. He introduced (without one act of inhumanity) such regularity and exactness of discipline into his corps, that, as long as the six British battalions on the plains of Minden are recorded in the annals of Europe, so long will Kingsley's stand amongst the foremost of that day. Of that regiment he continued lieutenant-colonel, till Mr. Pitt, afterwards lord Chatham, who roused the sleeping genius of his country, called him forth into higher spheres of action. He was early in the most secret consultations for the attack upon Rochfort : and what he would have done there, and what he afterwards did at Louisbourg, are recorded in history, with due approbation. He was scarcely returned thence, when he was appointed to command the important expedition against Quebec. There his abilities shone out in their brightest lustre : in spite of many unforeseen difficulties, from the nature of the situation, from great superiority of numbers, the strength of the place itself, and his own bad state of health, he persevered with unwearied diligence, practising every stratagem of war to effect his purpose. At last, singly, and alone in opinion, he formed and executed that great, that dangerous, yet necessary, plan which drew out the French to their defeat, and will for ever denominate him the conqueror of Canada. When, however, within the grasp of victory, he received a ball through his wrist, which immediately wrapping up, he went on, with the same alacrity, animating his troops by precept and example : but, in a few minutes after, a second ball, through his body, obliged him to be carried off to a small distance in the rear. There, roused from fainting, in the last agonies, by the sound of "They run," he eagerly asked, "Who run?" and being told the French, and that they were defeated, he said, "then I thank God; I die contented;" and almost instantly expired, Sept. 13, 1759.

He was brought to England, and interred at Greenwich in the same grave with his father, who was buried on the second of April preceding. There is no memorial for him at Greenwich, but a cenotaph has been put up to his memory in Westminster Abbey at the public expence, and there is another at Westerham, the place of his nativity. [1]

WOLFE (JOHN), a learned compiler, was born Aug. 10, 1537, at Bergzabern in the duchy of Deux Ponts, and was educated in law and philosophy at Strasburgh, Wirtemberg, Tubingen, and other celebrated academies, and afterwards was entrusted with the education of some noblemen's sons, with whom he travelled in France, &c. from 1564 to 1567. Returning then to Dol, he took the degree of licentiate in civil law, and settled in practice at Spire, where two years after he was admitted into the number of assessors. In 1569 he attended Wolfgang, the elector Palatine, who came with an army to the assistance of the French protestants, and his highness dying a few months afterwards, Wolfe conducted his corpse back to Germany by sea, and it was interred at Meisenheim. For this melancholy duty and his other faithful services he grew in esteem with Philip Lewis and John, the electors Palatine, who thought him worthy of being sent twice on important business to queen Elizabeth of England, and once to the king of Poland. In 1573 Charles marquis of Baden made him one of his counsellors, and in 1575 appointed him governor of Mundlesheim, which office he held for twenty years, and received many honours and marks of favour from the Baden family. In 1594, finding his health exhausted by official fatigues, he retired to Hailbrun, where he passed the remainder of his days in study, and died of a very short illness, as had always been his wish, May 23, 1600, in the sixty-third year of his

1 First edit. of this Dict.—Annual Register—and Gent. Mag. for 1759.

age. He wrote " Clavis Historiarum ;" and a larger work
entitled " Lectionum memorabilium et reconditarum Cen-
turiæ XVI." 2 vols. fol. printed first in the year he died,
but there is an edition of 1671, which is not so much valued. Mr. Dibdin has accurately described this curious
work in his " Bibliomania," to which the reader is referred. [1]

WOLFE (JOHN CHRISTOPHER), a learned scholar, hitherto strangely overlooked by most foreign biographers,
was a native of Germany, born in 1683, but removed in
his youth to Hamburgh, where he was educated under Fabricius, and assisted him in his " Bibliotheca Græca," as
appears by vol. XIII. of that laborious work. He was a
Lutheran divine, and preached at Hamburgh, where he
was also professor of the Oriental languages, and where he
died in 1739. Many of his works are known in this country, and have been often quoted with approbation by biblical scholars and critics. Among them are, 1. " Historia
Lexicorum Hebraicorum," Wittem. 1705, 8vo. 2. " Dissertatio de Zabiis," ibid. 1706, 4to. 3. " Origenis Philoso-
phumena recognita et notis illustrata," Hamb. 1706, 8vo.
4. An edition of Phædrus, 1709. 5. " Dissertatio de Atheismi
falso suspectis," Wittem. 1710, 4to. 6. " Casauboniana,
sive Isaaci Casauboni varia de Scriptoribus, librisque ju-
dicia," Hamb. 1710, 8vo. 7. " Libanii epist. adhuc non
editarum centuria selecta Gr. cum versione et notis,"
Leipsic, 1711, 8vo. 8. " Anecdota Græca sacra et pro-
fana," Hamb. 1722, &c. 3 vols. 8vo. 9. " Curæ philolo-
gicæ et criticæ in omnes libros N. T." Hamb. 1725—1735,
but the best edition is that of Basil, 1741, 5 vols. 4to.
This work, says bishop Watson, has some resemblance, in
the manner of its composition, to Pool's " Synopsis," but
is written with more judgment, and contains the opinions
of many expositors who have lived since the publication
of Pool's work. Wolfe, moreover, has not followed Pool
in simply relating the sentiments of others, but has frequently animadverted on them with great critical discernment. Wolfe published other works, and new editions, all
which display great learning and critical acumen. His
brother John Christian, who died in 1770, was the author
of the " Monumenta typographica," Hamburgh, 1740, 8vo,
an edition of the fragments of Sappho, and other works. [2]

[1] Melchior Adam.—Freberi Theatrum.—Bibliomania.
[2] Saxii Onomast.—Bibl. German. vols. V. and VIII.

WOLLASTON (WILLIAM), a learned and ingenious writer, was born March 26, 1659, at Coton Clanford, in Staffordshire, where his father then resided, a private gentleman of small fortune, being descended from an ancient and considerable family in that county, where the elder branch always continued; but the second, in process of time, was transplanted into other counties. The head of it flourished formerly at Oncot, in the county of Stafford, though afterwards at Shenton, in Leicestershire; and was possessed of a large estate lying in those and other counties. Our author was a second son of a third son of a second son of a second son, yet notwithstanding this remarkable series of younger brothers, his grandfather, who stands in the midst of it, had a considerable estate both real and personal, together with an office of 700*l.* per annum. And from a younger brother of the same branch sprang sir John Wollaston, lord-mayor of London, well known in that city at the time of the grand rebellion.

At nine years old, Mr. Wollaston was sent to a master, who had opened a Latin school, at Shenstone in Staffordshire, where his father then resided. Here he continued near two years, and then removed to Lichfield; but had not been long at this school, when the magistrates of the city, in consequence of some dispute, turned the master out of the school-house. Mr. Wollaston, however, with many of the scholars, followed the ejected master, and remained with him till he quitted school, which was about three years, after which, the schism being ended, he returned into the free-school, and continued there about a year. The rudeness of a great school was particularly disagreeable to his natural disposition; and what was still worse, he began now to be much troubled with the headach, which seems to have been constitutional in him; yet his uncommon attention to his book, and eagerness to improve, had now rendered him fit for the university. Accordingly he was sent to Cambridge, and admitted a pensioner at Sidney-college, June 18, 1674, in the sixteenth year of his age. Here he laboured under some discouragements. He was come up a country lad from a country-school; had no acquaintance in his college, nor even in the university; few books or materials to work with; his allowance being by no means more than sufficient for bare necessaries; neither had he sufficient confidence to supply that defect by applying to others. Add to this that his state of health was not quite firm. However, under all these disadvantages, he acquired much reputation, and having taken his degree of B. A. at the regular time, he offered himself a candidate for a fellowship in his college, but missed of that preferment. In July 1681 he commenced M. A. and about this time seems to have entered into deacon's orders.

On Michaelmas-day following, he left the university, and having made a visit to the then head of this branch of the family, his cousin Wollaston of Shenton in Leicestershire, he went to pay his duty to his father and mother at Bloxwyche, where they then lived, and remained with them till May or June 1682. But seeing no prospect of preferment, he so far conformed himself to the circumstances of his family, as about this time to become assistant at Birmingham school to the head master, who readily embraced the opportunity of such a coadjutor, and considered Mr. Wollaston as one who had prudentially stooped to an employment beyond what he might reasonably have pretended to. This instance, however, of his humble industry was far from being displeasing to his cousin of Shenton, who had a great esteem for the head master, and in a short time, he got a small lecture at the distance of about two miles from Birmingham; but as he performed there the whole Sunday's duty, that fatigue, added to the business of a great free-school for about four years, began to break his constitution. But the old master being now turned out, in order to make way for a particular person to succeed him, our author was chosen second master only, under a pretence that he was too young to be at the head of so great a school, but some of the governors themselves owned that he was not well used in this affair.

However that may be, it is certain upon this occasion he took priest's orders in pursuance to the charter of that school, which being interpreted likewise so as to oblige the masters to take no church-preferment, he resigned his lecture. This happened in 1686, and was a considerable relief to him, while his new post was worth about 70*l*. per annum, which afforded him a tolerable subsistence. In the mean time the late chief master after his expulsion retired to his brother's house, which lying in the neighbourhood of Shenton, he once or twice waited upon Mr. Wollaston, of Shenton, and undoubtedly informed him of the character, learning, conversation, and conduct of our author, which he was very capable of doing, because they lived together, till the time of this old gentleman's leaving Birmingham. Mr. Wollaston, of Shenton, having now lately lost his only son, and never intending (as appears from his whole conduct) to give his estate to his daughters, pursued his father's design of continuing it in the male line of his family, and resolved to settle it upon our author's uncle and father, his own first cousins, and his nearest male-relations, in the same proportions and manner exactly as it had been entailed on them by his father. And accordingly he made such a settlement, subject however to a revocation.

Our author all this while applied himself to his business; and never waited upon his cousin, or employed any one to speak or act in his behalf (though many then blamed him for neglecting to do it); only one visit he made him in the November before his death, which was upon a Saturday in the afternoon. He gave him a sermon the next day, received his hearty thanks, and the next morning desired leave to return to the duties of his station; without speaking or even insinuating any thing respecting his estate. His cousin dismissed him with great kindness; and by his looks and manner seemed to have a particular regard for him, but discovered nothing of his intention by words. However, he used to employ persons privately to observe our author's behaviour (who little suspected any such matter), and his behaviour was found to be such, that the stricter the observations were upon it, the more they turned to his advantage. In fine, Mr. Wollaston, of Shenton, became so thoroughly satisfied of our author's merit, that he revoked the above-mentioned settlement, and made a will in his favour. In August following, that gentleman fell sick, and sending secretly to our author to come over to him, as of his own accord, without any notice of his illness, he complied with the message, and staid some days at Shenton. But while he was gone home, under a promise of returning, his cousin died, August 19, 1688.

By his relation's will, Mr. Wollaston found himself intitled to a very ample estate; but this change, sudden, and advantageous as it was to his affairs, wrought no change in his temper. The same firmness of mind, which had supported him under the pressure of a more adverse fortune, enabled him to bear his prosperity with moderation. In November following he came to London, and about a year after, on the 26th of that month, 1689, he married miss Catherine Charlton, daughter of Mr. Nicholas Charlton, an eminent citizen of London, a fine woman with a good fortune, and an excellent character. With this lady he settled in Charter-house square, in a private, retired, and studious life. His carriage was nevertheless free and open. He aimed at solid and real content, rather than show and grandeur, and manifested his dislike of power and dignity, by refusing one of the highest preferments in the church, when it was offered to him.

He had now books and leisure, and he was resolved to make use of them. He was perfectly acquainted with the elementary parts of learning, and with the learned languages, Latin, Greek, Hebrew, Arabic, &c. He thought it necessary to add to these such a degree of philology and criticism as seemed likely to be useful to him: and also mathematical sciences, or at least the fundamentals of them; the general philosophy of nature: the history and antiquities of the more known and noted states and kingdoms; and in order to attain the knowledge of true religion, and the discovery of truth, the points which he always had particularly in view, and to which he chiefly directed all his studies, he diligently inquired into the idolatries of the heathens; and made himself master of the sentiments, rites, and learning of the Jews; the history of the first settlement of Christianity, and the opinions and practice introduced into it since. In the mean time he exercised and improved his mind by using himself to clear images, observing the influence and extent of axioms, the nature and force of consequences, and the method of investigating truth. In general, he accustomed himself to much thinking as well as much reading. He likewise delighted in method and regularity: and chose to have his labours and refreshments periodical, and that his family and friends should observe the proper seasons of their revolution. He was most remarkably cheerful and lively in conversation, which rendered his company agreeable, and himself worthy to be courted by the learned and virtuous. But a general acquaintance was what he never cultivated, and it grew (as is mostly the case) more and more his aversion, so that he passed his days principally at home, with a few friends, with whom he could enjoy an agreeable relaxation of mind, and receive all the advantages of a sincere and open friendship.

Having thus fixed his resolution to deserve honours, but not to wear them, it was not long before he published a piece entitled, " The Design of Part of the Book of Ecclesiastes, or the Unreasonableness of Man's restless Contentions for the present Enjoyments, represented in an English poem," in 8vo. But as he had never made poetry his study, he was very sensible of the defects of this attempt, and was afterward very desirous to suppress it. This poem was printed in 1690. Notwithstanding he declined to accept of any public employment, yet his studies were designed to be of public use, and his solitude was far from being employed in vain and trifling amusements, terminating in himself alone. But neither in this last view, could his retirement be without some inconveniences. His intimates were dropping off, and their places remained unsupplied; his own infirmities were increasing; the frequent remission of study, growing more and more necessary; and his solitude at the same time becoming less and less agreeable, for want of that conversation which had hitherto supported it.

It was but a short time before his death that he published his celebrated treatise, entitled " The Religion of Nature delineated." He appears at first to have doubted the success of this work, and in 1722 printed only a few copies for the use of his friends, but when prevailed upon to publish it, it was so much approved that upwards of 10,000 copies were sold in a few years; and it has in all passed through eight or nine editions, five of which were in quarto.

Of the ingenuity of this work as a composition no doubts have been entertained, but its tendency was soon thought liable to suspicion. Some objected that he had injured Christianity by laying too much stress upon the obligations of truth, reason, and virtue; and by making no mention of revealed religion, nor even so much as dropping the least and most distant hints in its favour. This made him pass for an unbeliever with some; and the late lord Bolingbroke supposes Dr. Clarke to have had him in his eye when he described his fourth sort of theists. Wollaston held and has asserted the being and attributes of God, natural and moral; a providence, general and particular; the obligations to morality; the immateriality and immortality of the soul; a future state: and Clarke's fourth sort of theists held and asserted the same. But whether Wollaston, like those theists, rejected all above this in the system of revelation, cannot with any certainty be concluded, though at the same time the contrary perhaps may not appear; because, whatever might have been thought necessary to prevent offence from being taken, it was not essential to Wollaston's design to meddle with revealed religion. In the mean time, lord Bolingbroke has treated "The Religion of Nature delineated," as a system of theism; which it certainly is, whether Wollaston was a believer or not. His lordship calls it "strange theism, as dogmatical and absurd as artificial theology," and has spent several pages to prove it so; yet allows the author of it to have been "a man of parts, of learning, a philosopher, and a geometrician." The seventh edition of this work was printed in 1750 in 8vo, to which are added an account of the author, and also a translation of the notes into English. There is prefixed an advertisement by Dr. John Clarke, late dean of Salisbury, which informs us, that this work was in great esteem with her late majesty queen Caroline, who commanded him to translate the notes into English for her own use. Pope, who has taken some thoughts from it into his "Essay on Man," informs Mr. Bethel in one of his letters how much this work was a favourite with the ladies, but accompanies his information with a sueer at the sex, which we dare not transcribe.

Immediately after he had completed the revisal and publication of his "Religion of Nature delineated," Mr. Wollaston had the misfortune to break his arm; and as his health was before in a very infirm state, this accident accelerated his death, which happened Oct. 29, 1724. He was interred in Great Finborough church, Suffolk, in the same grave with his wife, who died in 1720.

He had begun several other works, but they being in an unfinished state, he had burnt, or ordered them to be burnt, some time before his death. The following, however, happened to be spared; but from the place in which they were deposited, and from some other circumstances, it is probable that they owed their escape to mere forgetfulness. They were in number thirteen (besides about fourscore sermons) viz. 1. "An Hebrew Grammar." 2. "Tyrocinia Arabica & Syriaca." 3. "Specimen Vocabularii Biblico-Hebraici, literis nostratibus, quantum fert Linguarum dissonantia, descripti." 4. "Formulæ quædam Gemarinæ." 5. "De variis generibus pedum, me-

trorum, carminum, &c. apud Judæos, Græcos, & Latinos."
6. "De Vocum Tonis Monitio ad Tyrones." 7. "Rudi-
menta ad Mathesin & Philosophiam spectantia." 8. "Miscellanea Philologica." 9. Opinions of the ancient Philosophers. 10. "Judaica: sive Religionis & Literaturæ Ju-
daicæ synopsis." 11. A collection of some antiquities and
particulars in the history of mankind; tending to shew,
that men have not been here upon this earth from eternity,
&c. 12. Some passages relating to the history of Christ,
collected out of the primitive fathers. 13. A treatise relating to the Jews, of their antiquities, language, &c.
What renders it the more probable, or indeed almost beyond doubt, that he would have destroyed these likewise,
if he had remembered them, is, that several of those which
remain undestroyed, are only rudiments or rougher sketches
of what he afterwards reconsidered and carried on much
farther; and which even after such revisal, he nevertheless committed to the flames, as being still (in his opinion)
short of that perfection, to which he desired and had intended to bring them, and accordingly none of them have
appeared.[1]

WOLSEY (THOMAS), a celebrated cardinal and statesman, but to be remembered with more respect as a benefactor to learning, was so obscure in his origin that scarcely
any historian mentions the names of his father and mother.
Their names, however, are preserved by Rymer (Fœd. vol.
XIV. p. 355), in the pope's bull of favours to those who
came to Cardinal college in Oxford, and prayed for the
safety of the said cardinal, and after his decease for the
souls of him, his father Robert, and his mother Joan. This
partly confirms the discovery of his zealous biographer, Dr.
Fiddes, that he was the son of one Robert Wolsey, a butcher of Ipswich, where he was born in March 1471. Fiddes
says that this Robert had a son whose early history corre-
sponds with that of the cardinal, and that he was a man of
considerable landed property. We may from other evidence conclude that his parents were either not poor, or
not friendless, since they were able to give him the best
education his native town afforded, and afterwards to send
him to Magdalen college. But in whatever way he was introduced here, it is certain that his progress in academical

[1] Life prefixed to the Religion of Nature, many particulars of which are taken from a narrative drawn up by himself, and printed for the first time in Mr. Ni-chols's "Illustrations of Literature," vol. I.—Biog. Brit.

studies was so rapid that he was admitted to the degree of bachelor of arts at the age of fifteen, and from this extraordinary instance of precocity, was usually named the *boy bachelor*.

No proofs are indeed wanting of his uncommon reputation as a scholar, for he was elected fellow of his college soon after taking his bachelor's degree, and proceeding to that of master, he was appointed teacher of Magdalen grammar school. In 1498, he was made bursar of the college, about which time he has the credit of building Magdalen tower. It is yet more in proof of his learning having been of the most liberal kind, and accompanied with a corresponding liberality of sentiment, that he became acquainted with Erasmus, then at Oxford, and joined that illustrious scholar in promoting classical studies, which were peculiarly obnoxious to the bigotry of the times. The letters which passed between Wolsey and Erasmus for some years imply mutual respect and union of sentiment on all matters in which literature was concerned; and their love of learning, and contempt for the monks, although this last was excited by different motives, are points in which we perceive no great disagreement. Yet as Erasmus continued to live the life of a mere scholar, precarious and dependent, and Wolsey was rapidly advancing to rank and honours, too many and too high for a subject, a distance was placed between them which Wolsey would not shorten, and Erasmus could not pass. Hence, while a courteous familiarity was preserved in Wolsey's correspondence, Erasmus could not help betraying the feelings of a client who has received little more than promises from his patron, and when Wolsey fell from his high state, Erasmus joined in the opinion that he was unworthy of it. For this he is severely censured by Fiddes, and ably defended by Knight and Jortin.

Wolsey's first ecclesiastical preferment was the rectory of Lymington in Somersetshire, conferred upon him in 1500, by the marquis of Dorset, to whose three sons he had acted as tutor, when in Magdalen college. On receiving this presentation he left the university, and resided for some time on his cure, when a singular circumstance induced, or perhaps rendered it absolutely necessary for him to leave it. At a merry meeting at Lymington he either passed the bounds of sobriety, or was otherwise accessary in promoting a riot, for which sir Amyas Paulet, a justice of peace, set him in the stocks. This indignity Wolsey remembered when it would have been honourable as well as prudent to have forgot it. After he had arrived at the high rank of chancellor, he ordered sir Amyas to be confined within the bounds of the Temple, and kept him in that place for five or six years.

On his quitting Lymington, though without resigning the living, Henry Dean, archbishop of Canterbury, made him one of his domestic chaplains, and in 1503, the pope, Alexander, gave him a dispensation to hold two benefices. On the death of the archbishop, in the same year, he was appointed chaplain to sir John Nanfan of Worcestershire, treasurer of Calais, which was then in the possession of the English, and by him recommended to Henry VII. who made him one of his chaplains. About the end of 1504, he obtained from pope Julius II. a dispensation to hold a third living, the rectory of Redgrave in Norfolk. In the mean time he was improving his interest at court by an affable and plausible address, and by a display of political talent, and quick and judicious dispatch in business, which rendered him very useful and acceptable to his sovereign. In February 1508, the king gave him the deanery of Lincoln, and two prebends in the same church, and would probably have added to these preferments had he not been prevented by his death in the following year.

This event, important as it was to the kingdom, was of no disadvantage to Wolsey, who saw in the young king, Henry VIII. a disposition that might be rendered more favourable to his lofty views; yet what his talents might have afterwards procured, he owed at this time to a court intrigue. Fox, bishop of Winchester and founder of Corpus Christi college, introduced him to Henry, in order to counteract the influence of the earl of Surrey (afterwards duke of Norfolk), and had probably no worse intention than to preserve a balance in the council; but Wolsey, who was not destined to play a subordinate part, soon rose higher in influence than either his patron or his opponent. He studied, with perfect knowledge of the human heart, to please the young king, by joining in indulgencies which, however suitable to the gaiety of a court, were ill becoming the character of an ecclesiastic. Yet amidst the luxuries which he promoted in his royal master, he did not neglect to inculcate maxims of state, and, above all, to insinuate, in a manner that appeared equally dutiful and disinterested, the advantages of a system of favouritism, which he secretly hoped would one day center in his own person. Nor was he disappointed, as for some time after this, his history, apart from what share he had in the public councils, is little more than a list of promotions following each other with a rapidity that alarmed the courtiers, and inclined the people, always jealous of sudden elevations, to look back on his origin.

In this rise, he was successively made almoner to the king, a privy counsellor, and reporter of the proceedings of the Star-chamber; rector of Turrington in the diocese of Exeter, canon of Windsor, registrar of the order of the garter, and prebendary and dean of York. From these he passed on to become dean of Hereford, and precentor of St. Paul's, both of which he resigned on being preferred to the bishopric of Lincoln; chancellor of the order of the garter, and bishop of Tournay in Flanders, which he held until 1518, when that city was delivered up to the French, but he derived from it afterwards an annual pension of twelve thousand livres*. In 1514, he was consecrated bishop of Lincoln, in the room of Smyth, founder of Brasen-nose college, and was chosen chancellor of the university of Cambridge. The same year he was promoted to the archbishopric of York, and created cardinal of St. Cecilia.

Yet in the plenitude of that political influence which he now maintained to the exclusion of the ancient nobility and courtiers, it appears that for some time he preserved the peace of the country, by a strict administration of justice, and by a punctuality in matters of finance, which admitted no very unfavourable comparisons between him and his predecessors. Perhaps the splendour and festivities which he encouraged in the court might, by a diffusion of the royal wealth among the public, contribute to a certain degree of popularity, especially when contrasted with the more economical habits encouraged by Henry VII. It was not until he established his legantine court, a species of English popedom, that the people had reason to complain of a vast and rapacious power, unknown to the constitution, boundless in its capricious decrees, and against which there was no redress. This court, however, could not have in-

* Dr. Fiddes allows that this piece of preferment partook of usurpation, as the former bishop of Tournay had been neither legally nor ecclesiastically deprived.

flicted many public injuries, as it formed no part of the complaints of parliament against him, when complaints might have been preferred with safety, and would have been welcomed from any quarter. At that time, the legality of the power was called in question, but not the exercise of it.

In the private conduct of this extraordinary man, while in the height of his prosperity, we find a singular mixture of personal pride and public munificence. While his train of servants rivalled that of the king, and was composed of many persons of rank and distinction, his house was a school where their sons were usefully educated, and initiated in public life. And while he was dazzling the eyes, or insulting the feelings of the people by an ostentation of gorgeous furniture and equipage, such as exceeded the royal establishment itself, he was a general and liberal patron of literature, a man of consummate taste in works of art, elegant in his plans, and boundless in his expences to execute them ; and, in the midst of luxurious pleasures and pompous revellings, he was meditating the advancement of science by a munificent use of those riches which he seemed to accumulate only for selfish purposes.

In the mean time, there was no intermission in his preferments. His influence was courted by the pope, who had made him a cardinal, and, in 1516, his legate in England, with powers not inferior to his own ; and by the king of Spain, who granted him a pension of three thousand livres, while the duchy of Milan bestowed on him a yearly grant of ten thousand ducats. On the resignation of archbishop Warham, he was appointed lord high chancellor. " If this new accumulation of dignity," says Hume, " increased his enemies, it also served to exalt his personal character, and prove the extent of his capacity. A strict administration of justice took place during his enjoyment of this high office ; and no chancellor ever discovered greater impartiality in his decisions, deeper penetration of judgment, or more enlarged knowledge of law or equity."

In 1518, he attended queen Catherine to Oxford, and intimated to the university his intention of founding lectures on theology, civil law, physic, philosophy, mathematics, rhetoric, Greek, and Latin ; and in the following year three of these, viz. for Greek, Latin, and rhetoric, were founded and endowed with ample salaries, and read in the hall of Corpus Christi college. He appointed for his lectures the ablest scholars whom the university afforded, or whom he could invite from the continent. The members of the convocation, about this time, conferred upon him the highest mark of their esteem by a solemn decree that he should have the revisal and correction of the university statutes in the most extensive sense, and it does not appear that they had any reason to repent of this extraordinary instance of their confidence. The same power was conferred upon him by the university of Cambridge, and in both cases, was accompanied by documents which proved the very high opinion entertained by these learned bodies of his fitness to reform what was amiss in the republic of letters.

In the same year the pope granted him the administration of the bishopric of Bath and Wells, and the king bestowed on him its temporalities. This see, with those of Worcester and Hereford, which the cardinal likewise farmed, were filled by foreigners who were allowed non-residence, and compounded for this indulgence by yielding a share of the revenues. The cardinal's aid, about this time, in establishing the College of Physicians of London, is to be recorded among the many instances of the very liberal views he entertained of every improvement connected with literature. In 1521, he evinced his zeal against the reformation which Luther had begun, by procuring his doctrines to be condemned in an assembly of divines held at his own house, published pope Leo's bull against him, and endeavoured to suppress his writings in this kingdom; but there is no favourable part of his character so fully established as his moderation towards the English Lutherans, for one article of his impeachment was his being remiss in punishing heretics, and showing a disposition rather to screen them.

In the same year he received the rich abbey of St. Alban's to hold in commendam, and soon after went abroad on an embassy. About this time also, he became a candidate for the papal chair, on the demise of Leo X. but was not successful. This disappointment, however, was compensated in some degree by the emperor, who settled a pension on him of nine thousand crowns of gold, and by the bishopric of Durham, to which he was appointed in 1523. On this he resigned the administration of Bath and Wells. The same year he issued a mandate to remove the convocation of the province of Canterbury from St.

Paul's to Westminster, one of his most unpopular acts, but which appears to have been speedily reversed. On the death of pope Adrian he made a second unsuccessful attempt to be elected pope; but while he failed in this, he received from his rival a confirmation of the whole papal authority in England.

In 1524, he intimated to the university of Oxford his design of founding a college there, and soon commenced that great work. About two years after he founded his school *, or college, as it has been sometimes called, at Ipswich, as a nursery for his intended college at Oxford, and this for a short time is said to have rivalled the schools of Winchester and Eton. As he mixed ecclesiastical dignity with all his learned institutions, he appointed here a dean, twelve canons, and a numerous choir. At the same time he sent a circular address to the schoolmasters of England, recommending them to teach their youth the elements of elegant literature, *literatura elegantissima,* and prescribed the use of Lily's grammar.

Of the immense riches which he derived from his various preferments, some were no doubt spent in luxuries which left only a sorrowful remembrance, but the greater part was employed in those magnificent edifices which have immortalized his genius and spirit. In 1514 he began to build the palace at Hampton Court, and having finished it, with all its sumptuous furniture, in 1528, he presented it to the king, who in return gave him the palace of Richmond for a residence. In this last mentioned year, he acceded to the bishopric of Winchester by the death of Fox, and resigned that of Durham. To Winchester, however, he never went. That reverse of fortune which has exhibited him as an example of terror to the ambitious, was now approaching, and was accelerated by events, the consequences of which he foresaw, without the power of averting them. Henry was now agitated by a passion not to be controuled by the whispers of friendship, or the counsels of statesmen, and when the cardinal, whom he had appointed to forward his divorce from queen Catherine and his marriage with Anne Boleyn, appeared tardily to adhere to forms, or scrupulously to interpose ad-

* On the site of the priory of St. Peter's, which was surrendered to the cardinal, March 6, 1527. Dr. William Capon was first and last dean, for this school was discontinued on the cardinal's fall. The foundation stone is now preserved in Christ Church.

vice, he determined to make him feel the weight of his resentment. It happened unfortunately for the cardinal that both the queen and her rival were his enemies, the queen from a suspicion that she never had a cordial friend in him, and Anne from a knowledge that he had secretly endeavoured to prevent her match with the king. But a minute detail of these transactions and intrigues belongs to history, in which they occupy a large space. It may suffice here to notice that the cardinal's ruin, when once determined, was effected in the most sudden and rigorous manner, and probably without his previous knowledge of the violent measures that were to be taken.

On the first day of term, Oct. 9, 1529, while he was opening the Court of Chancery at Westminster, the attorney-general indicted him in the Court of King's Bench, on the statute of provisors, 16 Richard II. for procuring a bull from Rome appointing him legate, contrary to the statute, by which he had incurred a *præmunire*, and forfeited all his goods to the king, and might be imprisoned. Before he could give in any reply to this indictment, the king sent to demand the great seal from him, which was given to sir Thomas More. He was then ordered to leave York-place, a palace which had for some centuries been the residence of the archbishops of York, and which he had adorned with furniture of great value and magnificence: it now became a royal residence under the name of Whitehall. Before leaving this place to go to Esher, near Hampton Court, a seat belonging to the bishopric of Winchester, he made an inventory of the furniture, plate, &c. of York-place, which is said to have amounted to the incredible sum of five hundred thousand crowns, or pounds of our money. He then went to Putney by water, and set out on the rest of his journey on his mule, but he had not gone far before he was met by a messenger from the king, with a gracious message, assuring him that he stood as high as ever in the royal favour, and this accompanied by a ring, which the king had been accustomed to send, as a token to give credit to the bearer. Wolsey received these testimonials with the humblest expression of gratitude, but proceeded on his way to Esher, which he found quite unfurnished. The king's design by this solemn mockery is not easily conjectured. It is most probable that it was a trick to inspire the cardinal with hopes of being restored to favour, and consequently to prevent his defending himself in the prosecution upon the statute of provisors, which Henry knew he could do by producing his letters patent authorising him to accept the pope's bulls. And this certainly was the consequence, for the Cardinal merely instructed his attorney to protest in his name that he was quite ignorant of the above statute; but that he acknowledged other particulars with which he was charged to be true, and submitted himself to the king's mercy. The sentence of the court was, that "he was out of the protection, and his lands, goods, and chattels forfeit, and his person might be seized."

The next step to complete his ruin was taken by the duke of Norfolk and the privy counsellors, who drew up articles against him, and presented them to the king; but he still affecting to take no personal concern in the matter, remained silent. Yet these probably formed the basis of the forty-four articles presented December 1, to the House of Lords, as by some asserted, or, according to other accounts, by the lords of the council to the House of Commons. Many of them are evidently frivolous or false, and others, although true, were not within the jurisdiction of the House. The cardinal had, in fact, already suffered, as his goods had been seized by the king; he was now in a *præmunire*, and the House could not go much farther than to recommend what had already taken place. The cardinal, however, found one friend amidst all his distresses, who was not to be alarmed either at the terrors of the court or of the people. This was Thomas Cromwell, formerly Wolsey's steward (afterwards earl of Essex), who now refuted the articles with so much spirit, eloquence, and argument, that although a very opposite effect might have been expected, his speech is supposed to have laid the foundation of that favour which the king afterwards extended to him, but which, at no very distant period, proved as fatal to him as it had been to his master. His eloquence had a yet more powerful effect, for the address founded on these articles was rejected by the Commons, and the Lords could not proceed farther without their concurrence.

During the cardinal's residence at Esher the king sent several messages to him, "some good and some bad," says Cavendish, "but more ill than good," until this tantalizing correspondence, operating on a mind of strong passions, brought on, about the end of the year, a sickness which was represented to the king as being apparently fatal. The king ordered his physician, Dr. Butts, to visit him, who confirmed what had been reported of the dangerous state of his health, but intimated that as his disease affected his mind rather than his body, a kind word from his majesty might prove more effectual than the best skill of the faculty. On this the king sent him a ring, with a gracious message that he was not offended with him in his heart; and Anne Boleyn sent him a tablet of gold that usually hung at her side, with many kind expressions. The cardinal received these testimonies of returning favour with joy and gratitude, and in a few days was pronounced out of danger.

Nor can we blame Wolsey for his credulity, since Henry, although he had stripped the cardinal of all his property, and the income arising from all his preferments, actually granted him, Feb. 12, 1530, a free pardon for all crimes and misdemeanors, and a few days after restored to him the revenues, &c. of the archbishopric of York, except York place, before-mentioned, and one thousand marks yearly from the bishopric of Winchester. He also sent him a present of 3000l. in money, and a quantity of plate and furniture exceeding that sum, and allowed him to remove from Esher to Richmond, where he resided for some time in the lodge in the old park, and afterwards in the priory. His enemies at court, however, who appear to have influenced the king beyond his usual arbitrary disposition, dreaded Wolsey's being so near his majesty, and prevailed on him to order him to reside in his archbishopric. In obedience to this mandate, which was softened by another gracious message from Henry, he first went to the archbishop's seat at Southwell, and about the end of September fixed his residence at Cawood castle, which he began to repair, and was acquiring popularity by his hospitable manners and bounty, when his capricious master was persuaded to arrest him for high treason, and order him to be conducted to London. Accordingly, on the first of November he set out, but on the road he was seized with a disorder of the dysenteric kind, brought on by fatigue and anxiety, which put a period to his life at Leicester abbey on the 28th of that month, in the fifty-ninth year of his age *. Some of his last words implied the awful and

---

* The cardinal had a bastard son called Thomas Winter. " Bulla Julii Pont. Rom. dilecti filio Thomæ Wulcy Rectori paroch. Eccl'iæ de Lymyngton

256 WOLSEY.

just reflection, that if he had served his God as diligently
as he had served his king, he would not have given him
over to his enemies. Two days after he was interred in
the abbey church of Leicester, but the spot is not now
known. As to the report of his having poisoned himself,
founded on an expression in the printed work of Cavendish,
it has been amply refuted by a late eminent antiquary, who
examined the whole of the evidence with much acuteness*.

Modern historians have formed a more favourable estimate of Wolsey's character than their predecessors, yet it
had that mixture of good and evil which admits of great
variety of opinion, and gives to ingenious party-colouring
all the appearance of truth. Perhaps Shakspeare, borrow-
ing from Holinshed and Hall, has drawn a more just and
comprehensive sketch of his perfections and failings than is
to be found in any other writer.

—— " This cardinal,
Though from an humble stock, undoubtedly
Was fashioned to much honour. From his cradle
He was a scholar, and a ripe and good one ;
Exceeding wise, fair spoken, and persuading ;
Lofty and sour to them that lov'd him not ;
But, to those men that sought him, sweet as summer.
And though he was unsatisfy'd in getting,
(Which was a sin) yet in bestowing, madam,
He was most princely : Ever witness for him
Those twins of learning that he raised in you,
Ipswich and Oxford ! one of which fell with him,
Unwilling to outlive the good that did it ;
The other, though unfinish'd, yet so famous,
So excellent in art, and still so rising,
That Christendom shall ever speak his virtue.
His overthrow heap'd happiness upon him :
For then, and not till then, he felt himself,
And found the blessedness of being little :
And, to add greater honours to his age
Than man could give him, he died, fearing God †."

The cardinal's biographers, in treating of the foundation of his college, begin with a very laboured defence of
his seizing the property and revenues of many priories and
nunneries, which were to serve as a fund for building and

Batho. Well. dioc. Magistrum in Ar
tibus pro Dispensatione ad tertium in-
compatibile. dat. Romæ. 1508. prid.
cal. Augusti Pont. n'ri anno quinto."
—Kennet's MSS. in Brit. Mus. obligingly communicated by Mr. Ellis.

* The learned Dr. Samuel Pegge.
See Gent. Mag. vol. XXV. p. 25, and
two very able articles on the cardinal's
impeachment, p. 299, 345.
† The speech of the " honest chronicler, Griffith," to queen Katherine.
Henry VIII. Act IV. Scene II.

endowment; and the zeal they display on this subject, if it cannot now enforce conviction, at least proves the historical fact that the rights of property even at that time were not to be violated with impunity, and that the cardinal's conduct was highly unpopular. At first it was objected to even by the king himself, although he soon afterwards converted it into a precedent for a more general dissolution of religious houses. Wolsey, however, ought not to be deprived of such defence as has been set up. It has been urged, that he procured bulls from the pope empowering him to seize on these priories; and that the pope, according to the notions then entertained of his supremacy, could grant a power by which religious houses might be converted into societies for secular priests, and for the advancement of learning. It has been also pleaded, that the cardinal did not alienate the revenues from religious service, but only made a change in the application of them; that the appropriation of the alien priories by Chichele and Waynflete was in some respects a precedent, and that the suppression of the Templers in the fourteenth century, might also be quoted. Bishop Tanner likewise, in one of his letters to Dr. Charlett, quotes as precedents, bishops Fisher, Alcock, and Beckington. But perhaps the best excuse is that hinted by lord Cherbury, namely, that Wolsey persuaded the king to abolish unnecessary monasteries that necessary colleges might be erected, and the progress of the reformation impeded by the learning of the clergy and scholars educated in them. The same writer suggests, that as Wolsey pleaded for the dissolution of only the small and superfluous houses, the king might not dislike this as a fair experiment how far the project of a general dissolution would be relished. On the other hand, by two letters still extant, written by the king, it appears that he was fully aware of the unpopularity of the measure, although we cannot infer from them that he had any remedy to prescribe.

Whatever weight these apologies had with one part of the public, we are assured that they had very little with another, and that the progress of the college was accompanied by frequent expressions of popular dislike in the shape of lampoons. The kitchen having been first finished, one of the satirists of the day exclaimed, *Egregium opus ! Cardinalis iste instituit Collegium et absolvit popinam.* Other

mock inscriptions were placed on the walls, one of which
at least, proved prophetic :

> " Non stabit illa domus, aliis fundata rapinis,
>      Aut ruet, aut alter raptor habebit eam."

By two bulls, the one dated 1524, the other 1525, Wol-
soy obtained of pope Clement VII. leave to enrich his college by suppressing twenty-two priories and nunneries, the
revenues of which were estimated at nearly 2000*l.*; but on
his disgrace some of these were given by the king for other
purposes. The king's patent, after a preface paying high
compliments to the cardinal's administration, enables him
to build his college principally on the site of the priory of
St. Frideswide; and the name, originally intended to be
" The College of Secular Priests," was now changed to
CARDINAL COLLEGE. The secular clergy in it were to be
denominated the " dean and canons secular of the cardinal
of York," and to be incorporated into one body, and subsist by perpetual succession. He was also authorised to
settle upon it 2000*l.* a year clear revenue. By other patents and grants to the dean and canons, various church
livings were bestowed upon them, and the college was to
be dedicated to the praise, glory, and honour of the Holy
Trinity, the Virgin Mary, St. Frideswide, and All Saints.

With respect to the constitution of this college, there is
a considerable variation between the account given by the
historian of Oxford, and that by Leonard Hutten, canon
of Christ Church, in 1599, and many years sub-dean. His
manuscript, now in the possession of the college, and quoted
in the Monasticon, states that, according to Wolsey's design, it was to be a perpetual foundation for the study of
the sciences, divinity, canon and civil law, also the arts,
physic, and polite literature, and for the continual performance of divine service. The members were to be, a
dean, and sixty regular canons, but no canons of the second order, as Wood asserts.

Of these Wolsey himself named the dean and eighteen
of the canons. The dean was Dr. John Hygden, president of Magdalen college, and the canons first nominated were all taken from the other colleges in Oxford,
and were men of acknowledged reputation in their day.
He afterwards added others, deliberately, and according
as he was able to supply the vacancies by men of talents,
whom he determined to seek wherever they could be found.
Among his latter appointments from Cambridge, we find

the names of Tyndal and Frith, the translators of the Bible, and who had certainly discovered some symptoms of *heresy* before this time. Cranmer and Parker, afterwards the first and second protestant archbishops of Canterbury, were also invited, but declined; and the cardinal went on to complete his number, reserving all nominations to himself during his life, but intending to bequeath that power to the dean and canons at his death. In this, however, he was as much disappointed as in his hopes to embody a force of learned men sufficient to cope with Luther and the foreign reformers, whose advantage in argument he conceived to proceed from the ignorance which prevailed among the monastic clergy.

The society, as he planned it, was to consist of one hundred and sixty persons, according to Wood, or omitting the forty canons of the second order, in the enumeration of whom Wood was mistaken, one hundred and forty-six; but no mention could yet be made of the scholars who were to proceed from his school at Ipswich, although, had he lived, these would doubtless have formed a part of the society, as the school was established two years before his fall. This constitution continued from 1525 to 1529-30, when he was deprived of his power and property, and for two years after it appears to have been interrupted, if not dissolved. It is to his honour that in his last correspondence with secretary Cromwell and with the king, when all worldly prospects were about to close upon him, he pleaded with great earnestness, and for nothing so earnestly, as that his majesty would be pleased to suffer his college at Oxford to go on. What effect this had, we know not, but the urgent entreaties of the members of the society, and of the university at large, were at length successful, while at the same time the king determined to deprive Wolsey of all merit in the establishment, and transfer the whole to himself. The subsequent history of Christ church it would be unnecessary to detail in this place.

An impartial life of cardinal Wolsey is perhaps still a desideratum in English biography*. Cavendish is minute and interesting in what he relates of the cardinal's domestic history, but defective in dates and arrangement, and not altogether free from partiality; which, however, in one so

---

* A Life of Wolsey has indeed been recently published by Mr. Galt, which the editor has not yet had an opportunity of perusing.

near to the cardinal, may perhaps be pardoned. Fiddes is elaborate, argumentative, and upon the whole useful, as an extensive collector of facts and authorities; but he wrote for a special purpose, and has attempted, what no man can effect, a portrait of his hero free from those vices and failings of which it is impossible to acquit him. Grove, with all the aid of Cavendish, Fiddes, and even Shakspeare, whose drama he regularly presses into the service, is a heavy and injudicious compiler, although he gives so much of the cardinal's contemporaries, that his volumes may be consulted with advantage as a series of general annals of the time. But Cavendish, on whom all who have written on the actions of Wolsey, especially our modern historians, have relied, has been the innocent cause of some of their principal errors. Cavendish's work remained in manuscript, of which several copies are still extant, until the civil wars, when it was first printed under the title of "The Negociations of Thomas Wolsey, &c." 1641, 4to, and the chief object of the publication was a parallel between the cardinal and archbishop Laud, in order to reconcile the public to the murder of that prelate. That this object might be the better accomplished, the manuscript was mutilated and interpolated without shame or scruple, and no pains having been taken to compare the printed edition with the original, the former passed for genuine above a century, nor until very lately has the work been presented to the public as the author left it, in Dr. Wordsworth's " Ecclesiastical Biography.[1]

WOMOCK (LAWRENCE), an English prelate, was a native of Norfolk, born in 1612, and the son of Lawrence Womock, B. D. rector of Lopham and Fersfield in that county. He was admitted pensioner of Corpus Christi, Cambridge, July 4, 1629, and in October following was chosen a scholar of sir Nich. Bacon's foundation. He took the degree of A. B. in 1632, was ordained deacon Sept. 21, 1634, and proceeded A. M. in 1639. He is supposed to have succeeded his father in the living of Lopham upon his diocese in 1642, but was ejected by the Norfolk committee for the examination of those who were deemed scandalous ministers, and appears to have been afterwards imprisoned for his principles of religion and loyalty, and to have suffered extreme hardships. After the restoration,

[1] Fiddes's and Grove's Lives.—Chalmers's Hist. of Oxford.

however, he was promoted by letters mandate to the degree of D. D. and made both archdeacon of Suffolk, Sept. 8, 1660, and a prebendary of Ely. In 1662 he was presented to the rectory of Horningsheath in Suffolk, and in 1663 to that of Boxford in the same county. He was at length promoted, but late in life, to the bishopric of St. David's, Nov. 11, 1683, a preferment which, owing to his short continuance in it, was detrimental to his relations. He died March 12, 1685, aged seventy-three, and was buried near the remains of his only daughter in the south aile of the church of St. Margaret, Westminster, where, on a small compartment affixed to the pillar next the west end, is an inscription to his memory.

He is said to have been a man of wit and learning, and possessed of a very noble library. He was attached with much firmness to the constitution in church and state, and rejected all compromise with the principles of the dissenters. He took an active part in the controversies of the times, and was esteemed an antagonist worth contending with. His chief publications, besides some single sermons, were, " Beaten Oyle for the lamps of the Sanctuarie," Lond. 1641, 4to, in defence of the liturgy. " The Examination of Tilenus before the Triers," London, 1658, 8vo. " Arcana Dogmatum Anti-Remonstrantium," 1659, against Baxter, Hickman, and the Calvinists. " The Result of False Principles," in several dialogues, published anonymously, 1661, 4to. " Uniformity re-asserted," 1661. "The Solemn League and Covenant arraigned and condemned," Lond. 1661, 4to. " An Antidote to cure the Calamities * of their trembling for fear of the Arke," Lond. 1663, 4to. "The Verdict upon the Dissenters' plot," 1681, 8vo. "Two Letters containing a farther justification of the Church of England," Lond. 1682. " Suffragium Protestantium, wherein our governors are justified in their impositions and proceedings against dissenters. Meisner also, and the verdict rescued from the cavils and seditious sophistry of Dr. Whitby's Protestant Reconciler," Lond. 1683, 8vo.[1]

WOOD (ANTHONY), an eminent English antiquary and biographer, was the son of Thomas Wood, bachelor of arts and of the civil law ; and was born at Oxford, December 17, 1632. He was sent to New-college school in that city

---

* Rather Calamites, or followers of Mr. Calamy.

[1] Masters's C.C.C.C.

in 1641; and three years after removed to the free-school
at Thame in Oxfordshire, where he continued till his admission at Merton, 1647.　His mother in vain endeavoured
to prevail on him to follow some trade or profession; his
prevailing turn was to antiquity: "heraldry, music, and
painting, he says, did so much crowd upon him, that he
could not avoid them; and he could never give a reason
why he should delight in those studies more than others;
so prevalent was nature, mixed with a generosity of mind,
and a hatred to all that was servile, sneaking, or advantageous, for lucre-sake."　He took the degree of B. A.
1652, and M. A. in 1655.　As he resided altogether at Oxford, he perused all the evidences of the several colleges
and churches, from which he compiled his two great works,
and assisted all who were engaged in the like designs; at
the same time digesting and arranging all the papers he
perused; thus doing the cause of antiquity a double service.　His drawings preserved many things which soon
after were destroyed.　In 1665, he began to lay the foundation of " Historia & Antiquitates Universitatis Oxoniensis;" which was published in 1674, in 2 vols. folio.　The
first contains the antiquities of the university in general,
and the second those of the particular colleges.　This work
was written by the author in English, and so well esteemed
that the university procured it to be translated into Latin,
the language in which it was published.　The author spent
eight years about it, and was, as we are told, at the pains
to extract it from the bowels of antiquity.　Of the Latin
translation, Wood himself has given an account.　He tells
us, that Dr. Fell, having provided one Peers, a bachelor of
arts of Christ-church, to translate it, sent to him for some
of the English copy, and set the translator to work; who,
however, was some time before he could make a version to
his mind.　" But at length having obtained the knack,"
says Wood, "he went forward with the work; yet all the
proofs, that came from the press, went through the doctor's hands, which he would correct, alter, or dash out, or
put in what he pleased; which created a great deal of
trouble to the composer and author, but there was no help.
He was a great man, and carried all things at his pleasure
so much, that many looked upon the copy as spoiled and
vitiated by him.　Peers was a sullen, dogged, clownish, and
perverse, fellow; and when he saw the author concerned
at the altering of his copy, he would alter it the more, and

study to put things in that might vex him, and yet please
his dean, Dr. Fell." And he afterwards complains, how
"Dr. Fell, who printed the book at his own charge, took
so much liberty of putting in and out what he pleased, that
the author was so far from dedicating or presenting the
book to any one, that he would scarcely own it." Among
the "Genuine Remains of Barlow, bishop of Lincoln, published by sir Peter Pett in 1693," 8vo, are two letters of
that prelate, relating to this work. In the first letter we
have the following passage: "What you say of our late
antiquities is too true. We are alarmed by many letters,
not only of false Latin, but false English too, and many bad
characters cast on good men; especially on the Anti-Armi-
nians, who are all made seditious persons, schismatics, if
not heretics: nay, our first reformers are made fanatics.
This they tell me; and our judges of assize, now in town,
say no less. I have not read one leaf of the book yet; but
I see I shall be necessitated to read it over, that I may
with my own eyes see the faults, and (so far as I am able)
endeavour the mending of them. Nor do I know any
other way but a new edition, with a real correction of all
faults; and a declaration, that those miscarriages cannot
justly be imputed to the university, as indeed they cannot,
but to the passion and imprudence, if not impiety, of one
or two, who betrayed the trust reposed in them in the ma-
naging the edition of that book." In the second letter,
after taking notice that the translation was made by the
order and authority of the dean of Christ-church; that not
only the Latin, but the history itself, is in many things
ridiculously false; and then producing passages as proofs
of both; he concludes thus: "Mr. Wood, the compiler of
those antiquities, was himself too favourable to papists;
and has often complained to me, that at Christ-church
some things were put in which neither were in his original
copy, nor approved by him. The truth is, not only the
Latin, but also the matter of those antiquities, being erroneous in several things, may prove scandalous, and give
our adversaries some occasion to censure, not only the university, but the church of England and our reformation.
Sure I am, that the university had no hand in composing
or approving those antiquities; and therefore the errors
which are in them cannot *de jure* be imputed to the university, but must lie upon Christ-church and the composer
of them." This work, however, is now in a great measure

rescued from misapprehension by the publication of Wood's MS. in English by the rev. John Gutch, 3 vols. 4to.

Mr. Wood afterwards undertook his more important work, which was published in 1691, folio; and a second edition in 1721, folio, with this title: "Athenæ Oxonienses. An exact history of all the writers and bishops who have had their education in the most ancient and famous university of Oxford, from the fifteenth year of king Henry the seventh, A. D. 1500, to the author's death in November, 1695; representing the birth, fortune, preferment, and death of all those authors and prelates, the great accidents of their lives, and the fate and character of their writings. To which are added, the Fasti, or annals of the said university. In two volumes. The second edition, very much corrected and enlarged; with the addition of above·500 new lives from the author's original manuscript." Impartiality and veracity being qualities so essential in an historian, that all other qualities without them cannot make a history good for any thing, Wood has taken some pains to prove, that these great qualities were not wanting in him; and for that purpose thought it expedient to prefix to his work the following curious account of himself. "As to the author himself," says he, "he is a person who delights to converse more with the dead than with the living, and has neither interest with, nor inclination to flatter or disgrace, any man, or any community of men, of whatever denomination. He is such a universal lover of all mankind, that he could wish there was such a standing measure of merit and honour agreed upon among them all, that there might be no cheat put upon readers and writers in the business of commendations. But, since every one will have a double balance herein, one for himself and his own party, and another for his adversary and dissenters, all he can do is, to amass and bring together what every side thinks will make best weight for themselves. Let posterity hold the scales and judge accordingly; *suum cuique decus posteritas rependat.* To conclude: the reader is desired to know, that this Herculean labour had been more proper for a head or fellow of a college, or for a public professor or officer of the most noble university of Oxford to have undertaken and consummated, than the author, who never enjoyed any place or office therein, or can justly say that he hath eaten the bread of any founder. Also, that it had been a great deal more fit for one who pretends to be a virtuoso, and to

know all men, and all things that are transacted; or for one
who frequents much society in common rooms, at public
fires, in coffee-houses, assignations, clubs, &c. where the
characters of men and their works are frequently discussed;
but the author, alas! is so far from frequenting such company and topics, that he is as it were dead to the world,
and utterly unknown in person to the generality of scholars
in Oxon. He is likewise so great an admirer of a solitary
and retired life, that he frequents no assemblies of the said
university, hath no companion in bed or at board, in his
studies, walks, or journeys; nor holds communication with
any, unless with some, and those very few, of generous and
noble spirits, that have in some measure been promoters
and encouragers of this work: and, indeed, all things considered, he is but a degree different from an ascetic, as
spending all or most of his time, whether by day or night,
in reading, writing, and divine contemplation. However,
he presumes, that, the less his company and acquaintance
is, the more impartial his endeavours will appear to the
ingenious and learned, to whose judgments only he sub-
mits them and himself."

But, as unconnected as Wood represents himself with
all human things and persons, it is certain that he had his
prejudices and attachments, and strong ones too, for certain notions and systems; and these prejudices and attachments will always be attended with partialities for or
against those who shall be found to favour or oppose such
notions or systems. They had their influence upon Wood,
who, though he always spoke to the best of his judgment,
and often with great truth and exactness, yet sometimes
gave way to prejudice and prepossession. Among other
freedoms, he took some with the earl of Clarendon, their
late chancellor, which exposed him to the censure of the
university. He had observed in the life of judge Glynne,
that " after the restoration of Charles II. he was made his
eldest serjeant at law, by the corrupt dealing of the then
chancellor," who was the earl of Clarendon: for which
expression, chiefly, the succeeding earl preferred an action in the vice-chancellor's court against him for de-
famation of his deceased father. The issue of the process
was a hard judgement given against the defendant; which,
to be made the more public, was put into the Gazette in
these words: " Oxford, July 31, 1693. On the 29th instant, Anthony Wood was condemned in the vice-chancel-

lor's court of the university of Oxford, for having written and published, in the second volume of his book, entitled 'Athenæ Oxonienses,' divers infamous libels against the right honourable Edward late earl of Clarendon, lord high chancellor of England, and chancellor of the said university; and was therefore banished the said university, until such time as he shall subscribe such a public recantation as the judge of the court shall approve of, and give security not to offend in the like nature for the future: and his said book was therefore also decreed to be burnt before the public theatre; and on this day it was burnt accordingly, and public programmas of his expulsion are already affixed in the three usual places." An historian who has recorded this censure says, that it was the more grievous to the blunt author, because it seemed to come from a party of men whom he had the least disobliged. His bitterness had been against the Dissenters; but of all the zealous Churchmen he had given characters with a singular turn of esteem and affection. Nay, of the Jacobites, and even of Papists themselves, he had always spoken the most favourable things; and therefore it was really the greater mortification to him, to feel the storm coming from a quarter where he thought he least deserved, and might least expect it. For the same reason, adds the historian, this correction was some pleasure to the Presbyterians, who believed there was a rebuke due to him, which they themselves were not able to pay. Wood was animadverted upon likewise by Burnet, in his " Letter to the bishop of Litchfield and Coventry, concerning a book of Anthony Harmer (alias Henry Wharton, called 'A Specimen of some Errors and Defects in the History of the Reformation,' &c." upon which, in 1693, he published a vindication of himself, which is reprinted before the second edition of his " Athenæ Oxonienses."

As a collector Mr. Wood deserves highly of posterity; indeed we know not any man to whom English biography is so much indebted, although we may allow, at the same time, that he is deficient in judgment and style. His errors, in other respects, have been corrected, and many valuable additions made, from genuine authorities, in the new edition (of which two volumes, quarto, have already been published), by Philip Bliss, Fellow of St. John's-college.

Mr. Wood died at Oxford Nov. 29, 1695, of a retention of urine, under which he lingered above a fortnight. The circumstances of his death are recorded in a letter of Dr. Arthur Charlett, rector of University-college, to archbishop Tenison : this letter, which was published by Hearne, in the appendix to his edition of "Johannis Confratris et Monachi Glastoniensis Chronica," Oxon. 1726, illustrates the character of this extraordinary person, by minutely describing his behaviour at the most important and critical of all seasons. He left his papers and books to the charge of Dr. Charlett, Mr. Bisse, and Mr. (afterwards bishop) Tanner, to be placed in the Ashmolean library. [1]

WOOD (ROBERT), a polite scholar, and under-secretary of state in 1764, has a right to a place here, for his very curious "Essay on the original Genius of Homer." Of the particulars of his life, the proper subject for our pages, we reluctantly confess ourselves ignorant ; but shall observe, that in 1751, he made the tour of Greece, Egypt, and Palestine, in company with Mr. Dawkins and Mr. Bouverie ; and at his return published a splendid work, in folio, entitled "The Ruins of Palmyra, otherwise Tedmor in the Desert," being an account of the ancient and modern state of that place ; with a great number of elegant engravings of its ruins by Fourdrinier, from drawings made on the spot. This was followed by a similar work respecting Balbec. Speaking of the abovementioned friends, he says, " Had I been so fortunate as to have enjoyed their assistance in arranging and preparing for the public the substance of our many friendly conversations on this subject (Homer) I should be less anxious about the fate of the following work : but, whatever my success may be in an attempt to contribute to the amusement of a vacant hour, I am happy to think, that, though I should fail to answer the expectations of public curiosity, I am sure to satisfy the demands of private friendship ; and that, acting as the only survivor and trustee for the literary concerns of my late fellow-travellers, I am, to the best of my judgment, carrying into execution the purpose of men for whose memory I shall ever retain the greatest veneration ; and though I may do injustice to those honest feelings which urge me to this pious task, by mixing an air of compliment in an act of duty, yet I must not disown a private, perhaps an idle consolation, which, if it be vanity to indulge, it would be in-

[1] Life written by himself, and other information prefixed to the first volume of Mr. Bliss's edition, and so copious as to render every other reference unnecessary.

gratitude to suppress, viz. that, as long as my imperfect descriptions shall preserve from oblivion the present state of the Troade, and the remains of Balbec and Palmyra, so long will it be known that Dawkins and Bouverie were my friends."

Mr. Wood was meditating future publications relating to other parts of his tour, especially Greece, when he was called upon to serve his country in a more important station, being appointed under-secretary of state in 1759, by the earl of Chatham; during the whole of whose prosperous administration, as well as in those of his two immediate successors, he continued in that situation.

Mr. Wood had drawn up a great part of his " Essay on Homer" in the life-time of Mr. Dawkins, who wished it to be made public. " But," says Mr. Wood, " while I was preparing it for the press, I had the honour of being called to a station, which for some years fixed my whole attention upon objects of so very different a nature, that it became necessary to lay Homer aside, and to reserve the farther consideration of my subject for a time of more leisure. However, in the course of that active period, the duties of my situation engaged me in an occasional attendance upon a nobleman (the late earl Granville), who, though he presided at his majesty's councils, reserved some moments for literary amusement. His lordship was so partial to this subject, that I seldom had the honour of receiving his commands on business, that he did not lead the conversation to Greece and Homer. Being directed to wait upon his lordship a few days before he died, with the preliminary articles of the treaty of Paris, I found him so languid, that I proposed postponing my business for another time; but he insisted that I should stay, saying, " it could not prolong his life, to neglect his duty:" and, repeating a passage out of Sarpedon's speech, dwelt with particular emphasis on a line which recalled to his mind the distinguishing part he had taken in public affairs. His lordship then repeated the last word several times with a calm and determined resignation; and, after a serious pause of some minutes, he desired to hear the treaty read; to which he listened with great attention; and recovered spirits enough to declare the approbation of a dying statesman (I use his own words) on the most glorious war, and most honourable peace, this country ever saw."

Mr. Wood also left behind him several MSS. relating to his travels, but not sufficiently arranged to afford any hopes of their being given to the public. The house in which he lived in Putney is situated between the roads which lead to Wandsworth and Wimbledon, and became the residence of his widow. Mr. Wood purchased it of the executors of Edward Gibbon, esq. whose son, the celebrated historian, was born there. The farm and pleasure-grounds which adjoin the house are very spacious, containing near fourscore acres, and surrounded by a gravel-walk, which commands a beautiful prospect of London and the adjacent country. Mr. Wood was buried in the cemetery near the upper road to Richmond. On his monument is the following inscription, drawn up by the hon. Horace Walpole, earl of Orford, at the request of his widow:

" To the beloved memory of Robert Wood, a man of supreme benevolence, who was born at the castle of Riverstown near Trim, in the county of Meath, and died Sept. 9, 1771, in the fifty-fifth year of his age ; and of Thomas Wood his son, who died August 25th, 1772, in his ninth year ; Ann, their once happy wife and mother, now dedicates this melancholy and inadequate memorial of her affection and grief. The beautiful editions of Balbec and Palmyra, illustrated by the classic pen of Robert Wood, supply a nobler and more lasting monument, and will survive those august remains." [1]

WOODFORD (SAMUEL), a divine and poet, eldest son of Robert Woodford, of Northampton, gent. was born in the parish of All-hallows on the Wall, London, April 15, 1636 ; became a commoner of Wadham college in 1653 ; took one degree in arts in 1656 ; and in 1658 returned to the Inner Temple, where he was chamber-fellow with the poet Flatman. In 1660, he published a poem " On the return of king Charles II." After that period, he lived first at Aldbrook, and afterwards at Bensted in Hampshire, in a married and secular condition, and was elected F. R. S. in Nov. 1664. He took orders from bishop Morley, and was soon after presented by sir Nicolas Stuart, bart. to the rectory of Hartley-Maudet in Hampshire. He was installed prebend of Chichester May 27, 1676 ; made D. D. by the diploma of archbishop Sancroft in 1677 ; and prebendary of Winchester, Nov. 8, 1680, by the favour of his great

[1] Nichols's Bowyer.—Lyson's Environs, vol. I.

patron, the bishop of that diocese. He died in 1700. His poems, which have some merit, are numerous. His " Paraphrase on the Psalms, in five books," was published in 1667, 4to, and again in 1678, 8vo. This " Paraphrase," which was written in the Pindaric and other various sorts of verse, is commended by R. Baxter in the preface to his " Poetical Fragments," 1681 ; and is called by others " an incomparable version," especially by his friend Flatman, who wrote a Pindaric ode on it, and a copy of verses on Woodford's " Paraphrase on the Canticles," 1679, 8vo. With this latter paraphrase are printed, 1. " The Legend of Love, in three cantos." 2. " To the Muse," a Pindaric ode. 3. " A Paraphrase upon some select Hymns of the New and Old Testament." 4. " Occasional compositions in English rhymes," with some translations out of Latin, Greek, and Italian, but chiefly out of the last ; some of which compositions and translations were before falsely published by a too-curious collector of them, from very erroneous copies, against the will and knowledge of their author. Dr. Woodford complains, that several of his translations of some of the moral odes had been printed after the same incorrect manner.[1]

WOODHEAD (ABRAHAM), whom Dr. Whitby pronounces " the most ingenious and solid writer of the Roman (catholic) party," and who merits some notice from his name occurring so frequently in the popish controversy at the latter end of the seventeenth century, was the son of John Woodhead of Thornhill in Yorkshire, and was born in 1608 at Meltham in the parish of Abbersbury, or Ambury, in that county. He had his academical education in University college, Oxford, where he took his degrees in arts, was elected fellow in 1633, and soon after entered into holy orders. In 1641 he served the office of proctor, and then set out for the continent as travelling tutor to some young gentlemen of family who had been his pupils in college. While at Rome he lodged with the duke of Buckingham, whom he taught mathematics, and is supposed about the same time to have embraced the communion of the church of Rome, although for a long time he kept this a profound secret. On his return to England he had an apartment in the duke of Buckingham's house in the Strand, and was afterwards entertained in lord Capel's

<hr>

[1] Ath. Ox. vol. II.—Nichols's Poems.

family. In 1648 he was deprived of his fellowship by the parliamentary visitors, but merely on the score of absence, and non-appearance, when called. After the restoration he was reinstated in his fellowship, but finding it impossible any longer to conform, he obtained leave to travel, with the allowance of a travelling fellowship. Instead, however, of going abroad, he retired to an obscure residence at Hoxton near London, where he spent several years, partly in instructing some young gentlemen of popish families, and partly in composing his works. Here he remained almost undiscovered, until a little while before his death, which happened at Hoxton, May 4, 1678. He was buried in St. Pancras church-yard, where there is a monument to his memory.

Woodhead was considered as one of the ablest controversial writers, on the popish side, in his time, and some protestants have paid respect to his abilities and candour. Most of his works were printed at Mr. Obadiah Walker's private press, and some of them have been attributed to him. Wood gives a long list of about twenty-three articles, some of which are translations. The principal of his original writings is his " Guide in controversies," or more fully, " A rational account of the doctrine of catholics, concerning the ecclesiastical guide in controversies of religion : reflecting on the late writings of protestants, particularly of archbishop Laud, and doctor Stillingfleet, on this subject; in four discourses ;" under the initials R. H. 1666, 1667, and 1673, 4to. Wood adds, " Many stick not to say, which is a wonder to me, that he was the author of " The Whole Duty of Man ;" and of all that goes under the name of that 'author." The protestant writers with whom he was involved in controversy, and in whose lives or writings his name occurs, were, Peter Heylyn, Stillingfleet, archbishop Wake, Drs. Aldrich, Smalridge, Harrington, Tully, Hooper, and Whitby.[1]

WOODWARD (JOHN), an eminent natural philosopher, was descended from a good family, originally of Gloucestershire, and was born in Derbyshire, May 1, 1665. He received the first part of his education at a school in the country, where he made a considerable progress in the Latin and Greek languages ; but his father designing him for trade, he was taken from school, before he was sixteen

---

[1] Ath. Ox. vol. II.—Dodd's Ch. Hist.—Biog. Brit. art. Wake.

years old, and put apprentice, as is said, to a linen-draper in London. This way of life, however, was so contrary to his natural thirst for knowledge and love of books, that he quitted it in a few years, and devoted himself entirely to literary pursuits. His studies were directed to philosophical objects, and the progress he made soon attracted the notice of some persons of eminence in the learned world. Amongst others he was honoured with the particular friendship of that distinguished scholar and physician Dr. Peter Barwick, who was so pleased with his ingenuity and industrious application, that he took him under his immediate tuition in his own family. In this advantageous situation he prosecuted his studies in philosophy, anatomy, and physic, with the utmost ardour.

During his residence here, sir Ralph Dutton, who was Dr. Barwick's son-in-law, invited Mr. Woodward to accompany the doctor on a visit to his seat at Sherborne, in Gloucestershire. He probably made some stay here, for we are told that he was now first led to inquire into that branch of natural philosophy, which became afterwards the favourite object of his studies, and the foundation of the fame which he acquired. The country about Sherborne, and the neighbouring parts of Gloucestershire, to which he made frequent excursions, abounded with stone; and there being quarries laid open almost every where, he was induced to visit them, and to examine the nature and condition of the stone. In these visits he was struck with the great variety of sea-shells, and other marine productions, with which the sand of most of this stone was incorporated; and being encouraged by the novelty, and as he judged, the singular importance of this speculation, he resolved to pursue it through the remote parts of the kingdom. In consequence of this resolution, he travelled throughout almost all England, in order to inform himself of the present condition of the earth, and all bodies contained in it, as far as either grottoes, caverns, mines, quarries, &c. led him into a knowledge of the interior, and as far as his best observations could extend in respect to the exterior surface, and such productions as any where occurred, plants, insects, sea, river, and land-shells. He directed his attention likewise to the fluids; as well those within the surface of the earth, the water of mines, grottoes, caverns, &c. as those upon the surface, the sea, rivers, and springs; and in making these observations, he entered every curious circumstance, with great care, in a journal. When he had finished these researches, and had returned to London, he would gladly have gone to the continent on the same pursuit, but was prevented by the war which at that time disturbed the quiet of Europe. In order, however, to supply this defect as far as possible, he applied to gentlemen who had travelled, and were likely to give him information on the subject of his inquiries; and he also drew up a list of questions upon this subject, which he sent off to all parts of the world, whereever either himself, or any of his acquaintance, had any friends resident; the result of which was, that in time he was abundantly satisfied, that the circumstances after which he inquired, were much the same every where. Being now prepared with information, and, as it will appear, not unprovided with a theory, he published in 1695, in 1 vol. 8vo, " An Essay towards a natural history of the Earth and terrestrial bodies, especially minerals; as also of the sea, rivers, and springs. With an account of the universal deluge, and of the effects that it had upon the earth." He called it an " Essay," because it was designed, as he said, to be followed by a large work upon the same subject, of which this was but a specimen.

Not only the account of the deluge in Genesis, and the traditions to the same effect preserved by all ancient nations, but the abundant remains of sea-shells and coral, found at great distances from the sea, at great heights, and intermixed with various rocks, have induced mineralogists, without exception, to agree that at some former period the whole of this earth was covered with the sea. Various hypothetical explanations of the way in which this deluge took place, have been from time to time published, and several of these are to be found in the Philosophical Transactions. It is not necessary to take notice of the old hypothesis of Burnet, who conceived that the ante-diluvian world consisted of a thin, smooth crust spread over the whole sea, and that this crust breaking occasioned the deluge, and the present uneven surface of the earth; nor of Whiston, who ascribed the deluge to the effect of the tail of a comet; because those opinions have many years ago lost all their supporters. Nor is any attention at present paid to the hypothesis of Buffon, who conceived the earth to have been splintered from the sun by the blow of a comet, and accounted for the deluge by suppositions equally arbitrary, and inconsistent with the phenomena. Dr.

VOL. XXXII.         T

Woodward was the first writer who acquired a splendid reputation by his theory; and his opinions, though not always correct, generally prevailed in his time, and after. In the work above mentioned, which he afterwards considerably augmented and improved, after refuting the hypotheses of his predecessors, he proceeds to shew, that the present state of the earth is the consequence of the universal deluge; that the waters took up and dissolved all the minerals and rocks, and gradually deposited them along with the sea-shells; and he affirms that all rocks lie in the order of their specific gravity. Although this theory has long lost its authority, several of the positions which he laid down continue still to find a place in every theory which has succeeded him.

In the mean time Woodward's " Essay" occasioned no small controversy. Some of its errors were pointed out by Dr. Martin Lister, in three distinct pieces; and Mr. Robinson, a clergyman of Cumberland, soon after published some "'Observations on the natural history of the world of matter, and the world of life," in which 'he accused Woodward of plagiarism, and mentioned the authors from whom, as he said, he had borrowed most of his notions. But these different works received an answer in a single treatise published by Mr. Harris, in 1697; and the dispute was compromised that same year, in a pamphlet written by Dr. Arbuthnot, in which, after an impartial examination of Woodward's hypothesis, he decided that though it seemed liable to many just exceptions, yet the whole was not to be exploded. Hitherto the author himself had made no reply to any of the objections against his " Essay;" but in 1704, a Latin translation of it being published at Zurich, he was led into a controversy, by letters on the subject, with some of his learned correspondents abroad, and particularly with the celebrated Leibnitz. This controversy continued some years, and when ended, a fresh attack was made on our author's hypothesis, by Elias Camerarius, professor of physic at Tubingen, in some Latin dissertations printed in 1712. On this Dr. Woodward published in 1714, " Naturalis historia telluris illustrata et aucta," in the preface to which he declares, that what had been urged by his antagonists, before Camerarius, was not of such force as to deserve a distinct reply; that every thing considerable in their objections was now proposed by Camerarius, with some additions of his own entirely new, and that the present might be considered as a general answer. In this work, therefore, he supplied the main defects and omissions of his Essay, and endeavoured to vindicate his hypothesis. The dispute with Camerarius was closed in a very friendly address from that learned professor, which was published in the German Ephemerides in 1717, though not without some intimation of his continuing still in his first sentiments. In 1726, Mr. Benjamin Holloway, F. R. S. having translated the " Naturalis Historia telluris" into English, doctor Woodward readily embraced this opportunity of strengthening his opinion by some additional papers with which he furnished the translator.

The connexion of all the circumstances of Dr. Woodward's publication with each other, rendered it necessary to give the above account of the whole in succession; but we must now return to other transactions in his progress towards the reputation he had acquired, and which was not altogether unmixed. In the interval between his visit to sir Ralph Hutton, and the publication of his first " Essay," he had been elected professor of physic in Gresham college, to which place he was recommended by some persons of consequence in the learned world, and particularly by Dr. Barwick. This preferment, which he obtained in 1692, was soon followed by other honours. In 1693 he was elected a fellow of the Royal Society, and was frequently afterwards one of their council. In 1695 he was created M. D. by archbishop Tenison, and in the following year he was admitted of Pembroke-hall, Cambridge, and honoured with the same degree in that university. In 1698 he was admitted a candidate of the college of physicians, and was chosen a fellow in 1702.

In 1699 he published, in the Philosophical Transactions, " Some thoughts and experiments concerning Vegetation." These experiments have acquired great celebrity, and are constantly referred to by all writers on vegetable physiology. They consist in putting sprigs of vegetables into the mouths of phials filled with water, allowing them to vegetate for some time, and then determining the quantity of water which they have imbibed, and the quantity of weight which they have gained. The difference obviously indicates the quantity of moisture exhaled by the plant. About 1693, Dr. Woodward's attention was directed to an object of a very different kind. He had purchased from the museum of a deceased friend, a small, but very curious

iron shield of a round form; on the concave side of which
were represented, in the upper part, the ruins of Rome
when burnt by the Gauls; and below, the weighing out
the gold to purchase their retreat, together with the arrival
of Camillus, and flight of the Gauls; and in the centre
appeared a grotesque mask with horns very large and prominent; the figures all executed in a spirited and beautiful
manner.    Mr. Conyers, in whose collection this curiosity
was, had purchased it of a brazier, who bought it among
some brass and iron fragments which came out of the ar-
moury in the Tower of London, near the end of Charles
II.'s reign.    As soon as it came into the possession of Dr.
Woodward, many inquisitive persons came to see it, and
in order to enable others, who had not that opportunity,
to form a judgment of it, he not only had several casts
made of it, but also, in 1705, had it engraven at Amsterdam, on a copper-plate of the size of the original; copies
of which were transmitted to many learned foreigners, for
their opinion.   Antiquaries, however, could not agree as
to its age.    The professors and other critics in Holland, in
general, pronounced it antique; but those in France thought
otherwise, and Woodward wrote against their opinion a
letter to the abbé Bignon, which is published by Dr. Ward
in the appendix to his " Lives of the Gresham Professors."
Dodwell wrote a " Dissertatio de Parma equestri Wood-
wardiana," which was published by Hearne (See HEARNE)
in 1713.    Dodwell supposed this shield came out of some
public collection; such as the *Shield Walk* in Whitehall-
palace, from Henry VIII.'s time to Charles I.    Theophilus
Downes, fellow of Baliol college, differed from him as to
the antiquity of this monument; and after his death were
published, in two leaves, 8vo, his " De clypeo Woodwar-
diano stricturæ breves."    Ainsworth abridged Dodwell's
dissertation, and inserted it at the end of the " Museum
Woodwardianum," or catalogue of the doctor's library and
curiosities, sold by auction at Covent-garden in 1728.    He
afterwards enlarged the piece, considered the objections, and
reprinted it with the title, " De Clypeo Camilli antiquo,"
&c. 1734, 8vo.    Spanheim and Abr. Seller had both begun
to write dissertations on it, but were prevented by death.
Ward was the last who made any remarks on it, and those
in favour of its antiquity; but Moyle's objection to its antiquity from the ruins of an amphitheatre has not been removed by Dr. Ward.    No ancient artist, Mr. Gough ob-

serves, could be so ignorant as to ascribe such buildings to that period. At Dr. Woodward's sale, this shield was purchased by Col. King, one of his executors, for 100*l.*, and at the sale of the colonel's effects, in 1768, it was sold to Dr. Wilkinson for forty guineas, along with the letters, &c. relating to it.

In 1707, Dr. Woodward published "An account of some Roman urns, and other antiquities, lately digged up near Bishopsgate; with brief reflections upon the ancient and present state of London, in a letter to sir C. Wren," &c. This was reprinted at London and Oxford, 1713 and 1723, 8vo, with a letter from the doctor to the editor. It was printed first at the desire of sir Christopher, whose observations have since appeared in the "Parentalia." Wren could not be persuaded that the temple of Diana stood on the scite of St. Paul's, though Woodward had prepared a dissertation on her image dug up near that cathedral. This dissertation, never printed, is now in the possession of the editor of this Dictionary.

In the midst of those researches into antiquity, Dr. Woodward did not neglect his medical profession, although it cannot be said that he was eminently successful. In 1718 we find him involved in a controversy with two of the greatest physicians of his time, Dr. Freind and Dr. Mead. In a learned work which Dr. Freind published, about this time, he had advanced several arguments in favour of purging upon the access of the second fever, in some dangerous cases of the confluent small-pox. This practice was warmly opposed by Dr. Woodward, who, on the contrary, strenuously recommended the use of emetics in such cases; and in the following year printed his "State of Physic and of Diseases, with an Inquiry into the Causes of the late increase of them; but more particularly of the Small-pox. With some considerations upon the new practice of purging in that disease:" &c. in 8vo. This laid the foundation of a bitter controversy; and Dr. Mead retained a sense of the injury, as he thought it, for many years after, as appears from the preface to his treatise on the small-pox; where he gives a short history of the affair, and also throws some personal reflections on Dr. Woodward, which would have been inexcusable in the heat of the controversy, and were certainly much more so near thirty years after. Pope, Arbuthnot, and other wits, attempted also to turn Dr. Woodward into ridicule, and there appears to have been something of irascibility in his tem-, per, which afforded his enemies considerable advantage in this way.

Dr. Woodward declined in his health a considerable time before he died; and though he had all along continued to prepare materials for his large work, relating to the Natural History of the Earth, yet it was never finished; but only some collections, said to have been detached from it, were printed at different times, as enlargements upon particular topics in his essay. He was confined first to his house, and afterwards to his bed, many months before his death. During this time, he not only drew up instructions for the disposal of his books and other collections, but also completed and sent to the press his " Method of Fossils," in English; and lived to see the whole of it printed, except the last sheet. He died in Gresham-college April 25, 1728; and was buried in Westminster-abbey, where is a monument to his memory. After his death, the two following works were published, 1. " Fossils of all kinds, digested into a Method suitable to their mutual relation and affinity," &c. 8vo. 2. " A Catalogue of Fossils in the Collection of John Woodward, M. D." in 2 vols. 8vo. By his last will, he founded a lecture in the university of Cambridge, to be read there upon his " Essay towards the Natural History of the Earth, his Defence of it, his Discourse of Vegetation, and his State of Physic;" for which he ordered lands of 150l. per annum in South-Britain to be purchased and conveyed to that university, and out of this a hundred pounds per annum to the lecturer, who, after the death of his executors Dixie Windsor, Hugh Bethel, Richard Graham, esqrs. and colonel Richard King, is to be chosen by the archbishop of the province, the bishop of the diocese, the presidents of the College of Physicians and of the Royal Society, the two members of parliament, and the whole senate of the university. This lecturer to be a bachelor; to have no other preferment; to read four lectures a year in English or Latin, of which one is to be printed; to have the custody of the two cabinets of fossils given by the doctor to the university, to shew them three days in each week gratis; and to be allowed ten pounds per annum for making experiments and observations, and keeping correspondence with learned men. Some of these conditions it would not be easy to fulfil, yet the professorship continues, and has been held by men of talents. Dr.

Conyers Middleton was the first appointed to the office, who opened the lectures with an elegant Latin oration in praise of the founder, and upon the usefulness of his institution.

Dr. Woodward left a great many manuscripts, enumerated by Dr. Ward, some of which he ordered to be burnt, but others came into the possession of his executor, colonel Richard King, and were sold in 1768 with the rest of the colonel's collection. Dr. Woodward was in many respects a visionary and an enthusiast, but the extent of his ingenuity and learning cannot well be called in question, and it ought not to be forgot that the circumstances of his youth were discouraging, and that he had no help in his progress from academical instruction. [1]

WOOLLETT (WILLIAM), one of the most eminent of modern engravers in England, was born at Maidstone, in Kent, Aug. 27, 1735. Of his early history few particulars have been preserved, and those mostly traditionary. His father was a thread-maker, and long time a foreman to Mr. Robert Pope. The family is said to have come originally from Holland; and there is a tradition that Woollett's great grandfather escaped from the battle fought by the parliamentary forces against the royalists near Maidstone. Our artist was educated at Maidstone under Mr. Simon Goodwin, who used to notice his graphic talents. Once having taken on a slate the likeness of a schoolfellow named Burtenshaw, who had a prominent nose, his master desired him to finish it on paper, and preserved the drawing. He was also in the habit of drawing the likenesses of his father's acquaintances. His earliest production on copper was a portrait of a Mr. Scott, of Maidstone, with a pipe in his mouth. These are perhaps trifles, but they compose all that is now remembered of Woollett's younger days. His first attempts having been seen by Mr. Tinney, an engraver, he took him as an apprentice at the same time with Mr. Anthony Walker and Mr. Brown. His rise in his profession was rapid, and much distinguished, for he brought the art of landscape engraving to great perfection. With respect to the grand and sublime, says Strutt, "if I may be allowed the term in landscapes, the whole world cannot produce his equal." Woollett, however, did not confine him-

[1] Ward's Lives of the Gresham Professors.—Biog. Brit.—Thomson's Hist. of the Royal Society.—Gough's Topography.

self to landscapes, he engraved historical subjects and portraits with the greatest success. The world has done
ample justice to his memory, and the highest prices still
continue to be given for good impressions of all his prints,
but particularly of his " Niobe" and its companion " Phae-
ton," his " Celadon and Amelia," and " Ceyx and Al-
cyone;" and " The Fishery," all from Wilson, whose peculiar happiness it was that his best pictures were put into the
hands of Woollett, who so perfectly well understood and
expressed the very spirit of his ideas upon the copper.
To these we may add the portrait of Rubens, from Van-
dyke, and, what are in every collection of taste, his justly
celebrated prints from the venerable president of the academy, " The Death of General Wolfe," and " The Battle
of the Boyne."

Mr. Woollett died at his house, Upper Charlotte-street,
Rathbone-place, May 23, 1785, aged fifty; and the record of his death is given in these words: " To say he
was the first artist in his profession would be giving him his
least praise, for he was a good man.——Naturally modest
and amiable in his disposition, he never censured the works
of others, or omitted pointing out their merits; his patience
under the continual torments of a most dreadful disorder
upwards of nine months was truly exemplary; and he died
as he had lived, at peace with all the world, in which he
never had an enemy. He has left his family inconsolable
for his death, and the public to lament the loss of a man
whose works (of which his unassuming temper never boast-
ed) are an honour to his country." An elegant monument
was afterwards put up to his memory in the cloisters, Westminster abbey. [1]

WOOLSTON (THOMAS), an English divine, very notorious in his day for the pertinacity with which he published the most dangerous opinions, was born in 1669, at
Northampton, where his father was a reputable tradesman.
After a proper education at a grammar-school, he was entered of Sidney college, in Cambridge, in 1685, where he
took both the degrees in arts, and that of bachelor of divinity, and was chosen fellow of his college. From this
time, in conformity to the statutes of that society, he applied himself to the study of divinity; and entering into

[1] Strutt's Dict.——Some MS memorandums purchased at the late Mr. Alexander's sale, by Mr. J. B. Nichols, and obligingly communicated to the editor.

holy orders, soon, we are told, became distinguished and
esteemed for his learning and piety. Of what sort the latter was, his life will shew. It appears that he had very
early conceived some of those notions which afterwards so
much degraded his character. His first appearance as an
author was in 1705, when he printed at Cambridge a work
entitled " The old Apology of the Truth for the Christian
Religion against the Jews and Gentiles revived," 8vo. The
design of this work, which is an octavo of near 400 pages,
is to prove that all the actions of Moses were typical of
Christ, and to shew that some of the fathers did not think
them real, but typical relations of what was to come. This
allegorical way of interpreting the scriptures of the Old
Testament our author is said to have adopted from Origen,
whose works, however, he must have studied very inju-
diciously; yet be became so enamoured of this method of
interpretation, that he not only thought it had been unjustly neglected by the moderns, but that it might be useful, as an additional proof of the truth of Christianity.
He preached this doctrine first in the college chapel, and
afterwards before the university at St. Mary's, to the great
surprise of his audience. Yet, as his intentions seemed
to be good, and his character respected, and as he had not
yet begun to make use of the indecent language which
disgraced his subsequent works, no opposition was raised;
and when the volume appeared in print, though there
were some singular notions advanced, and a new manner
of defending Christianity proposed, yet there was nothing
that gave particular offence, and many things which shewed
great ingenuity and learning. He still continued to reside
at Cambridge, applying himself indefatigably to his studies,
in a quiet and retired way, until 1720, when he published
a Latin dissertation entitled " De Pontii Pilati ad Tiberium
Epistola circa res Jesu Christi gestas; per Mystagogum,"
8vo, in which he endeavours to prove that Pontius Pilate
wrote a letter to Tiberius Cæsar concerning the works of
Christ; but that the epistle delivered down to us under
that name among the writings of the fathers, was forged.
The same year he published another pamphlet in Latin,
with the title of " Origenis Adamantii Renati Epistola ad
Doctores Whitbeium, Waterlandium, Whistonium, aliós-
que literatos hujus sæculi disputatores, circa fidem vere
orthodoxam et scripturarum interpretationem;" ahd, soon
after, a second epistle with the same title. The rage of

allegorizing the letter of the holy scriptures into mystery, with which this writer was incurably infected, began now to shew itself more openly to the world than it had hitherto done. In 1720 and 1721, he published two letters to Dr. Bennet, rector of St. Giles's, Cripplegate, London; one upon this question, "Whether the people called quakers do not the nearest of any other sect of religion resemble the primitive Christians in principles and practice?" by Aristobulus; the other, "In defence of the Apostles and Primitive Fathers of the Church, for their allegorical interpretation of the law of Moses, against the ministers of the letter and literal commentators of this age;" and, soon after, he himself published an answer to these two letters; in all which his view appears to have been rather to be severe upon the clergy than to defend either apostles, fathers, or quakers. At what time he left college does not appear, but he had about this time absented himself from it beyond the time limited by the statutes. The society and his friends, however, compassionating his case, and judging it to be in some degree the effect of a bodily distemper, allowed him the revenues of his fellowship for a support. The supposition hurt his pride, and he went directly to Cambridge to convince the gentlemen of his college that he laboured under no disorder, and as he at the same time refused to reside, he lost his fellowship.

After this his brother, an alderman of Northampton, allowed him thirty pounds a year, besides other occasional assistance, and on this he supported himself, being a man of great temperance, in London. In 1722 he published a piece entitled "The exact fitness of the time in which Christ was manifested in the Flesh, demonstrated by reason, against the objections of the old Gentiles, and of modern Unbelievers." This was well enough received, as shewing much learning displayed in a temperate manner, and having in it some valuable remarks. It was written twenty years before its publication, and delivered as a public exercise both in Sidney college chapel, and in St. Mary's church, as Woolston himself observes in his dedication of it to Dr. Fisher, master of Sidney college. But he did not long abstain from his intended attack on the clergy and religion. In 1723 and 1724 came out his four "Free Gifts to the Clergy," and his own "Answer" to them, in five separate pamphlets; in which he attacks the clergy with the greatest contempt, and, as it would appear, without any provocation. Yet, though he treated them in this manner, he expressed a very great regard for religion; and did what some thought more than necessary to defend it, when in 1726 he published "A Defence of the Thundering Legion, against Mr. Moyle's Dissertations."

The "Four free gifts" were scarcely published, when, the controversy with Collins going on at this time, Mr. Woolston, under pretence of acting the part of an impartial inquirer, published his "Moderator between an Infidel and Apostate," and two "Supplements to the Moderator." In these pieces, he pursued his allegorical scheme, to the exclusion of the letter; and, with regard to the miracles of Christ, not only contended for sublime and mystical interpretations of them, but also asserted that they were not real, or ever actually wrought. As he conducted this attempt with greater rudeness and insolence than any of those that had appeared before him, his presumption was not likely to be unnoticed in a Christian country, and he was prosecuted by the attorney-general; but the prosecution was stopped at the intercession of Mr. Whiston *. In 1727, 1728, 1729, and 1730, were published his "Six Discourses on the Miracles of Christ," and his two "Defences" of them. The six discourses are dedicated to six bishops: Gibson, of London; Chandler, of Litchfield; Smalbroke, of St. David's; Hare, of Chichester; Sherlock, of Bangor; and Potter, of Oxford, who are all treated with the utmost rudeness. What he undertakes to prove is, that the miracles of our Saviour, as we find them in the Evangelists, however related by them as historical truths, were not real, but merely allegorical; and that they are to be interpreted, not in literal but only in mystical senses. His pretence is, that the fathers of the church considered our Saviour's miracles in the same allegorical way that he does; that is, as merely allegorical, and excluding the letter: but this is not so. Some of the fathers, indeed, and Origen in particular, did not confine themselves to the bare letter, but endeavoured, upon the

---

* It does not appear very clearly whether this was at the intercession of Whiston. Whiston informs us of his having applied to the attorney-general, sir Philip Yorke, who said that he would not proceed unless the secretary of state sent him an order so to do. "I then," adds Whiston, "went to Dr. Clarke, to persuade him to go with me to lord Townsend (the secretary of state) but he refused, alledging that the report would then go abroad, that the king supported blasphemy. However, no farther progress was made in Mr. Woolston's trial.

foundation of the letter, to raise spiritual meanings, and to allegorize by way of moral application; and they did this, not only upon the miracles of Christ, but upon almost all the historical facts of the Old and New Testament: but they never denied the miracles or the facts. This strange and enthusiastic scheme of Woolston was offensive enough of itself, but infinitely more so from his manner of conducting it; for he not only argues against the miracles of Christ, but treats them in a most ludicrous and outrageous way: expressing himself in terms of astonishing insolence and scurrility. Such conduct raised a general disgust: and many books and pamphlets, both from bishops and inferior clergy, appeared against his discourses; and a second prosecution was commenced and carried on with vigour, against which there seemed to be now little or no opposition, he having by his disingenuity of argument and scurrility of manner, excluded himself from all the privileges of a fair reasoner. At his trial in Guildhall before the lord chief-justice Raymond, he spoke several times himself; and among other things urged, that "he thought it very hard to be tried by a set of men, who, though otherwise very learned and worthy persons, were yet no more judges of the subjects on which he wrote than he himself was a judge of the most crabbed points of law." He was sentenced to a year's imprisonment, and to pay a fine of 100l. He purchased the liberty of the rules of the King's Bench, where he continued after the expiration of the year, being unable to pay the fine. Dr. Samuel Clarke had begun his solicitations at court for the releasement of Woolston, declaring that he did not undertake it as an approver of his doctrines, but as an advocate for that liberty which he himself had always contended for; but he was hindered from effecting it by his death, which happened soon after Woolston's commitment. The greatest obstruction to his deliverance from confinement was the obligation of giving security not to offend by any future writings, he being resolved to write again as freely as before. While some supposed this author not in earnest, but meaning to subvert Christianity under a pretence of defending it; others believed him disordered, and not perfectly in his right mind: and many circumstances concurred to persuade to the latter of these opinions; but how, in either case, a prosecution for blasphemy comes to be considered as persecution for religion, remains yet to be explained. Such a construction, however, appears to have been put upon it by the Clarkes and Lardners of those days, and by their successors in our own. As the sale of Woolston's books was very great (for such blasphemies will find readers as well as advocates for the publication of them), his gains arising from them must have been proportionable; but he defrayed all the expences, and those not inconsiderable, to which his publishers were subjected by selling. He died January 27, 1732-3, after an illness of four days; and, a few minutes before his death, uttered these words: " This is a struggle which all men must go through, and which I bear not only patiently, but with willingness." His body was interred in St. George's church-yard, Southwark. [1]

WOOLTON (JOHN), bishop of Exeter in queen Elizabeth's reign, was born at Wigan in Lancashire, in 1535; he was nephew to the celebrated dean Nowell. He entered a student of Brasen-nose college, Oxford, in 1553, whence in 1555 he fled to his uncle and the other exiles in Germany. On his return in the beginning of queen Elizabeth's reign, he was made canon residentiary of Exeter, where he read a divinity lecture twice a week, and preached twice every Lord's day; and in the time of the great plague, he only with one more remained in the city, preaching publicly as before, and comforting privately such as were infected with the disease. Besides his residentiaryship, he had the living of Spaxton in the diocese of Wells, and in 1575 became Warden of Manchester college. In 1579 he was consecrated bishop of Exeter, and, as he had been before esteemed a pious, painful, and skilful divine, he was now a vigilant and exemplary prelate. His character in this last respect excited some animosity, and a long string of accusations was presented against him to archbishop Parker, which Strype has recorded at length in his appendix to the life of that celebrated primate, all which bishop Woolton satisfactorily answered.

Bishop Godwin, the biographer, who married one of his daughters, and seems to have been with him in his last moments, says, he dictated letters, not two hours before his death, on subjects of importance, full of the piety and prudence of a man in health and vigour; and being reminded to consult his health, he repeated and applied the saying of Vespasian, that " a bishop ought to die upon his legs;"

[1] Biog. Brit.—Leland's Deistical Writers.—Whiston's Life.

which in him, as before in the emperor, was verified, for as he was supported across the room (his complaint being an asthma) he sunk, and expired almost before he touched the ground, in the fifty-ninth year of his age.  He was interred in Exeter cathedral, with a Latin inscription by his son.  He composed many theological tracts, monitory and practical, which were all printed and published in the space of about twelve months, in the years 1576 and 1577.   1. " Anatomie of the whole man."   2. " Christian manual." 3. " Of Conscience."   4. " Armour of proofe."   5. " Immortalitie of the soule."   6. " Fortresse of the Faithfull," and 7. " David's Chain," which last is not mentioned by Wood or Ames. [1]

WORCESTER (WILLIAM).   See BOTONER.

WORLIDGE (THOMAS), an artist of considerable merit, was a native of England, born in 1700, and for the greater part of his life painted portraits in miniature : he afterwards, with worse success, performed them in oil ; but at last acquired reputation and money by etchings, in the manner of Rembrandt, which proved to be a very easy task, by the numbers of men who have counterfeited that master so as to deceive all those who did not know his works. Worlidge's imitations and his heads in black-lead have grown astonishingly into fashion.  His best piece is the whole-length of sir John Astley, copied from Rembrandt, and his copy of the hundred Guilder print ; but his print of the theatre at Oxford and the act there, and his statue of lady Pomfret's Cicero, are very poor performances.  His last work was a book of gems from the antique. He died at Hammersmith, Sept. 23, 1766, aged sixty-six. [2]

WORMIUS (OLAUS), a learned physician of Denmark, was born May 13, 1588, at Arhusen, a city of Jutland, where his father was a burgomaster of an ancient family. He began his studies in his native place ; but was sent, when very young, to the college of Lunenburg ; and thence to Emmeric, in the duchy of Cleves.  Having spent four years at these places, he was removed to Marpurg in 1605 ; and two years after to Strasburg, where he applied himself to physic, to which profession he had now given the preference, and going to Basil studied some time with advantage under Platerus and others.  In 1608, he went to Italy, and

[1] Ath. Ox. vol. I.—Strype's Whitgift, p. 220.—Churton's Life of Nowell.— Fuller's Worthies.
[2] Walpole's Anecdotes.—Pilkington and Strutt's Dictionaries.

during a residence of some months at Padua, his uncommon parts and learning procured him singular honours. He visited other cities of Italy, and passed thence into France, remaining three months at Sienna, and four at Montpelier; after which his design was, to make a long abode at Paris; but the assassination of Henry IV. in 1610, about two months after his arrival, obliging him as well as other strangers to retire from that city, he went to Holland, and thence to Denmark. He had not yet visited the university of Copenhagen, so that his first care was to repair thither, and to be admitted a member of it. He was earnestly entreated to continue there; but his passion for travelling was not yet satiated, and he resolved to see England first. The chemical experiments that were then carrying on at Marpurg made a great noise; and he went thither in 1611, with a view of perfecting himself in a science of great importance to a physician. Thence he journeyed to Basil, where he took the degree of doctor in physic; and from Basil to London, in which city he resided a year and a half. His friends grew now impatient to have him at home, where he arrived in 1613: and was scarcely settled, when he was made professor of the belles-lettres in the university of Copenhagen. In 1615, he was translated to the chair of the Greek professor; and, in 1624, to the professorship of physic, in the room of Caspar Bartholin, which he held to his death. These occupations did not hinder him from practising in his profession, and from being the fashionable physician. The king and court of Denmark always employed him; and Christian IV. as a recompence for his services, conferred on him the canonry of Lunden. He died Aug. 31, 1654, aged sixty-six.

Wormius had three wives, who brought him a family of sixteen children. He published some works on subjects relating to his profession, several in defence of Aristotle's philosophy, and several concerning the antiquities of Denmark and Norway. For these last he is principally remembered now, and they are esteemed very learned and correct; particularly his, 1. "Fasti Danici," 1626. 2. "A History of Norway," 1633, 4to. 3. "Litteratura Danica antiquissima, vulgo Gothica dicta, & de prisca Danorum Poesi," 1636, 4to. 4. "Monumentorum Danicorum libri VI." 1643, folio. 5. "Lexicon Runicum, & Appendix ad Monumenta Danica," 1650, folio. 6. "Series Regum

Daniæ duplex, & limitum inter Daniam & Sueciam Descriptio," 1642, folio. 7. " Talshoi, seu Monumentum
Stroense in Scania," 1628, 4to. 8. "Monumentum Try-
gvvaldense," 1636, 4to. All printed at Hafnia, or Copenhagen. [1]

WORTHINGTON (Dr. John), an excellent divine of
the church of England, was born at Manchester, in the beginning of Feb. 1617-18, and was the son of Roger Worthington, a person of " chief note and esteem" in that town.
His mother was Mary, the daughter of Christopher Whichcote, esq. and niece to sir Jeremy Whichcote, bart. He
was educated at Emanuel college, Cambridge, of which he
became a fellow, was created B.D. in 1646, and D.D. in
1655. He was afterwards chosen master of Jesus college,
vacant by the ejectment of Dr. Richard Sterne, afterwards
archbishop of York, but was with some difficulty prevailed
upon to submit to the choice and request of the fellows, his
inclination being to a more private and retired life; and
soon after the restoration he resigned that mastership to
Dr. Sterne. In the mean time he was successively rector
of Horton in Buckinghamshire, Gravely and Fen Ditton in
the county of Cambridge, Barking, with Needham, in the
county of Suffolk, and Ingoldsby in Lincolnshire. During
the years 1660 and 1661 he cultivated a frequent correspondence by letters with that great promoter of all useful learning, Mr. Samuel Hartlib; four and twenty of Dr.
Worthington's being published at the end of his Miscellanies; and several others by bishop Kennet in his Register
and Chronicle. In 1663, he was collated to the sinecure
rectory of Moulton All Saints, in Norfolk. He entered
upon the cure of St. Bene't Fink in June 1664, under Dr.
George Evans, canon of Windsor, who held a lease from
that college of the rectory; and he continued to preach
there during the plague-year 1665, coming thither weekly
from Hackney, where he had placed his family: and from
February 18, 1665-6, till the fire in September, he preached
the lecture of that church, upon the death of the former
lecturer. Soon after that calamity, he was presented by
Dr. Henry More, of Christ's college in Cambridge, to the
living of Ingoldsby, before mentioned, and to the prebend
of Asgarby in the church of Lincoln, procured him by
archbishop Sheldon, who had a great esteem for him.

---

[1] Niceron, vol. IX.—Saxii Onomast.

From Ingoldsby he removed to Hackney, being chosen lecturer of that church with a subscription commencing from Lady-day 1670 ; and, the church of St. Bene't Fink being then rebuilding, he made suit to the church of Windsor to have his lease of the cure renewed to him, being recommended by the archbishop to Dr. Ryves, dean of that church. This was granted him ; but some difficulties arising about the form of the lease, with regard to the parsonage house, agreed to be rebuilt, he did not live to execute it, dying at Hackney Nov. 26, 1671. He was interred in the church there.

His funeral-sermon was preached by Dr. Tillotson at Hackney, on the 30th of Nov. 1671, on John ix. 4. printed, as it was preached on another occasion, in the third volume of his posthumous sermons, published by Dr. Barker. But the character of Dr. Worthington, which was the conclusion of that sermon, and omitted in that edition, is inserted in the preface to that learned man's "Miscellanies," published at London in 1704 in 8vo, by Dr. Fowler, bishop of Gloucester, and prefixed to Dr. Worthington's "Select Discourses," revised and published by his son John Worthington, M.A. at London, 1725, in 8vo. [1]

WORTHINGTON (WILLIAM), a learned English divine, was born in Merionethshire in 1703, and educated at Oswestry-school, whence he came to Jesus-college, Oxford, where he made great proficiency in learning. From college he returned to Oswestry, and became usher in that school. He took the degree of M. A. at Cambridge in 1742 ; was afterwards incorporated at Jesus-college, Oxford, July 3, 1758 ; and proceeded B. and D. D. July 10, in that year. He was early taken notice of by that great encourager of learning bishop Hare, then bishop of St. Asaph, who presented him first to the vicarage of Llanyblodwell, in the county of Salop, and afterwards removed him to Llanrhayader, or Llanrhadra, in Denbighshire, where he lived much beloved, and died Oct. 6, 1778, much lamented. As he could never be prevailed upon to take two livings, bishop Hare gave him a stall at St. Asaph, and a sinecure, "to enable him," he said, " to support his charities" (for charitable he was in an eminent degree). Afterwards archbishop Drummond (to whom he had been

[1] Barwick's Life.—Birch's Life of Tillotson.—Gent. Mag. vols. XLII. XLIII. and XLVI.

VOL. XXXII. U

chaplain for several years) presented him to a stall in the
cathedral of York. These were all his preferments. He
was a studious man, and wrote several books, of which the
principal are here enumerated. 1. "An Essay on the
Scheme and Conduct, Procedure and Extent, of Man's
Redemption; designed for the honour and illustration of
Christianity. To which is annexed, a Dissertation on the
Design and Argumentation of the Book of Job," by William Worthington, M. A. vicar of Blodwel in Shropshire,
London, 1743, 8vo. 2. "The historical Sense of the Mo-
saic Account of the Fall proved and vindicated," 17....,
8vo. 3. "Instructions concerning Confirmation," 17....,
8vo. 4. "A Disquisition concerning the Lord's-Supper,"
17...., 8vo. 5. "The Use, Value, and Improvement, of various Readings shewn and illustrated, in a Sermon preached
before the University of Oxford, at St. Mary's, on Sunday
Oct. 18, 1761," Oxford, 1764, 8vo. 6. "A Sermon
preached in the parish-church of Christchurch, London, on
Thursday April the 21st, 1768; being the time of the
yearly meeting of the children educated in the charity-
schools in and about the cities of London and Westminster," 1768, 4to. 7. "The Evidences of Christianity,
deduced from Facts, and the Testimony of Sense, throughout all Ages of the Church, to the present Time. In a
series of discourses, preached for the lecture founded by
the hon. Robert Boyle, esq. in the parish-church of St.
James, Westminster, in the years 1766, 1767, 1768;
wherein is shewn, that, upon the whole, this is not a decaying, but a growing, Evidence," 1769, 2 vols. 8vo. 8.
"The Scripture Theory of the Earth, throughout all its
Revolutions, and all the periods of its existence, from the
creation to the final renovation of all things; being a sequel to the Essay on Redemption, and an illustration of the
principles on which it is written," 1773, 8vo. 9. "Ire-
nicum; or, the Importance of Unity in the Church of
Christ considered, and applied towards the healing of our
unhappy differences and divisions," 1775, 8vo. 10. "An
Impartial Enquiry into the Case of the Gospel-Demoniacs;
with an appendix, consisting of an Essay on Scripture-
Demonology," 1777, 8vo. This last was a warm attack
on the opinion held out by the Rev. Hugh Farmer, in his
"Essay on the Demoniacs," 1775, 8vo. and, having produced a spirited reply in 1778, Dr. Worthington prepared
for the press (what by the express directions of his will

was given to the public after his death) " A farther Enquiry into the case of the Gospel-Demoniacs, occasioned by Mr. Farmer's on the subject," 1779, 8vo. [1]

WOTTON (ANTHONY), ranked by Fuller among the learned writers of King's-college, Cambridge, was born in London, about the latter part of the sixteenth century, and educated at Eton, whence, being elected to King's-college, he was entered, Oct. 1, 1579, commenced B. A. in 1583, M. A. in 1587, and B. D. in 1594. He was also fellow of that college, and some time chaplain to Robert earl of Essex. On the death of Dr. Whitaker in 1596 he stood candidate for the king's professorship of divinity in Cambridge, with Dr. John Overall of Trinity-college; but failed, by the superior interest of the latter, although he performed his probationary exercises with general ap= plause. In March 1596 he was chosen professor of divinity in Gresham-college, upon the first settlement of that foundation, and in 1598 quitted his fellowship at Cambridge, and marrying soon after, resigned also his professorship. He was then chosen lecturer of Allhallows Barking; but in 1604 was silenced by Dr. Bancroft, bishop of London, for some expressions used either in a prayer or sermon, which were considered as disrespectful to the king; but it does not appear that he remained long under suspension; at least, in a volume of sermons printed in 1609 he styles himself minister of Allhallows.

His next trouble arose from his brethren in London, of the puritan stamp, with which he is usually classed. He was accused of holding an erroneous opinion concerning the doctrine of justification, which, according to him, con= sisted in the forgiveness of sins. His principal accuser was the Rev. George Walker, minister of St. John the Evangelist in Watling-street, who went so far as to bring forward a charge of Socinianism, heresy, and blas= phemy. This produced a conference between eight di= vines of eminence, four for each party; and the result was, that although these judges differed from Mr. Wotton " in some points of the former doctrine of justification, contained in his expositions," yet they held " not the dif= ference to be so great and weighty, as that they are to be justly condemned of heresy and blasphemy."

In 1624, as Mr. Wotton had promised to explain himself more fully on the subject in dispute, he published his Latin treatise "De reconciliatione peccatoris," thinking it more advisable to discuss the question in a learned language, than to hazard differences among common Christians by printing his opinion in English. In this work he professed to agree with the Church of England, the generality of the first reformers, and particularly Calvin, and to oppose only the opinion of Flaccus Illyricus, Hemmingius, &c. and that of the Church of Rome, as declared in the Council of Trent. Walker, however, returned to the charge, but did not publish any thing until after Mr. Wotton's death. This obliged his friend Mr. Gataker, one of the eight divines who sat in judgement on him, to write a narrative of the conference, which was published by Mr. Wotton's son in 1641.

As Mr. Wotton was a zealous advocate for the reformation, he published several books in defence of it, which exposed him to the resentment of a different party. He entered particularly into the controversy with Dr. Montague, afterwards bishop of Chichester, whose work entitled "Appello Cæsarem" met with a host of opponents, on account of its leaning towards Arminianism and popery. Wotton did not long survive this performance. Though a man acknowledged by all parties to be learned and able, it does not appear he had any other preferment than the lectureship of Allhallows, where, according to the register, he was buried Dec. 11, 1626.

His writings are, 1. "An answer to a popish pamphlet, &c. entitled 'Certain Articles,' &c." Lond. 1605, 4to. 2. "A defence of Mr. Perkins' booke called A Reformed Catholike, &c." ibid. 1606, 4to. 3. "The tryal of the Roman Clergy's title to the Church," ibid. 1608, 4to. 4. "Sermons on part of chapter first of St. John's Gospel," ibid. 1609, 4to. 5. "Run from Rome; or, The necessity of separating from that Church," ibid. 1624, 4to. 6. "De reconciliatione peccatoris, &c." Basil. 1624, 4to. 7. "An answer to a book, entitled Appello Cæsarem, written by Mr. Richard Mountague," ibid. 1626. 8. "The art of Logick," ibid. 1626, 8vo. This is an English translation of Ramus's logic, made by his son, and with a dedication by our author. This son, Samuel, who died in 1680, was rector of East and West Wretham in Norfolk. [1]

[1] Ward's Gresham Professors.—Harwood's Alumni Etonenses, pp. 189 and 221.

WOTTON (EDWARD), an eminent physician, celebrated by Leland in his " Encomia," by the name of ODODUNUS, was the son of Richard Wotton, superior beadle of divinity in the university of Oxford, and was born there in 1492, and educated at the school near Magdalen-college, of which college he became *demy*, and took a bachelor's degree in 1513. Bishop Fox, founder of Corpus Christi college, was his patron, by whose interest he was appointed *socius compar* and Greek lecturer of that new foundation, and continued there till 1520, when he obtained leave to travel into Italy for three years. It appears that he studied physic on the continent, for he had a doctor's degree conferred upon him at Padua. After his return he resumed his lectureship, and was incorporated doctor of physic towards the end of 1525. He became very eminent in his profession, first about Oxford, and then in London ; and was a member of the college of physicians, and physician to Henry VIII. He died October 5, 1555, and lies buried in St. Alban's church, London. He was the first of our English physicians who particularly applied to the study of natural history. He made himself famous at home and abroad by his book, entitled " De Differentiis Animalium, lib. X." Paris, 1552 ; on which Gesner and Possevin have bestowed much praise. It was afterwards considerably improved by Moufet in his " Minimorum Animalium Theatrum," Lond. 1634. Wotton left many children, of whom his son Henry became also a physician of eminence. [1]

WOTTON (Sir HENRY), an Englishman, eminent for learning and politics, was descended from a gentleman's family by both parents, and was born at Boughton-hall in Kent, March 30, 1568. The Wottons were of no inconsiderable distinction, having possessed this lordship for nearly three centuries. Sir Edward Wotton, our statesman's grandfather, was treasurer of Calais, and of the privy-council to king Henry VIII. and was elder brother to the celebrated Dr. Nicholas Wotton, dean of Canterbury, the subject of our next article. Sir Robert Wotton, the father of these, was entrusted by king Edward IV. with the lieutenancy of Guisnes, and was knight-porter and comptroller of Calais ; where he died and lies buried. Sir Henry's elder brother, who was afterwards raised by king James I.

---

[1] Ath. Ox. vol. I.—Aikin's Biog. Memoirs of Medicine.

to the peerage by the title of lord Wotton, was in 1589
sent by queen Elizabeth ambassador to that monarch in
Scotland; and Dr. Robertson speaks of him, as "a man,
gay, well-bred, and entertaining; who excelled in all the
exercises, for which James had a passion, amused the
young king by relating the adventures which he had met
with, and the observations he had made during a long residence in foreign countries; but under the veil of these su-
perficial qualities," Dr. Robertson adds, that "he concealed a dangerous and intriguing spirit. He soon grew in
favour with James; and while he was seemingly attentive
only to pleasure and diversions, he acquired influence over
the public councils, to a degree, which was indecent for
strangers to possess."

Sir Henry was the only son of the second marriage of his
father Thomas Wotton, esq. with Eleanora, daughter of
sir William Finch, of Eastwell in Kent (ancestor to lord
Winchelsea), and widow of Robert Morton, of the same
county, esq. He was educated first under private tutors,
and then sent to Winchester-school; whence, in 1584, he
was removed to New-college in Oxford. Here he was
entered as a gentleman-commoner, and had his chamber
in Hart-hall adjoining; and, for his chamber-fellow, Richard Baker, his countryman, afterwards a knight, and author of the well known "Chronicle" which goes by his
name. Wotton did not continue long there, but went to
Queen's-college, where he became well versed in logic
and philosophy; and, being distinguished for his wit, was
solicited to write a tragedy for private acting in that society.
The name of it was "Tancredo:" and Walton relates,
"that it was so interwoven with sentences, and for the method and exact personating those humours, passions, and
dispositions, which he proposed to represent, so performed,
that the gravest of the society declared, he had in a slight
employment given an early and solid testimony of his future abilities." In 1588 he supplicated the congregation
of regents, that he might be admitted to the reading of any
of the books of Aristotle's logic, that is, be admitted to the
degree of bachelor of arts; but "whether he was admitted
to that or any other degree doth not appear," says Wood,
"from the university registers;" although Walton tells us,
that about his 20th year he proceeded master of arts, and
at that time read in Latin three lectures *de oculo*, on the
blessing of sight, which he illustrated by some beautiful
passages and apt reflexions.

In 1589 he lost his father, and was left with no other provision than a rent-charge of 100 marks a-year. Soon after, he left Oxford, betook himself to travel, and went into France, Germany, and Italy. He stayed but one year in France, and part of that at Geneva; where he became acquainted with Beza and Isaac Casaubon. Three years he spent in Germany, and five in Italy, where both in Rome, Venice, and Florence, he cultivated acquaintance with the most eminent men for learning and all manner of fine arts; for painting, sculpture, chemistry, and architecture; of all which he was an amateur and an excellent judge. After having spent nine years abroad, he returned to England highly accomplished, and with a great accumulation of knowledge of the countries through which he had passed. His wit and politeness so effectually recommended him to the earl of Essex that he first admitted him into his friendship, and afterwards made him one of his secretaries, the celebrated Mr. Henry Cuff being the other. (See CUFF.) He personally attended all the councils and employments of the earl, and continued with him till he was apprehended for high treason. Fearing now lest he might, from his intimate connexion, be involved in his patron's ruin, he thought proper to retire, and was scarcely landed in France, when he heard that his master Essex was beheaded, and his friend Cuff hanged. He proceeded to Florence, and was received into great confidence by the grand duke of Tuscany. This place became the more agreeable to him, from his meeting with signor Vietta, a gentleman of Venice, with whom he had been formerly intimately acquainted, and who was now the grand duke's secretary. It was during this retreat that Mr. Wotton drew up his "State of Christendom, or a most exact and curious discovery of many secret passages, and hidden mysteries of the times." This was first printed, a thin fol. in 1657, and afterwards in 1677, with a small alteration in the title. It was here also that the grand duke having intercepted letters which discovered a design to take away the life of James VI. of Scotland, dispatched Wotton thither to give him notice of it. Wotton was on this account, as well as according to his instructions, to manage this affair with all possible secrecy: and therefore, having parted from the duke, he took the name and language of an Italian; and to avoid the line of English intelligence and danger, he posted into Norway, and from that country to Scotland. He found the king at Stirling, and was admitted to him under the name of Octavio Baldi. He delivered his message and his letters to the king in Italian : then, stepping up and whispering to his majesty, he told him he was an Englishman, requested a more private conference with him, and that he might be concealed during his stay in Scotland. He spent about three months with the king, who was highly entertained with him, and then returned to Florence, where, after a few months, the news of queen Elizabeth's death, and of king James's accession to the crown of England, arrived.

Sir Henry Wotton then returned to England, and, as it seems, not sooner than welcome, for king James, finding, among other officers of the late queen, sir Edward, who was afterwards lord Wotton, asked him, " if he knew one Henry Wotton, who had spent much time in foreign travel?" Sir Edward replied, that " he knew him well, and that he was his brother." Then the king asking, "Where he then was?" was answered, " at Venice, or Florence; but would soon be at Paris." The king ordered him to be sent for, and to be brought privately to him; which being done, the king took him into his arms, and saluted him by the name of Octavio Baldi. Then he knighted him, and nominated him ambassador to the republic of Venice; whither he went, accompanied by sir Albertus Morton, his nephew, who was his secretary, and Mr. William Bedel, a man of great learning and wisdom, and afterwards bishop of Kilmore in Ireland, who was his chaplain. He continued many years in king James's favour, and indeed never entirely forfeited it, although he had once the misfortune to displease his majesty, by an apparently trifling circumstance. In proceeding as ambassador to Venice, he passed through Germany, and stayed some days at Augsburg; where, happening to spend a social evening with some ingenious and learned men, whom he had before known in his travels, one Christopher Flecamore requested him to write some sentence in his Album, a paper book which the German gentry used to carry about with them for that purpose. Sir Henry Wotton, consenting to the motion, took occasion from some incidental discourse of the company, to write a definition of an ambassador in these words: " Legatus est vir bonus peregre missus ad mentiendum Reipublicæ causa:" which Walton says he would have interpreted thus: " An ambassador is an honest man sent to *lie* abroad for the good of his country." The word *lie* was the hinge on which this conceit turned, yet it was no conceit at all in Latin, and therefore could not bear the construction sir Henry, according to Walton, wished to have put upon it: so that when the Album fell afterwards into the hands of Gaspar Scioppius (See SCIOPPIUS), he printed it in his famous book against king James, as a principle of the religion professed by that king, and his ambassador sir Henry Wotton; and in Venice it was presently after written in several glass windows, and spitefully declared to be sir Henry's. This coming to the knowledge of king James, he apprehended it to be such an oversight, such weakness, or worse, that he expressed much anger against him; which caused sir Henry to write two apologies in Latin; one to Velserus at Augsburg, which was dispersed into the cities of Germany, and another to the king " de Caspare Scioppio." These gave such satisfaction that the king entirely forgave sir Henry, declaring publicly, that " he had commuted sufficiently for a greater offence."

After this embassy, he was sent twice more to Venice, once to the States of the United Provinces, twice to Charles Emanuel duke of Savoy, once to the united princes of Upper Germany; also to the archduke Leopold, to the duke of Wittemberg, to the imperial cities of Strasburgh and Ulm, and lastly to the emperor Ferdinand II. He returned to England the year before king James died; and brought with him many servants, of which some were German and Italian artists, and who became rather burthensome to him; for notwithstanding the many public services in which he had been employed, he had by no means improved his private fortune, which was also impaired by his liberality and want of œconomy. As some recompense, which may at first appear rather a singular one for a man who had spent his days as a courtier and ambassador, he was in 1623 appointed provost of Eton-college. But in, fact this situation was very agreeable to him, for he was now desirous of retiring from the bustle of life, and passing the evening of his days in studious pursuits. Whoever peruses his " Remains," must perceive that he had much of the literary character, and finding now that the statutes of the college required the provost to be in holy orders, he was ordained deacon, and seemed to begin a new life. His usual course now was, after his customary public de-

votions, to retire into his study, and there daily spend
some hours in reading the Bible, and works of divinity,
closing those studies with a private prayer. His afternoons
he spent partly in philosophical studies, and partly in conversation with his friends, or in some recreation, particularly angling. His sentiments and temper during his latter days will best appear by what he said, on one occasion,
when visited by the learned John Hales, then a fellow of Eton.
" I have in my passage to my grave met with most of those
joys of which a discursive soul is capable; and have been
entertained with more inferior pleasures than the souls of
men are usually made partakers of. Nevertheless, in this
voyage I have not always floated on the calm sea of content; but have often met with cross winds and storms, and
with many troubles of mind and temptations to evil And
yet though I have been, and am a man compassed about
with human frailties, Almighty God has by his grace prevented me from making shipwreck of faith and a good conscience; the thought of which is now the joy of my heart,
and I most humbly praise him for it. . And I humbly acknowledge, that it was not myself, but he that hath kept
me to this great age, and let him take the glory of his great
mercy. And, my dear friend, I now see that I draw near
my harbour of death; that harbour will secure me from all
the future storms and waves of this restless world; and I
praise God I am willing to leave it, and expect a better;
that world wherein dwelleth righteousness; and I long
for it."

Sir Henry Wotton died in December 1639, and was buried in the chapel belonging to the college. In his will he
appointed this epitaph to be put over his grave: " Hic
jacet hujus sententiæ primus auctor, *Disputandi Pruritus
Ecclesiæ Scabies.* Nomen alias quære:" that is, " Here
lies the first author of this sentence: ' The itch of disputation is the scab of the church.' Seek his name elsewhere."

Sir Henry Wotton was a man of eminent learning and
abilities, and greatly esteemed by his contemporaries. His
knowledge was very extensive, and his taste perhaps not inferior to that of any man of his time. Among other proofs
of it, he was among the first who were delighted with Milton's mask of Comus; and although Mr. Warton has pronounced him to be " on the whole a mixed and desultory
character," he has found an able defender in a living author of equal taste and judgment, who observes on Mr.

Warton's expression, that "this in a strict sense may be true, but surely not in the way of censure. He mingled the character of an active statesman with that of a recluse scholar; and he wandered from the crooked and thorny intrigues of diplomacy into the flowery paths of the muses. But is it not high praise to have been thus desultory?" The same writer says of sir Henry as a poet, "It may be true, that sir Henry's genius was not suited to the higher conceptions of Milton. His mind was subtle and elegant rather than sublime. In truth the habits of a diplomatist, and of a great poet, are altogether incompatible," but "for moral and didactic poetry, the experience of a states-man does not disqualify him," and of this species, sir Henry has left some exquisite specimens. He seems to have lived in a perpetual struggle between his curiosity respecting the world, fomented by his ambition, and his love of books, contemplation, and quiet. His letters to sir Edmund Bacon, who married his niece, prove his strong family affections. His heart appears to have been moulded with a high degree of moral tenderness. This, both the sentiments attributed to him by Walton, and the cast of his poems, sufficiently evince.

He was a great enemy to wrangling and disputes about religion; and used to cut inquiries short by witticisms. To one who asked him, "Whether a Papist may be saved?" he replied, "You may be saved without knowing that: look to yourself." To another, who was railing at the papists with more zeal than knowledge, he gave this ad-vice: "Pray, Sir, forbear, till you have studied the points better; for, the wise Italians have this proverb, ' He that understands amiss concludes worse;' and beware of think-ing, that, the farther you go from the church of Rome, the nearer you are to God." One or two more of his bons mots are preserved. A pleasant priest of his acquaintance at Rome invited him one evening to hear their vesper-music, and seeing him standing in an obscure corner of the church, sent a boy to him with this question, writ upon a scrap of paper, "Where was your religion to be found before Luther?" To which sir Henry sent back under-written, "Where yours is not to be found, in the written word of God." Another evening, sir Henry sent a boy of the choir with this question to his friend: "Do you be-lieve those many thousands of poor Christians damned who were excommunicated because the pope and the duke of

Venice could not agree about their temporalities?" To which the priest underwrit in French, " Excusez moi, Monsieur."

Sir Henry Wotton had proposed, after he was settled at Eton, to write the " Life of Martin Luther," and in it " The History of the Reformation," as it was carried on in Germany. He had made some progress in this work, when Charles I. prevailed with him to lay that aside, and to apply himself to the writing of a history of England. He proceeded to sketch out some short characters as materials, which are in his " Reliquiæ," but proceeded no farther.

His works separately or collectively published were, 1. " Epistola de Caspare Scioppio," Amberg, 1613, 8vo. 2. " Epistola ad Marcum Velserum duumvirum Augustæ Vindelic. ann. 1612." 3. "The Elements of Architecture," Lond. 1624, 4to, a treatise still held in estimation. It was translated into Latin, and annexed to the works of Vitruvius, and to Freart's " Parallel of the ancient architecture with the modern." 4. " Plausus et Vota ad regem è Scotia reducem," Lond. 1633, small folio, reprinted in Lamphire's " Monarchia Britannica," Oxford, 1681, 8vo. 5. " Parallel between Robert earl of Essex and George late duke of Bucks," London, 1641, 4to, not remarkable for the judgment displayed. There were scarcely any parallelisms in the two characters. 6. " Short View of the life and death of George Duke of Bucks," London, 1642, 4to. 7. " Difference and disparity between the estates and conditions of George duke of Bucks and Robert earl of Essex." 8. " Characters of, and observations on some kings of England." 9. " The election of the new duke of Venice after the death of Giovanni Bembo," 10. " Philosophical Survey of Education, or moral Architecture." 11. " Aphorisms of Education." 12. " The great Action between Pompey and Cæsar extracted out of the Roman and Greek writers." 13. " Meditations on the 22d chapter of Genesis." 14. " Meditations on Christmas day." 15. " Letters to and characters of certain personages." 16. " Various Poems." All or most of these pieces are published together in a volume entitled " Reliquiæ Wottonianæ," at London, 1651, 1654, 1672, and 1685, in 8vo. 17. " Letters to sir Edmund Bacon," London, 1661, 8vo, reprinted with some editions of " Reliquiæ Wottonianæ." 18. " Letters to the Lord Zouch," printed at the end of " Reliquiæ Wottonianæ" in the edition of 1685. 19. " The State of Christendom; or a more exact and curious discovery of many secret passages and hidden mysteries of the times," London, 1657, folio, reprinted at London in 1667, folio, with this title; "The State of Christendom, giving a perfect and exact discovery of many political intrigues' and secret mysteries of state practised in most of the courts of Europe, with an account of their several claims, interests, and pretensions." 20. He hath also several letters to George duke of Bucks in the " Cabala, Mysteries of State," London, 1654, 4to, and in " Cabala, or Scrinia sacra," London, 1663, folio. 21. "Journal of his Embassies to Venice," a manuscript fairly written, formerly in the library of Edward lord Conway. 22. " Three propositions to the Count d'Angosciola in matter of duel, comprehending (as it seems) the latitude of that subject;" a manuscript some time in the library of Ralph Sheldon, esq.; and since in that of the college of arms.[1]

WOTTON (NICHOLAS), an eminent statesman and dean of Canterbury, was, as we have already noticed, grand uncle to the preceding sir Henry. He was the fourth son of sir Robert Wotton, knt. by Anne Belknapp, daughter of sir Henry Belknapp, knt. and was born about 1497. He was educated in the university of Oxford, where he studied the canon and civil law, his skill in which recommended him to the notice of Tunstall, bishop of London, to whom he became official in 1528, being at that time doctor of laws. Having entered into the church, he was collated by archbishop Warham to the rectory of Ivychurch in the county of Kent. But this benefice he resigned in 1555, reserving to himself a pension of twenty-two marks, one third of its reputed value, during his life. He continued to act as a civilian; and in 1536, when sentence was pronounced upon Anne Boleyn, he appeared in court as her proctor.

In 1538 archbishop Cranmer constituted him commissary of his faculties for the term of his natural life. About the same time he became chaplain to the king, who in 1539 nominated him to the archdeaconry of Gloucester, then vacant by the promotion of archdeacon Bell to the see of Worcester. His next promotion was to the deanery of Canterbury in 1541; in addition to which he obtained in

1544 the deanery of York, and was the only person who ever possessed at the same time the deaneries of the two metropolitan churches. In 1545 he was presented to the prebend of Osbaldwick in York cathedral. In 1553 he resigned the archdeaconry of Gloucester, and was presented in 1557 to the treasuryship of the church of Exeter, which he also relinquished the succeeding year.

Such were the appointments which Wotton obtained, but in 1539 he had refused a bishopric, and it is said that he refused the see of Canterbury, so that whatever he might be as a courtier, he was an unambitious ecclesiastic. His talents indeed were better suited to political negociation, and accordingly he was often employed on foreign embassies. His first service abroad is thought to have been his embassy to Cleves in 1539, in order to carry on the treaty of marriage between Henry and the lady Anne ; and it fell to his lot afterwards to acquaint the duke of Cleves with Henry's repudiation of his sister. In 1546 he was one of the commissioners who met at Campe, a small place between Ardres and Guisnes, in order to negociate peace between England, Scotland, and France. In September following he obtained the royal dispensation for non-residence on his preferments, being then the king's ambassador in France, and was there at the death of Henry, by whose will he was appointed one of the executors to whom, during the minority of his son Edward VI. he entrusted the government of the kingdom.

During the reign of Edward, the abilities of Wotton were exercised not only abroad, but also in his own country ; as he held, for a short time, the distinguished office of principal secretary of state, to which he was appointed in 1549, but resigned it in 1550 to Cecil. He was one of the council who, on Oct. 6, 1549, seceded from the protector, and who addressed a memorial to the young king on the encroachments of that unfortunate nobleman. In 1551, he was sent ambassador to the emperor, in order to explain that no absolute assurance had ever been made to the lady Mary, in respect to the exercise of her religion, but that only a temporary connivance had been granted under the hope of her amendment. Mary had been threatened, as well as pressed, on the point of conformity, and she did not fail to represent in the most odious lights these proceedings to her kinsman Charles, who, by his ambassador, remonstrated to the English court on her behalf, and Edward, prevailed upon by his council, sent Wotton to continue a good correspondence with his imperial majesty. At the death of Edward, Wotton, sir William Pickering, and sir Thomas Chaloner, were ambassadors in France, whence they wrote to Mary on her accession to the throne, acknowledging her queen, and ceasing to act any further in their public character. But in this capacity she thought proper to continue Wotton, with whom she joined sir Anthony St. Leger.

From France the dean is said to have written to the queen in 1553, on the following subject. He *dreamed* that his nephew Thomas Wotton was inclined to be a party in such a project, as, if he were not suddenly prevented, would turn out both to the loss of his life, and the ruin of his family. Accordingly he resolved to use such a preventive, as might be of no inconvenience either to himself or his nephew. He therefore wrote to Mary, requesting that his nephew might be sent for out of Kent, and that he might be interrogated by the lords of the council in some such feigned speeches, as would give a colour to his commitment to a *favourable prison*. He added, that he would acquaint her majesty with the true reason of his request, when he should next become so happy as to see and speak to her. It was accordingly done as he desired, but whether he gave her majesty " the true reason," we are not informed. The subject dwelling much on the dean's mind, he might have had a *dream*, yet the whole was probably an ingenious precaution to prevent his nephew from being involved in Wyat's rebellion (which broke out soon after), and which he was afraid might be the case, from the ancient friendship that had subsisted between the families of Wotton and Wyat.

The last important service Wotton performed in the reign of queen Mary was in 1557, when he detected the rebellious plot of Thomas Stafford, the consequence of which was Stafford's defeat and execution, and a declaration of war against France. At the queen's death he was acting as one of the commissioners to treat of a peace between England, Spain, and France, and in this station queen Elizabeth retained him (having also appointed him a privy-counsellor), and after much negociation peace was concluded at Chateau-Cambresis April 2, 1559. He was afterwards commissioned with lord Howard and sir Nicholas Throgmorton to receive from the French king the confirmation of the treaty.

This peace, however, was of short duration. The ambitious proceedings of the French court in 1559, and the success of their arms against the Scotch protestants, were sufficient to excite the vigilance of Elizabeth. Her indignation at the claim of Mary (queen of Scots) to the English crown, a claim which the French hoped to establish, and the declining affairs of the reformers who solicited her assistance, at length determined her to send a powerful force to Scotland. In the event of this quarrel the French were obliged to capitulate, and commissioners were appointed to treat of peace. Those on the part of England were dean Wotton and sir William Cecil; on that of France, Mouluc bishop of Valence, and the Sieur de Raudan. The interests of the English and French courts were soon adjusted; but to a formal treaty with the Scots, the French ambassador considered it derogatory from the dignity of their sovereign to accede. The redress of their grievances was, however, granted in the name of Francis and Mary, and accepted by the Scots, as an act of royal indulgence. And whatever concessions they obtained, whether in respect to their personal safety, or their public demands, the French ambassadors agreed to insert in the treaty with Elizabeth; so that they were sanctioned, though not with the name, yet with all the security of the most solemn negociation. The treaty was signed at Edinburgh, July 6, 1560.

The public services of Wotton were afterwards employed in regard to the trade of the English merchants, who had been ill-treated not only in Spain, but more particularly in the Netherlands, upon pretence of civil differences, but in fact out of hatred to the protestant religion. They therefore removed their mart to Embden in East Friesland. But Guzman de Sylva (canon of Toledo), then the Spanish ambassador in England, endeavoured to compose these differences, which he found materially to affect the interests of the Netherlands. At length Elizabeth, and the duchess of Parma, regent of the Low Countries, exchanged in Dec. 1564, a mutual agreement, by which the commerce between the two countries was restored, and viscount Montague, dean Wotton, and Dr. Haddon, were sent commissioners to Bruges in order to a full discussion of the subject. But, in the following year, the troubles in the Netherlands put a stop to their farther conference, after it had been agreed, that there should be an open trade, till one prince denounced war against the other; and in that case, the merchants should have forty days notice to dispose of themselves and their effects.

This was probably the last employment of the dean, which indeed he did not long survive. He died at his house in Warwick-lane, Jan. 25, 1566, aged about seventy, and was interred in Canterbury cathedral, in the chapel of the Holy Trinity, where is a beautiful and much admired monument, part, if not the whole of which, was executed at Rome. He is represented kneeling at his devotions; the head is said to have been carved by his own order, while living. Over his figure is a very long Latin inscription, containing many particulars of his life. As he died unmarried, he left his nephew Thomas Wotton his heir.

The dean's life, we have seen, was chiefly devoted to political affairs, yet he was not wholly unemployed as a divine. In 1537, the more learned ecclesiastics of that period were called together in order to the composition of the book entitled "The godly and pious institution of a Christian man;" among these was Dr. Wotton. To their discussion and judgment many of the principal points of religion were submitted. From his compliance under the differing reigns of Henry, Edward, Mary, and Elizabeth, he has been concluded to be a time-server, and a man of no decided religious principle; and he certainly is rather to be considered as a politician than an ecclesiastic, for it was in the former character principally that his services were required by his respective sovereigns. His learning is said to have been profound and extensive, and to have been displayed to the greatest advantage in the force of his arguments, and in the easiness of his elocution. In council his sentiments were delivered with admirable discretion, and maintained with undaunted resolution. The vigilance of his political conduct, both at home and abroad, distinguished him as an exemplary statesman; and the facility with which he could discuss the merits of a cause (his method being exact, and his memory tenacious), marked him as an acute civilian. His knowledge of trade and commerce was no less conspicuous, and in an acquaintance with the polity of nations he was inferior to none. To the greatness of his character Holinshed and Camden have bequeathed their testimonies; and Henry VIII. is said to have thus addressed him, when he was about to depart on an embassy, " Sir, I have sent a *head* by Cromwell, a *purse* by Wolsey, a *sword* by Brandon, and I must now send the *law* by you to treat with enemies."[1]

WOTTON (WILLIAM), an English divine of uncommon parts and learning, was the son of Mr. Henry Wotton, rector of Wrentham, in Suffolk, a man of considerable learning also, and well skilled in the Oriental tongues. He was born at Wrentham the 13th of August, 1666, and was educated by his father. He discovered a most extraordinary genius for learning languages; and, though what is related of him upon this head may appear wonderful, yet it is so well attested that we know not how to refuse it credit. Sir Philip Skippon, who lived at Wrentham, in a letter to Mr. John Ray, Sept. 18, 1671, writes thus of him: "I shall somewhat surprise you with what I have seen in a little boy, William Wotton, five years old the last month, the son of Mr. Wotton, minister of this parish, who hath instructed his child within the last three quarters of a year in the reading the Latin, Greek, and Hebrew languages, which he can read almost as well as English; and that tongue he could read at four years and three months old as well as most lads of twice his age. I could send you many particulars about his rendering chapters and psalms out of the three learned languages into English," &c. Among sir Philip's papers was found a draught of a longer letter to Mr. Ray, in which these farther particulars are added to the above: "He is not yet able to parse any language, but what he performs in turning the three learned tongues into English is done by strength of memory; so that he is ready to mistake when some words of different signification have near the same sound. His father hath taught him by no rules, but only uses the child's memory in remembering words: some other children of his age seem to have as good a fancy and as quick apprehension." He was admitted of Catharine Hall, Cambridge, in April 1676, some months before he was ten years old; and upon his admission Dr. John Eachard, then master of the college, gave him this remarkable testimony: *Gulielmus Wottonus infra decem annos nec Hammondo nec Grotio secundus.* His progress in learning was answerable to the expectations conceived of him; and Dr. Duport, the master of Magdalen-college, and dean of Peterborough, has de-

1 Todd's Account of the Deans of Canterbury.—Lodge's Illustrations.—Walton's Life of Sir Henry Wotton, Zouch's edition.—Coote's Catalogue of Civilians.

scribed it in an elegant copy of verses; "In Gulielmum Wottonum stupendi ingenii et incomparabilis spei puerum vixdum duodecim annorum." He then goes on to celebrate his skill in the languages, not only in the Greek and Latin, which he understood perfectly, but also in the Hebrew, Arabic, Syriac, Chaldee; his skill too in arts and sciences, in geography, logic, philosophy, mathematics, chronology.

In 1679 he took the degree of B. A. when he was but twelve years and five months old; and, the winter following, was invited to London by Dr. Gilbert Burnet, then preacher at the Rolls, who introduced him to almost all the learned; and among the rest to Dr. William Lloyd, bishop of St. Asaph, who was so highly pleased with him, that he took him as an assistant in making the catalogue of his library, and carried him the summer following to St. Asaph. Upon his return, Dr. Turner, afterwards bishop of Ely, procured him by his interest a fellowship in St. John's colege, where he took his degree of M. A. in 1683, and in 1691 he commenced bachelor of divinity. The same year bishop Lloyd gave him the sinecure of Llandrillo, in Denbighshire. He was afterwards made chaplain to the earl of Nottingham, then secretary of state, who in 1693 presented him to the rectory of Middleton Keynes, in Buckinghamshire. In 1694 he published "Reflections upon Ancient and modern Learning;" and dedicated his book to his patron the earl of Nottingham. To settle the bounds of all branches of literature, and all arts and sciences, as they have been extended by both ancients and moderns, and thus to make a comparison between each, was a work too vast, one should think, for any one man, even for a whole life spent in study; yet it was executed with very considerable ability by Mr. Wotton at twenty-eight years of age; and if it did involve him somewhat in the controversy between Boyle and Bentley, that was rather owing to his connections with Bentley, whose "Dissertations upon Phalaris," &c. were printed at the end of the 2d edition of his book in 1697, than to any intermeddling of his own. Boyle himself acknowledged that "Mr. Wotton is modest and decent, speaks generally with respect of those he differs from, and with a due distrust of his own opinion. His book has a vein of learning running through it, where there is no ostentation of it." This and much more is true of Wotton's performance; yet it must not be dissembled,

x 2

that this, as it stands in Boyle's book, appears to have been said rather for the sake of reflecting on Bentley than to commend Wotton. Wotton suffered, as is well known, under the satirical pen of Swift; and this induced him to write "A Defence of the Reflections upon Ancient and Modern Learning, in answer to the objections of sir William Temple and others;" with "Observations upon the Tale of a Tub;" reprinted with a third corrected edition of the "Reflections," &c. in 1705, 8vo. He says that this "Tale is of a very irreligious nature, and a crude banter upon all that is esteemed as sacred among all sects and religions among men;" and his judgment of that famous piece is confirmed by that of Mr. Moyle, in the following passage: "I have read over the 'Tale of a Tub.' There is a good deal of wild wit in it, which pleases by its extravagance and uncommonness; but I think it, upon the whole, the profanest piece of ribaldry which has appeared since the days of Rabelais, the great original of banter and ridicule."

His "Reflections" were published, as already noticed, in 1694. In 1695 he published, in the "Philosophical Transactions," an "Abstract" of Agostino Scilla's book concerning marine bodies which are found petrified in several places at land; and in 1697, a "Vindication" of that abstract, which was subjoined to Dr. John Arbuthnot's "Examination of Dr. Woodward's Account of the Deluge," &c. In 1701, he published "The History of Rome from the death of Antoninus Pius to the death of Severus Alexander," in 8vo. He paid great deference to the authority of medals in illustrating this history, and prefixed several tables of them to his book, taken chiefly from the collections of Angeloni, Morell, and Vaillant. This work was undertaken at the direction of bishop Burnet, and intended for the use of his lordship's royal pupil, the duke of Gloucester, who, however, did not live to see it finished. It was therefore dedicated to the bishop, to whom Wotton had been greatly obliged in his youth, and who afterwards, in 1705, gave him a prebend in the church of Salisbury. This history was esteemed no inconsiderable performance: M. Leibnitz immediately recommended it to George II. his late majesty, then electoral prince of Hanover; and it was the first piece of Roman history which he read in our language.

In 1706 Wotton preached a visitation-sermon, at Newport-Pagnel in Bucks, against Tindal's book of " The Rights of the Christian Church," and printed it. This was the first answer that was written to that memorable performance; and it was also the first piece which Wotton published as a divine. In 1707, archbishop Tenison presented him with the degree of doctor of divinity. In 1708 he drew up a short view of Dr. Hickes's " Thesaurus;" but the appendix and notes are Hickes's own. In 1714 the difficulties he was under in his private fortune, for he had not a grain of œconomy, obliged him to retire into South Wales, where, though he had much leisure, he had few books. Yet, being too active in his nature to be idle, he drew up, at the request of Browne Willis, esq. who afterwards published them, the " Memoirs of the Cathedral Church of St. David," in 1717, and of " Landaff " in 1719. Here he also wrote his " Miscellaneous discourses relating to the traditions and usages of the Scribes and Pharisees," &c. which was printed 1718, in 2 vols. 8vo. Le Clerc tells us that " great advantage may be made by reading the writings of the Rabbins; and that the public is highly obliged to Mr. Selden, for instance, and to Dr. Lightfoot, for the assistances which they have drawn thence, and communicated to those who study the holy scripture. Those who do not read their works, which are not adapted to the capacity of every person, will be greatly obliged to Dr. Wotton for the introduction which he has given them into that kind of learning." In 1719 he published a sermon upon Mark xiii. 32, to prove the divinity of the Son of God from his omniscience.

After his return from Wales he preached a sermon in Welsh before the British Society in 1722; and was, perhaps, the only Englishman who ever attempted to preach in that language. The same year, his account of the life and writings of Mr. Thomas Stanley was published at Eysenach, at the end of Scævola Sammarthanus's " Elogia Gallorum." In 1723 he printed in the " Bibliotheca Literaria" an account of the " Caernarvon Record," a manuscript in the Harleian library. This manuscript is an account of several ancient Welsh tenures, and had some relation to the Welsh laws, which he was busy in translating. He undertook that laborious work at the instance of Wake, who knew that the trouble of learning a new and very difficult language would be no discouragement to Dr. Wotton. It was published in 1730, under this title, " Cysreithjeu Hywel Dda, ac erail;

ceu, Leges Wallicæ Ecclesiasticæ et Civiles Hoeli Boni, et aliorum Walliæ principum, quas ex variis Codicibus Manuscriptis eruit, interpretatione Latina, notis et glossario illustravit Gulielmus Wottonus," in folio.   But this was a posthumous work, for he died at Buxted, in Essex, Feb. 13, 1726.   He left a daughter, who was the wife of the late Mr. William Clarke, canon-residentiary of Chichester. After his death came out his " Discourse concerning the Confusion of Languages at Babel," 1730, 8vo ; as did the same year his " Advice to a young Student, with a method of study for the four first years."   He was likewise the author of five anonymous pamphlets : 1. " A Letter to Eusebia," 1707.   2. " The case of the present Convocation considered," 1711.   3. " Reflections on the present posture of Affairs, 1712.   4. " Observations on the State of the Nation," 1713.   5. " A Vindication of the Earl of Nottingham," 1714.

What distinguished him from other men chiefly was his memory : his superiority seems to have lain in the strength of that faculty ; for, by never forgetting any thing, he became immensely learned and knowing; and, what is more, his learning (as one expresses it) was all in ready cash, which he was able to produce at sight.   When he was very young he remembered the whole of almost any discourse he had heard, and often surprised a preacher with repeating his sermon to him.   This first recommended him to bishop Lloyd, to whom he repeated one of his own sermons, as Dr. Burnet had engaged that he should.   But above all, he had great humanity and friendliness of temper.   His time and abilities were at the service of any person who was making advances in real learning.   The narrowness of a party-spirit never broke in upon any of his friendships; he was as zealous in recommending Dr. Hickes's great work as if it had been his own, and assisted Mr. Spinkes in, his replies to Mr. Collier in the controversy about the necessity of mixing wine and water in the sacrament, in 1718 and 1719.   He was a great lover of etymology ; and Mr. Thwaites in his Saxon Grammar, takes notice of his skill and acuteness that way, which he was extremely well qualified for, by knowing most of the languages from east to west.   Mr. John Chapman, chaplain to the archbishop of Canterbury (in " Remarks upon the Letter to Dr. Waterland in relation to the natural account of Languages," pag. 8, 9.) has done him the honour to place him in a list of great names after Bochart, Walton, Vossius, Scaliger, Duret, Heinsius, Selden, &c. all men of letters and tracers of languages. Wotton lived at a time when a man of learning would have been better preferred than he was; but it is supposed that some part of his conduct, which was very exceptionable, prevented it. [1]

WOUVERMANS (PHILIP), an eminent artist of Holland, was born at Haerlem, in 1620, and was the son of Paul Wouvermans, a tolerable history-painter, of whom, however, he did not learn the principles of his art, but of John Wynants, an excellent painter of Haerlem. It does not appear that he ever was in Italy, or ever quitted the city of Haerlem; though no man deserved more the encouragement and protection of some powerful prince than he did. He is one instance, among a thousand, to prove that oftentimes the greatest merit remains without either recompence or honour. His works have all the excellences we can wish; high finishing, correctness, agreeable composition, and a taste for colouring, joined with a force that approaches to the Caracci's *. The pieces he painted in his latter time have a grey or blueish cast; they are finished with too much labour, and his grounds look too much like velvet: but those he did in his prime are free from these faults, and equal in colouring and correctness to any thing Italy can produce. Wouvermans generally enriched his landscapes with huntings, halts, encampment of armies, and other subjects where horses naturally enter, which he designed better than any painter of his time: there are also some battles and attacks of villages by his hand. These beautiful works, which gained him great reputation, did not make him rich; on the contrary, being charged with a numerous family, and but indifferently paid for his work, he lived very meanly; and, though he painted very quick, and was very laborious, had much ado to maintain himself. The misery of his condition determined him not to bring up any of his children to painting. In his last hours, which happened at Haerlem in 1688, he burnt a box filled with his studies and designs; saying, I have been so ill-paid

* Many of the best works of Wouvermans were in the gallery of the prince of Orange at the Hague. "One of the most remarkable of them is known by the name of the Hay-cart; another in which there is a coach and horses is equally excellent," &c. "Upon the whole, he is one of the few painters whose excellence in his way is such as leaves nothing to be wished for."
Sir Joshua Reynolds's Works, vol. II. p. 343, &c.

[1] Gen. Dict.—Nichols's Bowyer.—Swift's Works.

for my labours, that I would not have those designs engage my son in so miserable a profession." Different authors, however, ascribe the burning of his designs to different motives. Some say it proceeded from his dislike to his brother Peter, being unwilling that he should reap the product of his labours; others allege that he intended to compel his son (if he should follow the profession) to seek out the knowledge of nature from his own industry, and not indolently depend on copying those designs; and other writers assign a less honourable motive, which seems to be unworthy of the genius of Wouvermans, and equally unworthy of being perpetuated.

Houbraken observes, that the works of Wouvermans and Bamboccio were continually placed in competition by the ablest judges of the art; and the latter having painted a picture which was exceedingly admired, John De Witt prevailed on Wouvermans to paint the same subject, which he executed in his usual elegant style. These pictures being afterwards exhibited together to the public, while both artists were present, De Witt said (with a loud voice), " All our connoisseurs seem to prefer the works of those painters who have studied at Rome; and observe only, how far the work of Wouvermans, who never saw Rome, surpasses the work of him who resided there for several years!" That observation, which was received with general applause, was thought to have had too violent an effect on the spirits of Bamboccio; and by many it was imagined that it contributed to his untimely death. [1]

WRAY (DANIEL), a man of taste and learning, was born Nov. 28, 1701, in the parish of St. Botolph, Aldersgate. His father, sir Daniel Wray, was a London citizen, who resided in Little Britain, made a considerable fortune in trade (as a soap-boiler), and purchased an estate in Essex, near Ingatestone, which his son possessed after him. Sir Daniel served the office of sheriff for that county, and was knighted in 1708 on presenting a loyal address to queen Anne. His son was educated at the Charter-house, and was supposed in 1783 to have been the oldest survivor of any person educated there. In 1718 he went to Queen's college, Cambridge, as a fellow commoner. He took his degree of B.A. in 1722, after which he made the tour of Italy, accompanied by John, earl of Morton, and Mr. King,

[1] Argenville, vol. III.—Pilkington.—Sir J. Reynolds's Works.

the son of lord chancellor King, who inherited his title.
How long he remained abroad between 1722 and 1728 is
not precisely ascertained, except by the fact that a cast in
bronze, by Pozzo, was taken of his profile, in 1726, at
Rome. It had this inscription upon the reverse, "Nil ac-
tum reputans, si quid superesset agendum," which line is
said to have been a portrait of his character, as he was in
all his pursuits a man of uncommon diligence and perseverance. After his return from his travels, he became
M. A. in 1728, and was already so distinguished in philosophical attainments, that he was chosen a fellow of the
Royal Society in March 1728-9. He resided however generally at Cambridge, though emigrating occasionally to
London, till 1739, or 1740, in which latter year, January
1740-41, he was elected F. S. A. and was more habitually a
resident in town. In 1737 commenced his acquaintance
and friendship with the noble family of Yorke; and in 1745,
Mr. Yorke, afterwards earl of Hardwicke, as teller of the
exchequer, appointed Mr. Wray his deputy teller, in which
office he continued until 1782, when his great punctuality
and exactness in any business he undertook made the constant attendance of the office troublesome to him. He was
an excellent critic in the English language; an accomplished judge of polite literature, of virtû, and the fine
arts; and deservedly a member of most of our learned societies; he was also an elected trustee of the British Museum. He was one of the writers of the "Athenian Letters" published by the earl of Hardwicke; and in the first
volume of the Archæologia, p. 128, are printed "Notes on
the walls of antient Rome," communicated by him in 1756;
and "Extracts from different Letters from Rome, giving an
Account of the Discovery of a most beautiful Statue of Ve-
nus, dug up there 1761." He died Dec. 29, 1783, in his
eighty-second year, much regretted by his surviving friends,
to whose esteem he was entitled by the many worthy and
ingenious qualities which he possessed. Those of his heart
were as distinguished as those of his mind; the rules of religion, of virtue, and morality, having regulated his conduct from the beginning to the end of his days. He was
married to a lady of merit equal to his own, the daughter
of —— Darrel, esq. of Richmond. This lady died at Richmond, where Mr. Wray had a house, in May 1803. Mr.
Wray left his library at her disposal; and she, knowing his
attachment to the Charter-house, made the governors an

offer of it, which was thankfully accepted : and a room was fitted up for its reception, and it is placed under the care of the master, preacher, head schoolmaster, and a librarian. The public at large, and particularly the friends of Mr. Wray, will soon be gratified by a memoir of him written by the late George Hardinge, esq. intended for insertion in Mr. Nichols's "Illustrations of Literature." This memoir, of which fifty copies have already been printed for private distribution, abounds with interesting anecdotes and traits of character, and copious extracts from Mr. Wray's correspondence, and two portraits, besides an engraving of the cameo. [1]

WREN (MATTHEW), a learned bishop of Ely, was descended of a very ancient family, which came originally from Denmark. His father, Francis, citizen and mercer of London, was the only son of Cuthbert Wren, of Monkskirby in Warwickshire, second son of William Wren of Sherburne-house and of Billy-hall in the bishopric of Durham : but the chief seat of the family was at Binchester in that county. Our prelate was born in the parish of St. Peter-cheap, London, Dec. 23, 1585. Being a youth of promising talents, he was much noticed while at school by bishop Andrews, who being chosen master of Pembroke-hall in Cambridge, procured his admission into that society June 23, 1601, and assisted him in his studies afterwards, which he pursued with such success as to be chosen Greek scholar, and when he had taken his batchelor's degree was elected fellow of the college Nov. 9, 1605. He commenced M. A. in 1608, and having studied divinity was ordained deacon in Jan. and priest in Feb. 1610. Being elected senior regent master in Oct. 1611, he kept the philosophy act with great applause before king James in 1614, and the year following was appointed chaplain to bishop Andrews, and was presented the same year to the rectory of Teversham in Cambridgeshire. In 1621 he was made chaplain to prince (afterwards king) Charles, whom he attended in that office to Spain in 1623. After his return to England, he was consulted by the bishops Andrews, Neile, and Laud, as to what might be the prince's sentiments towards the church of England, according to any observations he had been able to make. His answer was, "I know my master's learning

[1] Memoir, as above, a copy of which we have to acknowledge among the many obligations we owe to Mr. Nichols's steady and friendly attention to this work, and to its editor.

is not equal to his father's, yet I know his judgment is very
right : and as for his affections in the particular you point
at (the support of the doctrine and discipline of the church)
I have more confidence of him than of his father, in whom
you have seen better than I so much inconstancy in some
particular cases." Neile and Laud examined him as to his
grounds for this opinion, which he gave them at large; and
after an hour's discussion of the subject, Andrews, who had
hitherto been silent, said, " Well, doctor, God send you
may be a true prophet concerning your master's inclination, which we are glad to hear from you. I am sure I shall
be a true prophet : I shall be in my grave, and so shall you,
my lord of Durham (Neile), but my lord of St. David's (Laud)
and you, doctor, will live to see the day, that your master
will be put to it upon his head and his crown, without he
will forsake the support of the church."

In 1624, the rectory of Bingham in Nottinghamshire was
conferred upon Mr. Wren, together with a stall in the church
of Winchester. In July 1625 he was chosen master of Pe-
terhouse, in Cambridge, to which he became a great benefactor, building a great part of the college, putting their
writings and records into order, and especially contributing
liberally, and procuring the contributions of others towards
the beautiful chapel, which was completed and dedicated
by him in 1632. In July 1628 he was promoted to the dignity of dean of Windsor and Wolverhampton. The same
year he served the office of vice-chancellor, and was made
register of the garter. While he held this office, he composed in Latin, a comment upon the statutes of Henry VIII.
respecting the order. This was published by Anstis, in the
" Register of the most noble order of the Garter." Ash-
mole had a high opinion of this work, and regretted that
he had not met with it before he had almost finished his
" Institution of the order of the Garter."

In April 1629, Mr. Wren was sworn a judge of the star-
chamber for foreign causes. In 1633, he attended Charles
I. in his progress to Scotland, and he had some hand in composing the ill-fated form of liturgy for that country. On
his return home he was made clerk of the closet to his majesty, and was about the same time created D. D. at Cambridge. In 1634 he was installed a prebendary of Westminster, and the same year promoted to the bishopric of
Hereford, which he held only until the following year,
when he was translated to the see of Norwich, in which he

sat two years and a half, and appears to have been very unpopular with the puritan party. Lord Clarendon informs
us that he "so passionately and warmly proceeded against
the dissenting congregations, that many left the kingdom,
to the lessening of the wealthy manufacture there of ker-
seys and narrow cloths, and, which was worse, transporting
that mystery into foreign parts." But the author of the
"Parentalia" says, "that this desertion of the Norwich
weavers was chiefly procured through the policy and management of the Dutch, who, wanting that manufacture,
(which was improved there to great perfection) left no
means unattempted to gain over these weavers to settle in
their towns, with an assurance of full liberty of conscience,
and greater advantages and privileges than they had obtained
in England." This author commends his modesty and humility, particularly in never seeking preferment : but he
says too little of his zeal, which was indeed, ardent and
active. This drew upon him the unjust imputation of popery. Nothing seems to have rendered him more hateful
and invidious to the parliament, than his standing high in
the favour of his sovereign.

In 1636 he succeeded Juxon, as dean of his majesty's
chapel, and in May 1638 was translated to the bishopric
of Ely. He had not enjoyed this above two years, when in
Dec. 1640, the day after the impeachment of Laud, Hamp-
den was sent by the Commons with a message to the House
of Peers, acquainting their lordships that the Commons had
received informations of a very high nature against Matthew Wren, bishop of Ely, for setting up idolatry and superstition in divers places, and acting some things of that
nature in his own person, and also to signify, that because
they hear of his endeavouring to escape out of the kingdom, some course might be taken for his putting in security to be forthcoming, &c. Their lordships fixed his bail
at 10,000l.; and this being given, he was impeached July 5,
1641, of high crimes and misdemeanours. These were
contained in twenty-four articles, the sum total of which
amounts to a zeal he shewed in enforcing the observances
of the church. Against these he composed a long and spirited defence, in consequence of which his enemies declined
trying him for his life, which they commuted for an order
to keep him in prison in the Tower during their pleasure.
This lasted full eighteen years, during which he employed
himself chiefly in study and in composing some of his

works. He had offers of release from Cromwell, but he disdained the terms, which were an acknowledgment of the favour, and submission to the usurper. When the restoration drew nigh, he was released in March 1659, and returned to his palace at Ely in 1660. In May 1661, he introduced to the convocation the form of prayer and thanksgiving which is still in use on May 29. In 1663 he built a new chapel at Pembroke-hall, Cambridge, at his own expence, and settled an estate upon the college for the perpetual support of the building.

Bishop Wren died at Ely-house, London, April 24, 1667, in his eighty-second year, and was buried in Pembroke-hall chapel. He was a man of unquestionable learning, and sincere in his attachment to the doctrines and discipline of the church, of great courage in suffering for his principles, but of a most intolerant spirit. No prelate's name occurs oftener in the accounts of the prosecutions of the puritans. He resembled Laud in many respects, and narrowly escaped his fate. He distinguished himself by some publications; as, 1. "Increpatio Bar Jesu, sive Polemicæ adsertiones locorum aliquot Sacræ Scripturæ ab imposturis perversionum in Catechesi Racoviana," Lond. 1660, in 4to, and reprinted in the ninth volume of the "Critici Sacri." 2. "The abandoning of the Scots Covenant, 1661," 4to. 3. "Epistolæ Variæ ad Viros doctissimos;" particularly to Gerard John Vossius. 4. Two "Sermons;" one printed in 1627, the other in 1662. Dr. Richardson made use of some of his MSS. in his "De Presulibus Angliæ." [1]

WREN (MATTHEW), eldest son of the preceding, was born Aug. 20, 1629, at Peter-house, Cambridge, at which time his father was master of that college. His first education was in that university, being admitted of St. Peter's-college in 1642, whence he removed to Oxford, where he was a student, not in a college or hall, but in a private house, as he could not conform to the principles or practises of the persons who then had the government of the university. At the restoration he was elected burgess of St. Michael in Cornwall, in the parliament which began May 8, 1661, and was appointed secretary to the earl of Clarendon, lord high chancellor of England, who visiting the university of Oxford, of which he was chancellor, in Sept. 1661, Mr. Wren was there created master of arts.

[1] Wren's Parentalia.—Biog. Brit.

He was one of the first members of the Royal Society, when they began their weekly meetings at London, in 1660. After the fall of his patron, the earl of Clarendon, he became secretary to James duke of York, in whose service he continued till his death, June 11, 1672, in the forty-third year of his age. He was interred in the same vault with his father, in the chapel of Pembroke-hall, Cambridge. He wrote, 1. " Considerations on Mr. Harrington's Commonwealth of Oceana, restrained to the first part of the preliminaries, London, 1657," in 8vo. To this book is prefixed a long letter of our author to Dr. John Wilkins, warden of Wadham-college in Oxford, who had desired him to give his judgment concerning Mr. Harrington's " Oceana." Harrington answered this work in the first book of his " Prerogative of popular government," 1658, 4to, in which he reflects on Mr. Wren as one of those virtuosi, who then met at Dr. Wilkins's lodgings at Wadham-college, the seminary of the Royal Society, and describes them as an assembly of men who " had an excellent faculty of magnifying a louse, and diminishing a commonwealth." Mr. Wren replied in 2. " Monarchy asserted; or, the State of Monarchical and Popular Government, in vindication of the considerations on Mr. Harrington's ' Oceana,' London, 1659," in 8vo. Harrington's rejoinder was an indecent piece of buffoonery, entitled " Politicaster: or, a Comical Discourse in answer to Mr. Wren's book, entitled ' Monarchy asserted, &c.' " 1659, 4to. Sir Edward Hyde, afterwards earl of Clarendon, in a letter to Dr. John Barwick, dated at Brussels the 25th of July, 1659, and printed in the appendix to the doctor's " Life," was very solicitous, that Mr. Wren should undertake a confutation of Hobbes's " Leviathan:" " I hope," says he, " it is only modesty in Mr. Wren, that makes him pause upon undertaking the work you have recommended to him; for I dare swear, by what I have seen of him, he is very equal to answer every part of it: I mean, every part that requires an answer. Nor is there need of a professed divine to vindicate the Creator from making man a verier beast than any of those of the field, or to vindicate scripture from his licentious interpretation. I dare say, he will find somewhat in Mr. Hobbes himself, I mean, in his former books, that contradicts what he sets forth in this, in that part in which he takes himself to be most exact, his beloved philosophy. And sure there is somewhat due to Aristotle and Tully, and to our universities, to free them from his reproaches; and it is high time, if what I hear be true, that some tutors read his Leviathan, instead of the others, to their pupils. Mr. Hobbes is my old friend, yet I cannot absolve him from the mischiefs he hath done to the king, the church, the laws, and the nation; and surely there should be enough to be said to the politics of that man, who, having resolved all religion, wisdom, and honesty, into an implicit obedience to the laws established, writes a book of policy, which, I may be bold to say, must be, by the established laws of any kingdom or province in Europe, condemned for impious and seditious: and therefore it will be very hard if the fundamentals of it be not overthrown. But I must ask both yours and Mr. Wren's pardon for enlarging so much, and antedating those animadversions he will make upon it."

Besides the above works, Mr. Wren wrote a kind of historical essay "On the origin and progress of the revolutions in England," printed in vol. I. of Mr. Gutch's "Collectanea Curiosa," 1781, from a transcript in the hand-writing of archbishop Sancroft. [1]

WREN (CHRISTOPHER), a learned and illustrious English architect and mathematician, was nephew to bishop Wren, and the son of Dr. Christopher Wren, who was fellow of St. John's college, Oxford, afterwards chaplain to Charles I. and rector of Knoyle in Wiltshire; made dean of Windsor in 1635, and presented to the rectory of Hasely in Oxfordshire in 1638; and died at Blechindon, in the same county, 1658, at the house of Mr. William Holder, rector of that parish, who had married his daughter. He was a man well skilled in all the branches of the mathematics, and had a great hand in forming the genius of his only son Christopher. In the state papers of Edward, earl of Clarendon, vol. I. p. 270, is an estimate of a building to be erected for her majesty by dean Wren. He did another important service to his country. After the chapel of St. George and the treasury belonging to it had been plundered by the republicans, he sedulously exerted himself in recovering as many of the records as could be procured, and was so successful as to redeem the three registers distinguished by the names of the Black, Blue, and Red, which were carefully preserved by him till his death.

[1] Gen. Dict.—Parentalia.—Birch's Hist. of the Royal Society.—Cole's MS. Athenæ in Brit. Mus.

They were afterwards committed to the custody of his son, who, soon after the restoration, delivered them to Dr. Bruno Ryves, dean of Windsor.

His son Christopher, who is the subject of this article, was born at Knoyle Oct. 20, 1632 ; and, while very young, discovered a surprising turn for learning, especially for the mathematics. He was sent to Oxford, and admitted a gentleman-commoner at Wadham college, at about fourteen years of age : and the advancements he made there in mathematical knowledge, before he was sixteen, were, as we learn from Oughtred, very extraordinary, and even astonishing. His uncommon abilities excited the admiration of Dr. Wilkins, then warden of his college, and of Dr. Seth Ward, Savilian professor of astronomy, who then resided in Wadham. By Dr. Wilkins he was introduced to Charles, elector palatine, to whom he presented several mechanical instruments of his own invention. In 1647 he became acquainted with sir Charles Scarborough, at whose request he undertook the translation of Oughtred's geometrical dialling into Latin. He took a bachelor of arts degree in 1650 ; and in 1651 published a short algebraical tract relating to the Julian period. In 1652 he took his master's degree, having been chosen fellow of All Souls' college. Soon after, he became one of that ingenious and learned society, who then met at Oxford for the improvement of natural and experimental philosophy.

Aug. 1657, he was chosen professor of astronomy in Gresham college ; and his lectures, which were much frequented, tended greatly to the promotion of real knowledge. In his inaugural oration, among other things, he proposed several methods, by which to account for the shadows' returning backward ten degrees on the dial of king Ahaz, by the laws of nature. One subject of his lectures was upon telescopes, to the improvement of which he had greatly contributed ; another was on certain properties of the air and the barometer. In 1658, he read a description of the body and different phases of the planet Saturn, which subject he proposed to pursue ; and the same year communicated some demonstrations concerning cycloids to Dr. Wallis, which were afterwards published by the doctor at the end of his treatise upon that subject. About that time also, he solved the problem proposed by Pascal, under the feigned name of John de Montfort, to all the English mathematicians ; and returned another to the mathematicians in France, formerly proposed by Kepler, and then solved likewise by himself, of which they never gave any solution. He did not continue long at Gresham college; for, Feb. 5, 1660-1, he was chosen Savilian professor of astronomy at Oxford, in the room of Dr. Seth Ward. He entered upon it in May; and in September was created doctor of civil law.

Among his other eminent accomplishments, he had gained so considerable a skill in architecture, that he was sent for the same year from Oxford, by order of Charles II. to assist sir John Denham, surveyor-general of his majesty's works. In 1663, he was chosen fellow of the Royal Society; being one of those who were first appointed by the council after the grant of their charter. Not long after, it being expected that the king would make the society a visit, the lord Brounker, president, by a letter desired the advice of Dr. Wren, who was then at Oxford, concerning the experiments which might be most proper for his majesty's entertainment: to whom the doctor recommended principally the Torricellian experiment, and the weather-needle, as being not bare amusements, but useful, and likewise neat in the operation, and attended with little incumbrance. Dr. Wren did great honour to this illustrious body, by many curious and useful discoveries in astronomy, natural philosophy, and other sciences, related in the "History of the Royal Society;" where the author Sprat, who was a member of it, has inserted them from the registers and other books of the society to 1665. Among other of his productions there enumerated is a lunar globe, representing not only the spots and various degrees of whiteness upon the surface, but the hills, eminences, and cavities; and not only so, but it is turned to the light, shewing all the lunar phases, with the various appearances that happen from the shadows of the mountains and valleys. The lunar globe was formed, not merely at the request of the Royal Society, but likewise by the command of Charles II. whose pleasure, for the prosecuting and perfecting of it was signified by a letter under the joint hands of sir Robert Moray and sir Paul Neile, dated from Whitehall, the 17th of May, 1661, and directed to Dr. Wren, Savilian professor at Oxford. His majesty received the globe with satisfaction, and ordered it to be placed among the curiosities of his cabinet. Another of these productions is a tract on the doctrine of motion that arises from the impact between two bodies, illustrated by experiments. And a third is, the history of the seasons, as to the temperature, weather, productions, diseases, &c. &c. For which purpose he contrived many curious machines, several of which kept their own registers, tracing out the lines of variations, so that a person might know what changes the weather had undergone in his absence: as wind-gages, thermometers, barometers, hygrometers, rain-gages, &c. &c. He made also great additions to the new discoveries on pendulums; and among other things shewed, that there may be produced a natural standard for measure from the pendulum for common use. He invented many ways to make astronomical observations more easy and accurate. He fitted and hung quadrants, sextants, and radii more commodiously than formerly: he made two telescopes to open with a joint like a sector, by which observers may infallibly take a distance to half minutes, &c. He made many sorts of retes, screws, and other devices, for improving telescopes to take small distances, and apparent diameters, to seconds. He made apertures for taking in more or less light, as the observer pleases, by opening and shutting, the better to fit glasses for crepusculine observations. He added much to the theory of dioptrics; much to the manufacture of grinding good glasses. He attempted, and not without success, the making of glasses of other forms than spherical. He exactly measured and delineated the spheres of the humours of the eye, the proportions of which to one another were only guessed at before: a discussion shewing the reasons why we see objects erect, and that reflection conduces as much to vision as refraction. He displayed a natural and easy theory of refractions, which exactly answered every experiment. He fully demonstrated all dioptrics in a few propositions, shewing not only, as in Kepler's Dioptrics, the common properties of glasses, but the proportions by which the individual rays cut the axis, and each other, upon which the charges of the telescopes, or the proportion of the eye-glasses and apertures, are demonstrably discovered. He made constant observations on Saturn, and a true theory of that planet, before the printed discourse by Huygens, on that subject, appeared. He made maps of the Pleiades and other telescopic stars: and proposed methods to determine the great question as to the earth's motion or rest, by the small stars about the pole to be seen in large telescopes. In navigation he made many improvements. He framed a magnetical terella, which he placed in the midst of a plane board with a hole, into which the terella is half immersed, till it be like a globe with the poles in the horizon: the plane is then dusted over with steel filings from a sieve : the dust, by the magnetical virtue, becomes immediately figured into furrows that bend like a sort of helix, proceeding as it were out at one pole, and returning in it by the other ; the whole plane becoming figured like the circles of a planisphere. It being a question in his time among the problems of navigation, to what mechanical powers sailing against the wind was reducible ; he shewed it to be a wedge : and he demonstrated, how a transient force upon an oblique plane would cause the motion of the plane against the first mover : and he made an instrument mechanically producing the same effect, and shewed the reason of sailing on all winds. The geometrical mechanism of rowing, he shewed to be a lever on a moving or cedent fulcrum : for this end, he made instruments and experiments, to find the resistance to motion in a liquid medium; with other things that are the necessary elements for laying down the geometry of sailing, swimming, rowing, flying, and constructing of ships. He invented a very speedy and curious way of etching. He started many things towards the emendation of waterworks. He likewise made some instruments for respiration, and for straining the breath from fuliginous vapours, to try whether the same breath, so purified, will serve again. He was the first inventor of drawing pictures by microscopical glasses. He found out perpetual, or at least long-lived lamps, for keeping a perpetual regular heat, in order to various uses, as hatching of eggs and insects, production of plants, chemical preparations, imitating nature in producing fossils and minerals, keeping the motion of watches equal, for the longitude and astronomical uses. He was the first author of the anatomical experiment of injecting liquor into the veins of animals. By this operation, divers creatures were immediately purged, vomited, intoxicated, killed, or revived, according to the quality of the liquor injected. Hence arose many other new experiments, particularly that of transfusing blood, which has been prosecuted in sundry curious instances. Such is a short account of the principal discoveries which Dr. Wren presented, or suggested, to the Royal Society, or were improved by him. We now return to his progress as an architect.

In 1665, he went over to France, where he not only surveyed all the buildings of note in Paris, and made excursions to other places, but took particular notice of what was most remarkable in every branch of mechanics, and contracted acquaintance with all the considerable virtuosi[*]. Upon his return home, he was appointed architect and one of the commissioners for the reparation of St. Paul's cathedral; as appears from Mr. Evelyn's dedication to him of "The Account of Architects and Architecture," 1706, folio, where we have the following account. "I have named St. Paul's, and truly not without admiration, as oft as I recall to mind, as I frequently do, the sad and deplorable condition it was in; when, after it had been made a stable of horses, and a den of thieves, you, with other gentlemen and myself, were by the late king Charles named to survey the dilapidations, and to make report to his majesty, in order to a speedy reparation. You will not, as I am sure, forget the struggle we had with some who were for patching it up any how, so the steeple might stand, instead of new building; when, to put an end to the contest, five days after, that dreadful conflagration happened, out of whose ashes this phœnix is risen, and was by providence designed for you." Within a few days after the fire, which began Sept. 2, 1666, he drew a plan for a new city, of which Oldenburg, the secretary of the Royal Society, gave an account to Mr. Boyle. "Dr. Wren," says he, "has drawn a model for a new city, and presented it to the king, who produced it himself before his council, and manifested much approbation of it. I was yesterday morning with the doctor, and saw the model, which methinks does so well provide for security, conveniency, and beauty, that I can see nothing wanting as to these three main articles: but whether it has consulted with the populousness of a great city, and whether reasons of state would have that consulted with, is a quære with me," &c. The execution of this noble design was unhappily prevented by

---

* "The great number of drawings he made there from their buildings, had but too visible influence on some of his own, but it was so far lucky for sir Christopher, that Louis XIV. had erected palaces only, no churches. St. Paul's escaped, but Hampton court was sacrificed to the god of false taste. Yet I have been assured by a descendant of sir Christopher, that he gave another design for Hampton court in a better taste, which queen Mary wished to have executed, but was overruled." Walpole.

the disputes which arose about private property, and the haste and hurry of rebuilding; though it is said that the practicability of Wren's whole plan, without infringement of any property, was at that time demonstrated, and all material objections fully weighed and answered.

Upon the decease of sir John Denham, in March 1688, he succeeded him in the office of surveyor-general of his majesty's works. The theatre at Oxford will be a lasting monument of his great abilities as an architect; which curious work was finished by him in 1669. As in this structure the admirable contrivance of the flat roof, being eighty feet over one way, and seventy the other, without any arched work or pillars to support it, is particularly remarkable, it has been both largely described, and likewise delineated, by the ingenious Dr. Plott, in his " Natural History of Oxfordshire." But the conflagration of the city of London gave him many opportunities afterwards of employing his genius in that way; when, besides the works of the crown, which continued under his care, the cathedral of St Paul, the parochial churches, and other public structures, which had been destroyed by that dreadful calamity, were rebuilt from his designs, and under his direction; in the management of which affair he was assisted in the measurements and laying out of private property by the ingenious Mr. Robert Hooke. The variety of business in which he was by this means engaged requiring his constant attendance and concern, he resigned his Savilian professorship at Oxford in 1673; and the year following he received from the king the honour of knighthood. He was one of the commissioners who, at the motion of sir Jonas Moore, surveyor-general of the ordnance, had been appointed by his majesty to find a proper place for erecting a royal observatory; and he proposed Greenwich, which was approved of. On Aug. 10, 1675, the foundation of the building was laid; which, when finished under the direction of sir Jonas, with the advice and assistance of sir Christopher, was furnished with the best instruments for making astronomical observations; and Mr. Flamsted was constituted his majesty's first professor there.

About this time he married the daughter of sir Thomas Coghill, of Belchington, in Oxfordshire, by whom he had one son of his own name; and, she dying soon after, he married a daughter of William lord Fitzwilliam, baron of Lifford in Ireland, by whom he had a son and a daughter

In 1680, he was chosen president of the Royal Society; afterwards appointed architect and commissioner of Chelsea-college; and, in 1684, principal officer or comptroller of the works in the castle of Windsor. He sat twice in parliament, as a representative for two different boroughs; first, for Plympton in Devonshire in 1685, and again in 1700 for Melcomb-Regis in Dorsetshire. He was employed in erecting a great variety of churches and public edifices, when the country met with an indelible disgrace in a court intrigue, in consequence of which, in April 1718, his patent for royal works was superseded, when this venerable and illustrious man had reached his eighty-sixth year, after half a century spent in a continued, active, and laborious service to the crown and the public. Walpole has well said that "the length of his life enriched the reigns of several princes, and disgraced the last of them." Until this time he lived in a house in Scotland-yard, adjoining to Whitehall; but, after his removal from that place in 1718, he dwelt occasionally in St. James's-street, Westminster. He died Feb. 25, 1723, aged ninety-one, and was interred with great solemnity in St. Paul's cathedral, in the vault under the south wing of the choir, near the east end. Upon a flat stone, covering the single vault, which contains his body, is a plain English inscription; and another inscription upon the side of a pillar; in these terms:

> " Subtus conditur,
> Hujus Ecclesiæ et Urbis conditor,
> CHRISTOPHERUS WREN:
> Qui vixit annos ultra nonaginta,
> Non sibi, sed bono publico.
> Lector, si monumentum requiris,
> Circumspice.
> Obiit 25 Feb. ann. MDCCXXIII. ætat. XCI."

As to his person, he was of low stature, and thin; but, by temperance and skilful and management, for he was not unacquainted with anatomy and physic, he enjoyed a good state of health to a very unusual length of life. He was modest, devout, strictly virtuous, and very communicative of what he knew. Besides his peculiar eminence as an architect, his learning and knowledge were very extensive in all the arts and sciences, and especially in the mathematics. Mr. Hooke, who was intimately acquainted with him, and very able to make a just estimate of his abilities, has comprised his character in these few but comprehensive words : "I must affirm," says he, "that since the time of Archimedes, there scarcely ever has met in one man, in so great a perfection, such a mechanical hand, and so philosophical a mind." And a greater than Hooke, even the illustrious and immortal Newton, whose signet stamps an indelible character, speaks thus of him, with other eminent men : " D. Christophorus Wrennus, Eques Auratus, Johannes Wallisius, S. T. D. et D. Christianus Hugenius, hujus ætatis Geometrarum facile principes." Mr. Evelyn, in the dedication referred to above, tells him, that " he inscribed his book with his name, partly through an ambition of publickly declaring the great esteem I have ever had," says he, "of your virtues and accomplishments, not only in the art of building, but through all the learned cycle of the most useful knowledge and abstruser sciences, as well as of the most polite and shining ; all which is so justly to be allowed you, that you need no panegyric, or other history, to eternize them, than the greatest city of the universe, which you have rebuilt and beautified, and are still improving : witness the churches, the royal courts, stately halls, magazines, palaces, and other public structures; besides that you have built of great and magnificent in both the universities, at Chelsea, and in the country ; and are now advancing of the royal Marine-hospital at Greenwich : all of them so many trophies of your skill and industry, and conducted with that success, that, if the whole art of building were lost, it might be recovered and found again in St. Paul's, the historical pillar, and those other monuments of your happy talent and extraordinary genius."

The note below * contains a catalogue of the churches

* St. Paul's Cathedral.
Allhallows the Great
Allhallows, Bread-street,
Allhallows, Lombard-street.
St. Alban, Wood street.
St. Anne and Agnes.
St. Andrew, Wardrobe.
St. Andrew. Holborn.
St. Ancholin.
St. Au tin.
St. Bene't, Grasschurch.
St. Bene't, Paul's Wharf.
St. Bene't. Fink.
St. Bride.
St. Bartholomew.
Christ-Church.
St. Clement. East-cheap.
St. Clement Danes.

St. Dionis, Back-church.
St. Edmund the King.
St. George, Botolph-lane.
St. James, Garlic-hill,
St. James, Westminster.
St. Lawrence Jewry.
St. Michael, Basing-hall.
St. Michael Royal.
St. Michael, Queenhithe.
St. Michael, Wood-street.
St. Michael, Crooked-lane.
St. Martin, Ludgate.
St. Matthew, Friday-street.
St. Michael, Cornhill.
St. Margaret, Lothbury.
St. Margaret Pattens.
St. Mary Abchurch.
St. Mary Aldermanbury.

of the city of London, royal palaces, hospitals, and public edifices, built by sir Christopher Wren, surveyor-general of the royal works during fifty years, viz. from 1668 to 1718.

Among the many public buildings erected by him in the city of London, the church of St. Stephen in Walbroke, that of St. Mary-le-Bow, the Monument, and the cathedral of St. Paul, have more especially drawn the attention of foreign connoisseurs. "The church of Walbroke," says the author of the 'Critical Review of the public buildings, &c. of London,' "so little known among us, is famous all over Europe, and is justly reputed the master-piece of the celebrated sir Christopher Wren. Perhaps Italy itself can produce no modern building that can vie with this in taste or proportion. There is not a beauty which the plan would admit of, that is not to be found here in its greatest perfection; and foreigners very justly call our judgment in question, for understanding its graces no better, and allowing it no higher a degree of fame." The steeple of St. Mary-le-Bow, which is particularly grand and beautiful, stands upon an old Roman causey, that lies eighteen feet below the level of the present street; and the body of the church on the walls of a Roman temple. The Monument is a pillar of the Doric order, the pedestal of which is forty feet high and twenty-one square, the diameter of the column fifteen feet, and the altitude of the whole 202; which is a fourth part higher than that of the emperor Trajan at Rome. It was begun in 1671, and finished in 1677. But St. Paul's will probably be considered as the greatest monument of sir Christopher's genius. He died, says Walpole, at the age of ninety-one, having lived to see the completion of St. Paul's; a fabric and an event, which one

St. Mary-le-Bow.
St. Mary Magdalen.
St. Mary Somerset.
St. Mary at Hill.
St. Nicholas Cole Abbey.
St. Olave Jewry.
St. Peter, Cornhill.
St. Swithin, Cannon-street.
St. Stephen, Walbrooke.
St. Stephen, Colman-street.
St. Mildred, Bread-street.
St. Magnus, London-bridge.
St. Foster's Church.
St. Mildred, Poultry.
Westminster Abbey, repaired.

St. Christopher.
St. Dunstan in the East.
St. Mary Aldermary.
St. Sepulchre's.
The Monument.
Custom-House, London.
Winchester-Castle.
Hampton-Court.
Chelsea-Hospital.
Greenwich-Hospital.
Theatre at Oxford.
Trinity-college Library, Cambridge,
Emanuel-college Chapel, Cambridge,
&c. &c.

cannot wonder left such an impression of content on the mind of the good old man, that, being carried to see it once a year, it seemed to recall a memory that was almost deadened to every other use." The same writer observes, that " so many great architects as were employed on St. Peter's (at Rome) have not left it, upon the whole, a more perfect edifice than this work of a single mind "

Sir Christopher Wren never printed any thing himself; but several of his works have been published by others': some in the " Philosophical Transactions," and some by Dr. Wallis and other friends; while some are still remaining in manuscript, and several volumes of his designs are in the library of All Souls college. The title of one of them is, " Delineationes novæ fabricæ templi Paulini juxta tertiam propositionem et ex sententia regis Caroli II. sub privato sigillo expressæ 14 Maii, ann. 1678." By this it appears that he floated very much in his designs for St. Paul's. One of them is very much like that of San Gallo for St. Peter's at Rome. In another, the dome is crowned with a pine-apple, and it is curious to observe how every design for the present beautiful dome excels the other. The favourite design, however, of the great architect himself was not taken.

Sir Christopher was succeeded in his estate by his son and only surviving child, Christopher Wren, esq. This gentleman was born Feb. 16, 1675 (the year St. Paul's was founded), and was educated at Eton school and Pembroke' hall, Cambridge. In 1694, sir Christopher procured him the office of deputy-clerk engrosser; but this preferment did not prevent him from making a tour through Holland, France, and Italy. On his return from the continent he was elected member of parliament for Windsor in 1712 and 1714. He died Aug. 24, 1747, aged seventy-two, and was buried in the church of Wroxhall, adjoining to his seat at Wroxhall in Warwickshire. He was a man very much esteemed, and was equally pious, learned, and amiable. He had made antiquity his particular study, well understood it, and was extremely communicative. He wrote and published in 1708, in 4to, a work entitled " Numismatum antiquorum sylloge, populis Græcis, municipiis et coloniis Romanis cusorum, ex chimeliarcho editoris." This, which he dedicated to the Royal Society, contains representations of many curious Greek medallions in four plates, and two others of ancient inscriptions; these are followed by the legends of imperial coins in the large and middle size, from Julius Cæsar to Aurelian, with their interpretations : and subjoined is an appendix of Syrian and Egyptian kings, and coins of cities, all collected by himself.  He also collected with so much care and attention, as to leave scarcely any curiosity ungratified, memoirs of the life of bishop Wren, Dr. Christopher Wren, dean of Windsor, and his illustrious father ; with collections of records and original papers.  These were published in fol. under the title of " Parentalia," by his son Stephen, a physician, assisted by Mr. Ames, in 1750, and are illustrated by portraits and plates.  Mr. Wren married twice ; in May 1706 to Mary, daughter of Mr. Musard, jeweller to queen Anne, who died in 1712 ; he afterwards married in 1715 dame Constance, widow of sir Roger Burgoyne, bart. and daughter of sir Thomas Middleton, of Stansted Montfitchet, Essex, who died in 1734.  By each marriage he had one son, Christopher, and Stephen.  Christopher, the eldest, an eccentric humourist, was the poetical friend of lady Luxborough and Shenstone.  Displeasing his father, all the unentailed estates were given from him to sir Roger Burgoyne, bart. son of sir Roger.  Wroxall is still in the family, and owned by Christopher Wren, esq. now (1806) in the East Indies, who is the sixth Christopher Wren in succession from the father of sir Christopher.[1]

WRIGHT (ABRAHAM), a learned and loyal divine of the seventeenth century, was the son of Richard Wright, citizen and silk-dyer of London, who was the son of Jeffrey Wright, of Loughborough, in Leicestershire.  He was born in Black-Swan alley, Thames-street, in the parish of St. James's, Garlick Hythe, London, Dec. 23, 1611, and educated partly at Mercers'-chapel school, but principally at Merchant Taylors, whence he was elected scholar of St. John's-college, Oxford, in 1629, by the interest of Dr. Juxon, then president, who became his patron.  He was much admired at this time for a natural eloquence, and a love of polite literature.  In 1632 he was elected fellow, and while bachelor of arts, made a collection of modern Latin poetry, which he published afterwards under the title of " Delitiæ delitiarum, sive epigrammatum ex optimis quibusque hujus novissimi seculi Poetis in amplissima illa

1 Parentalia.—Biog. Brit.—Walpole's Anecdotes.—Seward's Anecdotes.—Noble's Continuation of Granger.—Ward's Gresham Professors. — Hutton's Dictionary.

Bibl. Bodleiana, et pene omnino alibi extantibus anthologia in unum corollum connexa," Ox. 1637, 12mo. In 1636, when archbishop Laud entertained the royal family at St. John's-college, Mr. Wright was selected to make an English address, and afterwards distinguished himself as a performer in a comedy called "Love's Hospital," which was acted before their majesties in the hall, by a company of St. John's men.

In Sept. 1637, and 1639, he took deacon's and priest's orders, and was so much admired as an eloquent preacher as to be frequently called upon to preach at St. Mary's, St. Paul's, London, &c. In 1645 he became vicar of Okeham in Rutlandshire, by the interest of his patron Juxon, now bishop of London, and received institution, but refused induction, because in that case he must have taken the covenant, which was altogether repugnant to his principles, and therefore a nonconformist was placed in his living, one Benjamin King. Mr. Wright then went to London, and lived retired till after the death of the king, when he was hospitably received into the family of sir George Grime or Graham at Peckham, and while here he instructed sir George's sons in Latin and Greek, and read the Common-prayer on all Sundays and holidays, and preached and administered the sacrament. About 1655 he returned to London, on being chosen by the parishioners of St. Olave, Silver-street, to be their minister. In this office he remained for four years, and was in fact rector, but would not take possession on account of the republican oaths and obligations necessary. He performed all his duties, however, according to the forms of the Church of England, although at some risk. On the restoration Benjamin King, who had been put into his living at Okeham, resigned, by his hand and seal, all title to it, and Mr. Wright took possession and retained it to his dying day, refusing some other preferments. He lived here to a very advanced age, and died May 9, 1690, and was buried in Okeham church.

Besides the "Delitiæ poetarum" already mentioned, he published 1. "Five Sermons in five several stiles or ways of preaching," Lond. 1656, 8vo. The object of this curious collection is to exhibit the advantages of education in fitting for the ministry, as well as the different styles of some eminent men of that period, viz. bishop Andrews, bishop Hall, Dr. Mayne, and Mr. Cartwright. Dr. Birch is mistaken in calling this an *imitation* of different styles;

it is a selection from the works of the respective authors.
2. "A practical commentary, or exposition on the book of
Psalms," Lond. 1661, fol.   3. "Practical Commentary on
the Pentateuch," ibid. fol.   4. "Parnassus biceps, or several choice pieces of poetry, composed by the best wits
that were in both the universities before their dissolution,"
ibid. 1656, 8vo.   He wrote some other works which have
not been printed.

He left a son, JAMES WRIGHT, known to dramatic antiquaries, as one of the earliest historians of the stage, and
perhaps one of the first collectors of old plays after Cartwright, whose collection was at Dulwich-college.   His
work on this subject, which is extremely scarce, is entitled
" Historia Histrionica ; an historical account of the English
stage, shewing the ancient use, improvement, and perfection, of dramatic representations in this nation.   In a dialogue of plays and players," Lond. 1699, 8vo.   It was first
brought forward by Oldys, who quoted it in his life of
Alleyn the player in the Biographia Britannica.   By Warburton's recommendation it was prefixed to Dodsley's
" Old Plays," but the preface has been omitted which
Warton says is a sensible one, and certainly points out the
only use of most old plays, as exhibiting the manners of
the times.   Wright wrote likewise " Country conversations,
being an account of some discourses that happened on a
visit to the country last summer, on divers subjects ; chiefly,
of the modern comedies, of drinking, of translated verse,
of painting and painters, of poets and poetry," Lond. 1694,
12mo.   He appears also to have been a skilful antiquary,
and had formed a very curious collection, which was unfortunately consumed in a fire in the Middle Temple in 1698.
Among his MSS. was an excellent transcript of Leland's
" Itinerary," of the age of queen Elizabeth, and consequently made before the present mutilations and corruptions.   On this he had much correspondence with Hearne.
His other works were, 1. " A poem, being an Essay on
the present ruins of St. Paul's cathedral," Lond. 1668, 4to.
2. " History and Antiquities of the county of Rutland,"
ibid. 1684, fol. soon followed by " Additions" in 1687, and
" Farther Additions," 1714.   This is a work of much labour and research, although not perfect.   3. "A new description of the city of Paris, in two parts, out of the
French," ibid. 1687, 8vo.   4. " Verses anniversary to the
venerable memory of his ever honoured father, &c." 1690,

8vo. 5. " Monasticon Anglicanum, &c." an accurate epitome in English of Dugdale's "Monasticon," ibid. 1693,
fol. 6. " Three poems of St. Paul's cathedral, viz. The
Ruins (mentioned above), The re-building, The Choir,"
1697, fol. 7. " Phœnix Paulina, a poem on St. Paul's
cathedral," 1709, 4to. 8. " Burley on the hill, a poem,"
4to, no date, but reprinted in his last additions to his Rutlandshire. Hearne, who knew and respected Wright, informs us, that he wrote strictures on Wood's "Athenæ,"
but that they remained in manuscript. Wright, a few years
before his death, gave Hearne a complete catalogue of his
works, which on application he had refused to Wood, " as
an injudicious biographer."

Wright, who was born about 1644, was probably educated at Merchant Taylors' school, but was not of either
university. In 1666 he became a student of New Inn, and
in three years removed to the Middle Temple, and was at
length called to the bar. He died about 1715.[1]

WRIGHT (EDWARD), a noted English mathematician,
who flourished in the latter part of the sixteenth century
and beginning of the seventeenth, is thus characterised in
a Latin paper in the library of Gonvile and Caius college,
Cambridge : " This year (1615) died at London, Edward
Wright, of Garveston, in Norfolk, formerly a fellow of
this college ; a man respected by all for the integrity and
simplicity of his manners, and also famous for his skill in
the mathematical sciences ; so that he was not undeservedly
styled a most excellent mathematician by Richard Hack-
luyt, the author of an original treatise of our English na-
vigations. What knowledge he had acquired in the science
of mechanics, and how usefully he employed that knowledge to the public as well as to private advantage, abundantly appear both from the writings he published, and
from the many mechanical operations still extant, which
are standing monuments of his great industry and ingenuity.
He was the first undertaker of that difficult but useful work,
by which a little river is brought from the town of Ware
in a new canal, to supply the city of London with water ;
but by the tricks of others he was hindered from completing the work he had begun. He was excellent both in
contrivance and execution, nor was he inferior to the most

---

[1] Ath. Ox. vol. II —Birch's Life of Tillotson.—Warton's edition of Milton's
Poems.—Wilson's Hist. of Merchant Taylors' school.

ingenious mechanic in the making of instruments, either of brass or any other matter. To his invention is owing whatever advantage Hondius's geographical charts have above others; for it was Wright who taught Jodocus Hondius the method of constructing them, which was till then unknown; but the ungrateful Hondius concealed the name of the true author, and arrogated the glory of the invention to himself. Of this fraudulent practice the good man could not help complaining, and justly enough, in the preface to his treatise of the "Correction of Errors in the art of Navigation;" which he composed with excellent judgment and after long experience, to the great advancement of naval affairs. For the improvement of this art he was appointed mathematical lecturer by the East India company, and read lectures in the house of that worthy knight sir Thomas Smith, for which he had a yearly salary of fifty pounds. This office he discharged with great reputation, and much to the satisfaction of his hearers. He published in English a book on the doctrine of the sphere, and another concerning the construction of sun-dials. He also prefixed an ingenious preface to the learned Gilbert's book on the loadstone. By these and other his writings, he has transmitted his fame to latest posterity. While he was yet a fellow of this college, he could not be concealed in his private study, but was called forth to the public business of the nation by the queen, about 1593. He was ordered to attend the earl of Cumberland in some maritime expeditions. One of these he has given a faithful account of, in the manner of a journal or ephemeris, to which he has prefixed an elegant hydrographical chart of his own contrivance. A little before his death he employed himself about an English translation of the book of logarithms, then lately discovered by lord Napier, a Scotchman, who had a great affection for him. This posthumous work of his was published soon after by his only son Samuel Wright, who was also a scholar of this college. He had formed many other useful designs, but was hindered by death from bringing them to perfection. Of him it may truly be said, that he studied more to serve the public than himself; and though he was rich in fame, and in the promises of the great, yet he died poor, to the scandal of an ungrateful age." So far the memoir; other particulars concerning him are as follow:

Mr. Wright first dicovered the true way of dividing the

meridian line, according to which the Mercator's charts are constructed, and upon which Mercator's sailing is founded. An account of this he sent from Caius college, Cambridge, where he was then a fellow, to his friend Mr. Blondeville, containing a short table for that purpose, with a specimen of a chart so divided, together with the manner of dividing it. All which Blondeville published in 1594, among his " Exercises." And, in 1597, the rev. Mr. William Barlowe, in his " Navigator's Supply," gave a demonstration of this division as communicated by a friend.

At length, in 1599, Mr. Wright himself printed his celebrated treatise entitled " The Correction of certain Errors in Navigation," which had been written many years before; where he shews the reason of this division of the meridian, the manner of constructing his table, and its uses in navigation, with other improvements. In 1610 a second edition of Mr. Wright's book was published, and dedicated to his royal pupil, prince Henry; in which the author inserted farther improvements; particularly he proposed an excellent way of determining the magnitude of the earth; at the same time recommending, very judiciously, the making our common measures in some certain proportion to that of a degree on its surface, that they might not depend on the uncertain length of a barley corn. Some of his other improvements were—the table of latitudes for dividing the meridian, computed as far as to minutes: an instrument, he calls the sea-rings, by which the variation of the compass, the altitude of the sun, and the time of the day, may be readily determined at once in any place, provided the latitude be known; the correcting of the errors arising from the eccentricity of the eye in observing by the cross-staff; a total amendment in the tables of the declinations and places of the sun and stars, from his own observations, made with a six-foot quadrant, in 1594, 95, 96, 97; a sea-quadrant, to take altitudes by a forward or backward observation; having also a contrivance for the ready finding the latitude by the height of the polar-star, when not upon the meridian. And that this book might be the better understood by beginners, to this edition is subjoined a translation of Zamorano's Compendium; and added a large table of the variation of the compass as observed in very different parts of the world, to shew it is not occasioned by any magnetical pole. The work has gone through several other editions since. And, beside the books above mentioned, he wrote another on navigation, entitled "The Haven-finding Art." Some accounts of him say also, that it was in 1589 that he first began to attend the earl of Cumberland in his voyages. It is also said that he made for his pupil, prince Henry, a large sphere with curious movements, which, by the help of spring-work, not only represented the motions of the whole celestial sphere, but shewed likewise the particular systems of the sun and moon, and their circular motions, together with their places and possibilities of eclipsing each other : there is in it a work for a motion of 17,100 years, if it should not be stopped, or the materials fail. This sphere, though thus made at a great expence of money and ingenious industry, was afterwards in the time of the civil wars cast aside, among dust and rubbish, where it was found in 1646, by sir Jonas Moore, who at his own expence restored it to its first state of perfection, and deposited it at his own house in the Tower, among his other mathematical instruments and curiosities. [1]

WRIGHT (JOSEPH), commonly called Wright of Derby, a very distinguished painter, was born at Derby, September 3, 1734. His father was an attorney there. In early life, he gave indications of a taste for mechanics, and those habits of attentive observation, which generally lead to perfection in the fine arts. In 1751, he came to London, and was placed with Hudson, the most eminent portrait-painter of the day, and who, lord Orford tells us, pleased the country gentlemen with " his honest similitudes, fair tied wigs, blue velvet coats, and white sattin waistcoats, which he bestowed liberally on his customers." Wright used to lament that he could not receive much instruction from this master, but it is certain he at this time painted both portraits and historical pieces in a very capital style, of which his " Blacksmith's forge," " Air-pump, &c." are proofs. In 1773, after marrying, he visited Italy, and made great advances in his profession. In 1775, he returned to England, and settled for two years at Bath, after which his residence was entirely at Derby.

His attention was directed for some years to portrait painting ; and from the specimens he has left, there can be no doubt that he would have stood in the first rank in

[1] Hutton's Dict.—Martin's Biog. Philosophica.

this branch of the art, had he chosen to pursue it; but his genius was not to be circumscribed within such narrow limits, and therefore, at a mature age, he visited Italy, to study the precious remains of art which that country possessed. His fine drawings, after Michael Angelo (which have scarcely been seen except by his particular friends), and the enthusiasm with which he always spoke of the sublime original, evinced the estimation in which he held them; and from their extreme accuracy, they may be considered as faithful delineations of the treasures of the Capella Sestina. In 1782 he was elected an associate of the Royal Academy; but offended at Mr. Garvey's being chosen royal academician before himself, he resigned his associate's diploma in disgust, yet continued to exhibit at intervals with that society. In 1785 he made an exhibition of his own pictures at the auction room, now Robins's, in the Great Piazza, Covent Garden. The collection consisted of twenty four pictures.

During his abode in Italy he had an opportunity of seeing a very memorable eruption of Vesuvius, which rekindled his inclination for painting extraordinary effects of light; and his different pictures of this sublime event stood decidedly *chef d'œuvres* in that line of painting; for who but Wright ever succeeded in fire or moonlights? His later pictures were chiefly landscapes, in which we are at a loss, whether most to admire the elegance of his outline, his judicious management of light and shade, or the truth and delicacy of his colouring; but of those, the greatest part have never been exhibited, as they were always purchased from the easel by amateurs who knew how to appreciate their value: a large landscape (his last work) now at Derby, being a view of the head of Ullswater, may be considered amongst the finest of his works, and deservedly ranks with the most valued productions of Wilson, or even Claude himself.

In the historical line, the Dead Soldier, which is now known by Heath's admirable print, would alone establish his fame, if his Edwin (in the possession of J. Milnes, esq. of Wakefield, who has also his Destruction of the Floating Batteries off Gibraltar, and some of his best landscapes), the two pictures of Hero and Leander, Lady in Comus, Indian Widow, and other historical subjects, had not already ascertained his excellence. His attachment to his native town, added to his natural modesty, and his severe application both to the theory and practice of painting, prevented his mixing with promiscuous society, or establishing his reputation by arts which he would never descend to practise. His friends long urged him to reside in London ; but his family attachments, and love of retirement and study were invincible, and he fell a victim to his unwearied attention to his profession. He died of a decline, Aug. 29, 1797.

His pictures have been so much in request, that there is scarcely an instance of their ever having come into the hands of dealers ; neither have his best works ever been seen in London ; a strong proof of their intrinsic worth, and that no artifices were necessary to ensure their sale. It is with pleasure therefore that we record, that his pecuniary circumstances were always affluent, and shew that the world has not been unmindful of his extraordinary talents, and also that, as a man, he enjoyed the friendship and esteem of all who had the pleasure of his acquaintance. [1]

WRIGHT (NATHAN), of Barwell, Leicestershire, barrister at law, was elected recorder of Leicester in 1680 ; called by writ, April 11, 1692, to take the degree of serjeant at law ; knighted Dec. 30, 1696, and made king's serjeant. On the refusal of the lords chief justices Holt and Treby, and Trevor the attorney-general, to accept the great seal, which was taken from lord Somers, it was delivered to sir Nathan, with the title of lord-keeper, May 21, 1700. As he was raised to this situation by the tories, so he seems to have acted in conformity to the views of that party. Burnet says, that many gentlemen of good estates and ancient families were put out of the commission of the peace by him, for no other visible reason but because they had gone in heartily to the revolution, and had continued zealous for king William ; and, at the same time, men of no worth nor estate, and known to be ill-affected to queen Anne's title, and to the protestant succession, were put in. He adds, that the lord-keeper was a " zealot to the party, and was become very exceptionable in all respects. Money, as was said, did every thing with him ; only in his court, I never heard him charged for any thing but great slowness, by which the chancery was become one of the heaviest grievances of the nation." The same author likewise says, that the lord-keeper " was sor-

[1] Edwards's Anecdotes.—Gent. Mag. for 1797.

didly covetous, and did not at all live suitable to that high
post: he became extremely rich, yet I never heard him
charged with bribery in his court." One of the most remarkable events that happened while he was in office, was
his sentence for dissolving the Savoy, July 13, 1702; and
in the same year, Nov. 30, he reversed a decree of his
great predecessor, lord Somers. Sir Nathan's removal,
however, which happened in May 1705, is said to have "been
a great loss to the church." He passed the remainder
of his days in retirement, beloved and respected, at Chal-
decot-Hall, in Warwickshire, where he died Aug. 4, 1721.[1]

WRIGHT (SAMUEL), an eminent dissenting clergyman,
was born Jan. 30, 1682-3, being eldest son of Mr. James
Wright, a nonconformist minister at Retford, in the county
of Nottingham, by Mrs. Eleanor Cotton, daughter of Mr
Cotton, a gentleman of Yorkshire, and sister to the rev.
Mr. Thomas Cotton of Westminster, whose funeral-sermon
his nephew preached and published. At eleven years old
he lost his father, being then at school at Attercliffe, in
Yorkshire, whence he removed to Darton, in the same
county, under the care of his grandmother, and his uncle
Cotton. At sixteen he studied under the care of the rev.
Mr. Jollie, at Attercliffe, whom about the age of twenty-
one he quitted, and went to his uncle's house at the Haigh,
where he officiated as his chaplain; and after his death he
came to London, having preached only three or four sermons in the country. He lived a little while in his uncle's
family at St. Giles's, and thence went to be chaplain to
lady Susannah Lort, at Turnham-green, and was chosen
to preach the Sunday evening-lecture at Mr. Cotton's, at
St. Giles's. Being soon after invited to assist Dr. Grosvenor at Crosby-square meeting, he quitted lady Lort and
St. Giles's, and was soon after chosen to carry on the
evening-lecture in Southwark, in conjunction with the rev.
Mr. Haman Hood, who soon quitting it, it devolved on
Mr. Wright, then only twenty-three. On the death of
Mr. Matthew Sylvester, 1708, he was chosen pastor of the
congregation at Blackfriars, which increased considerably
under his care, and where he continued many years, till
he removed to Carter-lane, which meeting-house was built
for him, and opened by him Dec. 5, 1734, with a sermon
on 2 Chron. vi. 40. His sermons, printed singly, amount

[1] Nichols's Hist. of Leicestershire, art. Hinckley.

to near forty. But his most considerable work was his "Treatise on the New Birth, or, the being born again, without which it is impossible to enter into the kingdom of God," which had gone through fifteen editions before his death. Dr. Wright is traditionally understood to have been the author of the song, "Happy Hours, all Hours excelling." He was remarkable for the melody of his voice and the beauty of his elocution. Archbishop Herring, when a young man, frequently attended him as a model of delivery, not openly in the meeting house, but in a large porch belonging to the old place in Blackfriars. He married, in 1710, the widow of his predecessor, Mr. Sylvester, daughter of the rev. Mr. Obadiah Hughes, minister of the dissenting congregation at Enfield, aunt to the late Dr. Obadiah Hughes, by whom he had one son, since dead, a tradesman in the city, and one daughter, married to a citizen in Newgate-street, a most accomplished woman, but who became the victim of her own imprudence. He died April 3, 1746, at Newington-green, which was his residence. His funeral-sermon was preached at Carter-lane meeting by Dr. Milner; and another at the same place, by Dr. Obadiah Hughes, who wrote his epitaph. [1]

WYATT (JAMES), an eminent modern architect, was born at Burton, in the county of Stafford, about 1743, of a respectable family, which is now become perfectly patriarchal in its numerous and extensive branches. His education, till the age of fourteen, was such as a country town afforded, but having at that period, exhibited a fondness for architectural design, though in humble and rude attempts, his friends had the happiness to succeed in introducing him into the suite of lord Bagot, then about to depart for Rome as the ambassador of Great Britain at the Ecclesiastical States. That genius which first budded spontaneously in its own obscure, native territory, could hardly fail to shoot forth in strength and beauty when transplanted to the classic and congenial soil of Italy. Amid the architectural glories of the West, the fallen temples of the World's fallen mistress, our young student stored up that transcendant knowledge of the rules of his profession, and that exquisite taste for the developement of those rules, which, in after-years, placed him without a professional rival in his own country.. Brilliant, quick, and intuitive, as

---

[1] Wilson's Hist. of Dissenting Churches.—Nichols's Bowyer.

was his genius, he was never remiss in investigating and making himself master of the details and practical causes by which the great effective results of architecture are produced. He has been heard frequently to state that he measured with his own hand every part of the dome of St. Peter's, and this too at the imminent danger of his life, being under the necessity of lying on his back on a ladder slung horizontally, without cradle or side-rail, over a frightful void of 300 feet. From Rome he departed for Venice, where he remained above two years a pupil of the celebrated Viscentini, an architect and painter. Under this master he acquired a very unusual perfection in architectural painting; and he has executed a few, and but a few, paintings in that line, which equal any by Panini. At the unripe age of twenty, when few young men have even commenced their pupilage to a profession of so much science and taste, Mr. Wyatt arrived in London with a taste formed by the finest models of ancient Rome, and the instruction of the best living masters in Italy. To him then nothing was wanting but an opportunity to call forth his powers into action, nor was that long withheld. He was employed to build the Pantheon in Oxford-street, a specimen of architecture which attracted the attention and commanded the admiration of all persons of taste in Europe, by its grandeur of symmetry, and its lavish but tasteful richness of decoration. Never, perhaps, was so high a reputation in the arts obtained by a first effort. Applications now poured in upon Mr. Wyatt, not only from all parts of England, Ireland, and Scotland, but also from the Continent. The empress of Russia, that investigator and patron of talent in all departments, desirous to possess the architect of the Pantheon, and to exercise his genius in a projected palace, offered him (through her ambassador at London) a *carte blanche*, as to remuneration, if he would settle at St. Petersburg; but he was recommended by his friends to decline the offer of the munificent Catherine. From this period it may well be supposed that he ranked foremost in his profession, and executed most of the important and costly works of architecture which were undertaken. On the death of sir William Chambers he received the most flattering and substantial proof of the king's great estimation, by being appointed surveyor-general to the Board of Works, which was followed by appointments to almost all the important offices connected with his profession in the government departments; and a dispute having arisen in the Royal Academy, which induced Mr. West to relinquish the president's chair, Mr. Wyatt was elected, and reluctantly obeyed his majesty's command to accept the vacant office, which he restored to Mr. West the ensuing year. From the building of the Pantheon to the period of his death, this classical architect erected or embellished some of the most considerable mansions, palaces, and other buildings, in the United Kingdom; among which are, the palace at Kew, Fonthill-abbey, Hanworth church, House of Lords, Henry the Seventh's chapel, Windsor castle, Bulstrode, Doddington hall, Cashiobury, Ashridge hall, &c. &c. The writer of his life says, that although Mr. Wyatt was educated a Roman architect, and made his grand and successful debut in England in that character, yet his genius was not to be bounded in a single sphere, and it afterwards revived in this country the long-forgotten beauties of Gothic architecture. It is, however, a more general opinion that Mr. Wyatt was far from successful either in his original attempts, or in his restorations of the pure Gothic*.

A man who walked foremost in the ranks of a lucrative profession (in a country filled with a rich and liberal aristocracy) for near 48 years, a considerable portion of which he was honoured with the royal favour, might naturally be supposed to have amassed a fortune almost princely; but, Mr. Wyatt bequeathed to his family little more than a name universally beloved and regretted, and a reputation which will live as long as the liberal arts continue to embellish and ennoble human life. To account for this, says his biographer, it is only necessary to observe, that, if to superior and all-powerful genius were added conduct and prudence equivalent, every individual so gifted would become a Napoleon or a Wellington——the destroyer or the saviour of nations: but infinite wisdom having ordained that such instances should be most rare, and that the mass of mankind should live in a great degree equalized in power, we commonly find that genius and great parts are paralyzed by an inattention to the minor considerations and details of calculating prudence, while a slow and dull intellect is often compensated by industry and worldly caution. Mr. Wyatt's genius achieved for him greatness at an early age, without the humbler aids last alluded to, and

* See on this subject Gent. Mag. vols. LXVII and LXVIII.

those discreet handmaids to wealth and permanent prosperity were never afterwards found in his train. He died Sept. 5, 1813, aged about seventy. He was proceeding to London with Mr. Codrington, in that gentleman's carriage, when it was overturned near Marlborough. The suddenness and violence of this accident was fatal to Mr. Wyatt: it is supposed to have produced a concussion of the brain. His death was instantaneous. The suavity of manners, the kind and obliging disposition, and the intelligent mind of Mr. Wyatt, attracted and retained the notice and friendship of some of the most illustrious persons in this kingdom; among whom are to be ranked the sovereign, and almost every branch of the royal family. No one, indeed, ever obtained more friends, or created fewer enemies. Mr. Wyatt left a widow and four sons, the eldest of whom, Mr. Benjamin Dean Wyatt, already has attained great fame in the profession of architecture. [1]

WYAT (SIR THOMAS), a statesman and poet, the only son and heir of sir Henry Wyat of Allington-castle, in Kent, was born in 1503. His mother was the daughter of John Skinner, of the county of Surrey. His father was imprisoned in the Tower in the reign of Richard III. when he is said to have been preserved by a cat which fed him while in that place, for which reason he was always pictured with a cat in his arms, or beside him. On the accession of Henry VII. he had great marks of favour shewn him, among which was the honour of knighthood, and a seat in the privy-council. One of the last services in which he was employed by that king, was conducting to the Tower the unfortunate earl of Suffolk, who was afterwards beheaded by Henry VIII. He was also a member of Henry VIII.'s privy-council, master of the jewel-office, and of the vanguard of the army, commanded by the king in person, which fought the memorable *battle of the Spurs.* He died in 1533.

The honours of educating sir Thomas has been claimed for both universities; by Carter for St. John's-college, Cambridge, and by Anthony Wood for Oxford, because he resided for some time on the establishment of cardinal Wolsey's new college, now Christ-church. He then set out on his travels according to the custom of that age, and returned after some years, a gentleman of high accomplish-

1 Gent. Mag. vol. LXXXIII.

ments and elegant manners, and of such conversation talents both as to sense and wit as to have attracted the admiration of all ranks, and particularly of his sovereign, who
bestowed on him the order of knighthood, and employed
him in various embassies. Mr. Warton appears offended
with Wood for saying that " the king was in a high manner delighted with his witty jests," while he allows that
Henry was probably as much pleased with his repartees as
his politics. Lloyd, whom Mr. Gray and lord Orford have
adopted as an authority, reports enough of his wit, to convince us that he might delight a monarch of Henry's fickle-
ness and passionate temper. Persons of this character are
often more easily directed or diverted by a striking expression, than by a train of argument.

According to Lloyd, he was frequently honoured with
the king's familiar conversation, which never put Wyat so
much off his guard as to betray him into any fooleries inconsistent with his character. When urged by the king to
dance at one of the court-balls, he replied that, " He who
thought himself a wise man in the day-time, would not be
a fool at night." His general deportment is said to have
been neither too severe for Henry VIII.'s time, nor too
loose for Henry VII.'s, with whose court, however, he could
have little acquaintance. In him also was said to have
been combined the wit of sir Thomas More, and the wisdom of sir Thomas Cromwell. It is no small confirmation
of this character that his friend Surrey describes him as of
" a visage stern and mild," a contrariety which seems to
be very happily preserved in Holbein's incomparable drawing lately published by Mr. Chamberlain.

But his wit was not evanescent. We are told that he
brought about the reformation by a *bon mot*, and precipi-
tated the fall of Wolsey by a seasonable story. When the
king was perplexed respecting his divorce from queen Catherine, which he affected to feel as a matter of conscience,
sir Thomas exclaimed, " Lord! that a man cannot repent
him of his sin without the pope's leave!" A truth thus
wittily hinted was afterwards confirmed by the opinion of
Cranmer and of the universities, and became a maxim of
church and state. The story by which he promoted the
fall of Wolsey has not descended to our times. Lloyd
merely says that when the king happened to be displeased
with Wolsey, " sir Thomas ups with the story of the curs
baiting the butcher's dog, which contained the whole

method of that great man's ruin," alluding to the common report of Wolsey's being the son of a butcher at Ipswich.

In the early state of the reformation, the clergy were discontented, because afraid of losing their valuable lands. "Butter the rooks nests," said sir Thomas, "and they will never trouble you." The meaning, not very obvious, was that the king should give the church lands to the great families, whose interest it would then be to prevent the re-establishment of popery. The wit, however, of this advice is more remarkable than the wisdom, for notwithstanding the robbery of the church, which has hept her poor ever since, popery was effectually re-established in queen Mary's reign. The liberality of the only other *bon mot* recorded of sir Thomas may be questioned. One day he told the king that he had found out a living of 100*l.* a year more than enough, and prayed him to bestow it on him, and when the king answered that there was no such in England, sir Thomas mentioned " the provost-ship of Eaton, where a man hath his diet, his lodging, his horsemeat, his servant's wages, his riding charge, and an hundred pounds *per annum* besides."

Sir Thomas was a man whose acquaintance was much courted, for his splendid entertainments, his knowledge of the political relations of the kingdom, his discernment in discovering men of parts, and his readiness to encourage them; and for the interest he was known to possess at court. It became a proverb, when any person received preferment, that " he had been in sir Thomas Wyat's closet." To this may be added, that his conversation had that happy mixture of the grave and gay which excludes dullness as well as levity, and his manners were so highly polished that he differed in opinion with the utmost civility, and expressed his doubts as if he needed the information which he was able to impart.

Amidst this prosperous career, he had the misfortune, like most of the eminent characters of this reign, to fall under the severe displeasure of the king, and was twice imprisoned, but for what offences his biographers are not agreed. Fuller says he had heard that he fell into disfavour about the business of queen Anne Bullen. Lloyd insinuates the same, and some have gone so far as to accuse him of a criminal connection with her, but all this is in part erroneous. From the oration which he delivered on his second trial, and which lord Orford has printed in his " Miscellaneous Antiquities," he expressly imputes his first imprisonment to Charles Brandon, duke of Suffolk. " His first misfortune flowed from a court-cabal; the second from the villainy, jealousy, and false accusation of that wretch Bonner, bishop of London, whose clownish manners, lewd behaviour, want of religion, and malicious perversion of truth, sir Thomas paints with equal humour and asperity."    Bonner accused him of a treasonable correspondence with cardinal Pole, and this, with some treasonable expresssions concerning the king, formed the principal charges against him, which he repelled with great spirit, ease, and candour.   The words which he was accused of having uttered were, " that the king should be cast out of a cart's a———e ;—and that by God's blood, if he were so, he was well served, and he would he were so."   Sir Thomas acknowledged the possibility of his having uttered the first part of this sentence, and explained his meaning, viz. that between the emperor and the king of France, his master Henry would probably be left in the lurch.

He was tried for this by a jury before a committee of the council, and probably acquitted, as we find that he regained the confidence of the king, and was afterwards sent ambassador to the emperor.   His eagerness to execute this commission, whatever it was, proved fatal, for riding post in the heat of summer, he was attacked by a malignant fever, of which he died at Shirebourne in Dorsetshire, 1541, in the thirty-eighth year of his age, and was buried in the great conventual church there *.

Lord Orford informs us that in Vertue's manuscript collections he found that Vertue was acquainted with a Mr. Wyat, who lived in Charterhouse-yard, and was the representative descendant of that respectable family.   In 1721, and at other times, Vertue says, at that gentleman's house, he saw portraits of his ancestor for seven descents, and other pictures and ancient curiosities †.   Sir Thomas has usually been termed sir Thomas Wyat *the elder*, to distinguish him from sir Thomas Wyat, his son, who suffered

---

* Lord Orford contradicts Anthony Wood's account of sir Thomas's death, by playing in his usual way upon words, but unfortunately upon words which are not to be found in the Athenæ. See Misc. Antiquities, p. 18, note, and compare with Wood, vol. I. col. 57.

† " Drayton, in his verses to master George Sandys, treasurer for the English colony in Virginia, mentions the name of a Wyat, who probably might be a descendant of our poet's. Sandys was related to the Wyat family." Headley's Beauties, I. lxvi.

death for high treason in the reign of queen Mary. His lady, according to Wood, was Elizabeth, daughter of Thomas Brooke, lord Cobham *. His son left issue, by Jane his wife, daughter and co-heir of William Hawte of Bourne, knight, a son named George Wyat of Boxley in Kent, restored 13 Elizabeth.

Sir Thomas's biographers are in general silent on the subject of his connection with lord Surrey. It is known, however, that they were closely allied by friendship, and similarity of taste and studies. Surrey's character of Wyat is a noble tribute to his memory. The year following his death, Leland published a volume of elegiac verses, some of which are very elegant, and all highly encomiastic, entitled " Næniæ in mortem Thomæ Viati, Equitis incomparabilis, Joanne Lelando Antiquario, Auctore," 4to. This scarce pamphlet has a wood cut of Wyat, supposed to be by Holbein, but represents him as a much older man than he was, and with a huge bushy beard hiding more than half his features. The copy in the British Museum is dated 1552.

His poems were first published by Tottel, along with Surrey's and the collection by uncertain authors. The authenticity of Surrey's and Wyat's poems seems to be confirmed by this care of Tottel to distinguish what he knew from what he did not know, and what, from the ignorance of an editor of so much taste, we apprehend were not generally known. Mr. Warton has favoured us with a very elaborate and elegant criticism on Wyat, but has found it impossible to revive his poetical fame. He contributed but little to the refinement of English poetry, and his versification and language are deficient in harmony and perspicuity. From a close study of the Italian poets, his imagination dwells too often on puerile conceits and contrarieties, which, however, to some are so pleasing that they are not to this day totally excluded from our poetry. As a lover, his addresses are stately, and pedantic, with very little mixture of feeling or passion, and although detached beauties may be pointed out in a few of his sonnets, his genius was ill adapted to that species of poetry. In all respects he is inferior to his friend Surrey, and claims a place in the English series chiefly as being the first moral satirist,

* She afterwards married sir Edward Warner, bart. Hasted's Kent, vol. II. p. 183.

and as having represented the vices and follies of his time in the true spirit of the didactic muse.

Lord Surrey, we have seen, praises his version of David's Psalms, a work about the existence of which bibliographers are not agreed. No copy is known to be extant, nor is it noticed in any history of the English press, nor in any library printed or manuscript. In 1549, were published "Certayne Psalms," a transcript of which appeared in the last edition of the "English poets," without, perhaps, adding much to the author's reputation. Mr. Warton observes that the pious Thomas Sternhold and John Hopkins are the only immortal translators of David's Psalms. But indifferent as they are now thought, there is nothing to be found of a superior kind before their time. In the library of Bene't college, Cambridge, is a manuscript translation of the Psalms into Scotch metre of the fourteenth century.[1]

WYCHERLEY (WILLIAM), an English comic poet, eldest son of Daniel Wycherley, of Cleve, in Shropshire, esq. was born about 1640. At fifteen years of age he was sent to France, in the western parts of which he resided, upon the banks of the Charante, where he was often admitted to the conversation of one of the most accomplished ladies of the court of France, madame de Montausier, celebrated by Voiture in his "Letters." A little before the restoration of Charles II. he became a gentleman-commoner of Queen's-college in Oxford, where he lived in the provost's lodge, and was entered in the public library, under the title of "Philosophiæ Studiosus," in July 1660. He left the university without being matriculated, or any degree conferred on him; having, according to Wood, been by Dr Barlow, reconciled to the Protestant Religion, which he had a little before deserted in his travels. He afterwards entered himself of the Middle Temple; but, making his first appearance in town in a reign when wit and gaiety were the favourite distinctions, he soon quitted the dry study of the law, and pursued things more agreeable to his own genius, as well as to the taste of the age. As nothing was likely to succeed better than dramatic performances, especially comedies, he applied himself to the writing of

[1] A Life of Sir Thomas Wyat appeared in the Second Number of Lord Orford's Miscellaneous Antiquities, from materials collected, in the British Museum, by his friend Gray, the poet, and augmented by his lordship from other writers, particularly Anthony Wood and Lloyd, but not without some inaccuracy. A few notices are now added of more recent authority.—See also a life of Wyat in the Bibliographer, vol. I.

these ; and in about the space of ten years published four : " Love in a Wood, or St. James's Park," in 1672 ; " The Gentleman-Dancing-Master," 1673 ; " Plain Dealer," in 1678 ; and " Country-Wife," in 1683. These were collected and printed together in 1712, 8vo.

Upon the publication of his first play, he became acquainted with several of the wits, both of the court and town ; and likewise with the duchess of Cleveland, by whom, according to Mr. Dennis, and the secret history of those times, he was admitted to the last degree of intimacy. Villiers duke of Buckingham had also the highest esteem for him ; and, as master of the horse to the king, made him one of his equerries ; and, as colonel of a regiment, captain-lieutenant of his own company, resigning to him, at the same time his own pay as captain, with many other advantages. King Charles likewise shewed him signal marks of favour ; and once gave him a proof of esteem which perhaps never any sovereign prince before had given to an author who was only a private gentleman. Wycherley happened to fall sick of a fever at his lodgings in Bowstreet, Covent-Garden, when the king did him the honour to visit him ; and, finding his body extremely weakened, and his spirits miserably shattered, and his memory almost totally gone, he commanded him, as soon as he should be able to take a journey, to go to the south of France, believing that the air of Montpelier would contribute to restore him as much as any thing ; and assured him, at the same time, that he would order him 500l. to defray the charges of the journey. Wycherley accordingly went into France, and, having spent the winter there, returned to England in the spring, entirely restored to his former vigour both of body and mind. The king, it is said, shortly after his arrival told him, that " he had a son, who he had resolved should be educated like the son of a king ; and that he could not chuse a more proper man for his governor than Mr. Wycherley ;" for which service 1500l. per annum should be settled upon him. But there seems no solid foundation for this report.

Wycherley, however, soon lost the favour of the king and of the courtiers. Dennis relates, that, immediately after he had received the preceding offer from the king, he went down to Tunbridge, to take either the benefit of the waters, or the diversions of the place ; when, walking one day upon the Wells-walk with his friend Mr. Fairbeard, of

Gray's-Inn, just as he came up to the bookseller's shop,
the countess of Drogheda, a young widow, rich, noble,
and beautiful, came to the bookseller, and inquired for
"The Plain Dealer." "Madam," says Mr. Fairbeard,
" since you are for ' The Plain Dealer,' there he is for
you," pushing Wycherley towards her. "Yes," says Wycherley, "this lady can bear plain dealing; for she appears
to be so accomplished, that what would be compliment
said to others, spoken to her would be plain dealing."
" No truly, sir," said the countess, "I am not without my
faults, any more than the rest of my sex; and yet I love
plain dealing, and am never more fond of it than when it
tells me of them." "Then, madam," says Mr. Fairbeard,
" you and the Plain Dealer seem designed by heaven
for each other." In short, Wycherley walked with the
countess upon the walks, waited upon her home, visited
her daily at her lodgings while she was at Tunbridge, and at
her lodgings in Hatton-garden, after she went to London;
where, in a little time, he got her consent to marry her,
which he did without acquainting the king.

But this match, so promising in appearance both to his
fortunes and to his happiness, was the actual ruin of both.
As soon as the news of it came to court, it was looked upon
as an affront to the king, and a contempt of his majesty's
orders; and Wycherley's conduct after marriage occasioned
this to be resented more heinously; for he seldom or never
went near the court, which made him be thought ungrateful. But the true cause of his absence was not known: in
short, the lady was jealous of him to distraction; jealous
to that degree, that she could not endure him to be one
moment out of her sight. Their lodgings were in Bowstreet, Covent-garden, over against a tavern, whither if
he at any time went with friends, he was obliged to leave
the windows open, that his lady might see there was no
woman in company; or she would immediately put on the
airs of a frantic woman. At last she died, and settled her
fortune on him; but his title being disputed after her death,
the expence of the law and other incumbrances so far reduced him, that, not being able to satisfy the importunity
of his creditors, he was thrown into prison.

In this confinement he languished seven years; nor was
he released till James II. going to see his "Plain Dealer,"
was so charmed with the entertainment, that he gave immediate orders for the payment of his debts; adding a

pension of 200*l.* per annum while he continued in England. But the bountiful intentions of that prince had not the designed effect, purely through his modesty; he being ashamed to give the earl of Mulgrave, whom the king had sent to demand it, a full account of his debts. He laboured under the weight of these difficulties till his father died; and then, too, the estate that descended to him was left under very uneasy limitations, since, being only a tenant for life, he could not raise any money for the payment of his debts. However, he took a method of doing it that was in his power, though few suspected it to be his choice, and this was, making a jointure. He had often declared, as major Pack says, that " he was resolved to die married, though he could not bear the thoughts of living married again;" and accordingly, just at the eve of his death, married a young gentlewoman of 1500*l.* fortune, part of which he applied to the uses he wanted it for. Eleven days after the celebration of these nuptials, Jan. 1, 1715, he died, and was interred in the vault of Covent-garden church. He is said to have requested very gravely of his wife upon his death-bed, that she " would not take an old man for her second husband."

Besides the plays abovementioned, he published a volume of poems in 1704, folio, of very inferior merit; and in 1728, his " Posthumous Works in prose and verse" were published by Theobald, in octavo. His curious correspondence with Pope may be seen in that poet's works, with many anecdotes of Wycherley, who appears to have been a libertine through the whole course of his life; nor are his works free from the licentiousness, so much encouraged when he was the favourite of Charles and James II. [1]

WYDEVILLE, WIDVILLE, or WOODVILLE (ANTHONY, EARL RIVERS), a very accomplished nobleman of the fifteenth century, was the son of sir Richard Wydeville, by Jaqueline of Luxembourg, duchess dowager of Bedford. He was born about 1442, and in his seventeenth year accompanied his father, who was now created lord Rivers, to Sandwich, where he had been sent to equip a strong squadron, in order to deprive Richard Nevil earl of Warwick, of his government of Calais; but that noble-

[1] Biog. Brit.—Bowles's edition of Pope's Works.—Major Pack's Works. p. 179.—Spence's Anecdotes, MS.—Malone's Dryden, vol. I. p. 190. vol. III. p. 37. and IV. p. 163. 335.—House and family, Gent. Mag. vol. LXXXI. and LXXXII.

man contrived to surprize lord Rivers in port, and took him and all his ships, together with his son Anthony, to Calais, where they were for some time detained as prisoners. From this it appears that both father and son were engaged in the interest of the house of Lancaster, and in opposition to that of York. But king Edward IV. being raised to the throne, and afterwards espousing lady Elizabeth Gray, daughter to lord Rivers, and sister to Anthony Wydeville, the former attachment of the Wydeville's to the Lancastrian interest was forgotten, and they began almost solely to engross the favour of king Edward.

Anthony Wydeville distinguished himself both as a warrior and statesman in king Edward's service. The Lancastrians making an insurrection in Northumberland, he attended the king into that country, and was a chief commander at the siege of Alnwick castle; soon after which he was elected into the order of the garter. In the tenth of the same reign, he defeated the dukes of Clarence and Warwick in a skirmish near Southampton, and prevented their seizing a great ship called the Trinity, belonging to the latter. He attended the king into Holland on the change of the scene, returned with him, and had a great share in his victories, and was constituted governor of Calais, and captain-general of all the king's forces by sea and land. He had before been sent ambassador to negociate a marriage between the king's sister and the duke of Burgundy; and in the same character concluded a treaty between king Edward and the duke of Bretagne. On prince Edward being created prince of Wales, he was appointed his governor, and had a grant of the office of chief butler of England; and was even on the point of attaining the high honour of espousing the Scottish princess, sister to king James III.; the bishop of Rochester, lord privy-seal, and sir Edward Wydeville, being dispatched into Scotland to perfect that marriage.

A remarkable event of this earl's life was a personal victory he gained in a tournament, over Anthony count de la Roche, called the bastard of Burgundy, natural son of duke Philip the Good. This illustrious encounter was performed in a solemn and most magnificent tilt held for that purpose in Smithfield. Our earl was the challenger; and from the date of the year, and the affinity of the person challenged, this ceremony was probably in honour of the afore-mentioned marriage of the lady Margaret, the king's sister, with Charles the Hardy, last duke of Burgundy. Nothing, lord Orford observes (whose narrative we follow), could be better adapted to the humour of the age, and to the union of that hero and virago, than a single combat between two of their near relations. A long account of this affair is given in a note in the Biog. Brit. art. Caxton, vol. III. new edit. It may be sufficient for our purpose to say that Wydeville was victorious.

On the death of king Edward, the queen sent a messenger to her brother earl Rivers, desiring him to assemble a body of troops in Wales, and with them to bring the young king immediately to London to be crowned ; but this design was defeated by the intrigues of Richard duke of Gloucester, afterwards Richard III. who by treachery got possession of the earl's person, as well as that of the young king, and next day earl Rivers, with lord Richard Gray, and sir Thomas Vaughan, was conveyed as a prisoner to the castle of Pontefract. They were all soon after beheaded by order of the usurper, and without any form of trial, on the very same day that lord Hastings was by the same order beheaded in the Tower of London.

Earl Rivers was at this time (1483) in the forty-first year of his age. He was without dispute one of the most accomplished noblemen of his time. Sir Thomas More asserts that *" Vir haud facile discernas, manuve aut consilio promptior,"* equally able to advise, and to execute in affairs of state. Lord Orford observes, that " the credit of his sister (the queen), the countenance and example of his prince, the boisterousness of the times, nothing softened, nothing roughened the mind of this amiable lord, who was as gallant as his luxurious brother-in-law, without his weaknesses ; as brave as the heroes of either Rose, without their savageness ; studious in the intervals of business, and devout after the manner of those whimsical times, when men challenged others whom they never saw, and went barefoot to visit shrines, in countries of which they scarce had a map."

The works of this gallant and learned nobleman were (with the exception of a ballad in Percy's collection) translations, published in the infancy of English printing by Caxton : 1. " The Dictes and Sayinges of the Philosophers, translated out of Latyn into Frenshe by a worshipful man called Messire Jehan de Teonville, sometyme provost of Parys," and thence rendered into English by lord Rivers.

It is supposed to have been the second book ever printed in England by Caxton. The date is Nov. 18, 1477. 2. "The morale Proverbes of Christyne of Pyse." 3. "The boke named Cordyale or Memorare novissima," a third translation from the French, the original author not named, dated 1480. Caxton says that lord Rivers "made divers balades ayenst the seven dedely synnes." All these curiosities will be found amply described in Mr. Dibdin's "Typographical Antiquities." Hume says that earl Rivers "first introduced the noble art of printing into England," but this is evidently a mistake. He did indeed countenance and employ Caxton, and appears to have introduced him to Edward IV.; and both he and Tiptoft, earl of Worcester (See TIPTOFT), contributed very much, by their example and patronage, to the restoration of learning in this kingdom. From various causes, however, England was long behind other nations on the continent in real learning, or a wish for it; and we have no great pleasure or pride in contemplating the productions of our first printers.[1]

WYKEHAM (WILLIAM, or WILLIAM OF), the illustrious founder of New college, Oxford, was born at Wykeham in Hampshire, in 1324. Whether Wykeham was his family name, seems doubtful. He mentions his father and mother only by their Christian names, John and Sybill, or Sybilla. Some of his biographers are inclined to think that his father's name was *Long*, and others *Perrot*, but there is no direct evidence for either, and we know by many other instances that nothing was more uncertain at the period of his birth than the state of family names.

His parents were of good reputation and character, but in mean circumstances when he was born; yet from the number of his contemporary relations, whose names and situations are upon record, it is probable that the family was not of mean extraction. Of their poverty there is less reason to doubt the report, as they could not afford to give their son a liberal education. He soon, however, found a patron, supposed to be Nicholas Uvedale, lord of the manor of Wykeham, and governor of Winchester castle, who must have discovered some talents worth improving, since he maintained him at Winchester school, where he was instructed in grammatical learning, and where he gave early

[1] Biog. Brit. vol. III. art. Caxton.—Park's edition of the Royal and Noble Authors.—Dibdin's Antiquities, vol. I.

proofs of piety and diligence, employing his leisure hours in acquiring a knowledge of arithmetic, mathematics, logic, divinity, and the canon and civil law. He was afterwards employed by his patron, in quality of secretary, and either by him, or by Edyngdon, bishop of Winchester, or by both, was recommended to the notice of Edward III.

This circumstance, however honourable to his talents, appears to have limited the progress of what was then deemed education, and disposed him to a life of business rather than of study, but can never be advanced to justify the opinion that he was deficient in useful learning. He certainly did not study at Oxford, and escaped the contests prevailing between the disciples of Occham and of Duns Scotus, which seem to have formed the only learning then in vogue ; but that one who dignified every office civil and ecclesiastical with the wisdom, talents, and popularity of Wykeham, should have been illiterate, is an absurdity too gross to require refutation, and would have passed unnoticed, had it not been, as far as his architectural abilities are concerned, in some measure countenanced by the Wartons.

He was about twenty-two, or twenty-three years of age when first introduced at court, but in what employment has not been ascertained, although it was probably of the same nature with those which he afterwards so ably filled. There is every reason to think that his skill in drawing recommended him to a sovereign who was bent on adding to his country the ornament and utility of magnificent and durable structures. The first office he held, or the first of which we read, had evidently a reference to this object. In May 1356, he was appointed clerk of all the king's works at the castle, and in the park of Windsor. It was by his advice that the king was induced to pull down great part of this castle, and by his skill that it was rebuilt nearly in the manner in which we find it. His other great work was Queenborough castle ; and although in these military structures he had little scope for the genius displayed afterwards at Oxford and Winchester, they would have been sufficient to prove that he had already reached that degree of architectural skill which modern art can but poorly imitate.

With a sovereign of Edward III.'s magnificent taste, it was but natural that Wykeham should now become a favourite, and accordingly we find that his majesty wished to

distinguish him by many marks of royal favour.    In order
to facilitate this, it was necessary he should take orders,
as ecclesiastical promotion was more particularly within his
majesty's power, where the pope did not think proper to
interfere ;  but this part of Wykeham's history is not so
clearly detailed as could be wished.    There is, on the contrary, some reason to think that he was in the church before he had given proof of his talents at Windsor and
Queenborough.    In all the patents for the offices he held,
he is styled Clericus, but, as his biographer supposes, he
had as yet only the clerical tonsure, or some of the lower
orders, while the historian of Winchester thinks he was
ordained  priest  by bishop Edyngdon.    The first preferment bestowed on him was the rectory of Pulham in Norfolk, in 1357, and as the court of Rome threw some obstacles in the way which kept him for a time out of that
living, the king, in 1359, granted him two hundred pounds
a year over and above all his former appointments, until he
should get quiet possession of Pulham, or some other benefice, to the value of one hundred marks.    But the dispro-
portion between the worth of the living, and the compensation for delay, is so very striking as to incline us to think,
either that Dr. Lowth has by mistake inserted 200*l.* for 20*l.*
or that the king took this opportunity to shew a special
mark of his favour, for which the loss of the living should
be the ostensible motive.    In the mean time he was presented to the prebend of Flixton in the church of Lichfield, which he afterwards exchanged for some other benefice, and in 1359 he was constituted chief warden and surveyor of the king's castles of Windsor, Leedes, Dover, and
Hadlam ;  and of the manors of old and new Windsor, Wi-
chemer, and several other castles, manors, and houses,
and of the parks belonging to them.    In 1360, the king
granted him the deanery of the royal free chapel, or colle-
giate church of St. Martin le Grand, London, which he
held about three years ;  during which he rebuilt, at his
own expense, the cloister of the Chapter-house, and the
body of the church.    This is the first instance on record
in which he is noticed as a public benefactor.    In 1361 he
was quietly settled in the rectory of Pulham, and in less
than two years received many other ecclesiastical preferments, specified by Dr. Lowth.    The annual value of his
livings, for some years before he became bishop of Winchester, amounted to 842*l.* but " he only received the

revenues of the church with one hand, to expend them in her service with the other."

His civil promotions were not less rapid and honourable. He was made keeper of the privy seal in 1364, and soon after secretary to the king, and chief of the privy council, and governor of the great council. These last terms his biographer supposes were not titles of office, but were used to express the influence he now possessed in the management of affairs of state, and which was so great, that, according to Froissart, "every thing was done by him, and nothing was done without him."

On the death of his old friend and patron William de Edyngdon, bishop of Winchester, in 1366, Wykeham was immediately and unanimously elected by the prior and convent to succeed him. Some delay having taken place before he could be admitted into possession, it has been supposed that he was objected to by the king on account of his want of learning. But this is utterly destitute of foundation, as it was by the king's express desire that he was chosen, and what is yet more in point, the pope's bull, contrary to the official language used at that time, and in which there was frequently no mention of learning, declares that Wykeham was recommended to his holiness, " by the testimony of many persons worthy of credit, for his knowledge of letters, his probity of life and manners, and his prudence and circumspection in affairs both spiritual and temporal." The real cause of the delay is stated at great length by Dr. Lowth, and depended on circumstances belonging to the history of that age, connected with the general state of ecclesiastical patronage.

His advancement to the bishopric was followed by his being appointed chancellor of England. In his speeches to parliament, it has been observed that he innovated on the practice of his clerical predecessors whose oratory savoured more of the pulpit than the bench, by introducing a style and manner wholly political. In 1371, when the parliament, become jealous of churchmen, requested that secular men only should be appointed to offices of state, Wykeham resigned the seal, but without any loss of favour on the part of the king, the commons, or the public at large. The king was obliged to comply with the request to dismiss churchmen from the high offices of state, but soon found it necessary to have recourse to the only persons of that age whose education and talents seemed to fit them for such preferments.

Soon after his being settled in the bishopric of Winchester, he began to employ his architectural skill in the repairs of the cathedral, the whole expense of which was defrayed by himself, but his more enlarged designs for this edifice were delayed to a more distant period. The care he bestowed on other parts of his episcopal duty, in reforming abuses, and establishing discipline, was not less exemplary, and in the case of his visitation of the Hospital of St. Cross, involved him in a long and troublesome dispute, which ended greatly to the benefit of that institution, and clearly to the honour of his firmness, judgment, and integrity. His mind appears now to have been deeply impressed by sentiments of enlarged liberality, and wholly influenced by those motives which determined him to become a benefactor to his country upon a most munificent scale.

The foundation of a college, or of some institution for the education of youth, had probably been revolved for a considerable time. About two years after he entered on the bishopric of Winchester, he began to make purchases in the city of Oxford with that view, and he connected with it the plan of a college at Winchester, which should be a nursery for that of Oxford. As early as 1373 he established a school at Winchester, in which he placed certain poor scholars who were to be instructed in grammatical learning, by one Richard de Herton, with an assistant. But the progress of this generous plan was for some time impeded by the intrigues of a party, headed by the duke of Lancaster, in the last year of the reign of Wykeham's friend and master Edward III. An accusation, branching into eight articles, was brought against him, but upon a fair trial, seven were found destitute of proof, and the eighth only was laid hold of, as a pretext for seizing into the king's hands the temporalities of the bishopric of Winchester, excluding the bishop from parliament, and removing him from court. A measure so violent, and justified upon such slight grounds, was not to be overlooked even in those days of popular acquiescence. At the ensuing convocation, the bishop of London, William Courtney, had the spirit to oppose any subsidy to the king until satisfaction should be made for the injury done to the whole body of the clergy, in the person of the bishop of Winchester; and he was so firmly supported by the convocation, that the archbishop of Canterbury, though a warm partizan of the duke of Lancaster, was obliged to admit Wykeham into their assembly, where he was received by every member with all possible marks of respect. Nor was he less a favourite with the people, who, when they rose in the affair of Wickliffe, demanded that the duke of Lancaster should allow the bishop to be brought to a fair trial. Wykeham was soon after restored to his temporalities, but with the ungracious condition, that he should fit out three ships of war for a certain time, or if they were not wanted, pay the amount of the probable expense to the king—that king who had formerly heaped so many marks of favour on him, but who, although in some measure reconciled to him, was now too much enslaved by a party to act with his wonted liberality

Edward III. died June 21, 1377; and on the accession of Richard II. Wykeham was released from all his difficulties, and by a solemn declaration of the privy council, most honourably acquitted of the accusations formerly preferred against him by the Lancaster party. This new reign, however, was a period of turbulence, faction, and bloodshed, and it required all the wisdom and circumspection of his steady mind to preserve the favour of the king, and the confidence of the people. Yet in both he was in a considerable degree successful. It was not long before the parliament appointed him one of the commissioners to inquire into the abuses of the former reign, and in their other proceedings they appear to have looked up to him as a statesman of inflexible integrity; nor was he less consulted in all matters of difficulty by the king and council. But notwithstanding such encouragement, the part he had to act was extremely arduous: the new reign was distracted by contending factions, and in the conflict of factions men of independent minds can seldom be safe; but what rendered the danger greater was, that the king, as he grew up, listened more to flatterers and favourites, than to the legitimate advisers of the crown.

When Richard assumed the reins of government, on coming of age, one of his first measures was to appoint Wykeham lord chancellor, and to dismiss the administration which had the care of public affairs during his minority. The new ministers, however, unwilling to be suspected of owing their appointments to a fit of caprice, after a short time, professed to resign, that their conduct might be investigated in parliament; and what they wished, actually happened. The commons declared in favour of their conduct, and they were all restored. In conjunction with them, Wykeham had the satisfaction of being very instrumental in promoting public tranquillity, until his resignation of the great seal in 1391. After this he seems to have kept at a distance from the management of public affairs, and thus avoided the risk of countenancing those ruinous proceedings which led to the deposition of the king; and during the succeeding reign his age and infirmities afforded an excuse for his no longer attending as a peer of parliament.

If we consider the importance of the undertaking begun at Oxford, and connected with a similar plan at Winchester, it will not appear surprising that he should, during the greater part of the reign of Richard II. have been disposed to bestow his whole attention on objects so dear to his heart. What he projected was certainly sufficient for the attention of any one man, and enough to immortalize the greatest. The design, bishop Lowth has eloquently expressed, was noble, uniform, and complete. " It was no less than to provide for the perpetual maintenance and instruction of two hundred scholars, to afford them a liberal support, and to lead them through a perfect course of education, from the first elements of letters, through the whole circle of the sciences ; from the lowest class of grammatical learning to the highest degrees in the several faculties." A design so enlarged, so comprehensive, so munificent, had not yet been conceived by the most illustrious of our English founders. In bringing it to perfection, we have not only to admire the generosity which supplied the means (for opulence may sometimes be liberal at a small expense), but that grasp of mind which at once planned and executed all that can be conceived most difficult in such a vast undertaking, and which enabled him to shine with equal lustre as benefactor, legislator, and architect, and give a lesson and example which could never be exceeded by the wisest of his posterity.

It has already been mentioned, that in 1373, he had begun his preparatory school at Winchester, and about the same time, having purchased tenements for the purpose, he established a similar institution at Oxford, appointing a governor, and acting in other respects towards his infant society in such a manner, that its constitution might be matured by the test of experience, and "that the life and soul, as it were, might be ready to inform and animate the body of his college, as soon as it could be finished."

Within less than three years from this commencement of his plan, the society consisted of a warden and seventy fellows, who were called *Pauperes Scholares Venerabilis Domini Domini Wilhelmi de Wykeham Wynton. Episcopi.* The warden had a salary of 20*l.* a year, and the fellows were lodged in the places hired for them, and then known by the names of Blake-hall, Hert-hall, Shule-hall, Mayden-hall, and Hamer-hall. The annual expense of their lodging amounted to 10*l.* 13*s.* 4*d.*; and each was allowed 1*s.* and 6*d.* a week for commons.

In 1379, having completed the several purchases of land necessary for the scite of the college, he obtained the king's patent or licence to found, dated June 30, of that year; and likewise the pope's bull to the same effect. In his charter of foundation which he published on November 26 following, his college is entitled *Seinte Marie College of Wynchestre in Oxenford.* But it is rather remarkable that the name of New college, which was then given in common speech without much impropriety, should be by some means continued until the present day, when it is in reality the oldest as to its principal buildings, and the seventh in the order of foundation. The foundation-stone was laid March 5, 1380, and the whole completed in six years; and on April 14, 1386, the society took possession by a public entrance accompanied with much solemnity.

According to the statutes, the society consisted of a warden and seventy poor scholars *, clerks, students in theology, canon and civil law, and philosophy; twenty were appointed to the study of laws, ten of them to that of the canon, and ten to that of the civil law; the remaining fifty were to apply themselves to philosophy, or arts, and theology; two to the study of medicine, and two to astronomy;

---

* Among the seventy poor scholars the founder orders that his next of kin should have the preference, and that immediately on their admission they should become fellows without undergoing the two years of probation, as is the case with the others; and even should there be no vacancies at New college, they are allowed to stay at the college at Winchester till they have attained their thirtieth year, for the chance of a vacancy, provided they have good characters, and have been proved by the electors to be sufficiently versed in grammar. By the injunctions of visitors the number of founders' kin as eligible for New college is now confined to two, but in defect of such kinsmen only, the choice by the founder was extended to others, according to the counties directed in the statute, from which boys were to be admitted upon the foundation at Winchester.

all of whom were obliged to be in priest's orders within a certain time, except in case of lawful impediment. Besides these there were ten priests, three clerks, and sixteen boys or choristers, to minister in the service of the chapel. The body of statutes, which was entirely of his composition, underwent many revisions and corrections, the result of experience and profound thinking on a subject which appears to have engrossed his whole mind, and although some of the latter revisions left an opening for irregularities which the society have not always been able to prevent, these statutes upon the whole are considered as highly judicious and complete, and have been very closely copied by succeeding founders *.

During the progress of the building, he established in form that society at Winchester which was to supply New college with its members. The charter of foundation is dated Oct. 20, 1382, and the college named *Seinte Marie College of Wynchestre*. The year after New college was finished he began this other upon the scite where stood the school at which he received his early education. This, likewise, was completed in six years, with a magnificence scarcely inferior to that of New college, and was opened for the reception of its intended inhabitants, March 28, 1393. The society resembles that of his other institution, consisting of a warden, seventy scholars, to be instructed in grammatical learning, ten secular priests, perpetual fellows, three priests, chaplains, three clerks, and sixteen choristers: and for the instruction of the scholars, a schoolmaster, and an undermaster or usher. The founder of Queen's college, by his twelve fellows, and seventy scholars, intended to allude to the apostles and disciples. The historian of Winchester informs us that the same design entered into the contemplation of Wykeham. The warden and ten priests represented the apostles, with the omission of Judas. The head master and second master, with the seventy scholars, denoted the seventy-two disciples, as in the vulgate, for the English bible, which is translated from the Greek, has only seventy; the three chaplains, and three

* Particularly Henry VI. who founded the two colleges of Eton and King's coll. Cambridge, entirely upon Wykeham's plan, transcribing the statutes of the latter without any material alteration. In 1464, a treaty of union for mutual defence was concluded between these two colleges and Wykeham's two. It was entitled " Concordia amicabilis sive Compositio Collegiorum Regalium Cantabrigiæ et Etonæ et Wiechamicorum Oxon. et prope Winton."

inferior clerks marked the six faithful deacons; Nicholas, one of the number, having apostatized, has therefore no representative; and the sixteen choristers represented the four greater, and the twelve minor prophets.

From this school the society at Oxford was to be supplied with proper subjects by election, and the college at Winchester was to be always subordinate, both in government and discipline, use and design, to that at Oxford, and subject to a yearly visitation from the warden and two fellows of the latter. This visitation, and the annual elections from Winchester to New-college, generally take place in the second week of July. The warden of Winchester is elected by the fellows of New-college, who for some years chose their own warden for that office; but in Wykeham's time, and for many years after, the wardenship of New-college was far superior in value *. The first instance of a warden of New-college being preferred to Winchester is that of Dr. Nicholas in 1679, and the last, Dr. Coxed.

Among the special privileges secured by the founder to New college, one was, that the fellows should be admitted to all degrees in the university without asking any grace of the congregation of masters, or undergoing any examination for them in the public schools, provided they were examined in their own college according to the form of the university, and had their graces given them in the same manner by the government of the house. In 1608 this was disputed; but archbishop Bancroft, then chancellor of the university, decided in favour of the college.

Wykeham lived long enough to witness the prosperity of both his institutions, and almost to see others emanating from them. He died in 1404, in his eightieth year, leaving in his will a continuation of those acts of munificence and pious charity which he had begun in his life. He was interred in the beautiful chantry which he had built for himself in Winchester cathedral. In this cathedral we still see the triumphs of his skill in the main body of the edifice from the tower to the west end, but more particularly in his chantry, which, with his monument, is kept in repair at the joint expence of his two colleges. [1]

WYNDHAM (SIR WILLIAM), an eminent statesman, chancellor of the exchequer in the reign of queen Anne,

---

* This superiority is again restored, and the three last wardens of Winchester were not wardens of New college.

[1] Life by Lowth.—Milner's Hist. of Winchester.—Chalmers's Hist. of Oxford.

was descended from a very ancient family, which derives its descent from Ailwardus, an eminent Saxon, in the county of Norfolk, soon after the Norman conquest, who being possessed of lands in Wymondham, or Wyndham, in that county, assumed his surname thence. Sir John Wyndham, who was knighted at the coronation of king Edward VI. had the estate of Orchard, in the county of Somerset, in right of his wife, Elizabeth, daughter and co-heir of John Sydenham, of Orchard, esq. His great grandson John married Catharine, daughter of Robert Hopton, esq. sister and co-heir to Ralph lord Hopton, by whom he had issue sir William Wyndham, advanced to the dignity of a baronet by king Charles II. whose eldest son, Edward, married Catharine, daughter of sir William Levison Gower, bart. and by that lady had one daughter, Jane, wife of sir Richard Grosvenor, of Eton, in Cheshire, bart. and an only son, the subject of this article, who was born about 1687; and upon the decease of his father, while he was very young, succeeded to the title and estate. He was educated at first at Eton school, and thence removed to Christ Church, Oxford, where his excellent genius soon discovered itself, and afterwards received great advantage from his travels into foreign countries. Upon his return to England he was chosen knight of the shire for the county of Somerset, in which station he served in the three last parliaments of queen Anne, and all the subsequent ones till his death. This public scene of action soon called forth his eminent abilities, and placed him in so conspicuous a point of light, that, after the change of the ministry under that queen in the latter end of 1710, he was first appointed master of her majesty's hart and buck hounds, then secretary at war, and at last, about August 1713, was advanced to the important post of chancellor of the exchequer. In this station he had an opportunity of appearing in his judicial capacity in a cause of Dr. Hooper, bishop of Bath and Wells, in which he gave sentence, and at the same time explained the grounds of it with a perspicuity, force of reasoning, and extent of knowledge worthy the most experienced judge. In May the year following he brought into the House of Commons, and carried successfully through it, the "Bill to prevent the growth of schism, and for the future security of the Church of England," &c. and was appointed to carry it up to the House of Lords, where also it passed. Upon the breach between the earl of Oxford, lord high treasurer, and lord Bolingbroke, secretary of state, in July 1714, sir William adhered to the interests of the latter.

Upon the death of queen Anne, on the 1st of August 1714, he signed with others the proclamation of his majesty king George I. and on the 13th of that month seconded a motion made in the House of Commons by Horatio Walpole, esq. for the payment of the arrears due to the Hanoverian troops in the English service. However, in October following he was removed from his post of chancellor of the exchequer, which was conferred upon sir Richard Onslow. In the next parliament, which met on the 17th of March 1714-15, he appeared very vigorous in opposition to the measures of the administration, and in defence of the peace of Utrecht; and on the 6th of April made a motion, that the House would appoint a day to take into consideration his majesty's proclamation of the 15th of January, for calling a new parliament, which reflected on the conduct of the last ministry of queen Anne, and which he represented as unprecedented and unwarrantable, and even of dangerous consequence to the very being of parliament; expressions which gave such offence to the majority of the house, that he was ordered to receive a reprimand from the speaker. He spake likewise in favour of the duke of Ormond and the earls of Oxford and Strafford, when they were impeached in that house. But, upon the breaking out of the rebellion in Scotland under the earl of Mar, in August 1715, sir William fell under suspicion; on which account he was seized on the 21st of September at his house at Orchard Wyndham, in Somersetshire, by colonel Huske, and one of his majesty's messengers; from whom making an escape, a proclamation was issued out for his apprehension. Soon after this he surrendered himself to the government; and, being examined by the privy council, was committed to the Tower, but was never brought to a trial.

After he had regained his liberty he continued his opposition to the several administrations under which he lived, though he is believed to have altered his opinion with respect to government itself, from the Jacobite notions which he might formerly have espoused, to a more large and popular system; and that upon this ground he afterwards formed his whole political conduct. It was universally allowed that he possessed all the qualifications requisite to

form an able senator; sagacity, to discern the strength or
weakness of every question, and eloquence, to enforce
the one and expose the other; skill and address, to seize
every advantage in the course of a debate, without affording any; and a proper degree of warmth and vivacity in
speaking, necessary to secure the attention of the audience,
without such an excess of it as might embarrass himself,
and expose him to the cooler observation of his antagonists.
And if we descend to the consideration of him in the more
familiar light of his private conversation, we shall find it
equally distinguished by an unaffected civility and politeness, enlivened by an easy flow of elegant wit, and supported by a various and extensive fund of useful knowledge.
To so imperfect a character of him, it will be but justice to
subjoin that which has been given by Pope, with whom he
lived in great intimacy.

—— " Wyndham, just to freedom and the throne,
The master of our passions, and his own."

He died at Wells, in Somersetshire, after an illness of a
few days, June 17, 1740.   He was twice married; first,
July 21, 1708, to the lady Catharine Seymour, second
daughter of Charles, duke of Somerset; by whom he had
issue two sons, Charles and Percy, and two daughters,
Catharine, who died in April 1734, and Elizabeth.   His
second lady was Maria Catharina, relict of the marquis
of Blandford, sister to the countess of Denbigh, and
daughter of M. De Jong, of the province of Utrecht, in
Holland.

He was succeeded in dignity and estate by his eldest
son, sir CHARLES WYNDHAM, who succeeded to the titles of
earl of Egremont, and baron of Cockermouth, by the
death of his grace, Algernon, duke of Somerset, without
heir male, who had been created earl of Egremont, and
baron of Cockermouth, in the county of Cumberland, by
George II. with limitation of these honours to sir Charles
Wyndham.   His lordship, whilst he was a commoner, was
elected to parliament as soon as he came of age, for the
borough of Bridgewater in Somersetshire.   He sat afterwards for Appleby, in Westmoreland, Taunton, in Somersetshire, and Cockermouth, in Cumberland.   In 1751
he was appointed lord lieutenant and custos rotulorum of
the county of Cumberland.   In April 1761 he was nominated the first of the three plenipotentiaries on the part
of Great Britain to the intended congress at Augsburg, for

procuring a general pacification between the belligerent powers; and in the same year was constituted one of the principal secretaries of state, in which it was his disadvantage to succeed Mr. Pitt (afterwards lord Chatham). In 1762 he was made lord lieutenant and custos rotulorum of the county of Sussex. He died of an apoplectic fit in June 1763. He was succeeded by his son, George, the second and present earl of Egremont.[1]

WYNNE (EDWARD), a learned barrister and law-writer, was born in 1734. He was the grandson of Owen Wynne, esq. LL. D. sometime under-secretary of state to Charles II. and James II. and son of William Wynne, esq. by his wife, Grace, one of the daughters of William Brydges, esq. serjeant at law. He followed his father's profession, and was called to the bar; but, whatever his success, seems to have devoted a considerable portion of his time to study and to the composition of some works, which unite great elegance of style to great legal knowledge and acuteness. In his private character he was noted for many virtues, and extensive liberality and charity. He died at his house at Chelsea, of that dreadful disorder, a cancer in the mouth, Dec. 26, 1784, in the fiftieth year of his age.

His first work was printed, but not generally published, under the title of "A miscellany containing several law tracts," 1765, 8vo. These were, 1. "Observations on Fitzherbert's *natura brevium*, with an introduction concerning writs, and a dissertation on the writ *De non ponendis in assisis et juratis*, and on the writ *De leprose amovendo*. 2. An inquiry concerning the reason of the distinction the law has made in cases between things annexed to the freehold, and things severed from it. 3. Argument in behalf of unlimited extension of collateral consanguinity, with extracts from the statutes on which the question arose. 4. Account of the trial of the Pix; and observations on the nature and antiquity of the court of claims. 5. An answer to two passages in the 'Catalogue of Royal and Noble Authors.' 6. Observations on the antiquity and dignity of the degree of serjeant at law." These two last were written by his father, who in the former refuted an aspersion cast on his character by Walpole (lord Orford) in his article of Philip duke of Wharton. After relating the story

[1] Birch's Lives.—Collins's Peerage, by sir E. Brydges.—Swift's and Pope's Works.—Coxe's Memoirs of sir Robert Walpole.—Gent. Mag. vol. LIV.

of Wharton's cheating the minister out of his arguments against bishop Atterbury, and replying to them, by anticipation, in a speech *for* Atterbury, Walpole added in a note that " Serjeant Wynne served the bishop in much the same manner ; being his counsel, he desired to see the bishop's speech, and then spoke the substance of it himself." This calumny Mr. Wynne refuted with so much spirit, that Walpole thought proper to omit the note in the subsequent editions of his " Catalogue."

In 1774 Mr. Wynne published (but like the former, without his name) " Eunomus, or Dialogues concerning the Law and Constitution of England. With an Essay on Dialogue," 4 vols. 8vo. This scientific work, says Mr. Bridgman, would probably have been held in higher estimation had it been better known ; but having been written before, and published after the commentaries of sir William Blackstone, its acknowledged merits have been obscured, though not totally eclipsed by the splendour of that great performance : it is, however, highly valued, as having very much illustrated the principles of our laws and constitution, and given an instructive and rational account of the several branches into which the practice of the law is divided, and as having recommended, with much learning, a liberal and enlarged method of study in that science, pointing out its necessary connexion with the other branches of literature. Mr. Hargrave has further observed, that this work treats incidentally of the character and authority of the several law writers, and more professedly on the origin and progress of the most important subjects and branches of the law, and their connexion with the history and constitution of England. A second edition of this work appeared after the author's death, in 1785, but without any alteration.[1]

WYNNE (JOHN HUDDLESTONE), a man of some original genius, but whose works will not entitle him to any very high rank in literature, was descended from a very respectable family in South Wales, where he was born in 1743. At what time he arrived in London, is not known, but for some time he gained his bread in the printing business, with which he became disgusted, and had interest enough to obtain an appointment in a regiment about to go abroad. Such was the perverseness of his temper while on ship-

[1] Gent. Mag. 1785.—Atterbury's Correspondence.—Bridgman's Legal Bibliography.

board with his brother officers, that they refused to associate with him, and actually left him behind when the ship arrived at its first place of destination. From thence he contrived to return to England, where be married a young woman of some property. This was probably soon spent, as about this time he commenced author by profession, but either his works or his employers were of the lowest order, for it was with difficulty he could procure the necessaries of life by his labours. In 1770, however, he began to aim at higher fame, and published "A General History of the British Empire in America: including all the countries in North America and the West-Indies ceded by the peace of Paris," 2 vols. 8vo. This as a compilation did him no discredit. In 1771 he published the "Prostitute, a Poem," 4to; in 1772 "Choice Emblems, natural, historical, fabulous, moral, and divine, for the improvement of youth; in verse and prose," 12mo. The same year appeared his principal work, "A general History of Ireland, from the earliest accounts to the present time," 2 vols. 8vo. This was more popular, from the nature of the subject, than his History of America, but far enough removed from the merit that would enrol him among historians. Next year he published "Fables of Flowers for the Female Sex," "Evelina, a poem;" and "The Four Seasons, a poem." In poetry he was ill-qualified to excel, although there are passages in some of his pieces that indicate superior talents, had be cultivated them at leisure, and been possessed of a mind better regulated. In 1787 he published a novel called "The Child of Chance;" and at different periods of his life supplied the magazines and newspapers with essays, poems, &c. generally with his name. All these were written to supply immediate wants, which they did but imperfectly. He died Dec. 2, 1788. It is mentioned to his honour that through a long life of poverty, be abhorred and avoided every mean and dishonest expedient to improve his finances, and was even so extravagant in his notions of independence that to do him an act of kindness unsolicited, was to incur his bitterest reproaches.

This unfortunate author had an uncle, the rev. RICHARD Wynne, M. A. rector of St. Alphage, London-wall, and Ayot St. Laurence, near Welwyn in Hertfordshire, where he died in 1799, in the eighty-first year of his age. He published in 1764, in 2 vols. 8vo, "The New Testament carefully collated with the Greek, and corrected, divided, and printed, according to the various subjects treated of by the inspired writers, with the common division in the margin; and illustrated with notes critical and explanatory." [1]

WYNTON, or WINTON (ANDREW), an ancient Scottish chronicler, was most probably born during the reign of David II. king of Scotland, which commenced in 1309, and terminated in 1370. He was a canon regular of St. Andrew's, and prior of the monastery of St. Serf, situated in the inch or island of Lochleven in the county of Kinross. In the chartulary of the priory of St. Andrew's, there are several public instruments of Andrew Wynton as prior of Lochleven, dated between the years 1395 and 1413. He was therefore contemporary with Barbour; to whose merit he has on various occasions paid a due tribute of applause. His " Orygynale Cronykil of Scotland" was undertaken at the request of sir John Wemyss, the ancestor of the present noble family of that name. Wynton's life must have been prolonged at least till 1420, for he mentions the death of Robert, duke of Albany, which happened in the course of that year.

The Chronicle of Wynton was suffered to remain in MS. for the space of several centuries, until in 1795 a splendid edition of that part of it which relates more immediately to the affairs of Scotland, was published by the late Mr. David Macpherson, in 2 vols. 8vo. The editor has added a copious glossary, a series of learned and valuable annotations, and other useful appendages. He says, with truth, that Wynton, not inferior to Fordun in historic merit, has also an equal claim to the title of an original historian of Scotland : for, though he survived Fordun, it is certain that he never saw his work; and his Chronicle has the advantage, not only of being completed to the period which he proposed, but even of being revised and greatly improved by himself in a second copy. It has also the further advantage, for such it surely ought to be esteemed, of being written in the language of the country

' Tyl ilke mannys wndyrstandyng ;

whereas the information contained in all the other histories of Scotland preceding the middle of the seventeenth century, if we except the brief chronicle subjoined to some manuscripts of Wyntown, and the translations of Ballenden

1 Europ. Mag. for Sept. 1804.—Nichols's Bowyer.—Gent. Mag. vol. LXIX.

and Read, was effectually concealed from the unlearned part of mankind under the veil of a dead or a foreign language. In Wyntown's Chronicle the historian may find what, for want of more ancient records, which have long ago perished, we must now consider as the original accounts of many transactions, and also many events related from his own knowledge or the reports of eye-witnesses. His faithful adherence to his authorities appears from comparing his accounts with unquestionable vouchers, such as the Fœdera Angliæ, and the existing remains of the Register of the priory of St. Andrew's, that venerable monument of ancient Scottish history and antiquities, generally coæval with the facts recorded in it, whence he has given large extracts, almost literally translated. All these we have hitherto been obliged to take at second or third hand in copies by Bower and others, with such additions and embellishments as they were pleased to make to Wyntown's simple and genuine narrative. An ecclesiastical historian of Scotland can no where find so good an account of the bishops of St. Andrew's, with occasional notices concerning the other sees, as from Wyntown, who in describing the churches, their buildings and paraphernalia, shews himself quite at home. The compiler of a Scottish peerage may obtain from Wyntown more true information concerning the ancient noble families of Scotland, than is to be found in any work extant, except the accurate and elaborate research made by the late lord Hailes in the celebrated Sutherland case, wherein he has repeatedly had recourse to our author for proofs of the laws and customs of succession. In this view the lawyer will also find the Chronicle of Wyntown an useful addition to his library, and may consult it with advantage, when called upon to adjust a disputed inheritance in an ancient family. Mr. Ellis, who allows that Wynton is highly valuable as a historian, adds that his versification is easy, his language pure, and his style often animated.[1]

WYRLEY, or WIRLEY (WILLIAM), Rouge-Croix pursuivant, was son of Augustine of Wyrley, of Nether Seile, in the county of Leicester, by Mary his wife, daughter of William Charnells of Snareston, in that county, esq. which Augustine was second son of William Wyrley, of Handsworth, in Staffordshire, esq. of an ancient family in that

[1] Macpherson's Edition.—Mackenzie's Scotch Writers.—Irvine's Lives of the Scotch Poets.—Ellis's Specimens.

county, which of late years expired in an heiress married into the family of Birch, of Birch, in Lancashire, who have since sold their ancient paternal estate in that county, and reside at the Wyrley seat in Staffordshire, having assumed the name and arms of that family. In early life he was noticed by the antiquary Sampson Erdeswick, of Sandon, who took him into his house; and Wyrley having for many years laboured in the study of heraldry, was, upon the 15th of May, 1604, appointed Rouge-Croix pursuivant of arms, which office he held, without higher promotion, till the beginning of February 1617-18, when he died in the Heralds' college, and was buried in the burial-place belonging to that corporation in the church of St. Bene't, Paul's Wharf, London. In 1592, he published a book, intituled, "The true Use of Armory shewed by History, and plainly proved by example. London," 4to; but the fame derivable from this work was somewhat injured by Erdeswick, in his dotage, laying claim to the authorship of it. Wyrley also made many collections for a history of his native county of Leicester, which Burton made use of. In 1569 he began to survey the churches there. His original MS. written by himself, containing also many churches in Warwickshire, is now in the library of the Heralds' college, bearing the mark V. 197. It appears also, that he afterwards accompanied Burton in his survey of the churches there, in the years 1603, 1608, &c. In V. No. 127, in the same library, is a fair and beautiful copy of their labours in this way, with the arms, monuments, and antiquities, well drawn. At the end of his "True Use of Armory" are two dull creeping metrical narratives, one on the life and death of lord Chandos, the other on Sir John de Gralhy, Capitall de Buz; but it seems doubtful whether these were the production of Erdeswick or of Wyrley. It is certain they are not worth contending for.[1]

[1] Noble's College of Arms.—Phillips's Theatrum Poetarum, by Sir E. Brydges.

# X,

XAVIER (St. Francis), commonly called the Apostle of the Indies, was born April 7, 1506, in Navarre, at the castle of Xavier. His father, Don John de Jasso, was one of the chief counsellors of state to John III. king of Navarre. Among their numerous family of children, of which Francis was the youngest, those that were elder bore the surname of Azpilcueta, the younger that of Xavier. Francis was sent to the university of Paris, in the eighteenth year of his age. He was afterwards admitted master of arts, and taught philosophy in the college of Beauvais, with an intention of entering the society of the Sorbonne; but having formed a friendship with Ignatius Loyola, he renounced all establishments, and became one of his first disciples. Xavier then went to Italy, where he attended the sick at the hospital of incurables at Venice, and was ordained priest. Some time after, John III. king of Portugal, having applied to St. Ignatius for some missionaries to preach the gospel in the East Indies, Xavier was chosen for that purpose, who, embarking at Lisbon, April 7, 1541, arrived at Goa, May 6, 1542. In a short time he spread the knowledge of the Christian religion, or, to speak more properly, of the Romish system, over a great part of the continent, and in several of the islands of that remote region. Thence in 1549 he passed into Japan, and laid there, with amazing rapidity, the foundation of the famous church which flourished during so many years in that vast empire. His indefatigable zeal prompted him to attempt the conversion of the Chinese, and with this view he embarked for that extensive and powerful kingdom, but died on an island in sight of China, Dec. 2, 1552. The body of this missionary lies interred at Goa, where it is worshipped with the highest marks of devotion. There is also a magnificent church at Cotati dedicated to Xavier, to whom the inhabitants of the Portuguese settlements pay the most devout tribute of veneration and worship. In 1747, the late king of Portugal obtained for Xavier, or rather for his memory, the title of protector of the Indies, from Benedict XIV.

There are two lives of this saint, the one by Tursellinus, and the other by Bouhours, but the latter is little more than a translation from Latin into French of the former, dressed out in a more elegant manner. They both contain the miracles ascribed to this saint, which are among the most absurd and incredible in the annals of superstition. For this, however, Xavier, who appears to have been only a zealous enthusiast, ought not to be censured. He claims no miracles for himself, nor were any such heard of for many years after his death ; on the contrary, in his correspondence with his friends, during his mission, he not only makes no mention of miracles, but disclaims all supernatural assistance. For the miracles, therefore, his biographers must be accountable, and we know of no evidence they have produced in confirmation of them. The life of Xavier is not unknown in this country. No less a person than our celebrated poet Dryden published a translation of Bouhours's Life of Xavier, in 1688, in consequence of the queen of James II. having, when she solicited a son, recommended herself to Xavier as her patron saint. Besides this, a Wesleyan preacher published, in 1764, an abridgment of Bouhours, as if he had intended to assist bishop Lavington in proving the alliance between the enthusiasm of the methodists and papists. Xavier's Letters were published at Paris, 1631, 8vo, with some lesser works ascribed to him.[1]

XENOCRATES, one of the most celebrated philosophers of ancient Greece, was born at Chalcedon, B. C. 400. He at first attached himself to Æschines, but afterwards became the disciple of Plato, and always retained a high degree of respect and attachment for that great man, whom he accompanied in a voyage to Sicily. When Dionysius the tyrant threatened Plato one day, saying, "that some person should behead him ;" " Nobody shall do that," said Xenocrates, "till they have first beheaded me." This philosopher studied under Plato at the same time with Aristotle, but did not possess equal talents : for he had a slow genius and dull apprehension, while Aristotle's genius was quick and penetrating, whence their master observed of them, "that one wanted a spur, and the other a bridle." But however inferior Xenocrates might be to Aristotle in genius, he greatly excelled him in the practice of moral philosophy.

[1] Lives as above.—Butler's Lives of the Saints.—Douglas's Criterion.—Mosheim.

He was grave, sober, austere, and of a disposition so serious, and so far removed from the Athenian politeness, that Plato frequently exhorted him to "sacrifice to the graces." He always bore his master's reproofs with great patience, and when persuaded to defend himself, replied, "He treats me thus only for my good." Xenocrates is particularly celebrated for chastity, and is said to have acquired so great a command over his passions, that Phryne, the most beautiful courtezan of Greece, who had laid a wager that she would seduce him, could not effect her purpose. Being afterwards laughed at, and the wager demanded, she replied, "I have not lost it ; for I undertook to seduce a man, and not a statue." The conduct of Xenocrates exhibited an equal example of temperance in every other respect. He cared neither for pleasures, wealth, or fame ; and was so moderate in his diet, that he often found it necessary to throw away his provisions because they were grown stale and mouldy ; whence the proverb among the Grecians, of *Xenocrates's cheese*, when they would describe any thing which lasted a long time. This philosopher succeeded Speusippus, who was Plato's immediate successor in the academy at Athens, in 339 B. C. He required his disciples to understand mathematics before they placed themselves under his care ; and sent back a youth who was ignorant of that science, saying, "that he had not the key of philosophy." So great was his reputation for sincerity and probity, that the magistrates accepted his testimony without an oath ; a favour granted to him alone. Polemo, a rich young man, but so debauched, that his wife had begun a prosecution against him for his infamous conduct, rambling through the streets, one day, with his dissolute companions, after they had drank freely, entered our philosopher's school, with an intention to ridicule and insult him. The audience were highly offended at this behaviour ; but Xenocrates continued perfectly calm, and immediately turning his discourse upon temperance, spoke of that virtue in terms so forcible, lofty, and elevated, that the young libertine made a sudden resolution to renounce his licentiousness, and devote himself to wisdom. From that moment, Polemo became the pupil of virtue, and a model of temperance, and at length succeeded Xenocrates in the philosophical chair. His conversion made much noise, and so increased the public veneration for Xenocrates, that when he appeared in the streets, no dissolute youths dared to remain there, but turned aside that they might avoid meeting him.   The Athenians sent this philosopher on an embassy to Philip, king of Macedon, and, a considerable time after, to Antipater; neither of whom could corrupt him by their presents, which circumstance made him doubly honoured.   Alexander the Great so highly esteemed Xenocrates, that he sent him fifty talents, a large sum then; and when his messengers arrived at Athens, Xenocrates invited them to eat with him, but gave them only his common fare. Upon their inquiring, next morning, to whom they should pay the fifty talents, he replied, "Has not last night's supper convinced you that I want no money?" intimating that he was contented with a little, and that money was necessary to kings, not to philosophers.   But at the earnest entreaties of Alexander's messengers, he accepted a small part of the sum, lest he should appear deficient in respect to that great monarch.   It is astonishing that the Athenians should suffer a philosopher of such exalted merit to be so ill treated by the collectors and receivers of their taxes; for though they were once fined for attempting to imprison Xenocrates, because he had not paid a certain tax imposed on foreigners, yet it is certain that the same collectors and receivers sold him at another time, because he had not enough to pay them.   But Demetrius Phalereus, detesting so base an action, purchased Xenocrates, gave him his freedom immediately, and discharged his debt to the Athenians.   This philosopher died about 314 B. C. aged eighty-two, in consequence of falling in the dark into a reservoir of water.   He wrote, at the request of Alexander, a small tract on the Art of Reigning; six books on Nature; six books on Philosophy; one on Riches, &c. but none of these have come down to us.   There is a tract on Death, under his name, in the Jamblicus of Aldus, 1497, folio. Xenocrates used to say, "That we often repent of having spoken, but never of having kept silence; that true philosophers are the only persons who do willingly, and by their own choice, what others are constrained to do by fear of the laws; that it is as great a crime to look into our neighbour's house as to enter it privately; that there was more necessity for putting iron-plates over the ears of children, to defend and preserve them from hearing vicious discourse, than of gladiators, to guard them from blows," &c.   As to his philosophical system, it was truly Platonic; but in his method of teaching he made use of the language of the

Pythagoreans. He made Unity and Diversity principles in nature, or gods; the former of whom he represented as the father, and the latter as the mother, of the universe. He taught, that the heavens are divine, and the stars celestial gods; and that besides these divinities, there are terrestrial dæmons, of a middle order between the gods and man, which partake of the nature both of mind and body, and are therefore, like human beings, capable of passions, and liable to diversity of character. After Plato, he probably conceived the superior divinities to be the Ideas, or intelligible forms, which immediately proceeded from the supreme Deity, and the inferior gods or dæmons, to be derived from the soul of the world, and therefore, like that principle, to be compounded of a simple and a divisible substance, or of that which always remains the same, and that which is liable to change. [1]

XENOPHANES, an eminent philosopher, was author of the Eleatic sect, so called because three of its most celebrated members, Parmenides, Zeno, and Leucippus, were natives of Elea, or Velia, a town in Magna Græcia. Xenophanes was a native of Colophon, and born probably about 556 B. C. He early left his country, and went to Sicily, where he supported himself by reciting verses against the theogonies of Hesiod and Homer. Thence he passed over into Magna Græcia, where he took up the profession of philosophy, and became a celebrated preceptor in the Pythagorean school. Indulging, however, a greater freedom of thought than was usual among the disciples of Pythagoras, he ventured to introduce new opinions of his own, and in many particulars to oppose the doctrines of Epimenides, Thales, and Pythagoras. This gave occasion to Timon, who was a severe satirist, to introduce him in ridicule as one of the characters in his dialogues. Xenophanes possessed the Pythagorean chair of philosophy about seventy years, and lived to the extreme age of an hundred years, that is, according to Eusebius, till the eighty-first Olympiad, or B C. 456.

In metaphysics, Xenophanes taught, that if ever there had been a time when nothing existed, nothing could ever have existed. That whatever is, always has been from eternity, without deriving its existence from any prior

[1] Diogenes Laertius.—Brucker.—Fenelon's Lives of the Philosophers.—Gen. Dict.

principle; that nature is one and without limit; that what is one is similar in all its parts, else it would be many; that the one infinite, eternal, and homogeneous universe, is immutable and incapable of change; that God is one incorporeal eternal Being, and, like the universe, spherical in form; that he is of the same nature with the universe, comprehending all things within himself; is intelligent, and pervades all things; but bears no resemblance to human nature either in body or mind.

In physics, he taught, that there are innumerable worlds; that there is in nature no real production, decay, or change; that there are four elements, and that the earth is the basis of all things; that the stars arise from vapours, which are extinguished by day, and ignited by night; that the sun consists of fiery particles collected by humid exhalations, and daily renewed; that the course of the sun is rectilinear, and only appears curvilinear from its great distance; that there are as many suns as there are different climates of the earth; that the moon is an inhabited world; that the earth, as appears from marine shells, which are found at the tops of mountains, and in caverns, far from the sea, was once a general mass of waters; and that it will at length return into the same state, and pass through an endless series of similar revolutions.

The doctrine of Xenophanes concerning nature is so imperfectly preserved, and obscurely expressed, that it is no wonder that it has been differently represented by different writers. Some have confounded it with the modern impiety of Spinoza, who supposed all the appearances in nature to be only modifications of one material substance. Others have endeavoured to accommodate it to the ancient system of emanation; and others, to the Pythagoric and Stoic notions of the soul of the world. But none of these explanations accord with the terms, in which the tenets of Xenophanes are expressed. Perhaps the truth is, that he held the universe to be one in nature and substance, but distinguished in his conception between the matter of which all things consist, and that latent divine force, which, though not a distinct substance, but an attribute, is necessarily inherent in the universe; and this is the cause of all its perfection. What Xenophanes maintained concerning the immobility and immutability of nature is to be understood of the universe considered as one whole, and not of its several parts, which his physical tenets supposed liable to change. If he asserted, that there is no motion in nature, he probably understood the term motion metaphysically, and only meant that there is no such thing in nature as passing from nonentity to entity, or the reverse. Perhaps the disputes among the ancients concerning motion, like many other metaphysical contests, were mere combats in the dark, for want of settling previously the meaning of terms. Brucker thinks that the notion ascribed to Xenophanes concerning the nature and origin of the celestial bodies, as meteors daily renewed, is so absurd as perhaps to have been defectively or unfairly stated ; and he is inclined likewise to suppose, that many of the fancies, ascribed to philosophers, are nothing more than the misconceptions of ignorant or careless biographers. [1]

XENOPHON, an illustrious philosopher, soldier, and historian, was an Athenian, the son of Gryllus, a person of high rank, and was born in the third year of the eighty-second Olympiad, or B. C. 450. Few particulars of his early life are known. Laertius tells us, that meeting Socrates in a narrow lane, after he was pretty well grown up, he stopped the philosopher with his staff; and asked him, "Where all kinds of meats were to be sold?" To which Socrates made a serious answer: and then demanded of him, "Where it was that men were made good and virtuous?" At which Xenophon pausing, "Follow me, then," said Socrates, "and learn :" from which time he became the disciple of that father-of ancient wisdom.

He was one of Socrates's most eminent scholars; but he did not excel in philosophy only; he was also famous for arms and military achievements. In the Peloponnesian war, he was personally engaged in the fight before Delium, the first year of the 89th Olympiad; in which the Boeotians overcame the Athenians. Here Xenophon, in the precipitation of flight, was unhorsed and thrown down; when Socrates, who having lost his horse was fighting on foot, took him upon his shoulders, and carried him many furlongs, till the enemy gave over the pursuit. This was the first essay of his military profession : afterwards he became known to the younger Cyrus, by means of Proxenus the Boeotian, who was favoured by that prince, and resided with him at Sardis. Proxenus, then Xenophon's friend, wrote to Athens, to invite him to come to Cyrus. Xeno-

[1] Gen. Dict.—Diog. Laertius.—Brucker.

phon shewed his letters to Socrates, desiring his advice. Socrates referred him to the oracle of Delphi, which Xenophon accordingly consulted : but, instead of asking whether he should go to Cyrus, he inquired how he should go to him; for which Socrates reprimanded him, yet advised him to go.   Being arrived at the court of Cyrus, he acquired at least as great a share of his favour as Proxenus himself; and accompanied that prince in his expedition to Persia, when he took up arms against his brother Artaxerxes, who had succeeded his father Darius in the kingdom.   Cyrus was killed : and Artaxerxes sent the day after to the Grecians, that they should give up their arms. Xenophon answered Phalinus, who brought the order, " that they had nothing left but their arms and valour; that as long as they kept their arms they might use their valour; but, if they surrendered them, they should cease to be masters of themselves."   Phalinus replied, smiling, " Young man, you look and speak like a philosopher ; but assure yourself, that your valour will not be a match for the king's power."   Nevertheless, ten thousand of them determined to attempt a retreat, and actually effected it with Xenophon at their head, who brought them from Persia to their own homes, remaining victorious over all who attempted to oppose his passage.   The history of this expedition, which happened in the 4th year of the 94th Olympiad, was written by himself; and is still extant.

After this retreat, Xenophon went into Asia with Agesilaus, king of the Lacedemonians ;. to whom he delivered for a sum of money the soldiers of Cyrus, and by whom he was exceedingly beloved.   Cicero says, that Xenophon instructed him; and Plutarch, that by his advice Agesilaus sent his sons to be educated at Sparta.   Agesilaus passed into Asia, the first year of the 96th Olympiad, and carried on the war successfully against the Persians; but the year after, was called home by the Lacedemonians, to assist his country, which was invaded by the Thebans and their allies, whom the Persian, with a view of drawing the war from his dominions, had corrupted.   During the absence of Xenophon, the Athenians proclaimed a decree of banishment against him; some say, for his going to Agesilaus ; others, because he took part against the king of Persia their friend, and followed Cyrus, who had assisted the Lacedemonians against them.   Whatever was the reason, he was obliged to fly ; and the Lacedemonians, to requite him for suffering in their cause, maintained him at the public charge. Then they built a town at Scilluntes in Elea, having driven the Eleans thence, and bestowed a fair house and lands upon Xenophon: upon which he left Agesilaus, and went thither, with his wife Philesia, and his two sons Diodorus and Gryllus. At this place of retirement, he employed himself in planting, hunting, and writing; and led a life truly philosophic, dividing his time between his friends, rural amusements, and letters.

At length, a war arising between the Eleans and Lacedemonians, the Eleans invaded Scilluntes with a great army; and, before the Lacedemonians came to their relief, seized on the house and lands of Xenophon. His sons, with some few servants, got away privately to Lepreus: Xenophon fled first to Elis, then to Lepreus to his sons, and lastly with them to Corinth, where he took a house, and continued the remainder of his life. During this time, the Argives, Arcadians, and Thebans, jointly opposed the Lacedemonians, and had almost oppressed them, when the Athenians made a public decree to succour them. Xenophon sent his sons upon the expedition to Athens, to fight for the Lacedemonians; for they had been educated at Sparta, in the discipline of that place. This enmity ended in a great battle at Mantinea, in the 2d year of the 104th Olympiad; when Epaminondas, the Theban general, though he had gained the victory, was yet slain by the hand of Gryllus. This Pausanias affirms to have been attested both by the Athenians and Thebans; but the glory was short-lived; for Gryllus himself fell in the same battle. The news of his death reached Xenophon, as he was sacrificing at Corinth, crowned with a garland; who immediately laid down the garland, and demanded in what manner he died? When being informed, that Gryllus was fighting in the midst of the enemy, and had slain many of them, he put on the garland again, and proceeded to sacrifice, without so much as shedding a tear, only saying, "I knew that I begot him mortal."

Xenophon, being extremely old, died at Corinth in the first year of the 105th Olympiad, or B. C. 360: leaving behind him many excellent works, of which a fine collection are happily come down to us. The principal of these are, the "Cyropædia," or the life, and discipline, and actions, of the elder Cyrus; seven books of the "Expedition of the younger Cyrus into Persia, and of the retreat of the

ten thousand Greeks under himself;" seven books of the
" Grecian History ;" four books of the " Memorabilia" of
Socrates, with the " Apologia Socratis." Cicero tells us,
probably grounding his opinion upon what he had read in
the third book of Plato " de legibus," that the " Cyropædia" is not a real history, but only a moral fable ; in which
Xenophon meant to draw the picture of a great prince,
without confining himself to truth, except in two or three
great events, as the taking of Babylon, and the captivity of
Crœsus : and in this he has been pretty generally followed,
though some have thought otherwise. The " Hellenica,"
or seven books of Grecian history, are a continuation of
Thucydides to forty-eight years farther ; and here is recorded an instance of Xenophon's integrity, who freely
gave the public the writings of Thucydides, which he might
either have suppressed, or made to pass as his own. The
smaller pieces of Xenophon are, " Agesilaus ;" of which
piece Cicero says, " that it alone surpasses all images and
pictures in his praise ;" " Oeconomics ;" with which Cicero was so delighted, that in his younger years he translated it, and when he was grown old, gave an honourable
testimony of it. The other writings of Xenophon are,
" The Republic of the Lacedemonians," and " The Republic of the Athenians ;" " Symposium ;" " Hiero, or, of
a Kingdom ;" " Accounts of the Revenues, of Horses, of
Horsemanship ;" and " Epistles."

Xenophon strictly adhered to the principles of his master
in action as well as opinion, and employed philosophy, not
to furnish with the means of ostentation, but to qualify him
for the offices of public and private life; and his integrity,
piety, and moderation, proved how much he had profited
by the precepts of his master. His whole military conduct
discovered an admirable union of wisdom and valour ; and
his writings, at the same time that they have afforded, to all
succeeding ages, one of the most perfect models of purity,
simplicity, and harmony of language, abound with sentiments
truly Socratic. Of all the disciples of Socrates, he is said,
by a recent critic, to be the only one who had the good
faith and good sense to report his master's opinions accurately without addition or disguise. When he teaches,
Xenophon is the most delightful of instructors; when he
narrates, the most fascinating of all narrators. When he
invents, he seasons his fictions with so much of his great
master's genuine philosophy, and so much of his own ex-

quisite taste, that it becomes impossible to decide, whether they are more instructive or more delightful; when he speculates as a politician, it is with a good sense and sagacity, which soar above the prejudices of his fellow citizens, and distinguish with correctness, the institutions which lead to virtue and happiness, from those which allow and encourage depravity. The most imperfect of his works, the " Hellenica," has yet many of the merits peculiar to the writer, and is, at the present day, an invaluable treasure.

The works of Xenophon have often been printed collectively by Junta, Florence, 1516, Gr. folio; by Aldus, Gr. at Venice, 1525, folio; by Henry Stephens, with a Latin version, in 1581, folio; by Wells, at Oxford, 1703, Gr. and Lat. in 5 vols. 8vo; and by Weisk, Lipsiæ, Gr. 1798—1802, 5 vols. 8vo. Separately have been published the " Cyropædia," Oxon. 1727, 4to, and 1736, 8vo; " Cyri Anabasis," Oxon. 1735, 4to, and 1747, 8vo; " Memorabilia Socratis," Oxon. 1741, 8vo, and 1804, 2 vols. 8vo, &c.[1]

XENOPHON, usually mentioned with the epithet Ephesius, from the place of his birth, to distinguish him from the above Xenophon Socraticus, is the author of five books " Of the loves of Habrocomes and Anthia," which are entitled " Ephesiaca," although they have no more to do with the town of Ephesus than the " Ethiopics of Heliodorus," which is a love-romance also, have with the affairs of Ethiopia. His late editor thinks that Xenophon lived about the end of the second, or the beginning of the third century of the Christian æra. It is at least very probable that he is one of the most ancient of the *Authores Erotici*, from the purity and simplicity of his style, in which there is little of those affected ornaments so common in writers of a later period. The only MSS. in which the history of Habrocomes and Anthia has been transmitted to posterity, is preserved in the Benedictine abbey of Monte Cassino, at Florence, and is written in so small a character, that the whole work is comprised in no more than nine leaves, 4to. The first person who copied it was Salvini, who likewise, in 1723, translated this romance into the Italian language. Of the Greek text itself, the first edition was prepared by the celebrated physician Anthony Cocchi, and published at London in 1726, 4to, although his late editor baron Lo-

[1] Diog. Laert.—Brucker.—Vossius de Hist. Græc.—Saxii Onomast.—Brit. Crit. vol. X.—Mitford's Hist. of Greece.

cella asserts that London was put in the title instead of
Florence.    But the fact was that it was printed at London
by Bowyer, as is proved in Mr. Nichols's life of that celebrated printer.   Two other editions, of 1781 and 1793, have
likewise appeared, but they are all incorrect.    At length
in 1796 the work was rendered not unworthy of the classical scholar, by baron Locella, a gentleman, not a philolo-
gist by profession, but a man of business, who dedicated
the leisure of his declining years to the Greek muses.    His
edition, which was elegantly printed at Vienna, 4to, is entitled, " Xenophontis Ephesii de Anthia et Habrocome
Ephesiacorum libri quinque, Gr. et Lat.    Recensuit et
supplevit, emendavit, Latine vertit, ad notationibus aliorum et suis illustravit, indicibus instruxit Aloys. Emeric.
Liber Baro Locella, S. C. R. A. M. a cons. aulæ."
     Politian is said to have been so much pleased with this
author, that he made no scruple to rank him with the Athenian Xenophon for sweetness and purity of style and manner.    Fabricius speaks of him nearly in as high terms, and
his style is certainly his chief merit.    In regard to antiquities, little can be learnt from him, and his geographical
knowledge is very limited.    The admirers of the Greek
language will think themselves greatly indebted to baron
Locella, since, in the earlier editions, nothing had been
done either to improve or illustrate the text; nor had any
proper use hitherto been made of the criticisms on this
work, by Hemsterhuis and Abresch, contained in the "Ob-
servat. Miscellan."    He had also access to the valuable collections of the learned Dorville, who was preparing an edition for the press. [1]
     XIMENES (FRANCIS), an eminent statesman and patron
of literature, was born in 1437, at Torrelaguna, in Old Castille, and was the son of Alphonso de Cisneros de Ximenes,
procurator of that city.    He was educated for the church,
at Alcala and Salamanca, and then went to Rome, but
having been robbed on his journey home, brought nothing
back with him, except a bull for the first prebend which
should be vacant.    This the archbishop of Toledo refused
to grant, and confined him in the tower of Uceda, where it
is said a priest, who had long been prisoner there, foretold
to him that he should, one day, be archbishop of Toledo.
Having recovered his liberty, he obtained a benefice in the

---

[1] Fabric. Bibl. Græc.—Brit. Crit. vol. X.—Saxii Onomast.

diocese of Siguenza, and cardinal Gonsalez de Mendoza, who was bishop there, made him his grand vicar. Ximenes entered soon after among the Franciscans of Toledo, and took the vows; but finding himself embarrassed by visits, he retired to a solitude called Castanel, where he studied the Oriental languages and divinity. On his return to Toledo, queen Isabella of Castille appointed him her confessor, and nominated him to the archbishopric of Toledo, 1495, without his knowledge. When Ximenes received the bulls from the hand of this princess, he only kissed them, returned them to her, unopened, saying, "Madam, these letters are not addressed to me," and went immediately back to his convent at Castanel, being determined not to accept the archbishopric. The queen was much pleased with this refusal; but when Ximenes still persisted in his refusal, an express command from the pope became necessary to overcome his resolution. Nor would he even then yield but upon the following conditions: "That he should never quit his church of Toledo; that no pension should be charged on his archbishopric (one of the richest in the world); and that no infringement of the privileges and immunities of his church should ever be attempted." He took possession of it in 1498, being received with unusual magnificence at Toledo. This prelate's first care was to provide for the poor, visit the churches and hospitals, and clear his diocese from usurers and licentious houses. Those judges who neglected their duty, he degraded, supplying their places with persons whose probity and disinterestedness were known to him. He held a synod afterwards at Alcala, and another at Talavera, where he made very prudent regulations for the clergy of his diocese, and laboured at the same time to reform the Franciscans throughout Castille and Arragon, in which he happily succeeded, notwithstanding the obstacles he had to encounter. Ximenes established a celebrated university at Alcala, and founded there in 1499, the famous college of St. Ildephonsus, built by Peter Gumiel, one of the best architects of that time. Three years after he undertook the great plan of a Polyglot Bible, for the execution of which he invited many learned men from Alcala to Toledo, who were skilled in Latin, Greek, Hebrew, Arabic, and other languages necessary for the perfect understanding the holy scriptures. This Bible, though began in 1502, was not printed till 1517, 6 vols. folio, at Alcala. It contains the Hebrew text of the Bible, the version of the LXX. with a literal translation, that of St. Jerome, and the Chaldee paraphrases of Onkelos on the Pentateuch only. In the original preface, addressed to pope Leo X. the learned archbishop says, " It is doing great service to the church to publish the scriptures in their original language, both because no translation can give a perfect idea of the original, and because, according to the opinion of the holy fathers, we should refer to the Hebrew text for the Old Testament, and to the Greek for the New Testament." The work was above fifteen years in finishing. Ximenes himself assisted in it with great assiduity, and paid the whole expence, which amounted to an immense sum. He purchased seven Hebrew copies, that cost four thousand crowns, and gave vast prices for ancient MSS. To the above-mentioned Bible, which is called the Polyglot of Ximenes, he added a dictionary of the Hebrew and Chaldee words in the Bible. In 1507 pope Julius II. gave him a cardinal's hat; and Ferdinand the catholic entrusted him with the administration of state affairs, from which moment cardinal Ximenes became the soul of all that was done in Spain. He began his ministry by delivering the people from an oppressive tax, which had been continued on account of the war of Grenada; and he laboured so zealously and successfully in the conversion of the Mahometans, that he made near three thousand proselytes, among whom was the prince of the blood royal of Grenada. This great multitude he baptized in a spacious square, and ordering all the copies of the Koran to be brought thither, set them on fire; which memorable day was afterwards kept as a festival in Spain. Cardinal Ximenes extended Ferdinand's dominion over the Moors, 1509, by the conquest of Oran, a city in the kingdom of Algiers. He undertook this conquest at his own expence, and marched himself at the head of the Spanish army in his pontifical habit, accompanied by a great number of ecclesiastics and monks, and at his return was met within four leagues of Seville by Ferdinand, who alighted to embrace him. Foreseeing afterwards an uncommon dearth, he ordered public granaries to be built at Toledo, Alcala, and Torrelaguna, and stored them with corn at his own cost; which made him so generally beloved, that his eulogy was engraved in the senate-house at Toledo, and in the public square, to perpetuate the memory of this noble action. King Ferdinand dying in 1516, appointed him regent of his dominious, and the archduke Charles (afterwards the emperor Charles V.) confirmed this appointment. No sooner was cardinal Ximenes established in the regency, than he became intent on exerting his authority. He introduced a reformation among the officers of the supreme council, and those of the court, ordered the judges to repress all extortions of the rich and of the nobility, and dismissed prince Ferdinand's two favourites. These changes excited murmurs among the grandees, and some officers asked the cardinal, by what authority he thus acted? Ximenes immediately showed them the soldiers who composed his common guard, and replied, that his power consisted in their strength; then shaking his cord of St. Francis, said, "This suffices me to quell my rebellious subjects." At the same time he ordered the cannon, which he kept behind his palace, to be fired, and concluded with these words: "Haec est ratio ultima regis;" i. e. This is the decisive argument of kings. He opposed the reformation of the inquisition; devoted himself, with indefatigable ardour, to the affairs of the church and state; and omitted nothing that he thought could contribute to the glory of religion, and the advantage of his sovereigns. At length, after having governed Spain twenty-two years, in the reigns of Ferdinand, Isabella, Jane, Philip, and Charles of Austria, he died November 8, 1517, as some think, by poison, in the eighty-first year of his age. His remains were interred in the college of Ildephonsus, at Alcala, where his tomb may be seen. This cardinal had settled several excellent foundations; among others, two magnificent female convents; one for the religious education of a great many young ladies of high rank, but destitute of fortune; the other to be an asylum for such poor maidens as should be found to have a real call to the monastic life. He also founded a chapel in his cathedral for the performance of divine service according to the Mozarabic rites. If we add the fountain of spring-water, which he conveyed to the town of Torrelaguna, for public use, to the other sums he expended there, it will appear that he laid out nearly a million in that one place.

Many anecdotes are related of the peculiar temper and virtues of this celebrated cardinal, by his biographers M. Flechier and M. Marsollier, each of whom published a life of him in 2 vols. 12mo, and there is a third by Gomez in folio. His family is generally represented to have been in

a low situation ; yet he is said, in the midst of his greatness, to have gone one summer to the village where he was
born, to have visited his kindred, and to have treated them
with all the marks of kindness and affection.　His humility
upon this head was very unaffected, and appeared sometimes very unexpectedly.　He was present once when doctor Nicolas de Pax was explaining the philosophy of Ray-
mund Lully ; and, in speaking to the question, whether
that famous man had the philosopher's stone or not, he
took notice of a passage in the Psalms which has been
thought to look that way : " he raiseth up the poor out of
the dust, and lifteth the needy out of the dunghill, that
he may set him with the princes, even with the princes of
his people."　That portion of scripture, said the cardinal,
may be much more naturally interpreted, for instance, in
my own case ; and then ran out in a long detail of his own
meanness, and the wonderful manner in which he had
been exalted.

He had a great contempt for what were styled the arts
of a court, and would never use them.　Don Pedro Porto
Carrero, who was with king Charles in Flanders, wrote to
him, that he had many enemies there, and advised him to
make use of a cypher.　He thanked him for his intelligence and friendship, but rejected the expedient : " I have
nothing," said he, " that I desire to conceal ; and, if I
write any thing that is amiss, I will not deprive my enemies
of their evidence."　He behaved sternly himself to the
nobility ; but he advised both Ferdinand and Charles not
to treat them with rigour.　" Ambition," said he, " is
their common crime ; and you will do well to make submission their only punishment."　His coadjutor Adrian
was miserably disturbed at the libels that flew about ; but
Ximenes, who was as little spared, bore them with great
temper : " We act," says he, " and we must give the
others leave to speak ; if what they say is false, we may
laugh ; if true, we ought to mend."　However, he sometimes searched the printers and booksellers shops ; but, as
he gave a previous notice, it may be presumed he did not
often meet with things that could give offence.

The great object of his care was the revenue of his archbishopric ; with which, however great, he did such things
as could scarcely be expected from it, especially as one
half of it was constantly distributed in alms, about which
he was so circumspect, that no fraud could be committed.
He was very plain in his habit and in his furniture ; but he

knew the value of fine things, and would sometimes admire them. He once looked upon a rich jewel, and asked its price. The merchant told him. "It is a very fine thing," said he, "and worth the money; but the army is just disbanded; there are many poor soldiers; and with the value of it I can send two hundred of them home, with each a piece of gold in his pocket." All his foundations, and other acts of generosity, were out of the other moiety. His regulations must have cost him at least as much thought as his buildings and endowments. He saw clearly that ignorance was the bane of religion, and the only thing that made the inquisition necessary; for, if men understood the Christian religion, there could be no need to fear either Judaism or Mohammedism. Upon the whole, we have great reason to believe that he spoke truth upon his deathbed, when he said, that, to the best of his knowledge, he had not misapplied a single crown of his revenue. Philip IV. was at great pains to have procured his canonization with the popes Innocent X. and Alexander VII. but we know not why he did not succeed. [1]

XYLANDER (WILLIAM), a German of great abilities and learning, was born at Augsburg in 1532, of very poor parents, and the love therefore of learning, which he discovered from his infancy, would have been fruitless if he had not met with a patron, in Wolfgang Relinger, a senator of Augsburg. This gentleman made him be supported at the public expence, till his progress in literature procured him admittance into the colleges, where the city maintained a certain number of students. In 1549 he was sent to the university of Tubingen, and afterwards to that of Basil, where he became an excellent Greek and Latin scholar. Melchior Adam affirms, that he took a master of arts degree at Basil in 1556; but Bayle is of opinion, that this date must be a mistake; for he thinks it improbable, that a man who had employed himself vigorously in study, and possessed such excellent natural talents, did not take that lower degree till his 24th year. Xylander certainly wrote his Latin version of Dion Cassius in 1557; at which time he was so good a scholar, that he employed but seven months in this work; for the truth of which he appeals to Mr. Herwat, a senator of Augsburg and his patron, to whom he dedicates it. Having given ample proof of his learning, and especially of his uncommon skill in the

[1] Chaufepie.—Dict. Hist.—Modern Univ. Hist.—Robertson's Hist. of Charles V.

Greek tongue, he was invited in 1558 to Heidelberg, to take possession of the Greek professor's chair, then vacant. In 1566, the elector-palatine Frederic III, and the duke of Wirtemberg, having called an assembly of the clergy to hold a conference upon the eucharist, about which there were great disputes, Xylander was chosen by the elector as secretary of the assembly, together with Osiander, who was named by the duke: he executed the same office upon a similar occasion in 1581. Excessive application to study is supposed to have brought an illness upon him, of which he died in February 1576, aged forty-three years.

He had a profound knowledge of the Greek language, and employed it in translating Greek authors into Latin: but his being always very poor, and obliged to labour for bread instead of fame, is the cause of many errors having crept into his versions; since, selling his sheets as fast as he wrote them, to the booksellers, he was naturally led to be more solicitous about the quantity than the quality of what was written. Of the many authors which he translated, the chief are, Dion Cassius, Marcus Antoninus, Plutarch (the very best translation), and Strabo.[1]

XYPHILIN (JOHN), a patriarch of Constantinople in the eleventh century, was a native of Trebisond. He distinguished himself by his learning and piety, and was raised to the see of Constantinople in 1064. He died Aug. 2, 1075. There is a sermon of his in the Bibl. Patrum. Andrew Scottus and Vossius erroneously imagined him to be the abridger of Dion Cassius: but it was a nephew of his name, as that nephew says himself in the history of Augustus. This nephew made, about the end of the eleventh century, a compendium of the last forty-five books of Dion, which contain the history of the emperors to the time of Alexander son of Mammea. It is probable he did not abridge the first five and thirty books, since there remains no trace or testimony of it: and, besides, he assures us, that even in his time there wanted something of the history of Dion. As to what remains, he has been very exact and faithful in following the sense, and often the very words of his author, as may appear by comparing the abridgment with the original. It has been printed sometimes with Dion Cassius, and sometimes separately, particularly at Paris, 1592, fol.[2]

1 Melchior Adam.—Moreri.—Gen. Dict.
2 Fabric. Bibl. Græc.—Moreri.—Saxii Onomast.

# Y.

**Y**ALDEN (Thomas), a divine and poet, the sixth son of Mr. John Yalden, of Sussex, was born at Exeter in 1671. Having been educated in the grammar-school belonging to Magdalen college, Oxford, he was, in 1690, at the age of nineteen, admitted commoner of Magdalen Hall, under the tuition of Josiah Pullen, a man whose name is still remembered in the university. He became next year one of the scholars of Magdalen college, where he was distinguished by a declamation, which Dr. Hough, the president, happening to attend, thought too good to be the speaker's. Some time after, the doctor, finding him a little irregularly busy in the library, set him an exercise, for punishment; and, that he might not be deceived by any artifice, locked the door. Yalden, as it happened, had been lately reading on the subject given, and produced with little difficulty a composition which so pleased the president that he told him his former suspicions, and promised to favour him. Among his contemporaries in the college were Addison and Sacheverell, men who were in those times friends, and who both adopted Yalden to their intimacy. Yalden continued throughout his life to think, as probably he thought at first, yet did not lose the friendship of Addison. When Namur was taken by king William, Yalden made an ode *. He wrote another poem, on the death of the duke

* " Of this ode mention is made in a humourous poem of that time, called 'The Oxford Laureat;' in which, after many claims had been made and rejected, Yalden is represented as demanding the laurel, and as being called to his trial, instead of receiving a reward.

His crime was for being a felon in verse,
  And presenting his theft to the king;
The first was a trick not uncommon or scarce,

But the last was an impudent thing :
Yet what he had stol'n was so little worth stealing,
  They forgave him the damage and cost ;
Had he ta'en the whole ode, as he took it piece-mealing,
  They had fin'd him but ten-pence at most.

The poet whom he was charged with robbing was Congreve."—Johnson's Lives.

of Gloucester. In 1700 he became fellow of the college, and next year entering into orders, was presented by the society with the living of Willoughby, in Warwickshire, consistent with his fellowship, and chosen lecturer of moral philosophy, a very honourable office. On the accession of queen Anne he wrote another poem; and is said, by the author of the "Biographia," to have declared himself one of the party who had the distinction of high-churchmen. In 1706 he was received into the family of the duke of Beaufort. Next year he became D. D. and soon after he resigned his fellowship and lecture; and, as a token of his gratitude, gave the college a picture of their founder. The duke made him rector of Chalton and Cleanville, two adjoining towns and benefices in Hertfordshire; and he had the prebends, or sinecures, of Deans, Hains, and Pendles, in Devonshire. In 1713 he was chosen preacher of Bridewell Hospital, upon the resignation of Dr. Atterbury. From this time he seems to have led a quiet and inoffensive life, till the clamour was raised about Atterbury's plot. Every loyal eye was on the watch for abettors or partakers of the horrid conspiracy; and Dr. Yalden, having some acquaintance with the bishop, and being familiarly conversant with Kelly his secretary, fell under suspicion, and was taken into custody. Upon his examination he was charged with a dangerous correspondence with Kelly. The correspondence he acknowledged; but maintained that it had no treasonable tendency. His papers were seized; but nothing was found that could fix a crime upon him, except two words in his pocket-book, "thorough-paced doctrine." This expression the imagination of his examiners had impregnated with treason; and the doctor was enjoined to explain them. Thus pressed, he told them that the words had lain unheeded in his pocket-book from the time of queen Anne, and that he was ashamed to give an account of them; but the truth was, that he had gratified his curiosity one day by hearing Daniel Burgess in the pulpit, and these words were a memorial hint of a remarkable sentence by which he warned his congregation to "beware of thorough-paced doctrine, that doctrine, which, coming in at one ear, paces through the head, and goes out at the other." Nothing worse than this appearing in his papers, and no evidence arising against him, he was set at liberty. It will not be supposed that a man of this character attained high dignities in the church; but he still retained

# YALDEN.


the friendship, and frequented the conversation of a very numerous and splendid body of acquaintance. He died July 16, 1736, in the sixty-sixth year of his age. Of his poems which have been admitted into Dr. Johnson's collection, his "Hymn to Darkness" seems to be his best performance, and is, for the most part, imagined with great vigour, and expressed with great propriety. His "Hymn to Light" is not equal to the other. On his other poems it is sufficient to say that they deserve perusal, though they are not always exactly polished, though the rhymes are sometimes very ill sorted, and though his faults seem rather the omissions of idleness than the negligences of enthusiasm. [1]

YELVERTON (HENRY), a distinguished lawyer, is said to have been born at Easton Mauduit, in Northamptonshire, June 29, 1566, but as the register of his baptism, July 5, of that year, occurs at Islington, it is more likely that he was born there, where his father, sir Christopher (then Mr. Yelverton, and a student at Gray's Inn) had, it is probable, country lodgings. He was educated for some time at Oxford, but removed afterwards to Gray's Inn for the study of the law. In 1606 he was elected Lent-reader, being then, Wood says, "accounted a religious gentleman, and a person well read in the municipal laws." In 1613 he was appointed solicitor-general, and received the honour of knighthood by the interest of Carr, earl of Somerset, and on March 17, 1616, was advanced to the higher office of attorney general; but having given offence, as it is said, to the favourite Buckingham, he was accused in the star-chamber of illegal proceedings in his office, and by a sentence of that court deprived of his place, imprisoned in the Tower, and heavily fined. Being afterwards brought before the lords, he made a speech which was so offensive to the king and his favourite, that he was fined 10,000 marks for the reflections which he had cast on his majesty, and 5000 for the insult offered to Buckingham. But by one of those unaccountable changes which occur among politicians of all ages, he became soon afterwards in great favour with the very man whose enmity had cost him so dear, and was, through his interest, made one of the justices of the king's bench, and afterwards of the common pleas, which last place he retained till his death;

[1] Johnson's Lives.—Cibber's Lives.—Nichols's Poems.

and had not the duke been untimely cut off, he would in all probability have been made lord-keeper of the great seal, as he was esteemed one of the first lawyers of his time. He died Jan. 24, 1630, at his house in Aldersgate-street, and was interred in the parish church of Easton Mauduit.

His " Reports of Special Cases in the King's Bench, from 44 Eliz. to 10 Jac. I." were originally published in French by sir W. Wylde, 1661, and 1674, and were afterwards carefully translated into English, and published in 1735, folio. Under his name there are extant in print, several speeches in parliament, and particularly one in Rushworth's collection ; also " The Rights of the People concerning Impositions," Lond. 1679 ; " Thirty-two Sermons of Mr. Edward Phillips," a puritan preacher, taken by him in short-hand. Some additional particulars concerning our author and his family and descendants may be seen in a long note to the article of Baroness Grey de Ruthyn, in Collins's Peerage. It is remarkable that sir Henry, who, we are inclined to think, was a man of independent spirit, fell under king James's displeasure in 1609, by his freedom of speech and conduct in parliament. His own narrative of this affair was lately communicated to the society of antiquaries, and is printed in the " Archæologia," vol. XV.[1]

YORKE (PHILIP, earl of HARDWICKE), an eminent lawyer, was the son of Philip Yorke, an attorney, and was born at Dover, in Kent, December 1, 1690 ; and educated under Mr. Samuel Morland, of Bethnal Green, in classical and general learning, which he ever cultivated amidst his highest employments. He studied the law in the Middle Temple under the instruction of an eminent conveyancer of the name of Salkeld ; and, being called to the bar in 1714, he soon became very eminent in his profession. In 1718 he sat in parliament as member for Lewes, in Sussex ; and, in the two successive parliaments, for Seaford. In March 1719-20, he was promoted to the office of solicitor-general by the recommendation of the lord-chancellor Parker ; an obligation he never forgot, returning it by every possible mark of personal regard and affection. He received also about the same time the honour of knighthood. The trial of Mr. Layer at the king's bench for high treason, gave him, in Nov. 1722, an opportunity of shew-

[1] Ath. Ox. vol. I.—Collins's Peerage, ubi supra.—Lyson's Environs.

ing his abilities; his reply, in which he summed up late at night the evidence against the prisoner, and answered all the topics of defence, being justly admired as one of the ablest performances of that kind extant. About the same time, he gained much reputation in parliament by opening the bill against Kelly, who had been principally concerned in bishop Atterbury's plot, as his secretary. In February 1723-4, he was appointed attorney-general, in the execution of which important office he was remarkable for his candour and lenity. As an advocate for the crown, he spoke with the veracity of a witness and a judge; and, though his zeal for justice and the due course of law was strong, yet his tenderness to the subject, in the court of exchequer, was so distinguished, that upon a particular occasion in 1733, the House of Commons assented to it with a general applause. He was unmoved by fear or favour in what he thought right and legal; and often debated and voted against the court in matters relating to the South-Sea company, when he was solicitor; and, in the affair of lord Derwentwater's estate, when he was attorney-general. Upon the resignation of the great seal by Peter lord King, in October 1733, sir Philip Yorke was appointed lord chief-justice of the king's bench. He was soon after raised to the dignity of a baron of this kingdom, with the title of lord Hardwicke, baron of Hardwicke, in the county of Gloucester, and called to the cabinet council. The salary of chief-justice of the king's bench being thought not adequate to the weight and dignity of that high office, was raised on the advancement of lord Hardwicke to it, from 2000*l.* to 4000*l.* per ann. to the chief-justice and his successors; but his lordship refused to accept the augmentation of it; and the adjustment of the two vacancies of the chancery and king's bench (which happened at the same time) between his lordship and lord Talbot, upon terms honourable and satisfactory to both, was thought to do as much credit to the wisdom of the crown in those days, as the harmony and friendship, with which they co-operated in the public service, did honour to themselves. In the midst of the general approbation with which he discharged his office there, he was called to that of lord high chancellor, on the decease of lord Talbot, February 17, 1736-7.

The integrity and abilities with which he presided in the court of chancery, during the space of almost twenty years, appears from this remarkable circumstance, that only three of his decrees were appealed from, and even those were afterwards affirmed by the House of Lords. On May 12th, 1740, he was nominated one of the lords justices for the administration of the government during his majesty's absence: also on April 21st, 1743, and in 1745. In 1746 he was appointed lord high steward of England, for the trials of the earls of Kilmarnock and Cromartie, and lord Balmerino: and in 1747 for the trial of lord Lovat. In 1748 he was again one of the lords justices; and on July 31, 1749, was unanimously chosen high steward of the university of Cambridge, on the resignation of the duke of Newcastle, who was elected chancellor; and the year after was again one of the lords justices, and the same in 1752.

After he had executed the high office of lord high chancellor about seventeen years, in times and circumstances of accumulated difficulty and danger, he was, in April 1754, advanced to the rank of an earl of Great Britain, with the titles of viscount Royston, and earl of Hardwicke. This favour was conferred unasked, by his sovereign, who treated him through the whole of his reign with particular esteem and confidence, and always spoke of him in a manner which shewed that he set as high a value on the man as on the minister. His resignation of the great seal, in November 1756, gave an universal concern to the nation, however divided at that time in other respects. But he still continued to serve the public in a more private station; at council, at the House of Lords, and upon every occasion where the course of public business required it, with the same assiduity as when he filled one of the highest offices in the kingdom. He always felt and expressed the truest affection and reverence for the laws and constitution of his country: this rendered him as tender of the just prerogatives invested in the crown, for the benefit of the whole, as watchful to prevent the least incroachment upon the liberty of the subject. The part which he acted in planning, introducing, and supporting, the "Bill for abolishing the heritable Jurisdictions in Scotland," and the share which he took, beyond what his department required of him, in framing and promoting the other bills relating to that country, arose from his zeal to the Protestant succession, his concern for the general happiness and improvement of the kingdom, and for the preservation of this equal and limited monarchy; which were the governing principles of his public conduct through life. And these, and other bills which might be mentioned, were strong proofs of his talents as a legislator. In judicature, his firmness and dignity were evidently derived from his consummate knowledge and talents; and the mildness and humanity with which he tempered it, from the most amiable disposition. He was wonderfully happy in his manner of debating causes upon the bench. His extraordinary dispatch of the business of the court of chancery, increased as it was in his time beyond what had been known in any former, was an advantage to the suitor, inferior only to that arising from the acknowledged equity, perspicuity, and precision, of his decrees. The manner in which he presided in the House of Lords added order and dignity to that assembly, and expedition to the business transacted there. His talents as a speaker in the senate as well as on the bench, were universally admired : he spoke with a natural and manly eloquence, without false ornaments or personal invectives ; and, when he argued, his reasons were supported and strengthened by the most apposite cases and examples which the subject would allow. His manner was graceful and affecting ; modest, yet commanding ; his voice peculiarly clear and harmonious, and even loud and strong, for the greater part of his time. With these talents for public speaking, the integrity of his character gave a lustre to his eloquence, which those who opposed him felt in the debate, and which operated most powerfully on the minds of those who heard him with a view to information and conviction.

Convinced of the great principles of religion, and steady in his practice of the duties of it, he maintained a reputation of virtue, which added dignity to the stations which he filled, and authority to the laws which he administered. His attachment to the national church was accompanied with a full conviction, that a tender regard to the rights of conscience, and a temper of lenity and moderation, are not only right in themselves, but most conducive in their consequences to the honour and interest of the church. The strongest recommendation to him of the clergy, to the ecclesiastical preferments in his disposal, was their fitness for the discharge of the duties of their profession. And that respectable body owes a particular obligation to his lordship, and his predecessor lord Talbot, for the opposition which they gave in the House of Lords to the " Act for the more easy recovery of Tithes, Church-rates, and other ecclesiastical Dues, from People called Quakers," which might have proved of dangerous consequences to the rights and property of the clergy ; though it had passed the other house, and was known to be powerfully supported. Many facts and anecdotes which do him honour may be recollected and set down, when resentments, partialities, and contests, are forgot.

The amiableness of his manners, and his engaging address, rendered him as much beloved by those who had access to him as he was admired for his great talents by the whole nation. His character indeed was never impeached until within a few years ago by an injudicious publication of a Mr. Cooksey, who professed to be compiling a life of him : but this had little other effect than to excite a portion of indignation, and to revive the respect in which lord Hardwicke's conduct had ever been held. Lord Hardwicke's constitution, in the earlier part of his life, did not seem to promise so much health and vigour as he afterwards enjoyed for a longer period than usually falls to the share of men of more robust habit of body. But his care to guard against any excesses secured to him an almost uninterrupted tenour of health : and his habitual mastery of his passions gave him a firmness and tranquillity of mind unabated by the fatigues and anxieties of business ; from the daily circle of which, he rose, to the enjoyment of the conversation of his family and friends, with the spirits of a person entirely vacant and disengaged. Till the latter end of his seventy-third year, he preserved the appearance and vivacity of youth in his countenance, in which the characters of dignity and amiableness were remarkably united : and he supported the tedious disorder which proved fatal to him, and which was of the dysenteric kind, with an uncommon resignation, and even cheerfulness, till the close of life. He died, in his seventy-fourth year, at his house in Grosvenor-square, March 6, 1764. His body lies interred at Wimple in Cambridgeshire, by that of his lady, Margaret, daughter of Charles Cocks, esq. of Worcestershire, and niece of lord-chancellor Sommers.

Lord Hardwicke, when a very young man, wrote a paper in the Spectator, (No. 364); and in 1727 published "The Legal Judicature in Chancery stated," which was republished with large additions in 1728.[1]

[1] Biog. Brit.—Collins's Peerage, by Sir E. Brydges.—Coxe's Memoirs of Sir R. Walpole.—Ann. Register for 1764.—Park's edition of the Royal and Noble Authors.

YORKE (Philip), earl of Hardwicke, the eldest son of the preceding, was born Dec. 20, 1720. At the school of Dr. Newcome, at Hackney, he received the first rudiments of his education, and from that seminary, on 26th May, 1737, was removed to Bene't college, Cambridge, under the tuition of the Rev. Dr. Salter. In the year following he was appointed one of the tellers of the exchequer, in the room of sir Charles Turner, bart. deceased. In 1740 he left college, and soon after married lady Jemima Campbel, only daughter of John lord viscount Glenorchy, by the lady Amabel Grey, eldest daughter of Henry duke of Kent, at whose decease she succeeded to the title of marchioness Grey and baroness Lucas of Crudwell. By this marriage he became possessed of a large part of the duke's estate, together with his seat of Wrest-house, near Silsoe, in Bedfordshire. He early engaged as a legislator. In 1741 he was chosen member for Ryegate, in Surrey, and in 1747 one of the representatives for the county of Cambridge, as he was also in 1754 and 1761. At the installation of the duke of Newcastle, as chancellor of the university of Cambridge, in 1749, he had the degree of LL.D. conferred upon him. In 1764 he succeeded his father in his title and estate; and after a strong contention for the office of lord high steward of the university, he obtained that honour against Lord Sandwich. The infirm state of his lordship's health, combined with his attachment to literary pursuits, prevented him from attending to, or joining in, the politics of the day. He had the honour, however, of a seat in the cabinet during the existence of that short-lived administration in 1765, of which lord Rockingham was the head, but without any salary or official situation; which, though repeatedly offered to him, he never would accept. He died May 16, 1790.

His lordship through life was attentive to literature, and produced several useful works, besides the assistance which he rendered on various occasions to authors who have acknowledged their obligations to him. On the death of queen Caroline, in 1738, he inserted a poem amongst the Cambridge verses printed on that occasion. Whilst a member of the university of Cambridge, he engaged with several friends in a work similar to the celebrated Travels of Anacharsis into Greece, by Monsieur Barthelemi. It was entitled "Athenian Letters; or the Epistolary Correspondence of an Agent of the King of Persia residing at Athens during the Peloponnesian War," and consisted of letters supposed to have been written by contemporaries of Socrates, Pericles, and Plato. A few copies were printed in 1741 by Bettenham, and in 1782 a hundred copies were reprinted; but still the work was unknown to the public at large. At length, an elegant, correct, and authenticated edition, under the auspices of the present earl of Hardwicke, was published in 1798, in two volumes, 4to, and an advertisement prefixed to the first volume, attributes its having been so long kept from the public to an ingenuous diffidence which forbad the authors of it, most of them extremely young, to obtrude on the notice of the world what they had considered merely as a preparatory trial of their strength, and as the best method of imprinting on their own minds some of the immediate subjects of their academical studies. The friends who assisted in this publication were, the hon. Charles Yorke, afterwards baron Morden, who died in 1770; Dr. Rooke, master of Christ's college, Cambridge; Dr. Green, afterwards bishop of Lincoln; Daniel Wray, esq., the rev. Mr. Heaton, of Bene't college; Dr. Heberden, Henry Coventry, esq., the rev. Mr. Laury, Mrs. Catherine Talbot, Dr. Birch, and Dr. Salter.

Though a good classical scholar, yet the object to which Lord Hardwicke, from his early youth, particularly directed his attention, was modern history. Accordingly he printed, in 4to. a small impression (not for sale) of the Correspondence of sir Dudley Carlton, Ambassador to the States General during the reign of James I. and prefixed to it an historical preface, containing an account of the many important negociations that were carried on during that interesting period. A second impression of fifty copies only was printed in 1775. In 1781 he is said to have printed for private distribution, "Walpoliana, or a few anecdotes of sir Robert Walpole."

The last publication of lord Hardwicke was entitled "Miscellaneous State Papers from 1501 to 1726," in two volumes, 4to, containing a number of select papers, such "as mark most strongly the characters of celebrated Princes and their Ministers, and illustrate some memorable æra or remarkable series of events." Collections of this kind have been frequently given to the public, but generally overladen with papers both tedious and trifling. The present avoids the errors of its predecessors, all the papers it contains being curious and important.[1]

YORKE (PHILIP), a relation of the Hardwicke family, and known also in the literary world, was the son of Simon Yorke, esq. of Erthig in Denbighshire, who died in 1767, leaving the subject of the present memoir, who was born in 1743, and admitted fellow-commoner of Bene't college, Cambridge, 1765; created M. A. by mandamus 1765; elected F. A. S. 1768; married Elizabeth youngest daughter of the speaker of the House of Commons, sir John Cust, by whom he had a son in 1771, afterwards M. P. for Grantham, and a daughter in 1772. She died 1779; and he took to his second wife, 1782, the relict of Owen Meyrick, esq. of Dyffrynaled, co. Denbigh. Mr. Yorke died Feb. 19, 1804. He was a gentleman of superior endowments and the most benevolent disposition. His hospitality, friendship, and charity, made the ample fortune he inherited a common benefit; whilst the peculiar mildness and suavity of his manners endeared him to his relatives, and to every one who had the honour of his acquaintance. He loved his country, and the constitution of its government, from a conviction of their excellence; and what he loved he was always ready to support, both in his public and private capacity, although constitutional diffidence would not allow him to speak in the House of Commons, where he sat as burgess for Helstone and Grantham. But Mr. Yorke had a cultivated as well as benevolent mind, being well versed in most branches of polite literature; which an accurate and retentive memory enabled him to apply with great advantage. Of late years he turned his attention a good deal to Welsh history and genealogy, in which, from the specimens given in his " Royal Tribes of Wales, 1799," 4to, he appears to have made great progress. This study, rather dry in itself, was, in his hands, enlivened by a variety of authentic and entertaining anecdotes, many of which had escaped preceding historians, as well as genealogical discussions; and his book was adorned with portraits of eminent persons of Wales, well engraved by the late Mr. Bond. He had collected materials for a longer work of the same kind, which has not yet appeared. His taste for natural beauties was very correct, of which the pleasure-grounds of Erthig are a decided proof. Of a character so respectable and amiable throughout, one of the most distinguishing traits was his talent for conversation. Whatever he advanced arose naturally from the occasion; and was expressed in such a happy manner and choice of words, as made him the very life and delight of society.[1]

YOUNG (EDWARD), a very celebrated and popular English poet, was born at Upham, near Winchester, in June 1681. He was the son of Edward Young, at that time fellow of Winchester college, and rector of Upham: who was the son of John Young of Woodbay, in Berkshire, styled by Wood, gentleman. In September 1682 the poet's father was collated to the prebend of Gillingham Minor, in the church of Sarum, by bishop Ward. When Ward's faculties were impaired by age, his duties were necessarily performed by others. We learn from Wood, that at a visitation of bishop Sprat, July 12, 1686, the prebendary preached a Latin sermon, afterwards published, with which the bishop was so pleased, that he told the chapter he was concerned to find the preacher had one of the worst prebends in their church. Some time after this, in consequence of his merit and reputation, and of the interest of lord Bradford, to whom, in 1702, he dedicated two volumes of sermons, he was appointed chaplain to king William and queen Mary, and preferred to the deanery of Salisbury, where he died in 1705, in the sixty-third of his age.

His son was educated, on the foundation, at Winchester-school, where he remained until the election after his eighteenth birth-day; but, for what reason his biographers have not determined, he did not succeed to a fellowship of New-college. In 1703, however, he was entered an independent member of that society, that he might live at little expence in the warden's lodgings, who was a particular friend of his father, till he should be qualified to stand for a fellowship at All-Souls. In a few months the warden died, and Mr. Young was then removed to Corpus college, the president of which, from regard also for his father, invited him thither, in order to lessen his academical expences. In 1708, he was nominated to a law fellowship at All-Souls, by archbishop Tenison, into whose hands it came by devolution. These exertions of patronage make it probable that his father did not leave behind him much wealth.

In April 1714, Young took his degree of bachelor of civil laws, and his doctor's degree in June 1719. His college appears to have set a value on his merit, both as a scholar and a poet, for in 1716, when the foundation of the present magnificent library of All-Souls was laid, he was appointed to speak the Latin oration, which, however, he desired to be omitted in the collection of his works published in 1741. It has been said, that when he first found himself independent, and his own master at All-Souls, he was not the ornament to religion and morality which he afterwards became. Yet he shewed a reverence for religion, and considerable warmth in defending it. The atheistical Tindal, who spent much of his time at All-Souls, used to say, " The other boys I can always answer, because I always know whence they have their arguments, which I have read an hundred times, but that fellow Young is continually pestering me with something of his own."

His first poetical flight was when queen Anne added twelve to the number of peers in one day. In order to reconcile the people to one at least of the new lords, Young published in 1712 " An Epistle to the Right Hon. George Lord Lansdowne," in which his intentions are said to have been of the ambitious kind ; but, whatever its intentions or merits, it is one of those of which he afterwards became ashamed, and rejected it from the collected edition of his works. He also declined republishing the recommendatory verses which he prefixed to Addison's " Cato" in 1713. In the same year appeared Young's " Poem on the Last Day," which is said to have been finished as early as 1710, before he was thirty, for part of it is printed in the " Tatler." It was inscribed to the queen, in a dedication, the complexion of which being political, he might have his reasons for dropping it in the subsequent edition of his works. From some lines of Swift's it has been thought that Young was at this time a pensioned writer at court :

" Where Young must torture his invention
To flatter knaves, or lose his pension."

and we have seen already, that either prudence, or more mature consideration, induced him to suppress a considerable part of what he had published. Before the queen's death appeared his " Force of Religion ; or, Vanquished Love," a poem founded on the execution of lady Jane Grey and her husband lord Guilford. This was ushered in by a flattering dedication to the countess of Salisbury, which he afterwards omitted, as he did soon after his extravagant panegyric on king George I.

As his connection with the profligate duke of Wharton has been thought a very objectionable part of his history, it is at least necessary to explain how it arose. His father had been well acquainted with lady Anne Wharton, the first wife of the marquis of Wharton, and she, who was celebrated by Burnet and Waller for her poetical talents, added some verses to dean Young's visitation sermon. Wharton, after the dean's death, was kind to Young, but died in 1715. Next year the young marquis, afterwards duke, began his travels, and the year following went to Ireland, and it is conjectured that our poet went with him. Whether this was the case or not, it is certain that he looked up to him afterwards as his patron.

From a paper in "The Englishman" it would appear that Young began his theatrical career so early as 1713, but his first play, "Busiris," was not brought upon the stage till 1719, and was dedicated to the duke of Newcastle, "because," he says, "the late instances he had received of his grace's undeserved and uncommon favour, in an affair of some consequence, foreign to the theatre, had taken from him the privilege of chusing a patron." This dedication also he afterwards suppressed. In 1721 his most popular tragedy, "The Revenge," made its appearance, and being left at liberty now to chuse his patron, he dedicated it to the duke of Wharton. That he ever had such a patron, Young took all the pains in his power to conceal from the world, by excluding this dedication from his works. He probably indeed was very soon ashamed of it, for while he was representing that wretched nobleman as an amiable character, Pope was perhaps beginning to describe him as "the scorn and wonder of his days," and it is certain that even at this time Wharton's real character was well known. His obligations to the duke of Wharton appear to have consisted both of promises and money. Young, about 1719, had been taken into the Exeter family as tutor to the young lord Burleigh. This circumstance transpired on a singular occasion. After Wharton's death, whose affairs were much involved, among other legal questions, the court of chancery had to determine whether two annuities granted by Wharton to Young, were for legal considerations. One was dated March 24, 1719, and the preamble stated that it was granted in consideration of advancing the public good by

the encouragement of learning, and of the love he bore to
Dr. Young, &c. This, as his biographer remarks, was
commendable, if not legal. The other was dated July 10,
1722; and Young, on his examination, swore that he
quitted the Exeter family, and refused an annuity of 100*l.*
which had been offered him for his life if he would continue
tutor to lord Burleigh, upon the pressing solicitations of
the duke of Wharton, and his grace's assurances of providing for him in a much more ample manner. It also appeared that the duke had given him a bond for 600*l.* dated
March 15, 1721, in consideration of his taking several
journeys, and being at great expences in order to be chosen
member of parliament at the duke's desire, and in consideration of his not taking two livings of 200*l.* and 400*l.* in
the gift of All Souls' college, on his grace's promises of
serving and advancing him in the world It was for Ciren-
cester that Young stood the unsuccessful contest. Such
were the obligations he owed to Wharton; how becoming
Young's character, may be left to the reader.

In 1719, Dr. Young published "A paraphrase on part
of the book of Job," prefixed by a dedication to the lord
chancellor Parker, which he omitted afterwards, and of
whom, says his biographer, he clearly appears to have had
no kind of knowledge. Of his "Satires" it is not easy to
fix the dates. They probably came out between 1725 and
1728, and were afterwards published collectively under the
title of "The Universal Passion." In his preface he says
that he prefers laughing at vice and folly, a different temper than that in which he wrote his melancholy "Night
Thoughts" These satires were followed by "The Install-
ment," addressed to sir Robert Walpole, but afterwards
suppressed: and by "Ocean, an Ode," accompanied by
an "Ode to the King, *pater patriæ*," an "Essay on Lyric
Poetry," both afterwards omitted by him. Perhaps no
writer ever rejected so many of his own performances, nor
were these juvenile effusions, for he was now forty-six or
forty-seven years old; and at this age, he entered into orders, April 1728, and was soon after appointed chaplain to
king George II. It is said by one of the biographers of
Pope, but the story is scarcely credible, that when he determined on the church, he did not address himself to any
eminent divine for instructions in theology, but to Pope,
who jocularly advised the diligent perusal of Thomas Aqui-
nas, and this, Ruffhead says, had almost brought on an

irretrievable derangement.    But as we have seen that Young
had once refused two livings in the gift of All Souls, it is
surely not improbable that he had then studied in the theological faculty, although at the duke of Wharton's persuasion, he had been induced to think of political life.    One
thing, after taking orders, he thought becoming his new
character.    He withdrew his tragedy of "The Brothers,"
which was already in rehearsal, and when at last it was performed in 1753, he made up the profits to the sum of 1000*l*
and gave the money to the society for the propagation of
the gospel in foreign parts.    We know not that that society
has been so *honoured* since, and it certainly never was so
before.

Not long after he took orders, he published in prose,
" A true Estimate of Human Life," and a sermon preached
before the House of Commons on Jan. 30, 1729, entitled
" An Apology for Princes, or the reverence due to government."    He soon became a very popular preacher, and was
very much followed for the grace and animation of his delivery.    According to his life in the " Biographia," he was
once in his life deserted by his oratorical talents.    As he
was preaching in his turn at St. James's, he plainly perceived it was out of his power to command the attention
of his audience.    This so affected his feelings, that he sat
back in the pulpit, and burst into tears.

In 1730 he resumed his poetical publications, but one
of them, his " Imperium Pelasgi, a naval lyric," he afterwards disclaimed.    This was followed by two epistles to
Pope " concerning the authors of the age."    In July of
the same year he was presented by his college to the rectory of Welwyn in Hertfordshire, and in May 1731 married lady Elizabeth Lee, daughter of the earl of Lichfield,
and widow of colonel Lee.    This lady died in 1741, and
her death is said to have contributed to the mournful tenour of his much celebrated " Night Thoughts," which
formed his next great publication, and that which will in
all probability preserve his name the longest.    The
" Nights" were begun immediately after his wife's death,
and were published from 1742 to 1744.    It has long been
a popular notion that his own son was the Lorenzo of this
poem, but this is totally inconsistent with the unquestionable fact that in 1741 this son was only eight years old.
Other persons have been conjectured with as little probability.    Why might he not have Wharton in his eye?

Of this work, we know of no more eloquent eulogium than that by Dr. Johnson. "In his Night Thoughts," says the critic, "he has exhibited a very wide display of original poetry, variegated with deep reflections and striking allusions, a wilderness of thought, in which the fertility of fancy scatters flowers of every hue and of every odour. This is one of the few poems in which blank verse could not be changed for rhime but with disadvantage. The wild diffusion of the sentiments, and the digressive sallies of the imagination, would have been compressed and restrained by confinement to rhyme. The excellence of this work is not exactness, but copiousness: particular lines are not to be regarded; the power is in the whole, and in the whole there is a magnificence like that ascribed to Chinese plantation, the magnificence of vast extent and endless diversity." By this extraordinary poem, written after he was sixty, it was the desire of Young to be principally known. He entitled the four volumes which he published himself, "The works of the Author of the Night Thoughts."

The composition of the "Night Thoughts" did not so entirely engross the author's mind as to prevent him from producing other compositions both in prose and verse, and some betraying a little of the same disposition to political ambition which he had reluctantly left. Among those of another kind, is his prose work, entitled "The Centaur not fabulous. In six letters to a friend, on the life in vogue," and well calculated to make the infidel and the voluptuary sensible of their error. This has often been reprinted, and the general strain of thought is strongly characteristic of the writer of the "Night Thoughts," notwithstanding an air of gaiety and even levity which is occasionally assumed.

He was now far advanced in years: but amidst the languors of age, he still occasionally employed his pen, producing in 1759, "Conjectures on original Composition." This was followed by "Resignation, a Poem," in which there is a visible decay of powers. In 1761 he was appointed clerk of the closet to her royal highness the princess dowager of Wales, which he did not long enjoy. He died at Welwyn, April 1765, in the eighty-fourth year of his age, and was buried under the communion-table of his parish church. After the death of his wife, he thought proper to entrust the whole management of his household affairs to a housekeeper, who is said to have attained an improper ascendancy over him, when his faculties began to decay. He left the bulk of his property to his son, of whom, as well as of his father, much additional information may be found in our references, and may yet be procurable perhaps elsewhere. Notwithstanding the narrative by sir Herbert Croft in Johnson's collection, which is not always candid, nor always perspicuous, there is room for a new life of Young, and a new appreciation of his character, both as a man and a writer. In his conduct there were great inconsistencies, but the foundation appears to have been good. He sought long for happiness, but seems to have found it at last, where only it can be found. [1]

YOUNG (MATTHEW), the very learned bishop of Clonfert and Kilmacduach, in Ireland, was of a respectable family in the county of Roscommon, where he was born in 1750. He was admitted of Trinity college, Dublin, in 1766, and was elected fellow of the college in 1775, and took orders. He became early an enthusiastic admirer of the Newtonian philosophy, and even at his examination for his fellowship, displayed an unexampled knowledge and comprehension of it; but although it was his favourite subject, his active mind, in rapid succession, embraced the most dissimilar objects; and these he pursued with unceasing ardour, amidst his various duties as a fellow and tutor, and the freest intercourse with society, which he was formed at once to delight and instruct. His love of literary conversation, and the advantages he experienced from it in the pursuit of science, led him early to engage in forming a society whose chief object was the improvement of its members in theological learning. It consisted of a small number of his most intimate college friends, and continued to exist for a series of years, with equal reputation and advantage. Out of this association grew another, somewhat more extensive, whose labours were directed to philosophical researches, and in the formation of which Dr. Young was also actively engaged: and this itself became the germ of the royal Irish academy, which owes its existence to the zeal and exertions of the members of that society, among whom Dr. Young was particularly distinguished. In the intervals of his severer studies, he applied himself to modern languages: and the result of his labours

[1] Biog. Brit.—Life in Johnson's Poets.—Swift's and Pope's Works. See Indexes.—Boswell's Tour and Life of Johnson.—Gent. Mag. vols. LX. LXVII. LXXI. LXXIII.—Forbes's Life of Beattie.—Spence's Anecdotes, MS.—Richardson's Correspondence.—Ruffhead's Life of Pope.—Warburton's Letters.—Nichols's Bowyer.

may be seen in the transactions of the royal Irish academy, to which he also contributed largely on mathematical and philosophical subjects. Besides these he published the following learned and ingenious works: 1. "The phenomena of Sounds and Musical Strings," 1784, 8vo. 2. "The force of Testimony," &c. 4to. 3. "The number of Primitive Colours in Solar light: on the precession of the Equinoxes; Principles of Natural philosophy," 1800, 8vo, being his last publication, and containing the substance of his lectures in the college.

In 1786, when the professorship of philosophy in Trinity college became vacant, he had attained so high reputation in that branch of science, that he was elected to the office without opposition. His "Essay on Sounds" had been published two years, and it was known that he was engaged in the arduous task of illustrating the "Principia" of Newton. He now devoted himself to the duties of his professorship: and the college having been enriched with the excellent apparatus of Mr. Atwood, Dr. Young improved the occasion of carrying his lectures to a degree of perfection unknown in the university of Dublin, and never perhaps exceeded in any other. He proceeded in the mean time in his great work, "The method of Prime and Ultimate Ratios, illustrated by a commentary on the first two books of the Principia," and had nearly completed it in English, when he was advised by his friends to publish it in Latin. He readily acquiesced, and thus had an opportunity, while translating it, of revising the whole, and rendering it fuller and more perfect. It was finished a year or two before his promotion to the see of Clonfert, at which time he was engaged in preparing it for the press. The circumstances of this promotion reflect equal honour on himself and on the lord lieutenant (earl Cornwallis) who conferred it. It was a favour as unsolicited as unexpected, unless the report made to his excellency by his principal secretary, on being consulted as to the properest person to fill the vacant see, may be called solicitation. His report was, that "he believed Dr. Young to be the most distinguished literary character in the kingdom."

His attention however was now diverted from his intended publication by the occupations incident to his new charge: and before he could return to it *, a cancer in his

---

* No part of this work has since appeared, but in 1803, was published at Dublin "An Analysis of the Principles of Natural Philosophy. By

mouth had made an alarming progress, and in about fifteen months, terminated fatally, Nov. 28, 1800.  He was at this time at Whitworth in Lancashire. [1]

YOUNG (PATRICK), an eminent scholar, was descended of an ancient Scotch family, and was born Aug. 29, 1584, at Seaton, in Lothian, then the residence of his father, sir Peter Young, knt. who, among other honourable offices, had been assistant tutor, with the celebrated Buchanan, to king James VI.  At the age of fifteen Mr. Young was sent to the university of St. Andrew's, where having completed the usual course of academical study, he received the degree of M. A. in 1603.  Soon after he accompanied his father to England, and being recommended to Dr. Lloyd, bishop of Chester, the latter assisted him in the study of divinity, as he was destined for the church.  He continued about a year with the bishop, and then went to Oxford, and his merit having strongly recommended him to some of the heads of houses, he was incorporated M. A. in July 1605.  He then took deacon's orders, and was chosen chaplain of New college, which office he held for three years, and during that time he employed himself chiefly in the study of ecclesiastical history, and in cultivating the Greek language, of which he at length acquired a profound knowledge.  Leaving Oxford, he went to London, where his object seems to have been advancement at court, and where his father, still living, had considerable interest. The first patron he acquired was Montague, bishop of Bath and Wells, by whose recommendation the king granted him a pension of 50l.  Having succeeded thus far, his next wish was to be appointed librarian to prince Henry, who had a very fine collection of books, and a museum of other curiosities ; and although he failed in this, he succeeded in obtaining the care of the royal library newly founded by the king, chiefly by the interest of his friend and patron, bishop Montague.  He had already drawn up a catalogue of the books by the king's express command, and after he obtained the place he employed himself in forming them into classes, as well as in making additions by purchases which he recommended to the king, parti-

Matthew Young, &c." an octavo volume containing a very imperfect collection of sixty-three lectures on various philosophical subjects, or rather such heads or minutes as a lecturer might use when addressing his pupils, and published as they were found among his papers.

[1] Hutton's Dict. new edit.—Gent. Mag. vol. LXX.

cularly of Isaac Casaubon's books. With the same view
he took journeys to Francfort, Holland, Paris, &c. In
the mean time his partiality to the Greek language induced
him to invite some of the natives of that country to England, and he contributed by himself or friends, to their
maintenance and education here. Such was his zeal in
this species of learned patronage, that bishop Montague
used to call him the "patriarch of the Greeks." He also
cultivated the Latin language, which he wrote elegantly,
and assisted Mr. Thomas Rhead, or Read, in translating
king James's works into that language. This volume appeared in 1619, and by his majesty's special command Mr.
Young was sent with a presentation copy to Oxford and
Cambridge.

In 1620 he married, and about the same time was presented to the rectories of Hayes, in Middlesex, and Llan-
nine, in Denbighshire, it being then lawful for persons who
were only in deacon's orders to hold parsonages. He was
also collated to a prebend of St. Paul's, of which church he
was made treasurer in 1621. Although he had hitherto
published nothing himself, he had been a very liberal con-
tributor to the labours of others. Among these was Selden,
whom he assisted in preparing for the press his edition of
the "Arundelian Marbles," and Selden was so sensible of
the value of his aid, that he dedicated the work to him.
The same year the famous Alexandrian MS. of the Old and
New Testament being placed in the king's library, Mr.
Young examined it with great attention, and furnished
the various readings, upon collation, to Usher, Grotius,
and other learned men. He had intended to have published a fac-simile of this MS.; but his many avocations, and
perhaps the confusions which ensued in the political world,
prevented him. In 1643, however, he printed a specimen
of his intended edition, containing the first chapter of Genesis, with notes; and left at his death scholia as far as the
15th chapter of Numbers. The future progress of such a
publication is noticed in our articles of GRABE and WOIDE.

In 1633, he published an edition of Clemens Romanus
reprinted in 1637, with a Latin version "Catena Græ-
corum patrum in Jobum, collectore Niceta Heracleæ Me-
tropolitæ," to which he subjoined, from the Alexandrian
MS. a continued series of the books of scripture, called
Poetici. This was followed, in 1638, by the "Expositio
in Canticum Canticorum Gilberti Folioti episc. Londini, una

cum Alcuini in idem Canticum compendio," with a dedication to bishop Juxon. He made preparations for publishing several other curious MSS. while he continued in the royal library, which was till near the death of Charles I. when it was seized by the republican party, and preserved, amidst many vicissitudes, with more care than could have been expected. Mr. Young now retired to Bromfield, in Essex, to the house of Mr. John Atwood, a civilian, who had married his eldest daughter. There he died Sept. 7, 1652, and was interred in the chancel of Bromfield church.

Respecting Mr. Young's learning there seems to have been no dispute. It was acknowledged by all the eminent scholars of his time, both at home and abroad, particularly Fronto-Ducæus, Sirmond, Petavius, Grotius, Salmasius, Vossius, Casaubon, Usher, Selden, &c. But it seems to be disputed whether he did not side with the republican party. Of this we have not discovered any direct proof, and his court connexions, and the friendships which subsisted between him and Juxon, Usher, Walton, Hammond, Pearson, &c. seem to afford a presumptive evidence that he was upon the whole more attached to monarchical than revolutionary principles.[1]

YRIARTE (JUAN DE), a learned and laborious Spanish writer, was born in the island of Teneriffe in 1702, and, at the age of eleven, was sent by his father to France, where he studied at Rouen and Paris for many years, till he was recalled, by the way of London, to the Canary islands, in order to be sent into Spain, where he intended him for the profession of the law. His father died before his arrival; but in pursuance of his design, Juan arrived at Madrid in 1724. Here he was admitted into the royal library, and patronized by many noblemen of the first rank. In 1729 he was appointed clerk, and in 1732, keeper of the royal library, which office he held for fifteen years, and being entrusted likewise with the augmentation of the library, he added 2000 manuscripts, and more than 10,000 printed volumes. At length he was appointed to the place of interpreter in the first secretaryship of state and dispatches, and chosen a fellow of the royal academy. He died at Madrid, Aug. 23, 1771.

That in his several employments he acquitted himself with great application and industry, appears from the cata-

[1] Smith's Vitæ quorundam erudit. virorum, 1707, 4to.—Ath. Ox. vol. I.— Usher's Life and Letters.—Biog. Brit.

logue of his works, which consist of " Regiæ Bibliothecæ Matritensis codices Græci MSS. Joan Yriarte ejusdem custos excussit, recensuit, notis, indicibus, anecdotis pluribus evulgatis illustravit," 1769, folio, vol. I. ; vol II. he left in manuscript ; " Regiæ Mat. Bibl. Geographica & Chronologica," 1729 ; " R. M. Bibl. Mathematica," 1730 ; corrections and improvements of Antonio's " Bibliotheca Hispana," and Don Miguel Casiri's " Bibl. Arabico-Hispana-Escurial ;" " Palæographia Græca," a MS. 4to ; his collection of Spanish treaties of peace ; near 600 articles intended for a Castilian Dictionary ; a treatise on the orthography and grammar of the Castilian idiom ; his immense collections of materials for a general alphabetical library, in many folios, of all the authors who have treated of the geography, history, politics, literature, biography, trade, &c. of Spain ; and for a history of the Canary islands, which was to consist of six quarto volumes at least. He wrote also a great number of articles inserted in the " Diario de los literatos," a critical journal. In 1774, his " Select Works" were published in 2 vols. 4to, " for the benefit of literature, at the expence of several noblemen, lovers of genius and merit." This collection, " Obras Sueltas," contains some works of imagination, his sacred and prophane Latin poems, or translations ; and his Latin translations of a number of Castilian proverbs, and of some oratorical and critical discourses.——Juan de Yriarte was probably related to Don Tomas de Yriarte, whose ingenious " Literary Fables" were published at Madrid in 1782, and were lately well translated into English verse by John Belfour, esq. ; but of this Don Tomas we have not found any biographical memoir. His poem " La Musica" has gone through many editions, and is much admired in Spain.[1]

YSBRAND (EBERARD IDES), a celebrated traveller, was a native of Gluckstad in Holstein, a man of ingenuity, activity, and enterprize, whose curiosity after voyages and discoveries led him to Moscow about the beginning of the reign of the czars John and Peter Alexiewitz. The latter, better known by the name of Peter the Great, discovered the talents of Ysbrand, took him into his service, and employed him on some regulations which he was about to form, and which laid the foundation for the commercial prosperity of Russia. Peter having afterwards a dispute with the emperor of China, respecting certain boundaries, considered Ysbrand as a very proper person to conduct a negociation, and therefore sent him to China, invested with the character of ambassador. He set off in March 1692, and returned in Jan. 1695, and afterwards published an account of his voyage, at Amsterdam in 1699, reprinted in 1704 and 1710. An English translation was published at London in 1704, 4to, with maps and plates, and is deemed a work of great curiosity and considerable value. It has also been translated into other languages. We have no farther notice of the author than that he was living in 1700.[f]

YVES. See IVES.

## Z

ZABARELLA, or DE ZABARELLIS (FRANCIS), an eminent cardinal, was born in 1339, at Padua. He taught common law in his native place and at Florence, where he acquired so much esteem, that when the archbishopric became vacant, he was chosen to fill it, but the pope had anticipated the election by giving it to another. Zabarella was afterwards invited to Rome by Boniface IX. and by John XXIII. who made him archbishop of Florence, and created him cardinal in 1411, from which time he had the title of the cardinal of Florence. The pope sent him on an embassy to the emperor Sigismund, who demanded a council, both on account of the Bohemian heresies, and the schism between the various candidates for the popedom; and the city of Constance having been fixed upon for this general council, Zabarella very much distinguished himself in its debates. He advised the deposition of John XXIII. and there is every reason to believe he would have been elected pope, had he not died, September 26, 1417, aged seventy-eight, six weeks before the election of Martin V. The emperor and the whole council attended his

[f] Chaufepie, in art. Isbrand.

obsequies, and Poggio spoke his funeral oration, exerting the full powers of his eloquence and learning. Zabarella's works are, "Commentaries on the Decretals and the Clementines," 6 vols. folio. "Councils," 1 vol. "Speeches and Letters," 1 vol. A treatise "De Horis Canonicis;" "De Felicitate, libri tres;" "Variæ Legum repetitiones;" "Opuscula de Artibus liberalibus ; et de naturâ rerum diversarum ;" "Commentarii in naturalem et moralem Philosophiam ;" "Historia sui temporis ;" "Acta in Conciliis Pisano et Constantiensi ;" lastly, "Notes" on the Old and New Testament, and a treatise "On Schism," Basil, 1565, folio, in which he ascribes all the misfortunes of the church, during his time, to the cessation of councils. . This treatise "On Schism" has been frequently reprinted by the protestants, because Zabarella speaks very freely in it of the popes and the court of Rome ; and for the same reason the book has been put into the index. Cardinal Zabarella had a nephew, BARTHOLOMEW Zabarella, who gave lectures in canon law at Padua, with reputation, and was afterwards archbishop of Florence, and referendary of the church under pope Eugenius IV. He died August 12, 1442, aged forty-six.[1]

ZABARELLA (JAMES), born Sept. 5, 1533, at Padua, was the son of Bartholomew Zabarella, mentioned in the preceding article. He took great pleasure in astrology, and amused himself with drawing several horoscopes. He taught logic at Padua during fifteen years, from 1564, and afterwards philosophy till his death. He was several times deputed to Venice, and spoke with great eloquence in the senate. He died at Padua, in October 1589, aged fifty-six. He bore the title of Count Palatine, which passed to his descendants. He left, "Commentaries on Aristotle." "Logica," 1597, folio. "De Animâ," 1606, folio. "Physica," 1601, folio. "De Rebus naturalibus," 1594, 4to ; from which he appears to have had much acuteness in clearing up difficult points, and comprehending the most obscure questions. He maintains, in these commentaries, but still more particularly in a short treatise "De Inventione Æterni Motoris" (which forms part of his works, Francfort, 1618, 4to), that, according to Aristotle's principles, no proof can be brought of the soul's immortality ; whence some writers accuse him of impiety.[2]

[1] Gen. Dict.—Dict. Hist.—Tiraboschi.—Saxii Onomast.
[2] Moreri.—Dict. Hist.—Saxii Onomast.

ZACCARIA (FRANCIS ANTHONY), an eminently learned
Italian Jesuit, was born in Venice, March 27, 1714, the
son of an eminent Tuscan lawyer, settled in the Venetian
states.    He received his education in the schools of the Jesuits in that metropolis, and, as early as the age of fifteen,
evinced such uncommon powers and attainments as to be
introduced into that society, already proverbial for its sagacity and conduct in discovering juvenile talents of every
kind.    In October 1731, he took the habit, went through
his noviciate in Vienna, and became soon after professor of
belles lettres in the college of his order at Govitz.    It was
not long before he was called by his superiors to Rome, ordained a priest in 1740, attached to the Roman province,
and sent on a mission to the Marche of Ancona.    He exercised similar functions also in Tuscany, Lombardy, and
almost the whole of northern Italy, with extraordinary success and fame, and without the least diversion from his favourite pursuit—the study of ecclesiastical, civil, and literary history.    He availed himself of these peregrinations
through the several capitals of Italy, in cultivating the
friendship of all the eminent literary characters he met
with, and in making every where those deep researches in
literature, antiquities, bibliography, and history, which
have supplied him with a great part of his literary history
of Italy, his annals of literature, and his several historical
and diplomatic collections.
    In 1752, he was recommended by the celebrated cardinal
Quirini as a director of the public library of Brescia, a recommendation which, however, had no effect.    But two
years after, his name being already known to the reigning
duke of Modena, under whose auspices he had undertaken
and continued his literary history of Italy, he was appointed
director of the Ducal library, a place formerly held by Muratori, and on his death tendered to the learned father Cor-
sini, of the university of Pisa, who had declined it, from
his invincible attachment to his native place.    He associated
to himself, in the direction of the Ducal library, those two
excellent friends and brothers, who were also co-operators
in the compilation of the Literary History, father Dominic
Troilo of Macerata, and father Joachim Gabardi of Carpi ;
who afterwards retained the same place under the celebrated father Granelli, and his successor, the illustrious
Tiraboschi.    Without any interruption to his higher literary pursuits, the improvements which he made in this

situation are recorded highly to the honour of Zaccaria: he enlarged the apartment devoted to the library; introduced a better classification of books, enriched it with new articles, and compiled a catalogue raisonné of every branch, which, to the regret of many intelligent persons, was never published.

His fame was already so great that the justly celebrated count Cristiani, then Austrian governor of Mantua, desired him to repair to that city, to superintend the then proposed establishment of an imperial library. He accepted the offer, with the permission of his master; and as soon as his business in Mantua was completed, he resumed his residence at Modena, and continued in the Ducal library, till the expulsion of the Jesuits from the several petty states of Italy obliged him to remove.

In 1768, he repaired to Rome, and was soon appointed librarian to the college of Jesus, and historiographer of the society for the literary department. Here a new field was open to his exertions. He became the champion of the holy see against the prevailing philosophy of the age, and against the encroachment of the secular powers on the church, for which he was rewarded with a pension by the then reigning and unfortunate pontiff Clement XIII. He did not long enjoy either this gift of fortune or his own tranquillity, as in 1773, by the dissolution of his order, after repeated risks of being confined in the castle of St. Angelo, he received a perpetual injunction not to go out of the gates of Rome without a licence from the magistrates. Pope Ganganelli esteemed and lamented him, though he could not restrain these violent measures. He had better days under the new pontificate, when Pius VI. not only restored liberty to Mr. Zaccaria, but increased the pension which had been formerly granted to him. He also appointed him governor to the newly established academy of noble clergymen, with a liberal salary; and as he had been, before that period, professor of ecclesiastical history in the Roman university, better known by the name of Sapienza, the pope gave him for the remainder of his life the dignity of ex-professor in that school, with the enjoyment of the same salaries as if he had retained the official post. In this situation he remained till his death, which took place October 10, 1795, in the eighty-second year of his age.

The mere list of the various works either written or edited by Zaccaria is sufficient to give him the character of an extraordinary man. Comprehensiveness of mind, depth of erudition, laboriousness of research, and celerity of execution, were happily combined in all his performances. In the earlier part of his life, he had entered the lists with the immortal Muratori and the illustrious Lami. Afterwards he had a great polemic dispute, on the pope's supremacy, with the celebrated German bishop, John Nicholas Hontheim, better known under the name of Justinus Febronius. In the latter part of his life, he corresponded with many sovereigns and princes, with many Italian academies, and many literary characters, on this side the Alps, among whom were the celebrated Stilting, a Bollandist; Mr. de Courcelles, editor of the Foreign Journal in Paris; the proprietors of the Literary Journal of Italy, published in Amsterdam; and that of the Encyclopedian Journal of Liege.

The number of his publications, original as well as others, amounts to 106, besides many unpublished manuscripts. The best of the former class are accounted his " Literary History of Italy," 14 vols. in 8vo; the " Literary Annals of Italy," 3 vols. in 8vo; the " Lapidary and Numismatic Institutions," 2 vols. 8vo; the " Library of ancient and modern Literary History," 6 vols. 4to. Some of his works, especially his polemic performances, were written in Latin, and it was remarked that in this language he wrote comparatively more elegantly than in Italian.

His moral character was excellent; frank, candid, humane, unassuming, and polite; cordial to his friends, and obliging to his pupils. In his opinions, however, he was too warm and passionate; and his works, especially those which he wrote for the support of the Roman catholic church, and of the papal prerogatives, are proverbial for intemperance and asperity.[1]

ZACCHIAS (PAUL), physician to pope Innocent X. was born in 1584, at Rome, and cultivated the belles lettres, poetry, music, painting, and all the sciences; which, however, did not prevent his being one of the best physicians of his time. He died 1659, at Rome, aged seventy-five. His works are, " Quæstiones Medico-legales;" of which there are several editions; among others, Lyons, 1726, 3 tom. folio. This is an excellent work; it contains great learning and judgment, with solid reasoning, and is very

[1] Baldwin's Lit. Journal for 1803.

necessary for divines and canonists, in cases where medicine and surgery are connected with the civil and ecclesiastical laws. He wrote also a treatise in Italian, entitled
"La Vita quadragesimale," for avoiding the dispensations
of Lent, Rome, 1673, 8vo; and three books, in the same
language, "On Hypochondriacal Diseases," Venice, 1665,
4to, &c.[1]

ZACUTUS, an eminent Spanish physician, was born
at Lisbon in 1575, and is usually called Lusitanus. He
studied both philosophy and medicine at Salamanca and
Coimbra, and took his degree of doctor in 1594 at Sagun-
tum, now called Morvedre, a famous university in Spain.
After this, he practised physic at Lisbon till 1624; when,
by an edict of Philip IV. who governed Spain with a high
hand, the whole race of Jews were interdicted the kingdom.
Zacutus, being a Jew, retired into Holland, practising
chiefly at Amsterdam and the Hague; at the former of
which places he died, in 1641 or 1642, aged about sixty-
six or seven. His works, written in Latin, were printed at
Lyons in France, in 1649, 2 vols. folio. Before the second
is placed what he calls "Introitus ad Praxin; or, An Introduction to Practice;" in which he displays the qualities
of a physician, moral as well as intellectual; and shews,
not only what are the qualifications necessary to the art,
but also what are the duties necessary to the man.[2]

ZANCHIUS (BASIL), one of the most learned men of
the sixteenth century, was a native of Bergamo. His real
name was Peter, which he exchanged for Basil, when he
became a canon regular. He was born in 1501. He appears to have studied at Rome and various other places, but
resided for the greater part of his life at Rome, where he
was highly honoured for his literary talents, and, as some
say (but this is disputed), was made keeper of the Vatican
library. He died there, however, in 1560. Paul Manu-
tius, in a letter to Gambara, the intimate friend of Zanchius, says that he was oppressed and persecuted in a very
cruel manner, and ended his days miserably, in consequence of a decree of the pope against those who did not
reside in their convents, but some have conjectured that
he might have probably become a convert to the reformed
religion, like his cousin Jerome, of whom we are next to

[1] Eloy, Dict. Hist. de Medecine.—Haller Bibl. Med.
[2] Eloy, Dict. Hist. de Medecine.—Manget Bibl.—Haller.

speak. It seems certain, however, that he died in prison, and that he was worthy of a better fate, being one of the most learned men, and best Latin poets of his age. His beautiful verses on the death of Sannazarius were translated into Italian by the great Torquato Tasso. His Latin poems were first printed at Rome in 1540, 4to, and were often reprinted. Serassi gave a new edition of them at Bergamo in 1747, with a life of the author. He wrote also observations on all the books of scripture, printed at Rome 1553, and twice reprinted. He is ranked among lexicographers, from having contributed to Nizolius's observations on Cicero, and from having added a great collection of words to Calepin, from the best and purest authors. He published also "Epithetorum commentarii," Rome, 1542, 4to, a work better known by the title of the second edition, "Dictionarium poeticum et epitheta veterum poetarum," &c. 1612, 8vo. [1]

ZANCHIUS (JEROME), an eminent divine, and ranked among the illustrious band of reformers, was a cousin of the preceding, and most probably born at Bergamo, Feb. 2, 1516, the year before the reformation appeared in Germany under Luther. He was deprived of both his parents, by death, when very young, and resolving on a monastic life, entered the society of the canons regular, where he found some of his relations, and where he had an opportunity of improvement in literature. Here he studied philosophy, the languages, and school divinity, for nineteen years. His first departure from the tenets of the Romish church may be dated from his having an opportunity of hearing Peter Martyr's lectures on the epistle to the Romans and on the Psalms, which he appears to have done along with count Maximinian and Tremellius, both afterwards converts to the reformed opinions. From this time he began to study the scriptures and the fathers, particularly St. Austin, and preached according to the new light he had received. In 1550, when Peter Martyr was no longer permitted to preach, and was obliged to leave Italy, eighteen of his disciples followed him, and among the rest Zanchius. He first went to the territory of the Grisons, and from that to Geneva, where, after he had resided about a year, he received invitation to fill a divinity professorship in England. This was probably at Oxford, where Peter

[1] Moreri.—Tiraboschi.—Gen. Dict.

Martyr was now settled, and had recommended him; but he preferred a similar invitation from Strasburgh, and in 1553, succeeded Caspar Hedio, as divinity professor there.

In this office he continued about eleven years, not without much opposition, which, however, was considerably moderated by the friendship of Sturmius, then at the head of the university. It was here that, in 1562, Zanchius presented to the senate the declaration of his faith concerning predestination, final perseverance, and the Lord's supper. But as the old divines and senators dropped off, his situation at Strasburgh became more and more uncomfortable, and at length he was required to subscribe the Augsburgh confession, on pain of losing his professorship. This he did, after mature deliberation, with a salvo that "it should be understood only in the orthodox sense;" but it would appear that he was not quite satisfied in his own mind, nor did his compliance prevent the divisions and dissentions which distracted the church of Strasburgh, and finally induced him to accept an invitation to become pastor of the church of Chiavenna, on the borders of Italy, and in the territory of the Grisons. Having therefore obtained the consent of the senate to resign his canonry of St. Thomas, and his professorship, he left Strasburgh in Nov. 1563, and entered on his charge at Chiavenna in January following. This he fulfilled for four years, interrupted only on one occasion by the plague, after which Frederick, elector Palatine, prevailed with him to accept a divinity professorship at Heidelberg, on the decease of Zachary Ursin. He entered on this new office in 1568, with an excellent oration on the means of preserving the pure word of God in the church. In the same year he received his doctor's degree, the elector Palatine and his son, prince Casimir, honouring the ceremony with their presence.

He had not been long settled in the Palatinate, when the elector strongly solicited him to take up his pen against the Socinians, who had fixed their head quarters in Poland and Transylvania, and were displaying every artifice to propagate their opinions. This produced Zanchius's two masterly treatises "De Dei natura," and "De tribus Elohim uno eodemque Jehovah." After this he retained his professorship at Heidelberg ten years, until the death of the elector, and the accession of a successor of different principles, who obliged him to remove to Newstadt, the residence of prince John Casimir, count Palatine. Here he remained upwards of seven years, and when excused, on account of his age and infirmities from public services, he removed once more to Heidelberg, where he died Nov. 19, 1590, in the seventy-fifth year of his age, and was interred in the college chapel of St. Peter. Zanchius, while one of the most learned of the reformers, was also one of the most pious, and distinguished for great moderation in controversy, united with sufficient firmness in maintaining what he considered to be the truth. His works were printed at Geneva in 1619, 9 vols. folio, usually bound in three. [1]

ZANOTTI (FRANCIS MARIA), an eminent Italian mathematician, was born at Bologna in January 1692, and was educated among the Jesuits. His first pursuit was the law, which he soon exchanged for philosophy, and particularly mathematics. In philosophy he was at first a Cartesian, but when sir Isaac Newton's discoveries were divulged, he was among the first to acknowledge his great superiority, particularly in optics and astronomy. He was made librarian and secretary to the academy of Bologna, and wrote a Latin history of its transactions continued down to 1766, and he also contributed many mathematical papers of great importance. But his talents were not confined to philosophy and mathematics: he was also a distinguished poet both in the Tuscan and Latin languages, and in the latter was thought a successful imitator of Catullus, Tibullus, Ovid, and Virgil. After a life honourably spent in those various pursuits, which procured him great fame, he died Dec. 25, 1777. He published a great many works, both in Italian and Latin, which are enumerated by Fabroni. [2]

ZANZALUS (JACOB), called also BARADÆUS, a monk of the sixth century, rendered himself conspicuous in the Eastern church by reviving the sect of the Monophysites, founded by Eutyches, and called from him Eutychians. Their doctrine was, that in Christ there is but one nature, that of the incarnate word. The sect was now reduced to very few, but these had ordained Zanzalus bishop of Edessa, and by his uncommon zeal and indefatigable labours, he left his sect, when he died in 588, in a most flourishing state in Syria, Mesopotamia, Armenia, Egypt, &c. and other countries, and such as exist in those countries are still called by the name of Jacobites in honour of him. [3]

ZEGEDIN, or SZEGEDIN, (STEPHEN DE), an eminent Lutheran divine, was born in 1505, at Zegedin, a city of Lower Hungary; his family name was Kis. He studied under Luther and Melancthon, at Wittemberg; taught and preached Lutheranism afterwards, in several cities in Hungary, and was taken prisoner by the Turks, who used him with great cruelty. Having recovered his liberty, he officiated as minister at Buda, and in many other places. He died at Reven, in Hungary, May 2, 1572, aged sixty-seven, leaving, "Speculum Roman. Pontificum Historicum," 1602, 8vo. "Assertio de Trinitate," 1573, 8vo. "Tabulæ Analyticæ in Prophetas, Psalmos, et Novum Testamentum," 1592, folio; a work very highly recommended for its utility by father Simon. [1]

ZEILER (MARTIN), an indefatigable German geographer, was born in Stiria in 1589. His father had been pupil of Melancthon, and minister at Ulm. He was appointed inspector of the German schools, and though with the disadvantage of having but one eye, was a very arduous and successful student, and wrote many works; the most esteemed among which are those relative to the modern geography of Germany, viz. "The Itinerary of Germany;" "The Topography of Bavaria;" "The Topography of Suabia," which is very accurate; "The Topography of Alsace;" "of the States of Brunswick;" and "of the Country of Hamburgh;" The "Itinerary of Italy," which is much esteemed; and a pretty good "Description of Hungary," &c. These compose almost all the whole topography of Merian, in 31 vols. folio. Zeiler also left two volumes of Historians, Geographers, and Chronologers, in which he has copied the whole of Vossius, and other authors, but without correcting their mistakes. He died Oct. 6, 1661, at Ulm, aged seventy-three. [2]

ZENO, the founder of the Stoic sect (a branch from the Cynic, and as far as respected morals, differing from it in words more than in reality), was a native of Cittius, a maritime town of Cyprus, and as this place was originally peopled by a colony of Phenicians, he is sometimes called a Phenician. His father, a merchant, encouraged him in the study of philosophy, and bought for him several of the writings of the most eminent Socratic philosophers, which he read with great avidity; and when he was about thirty

[1] Melchior Adam.—Freheri Theatrum.
[2] Freheri Theatrum.—Saxii Onomast.

years of age, determined to take a voyage to Athens, which was so celebrated both as a mart of trade and of science. Whether this voyage was in part mercantile, or wholly un-dertaken for the sake of conversing with those philosophers whose writings Zeno had long admired, is uncertain. If it be true, as some writers relate, that he brought with him a valuable cargo of Phenician purple, which was lost by shipwreck upon the coast of Piræus, this circumstance will account for the facility with which he at first attached him-self to a sect whose leading principle was the contempt of riches. Upon his first arrival in Athens, going accidentally into the shop of a bookseller, he took up a volume of the Commentaries of Xenophon, and formed so high an idea of the author, that he asked the bookseller, where he might meet with such men. Crates, the Cynic philosopher, hap-pening at that instant to be passing by, the bookseller pointed to him, and said, " Follow that man," which he did, and was so well pleased with his doctrine, that he became one of his disciples. But though he highly admired the general principles and spirit of the Cynic school, he could not easily reconcile himself to their peculiar manners ; nor would his inquisitive turn of mind allow him to adopt their indifference to scientific inquiry. He therefore attended upon other masters, who professed to instruct their dis-ciples in the nature and causes of things, and when Crates, displeased at this, attempted to drag him by force out of the school of Stilpo, Zeno said to him, " You may seize my body, but Stilpo has laid hold of my mind." After conti-nuing to attend upon the lectures of Stilpo several years, he passed over to other schools, particularly those of Xeno-crates and Diodorus Cronus. By the latter he was instructed in dialectics ; and at last, after attending almost every other master, he offered himself as a disciple of Polemo, who sus-pected that his design was to collect materials for a new system : nor was he mistaken. The place which Zeno chose for his school was called Στοα, or the Porch, and hence the name of Stoics. Zeno had advantages as the founder of a new sect; he excelled in that kind of subtle reasoning which was at that time popular, and while he taught a sys-tem of moral doctrine, his own morals were unexception-able. He therefore soon became much followed, and on account of his integrity the Athenians deposited the keys of their citadel in his hands, and honoured him with a golden crown and a statue of brass.

In his person Zeno was tall and slender; his aspect was severe, and his brow contracted. His constitution was feeble; but he preserved his health by great abstemiousness. The supplies of his table consisted of figs, bread, and honey; notwithstanding which, he was frequently honoured with the company of great men. It was a singular proof of his moderation, mixed indeed with that high spirit of independence which afterwards distinguished his sect, that when Democharis, son of Laches, offered to procure him some gratuity from Antigonus, he was so offended, that from that time he declined all intercourse with him. In public company, to avoid every appearance of an assuming temper, he commonly took the lowest place. Indeed, so great was his modesty, that he seldom chose to mingle with a crowd, or wished for the company of more than two or three friends at once. He paid more attention to neatness and decorum in external appearance, than the Cynic philosophers. In his dress indeed he was plain, and in all his expences frugal, which arose from a contempt of external magnificence. He showed as much respect to the poor as to the rich; and conversed freely with persons of the meanest occupations. He had only one servant, or, according to Seneca, none. Yet with all these virtues, several philosophers of great ability and eloquence employed their talents against him, and Arcesilaus and Carneades, the founders of the middle and new academy, were his professed opponents. Towards the latter end of his life he found another powerful adversary in Epicurus, whose temper and doctrines were alike inimical to the severe gravity and philosophical pride of the Stoic sect. Hence mutual invectives passed between the Stoics and other sects, to which little credit is due. At least it may be fairly presumed that Zeno, whose personal character was so exemplary, never countenanced gross immorality in his doctrine.

Zeno lived to the extreme age of ninety-eight, and at last, in consequence of an accident, voluntarily put an end to his life. As he was walking out of his school he fell down, and in the fall broke one of his fingers; upon which he was so affected with a consciousness of infirmity, that, striking the earth, he said, " Why am I thus importuned? I obey thy summons;" and immediately went home and strangled himself. He died in the first year of the hundred and twenty-ninth Olympiad, or B. C. 264. The Athenians, at the request of Antigonus, erected a monument to his memory in the Ceramicum.

From the particulars which have been related concerning Zeno, it will not be difficult to perceive what kind of influence his circumstances and character must have had upon his philosophical system. If his doctrines be diligently compared with the history of his life, it will appear that he compiled, out of various contemporary tenets, an heterogeneous system, on the credit of which he assumed to himself the title of the founder of a new sect; and, indeed, when he resolved, for the sake of establishing a school, to desert the philosophy of Pythagoras and Plato, it became necessary, either to invent opinions entirely new, or to give an air of novelty to old systems by the introduction of new terms and definitions. Of these two undertakings Zeno prudently made choice of the easier. Cicero says, concerning Zeno, that he had little reason for deserting his masters, especially those of the Platonic school, and that he was not so much an inventor of new opinions, as of new terms. In morals, the principal difference between the Cynics and Stoics was, that the former disdained the cultivation of nature, the latter affected to rise above it. [1]

ZENO, called the ELEATIC, to distinguish from the preceding, and from others, flourished about 463 B. C. He was a zealous friend of civil liberty, and is celebrated for his courageous and successful opposition to tyrants; but the inconsistency of the stories related by different writers concerning him, in a great measure destroys their credit. He chose to reside in his small native city of Elea, rather than at Athens, because it afforded freer scope to his independent and generous spirit, which could not easily submit to the restraints of authority. It is related that he vindicated the warmth with which he resented reproach, by saying, "If I were indifferent to censure, I should also be indifferent to praise." The invention of the dialectic art has been improperly ascribed to Zeno; but there can be no doubt that this philosopher, and other metaphysical disputants in the Eleatic sect, employed much ingenuity and subtlety in exhibiting examples of most of the logical arts which were afterwards reduced to rule by Aristotle and others.

[1] Diog. Laertius.—Brucker.—Fenelon's Lives of the Philosophers.

According to Aristotle, Zeno of Elea taught that nothing
can be produced either from that which is similar or dissimilar; that there is only one being, and that is God;
that this being is eternal, homogeneous, and spherical,
neither finite nor infinite, neither quiescent nor moveable;
that there are many worlds; that there is in nature no va-
cuum; that all bodies are composed of four elements, heat
and moisture, cold and dryness; and that the body of man
is from the earth, and his soul an equal mixture of these
four elements. He argued with great subtlety against the
possibility of motion. If Seneca's account of this philosopher deserves credit, he reached the highest point of
scepticism, and denied the real existence of external objects. The truth is, that after all that has been advanced
by different writers, it is impossible to determine whether
Zeno understood the term *one*, metaphysically, logically,
or physically; or whether he admitted or denied a nature
properly divine.[1]

ZENO (APOSTOLO), a learned poet, critic, and antiquary, was born in 1669, and descended from an illustrious
Venetian family, which had been long settled in the island
of Candia. He early applied himself to literature, and the
study of Italian history and antiquities. In 1696 he instituted at Venice the academy *Degli Animosi*, and was the
editor of the " Giornale de' Letterati d'Italia," of which he
published thirty volumes between the years 1710 and 1719.
His first musical drama, " L'Inganni Felici," was performed
at Venice in 1695, and between that time and his quitting
Vienna, whither he was invited by the emperor Charles VI.
in 1718, he produced forty-six operas, and seventeen oratorios, besides eighteen dramas, which he wrote jointly
with Pariati. His dramatic works were collected and published at Venice in 1744, in 10 vols. 8vo, by count Gozzi;
and in 1752 his letters were printed in 3 vols. by Forcellini, in which Dr. Burney, whom we principally follow in
this article, says, much sound learning and criticism are
manifested on various subjects. But one of the most useful of his critical labours seems to have been his commentary on the " Bibl. dell' Eloquenza Italiana di Fontanini,"
which was published in 1753, with a preface by his friend
Forcellini, chiefly dictated, however, by Zeno himself, just
before his death.

[1] Diog. Laert.—Gen. Dict.—Brucker.

After he was engaged as imperial laureat, he set out from Venice for Vienna in July 1718, but having been overturned in a chaise, the fourth day of his journey, he had the misfortune to break his leg, and was confined at an inn in the little town of Ponticaba, near Trevisa, till September. He arrived at Vienna, the 14th of that month, "safe," as he says, " if not sound and cured," after twelve days of excessive suffering on the road. Most of the dramas, sacred and secular, which he wrote for the imperial court, were set by Caldara, a grave composer and sound harmonist, to whose style Zeno seems to have been partial. But this excellent antiquary and critic seems never to have been satisfied with his own poetical abilities. So early as 1722, in writing to his brother from Vienna, he says, " I find more and more every day, that I grow old, not only in body, but in mind ; and that the business of writing verses is no longer a fit employment for me." And afterwards he expressed a wish that he might be allowed a partner in his labours, and was so just and liberal as to mention the young Metastasio as a poet worthy to be honoured with the emperor's notice. If the musical dramas of Apostolo Zeno are compared with those of his predecessors and contemporaries, they will be found infinitely superior to them in conduct, regularity, character, sentiment, and force. But Metastasio's refined sentiments, selection of words, and varied and mellifluous measures, soon obscured the theatrical glory of Zeno, who, after the arrival of his young colleague, seems to have attempted nothing but oratorios.

In 1731 he returned to Venice, and his place at court was entirely supplied by Metastasio, but the salaries of poet and historiographer were still continued to him. Zeno corresponded with the learned of Italy, and other countries; was an able antiquary, and had made an excellent collection of literary anecdotes. His candour, sincerity, affability, and other amiable qualities, rendered him universally esteemed, and highly agreeable in society. He died at Venice, November 11, 1750, in the eighty-second year of his age, and was buried at the convent of the Dominicans of the strict observance, to whom he had left his library. He is universally allowed to have possessed great talents for dramatic poetry, and is the first Italian poet who gave his countrymen good rules for tragedy, and taught them to consider music only as an embellishment. He discovers genius, spirit, and feeling; but his style, as has been remarked, is far inferior to that of Metastasio. Zeno also left a great number of works on Antiquities, &c. ; " Dissertationi Vossiani," 3 vols. 8vo ; " Letters," Venice, 1752, 2 vols. 4to. [1]

ZENOBIA, queen of Palmyra, and one of the most illustrious women that have swayed the sceptre, declared herself to be descended from the Ptolemies and Cleopatras. She was instructed in the sciences by the celebrated Longinus, and made such progress, that she spoke the Egyptian tongue in perfection, as well as the Greek. She also understood the Latin, although she scrupled to speak it. She protected learned men; and was so well acquainted with the history of Egypt, and that of the East, that she wrote an epitome of it. This princess had also read the Greek and Roman history, and was justly admired for her beauty, chastity, sobriety, and extraordinary courage. She married Odenatus, a Saracen prince, and contributed greatly to the most signal victories he gained over the Persians, which preserved the East to the Romans, when, after the taking of Valerian, it was highly probable that Sapor would dispossess them of all that country. Gallienus, in return for such important services, declared her Augusta, and, in the year 264, created Odenatus emperor. After her husband's death, Zenobia reigned with great bravery and glory ; for, her sons Herennianus and Timolaus, on account of their tender age, had only the name and ornaments of emperor. She preserved the provinces that had been under the obedience of Odenatus, conquered Egypt, and was preparing to make other conquests, when the emperor Aurelian made war against her ; and, having gained two battles, besieged her in Palmyra, where Zenobia defended herself with great bravery ; but at length, finding that the city would be obliged to surrender, she quitted it privately ; but the emperor, who had notice of her escape, caused her to be pursued with such diligence, that she was overtaken just as she got into a boat to cross the Euphrates. This happened in the year 272. Aurelian spared her life, although he made her serve to adorn his triumph, and gave her a country-house near Rome, where she spent the remainder of her life in tranquillity with her children. Her daughters formed noble alliances, and her

[1] Burney's History of Music, and Life of Metastasio.—Fabroni Vitæ Italorum, vol. IX.

race was not extinct in the fifth century. All historians bestow the most magnificent praises on this princess; and yet they suspect her of having consented that Mæonius should assassinate Odenatus, her husband, for shewing less fondness for her sons than for Herod, his son by another wife. She has also been censured for protecting Paulus Samosatenus, who had been condemned in the council of Antioch, and by that means preventing his being driven from his church so long as she reigned. But P. Jouve, who published her Life, 1758, 12mo, endeavours, not unsuccessfully, to clear her from all these imputations. She must be distinguished from Zenobia, wife of Rhadamistus, king of Iberia, who fled from the Armenians, and took her with him. This princess being near the time of her delivery, begged Rhadamistus to kill her. He reluctantly yielded to Zenobia's earnest entreaties, and wounded her with a sword; but she was found by some shepherds, who saved her life, in the year 51. Zenobia being afterwards conducted to Tiridates, he ordered her to be treated as a queen. [1]

ZEUXIS, a very famous painter of antiquity, flourished about 400 years before Christ, or about the 95th Olympiad. The particulars relating to his country are a little confused: for though Tully, Pliny, and Ælian, agree in affirming that he was of Heraclea, yet they have not, among the numerous cities of that name, told us the Heraclea in which Zeuxis was born. Pliny represents the art of painting, the rudiments of which had been discovered by Apollodorus, to have been carried to considerable perfection by this painter. Some authors relate, that he found out the manner of disposing lights and shades; and he is allowed to have excelled in colouring. Aristotle censured this defect in his paintings, that the manners or passions were not expressed in them; yet Pliny asserts the contrary with regard to the picture of Penelope; " in which Zeuxis," says he, " seems to have painted the manners."

This painter amassed immense riches; and he once made a shew of them at the olympic games, where he appeared in a cloak embroidered with gold letters expressing his name. When he found himself thus rich, he would not sell his works any longer, but gave them away, because, he said, no price could be set upon them. His Helen was his most celebrated picture. He wrote underneath this picture the three verses of the Iliad, in which Homer represents Priam and the venerable sages of his council confessing that the Greeks and Trojans were not to blame for having exposed themselves to so many calamities for the love of Helen; her beauty equalling that of the goddesses. It cannot be very well determined, whether this Helen of Zeuxis be the same as that which was at Rome in Pliny's time; or that which he painted for the inhabitants of Crotona, to be hung up in the temple of Juno. They had prevailed upon him to come among them, by giving him a large sum, in order to paint a great number of pictures, with which they intended to adorn this temple; and were not a little pleased when he told them, that he intended to draw the picture of Helen, as his chief excellence lay in painting women. This extraordinary picture he executed by combining the beauties of various living models; and this method of forming perfection he learned from Homer, whose mode of ideal composition was his rule.

Many curious particulars are recorded of this painter; among others we are told that he had painted some grapes so very naturally, that the birds used to come and peck them; and Parrhasius painted a curtain so artfully, that Zeuxis, mistaking it for a real curtain, which hid his rival's work, ordered it to be drawn aside, that he might see Parrhasius's painting; but, finding his mistake, he confessed himself vanquished; since he had only imposed upon birds, whereas Parrhasius had misled even those who were masters of the art. Another time, he painted a boy loaded with grapes, when the birds flew again to this picture, at which he was vexed; and frankly confessed, that it was not sufficiently finished, since, had he painted the boy as perfectly as the grapes, the birds would have been afraid of him. Archelaus, king of Macedon, made use of Zeuxis's pencil for the embellishment of his house; upon which Socrates made this reflection, as it is preserved by Ælian: "Archelaus," said he, " has laid out a vast sum of money upon his house, but nothing upon himself: whence it is, that numbers come from all parts of the world to see his house, but none to see him; except those who are tempted by his money and presents, and who will not be found among the worthiest of men."

One of Zeuxis's finest pieces was a Hercules strangling some dragons in his cradle, in the presence of his frighted mother: but he himself esteemed chiefly his athleta, or champion, under which he made a verse that became afterwards proverbial, viz. "that it would be easier to envy than to imitate that picture." It is probable, that he valued his Alcmena, since he presented it to the Agrigentines. He did not paint with rapidity; and used to say to those who reproached him with slowness, that "he was indeed a long time in painting, but that it was also to last a long time." Lucian has given us a description of a picture of Zeuxis, that of a female centaur. As to his death, we are told that having painted an old woman, he laughed so heartily at his performance that he died. This circumstance is related by Verrius Flaccus, under the word Pictor; but it is probably fabulous.[1]

ZIEGENBALG (BARTHOLOMEW), a very celebrated protestant missionary, was born at Pulnitz in Upper Lusatia, June 14, 1683. He began his education in the college of Camentz, where he first appears to have cherished that pious zeal which influenced his future conduct and labours. He then removed to Goerlitz, afterwards to Berlin, and lastly to Halle, where he studied divinity; but his excessive application to this and other learned pursuits injured his health and brought on a species of melancholy, to divert which he was advised to travel. He happened to visit Berlin in 1705, when missionaries were wanted by the king of Denmark to go to the East Indies, and resolving to be one of the number, he was recommended to Dr. Lutkens, whom his Danish majesty had employed to find out men of learning, zeal, and piety, suited to the work. Ziegenbalg being approved, and having settled his private affairs, went to Copenhagen, along with Mr. Henry Plutschau, another young missionary, where they received all necessary orders and instructions. On Nov. 29, 1709, they embarked on board the Sophia-Hedwige, and arrived on April 23 following at the Cape of Good Hope, where the deplorable state of the Hottentots excited their pity, and heightened their wishes for the conversion of the heathen. They left this place on May 8, and while pursuing their voyage, Ziegenbalg employed himself on a moral treatise, which he sent afterwards to be printed at Halle, under the title of "The School of Wisdom." They arrived at Tran-

1 Plin. Nat. Hist.—Junius de Pictura Veterum.—Gen. Dict.—Fuseli's Lectures, Lect. I.

quebar on July 9, but found their enterprise obstructed by many difficulties, one of which was their ignorance of the languages spoken in the country. Having, however, surmounted this by perseverance, and acquired a familiar knowledge of the Portuguese and Malabar languages, they made considerable progress in the great object of their mission, and by the month of January 1707, were enabled to teach the catechism in the Malabar language, and a few months afterwards baptised some young converts. In the same year they laid the foundation of a church for the sole use of the missionaries and their disciples, and with the assistance of some generous and charitable persons had completed it in the month of August, when it was dedicated by the name of the New Jerusalem. There they preached both in the Portuguese and Malabar, and catechised twice a week in the same languages. In Oct. 1708, Ziegenbalg began his version of the New Testament in the Malabar tongue, which was printed in 1714, at Tranquebar, under the title of "Nov. Test. D. N. Jesu Christi, ex originali textu in linguam Tamulicam versum, in usum gentis Malabaricæ, opera et studio Barth. Ziegenbalg, et Joannis Ernesti Grundleri, &c." 2 vols. 4to.

The opposition, however, to the labours of these missionaries, began to be very serious. Some time after he began his translation of the New Testament, he was arrested and sent as a prisoner to the castle of Tranquebar, in which he was confined about four months. During this time he was not permitted to carry on his translation, but he employed himself on some works of piety in German. In the beginning of 1709, the missionaries found themselves in a very embarrassing situation, having received no supplies from home, while the maintenance of their schools cost them fifty crowns *per* month. Some benevolent persons, however, having advanced about 200 crowns, they were enabled by prudent management to go on until the arrival of the fleet in July, which brought them very ample relief. They received, by these vessels, 2020 crowns from Denmark, 1700 from Germany, besides an apothecary, an ample stock of medicines, a collection of books, and three additional missionaries to assist them in their labours. The commander of Tranquebar at the same time received express orders from the king of Denmark, to protect the missionaries, and give them every aid and countenance. It was also about the same time that the missionaries received very great assistance from the London society for propagating the gospel in foreign parts.

One of Ziegenbalg's principal objects was to disperse in all the countries along the coast treatises in the Malabar language for the instruction of the heathen. In 1711 he made a voyage to Madras, and visited all the European establishments in that quarter. He also visited the territories of the Mogul, in which he preached the gospel, but had nearly lost his life by the bigotry of the natives on one of their festivals. The same year the king of Denmark assigned the missionaries a perpetual yearly pension, of 2000 crowns. They received also a fount of Malabar types, made at Halle, and thus in 1713 the printing-office of Malabar was in a condition to begin works in that language. Ziegenbalg in the mean time was preparing a translation of the Old Testament. In Oct. 1714 he embarked on board a Danish vessel to return to Europe on business concerning the mission, and during the voyage went on with his translation, which he had finished as far as the book of Joshua before they arrived at the Cape, in Jan. 1715. During the remainder of his voyage home, besides his labours on the Old Testament, he composed a grammar of the Malabar language, in Latin, which was printed at Halle in 1716, 4to. After the arrival of the ship, Ziegenbalg went to Copenhagen, where he was received with the highest respect by all classes, and, during his stay here, he succeeded in many necessary arrangements to place the mission on a better foundation. Before his departure the king of Denmark gave him the title of inspector of the mission. In 1716 he came to England, and was received with the greatest respect by archbishop Wake, had an audience of George I. and of the prince and princess of Wales, who promised him every aid and protection. Collections were also made for the benefit of the mission; and the society for the propagation of the gospel in foreign parts, obtained of the directors of the East-India company a passage to India for Ziegenbalg in one of their ships, free of all expence; and presented him also with fifty-five reams of paper, and a chest of books. He embarked at Deal March 4, and arrived at Madras in August of the same year (1716), whence he went to Tranquebar, and resumed his functions, inspirited by the encouragement he had met with in Europe. In 1718 he took an extensive journey by land, and was fulfilling the grand object of his mission with great zeal and success, when he was attacked by a disorder in the bowels, of which he died Feb. 23, 1719, lamented even by the heathen, whose affections he had gained, and particularly by his brethren and the friends of the mission.[1]

ZIEGLER (JAMES), a learned philosopher, mathematician, and divine, of the sixteenth century, was born at Laudshut, in Bavaria. He taught at Vienna for a considerable time, and resided afterwards near the bishop of Passau in Bavaria, where he died in 1549, leaving several works; which are different in their spirit, according as they were written before or after he quitted the Romish church. Among these, his notes on some select passages of the Holy Scriptures, Basil, 1548, folio, and his " Description of the Holy Land," Strasburg, 1536, folio, are particularly esteemed. There is an excellent life of Ziegler in Schelhorn's " Amœnitates."[2]

ZIEGLER (GASPAR), an eminent jurist, was born September 6, 1621, at Leipsic. He was professor of law at Wittemberg, afterwards counsellor to the appeals, and to the consistory; and the court of Saxony employed him in some affairs of importance. He died April 17, 1690, at Wittemberg. His works are, " De Milite Episcopo;" " De Diaconis et Diaconissis," Vitteberge, 1678, 4to; " De Clero Renitente;" " De Episcopis," Norimberg, 1686, 4to.; and critical notes on Grotius's treatise on " The Rights of War and Peace," &c.[3]

ZIGABENUS. See EUTHYMIUS.

ZIMMERMANN (JOHN GEORGE), an eminent physician and miscellaneous writer, was born December 8, 1728, at Brugg, a town in the German part of the canton of Bern. His father, the senator Zimmermann, was descended from a family which had been distinguished, during several ages, for the merit and integrity with which they passed through the first offices of the government. His mother, of the name of Pache, was the daughter of a celebrated counsellor at Morges, in the French part of the same canton; which accounts for the circumstance of the two languages, German and French, being equally familiar to him, although he had spent only a very short time in France. Young Zimmermann was educated at home till he had attained the age of fourteen, when he was sent to study the belles lettres at Bern. After three years had been thus employed, he was transferred to the school of philosophy, where the prolix comments on the metaphysics of Wolf seem to have much disgusted, without much enlightening, him. The death of both his parents leaving him at liberty to choose his destination in life, he determined to embrace the medical profession, and went to the university of Gottingen, in 1747. Here his countryman, the illustrious Haller, took him into his own house, directed his studies, and treated him as a son and a friend. Besides the proper medical professors, Zimmermann attended the mathematical and physical lectures, and acquired a knowledge of English literature. He spent four years in this university, part of the last of which he employed in experiments on the doctrine of irritability, first proposed by the English anatomist Glisson, and afterward pursued with so much success by Haller. Zimmermann made this principle the subject of his inaugural thesis, in 1751; and the clearness of the style and method with which he explained the doctrine, with the strength of the experimental proofs by which he supported it, gained him great reputation.

After a few months spent in a tour to Holland and France he returned to Bern, in 1752. Here he published an account of Haller, in a short letter to a friend, inserted in the journal of Neufchatel, and written in French. Though his only work in that language, it has much elegance of style; and it was the basis of his life of Haller, in German, which was published at Zuric in 1755. While at Bern he married madam Stek, a widow, who was a relation of Haller's, and a woman of a very amiable disposition and well-cultivated mind. Shortly after, he accepted the then vacant post of first physician to his native town. Here he earnestly devoted himself to the studies and duties of his profession; not neglecting, however, those literary pursuits which are necessary to fill up the time of a man of education, in a place which affords but few of the resources of suitable society. He amused himself occasionally with writing little pieces, which he sent to a journal published at Zuric under the title of "The Monitor." As his pleasures were almost exclusively confined to his family and his study, he here contracted that real or supposed love for solitude, which gave such a colour to his writings if not to his life. It seems, however, to have been rather the splenetic resource of a man who was dissatisfied with an obscure situation, which was not adequate to his talents and reputation. In this place his years passed on usefully for the improvement of his mind; but, as it appears, not very happily. His natural sensibility, for want of objects to divert it, preyed upon itself; and he was rendered miserable by a thousand domestic cares and anxieties which he would have felt more lightly in the tumult of public life. He took, however, the best method in his power for relief, by employing his pen with assiduity on professional and literary topics. In 1754, he sent to the physico-medical society of Basil, a case of spasmodic quinsey, together with some observations on the hysteric tumours of Sydenham. In 1755, he composed a short poem, in German, on the earthquake at Lisbon, which was much esteemed by adequate judges, and placed him among the earliest improvers of his native language. In 1756, appeared his first "Essay on Solitude;" a very short performance. Two years afterward, he began to enlarge its plan, and to collect materials for his more extended publication on this subject. He also formed the plan of his work on the "Experience of Medicine;" the first volume of which appeared in 1763. In 1758, he published his "Essay on National Pride;" which passed with rapidity through many editions, was translated into several foreign languages, and very much admired.

An epidemic fever, which reigned in Switzerland in 1763, 1764, and 1765, and which, in the latter year, changed into a dysentery, produced his "Treatise on the Dysentery," which gained him great reputation. This was the last medical work that he composed, though he continued to write short treatises on occasional topics. It should not be omitted, that his friend Dr. Tissot, by addressing to him his own letters on the prevailing epidemic, contributed to extend his professional fame. Nor was he less attentive to his interest, although in some efforts to serve him he was disappointed. At length, however, the vacant post of physician to the king of Great Britain at Hanover, which had been offered to Dr. Tissot, was, by his interest, procured for Zimmermann; and being accepted, he removed to Hanover in 1768. But this new situation was far from procuring the accession of happiness which was expected from it. A disorder which had commenced while he resided at Brugg (and which appears to have been a species of *hernia*), constantly increased, and was accompanied with acute pains, which sometimes rendered irksome the execution of his duty. Besides some incidental circumstances, which occasioned a number of those slight irritations he would not have felt when in health, but which the state of his nerves now rendered insupportable, he had the misfortune, in 1770, of losing his wife; a deprivation which affected him very sensibly. His complaint growing worse, his friend Tissot advised him to seek the best chirurgical assistance, and persuaded him, in 1771, to go to Berlin, and put himself under the care of the celebrated Meckel. He was received into this surgeon's house, and underwent a successful operation. The time of his convalescence was one of the most agreeable in his life. He made a number of acquaintances among distinguished characters at Berlin, was presented to the king, and was honoured by him with particular notice. His reception on his return to Hanover was equally pleasing. He now again plunged into business, and again professional and domestic cares brought on hypochondriacal complaints. In 1775, by way of vacation, he made a journey to Lausanne, where his daughter was placed for education, and spent five weeks with Dr. Tissot. As this was the first time that these intimate friends, of twenty years standing, had seen each other, it will be pleasing to translate some of Tissot, his biographer's, observations on this circumstance: "I had, at length, the pleasure of *seeing* him; I shall not say of *knowing* him. I found that I knew him already; the friend *conversing* reminded me every moment of the friend *writing*, and perfectly resembled the portrait which I had drawn of him. I saw the man of genius, who, with promptitude seizes an object under all its relations, and whose imagination knows how to present it under the most agreeable form. His conversation was instructive, brilliant, sprinkled with a number of interesting facts and pleasant narrations, and animated by an expressive countenance. He spoke of every thing with great precision. When medicine was our subject, as was frequently the case, I found his principles solid, and his notions clear. When I took him to see patients under severe indispositions, or read to him consultations on the most difficult cases, I always found in him the greatest sagacity in discovering causes, and explaining symptoms, great justice in forming indications, and an exquisite judgment in the choice of remedies, of which he employed few, but all efficacious.

In fine, on every occasion, I saw the man of sincerity, rectitude, and virtue. His stay was much shorter than I could have wished."

Dr. Zimmermann was unhappy in the fate of his children. His amiable daughter, whom he most tenderly loved, fell into a lingering malady soon after she left Lausanne: it continued five years, and then carried her off. His son, who, from his infancy, was troubled with an acrid humour, after various vicissitudes of nervous affections, settled in perfect idiotcy; in which state he remained at his father's death. To alleviate these distresses, a second marriage properly occurred to the mind of his friends, and they chose for him a most suitable companion, in the daughter of Dr. de Berger, king's physician at Lunenberg. This union took place in 1782, and proved the greatest charm and support of all his remaining life. His lady was thirty years younger than he; but she perfectly accommodated herself to his taste, and induced him to cultivate society abroad and at home more than he had hitherto done. About this time he employed himself in completing his favourite work on "Solitude," which, at the distance of thirty years from the publication of the first essay on the subject, appeared in its new form in the years 1784 and 1786, in four volumes. His ideas of solitude had probably been softened by so long an intercourse with the world; and as he now defined it, "that state of the soul in which it abandons itself freely to its reflections," it was not necessary to become either a monk or an anchorite, in order to partake of its benefits. Had it not been presented under such an accommodating form, a philosopher might have smiled at the circumstance of a recommendation of solitude from a court physician becoming the favourite work of one of the most splendid and ambitious of crowned heads. The empress of Russia sent her express thanks to the author for the pleasure which she had derived from the work, accompanied with a magnificent present, and commenced with him a regular correspondence, which subsisted, with great freedom on her part, till 1792, when she suddenly dropped it. She also gave him an invitation to settle at Petersburgh as her first physician; and, on his declining the offer, she requested his recommendation of medical practitioners for her towns and armies, and conferred on him the order of Wladomir.

One of the most distinguished incidents of Zimmermann's life was the summons which he received to attend the great Frederic in his last illness, in 1786. It was at once evident that there was no room for the exercise of his medical skill; but he improved the opportunity which he thus enjoyed of confidential intercourse with that illustrious character, whose mental faculties were pre-eminent to the last; and he derived from it the materials of an interesting narrative which he afterwards published. The partiality of this prince in his favour naturally disposed him to a reciprocal good opinion of the monarch; and, in 1788, he published " A Defence of Frederic the Great against the count de Mirabeau;" which, in 1790, was followed by " Fragments on Frederic the Great," in 3 vols. 12mo. All his publications relative to this king gave offence to many individuals, and subjected him to severe criticism; which he felt with more sensibility than was consistent with his peace of mind. His religious and political opinions, likewise, in his latter years, began to be in wide contradiction to the principles that were assiduously propagated all over Europe; and this added perpetual fuel to his irritability. The society of the *Illuminated*, coalesced with that of *Free-masons*, rose about this time in Germany, and excited the most violent commotions among men of letters and reflection. It was supposed to have in view nothing less than the abolition of Christianity, and the subversion of all constituted authorities; and, while its partizans expected from it the most beneficial reforms of every kind, its opponents dreaded from it every mischief that could possibly happen to mankind. Zimmermann was among the first that took alarm at this formidable accusation. His regard for religion and social order, and, perhaps, his connexions with crowned heads, made him see in the most obnoxious light all the principles of the new philosophers. He attacked them with vigour, formed counter associations with other men of letters, and, at length, addressed to the emperor Leopold a memoir, painting in the strongest colouring the pernicious maxims of the sect, and suggesting the means of suppressing it; means which are said to have depended on the decisive interference of civil authority. Leopold, who was well inclined to such measures, received his memoir very graciously, and sent him a letter and splendid present in return; but his death, soon after, deprived the cause of its most powerful protection. Zimmermann, however, in conjunction with M. Hoffman of Vienna, who had instituted a periodical work on the old principles, did not relax in his zeal. They attacked, and were attacked in turn ; and Zimmermann embroiled himself with the courts of law by a paper published in Hoffman's Journal, entitled " The Baron de Knigge unmasked as an Illuminate, Democrat, and Seducer of the People." As this charge was in part founded on a work not openly avowed by the baron, a prosecution was instituted against Zimmermann as a libeller, and he was unable to exculpate himself. This state of warfare may well be imagined to have been extremely unfriendly to an irritable system of nerves ; and the agitation of the doctor's mind was further increased by his personal fears on the approach of the French towards the electorate of Hanover in 1794 ; and his manner of expressing his fears announced the greatest depression. " I saw therein," says Tissot, " a mind whose springs began to fail, and which dared no longer say, as it could have justly done, ' I carry every thing with me.' I neglected nothing in order to raise his spirits, and entreated him to come to me with his wife, to a country that was his own, where he would have remained in the most perfect security, and enjoyed all the sweets of peace and friendship. He answered me in December, and one part of his letter resembled those of other times ; but melancholy was still more strongly marked, and the illness of his wife, which he unfortunately thought more serious than it really was, evidently oppressed him : he had been obliged to take three days to write me details which at another time would not have occupied him an hour, and he concluded his letter with, ' I conjure you, perhaps for the last time, &c.' The idea that he should write no more to his friend (and unfortunately the event justified him), the difficulty of writing a few pages, the still fixed idea of being forced to leave Hanover, although the face of affairs had entirely changed ; all, all indicated the loss I was about to sustain."

From the month of November he had lost his sleep, his appetite, his strength, and became sensibly thinner ; and this state of decline continued to increase. In January he was still able to make a few visits in his carriage ; but he frequently fainted on the stairs : it was painful for him to write a prescription : he sometimes complained of a confusion in his head, and he at length gave over all business. This was at first taken for an effect of hypochondria, but it was soon perceived, that his deep melancholy had destroyed the chain of his ideas. What has happened to so many men of genius, befell him. One strong idea masters every other, and subdues the mind that is no longer able either to drive it away, or to lose sight of it. Preserving all his presence of mind, all his perspicuity, and justness of thought on other subjects, but no longer desirous of occupying himself with them, no longer capable of any business, nor of giving advice, but with pain, he had unceasingly before his eyes the enemy plundering his house, as Pascal always saw a globe of fire near him, Bonnet his friend robbing him, and Spinello the devil opposite to him. In February he commenced taking medicines, which were either prescribed by himself or by the physicians whom he consulted; at the beginning of March he desired Tissot's advice; but he was no longer able himself to describe his disorder, and his wife wrote Tissot the account of it. Tissot answered her immediately; but there could be no great utility in the directions of an absent physician in a disorder whose progress was rapid, and with an interim of near a month between the advice asked, and the directions received. His health decayed so fast, that M. Wichman, who attended him, thought a journey and change of air would now be the best remedy. Eutin, a place in the dutchy of Holstein, was fixed upon for his residence. In going through Luneburgh on his way thither, M. Lentin, one of the physicians in whom he placed most confidence, was consulted; but Zimmermann, who, though so often uneasy on account of health, had, notwithstanding, the wisdom to take few medicines, and who did not like them, always had a crowd of objections to make against the best advice, and did nothing. Arrived at Eutin, an old acquaintance and his family lavished on him all the caresses of friendship. This reception highly pleased him, and he grew rather better. M. Hensler came from Kiel to see him, and gave him his advice, which was probably very good, but became useless, as it was very irregularly followed. At last, after a residence of three months, he desired to return to Hanover, where he entered his house with the same idea with which he had left it; he thought it plundered, and imagined himself totally ruined. Tissot wrote to intreat him to go to Carlsbad; but he was no longer capable of bearing the journey. Disgust, want of sleep, and weakness, increased rapidly; he took scarcely any nourishment, either on account of insurmountable aversion, or because it was painful to him; or perhaps, as M. Wichman believed, because he imagined he had not a farthing left. Intense application, the troubles of his mind, his pains, want of sleep, and of sufficient nourishment, had on him all the effects of time, and hastened old age: at sixty-six he was in a state of complete decrepitude, and his body was become a perfect skeleton. He clearly foresaw the issue of his disorder: and above six weeks before his death he said to this same physician, "I shall die slowly, but very painfully;" and fourteen hours before he expired, he said, "Leave me alone, I am dying." He expired Oct. 7, 1795. Most of the works mentioned above have been translated into English, and that on solitude particularly has acquired a considerable degree of popularity. [1]

ZINCKE (CHRISTIAN FREDERICK), an excellent enamel painter, was born at Dresden about 1684, and came to England in 1706, where he studied under Boit, and not only surpassed him, but rivalled Petitot. For a great number of years Zincke had as much business as he could execute; and when at last he raised his price from twenty to thirty guineas, it was occasioned by his desire of lessening his fatigue; for no man, so superior in his profession, was less intoxicated with vanity. He was particularly patronized by George II. and his queen, and was appointed cabinet-painter to Frederick, prince of Wales. Her late royal highness, the princess Amelia, had ten portraits of the royal family by him of a larger than his usual size. These she presented in 1783 to the prince of Wales, now Prince Regent. William, duke of Cumberland, bought several of his best works, particularly his beautiful copy of Dr. Mead's queen of Scots by Isaac Oliver.

In 1737 he made a visit to his own country; and after his return, his eyes failing, he retired from business, about 1746, to South Lambeth, with a second wife, by whom he had three or four children. His first wife was a handsome woman, of whom he had been very fond; there is a print of him and her; he had a son by her, for whom he bought a place in the six clerks office, and a daughter, who died a little before he retired to Lambeth. After his quitting business, madame Pompadour prevailed upon

[1] Life by Tissot.

him to copy, in enamel, a picture of the king of France, which she sent over on purpose. He died in March 1767.

Thus far from Walpole's "Anecdotes." What follows is from another authority. "When Zincke was in the greatest practice, he was in a very bad state of health; and being well respected by a number of the most celebrated physicians, had their assistance and advice. All of them pronounced that he was in a decline; but about the method of cure, they were not unanimous. Some prescribed one drug, and some another; and one of them recommended breast-milk. The drugs he swallowed; but the breast-milk he did not much relish the thought of. Finding himself grow rather worse than better; and being told that air and exercise were the best remedy for his complaint, he tasked himself to walk through the Park, and up Constitution-hill, every morning before breakfast. This did not relieve him; but from habit rather than hope, he still continued his perambulations. One summer morning, a handsome young woman, very meanly clad, with a child about six weeks old in her arms, asked his charity. He gave her some pence, and asked her how she came into her present distressed situation. Her history was short: she had been a servant; she became partial to a footman in the same house, and married him; they were both turned away; the man had no other resource but to enlist: he became a soldier; was sent abroad: she had never heard from him since; had been delivered of the child now at her breast, for whose support and her own she should beg till her infant was a few months older, when she should try to get some more reputable employment. ' Her frankness,' said Zincke, ' pleased me; her face pleased me; her complexion pleased me; I gave her my direction; she came to me; I took her infant into my house; I did bring myself to take her milk; it recovered me; I made inquiry after her husband, and found he was killed in the first engagement he was in, at the pillaging a village in Germany. I married her; and a better wife no man ever had.' With this woman he lived near twenty years. The soldier's child he educated for the army, and promised to get him a commission when he was twenty-one; but the boy died at fourteen. By Zincke she had two children, each of them were well provided for; and one of them was a very few years since alive, and well situated in a northern province." [1]

¹ Walpole's Anecdotes.—Anderson's Bee, vol. I.

ZINZENDORF (NICHOLAS-LEWIS), count de, founder, or restorer of the sect of the Moravian brethren, was descended from an ancient and noble family in Austria; but directly sprung from that Lutheran branch of it which flourished in Misnia. He was born in 1700, and even in his childhood, had formed a resolution of becoming a minister of the gospel, designing to collect a small society of *Believers*, who should altogether employ themselves in exercises of devotion, under his direction. Accordingly in 1721, when he became of age, he purchased the estate and village of Bertholsdorf, near Zittaw, in Upper Lusatia. Some time before this, in 1717, one Christian David visited the small remains of the church of the United Brethren, who had formed a society for religious exercises in a small village in Moravia, but finding their situation a precarious one, and them desirous of some more secure settlement, he recommended them to count Zinzendorf; and this scheme being perfectly compatible with the count's original design, the Moravian emigrants were permitted to settle here.

The count himself superintended the rising settlement. The first houses were built near the hill called the *Hutberg*, i. e. the Watch-Hill; and hence the new settlement was called *Herrnhut*, i. e. the Watch of the Lord; and the brethren were by some denominated (but very improperly) *Herrnhutters*. In 1724, more emigrants arrived at Herrnhut from Moravia, just as the brethren were beginning to lay the foundation of an edifice intended for the education of the children of the noblesse, for printing cheap Bibles, and preparing medicines for their neighbours, in which building was also to be a chapel.

Herrnhut soon became a considerable village; but it would far exceed our limits to recount the successive emigrations to Herrnhut, and the additions that were made by the preaching of the rev. Mr. Rothe, minister of Bertholsdorf, and by the zeal of Christian David. Among these settlers were persons of different opinions; a circumstance, which engaged the attention of count Zinzendorf, who endeavoured to establish a union among them in the fundamental truths of the protestant religion, and, in 1727, formed statutes for their government, in conformity to these truths.

From this period, in particular, when elders and wardens were chosen, and a union established between the brethren from Moravia, both among themselves, and with their Lutheran and Calvinistic brethren, the Moravian writers date the renewal of the "Unity of the Brethren." The whole congregation was divided into classes, called *choirs*, and one of their own sex and station in life appointed to have the special care of each choir under the inspection of the elders. The ministers were appointed by lot, according to the apostolic practice, which they have continued ever since. They have adopted also other primitive practices, as the foot-washing, the kiss of charity, and the celebration of the *agapæ*, or love feasts. All matrimonial contracts were subject to the direction and approbation of the elders. Their worship is directed principally to Jesus Christ ; and, in their religious services, they admit of instrumental as well as vocal music.

The Moravians retain the discipline of their ancient church, and make use of episcopal ordination, which has been handed down to them, in a direct line of succession for more than 300 years. In their doctrines they adhere to the confession of Augsburgh, which was drawn up by Melancthon, at the desire of the protestant princes then assembled in that city, and by them presented to the diet of the empire, in 1530*.

In 1732, count Zinzendorf determining to devote his whole time to the benefit of the brethren, and to the great work of preaching the gospel among the heathens, resigned his situation as one of the council of regency at Dresden. He had been appointed in 1727, one of the wardens of the congregation. These wardens, where necessary, were to patronize the congregation, and to have an eye to the maintenance of good order and discipline. To them, and to the elders in conjunction, the direction of the congregation, both internally and externally, was committed. This office he resigned in 1730, but upon the urgent entreaties of the congregation, resumed it in 1733. He entered into

* With respect to their doctrines, we refer the reader, for more ample information on the subject, to " An Exposition of Christian Doctrine, as taught in the Protestant Churches of the United Brethren, or ' Unitas Fratrum.' Written in German by Augustus Gottleib Spangenberg, and translated (with a Preface) by Benjamin La Trobe," 8vo, 1784.

Full information of the present Constitution of the Church of the Brethren may be likewise found in a small tract, entitled, " A concise historical Account of the present Constitution of the Unitas Fratrum,' or Unity of the Evangelical Brethren, &c." 1775; and, in 1779, was printed " A Summary of the Doctrine of Jesus Christ, to be used for the instruction of youth in the congregations of the United Brethren."

holy orders in 1734, at Tubingen, in the duchy of Wirtemberg; and in 1737, he received episcopal ordination, on which occasion he received a letter of congratulation from Dr. Potter, archbishop of Canterbury, and from this time we always find him called the Ordinary of the brethren. In 1741, he laid aside his episcopal function, as he believed it would be prejudicial to his intended labours in Pennsylvania, where he purposed to appear merely as a Lutheran divine.

The count was so zealous and indefatigable in the extension of his sect, that he travelled over all Europe, and was twice in America, in consequence of which numerous settlements of the Moravians were formed, and missionaries sent to all parts of the world. In the mean time the brethren had to encounter much serious opposition. From the count's writings, it was attempted to be proved that he had advanced the most pernicious notions, and recommended the most abominable practices; and with respect to the brethren at large, the language of their devotions was said to be licentious and obscene; and it was added, that no examples could be found of a fanaticism more extravagant, and a mysticism more gross and scandalous, than those of the Herrnhutters.

These accusations were first circulated in a pamphlet, published in 1753, entitled "A narrative of the rise and progress of the Herrnhutters, with a short account of their doctrines, &c." by Henry Rimius, Aulic counsellor to his late majesty the king of Prussia. The representations of this writer were confided in, and the character of the brethren was exhibited in the most odious colours. Bishops Lavington and Warburton, in particular, relying principally on the authority of Rimius, were distinguished as the most formidable of their antagonists. Bishop Lavington, in a pamphlet entitled "The Moravians compared and detected," instituted a curious parallel between the doctrines and practices of the Moravians and those of the ancient heretics; and Dr. Warburton, in his "Doctrine of Grace," wrote some very severe invectives against them. The count was at this time (1753) in England, and resided at an old mansion (called Lindsey house) which he had purchased at Chelsea. He was here witness to numerous libels against him. "To one of the first ministers of state," says Mr. Cranz, "who urged the prosecution of a certain libeller, and promised him all his interest in having him punished, he gave his reasons in writing, why he neither could nor would prosecute him. A certain eminent divine, who compared the brethren to all the ancient and modern heretics, and charged them with all their errors, though ever so opposite to each other, received from him a very moderate private answer."

Some Moravian writers, however, while they effectually refuted the calumnies against the brethren as a community or sect, very candidly acknowledged that the extravagant expressions and practices of some individuals among them, were indeed indefensible. "It may not be improper to observe," says Mr. La Trobe, in the preface to his translation of Spangenberg's Exposition of Christian doctrine, "that although the brethren have been very falsely traduced by their adversaries, and by misinformed people, who meant well, and that particularly the writings of the late count Zinzendorf have been used to prove, that the church, of which he was an eminent and the most distinguished minister, held the errors of the most fanatic, yea wicked heretics; and his writings have been, for this purpose, mutilated, falsely quoted, and translated; and, although the extravagant words and actions of individuals have been unjustly charged upon the whole body; yet it were to be wished that there had been no occasion given, at a certain period, to accuse the brethren of improprieties and extravagance in word or practice." Again, speaking of count Zinzendorf, he says, "He commonly delivered two or three discourses in a day, either publicly or to his family, which was generally large; and what he then uttered, was attended with a striking effect upon those who heard him. He spoke in the strictest sense extempore; and according to the state of the times in which, and the persons to whom he spoke. These discourses were commonly taken down as he uttered them; and the love and admiration of his brethren were so great, that they urged the publication of these discourses. His avocations were such, that he did not spend time sufficient in the revision; some were not at all revised by him, and some very incorrectly and falsely printed. Hence doctrines, of which he never thought, were deduced from his writings, and some of his transient private opinions laid to the charge of the whole brethren's church. I do not, and cannot, attempt to defend such publications, but relate the real state of the case.

" The count was so convinced of the impropriety of the

above proceedings, that he requested the reverend author of this exposition to extract all the accusations of his antagonists, and the adversaries of the brethren, and lay them before him. It was done; he answered all; and the charges, and his answers, were published in Germany, in the years 1751 and 1752. He finding positions in the writings under his name which he could not avow, declared in the public papers, that he could not acknowledge any books which had been published in his name, unless they were revised and corrected in a new edition by himself. He began this work in German; but the Lord took him to himself before he could get through many books.

" True it is, that at a certain time, particularly between 1747 and 1753, many of the brethren, in their public discourses, and in their hymns, which were published about that period, used expressions that were indefensible: the count himself laboured to correct both the theory and language; and he was successful, and they are no more in use among the brethren. The brethren's congregations do not take the writings of the count, or of any man, as their standard of doctrine; the Bible alone is their standard of truth, and they agree with the Augustan, or Augsburgh confession, as being conformable to it." It is evident from this acknowledgment that the objectionable language of which their opponents accused them, was actually to be found in the writings attributed to Zinzendorf, and the indignation, therefore, which they excited was just. Nor have they reason to regret the expression of that indignation, since it has produced a reformation which places the sect in a more unexceptionable light. " It is no more," says Mr. Wilberforce, " than an act of justice explicitly to remark, that a body of Christians, which, from the peculiarly offensive grossnesses of language in use among them, had, not without reason, excited suspicions of the very worst nature, have since reclaimed their character, and have excelled all mankind in solid and unequivocal proofs of the love of Christ, and of the most ardent, and active, and patient zeal in his service. It is a zeal tempered with prudence, softened with meekness, soberly aiming at great ends by the gradual operation of well adapted means, supported by a courage which no danger can intimidate, and a quiet constancy which no hardships can exhaust."

Count Zinzendorf died at Herrnhutt, May 9, 1760, and was interred in the burying-ground on the Hutberg. Mr.

Cranz has given the affecting particulars of his death and funeral in his History of the Brethren, p. 488—502. The count was married, about the year 1722, to the countess Erdmuth Dorothea Reuss, who died on the 19th of June, 1756, beloved and revered by all as a "faithful and blessed nursing-mother of the church of the Brethren." By her he had one son and three daughters. His son, count Christian Renatus of Zinzendorf, was educated at the university of Jena; in 1744 his father introduced him at Herrnhut as a co-elder of the single brethren: he wrote many poetical soliloquies and meditations; and died at Westminster, May 28, 1752. Of the three daughters, the eldest accompanied her father to America, and married the baron Johannes de Watteville, who, in 1743, was consecrated a co-bishop, at Gnadenfrey, in Silesia. [1]

ZISCA, or ZISKA (JOHN), whose proper name was De Trocznow, was a native of Bohemia, and was educated at the Bohemian court, in the reign of Wenceslaus. He went into the army very young, signalized himself on several occasions, and lost an eye in battle; whence he was called Zisca, which signifies one-eyed. Almost all Bohemia retaining the sentiments, and being shocked at the death of John Huss, Zisca became their leader, and soon saw himself at the head of 40,000 men, determined to rescue their country from civil and ecclesiastical tyranny; and with these troops he gained several victories over the catholics. He built a town in an advantageous situation, and named it Tabor, from which circumstance the Hussites were also called Taborites. Zisca lost his other eye, by an arrow, at the siege of Rubi; but this did not prevent his continuing the war, and obtaining great victories, particularly that of Aussig, on the Elbe, when 9000 catholics were left dead on the spot. The emperor Sigismond, alarmed by all this, privately offered Zisca very advantageous terms. Zisca accepted them, and set out to meet Sigismond; but died of the plague on his journey, in 1424, after having ordered, as is said, that his body should be left a prey to the birds and beasts, and that a drum should be made of his skin, at the sound of which, he assured his followers, the enemy would immediately fly. The Hussites, it is added, obeyed his command; and the news of this injunction made so strong an impression on the German catho-

[1] Life by Spangenberg.—Cranz's History of the Brethren.—Mosheim, vol. VI.

lies, who were not well disciplined, that they actually fled
in several battles, on hearing the drum made of John Zisca's
skin. The whole, however, is justly considered as an absurd fiction. Zisca has been ranked among the reformers,
and certainly may be considered as the successor of Huss
in the propagation of his opinions, but he was more of a
general than a divine, and makes a better figure in belligerent history than in that of the church. He was by no
means animated with that true spirit of Christianity which
his amiable master Huss had discovered on all occasions.
His fierce temper, says Gilpin, seems to have been modelled rather upon the Old Testament than the New; and
the genius of that religion in a great degree to have taken
hold of him, which in its animosities called down fire from
heaven. His military abilities were equal to what any age
has produced; and as such they are acknowledged by all
historians; nor was the end which he proposed unworthy
of his great actions. Utterly devoid both of avarice and
ambition, he had no aim but to establish, upon the ruins
of ecclesiastical tyranny, the civil and religious liberties of
his country. [1]

ZOILUS, a celebrated hypercritic, was born at Am-
phipolis, a city of Thrace, and lived about the year 270
B. C. He is supposed to have been of mean extraction.
He was a disciple of Polycrates, the sophist, who is said to
have been a critic of the same stamp, and particularly famous for an invective against the memory of Socrates. The
disposition of Zoilus appeared very early, in expressions
of general malignity, which he did not affect to conceal;
and being one day asked why he spoke ill of every one,
said, "It is because I am not able to *do* them ill." This
procured him the name of the rhetorical dog. While he
was in Macedon he employed his time in writing, and reciting what he had written in the schools of the sophists.
His subjects were the most approved authors, whom he
chose to abuse on account of their reputation. He censured Xenophon for affectation, Plato for vulgar notions,
and Socrates for incorrectness; Demosthenes, in his opinion, wanted fire, Aristotle subtlety, and Aristophanes humour; but he became most notorious for his attack on Homer, in a voluminous work which he entitled " The Censure of Homer," in the title of which are these words : " Zoi-

[1] Gilpin's Lives.—Univ. Hist.—Mosheim.

lus, the scourge of Homer, wrote this against that lover of fables." Of this work a few quotations only remain, sufficient to show the petulance of his spirit. Of his death there are various accounts, but all seem to agree that it was a violent one. Those who are desirous of farther information respecting his history, will find it in Parnell's Life of Zoilus, extracted from the best authorities, and enlivened with many just remarks on the descendants of the critic, who have inherited his name as well as his temper.[1]

ZOLLIKOFER (GEORGE JOACHIM), an eminent German divine, was born at St. Gall, in Switzerland, August 5, 1730. His father, a worthy practitioner of the law, withheld no expence in his education; and, after the usual progress through the school of his native town, being designed for the church, he was sent first to Bremen, and thence to the university of Utrecht, where the divinity professors are said to have been in high repute. Zollikofer was not, however, says his biographer, one of those who adhere pertinaciously to every thing instilled into them in a lecture-room, and are incapable of advancing a step beyond the routine of opinions, to which, from custom or articles, the tutors themselves are bound to accede. He was obliged, indeed, to attend lectures, as he once mentioned to a friend, on a systematic theology, resting solely on " unproved formularies, sophisms, technical and scholastic terms of the compendiums at that time in general use, instead of a sound exposition of the Bible, in connection with a strict investigation of ecclesiastical history:" but his sermons and books of devotion did not receive the least taint from the theology into which he became thus initiated. " The little that I know," said he, " I was obliged to teach myself chiefly after I was come to years of maturity; for I had but a miserable education."

Leaving the university, he became first a preacher at Murten in the Pays de Vaud, whence he was translated to Monstein, in the Grisons, and soon after was invited to Isenburg. None of these places enjoyed him long; for, at the age of eight-and-twenty, he was appointed to the office of preacher to the reformed church at Leipsic. This was a theatre worthy of his abilities; and his church was soon crowded with the chief people of the city, and the

[1] Life of Zoilus, in Parnell's Works.

members of the university. His attention was not confined to the pulpit. Psalmody and prayer formed, in his estimation, an essential part of public worship ; and his selection of hymns, in which the productions of the most esteemed modern poets of Germany—Gellert, Cramer, and Klopstock, were not forgotten, appeared in 1766. He was twice married ; but both marriages were childless. After having fulfilled the duties of his place till within a year of his decease, he formed the resolution of resigning his office ; but, at the united request of his congregation, who acceded to his preaching a discourse only once a fortnight, he was still induced to remain in his situation. A short time only elapsed before he was called from them, after an illness extremely painful, which he bore with the patience of a wise man, and the resignation of a Christian. He died Jan. 22, 1788, aged fifty-eight. The whole of his numerous congregation, together with some hundred students of the university, attended his body to the grave on the 25th, with every token of unfeigned sorrow.

Zollikofer, from the time that he quitted the university, studied the best models of composition, and was particularly attached to Cicero. At the same time, no part of moral or political knowledge escaped him ; and to continual study and meditation on the scriptures, he added an intimate acquaintance with profane history. His social and domestic conduct corresponded with the doctrines he taught from the pulpit. Entirely free from affected gravity, he was easy of access to all. The poor and indigent beheld in him a father and a friend ; and his bounty and his kindness were not confined within the limits of his own church and his own sect; they were extended to all who stood in need of his assistance. Cheerfulness reigned in his heart; his conversation was animated and entertaining ; and his raillery, in which he very rarely indulged, the mildest possible. Above all, he paid the strictest regard to veracity. " Whatever he said was true ; every word he uttered might be relied on, as conveying the real sentiments of his heart, and never did he commend or approve from complaisance any thing that was contrary to the conviction of his mind, or that he saw could not be approved upon the strictest rules of morality."

Eight volumes of Zollikofer's " Sermons," which are in the highest estimation in Germany, have lately been known in this country by a translation, of great purity and elegance, by the rev. William Tooke, F. R. S. who has pre-fixed some memoirs of the author to the " Sermons on the Dignity of Man," published in 1802.   In these sermons there is no display of the theological learning of their au-thor, and little that is explanatory in regard to peculiar texts of scripture ; they discuss not human creeds and systems of divinity : their aim is to explain the nature and grounds of Christian morality, and reconcile it with the best dictates of philosophy ; to reveal man to himself ; and they discover a talent seldom possessed—a knowledge of the human heart. [1]

ZONARAS (JOHN), a Greek historian, who lived about 1120, held some considerable posts at the court of the em-perors of Constantinople.   He afterwards entered the mo-nastic order of St. Basil.   He has left " Annals," to the death of Alexius Comnenus, 1118 ; the best edition of them is the Louvre, 1686 and 1687, 2 vols. fol. which form part of the Byzantine history ; but these " Annals," al-though valuable for their information, are written with little accuracy or critical skill, and discover too much cre-dulity.   President Cousin has translated into French what relates to the Roman history.   We have also some " Com-mentaries" by Zonaras, on the canons of the apostles and of the councils, Paris, 1618, folio ; and some " Tracts." [2]

ZOROASTER was an eminent philosopher, whose his-tory is involved in much obscurity, nor is it certain whether the name belongs to one or many.   Some have maintained that there was but one Zoroaster, and that he was a Per-sian.   Others have said that there were six eminent foun-ders of philosophy of this name.   Ham, the son of Noah, Moses, Osiris, Mithras, and others, both gods and men, have by different writers been asserted to have been the same with Zoroaster.   Many different opinions have also been advanced, concerning the time in which he flourished. Aristotle and Pliny fix his date at so remote a period as 6000 years before the death of Plato ; Hermippus says that he lived 5000 years before the Trojan war : idle tales, which are, doubtless, to be classed with the report of the Chaldeans concerning the antiquity of their astronomical observations.   According to Laertius, he flourished 600 years before the Trojan war ; according to Suidas, 500. In the midst of so much uncertainty, the probability may

[1] Memoirs as above.     [2] Vossius de Hist. Græc.—Fabric. Bibl. Græc.

he, that there was a Zoroaster, a Perso-Median, who flourished about the time of Darius Hystaspes, and that besides him there was another Zoroaster, who lived in a much more remote period among the Babylonians, and taught them astronomy. The Greek and Arabian writers are agreed concerning the existence of the Persian Zoroaster; and the ancients unanimously ascribe to a philosopher, whom they call Zoroaster, the origin of the Chaldean astronomy, which is certainly of much earlier date than the time of Hystaspes: it seems, therefore, necessary to suppose a Chaldean Zoroaster distinct from the Persian. Concerning this Zoroaster, however, nothing more is known than that he flourished towards the beginning of the Babylonish empire, and was the father of the Chaldean astrology and magic, which was probably nothing more than the performance of certain religious ceremonies, by means of which good dæmons were supposed to be prevailed upon to communicate supernatural properties and powers to herbs, stones, and other natural bodies, or to afford assistance, in other miraculous ways, to those who invoked them. In this art the kings of Chaldea and Persia were instructed, as one of the most useful instruments of government, among a people, whose ignorance and credulity rendered them proper subjects of imposture. The Chaldean magic was then a very different thing from a knowledge of the real properties of bodies; and it cannot be inferred, either from their magical or astrological arts, that the Chaldeans were eminent masters in any branch of natural science. All the writings which have been ascribed to the Chaldean Zoroaster, are unquestionably spurious.

As to the other Zoroaster, called ZARDUSHT, who revived philosophy among the Persians, he appears to have lived at a much later period than the former. It is probable that Zardusht was of Persian extraction, and was born in Media. What the Arabian writers report concerning his having been early instructed by the Jews, seems to be a fiction invented to obtain credit among the Jews and Christians, to the doctrines which they professed to have received from him. It is not, however, improbable, that he might have learned some things from the Israelites residing in Babylon, which might be of use to him in executing his design of correcting the doctrine of the Persian Magi, though it may not be easy to specify the particulars.

Several miracles are ascribed to Zoroaster, such as an artful impostor would naturally attempt, and would not perhaps find it difficult to perform. Having by these and other artifices established his credit, it is related that he undertook the revival and improvement of the religion of the ancient Magi, which had long before this time prevailed in Media and Persia, but which had been almost entirely supplanted by the worship of the stars, to which the Persians, with their king Darius, were addicted. Much is also said by the Arabian writers, concerning the learning which Zoroaster acquired from the Indian Brachmans; concerning the influence which he obtained with Darius, and the success with which he propagated his system; and lastly, concerning his assassination, by Argaspis, king of the Eastern Scythia, at the siege of Bactria. But the silence of the Greeks, who were at this time well acquainted with the affairs of Persia, and after Alexander's conquests must have become possessed of many Persian records, is a circumstance which casts a cloud of suspicion over these relations. Thus much, however, may be admitted as probable; that there was in Persia, in the time of Darius Hystaspes, a reformer, who, assuming the ancient name of Zoroaster, brought back the Persians from the worship of the stars, to their ancient worship of fire, with some innovations both in doctrine and ceremonies, and he might be acquainted with astronomy, medicine, and other branches of learning. This Lucian seems to confirm; and according to modern travellers, there is still, in the province of Carmania, a sect, who adhere to the doctrines of Zoroaster, and worship fire according to the institutions of the ancient Magi.

To Zardusht, or the Persian Zoroaster, many writings are ascribed. One of these, called the Zend, is said to be still remaining among the followers of Zoroaster, and is esteemed of sacred authority. It is written in the Persian language, and consists of two parts, one of which contains their forms of devotion and order of ceremonies; the other, the precepts of religion and morality. A portion of this book, or of a compendium of it, called the Sadder, is read to the people, on every sacred day, by their priests. There is, however, much reason to question, whether this book be of such ancient date as the time of Zoroaster: probably, it was written about the time when many Jews and Christians resided among the Persians, i. e. about the fourth or fifth century. Many other works have been attributed to Zoroaster, but they are all lost, and most of them were probably forgeries. Fragments of a work entitled "The Oracles" of Zoroaster are still extant. A small collection of them, consisting of only sixty verses, was published by Pletho, at Paris, 1538 and 1589, and at Amst. 1689. Patrizi afterwards made a much larger collection, containing 323 verses, with the commentaries of the Platonic philosophers. Several other editions of these verses have been published, and much pains has been taken by various writers to explain them. Stanley has subjoined to his account of "The Lives of Philosophers" a correct translation of them. They are quoted, with the highest respect, by all philosophers of the Alexandrian school, as genuine remains of Chaldean wisdom. But they abound so much in the ideas and language peculiar to that school, that it is probable they were written by some Platonist, about the beginning of the second century.

Hyde, Prideaux, and others, mention ancient books of Zoroaster, which are at this day extant among the Gheuri and other professors of the Zoroastrian superstition, and made use of in their sacred worship, copies from which have been brought over to England and France. A catalogue of these and other Persian MSS. lodged in the library of the king of France, was published by M. Anquetil du Perron, in his travels, and is copied in the Journal de Savans for July 1762. But these books, written partly in the Zendic or sacred, and partly in the vulgar Persian language, are, for the most part, a narrative of miracles and revelations, by which Zoroaster is said to have established his religion, or a collection of precepts for religious ceremonies. Some of them indeed treat of fundamental doctrines of theology, taught among the worshippers of fire : but it is probable, from the tenets contained in these books, many of which seem to have been borrowed from the Jews and Mahometans, from the entire silence of Greek authors who wrote after the time of Alexander concerning these books, and from other considerations, that they were written at a later period, for the purpose of appeasing the resentment of their Mahometan persecutors. [1]

ZOSIMUS, an ancient historian, who lived at the end of the fourth, and the beginning of the fifth, century, was a man of quality and place, having the title of count, and

---

[1] Brucker.—Gen. Dict.—Chaufepie.—Maurice's Indian Antiquities.

being advocate of the treasury. There are extant six books
of history, in the first of which he runs over the Roman
affairs in a very succinct and general manner, from Augustus to Dioclesian: the other five books are written more
largely, especially when he comes to the time of Theodosius the Great, and of his children Arcadius and Honorius,
with whom he was contemporary. Of the sixth book we
have only the beginning, the rest being lost. Zosimus drew
his narrative from historians now lost, viz. Dexippus, Euna-
pius, and Olympiodorus. His style is far superior to that
of the writers of the age in which he lived, and he is an historian of authority for his account of the changes introduced
by Constantine and Theodosius in the empire. He contains, however, many superstitious accounts, and being a
zealous pagan, he must be read with caution as to what relates to the Christian princes. Photius says, "that he barks
like a dog at those of the Christian religion:" and few
Christian authors till Leunclavius, who translated his history into Latin, made any apology for him. "To say the
truth," says La Mothe le Vayer, "although this learned
German defends him very pertinently in many things, shewing how wrong it would be to expect from a Pagan historian, like Zosimus, other sentiments than those he professed; or that he should refrain from discovering the vices
of the first Christian emperors, since he has not concealed
their virtues; yet it cannot be denied, that in very many
places he has shewn more animosity than the laws of history
permit." Some have said that his history is a perpetual
lampoon on the plausible appearances of great actions.
The six books of his "History" have been published, with
the Latin version of Leunclavius, at Frankfort, 1590, with
other minor historians of Rome, in folio; at Oxford, 1679,
in 8vo, and at Ciza the same year, under the care of Cel-
larius, in 8vo. This was dedicated to Grævius, and reprinted at Jena, 1714, in 8vo. But the best edition is that
of Jo. Frid. Reitemeier, Gr. and Lat. with Heyne's notes,
published at Leipsic in 1784, 8vo. The prolegomena are
particularly valuable. [1]

ZOUCH, or ZOUCHE (RICHARD), an eminent civilian,
descended from an ancient and noble family of that name,
was born at Ansley in Wiltshire about 1590. He was edu-

[1] Photii Bibliotheca.—Fabric. Bibl. Græc.—Reitemeier's edition.—Saxii Onomast.

cated, on the foundation, at Winchester school, whence in 1607 he was elected to New college, Oxford, and chosen fellow in 1609. Having studied the civil law, he took his bachelor's degree in that faculty, in June 1614, and in Jan. 1618 was admitted at Doctors' Commons, where he became an eminent advocate. In April 1619, he commenced LL. D. and upon the death of Dr. John Budden in June 1620, was appointed regius professor of law at Oxford. At the latter end of king James's reign, he was chosen more than once member of parliament for Hythe in Kent by the interest of Edward lord Zouche, warden of the cinque ports, to whom he was nearly related. In 1625 he was appointed principal of St. Alban's hall, being then chancellor of the diocese of Oxford, and afterwards made judge of the high court of admiralty by king Charles I. He had a considerable hand in drawing up the reasons of the university of Oxford against the solemn league and covenant and negative oath in 1647, having contributed the law part. Yet he chose to submit to the parliamentary visitors the following year, and therefore held his principal and professorship during the usurpation. In 1653, he was appointed by Cromwell to be one of the delegates in the famous cause of Don Pantaleon Sa, brother to the Portuguese ambassador, who in November of that year, had killed a gentleman in the New Exchange within the liberties of Westminster, for which he was afterwards executed. On this occasion Dr. Zouche wrote his celebrated piece, entitled "Solutio quæstionis de legati delinquentis judice competente," 1657, 8vo. In this he maintained, with Grotius, the general impunity of ambassadors, but denied the application of that rule to the case of Don Pantaleon.

On the death of Dr. Gerard Langbaine, he offered himself as a candidate against Dr. Wallis for the place of custos archivorum to the university, but was unsuccessful. (See WALLIS.) On the restoration he was reinstated in his post of judge of the admiralty, and was made one of the commissioners for regulating the university, but did not survive that year, dying at his apartments in Doctors' Commons, March 1, 1660. He was interred at Fulham church, Middlesex, near the grave of his eldest daughter, some time the wife of William Powell, alias Huison, esq. Wood says, " He was an exact artist, a subtle logician, expert historian, and for the knowledge in the practice of the civil law, the chief person of his time, as his works, much

esteemed beyond the seas (where several of them are reprinted) partly testify. He was so well versed in the statutes of the university, and controversies between the members thereof and the city, that none after (Bryan) Twine's
death went beyond him. As his birth was noble, so was
his behaviour and discourse; and as he was personable
and handsome, so he was naturally sweet, pleasing, and
affable."

His works were, 1. "The Dove, or certain passages of
Cosmography," Lond. 1613, 8vo, a poem composed in his
youth; but he was no great favourite of the muses. 2.
" Elementa jurisprudentiæ, definitionibus, regulis, et sen-
tentiis selectioribus juris civilis illustrata," Oxon. 1629, 8vo,
1636, 4to, and reprinted both at Leyden and Amsterdam.
3. " Descriptio juris et judicii feudalis, secundum consuetudines Mediolanæ et Normanniæ, pro introductione ad ju-
risprudentiam Anglicanam," Oxon. 1634, 1636, 8vo. 4.
" Descriptio juris et judicii temporalis, secundum consuetudines feudales et Normannicos," ibid. 1636, 4to. 5.
" Descriptio juris et judicii ecclesiastici, secundum canones
et consuetudines Anglicanas," ibid. 1636, 4to. These two
last were reprinted with Dr. Mocket's tract " De Politia
Ecclesiæ Anglicanæ," Lond. 1683, 8vo. 6. " Descriptiones juris et judicii sacri; juris et judicii militaris, et juris
et judicii maritimi," Oxon. 1640, 4to, reprinted at Leyden
and Amsterdam. 7. " Juris et judicii fecialis, sive juris inter gentes, &c. explicatio," Oxon. 1650, 4to. 8. " Cases
and questions resolved in civil law," ibid. 1652, 8vo. 9.
" Solutio questionis, &c." already mentioned, Oxon. 1657,
and Lond. 1717, 8vo. 10. " Eruditionis ingenuæ specimina, scilicet artium, logicæ dialecticæ," &c. Oxon. 1657.
11. " Questionum juris civilis centuria, in decem classes
distributa," Oxon. 1660, 8vo, Lond. 1682, the third edition. After his death, Dr. Timothy Baldwin, fellow of All
Souls, Oxford, published a posthumous work by Dr. Zouch,
entitled "The Jurisdiction of the Admiralty asserted against
sir Edward Coke's Articuli Admiralitatis, in the 22d chapter of his jurisdiction of Courts," Lond. 1663, 8vo. This
went through several editions. There is also ascribed to
Dr. Zouch an anonymous piece, entitled " Specimen
questionum juris civilis, cum designatione authorum," Oxon.
1653, 4to. [1]

[1] Ath. Ox. vol. II.—Biog. Brit.—Coote's Catalogue of Civilians.

ZOUCH (THOMAS), a learned divine, was born in 1737, at Sandal, near Wakefield, Yorkshire; and in 1757 removed from the school of the latter place to Trinity-college, Cambridge. In 1760, he was elected into one of lord Craven's scholarships, along with Mr. Joab Bates, celebrated afterwards for his skill in music. The year following, Mr. Zouch took his degree of B. A. and was classed as the third wrangler. Having been chosen fellow of his college in 1763, he was appointed assistant-tutor, which office he discharged with extraordinary credit; though his assiduity so much impaired his health, that he was obliged to quit the university; on which his college presented him in 1770 to the rectory of Wycliffe in the North Riding of Yorkshire. In this country retirement he continued till 1793, performing the office of a parish priest with great diligence, and augmenting his knowledge of natural history. His botanical excursions, in a pleasant and romantic part of Yorkshire, contributed not a little to invigorate his constitution. In 1791, he was appointed deputy commissary of the archdeaconry of Richmond; and in 1793 was chaplain to the master of the rolls, and rector of Scrayingham. By the death of his elder brother, the rev. Henry Zouch, in 1795, he succeeded to an estate at Sandal, where he resided till his death. On the demise of Dr. Smith, the master of Trinity college, one of the most learned mathematicians of his age, he was requested by the vice-master and senior fellows to deliver a Latin funeral oration in honour of his memory, which is said to have been much admired for the classical elegance of its language. In 1798, Mr. Pitt intended to have appointed him to the mastership of Trinity; but this design was set aside in favour of the present bishop of Bristol. On April 9, 1805, Mr. Pitt gave him the second prebend in the church of Durham, and in the same year he took his degree of D. D. In 1808, the see of Carlisle was offered to Dr. Zouch; but, in consequence of his advanced age and retired habits, he thought proper to decline the acceptance. Besides some anonymous publications, he was the author of, 1. "The Crucifixion, a Seaton prize poem," 1765, 4to. 2. "A Sermon preached at the primary visitation of William lord bishop of Chester, held at Richmond, in Yorkshire, August 21, 1789," 4to. 3. "An Inquiry into the Prophetic Character of the Romans, as described in Daniel viii. 23—25." 1792, 8vo. 4. "An Address to the Clergy of the Deaneries of

Richmond, Catterick, and Boroughbridge," 1792, 4to. 5.
" A Discourse delivered to the Clergy of the Deaneries of
Richmond, Catterick, and Boroughbridge, within the Diocese of Chester, at the visitation held June 20 and 25, 1793,
and published at their request," 4to. 6. " The good Schoolmaster, exemplified in the character of the rev. John Clarke,
M. A. formerly fellow of Trinity college, Cambridge, and
successively master of the Schools of Skipton, Beverley,
and Wakefield," 1798, 4to. 7. " An Attempt to illustrate
some of the Prophecies of the Old and New Testament,"
1800, 12mo. 8. " A Sermon preached in the Cathedral
Church of Durham, at the Assizes holden July 30, 1806,"
4to. 9. " Memoir of the Life and Writings of sir Philip
Sidney," 1808, 4to. 10. " Memoir of the Life of John
Sudbury, D. D. Dean of Durham," 1808, 4to.

Dr. Zouch was also the editor of, 1. " Love and Truth;
in two modest and peaceable letters concerning the dis-
tempers of the present times. Written from a quiet and
conformable citizen of London, to two busie and factious
shopkeepers in Coventry; with notes, and a preface by
the editor," 1795, 8vo. This edition of a tract written by
Isaac Walton, is dedicated to Mr. Henry Zouch. 2. " The
Lives of John Donne, sir Henry Wotton, Mr. Richard
Hooker, Mr. George Herbert, and Dr. Robert Sanderson;
by Isaac Walton; with notes, and the Life of the Author,"
1796, 4to. Of this excellent work an octavo edition appeared in 1798.

In a volume entitled " Odes on Peace and War, written
by many eminent and distinguished persons," London,
1795, are three poems, one by Henry Zouch, B. A. Trinity
college, and two by Thos. Zouch, B. A. fellow of the same
college, and university scholar. Mr. Henry Zouch died at
Sandal, June 17, 1795; he was the author of some valuable tracts on matters of police. [1]

ZUCCARELLI (FRANCIS), a royal academician and an
excellent artist, was born at Florence about 1710. In
early life he studied as an historical painter, but afterwards
confined his practice to the painting of landscape, with
small figures, in which he acquired a very beautiful manner, both of composing and executing his pictures. It has
been remarked, that among the figures which he introduced
in his landscapes, he frequently represented one with a

[1] Gent. Mag. vol. LXV. and LXXXVI.

*gourd* bottle at his waist, as is often seen in Italy. This is said to have been done intentionally, as a sort of pun on his own name, *Zucco* being the Italian word for a gourd. He is supposed to have come to England about 1752. On his way, the war raging in Europe, he was seized on the territories of one of the belligerent states, as a suspicious person. He told them his name and profession, and offered to confirm the fact by painting a picture, which was agreed to; the materials were procured, the picture painted, and Zuccarelli released.

In England he met with much encouragement, and several of his pictures were engraved by Vivares. By the advice of some of his friends, he executed a collection of drawings, which he disposed of by auction. They were well received, and produced a handsome sum. About 1773 he returned to Florence, and for some time relinquished his pencil, and lived upon his fortune; but part of that having been lost upon bad security, he again resumed his pencil, and was much employed by the English gentlemen who visited Italy. He died at Florence, at what time is not exactly known, but the event was confirmed to the Royal Academy in 1788. He was one of the original members, and consequently considered as one of the founders of the academy. The pictures of this artist have, in Mr. Edwards's opinion, infinite merit, particularly those which he painted in the early part of his life, when resident at Venice. They have an evident superiority over those he painted in England. He made several etchings, particularly of figures, from the originals of Andrea del Sarto, which are marked with his name, " Zuccarelli delin. et fecit.[1]

ZUCCHERO (TADDEO), an Italian painter, was born at St. Angelo in Vado, in the duchy of Urbino, in 1529; and was initiated in his art by his father, who was an ordinary painter. At fourteen years of age he was carried to Rome, and placed under Pietro Calabro, whose wife was so covetous, that she almost starved him, and forced him to look out for another master. However, he went to no other, but contented himself with contemplating Raphael's works and the antique sculptures: he improved himself also greatly by the study of anatomy. He excelled chiefly in a florid invention, a genteel manner of design, and in the

---

[1] Edwards's Anecdotes of Painting.

good disposition and œconomy of his pieces; but was not so much admired for his colouring, which was generally unpleasant, and rather resembled the statues than the life. He never worked out of Italy: Rome, Tivoli, Florence, Caparola, and Venice, were the places where he distinguished himself; but he left many pieces unfinished, being snatched away in his prime in 1566. [1]

ZUCCHERO (Frederico), an eminent painter, and brother of the preceding, was born in 1543, and carried to the Jubilee at Rome in 1550; when he was placed under his brother Taddeo, then in high reputation. He afterwards set up for a master painter, and finished many of his brother's pieces. Pope Gregory XIII. employed him: when Zucchero, having a difference with some of his officers, drew a picture of Slander, afterwards engraved by Cornelius Cort, in which he represented those who had offended him with ass's ears. He exposed it publicly over the door of St. Luke's church; but was obliged to leave Rome, in order to avoid the Pope's indignation. He worked in France for the cardinal of Lorrain, and in the Escurial for Philip II. without giving content to either the one or the other. He was more fortunate in England, where he drew the picture of queen Elizabeth, and of some other great personages, which gave great satisfaction. At last, returning to Italy, and having worked some time in Venice, Pope Gregory recalled and pardoned him. Soon after, he set up the academy of painting, by virtue of a brief obtained from this pope; of which being chosen the first president himself, he built a noble apartment for their meeting. He went afterwards to Venice, to print some books he had written on painting; thence passed on to Savoy; and, in a journey to Loretto, died at Ancona in 1616. He differed but little from his brother in his style and manner of painting; though in sculpture and architecture he was far more excellent. [2]

ZUERIUS. See BOXHORN.

ZUINGER, or ZWINGER (Theodore), a celebrated physician of Basil, was nephew, on the mother's side, to John Oporinus, the famous printer. He studied at Lyons, Paris, and Padua; and afterwards taught Greek, morality, politics, and physic, at his native place. He died in 1588,

[1] Argenville, vol. I.—Pilkington.
[2] Argenville, vol. I.—Pilkington.—Walpole's Anecdotes.

aged 54. His principal work is, the "Theatrum Vitæ humanæ," which had been begun by Conrad Lycosthenes, his father-in-law. Of this voluminous compilation there is a most splendid copy on vellum in the British Museum. Zwinger's family has produced many other illustrious men, and his descendants have distinguished themselves greatly in the sciences. James Zwinger, his son, who died in 1610, was also a skilful physician; he both enlarged and improved the "Theatrum Vitæ humanæ," Leyden, 1656, 8 vols. folio; and left other works. Theodore Zwinger, son of James, a learned protestant divine, married the daughter of Buxtorf the elder. He was pastor and physician when the city of Basil was afflicted with the plague in 1629. He wrote several works, and died in 1651, leaving a son, named John Zwinger, professor of Greek, and librarian at Basil, author of several works: he died in 1696. Theodore Zwinger, his son, professor of rhetoric, natural philosophy, and physic, at Basil, died in that city, 1724, leaving "Theatrum Botanicum," Basil, 1690, folio, in German. "Fasciculus Dissertationum," 1710, 4to; and "Triga Dissertationum," 1716, 4to, which are esteemed. John Rodolphus Zwinger, his brother, minister of several protestant churches, and professor of divinity, died 1708, leaving also some works.[1]

ZUINGLIUS (ULRICUS), an able and zealous reformer of the church, who laid the foundation of a division from Rome in Switzerland, at the time that Luther did the same in Saxony, was born at Wildehausen in the county of Tockenbürg (a distinct republic in alliance with the Switzers, or Helvetic body) in 1487. He was sent to school at Basil early, and thence removed to Berne, where he learned the Greek and Hebrew tongues. He studied philosophy at Vienna, and divinity at Basil, where he was admitted doctor in 1505. He began to preach with good success in 1506, and was chosen minister of Glaris, a chief town in the canton of the same name, where he continued till 1516. Then he was invited to Zurich, to undertake the principal charge of that city, and to preach the word of God there, where his extensive learning and uncommon sagacity were accompanied with the most heroic intrepidity and resolution. From his early years he had been shocked at several of the superstitious practices of the church of

[1] Moreri.—Freheri Theatrum.—Dict. Hist.

Rome, and now began to explain the Scriptures to the people, and to censure, though with great prudence and moderation, the errors of a corrupt church. He might have no doubt been animated by the example and writings of Luther, afterwards; but it appears that even now, he entertained very extensive views of a general reformation, while Luther retained almost the whole system of popery, indulgences excepted.

In 1519 a Franciscan of Milan, being sent from Leo X. as general visitor of his order, came to publish indulgences at Zurich, and preached according to the usual manner; namely, " That the pope had granted an absolute pardon of sins to those who purchased such indulgences with money, and that men might by this means deliver souls infallibly from purgatory." Zuinglius declaimed powerfully not only against the preacher, but even against the indulgences, or at least the use that was made of them. Hugh, bishop of Constance, supposing that he was displeased only with the abuse of them, exhorted him to go on, and promised him his patronage; but Zuinglius went farther, and solicited the bishop, and the pope's legate in Switzerland, to favour the doctrine he was about to establish, and which he called *evangelical truth*. The bishop and the legate refusing to hearken to his proposals, he told them, that he would oppose the errors of the court of Rome, and propagate his own doctrines, in defiance of them; and thus continued to preach, from 1519 to 1523, not only against indulgences, but other articles of the catholic church.

Zuinglius made no less progress with the reformation in Switzerland than Luther did in Saxony, yet, though by four years preaching he had prepared the magistrates and people, and knew that they were disposed to cast off the doctrine and discipline of the church of Rome, and to receive his new opinions, he would not attempt to make any alterations in the external worship without the concurrence of the civil powers, and to that end caused an assembly to be called of the senate of Zurich in 1523, that the differences among preachers in matters of religion might be composed. The senate, by their edict, invited all ecclesiastics of their canton, and gave the bishop of Constance notice of it, that he might either be present by himself or his deputies; and the assembly met at the day appointed. Here Zuinglius declared, " that the light of the gospel having been much obscured, and almost extinguished by human traditions, several persons of late had endeavoured to restore it by preaching the word of God in its purity; that he himself was one of that number; and, though he had for five years past taught nothing but what was contained in holy scripture, yet he had been treated as a heretic and seducer; that it was for this reason he had desired to give an account of his doctrines before the senate of Zurich, and the bishop of Constance, or his deputies; and, that they might the more easily understand them, he had drawn them out into sixty-seven propositions." The doctrine contained in these propositions may be reduced to the following articles: 1. "That the gospel is the only rule of faith." 2. "That the church is the communion of saints." 3. "That we ought to acknowledge no head of the church but Jesus Christ." 4. "That all traditions are to be rejected." 5. "That there is no other sacrifice but that of Jesus Christ." 6. "That we have need of no other intercessor with God but Jesus Christ." 7. "That all sorts of meat may be eaten at all times." 8. "That the habits of monks partake of hypocrisy." 9. "That marriage is allowed to all the world, and no man obliged to make a vow of chastity; and that priests are not at all debarred from the privilege of being married." 10. "That excommunication ought not to be inflicted by the bishop alone, but by the whole church; and that only notorious offenders ought to be excommunicated." 11. "That the power which the pope and bishops assume to themselves, is errant pride, and hath no foundation in scripture." 12. "That none can forgive sins but God; and that confession of sins to a priest is only to beg his ghostly advice " 13. "That the scripture teaches no such place as purgatory." 14. "That the character which the sacraments are said to impress, is a modern invention." 15. "That the scripture acknowledges none for priests and bishops but such as preach the word of God."

He also offered to deliver his judgment respecting tithes, the revenues of the church, the condition of infants not baptised, and confirmation, if any person should be willing to dispute with him upon those points. John Faber, one of the three deputies whom the bishop of Constance had sent, and his chief vicar, answered, that he was not come to dispute about ceremonials and customs, which had for many ages been used in the church; nor did he think fit to debate about that affair then, but would refer it to the general council, which was to meet shortly, according to the constitution of the diet of Nuremberg. Zuinglius replied, " that they ought not to regard how long a thing has been or has not been in use, but to observe only, whether or not it be agreeable to truth, or the law of God, to which custom could not be opposed; and that there were learned men in the present assembly who could very well determine the matters in question, without referring them to a council, since even private Christians, enlightened by the spirit of God, could discern between those that did and did not understand the Scripture." The result of this conference was in favour of Zuinglius; for the senate ordained by an edict, " that he should go on to teach and preach the word of God, and the doctrine of the gospel, after the same manner that he had hitherto done; and that no pastors, either in the city or country, should teach any thing that could not be proved by the gospel, and should also abstain from accusations of heresy."

After an edict so favourable, the doctrines of Zuinglius, which most of the pastors had before embraced, were preached under the name of Evangelical Truth in almost all the churches of the canton of Zurich; but, because the outward worship was contrary to their doctrines, images still remaining, and mass being celebrated, and they durst not abolish it without authority, Zuinglius, to complete his design, engaged the senate to call a new assembly in October the same year, when the bishops of Constance, Coine, and Basil, with the university of the latter city, and the twelve cantons of Switzerland, were invited to send their deputies. The senate assembled upon the day appointed, debates were held upon the points in question; and the result was an edict, by which the priests and monks were forbidden to make any public processions, to carry the holy sacrament, or to elevate it in the church, that it might be worshipped: reliques were taken out of the churches, and it was forbidden to play upon organs, to ring the bells, to bless palm-branches, salt, waters, or tapers, and to administer the supreme unction to the sick.

He appears to have aimed at establishing in his country, a method and form of divine worship, remarkable for its simplicity, and as far remote as could be from every thing that could have the smallest tendency to nourish a spirit of superstition. His design, says the translator of Mosheim, was certainly excellent; but in the execution of it, perhaps, he went too far, and consulted rather the dictates of reason than the real exigencies of human nature in its present state. The present union between soul and body, which operate together in the actions of moral agents, even in those that appear the most abstracted and refined, renders it necessary to consult the external senses, as well as the intellectual powers, in the institution of public worship. Besides, between a worship purely and philosophically rational, and a service grossly and palpably superstitious, there are many intermediate steps and circumstances, by which a rational service may be rendered more affecting and awakening without becoming superstitious. A noble edifice, a solemn music, a well-ordered set of external gestures, though they do not, in themselves, render our prayers more acceptable to the Deity, than if they were offered up without any of these circumstances, produce, nevertheless, a good effect. They elevate the mind, they give it a composed and solemn frame, and thus contribute to the fervour of its devotion.

Besides his public preaching, Zuinglius wrote several books in defence of his doctrines, which were published between 1522 and 1525 inclusive. In April 1525, he petitioned the senate of Zurich to abolish the mass and the adoration of the elements in the sacraments ; and he easily obtained what he petitioned. He explained the eucharist, and prescribed a form in celebrating the Lord's Supper, not only different from that of the church of Rome, but that of Luther also; and this engaged him in violent disputes and animosities even with his brethren, who were jointly labouring with him in the great work of reformation In the mean time, the other Swiss cantons, disallowing the proceedings of that of Zurich, assembled at Lucern in 1524, and decreed, that none should change the doctrines which had been established for 1400 years ; that they should not teach the doctrines of Zuinglius ; and that the magistrates should take care of the execution of this decree. They sent deputies at the same time to the senate of Zurich, to complain of the innovations they had made in their canton; who returned a firm answer, and stood with resolution to what they had done. They then called an assembly at Baden in 1526, where the most ingenious and able advocates of each side had the liberty of saying what they could, in justification of their respective doctrines ; and accordingly Oecolampadius maintained the part of Zuinglius, while

Eckius was representative for the catholics. Other assemblies were afterwards called; but things, instead of approaching nearer to peace and good order, tended every day more and more to tumult and civil discord.

In 1531 a civil war began in Switzerland, between the five catholic cantons, and those of Zurich and Bern. The Zurichese were defeated in their own territories, with the loss of four hundred men. Zuinglius, who accompanied them, was killed in this action, Oct. 11, 1531, in the forty-fourth year of his age. He was not present in the office of a soldier at this engagement, but with a view to encourage and animate, by his counsels and exhortations, the valiant defenders of the protestant cause. But had he, as the popish writers assert, been actually engaged, we must refer, for an apology to the manners of his country, all the inhabitants of which were trained to arms, and obliged to take the field when the defence of their country required it. In the time of Zuinglius this obligation was so universal, that neither the ministers of the gospel, nor the professors of theology, were exempted from military service. On receiving the mortal wound, he was heard to utter, " Can this be considered as a calamity? Well! they can indeed kill the body, but they are not able to kill the soul."

He was a man of acute parts and uncommon learning; and, in his character of Reformer, his zeal was tempered with a good degree of prudence. He held several notions peculiar to himself, and different from those of Luther, which produced no small misunderstanding between them; for Luther was not at all well affected to Zuinglius; nor did Zuinglius pay much deference to Luther. Their principal disagreement, however, was concerning the *manner* in which the body and blood of Christ were present in the eucharist. Luther and his followers, though they had rejected the doctrine of the church of Rome with respect to the transubstantiation, were still of opinion, that the partakers of the Lord's-supper received along with the bread and wine, the real body and blood of Christ. Zuinglius's doctrine, first maintained, although not so ably, by Carlostadt, who was Luther's colleague, amounted to this, that the body and blood of Christ were not really present in the eucharist; and that the bread and wine were no more than external signs or symbols, designed to excite in the minds of Christians the remembrance of the sufferings and death of the Saviour, and of the benefits which arise from it. This opinion was embraced by all the friends of the reformation in Switzerland, and by a considerable number of its votaries in Germany, who were termed Zuinglians, in contradistinction to the Lutherans.

Zuinglius also maintained doctrines respecting the divine decrees very opposite to those of some of his brethren, and had a system of his own concerning original sin, and contended for the salvation of infants dying without baptism, as well as of virtuous Pagans, both which points were rejected generally by the Protestants of his time. His works amounted to four volumes in folio, the greatest part of which were written in German, and afterwards were translated into Latin; they were printed at Basil in 1544, at Zurich in 1581, and at Basil again in 1593. They consist of Commentaries on various books of the Old and New Testament, and of controversial or theological tracts. His commentaries are said to have great merit, and he was one of the first of the reformers who reduced theology to a certain kind of order in his book " Concerning true and false Religion," which contains a brief exposition of the principal doctrines of Christianity. A few of his lesser pieces were translated into English, and published not many years after his death. His doctrines were afterwards spread into France, with some alterations by Calvin, Beza, and others, who were commonly called Calvinists; while the disciples of Zuinglius, who lived in Switzerland, retained the name of Zuinglians, or Sacramentarians.[1]

[1] Melchior Adam.—Mosheim and Milner's Ch. Hist.

# INDEX

### TO THE

## THIRTY-SECOND VOLUME.

Those marked thus * are new.
Those marked † are re-written, with additions.

GENERAL

# GENERAL INDEX

## TO THE

# LIVES

### CONTAINED IN THE

## THIRTY–TWO VOLUMES

### OF THE

## GENERAL BIOGRAPHICAL DICTIONARY.

Those marked thus * are new.
Those marked thus † are re-written, with additions.

<table>
<tr><td>†Aa, Peter Vander</td><td>*Abdollatiph</td><td>*Aboulola</td></tr>
<tr><td>*Aa, Chr. Ch. H. Van.</td><td>Abeille, Gaspar</td><td>*Abou-rihan</td></tr>
<tr><td>†Aagard, Christian</td><td>†——— Scipio</td><td>Abrabanel, Isaac</td></tr>
<tr><td>†——— Nicholas</td><td>*——— Lewis Paul</td><td>Abraham, Nicholas</td></tr>
<tr><td>*Aagesen, Suend</td><td>†Abel, Gaspar</td><td>†——— BenChaila</td></tr>
<tr><td>Aaron of Alexandria</td><td>*——— Fred. Gottfried</td><td>——— Usque</td></tr>
<tr><td>*——— St. a Briton</td><td>†——— Charles Fred.</td><td>*Abresch, Fred. Louis</td></tr>
<tr><td>†——— Hariscon</td><td>†Abela, John Francis</td><td>*Abriani, Paul</td></tr>
<tr><td>*——— Pietro</td><td>†Abelard, Peter</td><td>Abstemius, Laurent.</td></tr>
<tr><td>†Aarsens, Francis</td><td>*Abelin, John Philip</td><td>*Abucaras, Theodore</td></tr>
<tr><td>†Abáris</td><td>Abell, John</td><td>Abulfaragius, Greg.</td></tr>
<tr><td>*Abati, Anthony</td><td>†Abelli, Lewis</td><td>†Abulfeda, Ishmael</td></tr>
<tr><td>Abauzit, Firmin</td><td>†Abendana, Jacob</td><td>Abulgasi, Bayatur</td></tr>
<tr><td>†Abbadie, James</td><td>Aben-ezra</td><td>Abunowas</td></tr>
<tr><td>Abbas, Halli</td><td>Abengnefit</td><td>*Abundance, John</td></tr>
<tr><td>*Abbati, Nicolo</td><td>Abenmelek</td><td>†Abu, Temam</td></tr>
<tr><td>*Abbatius, Bald. Ang.</td><td>*Abercrombie, John</td><td>†Abydenus</td></tr>
<tr><td>†Abbo, Cernuus</td><td>*Abercromby, Patr.</td><td>Acacius, Luscus</td></tr>
<tr><td>†——— Floriacensis</td><td>*——— David</td><td>——— of Constant.</td></tr>
<tr><td>†Abbot, George</td><td>*——— Sir R.</td><td>——— of Berea</td></tr>
<tr><td>*——— G. his nephew</td><td>Abernethy, John</td><td>*——— of Amida</td></tr>
<tr><td>†——— Maurice</td><td>†Abgar</td><td>*——— of Melitene</td></tr>
<tr><td>†——— Robert</td><td>Abiosi</td><td>*Acca, St.</td></tr>
<tr><td>*——— R. of Cranbr.</td><td>†Able, Thomas</td><td>*Accarisi, Albert</td></tr>
<tr><td>*Abbt, Thomas</td><td>*Abney, Sir Thomas</td><td>*——— Francis</td></tr>
<tr><td>†Abdias</td><td>Abou-Hanifah</td><td>*——— James</td></tr>
<tr><td>Vol. XXXII.</td><td>3 A</td><td></td></tr>
</table>

# GENERAL INDEX.

GENERAL INDEX.

3 D

S D 2

# GENERAL INDEX.

# GENERAL INDEX.

# GENERAL INDEX.

## THE END.

Printed by Nichols, Son, and Bentley,
Red-Lion Passage, Fleet-Street, London.

Check Out More Titles From HardPress Classics Series In this collection we are offering thousands of classic and hard to find books. This series spans a vast array of subjects – so you are bound to find something of interest to enjoy reading and learning about.

Subjects:
Architecture
Art
Biography & Autobiography
Body, Mind &Spirit
Children & Young Adult
Dramas
Education
Fiction
History
Language Arts & Disciplines
Law
Literary Collections
Music
Poetry
Psychology
Science
…and many more.

Visit us at www.hardpress.net

CPSIA information can be obtained
at www.ICGtesting.com
Printed in the USA
BVHW080316270819
556819BV00007B/1180/P